Secondary Geography
HANDBOOK

Edited by David Balderstone

Geographical
Association

Acknowledgements

This project could not have been realised without the energy, enthusiasm, creativity and commitment of Diane Wright. Over the years, many people have had a significant influence on my own learning and teaching and therefore on shaping the principles underpinning this book. My own parents always provided me with the inspiration to learn and to become a teacher. I owe a huge debt of gratitude to David Lambert and David Jackson for their professional guidance, encouragement and support; for providing the conditions in which I, working with others, could take risks and explore new ideas and ways of educating young people through geography. Above all, they have always placed emphasis on the 'moral purpose' of education and the student-centred approaches that are both central to the vision for geography education outlined in this book. Creative energy and inspiration comes from having worked with Gene Payne, Rachel Henry and Chris Durbin amongst others. For me, learning and teaching geography has always been a collaborative activity. I therefore wish to acknowledge the contribution that every student, teacher and geography educator I have worked with has made to the thinking behind this book. Now it is over to you to develop the vision this book sets out for geography education in our schools and thus to make a real difference to the lives of the young people we work with.

The Geographical Association would like to thank the following individuals and organisations for providing images for this book: Dr Steve Banner (Wildlife and Wilderness Ltd), Bryan Ledgard, and Simon Scoones (Institute of Education).

Dedication

To Emily, Alex, Ben, Harry, Peter, Matthew, Thomas, Bethany, Erin, Sam, William and Oliver; and to every young geographer. Hoping that geography helps you to understand more about this world you live in and to make sense of your place within it, that it provides a key to your future.

ISBN 1 84377 165 9 [and CD-Rom] 1 84377 166 7
First published 2006
Impression number 10 9 8 7 6 5 4 3 2 1
Year 2009 2008 2007

Published by the Geographical Association, 160 Solly Street, Sheffield S1 4BF. Website: www.geography.org.uk E-mail: ga@geography.org.uk The Geographical Association is a registered charity: no 313129.

The Publications Officer of the GA would be happy to hear from other potential authors who have ideas for geography books. You may contact the Officer via the GA at the address above. The views expressed in this publication are those of the author and do not necessarily represent those of the Geographical Association.

Editing: Rose Pipes
Illustrations: Dave Howarth
Index: Jane Coulter
Front and back cover images: ©Steve Banner
Design and typesetting: Gloss Solutions, Dewsbury
Cartography: Paul Coles
Printing and binding: In China through Colorcraft Ltd, Hong Kong.

Secondary Geography HANDBOOK

Foreword

We want all young people to grow into informed citizens with a sound understanding of the human and natural processes that shape the globe and its people. Geography has a critical role in giving them an understanding of their place in the world.

Teaching such a dynamic and relevant subject can be challenging, but also richly rewarding for both students and teachers. This handbook is an excellent tool that will help bring teaching and learning to life for students of all ages and abilities. It offers useful insights into all aspects of secondary geography, from mapping to the media and from fieldwork to ICT. It brings together an impressive list of contributors from many different backgrounds, including classroom teachers, heads of geography, and teachers in higher education.

I thoroughly recommend this handbook to all secondary teachers of geography.

Andrew Adonis
Parliamentary Under Secretary of State for Schools

Contents

Visit the Secondary Geography handbook webpage: www.geography.org.uk/secondaryhandbook to download resources from this book and for updates on the weblinks mentioned at the end of each chapter.

Introduction

David Balderstone

> *To inspire is not to amaze. To inspire is to awaken the spirit of amazement in children* (Okri, 2002, p.30).

> *In our working lives as geography teachers we should never forget or abandon those ideals which draw us to the job in the first place. School geography has the potential to develop young people's understanding of their 'place' in the world and so help form their identity* (Huckle, 1997, p. 241).

> *In times of change, learners inherit the earth, while the learned find themselves beautifully equipped to deal with a world that no longer exists* (Eric Hoffer).

I have chosen to begin this book with the above quotations because, for me, they capture the spirit and purpose of what the contributors and myself are trying to achieve. They also provide worthy guiding principles for our work as teachers of geography.

'Learning' was the most frequently used word in, and a focus for the discussions that shaped the principles guiding the thinking behind this book, and the writing of the contributions. Our hope is that it will benefit everyone learning through geography in schools – young people and the teachers of geography who work with them. While geography is seen as a medium for education which can achieve worthwhile educational goals for young people, we must always remember that we, as teachers, are also learners – learning about the subject, about students' learning and about ways of devising activities that will bring about worthwhile learning through geography.

Our main aim when compiling this book was two-fold: to inspire and support the professional learning of geography teachers, and to promote worthwhile and stimulating learning through the subject. Margaret Roberts expressed the hope that the end-result would be 'more Rick Stein than Delia Smith', providing inspiration rather than guidance on 'how to do it'.

Providing inspiration for teachers is about renewing their faith in their own skills and understandings, and offering them encouragement to develop their own classroom practice. It does not have to be about 'big' ideas or totally new ways of doing things, though 'risk-taking' and creativity are clearly to be encouraged, rather than sticking to tired formulas and prescribed strategies. Being creative can transform teaching and learning. For teachers to have the opportunity to use their imagination and the freedom to innovate makes the process of teaching far more rewarding and motivating. It also helps teachers to become more open and responsive to change. For students, creative learning can help them to become more motivated, engaged and independent, resulting in higher levels of achievement.

The idea of encouraging young people to use their geographical imagination, and to connect with their lived experience, lies at the heart of the 'student-centred' view of teaching and learning in geography which has been a key guiding principle for this book. Intrinsic to this principle is the idea that the students themselves, and the ways in which they engage with geography, lie at the heart of planning and decision making in relation to teaching. This means that we must engage with our students in a very direct way, for example by asking them about their lifestyles, interests, views and beliefs, in order to find out what motivates them and what is relevant to them. And at all times we should try to bear in mind what Chris Durbin urged all the contributors to consider - namely, what, when reflecting back on what they have learnt in geography, students will consider geography to be; its essence and its value. The author Ben Okri describes the 'right inspiring' of young people as the 'hope of humanity'.

> *Education is an essential process in the eternally human quest for meaning and purpose in life and society ... It's not just jobs that children are being educated for; it is also, mainly, to be fulfilled human beings, people who have the tools to dispel their ignorance, their fears; and a desire to create a life worth living, a future* (Okri, 2002, p. 30).

To inspire students to learn we need to consider what we teach in geography, as well as the ways in which we enable young people to learn through the subject. Students need to be helped to learn the 'landscape' of the subject, how it works and its 'big' ideas. Providing for deeper understanding of these ideas, and learning how to use and apply students' skills, rather than focusing on 'performance', can raise their levels of attainment beyond what might be expected or predicted.

We (the contributors and myself) are optimistic in believing that geography teachers can create a geography curriculum that will excite students and stimulate relevant and worthwhile learning. To do so requires us all to have a dynamic view of the subject and its pedagogy, and constantly and rigorously to question what is worth teaching and how best to approach it. Romerty and Elberty Junior provide some interesting advice on this task:

> *Past successes pose a danger to person-centred education in geography. Once something works we tend to want to use the techniques over again in order to repeat the success ... If an approach works rejoice, but then approach the next situation freshly, on its own terms and seek a new perspective. Abandon 'techniques that get to feel like formulas, and search for freshness as if you have had no past experience. Mistakes? Yes, mistakes must continue to be made if progress is to continue. Failure to make mistakes generally means a failure to grow. Teachers must join their students in exploring all possible paths, including what may appear to be dead ends, if better paths are to be found. It is amazing how often a 'safe' path becomes a blind alley and an unlikely, overgrown trail leads to a previously unknown highway* (Romerty and Elberty Jr, 1984, p. 315).

Assessment has always been an integral part of teaching and learning and guidance is given in this book on ways of developing good practice. Assessment must not be allowed to become a barrier to learning and achievement. At a national level, much of the emphasis has been on summative assessment and the use of assessment data to report results, to compare schools' performance and to set targets. Such an emphasis on high-stakes assessment has resulted in 'teaching to the test' at the expense of learning, when what should be happening is that assessment is used as a means to help young people make progress in their learning, thereby improving their attainment.

An underlying assumption in the compiling of this book has been that teaching and learning geography is a collaborative activity, and that geography classrooms are learning communities in which the teacher has a productive and creative relationship with the subject which involves them in the process of 'curriculum making'. This is a challenging role, and while each teacher will draw on their own experience, imagination and unique ideas to develop their practice, they will inevitably look to the wider subject community as a source of ideas, strength and support. This handbook is a product of such a community of practice and the collaboration it supports, and will, we hope, play its part in helping school geography to realise its educational power both now and in the future.

References

Huckle, J. (1997) 'Towards a critical school geography' in Tilbury, D. and Williams, M. (eds) *Teaching and Learning Geography*. London: Routledge, pp. 241-54.

Okri, B. (2002) 'The best teachers awaken the spirit of amazement in children', *Report,* June, p. 30.

Romert, W. and Elberty Jr, W, (1984) 'On being a geography teacher in the 1980s and beyond' in Fien, J., Gerber, R. and Wilson, P. (eds) *The Geography Teacher's Guide to the Classroom*. Melbourne: Macmillan, pp. 306-16.

Finding your way around this book

Margaret Roberts

The Secondary Geography Handbook is rich in ideas to stimulate thinking about geographical education, almost all of which are illustrated with reference to possible application in the classroom or field. Many of these references are brief or are general and can be applied to many geographical themes.

There are, however, some references to practice that have been developed in reference to particular themes with examples of teaching frameworks, resources, activity sheets or students' work. In order to help users of this handbook to locate these specific examples easily, the grid below lists the themes and gives some indication of aspects of geography developed through the activities (many of the examples referred to can be downloaded from the GA's website).

Chapter	Figure/ Example	Theme, Activity or Enquiry	Economic	Environment/resources	Social	Place	Futures	Globalisation	Landscape	Climate/Weather	ICT/GIS	Fieldwork
6	Figure 6	Town trail for elderly visitors			✓	✓						✓
6	Figure 8	London Docklands	✓		✓	✓						
6	Case study 2	Investigating rural settlements			✓	✓						✓
7		Flooding: Ordnance Survey Mapzone - GIS							✓		✓	
9	Example 1, Figures 9 and 10	Recycling: an internet enquiry		✓							✓	
9	Example 2	Urban redevelopment: discussing a local plan			✓	✓	✓					
12	Figure 1	Life expectancy: using quantitative data			✓		✓					
12	Figure 5	Investigating snowfall using internet resources								✓	✓	
13	Figures 4 and 5	Should we buy the logos arguments for and against branded clothes	✓	✓	✓			✓				
13	Figure 6	Antarctica: discussing viewpoints	✓	✓	✓			✓				
13	Figure 8	The USA: an investigation				✓						
14	Figure 2	Lima, Peru: using contrasting texts			✓	✓						
15	Figure 1	The Blue Jeans Story: investigating an issue	✓		✓			✓				
15	Figures 4, 5 and 6	Should Nestor take the job: a moral dilemma	✓		✓			✓				
16	Figures 1, 4 and 7	Maps from memory: Europe				✓						
21	Figures 6, 7 and 8	Perceptions of crime and place: using photographs and OS maps			✓	✓						
21	Figures 10 and 11	Taking a year out: an independent investigation				✓						
22	Figures 2, 3 and 4	Physical processes: rift valleys and stacks sequencing activities							✓			
22	Figure 6	Glaciers: predictions using a model							✓			

Chapter	Figure/ Example	Theme, Activity or Enquiry	Economic	Environment/resources	Social	Place	Futures	Globalisation	Landscape	Climate/Weather	ICT/GIS	Fieldwork
23	Figure 6	Yorkshire Dales National Park: alternative futures	✓	✓	✓	✓	✓					
23	Figure 8	Climate change: investigating a possible scenario	✓	✓	✓		✓					
25	Figures 8-13	Counter-urbanisation: mystery, role play, web-page	✓	✓	✓						✓	
25	Figures 14-18	HIV/AIDS in Southern Africa: enquiry, role play, advertisement	✓		✓	✓						
26	Figure 4	Volcanoes: read, spell, know vocabulary sheet							✓			
26	Figures 10 and 11	Flooding in Bangladesh: a mystery	✓	✓	✓	✓			✓			
26	Figure 13	Earthquakes: concept map							✓			
26	Figure 15	The growth of Gateshead: a framework for enquiry			✓	✓						
27	Figure 5	Weather: categorising words related to weather								✓		
28	Figure 3	Development: Top Trumps cards	✓		✓							
28	Figure 4	Debt in Zambia: seminar cards			✓	✓						
28	Figures 7 and 8	Changes in the coal-mining industry: enquiry	✓	✓	✓							
28	Figure 9	Why do LEDCs suffer greater damage in earthquakes? Essay template	✓		✓				✓			
32	Figure 4	Regional differences in Italy: assessing learning				✓						
33	Figure 10	Should Aston Villa expand their football ground: end of unit assessment task	✓		✓							
34	Figure 4	Rainforest display: year 9 coursework task and assessment levels		✓								
35	Figure 4	How successful has the London Docklands redevelopment been? Investigation of key skills	✓		✓	✓						
37	Figure 4	Population issues in Malawi: framework for enquiry			✓	✓						

Contributors

The *Secondary Geography Handbook* could not have come into existence without the generosity of the following people, who freely gave their time, talent and experience.

Rachel Atherton is Head of Geography at Southfield Technology College, Workington.

David Balderstone is a Lecturer in Geography Education and Director of the Earth Science Centre at the Institute of Education, University of London. He previously taught geography at a comprehensive school in Bedfordshire where he was also Head of Geography.

Jeff Battersby is Dean and Head of ITT and PPD at Marjon, Plymouth, having taught geography in secondary schools for 25 years and spent 10 years training new teachers.

Mary Biddulph is a geography educator at the School of Education, University of Nottingham. She is co-editor of the *Theory into Practice* series, and a member of the *Teaching Geography* editorial board.

Dan Bloomer is a Senior Policy Officer at Cumbria County Council.

Paula Bradley-Smith teaches geography at Torquay Grammar School for Girls (Humanities Specialist Status) and teaches on the Citizenship with Humanities PGCE course at Exeter University.

Clare Brooks is Lecturer in Geography at the Institute of Education, University of London; and the GA's Website Editor.

Graham Butt is Senior Lecturer in Geography Education and Head of Curriculum and Pedagogy at the School of Education, University of Birmingham.

David Caton is Head of Geography at Shrewsbury Sixth Form College, Shropshire. He was formerly Head of Geography at Bridgnorth Endowed School, Shropshire.

Russell Chapman is Senior Tutor at University College School, London. He has authored several articles for students and teachers.

Jo Clarke has taught geography in the UK and in Africa

Bob Digby is Head of Geography at University College School, London. As well as authoring a number of school textbooks, he has considerable experience in examining and specification development.

Marielle Dow is Head of the EMAG Department at Sir John Cass Foundation School in Tower Hamlets.

Chris Durbin is the Secondary Education Adviser for English Schools Foundation, Hong Kong, China, and was formerly Inspector for Geography, Staffordshire Education Service and a BBC Education Officer.

Neil Enright is a Senior Teacher and Head of Geography Queen Elizabeth's School, Barnet, with whole-school responsibilities for assessment for learning and staff development.

Lynda Evans, formerly Head of Geography at Gosforth High School, is now Programme Manager for Teacher Education, Social Sciences and Humanities at Newcastle College.

Anne Flook teaches geography at Queen Elizabeth's School, Barnet, co-ordinates the A-level geography course and is the school's Duke of Edinburgh Award leader.

Denise Freeman is a Subject Leader for Geography in an outer London comprehensive school. She has contributed to a number of projects and publications including co-authoring a BBC geography revision guide, workbook and a website.

Emma Gobourn is a Geography Teacher at King Charles I School, Kidderminster, and writes geography textbooks.

Catherine Habgood teaches geography at Queen Elizabeth's School, Barnet, co-ordinates the GCSE Geography course and is involved in organising the school's PSHE programme.

Caroline Hare has been teaching geography for five years and is Head of Year 7 at Gravesend Grammar School for Girls in Kent.

Vicky Henn teaches geography and drama at Sir John Cass Foundation School in Tower Hamlets where she is also a professional learning leader.

Nicholas Hewlett is a Geography Teacher at Dulwich College, London.

Bob Holland is Tourism Education Consultant and Tourism Chief Examiner.

David Holmes is a part-time Geography Adviser to the Field Studies Council, and also teaches at King Edward VI College, Stourbridge.

John Hopkin is an Adviser with Birmingham local authority. He is a member of the GA's Assessment and Examinations Working Group and Chair of the Education Committee.

Neil Hornby is a Geography Teacher in a Worcestershire comprehensive and manages the integration of students with moderate learning difficulties.

Nic Howes is Head of Geography at the John Kyrle High School, and a member of the GA's AEWG.

Tom Inman is Head of Geography at Sharnbrook Upper School in Bedfordshire.

Roger Jeans is Education Manager at the Ordnance Survey, Southampton. Since 1993 he has introduced digital mapping and GIS to many teachers and PGCE students. Current editor of *Mapping News*, he is Ordnance Survey's expert in 'school GIS'.

Bob Jones has been Head of Geography at Alleynes High School, Staffordshire, for more years than anyone can remember.

Sheila King is Course Director of the Secondary PGCE at the Institute of Education, University of London, and subject leader of the MA 'Geography in Education'.

David Lambert is Chief Executive of the Geographical Association; and Research Associate at the Institute of Education, University of London.

David Leat is Director for the Centre for Learning and Teaching and a Reader in Curriculum Innovation at the University of Newcastle upon Tyne.

Janet Lewis teaches geography at Walton Priory Middle School, Staffordshire.

Rachel Lofthouse is the Geography Tutor and Director of Secondary PGCE in the Education, Communication and Language Sciences Department, University of Newcastle upon Tyne.

Fred Martin is Course Tutor for the PGCE course in Geography with ICT at Bath Spa University.

Alan Marvell is Senior Lecturer in Geography and Director for Tourism Management at Bath Spa University.

Doreen Massey is Professor of Geography at the Open University.

Michael McPartland is a part-time Geography Tutor in the School of Education, University of Durham.

Simon Miller is currently teaching geography in Adelaide, South Australia. He has co-authored the *BBC Bitesize* geography revision workbook.

Alun Morgan is currently Lecturer in Geography at the Institute of Education, University of London. He has previously worked as a secondary school teacher and teacher advisor for education for sustainable development.

John Morgan is Senior Lecturer in Education at the University of Bristol. He is author (with David Lambert) of *Geography: Teaching school subjects 11-19* (Routledge).

Adam Nichols is a Teaching and Learning Consultant with Sunderland Local Authority, formerly Lecturer in Geography Education at the University of Durham.

Eleanor Rawling was QCA Subject Adviser for Geography when her chapter for this book was written. She is now an Honorary Research Fellow at the University of Oxford and an independent educational consultant.

Margaret Roberts is Editor of *Teaching Geography*. Until September 2005, she was Senior Lecturer at the University of Sheffield where she co-ordinated the Geography PGCE course.

Keith Shuff is Head of Geography at Leigh City Technology College.

Deborah Smith is Head oF Geography at Walker technology College; an inner city comprehensive in Newcastle Upon Tyne. She was one of the contributors to 'Thinking Through Geography' (edited by David Leaf, 1998).

Diane Swift is Senior Lecturer in Continuing Professional Development at the University of Wolverhampton.

Liz Taylor co-ordinates the Geography PGCE course at Cambridge University and writes on various themes in geography education.

Linda Thompson is a Regional Adviser for the Secondary National Strategy. She is on the Assessment for Learning project team and is responsible for geography across the SNS.

Dennis Vickers teaches geography at Alleynes High School, Stone, having previously had a career as a PE teacher.

Mark Walker is a freelance Outdoor and Environmental Educator working on behalf of Plas Y Brenin, the Field Studies Council and individual clients.

Sue Warn is a Chief Examiner at A-level. She has written many textbooks on A-level geography including standard texts and specialist volumes on coral reefs, sport and tourism.

Paul Weeden is a Lecturer in Education at Birmingham University. His main research interest is assessment. He is secretary of the GA's Assessment and Examinations Working Group.

Emma Wellsted is a secondary school geography teacher. She recently completed an MA in Geography Education at the Institute of Education, University of London.

John Widdowson is a geography teacher and textbook writer. His latest series for key stage 3, *This is Geography*, is published by Hodder Murray.

Phil Wood is Subject Leader in Geography at the Deepings School, South Lincolnshire, and is also an Advanced Skills Teacher in Geography.

Section One
Geography Matters

Section one:
Geography Matters

"" Looked at objectively, it is surely perverse for a geography teacher not to be able to stimulate students, given that the essence of the subject matter is of such variety, dynamic change and interest (from Walford, R. (1998) 'Geography: the way ahead', *Teaching Geography*, 23, 2, p. 64).

"" Like most subjects, geography is difficult to teach well if you are not sure about what it offers and where it can take you (from Lambert, D. (2005) 'An axis to grind: What is worth teaching and why?', *Times Educational Supplement,* 4 March).

"" Geography is a dynamic subject; it responds to and seeks to describe and explain the world as it changes. Geography teachers are charged with the task of describing and explaining aspects of this changing world to young people they teach; being clear about the theoretical basis on which they base their teaching is the least we should expect (John Morgan, 2004, unpublished draft manuscript).

"" Place then is an important concept for geography. It overlaps with and sometimes substitutes for other key terms such as region, area and landscape but still adds a dimension of its own. Place can be studied in its own right as an identifiable segment of the Earth's surface with a particular set of identifying features. It can also be seen as a mirror of society, reflecting both the history and distributions of power of the context in which it has emerged. Place for geographers is part of the Earth's surface with a spatial identity and boundaries that separate it from other places. Some places are very clearly defined in these terms; others are more opaque (from Matthews, J. and Herbert, D. (2004) *Unifying Geography*. Abingdon: Routledge, p. 168).

Chapter 1

What's the point of learning geography?

David Balderstone

> ## Before reading this chapter consider the following questions:
>
> ■ What sense do your students make of learning geography?
>
> ■ What are the main influences on your approaches to the teaching and learning of geography?
>
> ■ When teaching the subject, in what ways do you try to connect with the personal geographies of your students and to make use of their interests and 'lived experiences'?

Some of the answers to the question posed in the title of this chapter can be found by listening to young people themselves. For example, Louise's experience of geography followed an unusual path: she dropped the subject at the age of 14, returned to it aged 16 and continued through to A-level. Her experience, which she describes in Figure 1, provided the inspiration for this chapter.

Louise's reflections provide an insight into what might motivate a young person to study, or not to study, a subject like geography. She noted an apparent lack of coherence in her experience of geography at key stage 3. Studying a series of 'fragmented' topics left Louise with no sense of where her learning in geography was going, and, moreover, it did not seem relevant to her. If significant numbers of young teenagers arrive at similar conclusions to Louise, this could help to explain the falling popularity of geography (see Westaway and Rawling, 2001; and Chapter 8). Inspection evidence supports Louise's observations, as noted by the Chief Inspector for Schools, David Bell:

> ❝ *in many schools, the key stage 3 curriculum is not made sufficiently relevant or stimulating to capture students' interest and persuade them to continue their learning at examination level* (2005, p. 13).

Reinvigorating geography

But it doesn't have to be this way. When trainee teachers first encounter the national curriculum I ask them to think of the aspect or experience of geography that excited or stimulated them most. After studying the key stage 3 programme of study, they consider

What's the point?' was my reaction to taking geography at GCSE level when the idea was suggested to me at options time. As far as I could see, there were far more interesting things to be learnt than how the odd rock formation came about, or where various volcanoes were. It all seemed so, well, fragmented, and for that reason I chose history instead: there was, after all, a story in history!

All too soon it was yet again time to choose my subject options, but this time for A-level. Now, I had to think about it carefully. A-levels are important exams, and one must choose subjects that are enjoyable and within one's capabilities. I chose geography at the very last minute because I realised on results day that perhaps history wasn't my thing because I hadn't done as well as I'd hoped. I could have done French, but I was already doing German and I didn't want two languages at A-level. So geography seemed to fill the gap. It was a general subject in which I did not have to learn equations and names of famous prime ministers. I must admit, though, that I was half expecting to be bored a lot of the time. But wait!

Geography, it turned out, was an interesting subject, partly because it is constantly changing. Those rock formations that I had hastily pushed aside were actually quite important to understand and the volcanoes I had never thought much about before caused havoc in the lives of those people that lived nearby. Geography is an incredibly broad subject encompassing social, political, environmental and economic aspects of what is happening in the world today. It has taught me to understand that we can be affected by events all over the world; for example, El Nino doesn't just affect the weather off the coasts of Peru and Australia, but it has in the past caused freak weather in most continents. Of course, geography is not just about weather, as I have already said. During the A-level course I also learnt about development and disparity in Los Angeles (the 'ecology of fear'), about wilderness areas and the threats towards them and (maybe most importantly) about poverty, how it comes about and how people try to deal with it.

In the last two years, I have learnt a lot about the world we live in and how it is changing, sometimes for better and other times for worse. Geography has taught me so much more than my other subjects, about the world and my future in it.

Figure 1 | *Louise's experience of geography at school.*

whether it provides possibilities for teaching young people about their 'favourite' piece of geography. In over ten years, I have yet to hear a negative reply. Yet, within a few weeks of working in key stage 3 classrooms, many trainees complain that the geography they are expected to teach to young teenagers does not reflect the exciting vision they had on entering the profession. Instead, they find themselves teaching, for example, about Burgess and Hoyt's land-use models to 12- and 13-year-olds. This results from the 'perceived need for teachers to "cover" a kind of authorised version of the geography curriculum' (Lambert, 2004, p. 79). The emphasis is on subject content and getting students to accumulate knowledge, which, according to Bell (2005), may account for geography's lack of 'relevance and appeal' at key stage 3.

For students to experience a worthwhile, relevant and enjoyable school geography, the teaching they receive should aim to achieve the following:

- Connect with students' 'lived experiences'
- Help students how to 'think geographically' about the world through studying real places
- Develop the 'geographical imagination' through a student-centred approach
- Relate learning to real-world contexts, such as the world of work
- Emphasise the importance and significance of effective communication, e.g. through the use of ICT.

Connecting with students' lived experiences

First on my agenda for reinvigorating geography is the need for teachers to find ways of ensuring that 'school geography' draws upon and reflects the 'lived experience' of young people. But who are these young people, and what are their interests, aspirations and needs? Herein lies the first, and probably one of the biggest challenges facing us as geography teachers, because meeting the interests of young people is far more difficult than it sounds.

In the past, curriculum development projects (e.g. GYSL, 16-19 Geography – see Rawling, 2001) in geography, and the 2004 Pilot GCSE, were prompted by concerns that school geography 'may not be meeting the needs of young people today or current thinking in geography'. It could be argued that school geography has failed to keep up with social and cultural change, and indeed developments in the wider discipline, though this problem is not confined to geography (see, for example, Buckingham, 2003).

So what are the perceptions and reflections of young people on their learning through geography? In their study of students' experiences of learning geography at key stage 3, Adey and Biddulph concluded that the teaching and learning activities employed were 'far more influential than subject content per se in shaping students' attitudes' (2001). A lack of variety limited students' enjoyment of geography, and tasks that employed extended periods of passive listening, copying or transforming information were criticised for reducing learning to 'a "seek and find mission" that should be completed as soon as possible, thereby resulting in surface learning' (Adey and Biddulph, 2001). This accords with the view of one 15-year-old who pleaded for change in a national newspaper:

> *Experiments that you know the answer to before starting; murdering books by over-analysis – and that's just Wednesday morning. That's right folks, Charles Clarke [the then Secretary of State for Education] is not wrong when he says school is no longer stimulating, [it] sucks! It is obsessed with results and league tables and what can be put on the front of the latest, perfectly photographed prospectus. Lessons are taken over by the textbook and his [sic] fat sidekick the worksheet whose influence has stifled creativity to the point where it exists only in non-academic subjects* (Greene, 2004, p. 3).

Adey and Biddulph (2001) found that more challenging tasks such as decision-making exercises were 'unanimously popular' as they were perceived to have more of a purpose and provided opportunities to work with a range of sources, undertake independent and group research and express opinions which had to be justified. Students enjoyed writing that resulted from their own research or, in shared activities, from peer discussion (see also Lord and Harland, 2000).

In a subsequent study of students' perceptions of geography at GCSE, Biddulph and Adey (2003) noted how the *purpose* of studying geography had not progressed significantly for many students since year 9. Only those who had a clear sense of their own future aspirations, and therefore an understanding of what they needed to achieve academically, could articulate the usefulness of geography to their own lives. Encouragingly, some interviewees were aware of the subject's wider contribution and valued the opportunities provided to gain a broader perspective on a range of social and cultural issues (see Figure 1). Using geographical concepts and terminology to express and justify opinions was viewed as both challenging stimulating. Students felt geography was more relevant to them when what they were studying was topical. They also valued investigative work, particularly fieldwork, group work and discussion at GCSE.

These students also enjoyed learning new aspects of geography. Interestingly, their views about progression contrasted sharply with those of their teachers. Studying the same issues, case studies and places at different levels of detail at different key stages apparently does not bring about the deeper levels of conceptual understanding envisaged by some educationists. Students find it repetitive and de-motivating. The emphasis of many examinations in geography on learning 'case studies' may have contributed to students' perception of the subject as being fragmented in nature. What they value more is the opportunity to broaden their horizons and gain a sense of the bigger picture because this will enable them to apply their learning in geography to a range of different situations and to tackle the complexity involved in understanding many concepts and processes or in solving problems.

Exploring the 'residuals' from adults' experiences of geography at school (i.e. what *remains* after leaving school) reinforces these observations and chimes with both Louise's reflections (Figure 1) and the perceptions of students outlined above. It can provide helpful insights into how we can try to make geography feel more relevant to young people (Durbin, 2004).

There are clear messages here about connecting what students are learning through geography to real-world situations. The need to provide challenging learning experiences and the value of fieldwork are highlighted, as are the dangers of delivering an 'issues-dominated' geography curriculum which paints an overly bleak and problematic view of the world. As a university student living in a vibrant Moss Side, Manchester, my experiences of life in the 'inner city' contrasted sharply with that in school geography textbooks. Although my experience was partial, it was not one acknowledged in textbooks I encountered as a teacher.

There is a need for geography in schools to 'connect' with such 'lived experience'. This may involve consulting students at key points in their learning, focused evaluation of specific curriculum units, or by exploiting the many opportunities for gaining feedback through the frequent use of formative assessment strategies in the classroom. Negotiated styles of enquiry where students, with support from the teacher, determine the focus of their geographical enquiry, devise the questions to be investigated, select relevant data, methods of analysis and interpretation, can empower students to take more ownership of their learning and to use a more extensive range of skills (Roberts, 2003).

Ensuring that school geography connects with and draws upon the lived experience of young people is to adopt a 'student-centred approach'. Because of their rather abstract and complex nature, introducing specific geographical concepts to young people can be challenging. Concepts like sustainability, for instance, may also appear disconnected from students' own lived experience. Daniel Raven-Ellison (2004) has developed a creative way of engaging young teenagers with sustainability through an enquiry into their own 'ecological footprints' at a range of scales.

Students begin by researching, calculating and mapping *their* individual ecological footprint. These ecological footprints are then compared with those of people in a range of countries, providing opportunities to use a variety of cross-curricular or generic skills including numeracy and reasoning. The students are encouraged to use their findings to speculate about how big an 'ecologically sustainable footprint' might be.

Next, students develop an action plan to attempt to reduce the size and impact of their ecological footprint, put their plan into action and, finally, evaluate their ability to reduce it (Figure 2). This approach empowers the students to take actions and monitor their results within a relatively short period of time. They are able to explore some of the links between environmental, social, political and economic aspects of changing consumption habits. The investigation provides opportunities for students to explore a range of concepts relating to education for sustainable development (Figure 3) and to use a range of skills in tackling real-life issues. Above all, they are using their own lived experience to develop their understanding of these concepts, which adds both motivation and meaning.

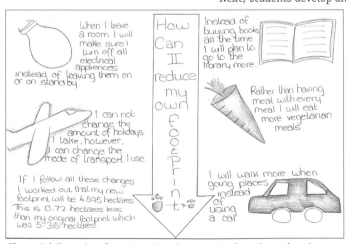

Figure 2 | *Examples of year 9 students' sustainable footprint action plans.*
Source: Daniel Raven Ellison

Concept	Description
Interdependence	Being aware of the global context within which trade, industry and consumption patterns operate
Citizenship and stewardship	Knowing how decisions about social, economic and environmental issues are made; that they have an impact on each other; and how they can be influenced locally and nationally through direct or indirect participation
Needs and rights of future generations	Being able to assess the sustainability of their own lifestyle
Diversity	Appreciating the nature of the changes that have affected economic, cultural and biological diversity in their locality over past generations
Quality of life	Understanding the difference between quality of life and standard of living
Sustainable change	Understanding the idea of sustainable consumption at individual and national levels
Uncertainty and precaution	Knowing how different cultures and belief systems influence how the environment and resources are viewed

Figure 3 | *Key concepts relating to education for sustainable development at key stage 3.*

Two significant features of this scheme of work help to reinforce the student-centred nature of the learning experience. First, the year 9 students have opportunities to use digital video technology to produce video journals of their investigations of ecological footprints. Second, they are also given a real purpose and audience for their work, i.e. they teach younger students about the sustainable use of resources. Peer teaching is a powerful learning strategy – in order to teach something, you have to understand it. This peer teaching enhances the use of formative assessment and, in having to articulate their understanding, students develop their use of language.

Daniel's approach to learning about sustainability displays the characteristics of 'purposeful creative enquiry' in geography (Durbin, 2003) in which young people are given responsibility for their learning, a motivating stimulus, the need to produce a creative response that demonstrates their understanding and skills, with an authentic (other public) audience. It clearly provided a memorable learning experience for these students.

Other examples of stimulating activities can be found throughout this book. For example, for a homework activity Denise Freeman and Simon Miller draw upon the fact that many young people will travel independently – they describe how students 'embark' on a gap year between key stage 3 and GCSE (see Chapter 21, pages 259-261).

Young people's cultures and 'thinking geographically'

There is substantial interest in the geographies of children and young people (for instance, see Skelton and Valentine, 1998; Holloway and Valentine, 2000). What this reminds us above all is that young people are not a homogenous group: the plurality of youth culture is evidenced by the fact that young people do not all listen to the same music, watch the same films or enjoy the same activities.

Nevertheless, the popular cultural experiences of young people provides opportunities for developing different approaches to school geography that might be helpful in increasing the perceived relevance of geography and engaging for these young people. In recent years, the geography of sport, fashion and music have appeared in the geography curriculum for this reason. Figure 4 shows one teacher's approach to using popular youth culture and consumption to develop stimulating and relevant geographical enquiries for 14-16 year olds (see also Pilot GCSE webpages on the unit 'People and consumption'). In developing these enquiries, Denise Freeman placed emphasis on the need to use authentic voices of young people in the resources students study. In doing so, she used a number of important principles to guide the selection and design of these resources:

■ Does the resource provide a plurality of voices?
■ Does the resource resist or expose stereotypes of young people?
■ Does the resource resist assumptions about young people?
■ Does the resource include commentaries and ideas from young people?

John Morgan (2003) argues that if school geography is to connect with the experiences of young people, it must provide them with opportunities to question cultural representations. John describes how the film *The Full Monty* provides opportunities for

Pets as an environmental concern

Students may be asked to assess the environmental impacts of keeping pets.

Why do they keep or not keep pets? How does the desire to keep some pets create conflict, e.g. parrots?

Possible links to exotic celebrity pets!

How do students use resources?

Students may consider their use of resources over time and space:

When do they use public/private transport systems?

How far do they go?

How much energy do **they** use?

What do **they** use electricity for?

What power **their** homes?

Where does this power come from?

Thinking about careers and futures

The students work as a class to gather data about their career aspirations and those of other students in other schools (nationally and internationally) using e-mail links.

Where do these careers fit into the classification of industry?

Students consider the role of family expectations, wealth, education and local trends in career choice, e.g. in some places some people may be expected to continue the family business, and in others young people may resist this expectation.

Why are people resisting these careers? What impact is it having on employment patterns?

Links to work on geographical futures.

i. changing distribution of economic activity and its impact, including:

types and classifications of economic activity

the geographical distribution of one or more economic activities [for example, farming, tourism]

how and why the distribution has changed and is changing [for example, the impact of new technologies], and the effects of such changes

j. environmental issues, including:

how conflicting demands on an environment arise

how and why attempts are made to plan and manage environments

effects of environmental planning and management on people, places and environment [for example, managing coastal retreat, building a reservoir]

k. resource issues, including:

the sources and supply of a resource

The mobile phone industry

How many students own a mobile phone?

Why do they own a phone? (Safety, fashion commodity, expectation, technological application, e.g. web access, peer pressure, text messaging.)

Where were their phones made?

How do young people in the country of production regard mobile phones?

Links to the geography of crime and fear: investigation of attacks on young people outside schools for their phone.

Globalisation links

Local development and conflict

Students identify a local development, either one that is being planned or has taken place.

The issue could be selected because it pleased or annoyed them:

Was it a good thing for the area and for them (e.g. a new shopping centre or cinema)?

Is it something that they are annoyed about (e.g. the loss of a leisure space for flats)?

The issue should be something relevant to them. Investigation of the issue can then lead t analysis of the wider interest groups involved.

Using films or soaps to explore environmental issues and conflict

Working in groups, students are asked to identify a film or television programme that has represented an issue of environmental conflict (real or fictional). Students map the issue. What is the issue? Where does it affect? Who is involved? What do different people think about the issue? Students may present the issue, using clips from the film or programme. Links can then be made to a local or national issue and the student analyse it using the skills learned in the previous example.

Alternatively, students may vote on one issue to be studied by the whole class. Either way the students are active in planning the learning process.

This avoids the problem of making assumptions about the cultural texts that interest students. Not all students watch soaps and students don't all watch the same films.

Figure 4 | *Using young people and their popular culture in geography at key stage 3.*

reflecting developments in the subject, particularly drawing upon cultural geography to look at:

- the 'invisible' forces that are shaping places like Sheffield,
- how places are represented in films,
- what people who live there may feel about these representations,
- the use of metaphors of 'stripping' in relation to the 'stripped' nature of the landscapes of industrialisation,
- gendered roles (the 'craft skills' of men no longer needed), and
- representations of 'working class communities' whose passing is being mourned, defined as being a 'community of men'.

(Morgan, 2003, p. 223).

Morgan's discussion highlights the value for teachers of exploring cultural geography in order to enrich school geography.

The attention given to developing students' thinking skills has brought a welcome focus on pedagogy (the art and science of teaching). However, is enough consideration being given to what students are learning in geography in some of these lessons? Sometimes the 'pedagogic adventure' has appeared to dominate (Lambert, 2005) at the expense of worthwhile geographical understanding. Questions about what it might mean to think geographically may therefore help geography teachers to develop students' higher order cognitive skills and conceptual understanding in the subject.

Developing students' geographical imaginations

In Chapter 4 Doreen Massey explores what it means to *think geographically* in ways that bring to the fore questions of space, place and nature. It is through our *geographical imagination* that we develop our sense of place and a sense of the global nature of places in which we live. As Allen and Massey emphasise: 'How we imagine the world to be, and how we represent it to others lie at the heart of geography' (1995). The plurality of geographies inside young people's minds is shaped by their direct and indirect experiences as well as by their cultural attitudes and values. The idea of the *geographical imagination* can stimulate creative ways of 'thinking geographically' about many parts of the subject and not just the cultural. In exploring the fear and wonder of mountain environments, Robert MacFarlane provides inspiring ways of stimulating students' interest in aspects of physical geography. In *Mountains of the Mind* MacFarlane argues that:

> *What we call a mountain is thus in fact a collaboration of the physical forms of the world with the imaginations of humans – a mountain of the mind. And the way people behave towards mountains has little or nothing to do with the actual objects of rock and ice themselves (2004).*

Given the spectacular scenery created by glaciers, it is surprising that glaciation is often viewed as a 'dry' topic. Dee Sandhu has employed the 'mountains of the mind' idea in order to stimulate student interest in glaciated environments. Dee screened a clip from *The Lord of the Rings* to show how one film director represented a mountain environment (Figure 5). After exploring how

Figure 5 | *The dramatic landscape of New Zealand provided the backdrop for the film trilogy* The Lord of the Rings. *Photo: ©Simon Scoones.*

the director might have used the dramatic scale and shape of a glaciated landscape to capture the imagination, students used *their* geographical imagination to explore their own experiences and views of mountain environments. This approach certainly captured the students' interest and provided an effective way into studying the processes that create such landscapes. But perhaps as important is the belief that young people growing up cannot possibly value the physical environment until and unless they have been given the chance to experience awe, wonder and even fear of the natural world.

Similarly, Peter Knight (2005) demonstrates how the study of glaciers can be used to encourage students to recognise the linkages both between global systems and local conditions and between past environments and present day landscapes. He points out how the internet can provide students with access to a range of resources for studying glaciers and glacial landscapes (see Knight, 2005).

Real places

A major challenge for teachers of geography is to stimulate young people's interest in contemporary issues and help them to develop a critical understanding of the world in which they live. As Lambert stresses, 'geography taught well can help people make sense of the world' and studying change in specific places is a 'supreme educational contribution of geography' (2004, p. 84). It could be well worth asking some pointed questions about real places and relevance in the geography curriculum. For example, when studying changes in global economic activity, is the industrial growth of China overlooked in favour of locations for manufacturing industry that are part of our history, rather than the present or future? Why is it that young people tend not to study the places where many significant contemporary issues today are being played out? Do specific areas of the world seem to be missing from school geography? – such as the Middle East, for example, which is constantly in the news. Yet, trying to locate information on the geography of this region – physical, environmental, economic, political, social or cultural – in the resources available to geography teachers is difficult. How can we help young people to make sense of the world if they do not have opportunities to study these issues and these places?

When Figure 6 was shown to students from diverse backgrounds in a school in inner London, it generated enthusiastic discussion. The students asked a range of questions that could form the basis of a geographical enquiry. For example:

■ Who is Samia?
■ Where does she live?
■ Why can't she find Palestine on a map?
■ Where is Palestine?
■ Who might have different views to Samia?

Figure 6 | *An advertising billboard at the side of a highway into Amman, Jordan, 2002. Photo: ©Tony Escritt.*

These students clearly wanted to know more about the Middle East, its geography (and its history) so that they could develop more informed insights into what is happening there. Some were concerned that they knew so little about Iraq and its surrounding region – which has dominated the media during 2005.

'Thinking geographically' might help them to make some sense of the region where this conflict was taking place. Young people need to learn about the geography of the Middle East (and the ways in which it is portrayed in the media) if they are to critically formulate, discuss and express their views. So why is such content not found more frequently in geography classrooms? After all, geography teachers often *claim* that it is through the study of controversial issues that geography contributes to the development of political literacy.

This example also demonstrates how conflicts take place in a spatial context and at a variety of scales. They are often very place specific. They indicate how geopolitical boundaries are often the source of conflicts, and changes in geographical conditions such as population and resources can be the source of great tension. In these ways it is clear to see that thinking geographically is a pre-requisite to understanding. If we truly believe that one of the significant contributions geography makes to a young person's education is the development of skills of critical enquiry, then we cannot close our classroom doors to the complex and controversial issues in the world.

Learning geography for the 'real' world

To make learning through geography stimulating and worthwhile there is a need to connect what is being learnt with real contexts. A former student who now works in the property development division of a major logistics company stated how geography was proving to be the most useful of his school subjects. He was able to articulate clearly the value of the problem-solving skills he had developed, as well as other geographical understanding and skills, in his current employment. The interpretation of the

Figure 7 | *'Living Futures: my home': (a) introduction to Eva's housing scenario, and (b) checklist for evaluating each housing scenario. Source: CABE Education website.*

(a)   *(b)*

Area of assessment	Criteria
Social Issues	Can people afford the housing? Does the housing create a sense of place or community? Does the housing meet the needs of a wide range of people? Will crime be a problem?
Technological Issues	Does the housing offer flexibility of lifestyle? Does the housing provide the technology for home working? Does the housing use efficient construction processes?
Economic Issues	Is the housing situated near places of employment? Has affordable housing been built alongside private homes? Does the housing address regional issues like the 'north-south divide'?
Environmental Issues	Is the housing energy efficient and sustainable? How will the housing cope with climate change? How well does the housing blend in with the environment; are there open areas and community facilities? Is public transport access built in to the design, or does the car still rule?
Political Issues	Does the housing meet the demand for new homes in different parts of the country? Do local authorities and local people have a say in the housing developments? Has NIMBYism been tackled? Is there community involvement in the design process?

geographic information, particularly that provided by geographical information systems (GIS), were skills that he could identify in the decision-making exercises he tackled through GCSE and A-level.

However, many students are not aware of the relevance of their geographical studies to their own aspirations for the future. One teenager who had ambitions to become an architect was surprised when I questioned his decision not to study geography at GCSE. He could only see the relevance of design and technology skills to his chosen profession, and argued that geography had not provided him with opportunities to recognise the application of specific skills and understanding. What a shame! He might well have found a visit to 'Housing Futures' insightful. Figures 7a and 7b shows an example of how the geography young people learn might be applied to real situations through 'Living Futures: My home'. This online decision-making activity, developed by the Commission for Architecture and the Built Environment (CABE), helps 11-14 year-olds to investigate visions of housing in 2003. It provides opportunities to learn about a range of geographical concepts associated with population distribution, settlement, environmental change and its impacts, and sustainability in relation to real issues affecting their futures (see also 'Where will I live?' webpages). Students investigate and evaluate six scenarios for future housing, considering what it might be like to live in the places envisioned in these scenarios.

Students can use the site to undertake wider research into the design, location and development of housing in the future with information provided about a variety of sustainable urban and rural housing developments as part of an online enquiry. Such enquiries can be enhanced through collaboration with art and design (creativity and graphic design skills), citizenship (participation and responsible action) and English (audience centred writing, speaking and listening). They also provide opportunities for involving planners, architects, local councillors and parents in order to introduce other relevant real world perspectives. Through this 'purposeful creative enquiry' students can respond to relevant issues, which they can then present to an appropriate audience in their own community.

It is widely acknowledged that geographers are amongst the most employable graduates. They combine an enormous breadth of knowledge with a wide range of skills and are therefore adaptable and well prepared for further learning. But the real strength of geography in education is the way it can help prepare people with the intellectual skills including decision making and problem solving, for sustainable future living (as Alan Morgan discusses in Chapter 23).

Exploiting the 'c' in ICT

This leads me to my final way of breathing new life into school geography – the need to use information communications technology (ICT) in purposeful and meaningful ways, which can be done by exploiting the opportunities for students to 'communicate' with others about their learning. Providing authentic audiences and purposes for students' learning improves their motivation and the opportunities for them to develop creative responses – essential if they are to achieve higher standards in geography and in the use of core skills of literacy, numeracy and ICT.

Figure 8 indicates how Olivia Stanton employed e-mail in an enquiry into the impacts of HIV/Aids in Uganda. Working in small groups, year 9 students wrote three questions to ask Olivia's contact in Uganda. Each student was required to summarise the response to one question and then 'teach' this to other students in the group who then produced a spider diagram to represent their understanding of these responses.

The message here is that ICT can be utilised to provide stimulating learning experiences for students, and the good news is that the range of digital media available

Write the answers to the following questions on your spider diagram:
- How is HIV transmitted?
- What is the difference between HIV and AIDS?
- Is there a cure for HIV/AIDS?
- How does it impact a family if the father has died from HIV and the mother is ill?
  - Work and income
  - Growing food
  - School fees
  - Children's future
  - Medicines

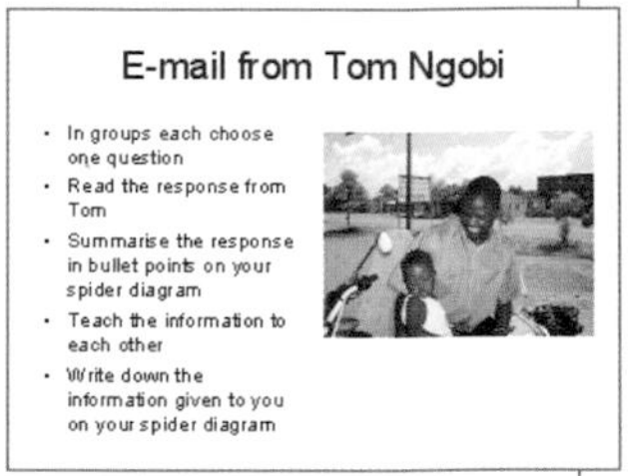

From: Tom Ngobi
Sent: 24 January 2005 15:31:35
To Miss Stanton
Subject: Re: my students

Hi Miss Stanton,

Here are the answers to your questions:

Q1: What percentage of people in our area have HIV/AIDS?
Answer: 17-22%. Majority of whom are women. This is so because women are more keen on going for HIV tests.

Q2: Why do so many people in Uganda have HIV?
Answer: There are several reasons but the most common ones are:
(a) Ignorance; most people in Uganda are illiterate and do not have access to correct information about the transmission and effects of HIV/AIDS apart from knowing that it is spread through sexual intercourse and the end result is death, (b) Bad cultural beliefs like female mutilation, circumcision of male, and body piercing using the same sharp object from one person to another, (c) Poverty; this leads to prostitution/commercial sex especially in urban areas, (d) Lack of self esteem especially amongst female youth seeking employment. They give to their would be bosses for possible chances, (e) Lack of information dissemination facilities to the grass roots/local people. (f) Not enough testing so people don't know they have it and keep spreading it.

Q3: What is like to live with HIV?
Answer: It is very bad. The infected person lives in perpetual fear throughout. It is very scary for mums and dads who worry about what will happen to their children when they die. There are no social services in Uganda to look after orphans. Many people cannot work because they are ill and so have no money and their children cannot go to school. They have to be very careful to stay healthy and not get diseases like malaria which they can die from. People with HIV are often ashamed of their illness and think they are a bad person. This isn't true but they feel really bad about it.

Q4: How do people cope?
Answer: HIV positive people cope by forming themselves into positive people groups popularly known as PHAS. Whilst there, they are assisted in many ways, e.g. they get free counselling, free treatment, at times they get free food and of late the central government is helping to educate the orphans, care for the AIDS patients, support the elderly guardians.

It is therefore important for one to test so that he/she can be assisted.

PHAS need love, care, protection, support and continuous counselling to cope. In Uganda Community Based Organisations, Local NGOS and International NGOS and the Central government are doing a good job to help PHAS cope. People need to eat healthy food, and stop themselves getting malaria and other diseases.

E-mail from Tom Ngobi
- In groups each choose one question
- Read the response from Tom
- Summarise the response in bullet points on your spider diagram
- Teach the information to each other
- Write down the information given to you on your spider diagram

Figure 8 | *Using e-mail to investigate the impacts of HIV/AIDS in Uganda. Source: Olivia Stanton, Fortismere School.*

will continue to expand. Already, the globe is available in astonishing detail via Google Earth Globe at almost zero cost. Acquiring the skills and strategies needed to develop our students' media literacy and how to handle such information, will probably be greater than the demands on our technical skills (see Chapter 19). However, this is a challenge we will need to overcome if we are to ensure that 'thinking geographically' using ICT becomes a key feature of learning for young people.

Summary

This chapter provides a framework within which geography teachers might begin to reflect on what makes learning through geography worthwhile for young people. The intention has been to raise some important questions and suggest ways in which geography teachers might respond creatively to the challenges. There are many reasons why curricula and the learning experience of young people can stagnate, but, as this chapter demonstrates, I frequently encounter innovative geography teachers finding creative ways of stimulating students' learning.

Nevertheless, this chapter has merely scratched the surface of the debate. Over the years, I have had the good fortune to observe and share the experience of young people from a diverse range of backgrounds (ethnically, socially and culturally) learning geography in a large number of schools across London, the south east of England and beyond. Increasingly, we need to develop a far more 'inclusive' geography education for young people if we are to meet the needs of our diverse student population. We need to 'infuse' our lessons with more student-centred perspectives on the subject that acknowledge difference and diversity as well as common experiences, and provide a space for young people to reference and explore their lived experience within their learning through geography.

What we decide to teach and how we design the learning experience of young people through geography is important. Geography turned out to be a worthwhile subject for Louise because 'it is constantly changing' and because it helped her to make sense of what is happening in the world today. The final word in this discussion belongs to a young person taught by one of the geography teachers described earlier.

> *Thanks for being my geography teacher! Geography has been a revelation for me. Your lessons have inspired me. Not just some lessons, but every lesson! Your geography lessons have done so much to open eyes, to what the world is like, and what it could be like. I will miss my geography lessons with you. Whatever you do, please keep on opening eyes in your lessons!*

Implications for practice

(a) Engage with the wider subject discipline and continue to develop your subject expertise.

Stimulate your own mind to 'think geographically'. Maintain a dynamic approach to the selection of subject content and pedagogy. What we teach in geography is important, so consider what is worthwhile for young people to learn through geography. Find time to engage with current thinking in the subject discipline through reading and participation in subject conferences. This will enable you to bring new perspectives on the subject into the geography curriculum. We are all learners, teachers and students alike!

(b) Value and exploit students' own 'lived experiences' when planning for learning through geography.

Student voices need to be heard and to influence the way in which geography develops as a subject in schools. Formative assessment provides feedback about students' experiences of geography and powerful learning strategies such as peer teaching can help to raise student achievement. Where possible, develop creative ways of engaging students with geography through their own 'lived experiences' and places they encounter, particularly through their popular cultural experiences. Ensure that authentic voices of young people are present in the resources used in geographical enquires.

(c) Stimulate students' interest in real issues in the world today.

Ensure that school geography reflects the changing landscape and issues of the day. Broaden the global coverage of the geography curriculum to provide students with a geographical framework within which to understand and interpret global patterns, processes and events. Developing a sense of place and an understanding of the geographical dimensions of issues helps students to develop skills of critical enquiry. Do not close the classroom door to the complex and controversial issues in the world today.

(d) Apply what students learn in geography to real world situations.

Make the value of the skills and understanding they are developing explicit. Students need to see the broader relevance and application of these skills and understanding to provide a creative purpose for what they are learning through geography. This can often be achieved through problem-solving and decision-making activities in which their understanding and skills can be used to tackle real questions, issues and problems.

(e) Use ICT in meaningful and purposeful ways to enhance geographical enquiry.

Exploit opportunities for students to 'communicate' with others about their learning through geography. This can provide them with real audiences and a real purpose for their learning, as well as opportunities to produce creative responses to real questions and problems. Using authentic personal accounts provides students with stimulating learning resources.

Related publications from the Geographical Association:

- Hall, T. (forthcoming) *Changing Geography: Everyday geographies*.
- Knight, P.G. (2005) (see below).
- Rawling, E. (2001) (see below).
- Roberts, M. (2003) (see below).

References

Print

Adey, K. and Biddulph, M. (2001) 'The influence of pupil perception on subject choice at 14+ in history and geography', *Educational Studies,* 27, 4, pp. 439-50.

Allen, J. and Massey, D. (1995) *Geographical Worlds.* Milton Keynes: The Open University

Bell, D. (2005) 'The value and importance of geography', *Teaching Geography,* 30, 1, pp. 12-13.

Biddulph, M. and Adey, K. (2003) 'Perceptions vs. reality pupils' experiences of learning history and geography at KS4', *Curriculum Journal,* 14, 3.

Buckingham, D. (2003) *Media Education: Literacy, learning and contemporary culture.* Cambridge: Polity Press.

Durbin, C. (2003) 'Creativity – criticism and challenge in geography', *Teaching Geography,* 28, 2, pp. 64-9.

Durbin, C. (2004) 'The good and the bad in geography', *Teaching Geography,* 29, 2 pp. 82-3.

Greene, T. (2004) 'School sucks. The reason? Textbooks', *The Independent Education,* 4 March, p. 3.

Holloway, S. and Valentine, G. (2000) *Children's Geographies: Living, playing, learning.* London: Routledge.

Knight, P.G. (2005) *Changing Geography: Glaciers and glacial landscapes* (series editor: Janet Speake). Sheffield: Geographical Association.

Lambert, D. (2004) 'Geography' in White, J. (ed) *Rethinking the School Curriculum: Values, aims and purposes.* London: Routledge Falmer.

Lambert, D. (2005) 'An axis to grind', *Times Educational Supplement,* 4 March.

Lambert, D. and Balderstone, D. (2000) *Learning to Teach Geography in the Secondary School.* London: Routledge Falmer.

Lord, P. and Harland, J. (2000) 'Pupils' experiences and perspectives of the national curriculum', *Research Review.* Windsor: NFER

MacFarlane, R. (2004) *Mountains of the Mind: A history of a fascination.* London: Granta.

Morgan, J, (2003) 'Cultural studies goes to school', *Geography,* 88, 3, pp. 217-24.

Raven-Ellison, D. (2004) 'Ecological footprints', unit 25. London: QCA.

Rawling, E. (2001) *Changing the Subject: The impact of national policy on school geography 1980-2000.* Sheffield: Geographical Association.

Roberts, M. (2003) *Learning through Enquiry: Making sense of geography in the key stage 3 classroom.* Sheffield: Geographical Association.

Skelton, T. and Valentine, G. (1998) *Cool Places: Geographies of youth cultures.* London: Routledge.

Westaway, J. and Rawling, E. (2001) 'The rise and falls of geography', *Teaching Geography,* 26, 3, pp. 108-10.

Electronic

CABE – www.cabe-education.org.uk

Power of Geography webpages – www.geography.org.uk/news/powerofgeography/

Pilot GCSE pages – www.geography.org.uk/pilotgcse

Where will I live? – www.geography.org.uk/projects/wherewillilive/

Chapter 2

what's the point of teaching geography?

David Lambert

Before reading this chapter consider the following questions:

- ■ Why do significant numbers of students have difficulty in seeing the point of geography?

- ■ Can school geography contribute to citizenship education at a deeper level than providing a description of the world and basic locational knowledge (important though these aspects are)?

- ■ What is the moral purpose of geography education?

- ■ How can school geography help 'frame' students' thinking about complex and controversial issues?

What's the point of studying geography?

To the 15-year-old having chosen to study geography, the question 'What's the point of studying geography?' may never arise. It is perhaps self-evident that geography is concerned with helping people make sense of the world. It achieves this partly through informing us about the world. Geography is useful in this sense, and an essential component of becoming an 'informed citizen'. The point of studying geography is clear.

On the other hand, I have always been slightly anxious about the somewhat complacent, and restricted, concept of geography that rests its case on the subject's 'obvious' utility – often summed up by popular slogans such as 'Geography is where it's at' or 'Geography is everywhere' and 'You know where you are with geography'. Others, such as 'Geography puts the knowing into seeing' attempt to suggest a deeper concept of the subject, but still need to be taken with a pinch of salt. Indeed, in his introductory discussion of geography and ethics, James Proctor (1999) cites the child in *The Little Prince* (de Saint-Exupéry, 1943) who discovers painfully that the things he cares most about (symbolised by a flower) mean nothing to adults – and geographers in particular – as they become hooked on what they believe to be 'matters of consequence'.

I grew up, as perhaps did many readers, with a sense of geography as one subject most to be avoided. 'A geographer', the man of the sixth planet explained to the Little Prince, 'is a scholar who knows the location of all the seas, rivers, towns, mountains, and deserts,' ... This is not the subject matter most of us would consider to be extremely compelling, intellectually, morally, or otherwise, and thank goodness there is more to say from the perspective of geography than that location counts (Proctor, 1999, p. 1).

This chapter provides a discussion of school geography in relation to the creation of an informed citizenry – and, to alter slightly Proctor's statement, thank goodness there is more to say from the perspective of school geography than that location counts! The chapter also urges you to clarify for yourself the educational purposes served by learning and teaching geography.

In what follows, the concept of citizenship education is explored and the role that geography can play in promoting an informed citizenship. I do not separate citizenship education from moral education; the former is a subset of the latter and if we want to clarify the role of geography in citizenship education we cannot avoid moral and ethical questions. Arising from such a perspective are questions concerning the *contents* of school geography (as the Little Prince found, much to his frustration), its *pedagogy* and the *assessment* of children's learning. This is a large agenda, which really boils down to a discussion about what influences the content of that 'school subject' called geography. In other words, I shall be concerned with a discussion of school geography from the point of view of its apparent moral purpose. Without this, it is very hard say what is 'the point' of studying geography.

A note about the 'UK space': geography and identities

The UK space may be perceived from the outside to be a given political entity on the world map. Whether for the Eurovision Song Contest or for the Olympic Games, the component countries of the United Kingdom present themselves as one. This is not so in the case of the (association) football World Cup, however. In this case, England, Wales, Scotland and Northern Ireland all compete separately and with each other, and of course with the Republic of Ireland, the other fully independent nation within the British Isles. In rugby, England, Scotland, Wales and Ireland compete internationally ... but *also* unite to compete as the British and Irish Lions. This is confusing in terms of 'national identities' and is likely to become even more so as a consequence of political devolution for Northern Ireland, Scotland and Wales. These measures are taking place within the context of Britain's membership of the European Union which itself is having complex impacts on national and regional identities and has recently expanded its membership substantially.

Thus, human beings have multiple identities. Some of these are inextricably tied up with territory, which links identity to concepts of citizenry. This is partly because of the tendency to describe citizenship in exclusive terms - that is by defining citizenry partly as a spatial belonging by excluding outsiders or 'others'. Geography lessons, surprisingly, do not explore such questions in as much depth as they perhaps could (but see Morgan and Lambert, 2003). For example, 'Where is the eastern edge of the continent of Europe?' and 'Does it coincide with the border of the enlarged European Union?' are tricky questions and can lead on to others that can challenge our view of the world which is inevitably shaped to some degree by preconceptions and prejudices arising from unexamined assumptions and use of language. Why, for example, is Europe, a peninsula of the Euro-Asian landmass, considered to be a continent while India, another peninsula of the Euro-Asian landmass, is considered to be a *sub*-continent?

Geography plays a distinctive role in citizenship education through performing a type of 'mapping' function that enables young people to locate themselves in relation to other people and other places. This function of geography needs to be understood, for like most educational transactions it needs to be undertaken with a conscious effort, a prerequisite for teaching in a 'morally careful' manner. This is how John Morgan has expressed the point:

> *Thus, in the academic division of labour, geography's particular role is to define social space and territory, since it is concerned with boundaries, zones of activity and notions of regionality [However], rather than simply providing pupils with an accurate and 'truthful' representation of the world, geography teachers are involved in the active construction of pupils' maps of meaning. Further, the maps of meaning that are constructed in school geography lessons cannot be seen as innocent and free from power relations. For instance, to reinforce the idea that pupils primarily 'belong' to a national space necessarily means that they are less likely to identify themselves as 'Europeans'* (Morgan, 2001, p. 89).

Compare this with the way 'school geography' has been framed in recent years. The first (1991) version of the national curriculum was unduly influenced by certain kinds of anxiety existing in policy circles at the time, possibly relating to a perceived deficit in the 'cultural literacy' of the population at large. The significance of the concept of cultural literacy is that without a shared information base, including a geographical locational knowledge framework (certain 'facts'), people are unable to function effectively as *national* citizens. The resulting national curriculum specification was full of 'content' – things students were thought to need to know, including a list of places and features, a division of the world into 'economically more developed' and 'less developed' countries, geographies of the superpowers (defined as USA, Japan and USSR [sic]), a geography of Britain, and the geography of the *home* region (or Wales!). The purpose of 'delivering' all this was left implicit, for there were no aims stated for this 'curriculum'. Lip service was paid to the intellectual skills of enquiry and there was a clear message to avoid values and values education strategies.

Though the successive revisions of the national curriculum have stepped decisively away from the absurdities of the 1991 specification – the curriculum is now oriented by explicit educational aims, the content has been sharply pruned, there is now more choice, and values education and enquiry are explicit – the story illustrates a certain kind of tension that follows whenever the State becomes directly involved in educational processes. If schooling is concerned with the cultural production of the nation, we should ask '*Whose* nation is being produced?' and 'For what purpose?' For although at one level the concept of nation is fairly straightforward (even though slightly unstable in the case of the UK space), composed of a recognisable group of people who feel a belonging to a distinctive territory or space, at another level the concept is highly political. Geography teachers are in the front line in that they prepare young people to function confidently in the culturally diverse and highly contested political world in which they live.

School geography and informed citizenship

The radical move, in 2002, to establish citizenship in the national curriculum for the very first time was partly in response to (especially young) people's apparent apathy towards or disengagement from the formal political process of voting. It is a concern because low turnouts at election time seriously damage the legitimacy of a 'democratically elected' government. This is how the government's educational quango, the Qualifications and

Curriculum Authority, expressed its intentions in the Final Report that guided the establishment of citizenship in the curriculum:

> *The benefits of citizenship education will be: for pupils – an entitlement in schools that will empower them to participate effectively as informed, critical and responsible citizens; ... for society – an active and politically literate citizenry convinced that they can influence government and community affairs at all levels* (QCA, 1998, p. 9).

But this still begs the question as to what information, knowledge, understanding and skills the 'informed, critical and responsible citizen' requires. The informed citizen is a person who can think about their rights and duties and the power of the State. As with thinking about any abstract idea it helps to have models and structures in which to 'frame' the mental effort. So, what of school geography – *what can geography lessons contribute to helping young people 'frame' their thoughts about the world and their place in it?*

I cannot respond fully to this question here – the rest of this book contains many of the answers. But I do want to argue that geography teachers need to take great care in what they claim their lessons are able to accomplish, particularly when measured against the creation of 'informed citizens'. It is precisely in this way that the idea of 'moral care' in teaching, opened up in the following section, gains purchase. Teachers need to be cautious and above all they need to be informed themselves. This is an obvious point at one level (teachers have to have something to think about and to teach!), but at another level it is seriously challenging. First, examine Figure 1.

Running through Figure 1, which shows a number of 'big concepts' in school geography, is the implied use of certain types of classroom strategies that can underpin *values education*.

Values	Concepts	Skills
Social/economic justice	Interdependence	Critical thinking
Sense of place	Sustainable development	Decision making
Sense of community	Place	Reflection
Empathy	Scale	Reconsideration
Diversity	Cultural diversity	Communication

Figure 1 | *Some values, concepts and skills shared by citizenship and geography education. The list is not intended to be read as exhaustive! Adapted from: Machon and Walkington, 2000.*

Considered in this way both geographical and citizenship education are concerned with developing values as well as skills and understanding. However, to what extent is the level of critique, reflection and communication among students raised beyond the level of immediate self-interest? For instance, let us consider the analysis of material inequalities in societies (indeed, across the world) – a popular topic in school geography. We know that capitalism works in a way that brings uneven well-being. Once established, uneven development brings to disadvantaged people inferior living space, poorer physical environments, poorer diets, poorer access to health services, schools and other amenities that help shape life chances. But in school geography, while it is relatively easy to map such inequalities, and to find students doing just this, it is much harder to provide explanations for the patterns, which articulate economic, social or political processes. (It is even harder to involve students in a spirit of genuine 'empowerment' when they may recognise themselves as being powerless, being themselves victims of poverty for example.)

In school geography it would do no harm to submit much of what is offered as 'explanation' to serious critical examination. In the same way as geography helps to 'map' students' identities, it can contribute to their maps of meaning by framing how they 'see' the world. Many of those concepts and values in geography that help us 'frame' what we see, such as those in Figure 1, are themselves underpinned by models and theories that often work at the level of assumption. Thus, sustainability is not a 'given'; its meaning is not self-evident, and this is true of all other concepts. It follows, for example, that scale, that most fundamental geographical concept, is also a social construction: as we have already considered, the regional, the national, the continental are all concepts that are contingent. Furthermore, the choice of what scale at which to study an issue or problem, from the local through to the global, certainly influences how the issue is understood and the nature of the investigation. For example, the case of industrial change in South Wales (and in particular the continued contraction of the steel industry) can be studied at the scale of people's daily lives or within the context of 'inevitable' forces of 'globalisation'. Take your pick, but it matters.

Geography education expressed in this way is ambitious in its educational goals, and to reiterate, it is vital that geography teachers – at least those who are offering subject leadership in schools – think carefully about how and what they teach contributes to these goals. I equate these goals with moral education, and the next section briefly shows why.

Geography, conversation and moral carelessness

It was indicated in the previous section that geography teachers need to exercise careful vigilance when considering the *assumptions* underpinning the conceptual 'frames' that school geography utilises. Teachers should be prepared to lay these assumptions bare with greater alacrity than is usually the case in standard textbooks. In this final section I provide examples to show what I mean and conclude with a discussion linking the subject 'expertise' of the geography teacher and his/her ability to avoid what I call 'moral carelessness' in their teaching.

To begin with, however, it is useful to reflect briefly on the very nature of what it means to prepare students for a morally healthy adult life. Moral education is largely to do with preparing students to deal with issues of right and wrong: according to Wilson (1992) this involves, in combination, the ability to make healthy allegiances and critical distinctions. In the (post)modern age this is truly a complex process, for it is believed by many that there is now a total breakdown in universal moral codes and that individuals need to act primarily in their own particular interests in a relativistic world. What do you teach, when 'anything goes'?

Well, it is certainly possible to reject the nihilism of such an extreme relativist world view (see, for example, Smith, 1998). Geography can operate with the 'dual vision' of both the universal and the *particular* at the same time by explicitly using its key big concepts of place and scale. In other words, students can be shown some universal (global) principles that do not necessarily exclude particular (local) differences in ways of life. In a similar manner, believing in the right for local communities and cultures to exist under their own particular codes does not necessarily mean that all ways of life have to be considered equally valid.

I have argued in this chapter that the moral duty of the education service is to ensure that students are given sufficient insight ('knowledge and understanding') and practice ('skills') to become informed citizens – in the sense that they can participate meaningfully in society's debates and struggles. This means that geography teachers need to be aware of the dangers inherent in operating only in an 'answer culture' (as in teaching to the test) instead of promoting a vigorous 'culture of argument'. The latter can be equated with an 'education for *conversation*', which signals students and teachers in a dialogic relationship with knowledge, and with each other. Thus, the only 'good causes' for geography (or citizenship) education are the goals of a healthy moral education, in which students are encouraged to ask questions, feel comfortable with scepticism and adopting a cautious approach to complexity, but feel enabled to make judgements of merit. This has been called a condition of 'confident uncertainty', and I think geography education can contribute to this entirely healthy state among students – though it may better describe the mental state of a switched-on geography teacher! – as the following paragraphs show.

The approach to moral/citizenship education outlined above is dependent on well-educated and trained teachers, for operating within the metaphor of 'conversation' requires subject specialists who are confident in their expertise (who can, so to speak, break away from 'teaching to the test' and can allow perspectives ignored by the textbook). For example, although the concentric rings of the 'Burgess model' are well-nigh ubiquitous in textbook chapters explaining urban land use, the assumptions underpinning the Chicago School's thinking are not so easy to find articulated. The ecological concepts of invasion and succession and the social Darwinist constructs of 'natural order' to human hierarchies and spatial patterns gives the model a certain kind of power. As in all questions involving power, it is good to question in whose interests the model serve(d)s. What is not acceptable is for an *informed citizen* to have been *taught* that 'transition zones' containing 'inner city slums' inhabited by 'immigrants' (sic) are inevitable in British cities (according to a model based on a 1920s sociological account of Chicago!).

In other words, while choosing teaching strategies is clearly important, we need to pay more attention to what is actually learned (and not simply from classroom encounters!). An example of how such an approach may have significance relates to some newly enrolled PGCE geography teachers who were asked to interview small groups of young, urban secondary students: part of learning about children's worlds. One PGCE group concluded that 'Black kids do not have a countryside'. This is a remarkable observation, especially when set against my own experience in a rural town not 32km away from where these conversations took place. In this tourist honeypot, in the heart of the English Peak District, there is a gift shop entitled (without irony) 'Truly English'; there was, interestingly, not a black face in sight in the entire town on the day I was there. At the very least these observations raise a legitimate question about the type of geography curriculum that might be suited to the needs of a multicultural society. To what extent, to echo McGuinness's (2000) discussion on 'race' and academic geography, is school geography really about whiteness? It could be, therefore, that in order to promote an informed citizenry, school geography teachers will have to pay greater attention to meeting the needs of all future citizens. This means teachers 'listening' to them as well as 'speaking'; that is, developing the art of teaching as 'conversation'. (See also Chapter 30.)

Some final thoughts

So what is the point of studying geography? My point is that any answer to this question worth listening to has to take us way beyond 'because it's there'. Furthermore, we need to be very careful about what we claim 'geography' can do. This chapter has not ducked what I believe to be a profound and difficult question: in what ways can geography contribute to the creation of an informed citizenry? My response has a number of facets, but in the end advocates a sophisticated view of the subject, one that inevitably makes reference to fundamental educational goals, summed up by the phrase 'education for conversation'. Every single geography teacher, because they are a geography teacher, has a part to play in generating this conversation.

An informed citizen must have an understanding of how the world works. This requires engagement with economic, social and political as well as physical and environmental processes. It also involves practice in the intellectual skills of reflection, reconsideration, communication and other forms of participation in decision making. And it requires teachers to maintain focused energy on the assumptions that frame (and can obscure) critical thinking. Not least, a sophisticated sense of scale can help students understand their role as global citizens who exercise daily (individual) local choices that can have global (universal) effects. Given the stasis recently apparent in the political leadership of the USA in relation to a range of international and global issues, there is arguably no more important subject of conversation in school geography lessons.

Related publications from the Geographical Association:

- DEA/GA (2004) *Geography: The global dimension (key stage 3)*. London/Sheffield: DEA/GA.
- Morgan, J. and Lambert, D. (2003) (see below).
- Rawling, E. (2001) *Changing the Subject: The impact of national policy on school geography 1980-2000*.
- Walkington, H. (1999) *Theory into Practice: Global Citizenship Education*.

References

de Saint-Exupéry, A. (1943) *The Little Prince*. (Pavilion Classics edition, 1997 (translated by Wakeman, A.; illustrations by Foreman, M.).

Machon, P. and Walkington, H. (2000) 'Citizenship: the role of geography?' in Kent, A. (ed) *Reflective Practice in Geography Teaching*. London: Paul Chapman Publishing, pp. 179-91.

McGuinness, P. (2000) 'Geography matters? Whiteness and contemporary geography', *Area*, 32, 2, pp. 225-30.

Morgan, J. (2001) 'The seduction of community: to which space do I belong?' in Lambert, D. and Machon, P. (eds) *Citizenship Education through Secondary Geography*. London: Routledge Falmer, pp. 87-97.

Morgan, J. and Lambert, D. (2003) *Theory into Practice: Place, 'Race' and Teaching Geography*. Sheffield: Geographical Association.

QCA (1998) *Education for Citizenship and the Teaching of Democracy in Schools*. London: Qualifications and Curriculum Authority.

Proctor, J. (1999) 'Introduction: overlapping terrains' in Proctor, J. and Smith, D. (eds) *Geography and Ethics: Journeys in a moral terrain*. London: Routledge, pp. 1-16.

Smith, D.M. (1998) 'Geography and moral philosophy: some common ground', *Ethics, Place and Environment*, 1, 1, pp. 7-34.

Wilson, J. (1992) 'Moral education, values education and prejudice reduction' in Lynch, J., Modgil, C. and Modgil, S. (eds) *Cultural Diversity and the Schools; Volume 2: Prejudice, polemic or progress*. London: Falmer.

Implications for practice

(a) The overarching question is 'what is the purpose of teaching and learning geography?'

Subject leaders, such as heads of department, may need to generate a conversation about the 'big concepts' or the 'guiding principles' of geography. Figure 1 may help start this off. How does geography help young people think more intelligently about the world? Such a conversation may help ward off a common issue noticed from research with secondary school students, namely that they say that geography appears fragmented or bitty. It is hard to knit the subject together in comparison with other subjects that may seem to have a clearer 'story'.

(b) The experience of school geography must not be limited to endless 'stuff'.

The classic 'problem with geography' is that it is, inevitably, content rich. The contents of the subject are potentially infinite. There is a need for another conversation (following that on purpose) on the balance between facts, organising concepts and values.

(c) Less explicit in the chapter, but nevertheless important, is the place of 'skills'.

Are there any skills that can be called 'geographical' or are we better off identifying those intellectual skills that geography is particularly good at developing – such as decision making, communication and synthesis?

(d) School geography plays a distinctive role in citizenship education by enabling young people to locate themselves in relation to other people and places.

(e) The other big idea that runs through this chapter is that of identity.

It is hard to imagine 'delivering' lessons on identity however, as students already have experiences and views on such matters. Students, in other words, are themselves significant agents in the teaching and learning process – which is why some lessons at least should be quite explicitly 'conversational' rather than one-way 'transmission'.

Chapter 3

Geography - a dynamic subject

John Morgan

> **Before reading this chapter consider the following questions:**
>
> ■ How similar or different is the geography you teach now from the geography you learned in your university course?
>
> ■ What strategies do you have for keeping abreast with developments in the subject?
>
> ■ What do you think it is important for students to learn about 'the world of work'?

How do geography teachers make sense of the inherent dynamism of geography as a subject? This chapter asks you to reflect upon the question of the proper relationship between the subject as taught in schools and studied in universities. As an example of the 'dynamic' nature of geographical knowledge and thought, consider the following example. I completed my degree in geography in 1987. One of the books I read in my final year was Ron Johnston's *Geography and Geographers* which detailed the story of Anglo-American human geography since 1945. By that time the book was in its second edition (the first edition was published in 1979). In 2004 the book was published in its sixth edition. The latest edition is considerably longer (527 pages compared with 264). It had a new co-author, brought in to broaden the expertise (and presumably handle the increased volume of writing about human geography), and the section on 'behavioural geography' was shortened to make space for new developments. These included the 'cultural turn', postmodern geographies and feminist geographies. Reading the latest edition, one is struck by the changes in subject matter, methodology and philosophy that characterise human geography. The same is true of physical geography, where Ken Gregory's *The Nature of Physical Geography* (published in 1984) has been up-dated by *The Changing Nature of Physical Geography* (2000).

These are not isolated examples. There is a burgeoning literature on the development of geographical thought and study. One of the advantages of these texts is that they remind us that geography is a dynamic subject. It responds to changes in the nature of the world and in turn influences the way we see the world. In more concrete terms, reading these texts reminds us that what is sometimes taught in school geography lessons (in the form of models, theories and concepts) as 'fact' is in reality less stable and fixed.

This alone requires that geography teachers remain vigilant in ensuring that they recognise the more or less 'arbitrary' nature of the school geography curriculum.

The question that this chapter seeks to highlight is how geography teachers, who are embroiled in the day-to-day activity of teaching the subject, can cope with the dynamic nature of geography as a discipline. It argues for a particular orientation or *stance* towards curriculum thinking in geography, one that recognises the dynamism of the subject.

The curriculum problem

I want to start with the intensely urgent and practical issue geography teachers face every day of their working lives – what am I going to try to get my students to learn?, how am I going to manage the situation to get them to learn?, and how am I going to evaluate the success or otherwise of what's happened? This is the 'curriculum problem' that is at the heart of teaching (Graves, 1975). I think it is possible to argue that, in the last two decades, as a community of geography educators we have focused less on the first part of the curriculum problem (what it is we are trying to get students to learn), and more on the other parts. There are many reasons for this, and I am not going to dwell on them here. However, I want to argue that the lack of attention to the first question has had quite catastrophic effects. This is because the question of what we want students to learn is not merely a technical issue – a matter of matching up the 'right' bits and rearranging them in a logical order – but involves profound moral and political choices. As Michael Apple put it in his book *Ideology and Curriculum*:

> *It should be made clear that curriculum design, the creating of educative environments in which students are to dwell, is inherently a political and moral process. It involves competing ideological, political, and intensely personal conceptions of valuable educational activity* (Apple, 1979, p. 111).

This is an extremely important idea that may be illustrated by an example. As a school student, I was taught physical geography. This was the early 1980s, and the approach followed was resolutely 'scientific', since school geography had been influenced by the study of processes which, according to Sims (2003), had become the 'Holy Grail' of geomorphology from the late 1960s onwards. Physical geography lessons contained a lot of hydrology, and focused on the study (often involving measurement) of drainage basins and catchments. There were exercises in which we had to measure correlations between stream order and variables such as gradient and channel roughness. There were studies of fluvial processes on hillslopes in small catchments measuring rates of infiltration and hypothesising about the role of vegetation in run-off. I learned to see glaciers as part of a system, with inputs, processes and outputs. This focus on processes was reflected in all branches of physical geography. Thus Pethick's *Introduction to Coastal Geomorphology* 'attempts to bring coastal geomorphology into the established framework of process studies' (1984, p. 1), and Cooke and Warrens' (1973) *Geomorphology in Deserts* and Sugden and John's (1976) *Glaciers and Landscape* attempted much the same in their respective fields.

As a 'young geographer' I was learning to see how geographers went about practising their subject (see Cloke *et al.*, 2004). At the time I had no way of seeing how such geographical knowledge reflected particular conditions of knowledge production. For instance, this approach to physical geography tends to break down the physical world into discrete parts and these are studied in their own right. I admit it is possible I may not have listened enough to my teachers, but there seemed to be little attempt to show how these parts were linked. In addition, the study of these processes tended to be quite small-scale. I remember doing 'stream studies' at various sites on a river, but the focus was on getting the 'data' to 'number-crunch' back in the classroom, rather than seeing how the river formed part of a wider landscape. Finally, the landforms we studied seemed to exist independently of people, or maybe people and what they were doing to the landscape came as an 'add-on' at the end of a series of lessons.

The point is that what seemed like a neutral, objective and scientific approach to the study of physical landforms in fact relied on some quite important assumptions about science, about meaningful educational activity, and about people-environment relations. I do not know if my geography teachers were aware of it. However, I want to argue that teachers who are able to recognise the way in which geographical knowledge is produced, and how it might be possible to produce it differently, are more likely to give a considered answer to the question of what it is they want students to learn. Though it is a little dated now, I still find David Pepper's (1985) article 'Why teach physical geography?' a useful starting point, and more recently physical geographers are explicitly reflecting on the 'meanings' and 'contexts' of their work (Trudgill and Roy, 2003). What we are describing here is the 'geographical imagination'. This is, more and more, a term used by geographers to refer to the idea that our understandings of the world are always partial and situated – we always come at the world from some angle, or, as Paul Cloke and colleagues recently put it:

> *For years now, many … geographers have reacted vehemently against the notion that they should operate as some white-coated automaton, carrying out their work in the supposed tyranny of supposed neutrality and objectivity* (Cloke *et al.*, 2004, p. 1).

The problem is, of course, that once we begin to talk about 'imagination' and 'envisioning' in geography, the idea of 'rational curriculum planning', or the notion that we could all agree what it is we want students to learn, is seriously weakened. I may be getting inflamed here, but I suspect that there is a certain comfort to be had in the idea that the 'what' question seems to have been answered by the 'national curriculum'. It saves us sitting down and having it out with colleagues, and though we may claim not to like it that much, it helps that publishers have commissioned people to write textbooks that 'cover' everything. It certainly makes it easier when the inspector calls. But I cannot help feeling that this leads to an impoverished and profoundly depressing view of the role of geography teaching. As Gregory and Walford wrote in their introduction to *New Horizons in Human Geography*:

> *If school geography were to become a limited-objective, narrow instrumental study, uninformed by the excitement and potential of contemporary research … then it would eventually lose its intellectual edge and its capacity to interest students* (1989, p. 6).

Imagining economic geographies

In the rest of this discussion I want to provide an example of the type of 'curriculum-thinking' I am proposing. My example is the theme of economic geography. As a starting point, you may want to 'map out' the theme and think about what 'facts', concepts, ideas, generalisations and case studies you think it would be important for students to learn. The Geography National Curriculum includes the following requirement:

> *Pupils should be taught …*
> *6h. the changing distribution of economic activity and its impact, including:*
> ■ *types and classifications of economic activity*
> ■ *the geographical distribution of one or more economic activities*
> ■ *how and why the distribution has changed and is changing, and the effects of such changes* (DfEE/QCA, 1999, p. 159).

You will have noticed that the wording of the national curriculum is very broad. It provides only the briefest guidance on the content and form of teaching about this topic. In addition, it does not offer teachers any guidance on the types of geographical explanation they might offer to students. This leaves considerable space for teachers to interpret the curriculum requirement. For example, changing patterns of industrial location could be explained by environmental determinism (flat, well-drained land), neoclassical economic theory (Weber's locational triangle), political economy (Marxist theory), and so on. The important point is that teachers have to make such judgements themselves, on the basis of their specialised understanding of the subject. John Fien (1989) makes this point in his discussion of planning and teaching a curriculum unit. He suggests that, faced with the prospect of teaching a unit of work (on economic activity, say) the first thing to decide is what *angle* you want to take on the topic:

> *Do not go to textbooks to see what they have on the topic at this early stage. The textbook author has answered the important curriculum questions of why, what and how to teach the topic, without reference to the local environment in which you are teaching, the individual needs of your students, or the specific relevance of the topic to them. Rather, as a first step, ask yourself the question, 'what about it?' in relation to the topic to be taught* (Fien, 1989, p. 348).

Bob was a geography teacher who was trained in the 1970s, a time when positivistic approaches were being introduced into school geography. He thinks that students should be introduced to important spatial concepts such as 'least cost location' and 'accessibility'. Bob believes that economic geography is all about introducing students to the general principles of location and the factors that explain why industries locate in particular places, and how changes in the location of industry can be explained by geographical factors.

Sara agrees with Bob that it is important that students understand the factors that explain the patterns of economic activity. However, she is not convinced that the various 'models' provide realistic explanations. In her teaching of economic geography Sara tends to stress the ways in which individuals make decisions based on less than perfect knowledge. Sara is also concerned that some approaches in economic geography

Photo: ©Alan Young.

tend to have a 'mechanistic' view of economic decision making, and attempts to get students to think about the consequences of changing patterns of economic activity. She asks the question of 'who gets what, where and why?' and tries to identify the impacts of changing patterns of economic activity.

John studied geography in the late 1980s where he encountered some of the ideas of 'radical' geographers such as David Harvey and Doreen Massey. He was also influenced by his own experience of economic change, as he grew up in a mining town which was affected by the miners' strike of 1984-85. John considers that much of the explanation offered in geography textbooks prevents students from understanding the real causes of economic change – the clash between capital and labour. In his teaching, John tries to get students to understand the historical context in which work takes place.

Like John, Mary studied geography in the 1980s. She was particularly influenced by the work of feminist geographers who argued that geography tended to ignore the experience of half the world's population – women. In teaching about economic geography Mary is concerned to question the distinction between paid and unpaid 'work' and provide studies of economic activities that are dominated by female labour.

Paulo is a recent graduate who has been influenced by some of the ideas in the new economic geography influenced by post-structural theory. In particular he is concerned that the types of representations of the economy found in school geography tend to offer a rather simple and 'cleaned up' version of economic reality. This has the effect of marginalising other accounts of economic life. In his teaching Paulo tries to offer students a set of different representations of economic life, stressing the many ways in which people make a living. For instance, he introduces 'case studies' of local economic trading systems and 'alternative' lifestyles based on co-operation.

Ayeesha finds that much of the economic geography she has taught in schools so far tends to focus on industries and activities far removed from the experiences of the students she teaches. There is also a focus on the patterns and processes of production. More recently Ayeesha has tried to refocus her teaching on the act of consumption (what people buy, where and why) and then trace back the links between the consumers and producers. In doing so, she finds that she spends time teaching about patterns of retailing and advertising and trying to help students to consider their consumption choices.

All the teachers described above are involved in the process of 'curriculum thinking'. They are all answering the question posed by John Fien – 'What about it?' It is possible to imagine that when faced with the prospect of teaching a series of lessons on economic geography teachers do not have a fixed set of lesson plans (perhaps based around textbooks) but construct their own 'map' of the topic based on a thorough knowledge of the subject and an understanding of the contexts in which geographical knowledge is produced (Paulo's choice of post-structuralist economic geography involves a rejection of what he sees as monolithic accounts of economic space). In addition, such teachers are aware of the social context in which they are teaching (John's teaching is clearly rooted in an understanding of why economic geography matters), and have insights into the lives of their students (Ayeesha's decision to focus on consumption reflects her developing understanding of the lived realities of the students she teaches). It is this type of thinking that I think Apple meant by the statement that curriculum design is 'an intensely political and moral process' (1979, p. 111). All the teachers described are making decisions about what, how and (crucially) why teach economic geography.

What I am describing here is the shift away from the idea that the task of geography teachers is simply to represent the 'facts' about economic geography. I am arguing that important messages are being passed on to students in these representations, and what's more, these messages matter – this is my way of saying that 'geography matters'. For example, neoclassical economic geography focuses on the rational decision making of individuals who produce a landscape that is ordered and predictable. Feminist geographers seem to offer an alternative perspective, one that stresses that much work is done for altruistic reasons and is undervalued. Radical or Marxist geographers tend to stress the deeper historical forces that shape landscapes – thus there are landscapes of accumulation.

Another way of putting this is to say that it is not the 'real world' that is being taught about in geography lessons but rather a discourse (or, maybe discourses) about the world – a representation of the world that is geographical. The problem is, of course, that this is denied because the school geography curriculum is based on a 'realist' view of both knowledge and the world. In other words, different groups of economic geographers create, within discourse, different economies – with different problems, different solutions, and so on.

So where does all this get us? It certainly does not offer 'easy' solutions to the curriculum problem. In his book on the philosophy of education, *Leaving Safe Harbors*, Denis Carlson describes in succinct terms the educational implications of this shift in thinking about knowledge:

> *The critical shift here is away from an understanding of knowledge or truth as something that exists prior to and independent of the language that describes and represents it … a recognition of the formative or generative role of language in producing the world both symbolically but also materially. All of this is linked to a language of paradigm shifts, transformative thinking, and the importance of learning to 'think' the world differently* (2002, pp. 179-80).

Carlson argues that educators are beginning to move beyond the idea that education is about the transmission of a corpus of knowledge to receptive students, towards the idea that education is a process by which knowledge or truth is actively constructed. We get into lots of tricky debates here. In suggesting that school knowledge does not simply mirror the 'real world', are we saying that there is no basis for teaching what we do? Is it a case of 'anything goes'? Should we make explicit the partiality of what we teach, and draw attention to the other possible representations that we are choosing not to offer? Of course, there are no clear-cut answers to such questions. However, they are exactly the types of arguments that are raised by even the most cursory engagement with debates within the subject of geography. As a final parting shot, you might consider the implications for geography teaching of the following statement:

> *All curricula come from somewhere. The 'somewhere' subject matter and modes of teaching come from is marked by particular understandings, philosophical assumptions, interpretations of information, cultural inscriptions. It is a subjective place where some interests are included and others excluded. A self-conscious curriculum, therefore, is aware of the power relations that shape it* (Kincheloe, 2003, p. 112).

Taking the subject forward

Most geography teachers come into the profession because they believe that they possess useful knowledge and understanding that they think it important to pass on to students. The problem is that their knowledge is not timeless – it passes its 'sell by' date. It is easy to understand why not much of a premium is placed on keeping up with the 'dynamism of geographical explanation'. There are the challenges of handling large and (sometimes) reluctant classes, with limited time for preparation and reflection. School managers do not always understand, especially when there are lots of 'initiatives' to work with. But I hope that the example of economic geographies shows why 'geography matters'. You will no doubt have noticed that this chapter has not really mentioned the role of students in all this. I do not have much space, but suffice to say that I am not arguing for geography teachers to be foisting upon students the latest trend in intellectual fashion. Curriculum planning – that political and moral process – is always done (or ought to be) with students in mind. The geography teacher, armed with a complex understanding of how geographical knowledge is produced, makes judgements about the needs of her/his students. What I have argued for in this chapter is a tall order – but it can be done. I hope this chapter will encourage you to think about the nature of teaching geography when the subject itself is characterised by dynamism and flux.

Implications for practice

(a) Geography matters!

This chapter is arguing for a particular stance towards geographical knowledge – one that rejects the view that what is taught and learned in geography can ever be a 'final' reflection of the world.

This stance requires that geography teachers ask themselves the questions: 'Where does this geographical knowledge come from?', 'Who produced it and why?' and 'Are there other possible ways of thinking about this knowledge?'

Geography teachers who routinely ask these questions are more likely to adopt a critical and reflective approach to curriculum planning – what I have called 'curriculum thinking' – and plan learning experiences that reflect the needs (in the widest educational sense) of the students they teach. Further examples of this type of curriculum thinking can be found in Morgan and Lambert (2005) *Teaching School Subjects: Geography* (particularly in Chapter 4).

(b) 'Subject knowledge' can never be 'secure'.

Instead, geography teachers are involved in a process of 'lifelong learning' in which their 'geographical mind' develops with further study, reflection and experience.

Related publications from the Geographical Association:

■ Rawling, E. (2001) *Changing the Subject: The impact of national policy on school geography 1980-2000.*

■ *Changing Geography* (1999-present) (a series edited by John Bale, and Janet Speake) – includes titles on *Disability, space and society, Sportscapes, Regenerating cities, Countryside conflicts and Citizen, state and nation.*

■ *Geography* (1901-present)

References

Apple, M. (1990) *Ideology and Curriculum* (second edition). London: Routledge.

Carlson, D. (2002) *Leaving Safe Harbors: Towards a new progressivism in American education and public life*. New York: Routledge Falmer.

Cloke, P., Cook, I., Crang, P., Goodwin, M., Painter, J. and Philo, C. (2004) *Practising Human Geography*. London: Arnold.

Cooke, R. and Warren, A. (1973) *Geomorphology in Deserts*. London: Batsford.

DfEE/QCA (1999) *The National Curriculum: Handbook for secondary teachers in England (KS3&4)*. London: DfEE/QCA.

Fien, J. (1989) 'Planning a curriculum unit' in Fien, J., Gerber, R. and Wilson, P. (eds) *The Geography Teachers' Guide to the Classroom*. Melbourne: MacMillan, pp. 346-8.

Graves, N. (1975) *Geography in Education*. London: Heinemann Educational.

Gregory, D. and Walford, R. (eds) (1989) *New Horizons in Human Geography*. Basingstoke: MacMillan.

Gregory, K. (1984) *The Nature of Physical Geography*. London: Edward Arnold.

Gregory, K. (2000) *The Changing Nature of Physical Geography*. London: Arnold.

Johnston, R. (1983) *Geography and Geographers: Anglo-American human geography since 1945* (second edition). London: Edward Arnold.

Johnston, R. and Sidaway, J. (2004) *Geography and Geographers: Anglo-American human geography since 1945* (sixth edition). London: Arnold.

Kincheloe, J. (2003) *Teachers as Researchers*. London: Routledge Falmer.

Morgan, J. and Lambert, D. (2004) *Teaching to Learn Geography*. London: Routledge Falmer.

Pepper, D. (1985) 'Why teach physical geography?', *Contemporary Issues in Geography and Education, 2*, 2, pp. 62-71.

Pethick, J. (1984) *Introduction to Coastal Geomorphology*. London: Arnold.

Sims, P. (2003) 'Previous actors and current influences; trends and fashions in physical geography' in Trudgill, S. and Roy, A. (eds) *Contemporary Meanings in Physical Geography: From what to why?* London: Arnold, pp. 3-23.

Sugden, D. and John, B. (1976) *Glaciers and Landscape*. London: Arnold.

Trudgill, S. and Roy, A. (eds) (2003) *Contemporary Meanings in Physical Geography: From what to why?* London: Arnold.

Chapter 4

The geographical mind

Doreen Massey

> **Before beginning this discussion of what it might mean to 'think geographically', consider your response to the following questions:**
>
> ■ Do local people have rights to, or over, their localities?
>
> ■ Should we open all borders and live without boundaries on a planet which belongs to us all?

A moment of discussion

Questions such as those above are often approached through particular cases, so let us eavesdrop on a discussion about one such. The subject is Amazonia and in what is already an unusual twist the focus is on the peoples rather than (or as well as) the forest itself. Both are precarious, under attack from outside forces. The discussion is lively and the tenor of the emerging consensus lies with the local people of Amazonia against the monied interests of loggers and ranchers and even against the invasion of other poor people (but from 'outside') who are also in search of somewhere to live. So far, probably, so predictable. I too am inclined to support the idea of some kind of rights to land and territory for the remaining ancient societies of Amazonia.

But on what grounds? Perhaps the argument is made on the grounds that these are local people and, in consequence of that, they have rights to this locality in the face of global forces. For this argument to be truly valid it must be a principle which is applicable in other situations too. And if that is really the way in which we want to argue the case then what is being proposed is a particular geographical imagination of the planet: as a world which is essentially divided into localities, or territories, within each of which dwell local people with local rights. (It proposes, of course, a lot more besides – notions of indigeneity being chief among them.)

When confronted with that background geographical imagination, defending the local people of Amazonia *on the grounds that they are local* begins to look less convincing. That is, after all, precisely the imagination which is mobilised in Europe, say, to justify strict controls against immigration, or in California against the people escaping north from the poverties and repressions of Latin America. These too, after all, are cases of local people defending their space against the pressure of global flows. These, though, are the localisms of the powerful. And it is remarkable how many of those who would argue for local rights in Amazonia will argue the opposite case when it comes to a question of immigrants and asylum seekers looking for entry to Europe. Here, the rights of immigrants are treated more sympathetically. *Another* set of principles is brought into play – about the right of movement perhaps, or about how this planet, after all, belongs to all of us. And behind those other principles lies another, very different, equally particular, geographical imagination – this time of a world which is, essentially, without borders.

There is a lot going on in this very simple example.

First it points to both the inevitability and the power of our geographical imaginations. They may be implicit but they are present and deeply implicated each time we argue about rights to migration, for instance, or have recourse (as we all do) to phrases like 'local people'. We all operate, all the time, all of us – students, teachers, all of us in our roles as member of the public or citizen – with background imaginations of how the world is organised, or might be organised in a better future. (And it is important to note immediately how these imaginations extend beyond the human world – the decision to cull certain animals in order to defend 'indigenous'(?) species is a case in point.) A first move for the enquiring geographer, therefore, is to make those geographical imaginations explicit, and to ask where they come from.

Second, and in part precisely because they are not usually examined explicitly, we often function in fact with a bundle of quite contradictory geographical imaginations – as individual people, as social groups, or as, for instance, political tendencies. The contradictory imaginations of 'local people', in Amazonia and Fortress Europe, in the foregoing paragraphs, are likely to be held by more 'progressive' tendencies. More 'conservative' groups are likely to defend Fortress Europe ('local people have rights to what they have built, you know') at the same time as advocating free trade ('the new world is

Photo: ©Simon Scoones.

one without boundaries; protectionism is to be avoided'). One of the most effective ways of disrupting the taken-for-grantedness of much received wisdom is to point to the contradictions between the geographical imaginations on which they are founded.

Third that crucial aim of education – to question rather than to accept without further thought – is particularly powerful when what is at issue is the nature of our geographical imaginations. The point of exposing the contradictions in the geographical imaginations mobilised in debates over local people/immigration/free trade is that neither 'local' nor 'global' is in *itself* good, whatever position one takes on the political spectrum. It is necessary to distinguish between the localism of the powerless and the localism of the powerful, and likewise with globalism (which may be that of trans-national corporations or military powers, but equally may be the new internationalisms of indigenous groups or trade unions). The argument is not that geography is not the answer but that in order to think geographically we must necessarily take account of (differential) power: the geographies (the power geometries) through which the world is constructed and, maybe, the more egalitarian power geometries through which it might be reconstructed. Taking seriously the geography underlying some of the major questions of our time both takes us to the heart of the issues and forces us to think geography more critically.

Fourth, this kind of example is one among many which point towards the specific intellectual contribution which can be made by geography as a discipline. One of the wonderful things about geography is certainly its breadth, the way it enables us to cross boundaries which hem other disciplines in; but that breadth should not obscure the fact that geography also has its own particular intellectual integrity, its own particular avenues to explore and propositions to present. The contribution which geography brings to the discussions just cited is a persistent rigour in the way in which we conceptualise two of the central concepts of modern life: space and place. Many others could be cited but I want for a moment to take further an exploration of these two particular concepts in pursuit of these notions of the geographical imagination and the geographical mind.

The geographical imagination

It is probably now well accepted, though it is still important to argue, that a lot of our 'geography' is in the mind. That is to say, we carry around with us mental images, of the world, of the country in which we live (all those images of the North/South divide), of the street next door. The New Yorker's mental map of the USA, Ronald Reagan's imagination of the world, became popular posters. All of us carry such images; they may sometimes be in conflict or even be the cause of conflict, and digging these things up and talking about them is one good way in to beginning to examine what it means to think 'geographically'. We can also examine how such imaginations are produced, whether that be through the nexus of powerful international media conglomerates or the persistent imagery deployed in local conversations ('that's not a very nice road, not as respectable as ours ...'). And we can explore, too, how such imaginations have powerful effects upon our attitudes towards the world and upon our behaviour. One of our (many) abilities as geography teachers is to unearth these taken-for-granted imaginations and subject them to questioning.

However, I would contend that what is at issue in debates over the rights of local people, or immigration, or the rights and wrongs of free trade, is an even deeper layer of geographical imagination. And it is one which, again, it is important to unearth and examine. To argue for the rights of Amazonian society *on the grounds that it is local* is to imagine space, implicitly, as a space of places, of territories. To argue for 'free trade' on the grounds that, in this age of globalisation *of course boundaries and borders must fall*, is to imagine space as, first and foremost, a space of flows. My argument above was that neither of these imaginations provides us with a principle, that each is likely to run into contradictions, and that one can only consider particular cases in relation to the power relations in which they are embedded. What we need is an imagination of space which incorporates the geometries of power which construct this highly unequal world. What is at issue is how, at quite a fundamental level, we think about the planet; indeed how we think about geographical space itself.

Let me take another example. One most important area of geography teaching is that which explores issues of 'development', whether the focus be on inequalities between first and third worlds (the terminology here is always inadequate) or within a country. There are many issues here of powerful geographical imaginations and both geographers and some aid agencies have fought to counter images of the third world as hapless victim, for instance. That is the layer of geographical imagination which focuses on images of places. Below that, however, is yet another imagination, which is that such places are somehow 'behind' the 'advanced' countries in their levels of development.

The very language which is used powerfully projects this imagination – terms such as advanced and backward (and while 'backward' is probably less in vogue, because of its pejorative implications, deploying the term 'advanced' has exactly the same effect – advanced as opposed to what?!). The terminology of development can have the same implications. Upgrading under-developed to the more optimistic 'developing' still places the developing country *behind* those which are already 'developed'. Moreover, exactly the same implicit positioning of some parts of the world as behind and others as in front is entailed in all the narratives of a singular 'modernisation' or a single path of 'progress'. There is a very important manoeuvre going on here, which again concerns how we imagine the planet, and how we conceive of geographical space itself.

The criticism most often made of such tales of development (or modernisation, or progress) is that they presume that such development can basically only take one form. Others must follow the path along which the West has led. This is a very important point in itself for it assumes that there can be only one kind of history. It is a global version of the infamous dictum that there is no alternative. But I would argue that to say there is only one history is to imply that there is no geography. To imagine places in terms of how far they are along this one-and-only path of development (or modernisation, or progress) is to imagine the differences between them only in terms of history. It is to turn geographical differences (real, coexisting differences) merely into places in the historical queue. It refuses to countenance the possibility that there are lots of histories *going on at the same time*; that other places have their own particular trajectories and, of even more political significance perhaps, the potential for their own particular futures. This is certainly a geographical imagination; it is clearly a way of imagining geographical space. But ironically its effect is almost to abolish that space; to turn it into time.

This is an imagination which has been quite characteristic of Western modernity, with its grand narratives of progress and change. And as with other geographical imaginations it is perpetually reproduced through political and popular discourses. As Chris Durbin argues in Chapter 19, the ability to diagnose such imaginations is an important, and *specifically geographical*, element of media literacy.

The geographical mind

That last geographical imagination, where geography is turned into history, is particularly interesting. When discourses of development and suchlike perform this operation, one of the crucial things they are doing is to undervalue difference. For the purposes of this argument, consider this very crude example: when we in our mind's eye place Chad, Brazil, and the United States of America in a historical sequence (under-developed, developing, developed) we are resisting a full recognition of the differences (historical, actual, and potential) which exist between them. The fact that these places might have distinct trajectories is obscured. It is only when we recognise that in fact these three countries do not form a historical sequence that we can investigate the full extent of their individual distinctiveness and, indeed, their interdependence. But that means recognising that they co-exist; that Chad is fully contemporary with the United States of America. And to do that, in turn, we must recognise that these differences are organised not historically but spatially. One of the implications of 'taking space (or geography) seriously', is the full recognition of the contemporaneous coexistence of different others. (To break into philosophy for a moment: if time is the dimension of sequence and change, space is the dimension of coexisting multiplicity.)

A real spatial awareness, on this argument, implies an outwardlookingness, a willingness to give full recognition to the existence of autonomous others. It has been called a recognition of 'coevalness'. Perhaps this is an aspect of a really 'geographical mind'.

Moreover, it has further implications. As hinted above, it is only with the recognition of contemporaneous coexistence that it is possible to begin to examine the many power-filled relations and interdependencies which bind these places together, and influence their evolving characters and trajectories. If we recognise (again using very crude examples) that Chad and the United States each has its own history, then the politics, and the big questions of their so-called under-development and development, lie also in the terms of their interdependence. Or again, and to come at things this time from the opposite direction, it is often argued that an emphasis on 'difference' (at personal, or group, or ethnic level, for instance) gets in the way of collectivity or solidarity. I would argue the contrary: that difference has to be acknowledged and negotiated before any meaningful solidarity or collectivity – or even that thing called 'society' – can be built. And a genuine recognition of difference requires a fully spatial, a geographical, turn of mind.

An example might help to illustrate the argument and to demonstrate its potential significance. The previous references have been at the global level so let us now focus in at a more local scale; for if the various cultures and societies of the world can be seen as having their own histories, and if the geographies we must explore are the power geometries of their interactions and interdependencies, the same is also true at the level of the local place. We have in geography done much work to undermine the rather romantic notion of places as simply coherent entities with singular, unproblematic, and often seemingly 'eternal', characteristics. We have, in various ways, argued that it is more helpful to understand places as complex, as internally differentiated, as 'meeting places'.

This replicates the wider argument. Places are meeting places of different people, different groups, different ethnicities. In human terms they are the entanglement, the meeting-up, of different histories, many of them without any previous connection to others. I live in a second-floor flat; there are two flats below mine. The occupants of these three dwelling-spaces arrived here, in this building now, from very different directions. But here we are, and now we must manage to live together, to get along. The area of the city in which I live replicates this on a larger scale, and one way of imagining whole cities is indeed as massively complex meeting-places of difference. (This difference does not have to be dramatic or ethnically-defined, for instance. We are each of us different.) The point is that 'places', from a house of flats to a whole city, in consequence require negotiation. On a daily basis, and in a hundred unremarkable ways, we manage to live together, to negotiate our difference. Or sometimes we do; sometimes there are chasms of inequality and/or incomprehension; there may be violence and confrontation.

The point is that there must be negotiation. And before there can be negotiation there must be recognition of and respect for difference. Now, this throws a spanner in the works of all those all-too-easy rhetorics of 'local community' which find their way into so many policy documents attempting to address, for instance, places of urban deprivation. What the analysis here means is that 'community', in the sense of unproblematical coherence that is usually implied, does not simply exist; rather it always has to be negotiated. And given that the internal power geometries of the space of local places can sometimes be almost as complex as those at global level, this negotiation will be difficult and ongoing. Indeed, since negotiation will never end, it is arguable not only that the static, romantic notion of local community is unachievable but also that a recognition of the internal power relations and negotiations is more politically healthy than a longing for a pacified conformity. A healthy democracy requires not the suppression of difference but an openness to it and a willingness to negotiate.

And my contention here is that 'a geographical mind' implies precisely an outwardlooking attitude which, by recognising difference, also necessarily enquires about the terms of negotiation. And one of the things a geographical *discipline*, as an intellectual exercise, can bring to that is a rigour in the way in which we imagine (and analyse the imaginations of) those essential geographical notions: space and place.

Reference

The ideas in this chapter are developed more fully in: Massey, D. (2005) *For Space*. London: Sage.

Implications for practice

(a) Geography can help young people to explore the contested nature of our world.

Geography as a discipline is in the school curriculum because of the value it offers to a young person's education. Thinking geographically can support students in understanding and interpreting their own reactions to people and places, and in reflecting on others' perspectives which may be different from their own. To enable students to 'think geographically' we must ensure that geographical enquiry necessarily takes account of (differential) power. This would lead to a consideration of the geographies (power geometries) through which the world is constructed and perhaps more egalitarian power geometries through which it might be reconstructed.

(b) Much of our 'geography' is in the mind – in the mental images we carry of the world.

Geographical enquiry should make students' 'geographical imaginations' explicit, and explore where they come from. It should also expose contradictions in the geographical imaginations on which much of the 'received wisdom' about many geographical issues is founded. Geography can thus fulfil that crucial aim of education – to question rather than to accept without further thought.

(c) Geography should help students to explore how places are complex and diverse.

It should do this through a variety of perspectives and give sufficient credence to students' own views. It is more helpful to think of places as complex, internally differentiated 'meeting places' of different people, different groups and different ethnicities. Difference has to be acknowledged and negotiated before any meaningful sense of community, or even of society, can be developed. By denying difference we can deny students opportunities to develop the higher-order thinking skills needed to produce deeper explanations of geographical phenomena.

Chapter 5

understanding landscape

Daniel Bloomer and Rachel Atherton

Before reading this chapter consider the following questions:

- What do you think of first when you look at a landscape or view that you have never seen before?

- How do these thoughts differ from those you experience when you are looking at a landscape or view with which you are very familiar?

- How do the ways you look at a landscape when you are on holiday compare with when you are carrying out physical geography fieldwork with your students?

The significance of landscape

Physical geography is essentially concerned with the study of landscape: Why does it look the way it does? How have the processes that operate upon it caused it to look this way? The aim of the specialist physical geographer is to provide rational and reasoned answers which explain how form and process combine to produce a given landscape. Human geographers, on the other hand, are concerned with the way in which people and society operate within these landscapes.

What is landscape?

Before considering ways in which to understand *landscape* it is worth considering what is meant by this term as it has witnessed much change both in the way it is perceived and how it is studied or read.

The term *landscape* is derived from the Dutch word *landschap* used during the Middle Ages to denote a 'region' or 'tract of land'. Its contemporary meaning is much broader and is associated with aspects of nature and art as well as the physical land itself. Landscapes are defined by both natural and human influences and are constantly changing. There is also significant variation in the way they are interpreted as a result of differences in society, culture and experience.

In the nineteenth century the relevance of the term landscape as a holistic concept was eroded as scientific disciplines became increasingly interested in studying the isolated components rather than the 'big picture'. Later, during the twentieth century, landscape re-emerged as an integrated framework requiring a multi-disciplinary approach. Advances in technology such as remote sensing and geographical information systems (GIS) (see Chapters 7 and 10) have provided a new perspective from which to view landscape and have encouraged a synthesis between subjects.

There are three key factors that combine to produce the landscapes we see. The first, 'form', refers to the underlying shape of the land. This could be a mountain, a floodplain or a valley. The second is 'process' which refers to the components that are active within the landscape. Processes could include a river flowing, vegetation growing or hikers walking along a path (see also Chapter 22). 'People', form the final part of the landscape and play the role of interpreting the processes and form into a holistic setting. The interplay between these three components varies over both space and time. In short, landscape is as applicable to a pristine, untouched wilderness as it is to an area heavily impacted by human activity such as a city. In this chapter we are interested in considering the way we see landscape and the world around us.

As teachers of geography it is important for us to recognise that our life experience and values influence the way we, together with students, look at the natural world around us. The context in which we are looking at the landscape can also play a crucial role. How these frames of reference combine can have a great impact on the way we interpret landscape. Perhaps an example will help to illustrate the point: look at a view that is very familiar to you. It might be a hill you can see from your house, something you pass on your way to work, or an old haunt from where you grew up. How does looking at this landscape make you feel? Do you think it is pretty or pleasant? Maybe it evokes childhood memories of happiness or reminds you that you are on your way to battle through another day of teaching. Perhaps it is a favourite view you gaze at when on holiday in a place you visit regularly. Each of you will have picked a different view and each view will promote different feelings and emotions. These feelings are, of course, based on past experience, but will also be moderated by how you are feeling today and by your own set of values regarding what makes an attractive (or ugly) landscape. To see how important these experiences and values are, ask someone who has not experienced the landscape in the same way you have how *they* feel about it. The chances are that their thoughts will be quite different from yours.

As a geographer you can explain to your companion observer how the landscape you are looking at was formed and how various geomorphological processes are operating within it. In geomorphology we study the physical shape of the land (its relief), often by

Landscape as:	Main focus of 'reading'	Example land system	Questions to ask
'Machine and system'	Here we are most concerned with why the landscape works like it does. We need to consider the processes that are operating today and how these processes interact with one another.	River drainage basin	How does the rain that falls on the catchment maintain the drainage pattern system that is present?
'Palimpsest'	Here we are interested in the form of the landscape by analysing the processes that have created it over time. The emphasis here is on evolution rather than contemporary processes.	De-glaciated valley	What processes have combined, in the past, to lead to the development of the landscape we can see today?
'Taste and value'	Our concern here is with how the aesthetic quality of a landscape is defined by a particular set of social and cultural values. In this case the person viewing the landscape is as important as the landscape itself in terms of how it is interpreted.	The Himalaya	Would someone from a different society, or with a different upbringing, view this landscape differently from me?
'Social process'	The key here is the impact that landscape can have on society rather than the current form of the landscape itself. The role that landscape has on the population living in the area is the main focus.	Valleys, which once contained inhabited villages, that have been flooded (e.g. Ladybower Reservoir in the Peak District) to provide water for large centres of population	What impact has the nature of the landscape had on the development of society in the local area?
'Text'	Here we are interested in the way in which landscapes are described and interpreted by a third party.	Any landscape described and recorded in a travel guide, e.g. Bill Bryson's *Neither Here Nor There* (1998).	Can I describe, or sketch, the landscape that is being illustrated in the text once I have put the book down?
'Identity'	How landscape impacts on the cultural identity of people. An important point here is how different cultures relate to and connect with their environment.	Lake District fell	How might the views of a local sheep farmer and a holidaying fell walker differ with regard to the Cumbrian mountains?
'Performance and movement'	The argument here is that landscape can only be properly appreciated by interacting with it directly rather than simply viewing it. The world of physical geography is inherently linked to the world of human geography and to understand this we must experience the landscape of interest first-hand.	Urbanised river floodplain	How does my interacting with this landscape impact on my perception of it?

Figure 1 | *Ways of reading the landscape.*

detailed analysis of *landforms*. The interesting aspect for the purposes of this discussion, is that the geomorphological processes that formed a *landscape* may only be part of what makes a landscape. Physical process may even be irrelevant to the emotions and feelings each individual has when looking at it – the systems within the landscape are the same, whoever is looking at it, and yet we can still regard the scene in different ways.

In this chapter we will introduce a number of different ways of looking at the world; different hats to wear while considering any landscape that interests us. We will also consider how the variations in experience and cultural values might manifest themselves, and how these can be used to introduce landscapes to students in alternative ways. We feel that this may help students and teachers alike to gain a broader understanding of the case studies they investigate and ensure that, where possible, the physical and human aspects of geography are considered in unison.

A note regarding scale

When investigating a new landscape, both in the classroom and the field, it may be helpful to think about the scale at which it is best viewed. An assessment of the time over which we want to consider the landscape and the spatial range we want to look at can help focus our analysis on the most relevant aspects that students must extract from a case study. This exercise is valuable not only when investigating landscape but also when exploring all aspects of the geography of the world around us. Are we most interested in what has happened over the last second, hour, or day right through to centuries or millennia? And should we focus on the very small scale, or the very large, or somewhere in between?

In most cases the choice is simple. Climate change, for example, is best considered over hundreds to tens of thousands of years. Global warming predictions, however, suggest more rapid changes over decades. If we are studying synoptic charts in meteorology then days become our most appropriate timescale, while for microclimatology we might consider changes occurring over a few hours.

For other situations it is less clear. During a flood we may consider the process of the entrainment of a grain of sand or fine gravel at a very small scale. Alternatively we may wish to look at the undercutting of the outer bank of a meander or how the river is spreading out across the whole of its flood plain. Looking at more than one scale does, or course, give us more information about the system we are interested in. However, some of this information may not be relevant for students, so a clear awareness of the most appropriate scale will ensure that the necessary information is extracted.

Ways of understanding landscape

Both in the classroom and the field we need to be clear about the key points that we are trying to communicate to students when investigating a new landscape. This will have a major impact on the way in which we approach the task:

- Do we want the students to understand the processes that are operating on and within the landscape?
- Perhaps we would like them to think about what has happened in the past to make the landscape look like it does today?
- Alternatively, should students try to imagine a landscape from the point of view of those who live within it?

Each of these questions can cause us to look at the landscape in different ways, and, as a result, to understand it in more detail. Also, varying the perspective in this way may make it easier to explain the intricacies of new landscapes to students, as well as adding interest.

Figure 1 describes some different ways of reading landscape, and provides an example land system in each case, as well as a question that could be asked by students to draw out the information they need from the case study. You will, no doubt, be able to think of specific examples of case studies or questions that fit better with your teaching style or curriculum.

Examples

Landscape as 'palimpsest' – a de-glaciated valley

Glaciation has a major impact on the landscape. To understand why a valley, which has been glaciated in the past, looks the way it does today we must understand how long-ceased processes used to operate. Because these processes are not operating today we must base our interpretations of the environmental history of the valley on the evidence that remains. An investigation of currently occurring processes will only provide a partial history. By looking at the imprint of past processes, however, it is possible to get a full picture of the evolution of the valley.

Lesson idea – work with students to list all the sources of evidence that they may wish to collect to understand the environmental history of a de-glaciated valley. This may include a record of changes in vegetation, soil development, current landforms, climate records and present day analogues. Then ask students to act as landscape detectives to evaluate the relative importance of each source of evidence.

Landscape as 'identity' *vs* landscape as 'taste and value' – the Himalaya

Traditionally the people who live near the large mountains of the Himalaya have revered the mountains and imagined them as the homes of the gods, the centre of the universe, or the abode of the dead. The deities were often regarded as the protectors of local communities. These beliefs formed part of their culture and *'identity'*. Because the peaks were considered sacred no local people scaled them – at least, not before the early twentieth century. However, Western ideas of *'taste and value'* resulted in the mountains being viewed as something to be conquered simply because of their scale. The indigenous mysticism of the sacred mountain sites is diminished by the climbers who come from all

Photo: ©Simon Scoones

over the world in an attempt to ascend to their summits. If mountains become the world's playgrounds, there is a risk that they will lose their identity within the culture of the mountain people. Many indigenous cultures draw vitality and cohesion from their relationship with mountains and other sacred features of the landscape. Destroying what makes such a site sacred may undermine a culture, resulting in negative social, economic and environmental impacts as the society decays and traditional controls of land are lost.

Photo: ©Mark Horrell.com

Lesson idea – The Sherpas of Khumbu in Nepal view the craggy, fortress-like peak of Khumbila as the seat of the warrior god who watches over their homeland and protects their yaks. Actions that would make such a mountain unsuitable as the abode of its deity, appearing to drive the god, spirit, or ancestor away, may leave nearby villagers feeling vulnerable. Ask the students to split into two groups, Sherpas and climbers, for a class debate. The Sherpa group should attempt to make the climbers aware of the impact that their actions will have on the culture and beliefs of Sherpa society. The other group, the climbers, should try and justify why they feel they should be allowed to continue with their ascent of Khumbila.

Landscape as 'machine and system' *vs* landscape as 'performance and movement' – a river drainage basin

An investigation into some aspect of a river drainage basin, be it stream ordering, hillslope erosion or river channel processes, will be taught to the majority of students at some stage in their schooling. To understand the landscape as *'machine and system'* we must begin to appreciate how the individual features and forms are linked together within the landscape. Once we have done this we can start to build up a picture of how the drainage basin is functioning at the present time. All of this can be achieved in the classroom by looking at textbooks and photographs. To understand the landscape processes in more detail, however, students will have to experience its *'performance and movement'* themselves first-hand. This could be achieved through fieldwork or on a visit undertaken in their own time.

Photo: ©David Holmes

Lesson idea – Study a drainage basin using a textbook and photographs. Ask the students to write a short report about how the processes operate to make the landscape look like it does. Then take the students out to experience a drainage basin first-hand. Once fieldwork is complete ask the students to write another report about the landscape processes. Comparing the differences between the two reports will reveal the different perspectives on the landscape that the students have experienced.

Acknowledgements

This chapter draws on and develops ideas laid out in Huggett and Perkins (2004).

Related publications from the Geographical Association:
- Holmes, D. and Farbrother, D. (2000) *A-Z Advancing Geography: Fieldwork.*
- Knight, P. (2005) *Changing Geography: Glaciers and glacial landscapes.*

References

Bryson, B. (1998) *Neither Here Nor There: Travels in Europe.* London: Black Swan.

Huggett, R. and Perkins, C. (2004) 'Landscape as form, process and meaning' in Matthews, J.A. and Herbert, D.T. (eds) *Unifying Geography: Common heritage, shared future.* London: Routledge.

Implications for practice

(a) Landscapes can be investigated and interrogated in various ways.

Before introducing a new landscape to students we, as teachers, should be clear about the spatial and temporal scale we would like to use. We then need to ensure that we are reading the landscape in the right way – wearing the right hat – in order to extract the information we need. The questions we encourage students to ask should be conditioned by a conscious awareness, on our part, of the way we would like students to read the landscape (as 'machine and system', as 'palimpsest', etc., or a combination).

(b) The experience of different individuals has an impact on how they view the same landscape.

People connect with landscapes in different ways. If a student is having trouble understanding a new landscape in a particular way, as 'machine and system' for example, try to help them look at the landscape in a different way by asking different questions. It is possible that the difficulties they are having with comprehension are due to a difference in past experience or the context in which they are viewing the landscape. For detailed case studies, encourage students to consider landscapes in as many different ways as possible to maximise awareness and reinforce learning.

(c) First-hand experience of landscape brings a new perspective and understanding.

An obvious way to build awareness of landscape is to provide young people with the opportunity to experience them in as many ways as possible. This could include textbooks, systems diagrams, photographs, videos, written descriptions or narratives of indigenous people. The best ways to gain an understanding of a particular landscape, however, is to experience it first-hand. This can be accomplished through organised fieldwork or by encouraging students to explore landscapes with friends or family.

(d) In any analysis of landscape it is very difficult to separate physical and human aspects of geography.

Through the act of looking at a landscape in several ways the inherent links between form, process and society become clear. Landscape impacts on human activity and vice versa. The more perspectives that landscape is viewed from the clearer these links become.

Chapter 6

Real world learning through geographical fieldwork

David Caton

Before reading this chapter consider the following questions:

■ What purposes can be achieved through fieldwork?

■ How can students be actively engaged in their learning?

■ Should fieldwork be concerned with how students feel about the places that they visited?

■ How can conceptual understanding be developed?

I would like us to begin by imagining a visit to Torcross, a small, coastal village in Start Bay, South Devon (Figure 1). This picturesque settlement spills from a hillside onto a shingle ridge running between the sea and Slapton Ley, a freshwater lake. The place is a gift for geography teachers, providing an interesting opportunity for investigating coastal management, rural settlement and ecology. The future prosperity of the village is threatened by the impact of easterly storm waves that occasionally batter seafront properties. Furthermore, the coastal road that runs along the ridge, providing a crucial link for both locals and tourists, was seriously damaged by waves in the winter of 2001. Debate currently rages over whether the road should remain open. The future management of this problem has huge implications for the village economy and community, as well as the precious ecosystem sheltering behind the shingle.

If you were leading a field visit to this site, what activities would you want your students to do? The choice of fieldwork methods for the majority of teachers would probably involve the collection of quantitative data, possibly to test a hypothesis or answer a set of questions (see also Chapters 18 and 31). It is a very fertile environment for this type of approach. Activities such as beach profiles, traffic flow counts, vegetation surveys and questionnaires could be used to develop understanding as well as practical skills. However, no matter how successfully these methods were employed, there would be aspects of this place that remained beyond the scope of such techniques. Quantitative data could at most only hint at the beauty of the landscape, the feeling of irritation at the cars that race through this tranquil scene, the strength of community spirit or the worry of a shopkeeper whose business is threatened.

Yet these emotions are at the heart of the connection that people have with their environment. If students can develop an appreciation of these more qualitative aspects of the environment, then they may begin to see the essence of a place that sets it apart from any other. Fieldwork might then become more than 'the study of *any* stream or *any* town, where the peculiarity of landscape or landscape features is subordinated to perceived generality' (Pocock, 1983, p. 319). Students may also move beyond seeing people in their stereotypical categories of 'environmentalist' or 'shopkeeper' and more as individuals.

A further justification for a qualitative approach to fieldwork is in the benefits of getting students to describe their own feelings about the place that they are visiting. When learning about Torcross, for example, students may appreciate the aesthetic qualities of the landscape, become concerned about the future of the village or feel frustration at the potential impact of the proposed coastal defences. Research by Harvey (1991) highlights how students might have strong feelings about the place that they visit, yet may find that their fieldwork activities do not embrace this type of emotional response. Might there be a case for incorporating experiential fieldwork activities into a field visit in order to encourage students to develop and express their own feelings? When fieldwork consists only of quantitative techniques there is a danger that students may leave the study area burdened with data but lacking in insight.

A variety of qualitative fieldwork activities are in use in some field centres, primary schools and university geography departments. However, their adoption by secondary school geography departments may have been more limited. Figure 2 introduces the range of approaches that might be used in the field. The main purpose of this chapter is to examine this debate over approaches to fieldwork in more detail. The starting point will be an evaluation of what the more traditional approaches have to offer, before exploring the main purposes and methods of qualitative fieldwork.

Field research

The hypothetico-deductive approach to fieldwork (known as 'field research') entered geography departments in the 1970s, amid the quantitative revolution within the subject. This method, which has now come to a position of dominance in secondary schools, uses a scientific approach to test models or expected trends (Job *et al.*, 1999). The study is limited to a particular theme in a small area in order to make the content more manageable for both teacher and learner.

Figure 1 | *Torcross and Start Bay, South Devon. Photo: ©Simon Lewis.*

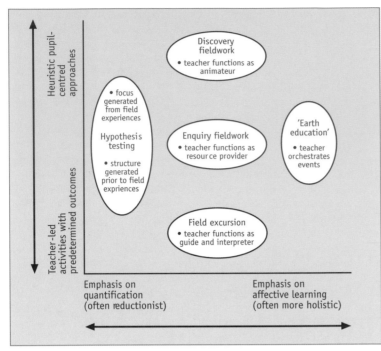

Figure 2 | *Some fieldwork strategies.*

The teacher, often in collaboration with the students, sets up the study by developing hypotheses or establishing questions to be answered through the fieldwork. These provide students with a clear structure and purpose as they work through a series of stages in order to find answers (Job, 1996). Quantitative fieldwork activities are used to collect evidence in the field, with an emphasis placed upon reducing bias. The students are therefore asked to distance themselves from their feelings about the place they are visiting in order to study it objectively. Once the data are collected they are presented and analysed before conclusions are drawn relating back to the initial aims of the project. Much of the process is directed by the teacher, which can reduce the feeling of ownership that students have over their work and prevent them from pursuing issues that catch their interest (Rynne, 1998; Job, 1999).

A strength of field research is the training it provides in a range of skills of data collection, presentation and analysis. Students are required to be actively involved in collecting data, which can be beneficial for developing both motivation and social skills. While in the 1970s this provided a significant departure from the more passive field excursions that preceded this approach, this has now become the norm in school fieldwork. However, the debate has now moved on to consider just how engaged students really are. A group of students noisily wielding equipment and calling out numbers while standing in a river may at first seem active, but this may overlook the limited contribution of some of its members and the repetitive nature of the task (Figure 3).

Questions have been raised about the levels of conceptual understanding achieved through field research. Although conceptual learning will undoubtedly take place, the emphasis of this approach is very much upon the research process and the use of skills within it (Rynne, 1998). Research by Harvey (1991) indicates that the transfer of conceptual learning from quantitative fieldwork to examinations can be poor. This can in part be attributed to having the main discussion of concepts in front of a set of data back in the classroom, rather than when the students are out in the field (Harvey, 1991; Rynne, 1998). It might also result from the lengthy process of data collection and presentation causing students to lose sight of the purposes of their investigation. Harvey (1991) also suggests that by focusing on one specific human or physical theme, students can be inhibited from appreciating the links between processes as well as the wider geographical context of their investigation. If developing knowledge and understanding is a priority for fieldwork, then there may be a case for re-evaluating the approaches that we use.

Further criticisms of field research concern the type of learning outcomes that tend to be encouraged. These investigations typically focus on patterns and processes, with values and opinions often given only superficial consideration (Job, 1996). For example, a study of urban social areas may show patterns of inequality yet may fail fully to engage students in a debate about the underlying causes of deprivation or what should be done to address this. Learning is also influenced by the reliance of field research on

Natural meandering channel – lower velocity, gradient and hydraulic radius

Channelised reach: straightened and re-sectioned. Increased gradient, hydraulic radius and velocity

Bank re-enforcement – rip-rap plus willow planting (more stable)

Collapse of rip-rap resulting in over bankfull discharge

Figure 3 | *Students investigate channel management. Source: Job, 2001.*

quantitative data. The subtleties of people and their interactions with the environment may be lost when they are reduced to numbers. While quantification can make it easier to see patterns and make comparisons, it can also oversimplify or even overlook qualities such as tension or beauty that make a place unique and interesting (Job, 1999).

Enquiry fieldwork

An attempt to address some of the limitations of hypothesis-testing fieldwork emerged in the late 1970s in the form of the enquiry-based approach (Job 1996). This adapts the hypothesis-testing framework to focus students on a geographical question or issue. Addressing issues such as 'Where should the bypass go?' or 'Where should a wind farm be built?' encourages students to examine people's opinions and values, and to develop their own. High levels of motivation can be generated when finding out about the conflicting points of view over an issue. This approach also involves students in examining a range of geographical factors within one investigation. This encourages them to see links between different strands of the discipline and work at different spatial scales, with subsequent benefits for conceptual understanding. Since this approach also includes quantitative fieldwork techniques, students will gain experience in similar skills to those developed by field research. Moreover, this values analysis will often allow them a greater role in planning fieldwork activities and also encourages the development of decision-making skills (Job, 1996).

Job (1996, 1999) identifies a number of limitations of the enquiry-based approach. First, many enquiries are limited to considering where a development should take place, rather than going further critically to consider whether it should take place at all, and

Strategy	Purposes	Characteristic activities
The traditional field excursion	■ Developing skills in geographical recording and intervention ■ Showing relationships between physical and human landscape features ■ Developing an appreciation of landscape and nurturing a sense of place	Students guided through a landscape by teacher with local knowledge, often following a route on a large-scale map. Sites grid-referenced and sketch maps to explore the underlying geology, topographical features, the mantle of soil and vegetation and the landscape history in terms of human activity. Students listen, record and answer questions concerning possible interpretations of the landscape.
Field research based on hypothesis testing	■ Applying geographical theory or generalised models to real world situations ■ Generating and applying hypotheses based on theory to be tested through collections of appropriate field data ■ Developing skills in analysing data using statistical methods in order to test field situations against geographical theory	The conventional deductive approach involves initial consideration of geographical theory, leading to the formulation of hypotheses which are then tested against field situations through the collection of qualitative data and testing against expected patterns and relationships. More flexible variants of this approach encourage students to develop their own hypotheses based on initial field observations, thereby incorporating an inductive element.
Geographical enquiry	■ Encouraging students to identify, construct and ask geographical questions ■ Enabling students to identify and gather relevant information to answer geographical questions and offer explanations and interpretations of their findings ■ Enabling students to apply their findings to the wider world and personal decisions	A geographical question, issue or problem is identified, ideally from student's own experiences in the field. Students are then supported in the gathering of appropriate data (quantitative or qualitative) to answer their key question. Findings are evaluated and the implications applied to the wider world and personal decisions where appropriate.
Discovery fieldwork	■ Allowing students to discover their own interests in a landscape (rather than through the teacher) ■ Allowing students to develop their own focus of study and methods of investigation ■ Encouraging self-confidence and self-motivation by putting students in control of their learning	Teacher assumes the role of animateur, allowing the group to follow its own route through the landscape. When students ask questions these are countered with further questions to encourage deeper thinking. A discussion and recording session then identifies themes for further investigation in small groups. This further work has arisen from students' perceptions and preferences rather than those of teachers.
Sensory fieldwork	■ Encouraging new sensitivities to environments through using all the senses ■ Nurturing caring attitudes to nature and empathy with other people through emotional engagement ■ Acknowledging that sensory experience is as valid as intellectual activity in understanding our surroundings	Structured activities designed to stimulate the senses in order to promote awareness of environments. Sensory walks, use of blindfolds, sound maps, poetry and artwork are characteristic activities. Can be used as an introductory activity prior to more conventional investigative work or to develop a sense of place, aesthetic appreciation or critical appraisal of environmental change.

Figure 4 | *Fieldwork strategies and purposes, Source: Job* et al., *1999.*

what alternatives there might be. Job also points out that fieldwork enquiries often require students to predict the outcomes of decisions, which can be difficult to do with any accuracy. Finally, he argues that since the questions on which enquiries are based rarely develop from the issues that concern individual students, they may not feel personally involved in their research. This may inhibit students from developing their own opinions and makes it less likely that they will be motivated enough to become actively involved with the issue that they have studied.

Purposes of fieldwork

By learning at first hand in the field, students will benefit in a wide variety of ways, but the choice of fieldwork approach will undoubtedly channel learning in a particular direction. For example, if field research is used it can be expected that the main outcomes will include learning how to use research procedures and developing skills of data collection and analysis. Similarly, enquiry fieldwork is likely to develop decision-making skills and help students to form geographical questions (Job et al., 1999) (Figure 4 provides more details of the purposes of different approaches to fieldwork). The key question that teachers need to ask themselves when planning fieldwork is 'What direction do you want to take your students in?' As the discussion so far has shown, critics of field research and enquiry-based learning have identified purposes and outcomes that are neglected to a greater or lesser extent by these methods. This concern has led to the development of a variety of alternative, more qualitative fieldwork approaches. These attempt to redress this perceived imbalance by encouraging outcomes such as:

- respect for nature
- aesthetic appreciation
- intimacy with the surroundings
- awe and wonder
- active participation
- getting into other people's shoes
- caring about a place and the people who live there
- having an encounter with a place
- improvement in literacy
- engagement with social, environmental and political issues
- developing practical skills
- challenging personal lifestyle decisions
- understanding how to have a more sustainable lifestyle
- seeing familiar places in a new way.

Inevitably each qualitative technique has slightly different aims, but an examination of their methods and purposes reveals recurring themes. Their methodology is characterised by a student-centred approach to learning. Students are encouraged to adopt a receptive, reflective manner in order to discover things for themselves. An affective response to the environment is encouraged, in which the emotions are engaged and feelings expressed. Learning is therefore opened up to become holistic, in which all aspects of a place are felt to be equally worthy of attention (Job, 1999).

The purposes of qualitative fieldwork methods fall into two, closely related camps. A first group of activities arose from the work of Steve Van Matre and others in the earth education strand of the environmental movement. Their aim is to develop love and respect for nature, in the hope that this might motivate students to care for their world more actively (Van Matre, 1979). A second group, largely focused upon urban environments, aim to develop a sense of place. This is driven by a desire to counter the growth of placelessness in the way that we perceive and learn about places (Goodey, 1982). Many of

Figure 5 | *Bark rubbing provides students with one way of 'getting in touch' with nature. Photo: ©David Caton.*

the activities across both of these genres have an underlying purpose that students might develop a greater understanding of their own perceptions, opinions and values.

While these methods resist being placed into neat categories, four groups can loosely be identified: sensory fieldwork, trails and expeditions, discovery and fieldwork for sustainable development.

Sensory fieldwork

Our reliance on sight leaves other senses underused, which can cause us to overlook many of the features that give a place its unique character (Pocock, 1983). Fieldwork methods that get students to close their eyes, use a blindfold or just listen carefully, can develop a sense of place by alerting them to aspects of an environment that they might otherwise have overlooked (Rogers, 2005; Figure 5). One effective technique is to use a sound map, where lines are made from a central point in the direction of any noise that is heard. At the end of the line, a note can be made as to what made the sound and whether it adds to or detracts from the environment. Sense of place might also be developed by activities such as feeling artefacts and surfaces, or smelling a baker's shop, factory or forest floor (Pocock, 1983; Job, 1999).

Trails and expeditions

In these related approaches, a variety of activities is used to encourage students to look closely and experience the place that they are visiting. The teacher facilitates this, but will step back as much as possible and allow the students to ask questions, follow their own impulses and find out for themselves. Activities are varied, but typically might include sketching, observing, describing and discussing (see, for example, Ward and Fyson, 1973; Goodey, 1982; Cosgrove and Daniels, 1989; Burgess and Jackson, 1992). One effective development of this method is for students to devise a trail for users with

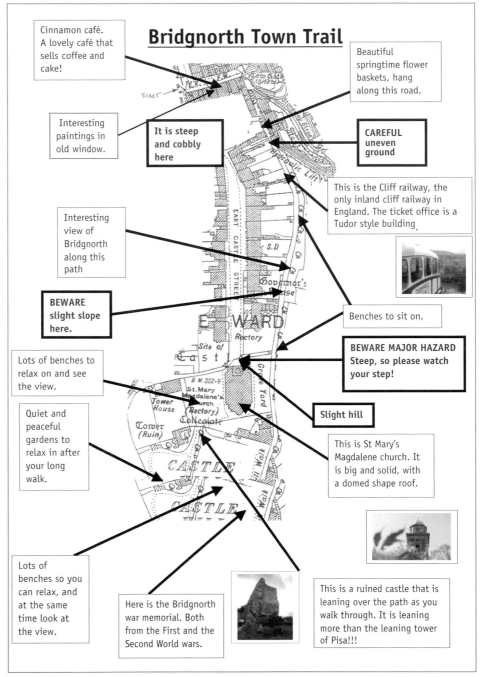

Figure 6 | *Town trail for elderly visitors to Bridgnorth. Source: Caton, 2001. Photos: ©David Caton.*

special needs (Dove, 1997). Figure 6 shows an annotated map that visitors with special needs could use to find a route through a town. Groups of year 7 students were first asked to decide what type of visitor they were aiming their map at (e.g. someone with a visual impairment, an elderly person with mobility impairment); and then to consider factors such as the hazards that particular visitors will encounter, what their needs might be and what features may be of interest to them. This encouraged the students to look closely at their surroundings and empathise with other people. Figure 6 shows the resulting town trail for elderly visitors to Bridgnorth.

Discovery

This approach, described by Hawkins (1987) and Job (1999), provides a framework for using experiential methods alongside quantitative techniques (Figure 7). The fieldwork starts with student-centred acclimatisation activities. These aim to get students to become more aware of their surroundings. Job's (1999) detailed account of discovery in Start Bay describes how students get to know the area by using drama, old photographs, chatting to locals and making landscape models with pebbles. Stimulating questions are written on 'Discovery cards', which are introduced as a further tool for acclimatisation. A discussion follows this initial stage, in which memorable experiences are shared. From these, issues and questions for a more conventional field study emerge. By doing fieldwork that arises out of the experiences and questions of the students, it is hoped that they might feel some attachment to the place they are learning about. This may make them feel more strongly about the issues that they have studied there and perhaps even encourage them to participate in improving things (Hawkins, 1987).

Fieldwork for sustainable development

A natural extension of this discovery approach is to place political awareness and action at the heart of the fieldwork. Since fieldwork will very often reveal a problem that may need resolving, this approach suggests continuing beyond the conclusion stage and taking practical action to make things better. Job (2001) illustrates this approach with a river study, in which quantitative fieldwork, combined with discussion within the group and with local people, leads to the students stabilising an eroding bank using traditional materials and techniques. A related approach is the demonstration of sustainable living through the hidden curriculum of fieldwork, such as by getting students to compost their waste, travel to their fieldwork site on a public service bus or learn about (and use!) composting toilets. One model of this approach is to use gardening as a way to learn about seasons, soil, plants and, more fundamentally, where our food comes from (Hutchinson, 1998).

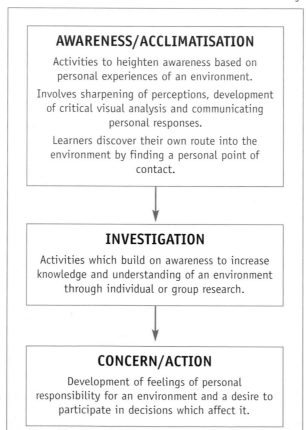

Figure 7 | A teaching-learning model for outdoor experience. After: Hawkins, 1987; Job, 1999.

AWARENESS/ACCLIMATISATION

Activities to heighten awareness based on personal experiences of an environment.

Involves sharpening of perceptions, development of critical visual analysis and communicating personal responses.

Learners discover their own route into the environment by finding a personal point of contact.

INVESTIGATION

Activities which build on awareness to increase knowledge and understanding of an environment through individual or group research.

CONCERN/ACTION

Development of feelings of personal responsibility for an environment and a desire to participate in decisions which affect it.

Figure 8 | 'We wondered what the dock workers would make of today's quiet, gentrified scene'. Photo: David Caton.

Using qualitative fieldwork methods

The following case studies – 'London Docklands' and 'Investigating rural settlements' illustrate some qualitative methods.

Case study 1: London Docklands

We enter the area travelling on the Docklands Light Railway. This offers us a chance to gaze at the mix of new and old, tidy and untidy outside the carriage, while rubbing shoulders with the office workers and local residents within. Travel around the study area is on foot, at a leisurely pace, occasionally taking a detour to answer questions such as 'What is through there?' or 'What is making that noise?' Stopping at some graffiti leads to discussion about whom it might have been written by, why they wrote it and what it might mean. A burned-out car provokes a similar debate.

In Wapping, old photographs showing hoards of men queuing for work at the very spot where we are standing lead us to think about what happened to people like these when the Docks closed. We wonder what they would make of today's quiet, gentrified scene (Figure 8). This theme is developed as we walk among the grand, confident architecture of an office development and its associated sculptures. Students who are studying for a GCSE in art enjoy the challenge of exploring their meanings. Some draw upon their previous geography lessons and begin to see how these rather plush modern buildings reflect the brash approach to redevelopment of the 1980s. Finally, the group is led towards the Cable Street Mural, where they reflect upon issues of race and conflict in East London's past and present.

Case Study 2: Investigating rural settlements

This trip involves visits to Craven Arms and Alveley, two small towns of similar size,

Craven Arms	Alveley
Shops and a car park People chat, Lorries roar past. A place to pass through.	Historic stone church Empty houses, open space. Where is everyone?

Figure 9 | *Students' haikus about the settlements of Craven Arms and Alveley in Shropshire*

located in different parts of Shropshire. A combination of qualitative and quantitative techniques is used to find out how and why these places are different from each other. An important sub-aim is to discover how much the pull of people to the West Midlands conurbation for jobs and services has influenced these settlements.

Initial quantitative surveys of services, the age of buildings, and traffic, as well as Census data and questionnaires, provide plenty of information about Craven Arms, the first place that we visit. Yet, there remains a feeling that we have ghosted through the settlement, collecting numbers as we go, without really pausing to reflect upon what this place is really like. A number of questions remain unanswered and my students are not as engaged as we would like. I wonder how much they would remember about this place in their far-off examination if we were to leave here without any further activities.

Qualitative techniques are employed in order to address these issues. We begin by listing the things that we observe people doing, however mundane they may appear. Later on, the bustling community in the centre of Craven Arms will be contrasted with the rather car-centred emptiness of Alveley, the dormitory settlement that we visit after lunch. I ask the students to write words that describe their perceptions of this place. After a minute, we begin to call out the words that best describe the town, so that we can hear what other people are thinking. I ask the students to use the words to write a haiku. These poems follow a strict structure of three lines, with five, seven, then five syllables (Figure 9).

They continue to develop and record their perceptions of Craven Arms by choosing one object that epitomises the place. Finally, we ask some local people to choose five words to describe the town. The words they use will later be sorted on a spreadsheet into 'positive', 'negative' and 'neutral'. This allows a quantitative comparison of perceptions of the settlement to be made, while phrases such as 'gossipy', 'a place you pass through' and 'one-horse border town' add greater depth of understanding and provoke discussion.

Ways forward

For some geography teachers, the approach described above will be novel. It might be helpful therefore to consider some of the other constraints that limit the use of qualitative fieldwork.

A crucial factor working against the use of qualitative methods with the 14-19 age group is the expectation of the awarding bodies that students will use either field research or enquiry for their coursework assignments. Teachers are understandably reluctant to risk their students' results by using alternative methods. Perhaps the most significant role for qualitative methods in this context could be to use them alongside traditional approaches in order to develop conceptual understanding and acclimatisation. Research by MacKenzie and White (1982) shows that fieldwork based upon memorable experiences and use of the senses is more beneficial for cognitive learning than a more passive, teacher-led approach. Slater (1994) and Reid (1986) develop this point by arguing that engaging feelings and emotions can help students to develop their objective understanding of concepts, as well as giving them a more rounded educational experience. By giving students greater awareness of the qualities of a place, qualitative fieldwork can provide a context for ideas, which is invaluable for linking thought and feeling and thus developing conceptual understanding (Slater, 1994).

Experiential methods might also have a role in GCSE and A-level coursework if they can be adapted to provide more objective forms of information. The use of sound maps in conjunction with a decibel meter and the aforementioned counting of positive and negative descriptive words provide two such examples. Furthermore, while quantitative techniques are likely to dominate at GCSE and A-level, there is a good deal more freedom to use qualitative approaches at key stage 3. Indeed, the focus that certain qualitative methods place upon themes such as sustainability, values and knowledge of places meets with some important priorities of the national curriculum. Moreover, certain activities might be used as a means to develop literacy skills and those involving practical activities might be incorporated into a citizenship programme (Job, 2001).

A further issue is that since qualitative techniques offer different ways of teaching and learning to field research and enquiry, they create new challenges for teachers. With such a student-centred approach, skilful management is required in order to guide the content gently towards worthwhile outcomes. It is also not uncommon for students to work at a fairly superficial, descriptive level when using these techniques. In their defence, it could be argued that the student who is writing good quality description, showing insight, empathy and well-developed literacy skills, may actually be working at quite a high level. Nevertheless, when leading qualitative fieldwork, the teacher should be mindful of the need to encourage explanation, perhaps with the use of questioning and thinking skills (Caton, forthcoming).

The future for geography fieldwork in secondary schools does not need exclusively to follow the well-trodden quantitative path. With a little imagination, geography departments can sometimes choose to take their students in a different direction. While the outcomes of these alternative methods are likely to be very different from those of field research and enquiry, they are nonetheless worthwhile, and they also complement these traditional approaches. It might be worthwhile for geography departments to take some time to discuss the approaches that they use in the field. Where quantitative methods are employed, a good deal of useful learning undoubtedly takes place. But it is also worth considering what can be offered by qualitative methods. If these can also be employed they may serve to heighten awareness, engage feelings and provoke questions, resulting in a richer, more varied educational experience.

Related publications from the Geographical Association:

■ Job *et al.*, 1999 (see below)
■ Holmes, D. and Farbrother, D. (2000) *A-Z Advancing Geography: Fieldwork*.
■ GA/FSC (2005) *Fieldwork File: Managing safe, successful fieldwork*.
■ *Teaching Geography* (2000) 'Focus on fieldwork', 25, 2, 52pp.

References

Burgess, J. and Jackson, P. (1992) 'Streetwork: an encounter with place', *Journal of Geography in Higher Education*, 16, 2, pp. 151-7.

Caton, D. (2001) 'An encounter with nature', *Teaching Geography*, 26, 3, pp. 139-41.

Caton, D. (forthcoming) *Theory into Practice: Reflections on fieldwork*. Sheffield: Geographical Association.

Cosgrove, D. and Daniels, S. (1989) 'Fieldwork as theatre: a week's performance in Venice and its region', *Journal of Geography in Higher Education*, 13, 2, pp. 169-83.

Dove, J. (1997) 'Perceptual geography through urban trails', *Journal of Geography in Higher Education*, 21, 1, pp. 79-88.

Goodey, B. (1982) 'Values in place: interpretations and implications from Bedford' in Gold, J. and Burgess, J. (eds) *Valued Environments*. London: Allen and Unwin, pp. 10-34.

GTIP webpages – www.geography.org.uk/gtip

Job, D. (1996) 'Geography and environmental education: an exploration of perspectives and strategies' in Kent, A., Lambert, D., Naish, M. and Slater, F. (eds) *Geography in Education: Viewpoints on teaching and learning*. Cambridge: Cambridge University Press, pp. 22-49.

Job, D. (1999) *New Directions in Geographical Fieldwork*. Cambridge: Cambridge University Press/Queen Mary Westfield College.

Job, D. (2001) 'Fieldwork for a change', *Teaching Geography*, 26, 2, pp. 67-71.

Job, D., Day, C. and Smyth, T. (1999) *Beyond the Bikesheds: Fresh approaches to fieldwork in the school locality*. Sheffield: Geographical Association.

Harvey, P.K. (1991) *The Role and Value of A Level Geography Fieldwork: A case study*. Unpublished PhD thesis, University of Durham.

Hawkins, G. (1987) 'From awareness to participation: new directions in the outdoor experience', *Geography*, 72, 1, pp. 217-22.

Hutchison, D. (1998) *Growing Up Green: Education for ecological renewal*. London: Teachers College Press.

MacKenzie, A.A. and White, R.T. (1982) 'Fieldwork in geography and long term memory structure', *American Education Research Journal*, 19, 4, pp. 623-32.

Pocock, D. (1983) 'Geographical fieldwork: an experiential perspective', *Geography*, 68, 4, pp. 319-25.

Reid, L.A. (1986) *Ways of Understanding and Education*. Oxford: Heinemann.

Rogers, J. (2005) 'Sensing places', *Teaching Geography*, 30, 1, pp. 38-9.

Rynne, E. (1998) 'Utilitarian approaches to fieldwork', *Geography*, 83, 3, pp. 205-13.

Slater, F. (1994) 'Education through geography: knowledge, understanding, values and culture', *Geography*, 79, 2, pp. 147-63.

Van Matre, S. (1979) *Sunship Earth: An acclimatisation programme for outdoor learning*. Martinsville IN: American Camping Association.

Ward, C. and Fyson, A. (1973) *Streetwork: The exploding school*. London: Routledge.

Implications for practice

(a) **There are a variety of ways of learning in the field, each has value but with different purposes and outcomes.**

Field research using quantitative techniques provides, among other things, experience in using research procedure. Enquiry is particularly helpful for developing values and decision-making skills. Qualitative methods can lead to a variety of outcomes, including developing a sense of place and care for the environment. Each method also has its limitations. To take account of this a department could usefully discuss the purposes that they have for a field visit prior to planning the trip. Very often a combination of approaches will ensure a more varied and fulfilling educational experience.

(b) **Qualitative fieldwork techniques can be used to enhance fieldwork in GCSE and A-level coursework.**

Acclimatisation activities can be used at the start of a coursework assignment to generate interest and awareness. If the aims of an investigation are developed from the student's own experience they may begin to care more about the place and issues that they are studying. Qualitative activities can also be used alongside quantitative fieldwork as a means of enhancing levels of conceptual understanding. Finally, some qualitative activities can be adapted to provide information that can be used as data in a conventional research project. Collaboration with other subject specialists can help geography teachers to develop their confidence and expertise in using qualitative approaches.

(c) **Teachers and students who are unfamiliar with qualitative fieldwork will benefit from finding ways to develop their experience of this approach.**

One way forward towards overcoming this is to work alongside specialist teachers from other subjects. For example, asking an English specialist to lead activities such as haiku poetry on a field visit can be a useful way to learn new teaching strategies while increasing awareness of the school's literacy objectives. Experience can also be gained for both teachers and students by adapting qualitative fieldwork activities for use within the classroom. Examples could include using poetry to describe the stages of a river or choosing an epitome of a place using photographs. Students learn what our subject involves from the content of their geography lessons. Teachers can engender in their students the belief that learning in geography involves emotions as well as objective understanding.

Chapter 7

Mapping for the future

Roger Jeans

> **Before reading this chapter consider the following questions:**
>
> ■ Are your students aware of when and why Britain was systematically and accurately mapped?
>
> ■ What functions have paper maps performed and what are the limits of using them with your students?
>
> ■ In what ways do geographical information systems (GIS) address these limits, and how can GIS as a resource in your classroom help to release the power of geography?

This chapter is concerned with the map resources of Britain, notably the contribution of the Ordnance Survey. Non-Ordnance Survey maps, such as those found in atlases, which are also vital for geography education, are not the main concern here (see also Chapter 11).

Introduction

Ordnance Survey was established in 1791 to provide accurate mapping of Great Britain for military purposes. Over the years that followed the mapping surveys were completed gradually by many different methods, culminating with the digitising of some 230,000 maps in 1995, making Britain the first country in the world to complete a programme of large-scale electronic mapping. Computers have transformed the map-making process, and electronic data are now routinely available to customers within 24 hours of being surveyed (see also Ordnance Survey website).

Many of the maps are used extensively in schools and for national examinations, such as GCSE and A-level, and are now produced from the digitised map data. In an article published in *Teaching Geography*, Vanessa Lawrence stated:

> *There cannot be a geography teacher in Great Britain who does not enthuse about the value of a good map. Maps are indispensable for a whole host of purposes. For business, administration and leisure, they have performed an essential role for centuries. Knowing how to read and interpret one not only helps ease a journey from A to B but also brings a landscape to life and can aid the understanding of the most complex social and economic issues ... Few maps are more familiar than those produced by Ordnance Survey at the many scales available to business and education. As the importance of geography grows, Ordnance Survey is at the heart of a revolution in mapping that is effectively bringing geographical information to life through sophisticated digital data (Lawrence, 2004, p. 116).*

Paper maps

There is an ongoing requirement for paper maps, especially for the leisure industry, and all the familiar scales continue to be available, although not always in the format of a folded map. Already it is possible to 'site-centre' and produce a plotted map with your required area in its centre.

Mapping at a wide variety of scales, from the 1870s to the present is available to schools either via the internet or from a growing network of suppliers across Great Britain. At the time of writing, Ordnance Survey is annually supplying a free 1:25,000-scale map to all year 7 students in Great Britain, thus ensuring that they have access to an appropriate resource for developing their mapping skills. To date, over a three-year period, Ordnance Survey has supplied over 2.3 million maps to schools for distribution to students.

Geographical information systems

With the completion of Ordnance Survey's digitising programme it became obvious that there were many uses for the new resources, in particular in relation to geographical information systems (GIS). This is an area that is expanding rapidly in the commercial and public sectors. It is widely acknowledged that such systems are invaluable for understanding and visualising information as well as the linking and analysing of disparate datasets. In the commercial sector GIS is playing an increasingly important role and is the must-have tool for all successful businesses.

Ordnance Survey data is already used by a range of public bodies [for many different purposes]: from analysing statistics in the last Census to locating suitable derelict land for house building; from identifying areas of deprivation to planning access to the countryside; and from controlling the flow of urban traffic to helping the police detect crime patterns. Its use commercially ranges from targeting marketing effort to calculating insurance risks; from managing property portfolios to developing in-car navigation systems; and from organising transport logistics to delivering real-time, location-based information on mobile phones. An independent study has calculated that around £100 billion worth of economic activity in Britain alone is dependent on Ordnance Survey data. Thus, GIS and associated digital data are clearly vital tools for geographers (Lawrence, 2004, p. 116).

From this it follows that geography teachers have an absolutely crucial role to play in ensuring that the next generation understands the power and relevance of geographical information (GI) – and in equipping young people with the skills and enthusiasm needed to pursue future careers with confidence. Encouragingly, employers increasingly need people with geographical skills, and Ordnance Survey recognises the responsibility it carries in supporting the teaching of the subject in schools. Even those young people that have no interest in geography may well find themselves working in an environment that uses GI indirectly. There are many software developers now producing GIS packages for schools that are designed to meet curriculum needs, some of which are described in the section on GIS packages.

Looking at how GIS can be used as a tool in business will help to explain the principles of using maps, GI software and geographical information the three necessary

Photo: ©Ordnance Survey.

Figure 1 | *GIS on properties. Note: All of the diagrams and data in this example are fictious and have been prepared to illustrate how a GIS works.*

Figure 2 | *The extent of previous floods in the same area.*

Flood Level - Autumn 1953

Flood Level - Winter 1971

elements of GIS. Below are two examples of how GIS is used in the commercial sector.

Example 1: Insurance

You may want to insure your car or property or perhaps buy a new house. There are many things that can affect what risk you represent to the insurance company, and these will be taken into consideration. But how does the insurance company make its assessment?

Suppose you want to insure your house. You telephone the chosen insurance company to ask for a quote and you are asked to supply your postcode details and house number. This is usually all the information the company needs to decide what risk they are prepared to insure you for. From the postcode, and using their GIS, they can immediately see precisely where your house is situated. They will have linked information about the site that could go back many years. They will also have statistics about incidents and maybe details of crimes committed around that locality, access to flooding records, subsidence, credit records and many other relevant datasets. They may also have information on proposed projects that might affect your property. All these factors are used to calculate your risk to them, and consequently what you will be charged for them to insure you. All the data and information are linked to the Ordnance Survey mapping data in their GIS. This will include a base map, from OS MasterMap®, to relate the data spatially, a postcode dataset such as Code-Point®, an address dataset, ADDRESS-POINT®, and maybe other layers of information such as historical mapping, a contour layer showing heights and geological information. In the figures below you can see how these data are linked to the mapping in order to identify the property in question.

Figure 1 shows each house identified by a blue circle. This is the seed in the GIS dataset that will be attached to information about each property. These identifying seeds have been produced using the Ordnance Survey ADDRESS-POINT dataset. A 1m contour dataset has also been overlaid on the mapping to aid identifying the height of the land surrounding the properties. This has been taken from Ordnance Survey's Land-Form PROFILE® dataset.

Figure 2 shows the extent of flooding in 1953, which was very abnormal, and 1971, less severe in the area shown in Figure 1. This would be one of the datasets held by the insurance company. You can see in this instance there was extensive flooding in 1953 that could happen again, unless substantial flood protection has been put in place since that date. With just this historical information you can see that a large number of properties have a much greater risk of flooding than others higher up the hill. Those properties that fall between the flood levels of 1953 and 1971 are at less risk than those falling below the 1971 levels so they would be a medium risk for the insurance company. Those falling below the 1971 levels would obviously be high risk as they will be the first to flood if the river water level were to rise. Check the flood levels against the contours in

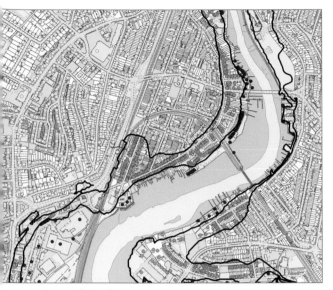

Figure 3 | *The flooding and housing data combined.*

Figure 1 as this shows the shape and height of the land on which the houses are built.

Combining the layers of information within the GIS will give an easily understood graphical image of the flooding risks to every property. Displaying complex databases visually in this way is a key element of GIS, well illustrated in Figure 3 where layers of data have been combined to show those houses most at risk from flooding, and consequently those with higher insurance premiums.

Flooding of properties in low-lying areas, such as river flood plains and coasts, appears to be on the increase in Britain and elsewhere, most probably due to global warming and related changes in climate and weather patterns across the world. Through using GIS to map actual and potential flood levels in relation to property and other data, insurance companies can plan ahead and formulate their policies in the light of possible future events. So too can local authorities, environment agencies and the government.

Example 2: Retail

The retail trade uses GIS to enable decisions to be made which help individual companies to run their business to greatest effect. The GIS of a company will hold information on all its store locations. Customer information is gathered at the checkouts and through the distribution of store and reward cards from the customers as they shop. Each time you shop at one of their stores and use your reward card, the information about you is entered into the system and stored. From this information a profile can be built of where you come from and how far you travelled to the store, how many times you use the store, what you buy, how much you spend, and so on. With this information collected from each customer a company is able to build a picture of its customer base, which can be used to aid marketing decisions and even to identify the best site to locate a new store. By interrogating the data it is possible for a company to identify how far customers travel to its shops, and also to identify those areas from which few or no customers travel.

By plotting all the gathered information on maps, using a GIS package, a company can easily identify spatial patterns in relation to customer behaviour. Such mapped data is invaluable in helping companies to reach critical decisions about a range of issues. For example, it helps them to identify: the best location for holding stock, or for a new store; regional differences in product purchase; areas where postal marketing would be most effective in boosting the customer base; and areas to target with new-product promotions. In summary, GIS is key to the future success of retail businesses.

GIS in schools

As mentioned earlier, the three main elements of GIS are digital map data, a GIS package, and information. Clearly, to make best use of GIS in schools the necessary hardware must be available.

Digital map data

The first thing that schools will need is Ordnance Survey map data and for LA-funded schools this can be obtained through the local authority. For all other schools, the latest information on where to acquire map data can be obtained from the Ordnance Survey website. The data most used in the software packages is Land-Line data, surveyed at

Figure 4 | *Land-Line available at 1:1250 or 1:2500 scale.*

1:1250 scale for urban areas (see Figure 4), 1:2500 for rural areas and 1:10,000 for mountain and moorland areas. However, this will be replaced by OS Mastermap in the near future. OS Mastermap is a far more sophisticated dataset that uses the full potential of GIS software.

Other map data downloaded from the internet can also be used free in most schools' GIS packages, providing it is used for teaching purposes. One example is the Ordnance Survey website under Get-a-Map™. Many other websites have useful map data, but it is always advisable to read the terms and conditions of use before downloading.

Schools GIS packages

Many GIS packages, to suit all levels of expertise, are available to schools for use in the classroom. All the packages incorporate a set of tools to enable you to work over the mapping base to create your own layers of information. Some link information such as databases, photographs and text can be added to the mapping to create interactive worksheets. Other packages have pre-designed symbols to drag and drop onto the mapping for specific projects, such as *Safe routes to school*. Almost all of them allow you to draw line work and create polygons to represent buildings, and some have measuring tools for measuring distances or calculating areas. A few new products on the market already incorporate mapping and datasets of your local area for you to use. They also include some 3D height data that brings the mapping to life. They all work on the same principles, i.e. enabling layers of information to be linked to a mapping base.

Deciding which is the best package for you is often the most difficult part of using GIS in the classroom. The list of available software shown at the end of this chapter offers some guidance. All of the companies listed will be able to send you a demonstration copy or literature for you to appraise before buying, and there are many more companies developing software all the time, so this list is not exhaustive. *Mapping news*, which is sent free to all schools by Ordnance Survey, will be updated every six months with the latest GIS packages available to schools, so this is a good source of information for helping you to decide what you need.

A number of Grids for Learning that are supported by the local authorities have a huge amount of map data and related datasets, so if you are within an area that has one of these it will provide you with a useful starting point for your entry to the world of GIS. These Grids are accessed through local networks, often by annual subscription, but offer the complete solution – including many lesson plans.

Web-based GIS

GIS Zone

The Ordnance Survey MapZone® website includes a dedicated section on GIS called GIS Zone. This explains GIS in simple terms and provides a series of GIS 'missions' for you and your students to have a go at, using GIS scenarios. The site is free to use and is not restricted, so can be used to provide a fun homework for those with internet access at home. The two sample screens (that you can work through on the GIS missions) are taken from the Flood mission. Here you need to use the information in conjunction with the mapping to decide the best three sites, out of the six given, to put the flood barriers to protect the areas from disaster. You will be given a score at the end, telling you how well you did ... or not!

Example 1: Flood mission

On this screen you choose your flood barriers using your knowledge and understanding of the terrain, and the information shown on the map. You are able to predict, using the contours, what will happen when your barriers are in place. In the list on the left you have many layers of information at your disposal, and you need to use these to help you to make your decisions.

Which barriers you choose will decide the success or failure of this mission! Can you save the area from flooding? Will you stay within budget? Is your solution viable? You then select, using a simple-to-use grading menu, three of the most suitable sites. Placing the barriers in the wrong locations will cause problems that will need to be overcome.

Example 2: Mission accomplished

This screen shot gives you an indication of how well you did in achieving the goals and gives you an opportunity to retry the mission.

Each of the missions can be developed further in the classroom in a wider context. All the missions touch on areas of citizenship, so possible follow-up activities might address questions such as:

■ What are the effects on the community?
■ What are the main issues – geographical or social?
■ What are the consequences of your decisions (e.g. in relation to flooding, or the siting of a wind farm)?
■ How could your chosen solution affect your local environment?

For the teacher there is a lesson plan for each scenario, and class activities and even a homework sheet for the students. There are many possibilities for extension work based around the different missions, and however they are used they will help students to understand the growing importance of GIS in the commercial world.

MapZone

This free site also provides opportunities for using maps in fun and enjoyable ways. It was developed with 7–16-year-old students in mind, and there are many useful free downloadable resources for the teacher to help with all map-reading skills. The site contains many educational games with a geographical theme, and there are competitions for students which use various parts of the information contained on the site. Students are taken through quizzes based on different themes, such as map symbols and grid references, gaining 'lives' as they go to enable them to move on to the fun parts. The more questions they answer correctly, the more 'lives' or turns they get to play the games. New games are added to the site periodically, so it is worth revisiting on a regular basis.

Augmented reality

Mapping in its present form is well established, either paper mapping or that available over the internet, but what is next? Ordnance Survey Research and Intelligence unit is looking hard at different ways of using the mapping databases that have already been produced. Some of these you may already be familiar with, such as in-car navigation

Figure 5 | *Picture as seen when viewed through the special glasses. The virtual labels are superimposed on the landscape.*

systems, or perhaps you have maps on your mobile phone that could be developed to include location-based information layers.

Technology moves forward at an ever increasing and, possibly for some, alarming rate, such that it is now feasible to combine datasets from many sources and link them with mapping to give a virtual reality image of that data. Imagine looking down your street through special glasses or the screen of a PDA to see how it looked before it was built, or as a set of a battle with aliens who are lurking in the doorways, or when you are walking or trekking being able to see virtual labels and way-finding information that augments the real landscape you are navigating (Figure 5).

Another recent advance in the technology enables special cameras to be used to plot selected points, from which visual images of planned buildings can be produced. Compare the two pictures shown in Figure 6 and work out which one shows the proposed new buildings.

GI development is heavily reliant on schools/universities producing GI-literate students, so ensuring a constant supply of expertise in this subject. In her speech at the 2004 Geographical Association Conference in Canterbury, Vanessa Lawrence Director General and Chief Executive of Ordnance Survey recognised the important part schools and teachers have to play.

> *Geography teachers have an absolutely crucial role in ensuring the next generation understands the power and relevance of geographical information and in equipping young people with the skills and enthusiasm needed to pursue future careers with confidence. Encouragingly, employers increasingly need people with geographical skills, and Ordnance Survey recognises the responsibility it carries in supporting the teaching of the subject in schools.*

GIS training for teachers

Ordnance Survey works closely with the Geographical Association and the Royal Geographical Society and, collectively, they are preparing training sessions for teachers for delivery through professional development units and conferences.

Figure 6 | *Spot the new 'virtual' building.*

Related publications from the Geographical Association:
- Phillipson, O. (2005) *Longman Student Atlas.* Pearson Longman/GA.
- Scoffham, S. (1997) *Atlaswise: Ideas and themes for atlas work.*
- Wright, D.J. (2000) *Theory into Practice: Maps with Latitude.*

References and resources

Print and electronic

Geographical Association – www.geography.org.uk (see projects section)

Lawrence, V. (2004) 'Mapping out the future', *Teaching Geography*, 29, 3, pp. 116-19.

MapZone – www.ordnancesurvey.co.uk/mapzone

Ordnance Survey – www.ordnancesurvey.co.uk

Royal Geographical Society (with IBG) – www.rgs.org

Producers of GIS software for schools

This list was correct at the time of writing, updates appear in *Mapping news* (Ordnance Survey) (see also Chapter 10 Resources list).

- Advisory Unit Computers in Education (tel: 01707 266714)
- Allied Integrated Technologies Ltd (tel: 0870 2406531)
- Anquet Technology Ltd (tel: 0845 2709020)
- Digital Worlds International Ltd (tel: 01303 297007)
- ESRI (UK) (tel: 01296 745500)
- EVO Distribution Ltd (tel: 0870 7409040)
- Intergraph (tel: 01793 492714)
- Pebbleshore (tel: 01273 483890)
- Soft Teach Educational (tel: 01985 840329)
- TrackLogs (tel: 01298 872537)
- WebBased Ltd (tel: 01752 764445)
- Wildgoose, Bluesky International Ltd (tel: 01530 518568)

Implications for practice

(a) Paper-based maps are not redundant.

Paper-based maps are cheap, flexible, robust, portable and 'fit for many purposes' in classroom and fieldwork contexts. Ordnance Survey now provides some free maps to schools, as well as site-centred mapping.

(b) Combine the use of paper-based maps and GIS technologies.

Devise ways of combining the use of printed maps and GIS technologies in investigations of the 'real world'. For example, make a telephone call, purchase an item from a supermarket, and your spatial (and other) behaviours can be mapped. It is possible to help students understand the basis on which GIS technology works, i.e. as layers of spatial data, as well as to grasp the implications of these technologies as a power for good and, potentially, for harm.

(c) Inspire students with mapping technology.

Many students can be inspired by the technology and it may be desirable well to develop this vocational skills 'pathway' as a popular application of geography education.

Chapter 8

Changing the subject – what's it got to do with me?

Eleanor Rawling

Before reading this chapter consider the following questions:

- Does the school geography curriculum provide a relevant and meaningful framework for your students' learning in the twenty-first century? If not why not?

- How did the school geography curriculum get the way it is? Does it matter to you and your students?

- What role can you and your subject colleagues play in changing and developing the curriculum?

Writing this chapter in the context of the recent Asian tsunami (December 2004-January 2005), and the major and horrifying consequences for human life and society, provided me with a stark reminder of the need for geographical education. No other school subject provides the overview, or the big picture, of the way in which the natural, social, economic and political worlds interact, often with devastating consequences. The kind of responsible and knowledgeable global citizenship which a good geographical education provides will never be more in demand than now – at the beginning of the twenty-first century.

And yet ... while we geographers know this to be true, the newspapers, a few weeks earlier bore headlines such as 'Geography teachers fail their students' and 'Students desert geography lessons'. How can this be true? What is happening to school geography?

The headlines were referring to a press release (24 November 2004) issued by the Chief Inspector of Schools, David Bell, in which he drew on evidence from school inspectors to report that:

> *geography lacks relevance and appeal because it focuses on subject content and factual recall rather than stimulating students' interest in the real world around them and the real issues which impact on their lives.*

Unfortunately other evidence from the subject associations and from the Qualifications and Curriculum Authority's monitoring programme seem to confirm that there are problems. In the primary curriculum, there is good practice but it is thinly spread because in many schools the subject has been marginalised by the focus on the literacy and numeracy strategies. At key stage 3, geography often seems to fail to grab students' attention or to result in high achievement, while at 14-19 we have the evidence of declining entries for GCSE and A-level since the mid-1990s to tell us that all is not well here either.

So who or what is to blame for this state of affairs? The newspapers in December 2004 almost all blamed the teachers. But the Chief Inspector, despite the press reporting, was actually drawing attention to the lack of curriculum time and professional support for geography teachers.

Each of these views may have an element of truth but they are only partial explanations. The real picture is much more complex. To understand the shape and character of the curriculum and the way it is interpreted in schools requires us to understand something of the mutual relationship between the subject, the role of teachers in schools and the national political context within which the curriculum operates. Let's start by exposing a few myths which seem to have penetrated surprisingly deeply within educational policy-making circles.

Myth 1: The school geography curriculum is a relatively static item ...

... deriving from a well-established and virtually unchanging block of knowledge and skills. The way it is packaged and the balance of content selected may vary slightly according to the concerns of society and the whims of policy makers, but overall it is unlikely to change dramatically. In this view, policy makers do not need curriculum planners considering the big picture, such as the aims of the curriculum and what a subject can contribute. It is assumed that, somehow, this is settled because geography is already in the curriculum. The task required is a low-level and technical one of neatly parcelling up the existing bits of geography into a national curriculum and GCSE/A-level specifications, and building in some kind of content progression from primary school to the end of secondary.

Myth 2: The role of the geography teacher is to deliver agreed content and skills ...

... as set out in the national frameworks prescribed by the state (as if they were the static packages described in myth 1). Because this is a statutory requirement, it is believed that there can be no debate about it. The role of the teacher is not to question, challenge or extend this framework but to know about it, to resource it, to teach it and to assess students' learning against standard measures. The appropriate support for such a role is that of training teachers in the required content and methods of delivery. Teaching is largely a technical task and hence it is quite possible to set up standardised systems and strategies for dealing with teaching methods and assessment practice.

Myth 3: School geography can be considered totally separately from academic geography.

...moreover, it is perfectly acceptable that they now seem far removed from each other in aims and character. School geography has developed in response to pressures from society for education to focus on employability, useful knowledge and a range of specific social and behavioural skills. Some apparently timeless aspects of basic geography can be used to develop these. Academic geography has expanded and diversified so that physical and human geography now have as strong links with cognate disciplines in the natural and social sciences as they do with each other. In addition, geographers have explored different perspectives on their discipline, becoming involved in philosophical debates and discussions about epistemology. None of this is relevant to school geography.

Photos: ©Diane Wright.

As presented here, the myths have been over-simplified, to make the case – but not a lot! Some examples from the current situation show how persistent they are:

■ Despite the opportunities provided by the two national curriculum reviews (1995 and 1999), the only changes that were allowed to geography were those of reduction, simplification and the addition of some new emphases promoted by the Labour Government (e.g. citizenship, numeracy, literacy, education for sustainable development). For GCSE and A-level, there has been an increasing number of structural and technical changes (e.g. modular format, new AS, synoptic assessment) but no curriculum reconsideration since the late 1980s (GCSE) and early 1990s (A-level). Effectively 15 years of regulation without curriculum development has left the national geography frameworks as static technical documents rather than representations of a dynamic subject discipline.

■ The Tomlinson Review of 14-19 qualifications (2004) might have provided an opportunity to reconsider the aims and purposes of the curriculum for this age group and to reassess the role of subjects and vocational learning areas within it. Instead the remit was narrowly focused on technical matters to do with qualification pathways and the mechanisms for merging and rationalising courses. Curriculum review was not undertaken and is unlikely to be a feature of the highly intensive programme of change following the 2005 White Paper. Geography has been filed away as a minor qualification under a social sciences heading, with no recognition of its full potential.

■ The Key Stage 3 Strategy has a mission to improve teaching and learning in schools and to raise standards of achievement. The preferred approach has been a technical, managerial one of focusing on generic teaching skills, apparently applicable to all subjects, and providing ring-binder manuals of 'how to do it', backed by heavily funded training programmes for teachers. While there is much potential and good practice in the materials (assessment for learning, thinking skills, etc.), the overall ethos of the strategy is that of training technicians to undertake a clearly defined task. The messy, but professionally satisfying, realities of dealing with dynamically evolving subjects, deep-seated subject-based professionalism and the power relations of schools and classrooms seem to be glossed over, buried within the smooth management-speak of target setting, auditing and coaching.

It is not just that these examples represent a different approach. The problem is that the direct consequence of basing policy on these myths is that it leads to the situation we now have for geography (and probably other subjects too). The school subject has lost dynamism and relevance. It fails to present a clear image and purpose to policy makers, the public and students; it fails to take on new perspectives from the academic subject that might illuminate current issues for young citizens; and it fails to motivate and attract students or their teachers. Inevitably students vote with their feet, as soon as they are able, and leave the subject. More significantly, a whole generation of young people is missing out on the distinctive understanding and perspectives that a geographical education can provide.

So what can be done about it? Figure 1 shows a rather different representation of the subject curriculum system. Ideally the State sets a minimum national framework, comprising overarching and agreed aims and intentions, suitable for the twenty-first century. Subjects can then consider their distinctive contribution to such a curriculum – asking 'What if my subject were not there? What would be missing?' A national subject framework can then be drawn up, ideally focusing on the concepts, big ideas and relevant skills and attitudes contributed by geographical education.

It is essential that the subject framework is minimal and flexible enough to enable schools and teachers to interpret and translate this framework (i.e. make the curriculum) as appropriate for their students and their community. This is a view of the subject as an

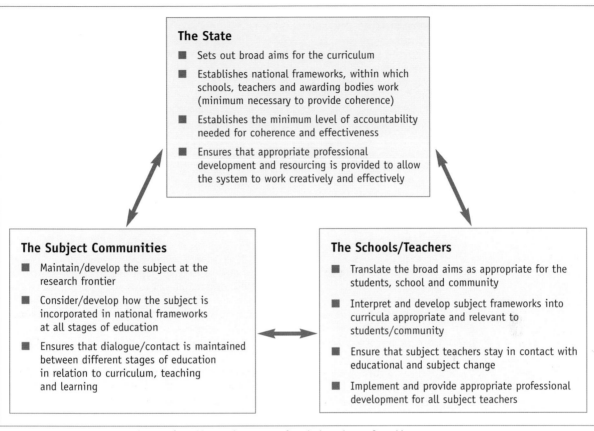

The State
- Sets out broad aims for the curriculum
- Establishes national frameworks, within which schools, teachers and awarding bodies work (minimum necessary to provide coherence)
- Establishes the minimum level of accountability needed for coherence and effectiveness
- Ensures that appropriate professional development and resourcing is provided to allow the system to work creatively and effectively

The Subject Communities
- Maintain/develop the subject at the research frontier
- Consider/develop how the subject is incorporated in national frameworks at all stages of education
- Ensures that dialogue/contact is maintained between different stages of education in relation to curriculum, teaching and learning

The Schools/Teachers
- Translate the broad aims as appropriate for the students, school and community
- Interpret and develop subject frameworks into curricula appropriate and relevant to students/community
- Ensure that subject teachers stay in contact with educational and subject change
- Implement and provide appropriate professional development for all subject teachers

Figure 1 | Looking at the process of curriculum change for subjects.

educational resource, in which subject expertise and subject specialism are more not less important as a foundation for the school curriculum. There will need to be appropriate levels of professional support, time and funding to facilitate school-based curriculum development. Dialogue with the wider geography subject community is essential to provide a dynamic flow of new ideas and new perspectives which can regenerate the national framework directly, clarify the public image and provide appropriate professional development opportunities for teachers.

This is all very well you may think – but isn't the direction of the next round of change already sewn up? How can the subject community or teachers individually make any difference? In fact, signs of change in the direction of Figure 1 are under way to some extent. For example, the QCA Futures Project was established in the autumn of 2004 with the aims of promoting a wide-ranging debate about the future curriculum, and of ensuring that the outcomes of this are fed into the changes taking place to the national curriculum and at 14-19 over the 2005-2010 period. QCA's Curriculum Division, which is leading this project, hopes to ensure that the debate will not just be conducted in terms of qualifications structures and technical procedural solutions. Discussions within subjects, via a series of subject summits, have been one of the first steps undertaken. The geography summit took place in January 2005, involving classroom teachers, the two geography subject associations, teacher educators and academic geographers. Figure 2 presents an early draft of the summit's thinking about geography's distinctive contribution to a future curriculum.

Figure 2 | *Geography's distinctive contribution. Source: ©QCA, Geography Futures.*

The key concepts (big ideas)

- Geographical imagination – a sense of place, identity and an ability to negotiate in and about place
- Spatial awareness – the importance of where things are and how they relate to other phenomena, and why it matters
- Interdependence – the interconnections and inter-relationships operating in a complex, diverse, interconnected world – explaining and coping with the dynamics of change
- Scale and scale linkages – how all scales from the personal and local to global are linked, and the importance of recognising this in the way we conduct our lives
- Interactions – the way in which geographers draw across the physical and human worlds to understand environmental change, sustainable development, social and cultural exchange, and to clarify the big picture for human society

The distinctive experiences, skills and attitudes

- Valuing and building on students' own experiences of their lives, their communities and the wider world
- Promoting an active and critical approach to enquiring about the world around them and so developing thinking skills, problem-solving approaches and the ability to recognise, clarify and confirm their own attitudes and values
- Contributing to political literacy by providing opportunities to explore the values dimension of issues concerning society and environment
- Emphasising fieldwork and outdoor learning, providing a distinctive opportunity to investigate and explore in the real world. Practical, social and behavioural skills developed
- Developing graphicacy and visual literacy through geography's distinctive use of maps, diagrams, computer images, multimedia, geographical information systems
- Promoting social awareness, environmental responsibility and understanding of cultural diversity through real-world issues at different scales, so assisting students in identifying personal routes for action – a unique contribution to global citizenship
- Developing young people's social and emotional development, e.g. through group work, fieldwork, individual enquiry and addressing real and significant questions and issues

Another encouraging development is the QCA/OCR Geography GCSE Pilot (see QCA and GA websites below). This has shown how a course can be conceptually based and more selective of content, how appropriate new developments from academic geography can enliven and refresh the school subject, and how students' own experiences can be drawn on in a rigorous and meaningful way. The geography pilot has also raised important questions for all subjects about future curriculum development. The QCA geography team was able to steer the pilot project in a very direct way, drawing on the subject associations, curriculum experts and geographers in higher education, and making funding available for teachers' professional development and support. Where are the mechanisms to ensure that this happens in the future? If curriculum content is being reviewed, it is vital to consider how curriculum development can become an integral part of the system rather than yet another temporary upheaval.

The Geographical Association and the Royal Geographical Society (with IBG) are also following their own subject-modernising agendas in closer collaboration than has been the case in recent years. Much of this work is making an input to policy, via, for instance, the Secretary of State's Geography Focus Group (2004-05) and the subsequent action programme supported by the DFES.

The message is that now is the time for geographers to make a difference. To move to a sounder system, in which the emphasis is on curriculum quality and teacher professionalism, will require nothing less than a culture change throughout the national education system. The bad news is that there is still a long way to go. The good news is that for the first time in about 20 years, things are beginning to move in the right direction. The geography community is already on the case and it needs your input!

Implications for practice

(a) How can my views on what geography has to offer to the curriculum make a difference?

- Liaise with subject colleagues at all levels to identify the fundamental aspects of the subject which you think should be at the heart of any curriculum. Concentrate on the big ideas and important skills. Selecting detailed content is a secondary issue. Contribute your ideas via subject association channels.

- Try to extend or re-establish dialogue with academic geographers in your area. Invite their involvement in school curriculum and teaching matters. Join in subject updating or discussion sessions.

- Involve yourself in important debates about the subject via the subject associations and their committees or local groups.

- Publicise the purpose and aims of geography widely to parents, students and other staff in the school. Be clear about geography's distinctive contribution to citizenship, global awareness, environmental understanding and sustainable development. Go for a simple and effective statement rather than a long list of topics or issues.

(b) How I can be involved in changing the curriculum culture?

- Consider the national frameworks for geography as minimal and flexible and redesign or reinterpret them for your students and schools – even now, before any reviews or changes take place. You may be surprised at how much flexibility there already is.

- Start from your students' prior experience and knowledge, as far as you can, in planning selection of content and teaching and learning activities. Young people's geographies are more extensive than we think and provide an excellent base on which to build more conventional geographical knowledge and understanding.

- Take part in local, regional or national curriculum initiatives if possible. For example, GA curriculum projects, the Pilot GCSE Geography, local school/higher education institution activities, specialist school developments in your region. You may even want to join or start a local GA Branch.

- Try to steer curriculum discussions in your school into seeing subjects as fundamental resources to be used in addressing any new initiatives, not as chunks of content for which room has to be found.

Related publication from the Geographical Association:
Rawling, E. (2001) (see below)
Scoffham, S. (ed) (2005) *Primary Geography Handbook*.

References

Final Report of the Working Group on 14-19 Reform (Tomlinson Report) www.14-19reform.gov.uk/reports

Geography GCSE Pilot – www.qca.org.uk/subjects/geography and www.geography.org.uk/pilotgcse

QCA *Futures: Meeting the Challenge* – www.qca.org.uk/futures

Rawling, E. (2001) *Changing the Subject: The impact of national policy on school geography 1980-2000.* Sheffield: Geographical Association.

Rawling, E. (2003) *Connecting Policy and Practice: Research in geographical education, a BERA professional user review*, British Educational Research Association.

Section two
Teaching and Learning geography

Section two: Teaching and Learning geography

❝ The distinctive aspect of a teacher's sense of purpose is that it is dominated by matters to do with children's learning (from Lambert, D. (2004) 'Geography' in White, J. (ed) *Rethinking the School Curriculum*. London: Routledge Falmer, p. 82).

❝ An enquiry approach to learning is consistent with a widely held theory of learning. Enquiry can be justified because of the emphasis it places on thinking and understanding, rather than on memorisation. Enquiry can also be justified because it can be used to achieve broader educational purposes (from Roberts, M. (2003) *Learning through Enquiry*. Sheffield: GA, p. 36).

❝ For a subject like geography, with its diverse content and roots in the wider world, it is also about learning from and building on students' experience, seeing them as integral parts of geographical enquiry, and blurring the distinction between in-classroom and out-of-classroom learning (from Rawling, E. (2001) *Changing the Subject*. Sheffield: GA, p. 177).

❝ To me, fieldwork is the heart of geography... It renews and deepens our direct experience of the planet and its diversity of lands, life and cultures, immeasurably enriching the understanding of the world that is geography's core pursuit and responsibility ... Without fieldwork, geography is secondhand reporting and armchair analysis, losing much of its involvement with the world, its original insight, its authority, its contributions for addressing local and global issues, and its reason for being (from Stevens, S. (2001) 'Fieldwork as commitment', *The Geographical Review*, 91, p. 66).

❝ Your view of this country has been built up through how the media have depicted the UK, through how you were taught at school to view human geography, and through what your friends and family told you. All these influences on your knowledge were in turn influenced by other events (from Dorling, D. (2005) *Human Geography of the UK*. London: Sage, p. 1).

Chapter 9

Geographical enquiry

Margaret Roberts

> ## Before reading this chapter consider the following questions:
>
> ■ What examples are there in your own classroom practice of 'geographical enquiry'?
>
> ■ In your classroom is geographical enquiry an occasional activity or an approach to learning?
>
> ■ What would be the best example of 'geographical enquiry' in your own classroom practice?

" *The first key to wisdom is constant questioning ... By doubting we are led to enquiry and by enquiry we discern the truth* (Peter Abelard, 1079-1142).

What is geographical enquiry?

What makes enquiry geographical?

There is nothing particularly new or geographical about the term 'enquiry' (or 'inquiry' as it is sometimes spelt). The term has been used for centuries in a variety of contexts and, in relation to secondary education in England, it is currently used across seven subjects of the national curriculum: citizenship, design and technology, geography, history, ICT, mathematics and science (DfEE/QCA, 1999a).

What makes an enquiry 'geographical' is **what** is being investigated and **the kinds of questions** being asked. Neighbour (1992) identified the emergence of five 'core' questions that he claims have:

" *received national and international recognition as the focus for geographical education at high school level:*
1. What is the phenomenon?
2. Where is it located?
3. Why is it located there?
4. What impact does its location have?
5. What changes should be made? What ought to be done? (Neighbour, 1992, p. 15).

Section A

What do you think are the characteristics of geographical enquiry? Look at each of the possible characteristics below (A1-A12) and decide whether it is essential for geographical enquiry or not.

	Geographical enquiry ...	Essential	Not essential
A1	■ incorporates the whole sequence of enquiry skills from questions through to evaluation (Figure 4)		
A2	■ includes some field work		
A3	■ includes the use of primary data		
A4	■ includes both physical and human aspects of geography		
A5	■ is related to an issue about which there are different viewpoints		
A6	■ is an approach to learning to be applied to all themes and places studied		
A7	■ includes the identification of questions		
A8	■ includes the suggestion of hypotheses		
A9	■ includes the collection of data		
A10	■ includes the analysis of data		
A11	■ includes evaluating information		
A12	■ requires students to give their own opinions		

Section B

How essential is students' involvement (B1-B10) in the different stages of geographical enquiry work?

	The students ...	Essential	Not essential
B1	■ choose the example to be studied (e.g. which volcano, which LEDC)		
B2	■ are involved in identifying key questions or hypotheses		
B3	■ devise the procedure for the study		
B4	■ locate sources of information		
B5	■ collect data		
B6	■ decide how to present data		
B7	■ analyse and interpret the data themselves		
B8	■ reach their own conclusions		
B9	■ evaluate the study		
B10	■ express their own views		

Figure 1 | *What do you think are the characteristics of geographical enquiry?*

Positive responses to:	Possible influences
A1-A3	GCSE and/or A-level specifications which refer to enquiry only in relation to the coursework investigation and not in relation to the content as a whole. Note: All geography GCSE and A-level specifications require candidates to collect first-hand primary data and to use the whole sequence of enquiry skills (Figure 3).
A4	GCSE and/or A-level specifications which emphasise a people/environment approach and in which physical geography is not studied as a separate entity.
A5	GCSE and/or A-level specifications that focus on issues.
A6	GCSE and A-level specifications that promote an investigative, enquiry-based approach to all the themes studied. This is also required by the geography national curriculum.
A7–A12	The sequence of enquiry skilled lists in the geography national curriculum and in GCSE and AS/A-level geography specifications. A positive response to only question A7 suggests a restricted view of enquiry, possibly influenced by the list of 'Thinking skills' in the introductory section of the *National Curriculum: Handbook for Secondary Teachers in England* (DfEE/QCA, 1999a). According to the Handbook, enquiry skills: *'enable pupils to ask relevant questions, to pose and define problems, to plan what to do and how to research, to predict outcomes and anticipate consequences, and to test conclusions and improve ideas'* (DfEE/QCA, 1999a, pp. 23-4). Other skills, in spite of being generally thought of as integral to geographical enquiry, are not included under the heading of enquiry skills but are categorised under different headings: ■ Suggesting hypotheses is included in 'Creative thinking skills' ■ Evaluating information is included in 'Evaluation skills' ■ Collecting data and analysing data are included in 'Information-processing skills' ■ Giving reasons for opinions and making judgments are included in 'Reasoning skills'.
B1–B5	GCSE and A-level specifications which require students to make decisions at all stages of an enquiry. Some specifications allow teacher to plan this part of the coursework investigation. Positive responses could also be influenced by the geography national curriculum which requires pupils to be taught to: 'Ask geographical questions, suggest appropriate sequences of investigation' (DfEE, 1999a, p. 22).
B6–B10	All GCSE specifications for coursework require students to be involved in these stages of the enquiry process, as does the geography national curriculum. The extent to which teachers enable students to make decisions depends on their interpretation of the geography national curriculum and of examination requirements and the extent to which they value more student centred approaches to learning.

Figure 2 | *Comments on questionnaire responses.*

A list of core questions can provide a supportive framework but should be open to scrutiny, debate, modification and extension because what geographers study and the questions they ask change over time. Neighbour's questions do not incorporate recent developments in human geography which take into account different geographies and perspectives. These might be addressed by a question such as *'How is space and place experienced and represented by different people?'*. Any set of questions in themselves, however, does not make it clear what geographical enquiry means in the context of the secondary school curriculum. Before we go any further, I invite you to clarify your own views by responding to the questionnaire in Figure 1 and by reading the comments on the questions in Figure 2.

Photo: ©*Margaret Roberts.*

Different understandings of geographical enquiry

Research has shown that people are uncertain of the meaning of 'enquiry' (Rawling, 2001; Roberts, 1998). This is hardly surprising as the term is used in two rather different ways, as is evident in the comments on the questionnaire.

First, the term is used to refer to a discrete piece of work, the kind of investigation required for GCSE and A-level geography coursework. Such investigations require the collection of primary data, usually in the field, and the use of the complete sequence of enquiry skills (Figure 3). The use of a similar sequence of enquiry skills in the geography national curriculum (DfEE/QCA, 1999b, p. 22) could lead people to think that what is required is something similar to an investigative course study.

The geography national curriculum, however, uses the term 'enquiry' to mean an approach to learning to be used for all themes and places studied. The enquiry approach to learning geography was first introduced by the three Schools Council geography projects of the 1970s and 1980s. Naish *et al.* (1987), writing about the Schools Council

Stage:	Skills
1	Planning the enquiry, identifying the issue, questions and/or hypotheses, and planning how to investigate
2	Collecting, recording and presenting data
3	Analysing and interpreting data
4	Reaching conclusions
5	Evaluating the enquiry

Figure 3 |
Sequence of enquiry skills.

16-19 geography project, wanted students 'to enquire actively into questions, issues and problems, rather than merely to accept passively the conclusions, research and opinions of others' (Naish *et al.,* 1987, p. 45). The Bristol Project wanted students to be engaged in 'activities which involve them in processes of inquiry [sic] similar to those which geographers themselves follow when attempting to solve problems' (Tolley and Reynolds, 1977, p. 21). The Geography for the Young School Leaver (GYSL) Project also emphasised students' active involvement in the learning process. The style of learning promoted by all three projects contrasted with a style of learning in which geographical information was transmitted or 'delivered' to students by the teacher. These projects have had a continuing influence on examination specifications. Four of the current GCSE specifications and two of the current A-level specifications explicitly promote an enquiry approach to the study of all the content specified (Figure 4) and set out what is to be studied under headings of key questions to be investigated rather than as content to be learnt.

Although what is written in this chapter is relevant to separate coursework investigations, its focus is on the second meaning of enquiry as an approach to learning.

Why is geographical enquiry important?

An enquiry approach to learning geography can be justified in relation to a theory of learning, in relation to how knowledge is constructed and in relation to the overall purposes of education.

1. It is an approach to learning which involves students in making sense of new information for themselves

According to constructivism, a widely accepted theory of learning, we can learn about the world only through actively making sense of it for ourselves (Barnes and Todd, 1995). Knowledge cannot be transmitted to us ready made; it cannot be 'delivered'. In order to learn we have to connect new knowledge with what we know already. The sense we make of new knowledge depends on our existing ways of thinking; on what Massey calls our 'geographical imaginations' (Allen and Massey, 1995). An enquiry approach provides scope for students to make connections with their existing knowledge and ways of thinking. It enables students to make sense of new data for themselves through their active involvement in analysis and interpretation. It can enable students to become aware of their own geographical imaginations through which they understand the world.

2. It acknowledges that geographical knowledge is not 'out there' as some absolute reality, but that it has been constructed by geographers

What counts as geographical knowledge has been constructed by people who have asked particular questions at particular times and in particular places. Geographers have developed ways of seeing the world and have constructed theories to understand it and stories to explain it. They search for new information in light of these stories. These ideas have been well expressed in relation to journalism by Claud Cockburn:

> *To hear people talking about facts, you would think that they lie about like pieces of gold ore in the Yukon days waiting to be picked up. There are no such facts. Or if there are, they are meaningless and entirely ineffective; they might, in fact, just as well not be lying about at all until the prospector – the journalist – puts them into relation with other facts: presents them in other words. They become as much a part of a pattern created by him [sic] as if he were writing a novel. In that sense all stories are written backwards. They are supposed to begin with the facts and develop from there, but in reality they begin with a journalist's point of view, a conception*
> (quoted in Wheen, 2002, p. xii).

(a) GCSE specifications

		AQA A	AQA B	AQA C	Edexcel A	Edexcel B	OCR A	OCR B	OCR C
Course work essential requirements	Use of primary data	■	■	■	■	■	■	■	■
	Use of complete sequence of enquiry skills	■	■	■	■	■	■	■	■
	Fieldwork	■	■	■	■	■	■	■	■
Characteristics of specification as a whole	Physical geography studied separately				■				
	Physical geography in people/environment context	■		■		■	■	■	■
	Emphasis on issues			■		■		■	■
	Decision making/ problem solving paper			■		■		■	■
	Enquiry approach encouraged for study of all themes			■		■		■	■
	Content framed by key questions			■		■		■	■

(b) AS/A2-level specifications

		AQA A	AQA B	Edexcel A	Edexcel B	OCR A	OCR A	OCR B	OCR B
Level at which examined		A2	A2	AS	AS	AS	A2	AS	A2
Characteristics of personal investigative study	Use of primary data	■	■	■	■	■	■	■	■
	Use of complete sequence of enquiry skills	■	■	■	■	■	■	■	■
	Fieldwork	■	■	■	■	■		■	
	Assessed by centre		■	■	■				■
	Examination alternative to presentation of coursework	■	■	■					
Characteristics of specification as whole	Physical geography studied separately	■	■	■					
	Physical geography studied in people/ environment context				■			■	
	Emphasis on issues				■			■	
	Decision making paper		■		■			■	
	Enquiry approach encouraged for study of all themes				■			■	
	Content framed by key questions				■			■	

Figure 4 | *Enquiry in geography (a) GCSE specifications, and (b) AS/A2 level specifications.*

Geographical stories, like journalists' stories, start with points of view, with geographical conceptions, and are created by geographers who put facts 'into relation with other facts' so that they are not 'meaningless'.

The enquiry approach to geographical education recognises this; by involving students in constructing geographical knowledge for themselves they can become aware of how such knowledge is created. It can make them aware of the selectivity of knowledge.

3. It has the potential to give students more control over their own learning

Students who are involved in geographical enquiry are learning how to learn at the same time as they are learning geography. By developing enquiry skills, students learn how to investigate an issue, how to select data, to be critical of data, to analyse and interpret data for themselves and to reach their own conclusions. Geographical enquiry can be an empowering process in which students gain greater awareness of how they learn and how knowledge is constructed and presented to them. This can only happen if the teacher allows students to participate in the decisions that are made in constructing knowledge. If teachers make all the decisions, then students learn to do little more than follow instructions. If we think it is important that students learn to take more control of their own learning, then we need to be aware of when and how and why we are controlling enquiry work and when and why and how we are enabling students to have control. Figure 5, based on a framework devised by Barnes *et al.* (1987) provides a structure for analysing the extent to which teachers control enquiry work and the extent to which students are enabled to participate in the construction of geographical knowledge.

	Closed	Framed	Negotiated
Content	Focus of enquiry chosen by teacher.	Focus of enquiry chosen by students within theme (e.g. choosing which volcano to study).	Student chooses focus of enquiry (e.g. choosing which LEDC to investigate).
Questions	Enquiry questions and sub-questions chosen by teacher.	Teacher devises activities to encourage students to identify questions or sub-questions.	Students devise questions and plan how to investigate them.
Data	All data chosen by teacher. Data presented as authoritative evidence.	Teacher provides variety of resources from which students select data using explicit criteria. Students encouraged to question data.	Students search for sources of data and select relevant data from sources in and out of school Students encouraged to be critical of data.
Making sense of data	Activities devised by teacher to achieve pre-determined objectives. Students follow instructions.	Students introduced to different techniques and conceptual frameworks and learn to use them selectively. Students may reach different conclusions.	Students choose their own methods of interpretation and analysis. Students reach their own conclusions and make their own judgements about the issue.
Summary	The teacher controls the construction of knowledge by making all decisions about data, activities and conclusions.	The teacher inducts students into the ways in which geographical knowledge is constructed. Students are made aware of choices and are encouraged to be critical.	Students are enabled, with teacher guidance, to investigate questions of interest to themselves and to be able to evaluate their investigation critically.

Figure 5 | *The participation dimension in geographical enquiry.*

What are the essential aspects of geographical enquiry?

There are four essential aspects of geographical enquiry that need to be considered in planning both schemes of work and individual lessons: creating a need to know; using data as evidence; making sense of data; and reflecting on learning. These aspects together with some of the thinking skills related to them are shown in Figure 6.

Creating the need to know

Geographical enquiry is about having an inquisitive attitude towards the world and to what we know and understand. It seems vital, if students are to learn anything in school, that they too have a 'need to know', that they too are made curious, are puzzled, and want to ask their own questions. Even when the key enquiry questions are identified by an examination specification or by the teacher, it is important that these questions and any subsidiary questions become the students' own questions.

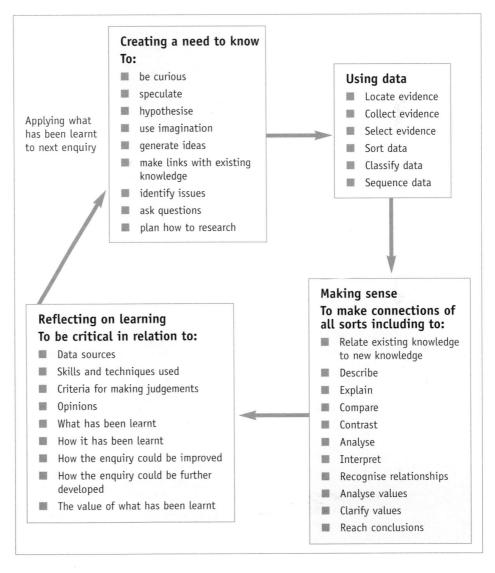

Creating a need to know
To:
- be curious
- speculate
- hypothesise
- use imagination
- generate ideas
- make links with existing knowledge
- identify issues
- ask questions
- plan how to research

Applying what has been learnt to next enquiry

Using data
- Locate evidence
- Collect evidence
- Select evidence
- Sort data
- Classify data
- Sequence data

Making sense
To make connections of all sorts including to:
- Relate existing knowledge to new knowledge
- Describe
- Explain
- Compare
- Contrast
- Analyse
- Interpret
- Recognise relationships
- Analyse values
- Clarify values
- Reach conclusions

Reflecting on learning
To be critical in relation to:
- Data sources
- Skills and techniques used
- Criteria for making judgements
- Opinions
- What has been learnt
- How it has been learnt
- How the enquiry could be improved
- How the enquiry could be further developed
- The value of what has been learnt

Figure 6 | *A framework for learning through enquiry.*

Text as data
- Textbook descriptions and accounts
- Non-fiction, e.g. travel writing
- Fiction
- Newspapers – articles, letters
- Magazines
- Brochures
- Advertisements

Visual data
- Photographs
- Paintings
- Drawings
- Diagrams
- Advertisements
- Video
- Cartoons

Statistical data
- Tables of figures
- Bar graph
- Pie chart
- Choropleth map
- Line graph
- Flood hydrograph
- Population pyramid
- Climate graph

Maps
- Ordnance Survey maps
- Atlas maps – political, physical and thematic
- Maps in use outside the classroom, e.g. in brochures and newspapers, football tickets
- Weather maps

Personal knowledge
- Memories of place including remembered images
- Memories of events
- Mental maps
- Personal theories and ways of seeing
- Personal knowledge gained indirectly

Objects
- E.g. bags of rubbish
- Artefacts
- Food
- Rocks

Figure 7 | Types of data that can be used as evidence in classroom enquiry work at key stage 3.

There are several ways of creating a need to know, these include:

1. **Stimulus** Teachers can provide some sort of stimulus to promote curiosity and questions (Davidson and Catling, 2000). The stimulus could be in the form of resources, e.g. photographs, or in the form of activities which invite students to speculate, e.g. intelligent guesswork (Roberts, 2003).
2. **Stance** Bruner (1986) contrasted two stances that a teacher could adopt in relation to what was being studied. A teacher could 'open wide a topic to speculation and negotiation' by suggesting doubt and uncertainty in his/her talk. Alternatively, a teacher could 'close down the process of wondering by flat declaration of fixed factuality'. One of the ways of creating a need to know is by recreating in the classroom the sense of the uncertainty that preceded what is now known. But how often do teachers convey uncertainty? When they do, it is memorable. For example I can still remember my biology teacher, Miss Page, being genuinely puzzled about how birds managed to migrate. Her 'stance' made us wonder and puzzle with her. In an enquiry approach to learning it is more appropriate at the start of a lesson or unit of work to establish the questions which are to frame the investigation than to inform a class of the outcomes of what is to be learnt. How can outcomes of enquiry work be anticipated with any degree of certainty?
3. **Choice** Enquiry work can be organised so that students investigate what interests them most. They could, for example, be given a choice of which volcano or earthquake or tourist destination to investigate.
4. **A motivating outcome** A need to know can be created by students having to present their findings to the class or to a wider audience: e.g. in a television presentation, in a *PowerPoint* presentation, in a role-play, on a display or in a letter or report which is actually going to be sent to someone.

Using data as evidence

Geographical enquiry needs good data that can be used as evidence in the investigation. But what constitutes 'good data' and how can data be used 'as evidence'? Good data for enquiry would:
- be relatively unprocessed, so that information has not already been extracted for them. The range of data that can be used in geography is vast (Figure 7);
- include data likely to be encountered in the world outside the classroom, e.g. publicity maps, televised weather forecasts, in order to help students make sense not only of geography resources but also of the world they live in;
- include some irrelevant information. Students need to learn to distinguish between relevant and irrelevant information and to select what is relevant;
- have the source of the data acknowledged.

The following activities would encourage students to use data as evidence rather than as 'fact':
- Locating information on the internet or in libraries. This can make students aware of the vast amount of data on any subject and of the presence of conflicting data.
- Selecting relevant information (from textbooks, libraries, the internet,

from mystery statements, see e.g. Chapter 26, page 344).

■ Extracting information from data, using a variety of note-taking frames. If students are introduced to a variety of note-taking frames they can learn how the same data can be used in different ways to produce different information.

■ Making inferences from data. Students should be encouraged in geography, as they are in history, to distinguish between what they can definitely say, what they can infer from a data source and what they cannot say from a given data source. The Layers of Meaning framework (Figure 8) can be used to develop these skills in relation to a variety of data sources, e.g. photograph, text, map, graph.

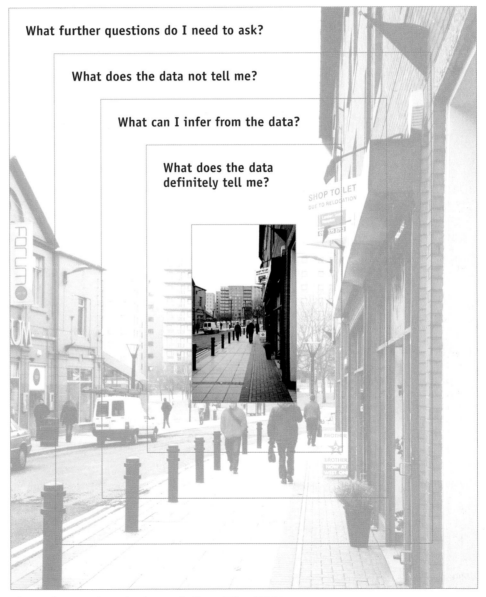

What further questions do I need to ask?

What does the data not tell me?

What can I infer from the data?

What does the data definitely tell me?

Figure 8 | *Layers of meaning framework. Photo: ©Diane Wright.*

Making sense

Making sense is at the heart of learning. Geographical enquiry is essentially about using the information collected from data to develop understanding and to construct geographical knowledge. There is a difference between information and knowledge. Students can find information from a wide range of data but that in itself is not enquiry. Enquiry is not simply about students finding information to answer a question and writing the correct answer in their books. It is about developing understanding. In order to do this, students need to do something with the information they have collected. They need to see relationships between different bits of information, to make all kinds of connections, to relate it to what they already know and to develop their own understanding of what they are studying.

Activities which help students to make connections and make sense include:
- Extended writing of all kinds, including personal writing
- Making oral presentations to others
- Creating a *PowerPoint* presentation
- Producing a video or a set of photographs
- Drama activities, including formal role-play
- Concept mapping (Leat and Chandler, 1996)
- Making displays.

Reflecting on learning

Another essential aspect of learning through enquiry is the process of reflecting on learning. This has two elements:
- Reflecting on *what* has been learnt
- Reflecting on *how* it has been learnt.

Reflecting on *what* has been learnt

Throughout enquiry work it is important to stand back and ask critical questions. All of the following should be open to scrutiny and evaluation:
- the questions posed at the outset;
- the way the data was collected and/or selected;
- the validity of the data;
- the reliability of the data;
- the ways in which the data have been presented;
- the ways in which the data have been analysed and interpreted; and
- the conclusions reached.

Students can be prompted to think critically about what they are doing throughout the enquiry process. Reflecting on what has been learnt pays critical attention to the way knowledge has been constructed and could be part of a planned debriefing activity.
- Are there any other questions we could have asked at the start of the enquiry?
- Which resources did you find most useful and why?
- Were these sources of information reliable? Why or why not?
- Would it have been useful to have some other sources of information? If so, what?
- Do you think you would have found out something different from different resources?
- What advice would you give to another class carrying out a similar enquiry?

Reflecting on *how* learning has taken place: 'going meta'

Psychologists are paying increasing attention to the role of metacognition in learning. Bruner describes this as 'going meta' or 'turning around on what one has learned' (1996, p. 88). 'Going meta' involves making students aware of their own thought processes. When students are 'going meta' they are attempting to put their thinking processes into words so that thinking processes can be shared, evaluated and developed further. Research has shown that students are capable of doing this and that 'going meta' improves learning (Bruner, 1996).

Students can be encouraged to 'go meta' both during individual or small group consultations with teachers or in whole-class plenary activities. Questions which encourage students to 'go meta' would vary according to the activity but might include:

- How did you set about doing this?
- What did you find easy/difficult? Why?
- What things did you consider when making that decision?
- What alternatives did you think of?
- What categories did you use?
- How did you set about combining information from different sources?

The questions above are only suggestions; questions need to be devised which are appropriate to particular enquiries. Such questions are important not only as plenary whole-class debriefing questions but also for the conversations that teachers have throughout a lesson with individuals and small groups. Some of the essential differences between an enquiry approach to learning and a transmission 'delivery' approach to teaching are in the kinds of conversations that teachers have with students. Research showed that it was these interactive conversations and not the activities themselves that were 'the difference that made the difference' in children's learning (Beveridge, 1995, p. 151). In the same way that a teacher can adopt a stance in creating a need to know, so a teacher can adopt a stance that encourages critical reflective thinking throughout the enquiry process. Critical reflective questions can be included in the planning process for geographical enquiry.

Example 1: Year 8 enquiry: recycling

In this series of lessons year 8 students investigated the theme of recycling. These lessons demonstrate the essential aspects of an enquiry approach to learning. The teacher created a need to know by inviting students to devise their own questions and by providing a wider audience for the outcome of their research. The students had to locate and select data from the internet and to make sense of the data by planning how to present their own work to create a newsletter. The plenary discussion sessions encouraged both the students and the teacher to reflect on the process of the enquiry and the adequacy of the data. The data could have been supplemented with resources on recycling in the area local to the school.

Lesson 1

Starter: Introduction to the enquiry
Introduce students to the topic being investigated: What shall we do about recycling?
Give students Task Sheet (Figure 9)

- Inform students about what they are going to do:
- Generate questions about recycling in groups
- Find out about recycling from the internet
- Use the information to produce a newsletter

Recycling - what can we do about it?

Aim of this series of lessons:
To produce a Tupton Hall Newsletter about what we can do about the recycling issue.
We could be:

- As individuals
- As a group
- As a family
- As a school
- Or a mix of all of the above

Tasks

1. Group work: Brainstorm the key question you wish to research (use the grid over the page to help you)
2. Individually/pairs: Use the internet to find out the answers to your key questions (Quick tip: each member of the group researches the answers to different key questions)
3. Group work: Gather back as a group and share your research answers
4. Individually: Using *PagePlus*, produce a newsletter about **'What we can do about recycling'** (Hint: use the why, what, where, how order for your newsletter)

Websites

www.alupro.org.uk www.foe.co.uk/campaigns/waste/issues/recycling www.epa.gov/recyclicity
www.wastepoing.co.uk/wasteconnect www.useitagain.org.uk/texts/green02b.html
www.bbc.co.uk (search recycling or go to 'where I live' then Leicester, then Links)

Figure 9 | *The year 8 recycling activity sheet.*

Activity 1: Devising questions (creating a need to know)

Students work in groups of 3 and 4. Each group devises four questions using note-taking frame (Figure 10). The group decides who should investigate each question.

Recycling - what can we do about it?

	Key Questions	Answers
Why?	■ ■ ■ ■	
What?	■ ■ ■ ■	
Where?	■ ■ ■ ■	
How?	■ ■ ■ ■	

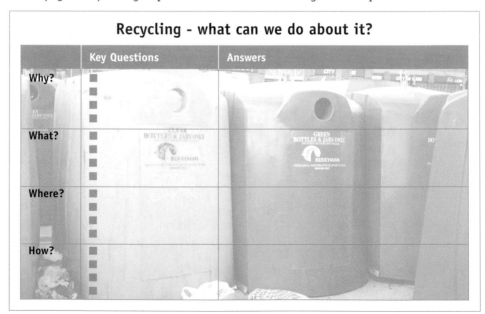

Figure 10 | *The note-taking frame. Photo: ©Diane Wright.*

Activity 2: Using data

Students work individually at computers. Teacher supports.

Plenary: Reflecting on learning

Feedback on enquiry so far:
What have they found out so far?
Which questions were easy to research? Which websites were good/not so good?
Which questions were difficult to research? Can these questions be re-phrased?

Lesson 2

Activity 1: Using data

Students continue their research using the internet. Teacher supports.

Activity 2: Making sense of data

Students reconvene in groups. Each student reports back on what he/she has found out.
The group decides how this information should be presented in a newsletter.
The group decide on what each person in the group will do.

Plenary: Making sense of data: scaffolding

Discussion of how to present and structure the newsletter.
What ideas have the groups had so far? What kinds of headings could be used?
How could the information be presented? What is the most important information to include?

Lesson 3

Activity 1: Making sense of data

Students work on the computers compiling the newsletter.

Plenary: Reflecting on learning

What have they learnt about recycling?
What kinds of things can be recycled? Which are the easiest for people to recycle?
Where is it possible to recycle? Is it important to recycle? If so, why?
What have they learnt from writing the newsletter? If they were starting the whole project again, what would they do differently? What advice would they give another class?
Follow up: the newsletters are displayed for everyone to see.

Example 2: Year 10 enquiry: urban redevelopment

This series of lessons was used with year 10 students studying for GCSE Geography (OCR specification B). Again, the essential aspects of an enquiry approach to learning were evident. The teacher created a need to know by asking the students to take part in a real-life consultation exercise about the town they lived in. Students' own local knowledge and their own opinions were highly relevant to the study. The teacher also created a need to know by providing a real audience for the students' reports; they were going to be read by Town Planners. They had access to real data from the world outside the classroom: Local Plans, consultation documents and Ordnance Survey maps.

They had to make sense of the data for themselves by responding to the consultation questions when writing their reports.

Lesson 1

Starter: introduction to the enquiry

Students were asked to think about their local town, Worksop, and to jot down any problems or issues that needed to be addressed. Their ideas were pooled on a spider diagram on the board. For a few of the issues raised, possible solutions were discussed briefly.

The class was then given the leaflet produced by Bassetlaw District Council entitled 'A new Local Plan for Bassetlaw: Your chance to shape the future of Bassetlaw'. They were told that the class would take part in the consultation process. Attention was drawn to some of the questions in the leaflet:

- How would you like to see your town change in the future?
- Are there any features that should be protected or kept just as they are now?
- Is more land needed for housing? If so where should this be?
- Is there a need for any environmental improvements?

Students were informed that they were going to work in groups to find out more information and to produce reports of their own recommendations. These would be submitted to Bassetlaw District Council within the period of the consultation and a Planning Officer from the Council would read them and report back to them.

Activity: Using data to find out about the Local Plan

Students worked in groups using copies of the Local Plan and copies of the local Ordnance Survey map to identify what they wanted to stay the same and what they wanted changed.

Lesson 2 and homework

Activity: Using data and making sense of data

Students continued to collect data for a report.
Students started to plan their reports, supported by the teacher.

Lesson 3 and homework

Activity: Using data and making sense of data

Students completed their reports which were then sent to the Council.

A few lessons later...

Activity: Plenary meeting with Planning Office

A Planning Officer from the Council visited the class, gave a talk on 'A planner's job and duties in relation to urban regeneration' and replied to all their suggestions. Each group had a chance to raise an important local issue to which the Planning Officer responded. Following the lesson, the Planning Officer wrote to the class commenting on their suggestions about:

- Removing the one-way traffic system
- Improving public transport
- Providing more CCTV cameras
- Providing better leisure activities
- Redeveloping the Mayfair Centre

The students' reports and suggestions were kept at the local council offices for later inspection together with any proposals made by other members of the general public.

Related publications from the Geographical Association:
Fisher, T. (2002) *Theory Into Practice: WebQuests in Geography.*
Roberts, M. (2003) (see below).

Acknowledgement

The author wishes to thank Jeanette Shipley, Tupton Hall School, Chesterfield, and Matt Podbury for permission to reproduce the series of lessons in Examples 1 and 2. Matt organised and developed the activities when he was a PGCE student on school experience at Valley Comprehensive School, Worksop.

Implications for practice

(a) How can I create a 'need to know' for my students?

It is all too easy for geographical enquiry to remain the teacher's enquiry, in which students have no real curiosity about what is being investigated. It is good to reflect on what creates a need to know for particular classes; to explore what provokes their curiosity, what makes them want to investigate. The three 'S's are important: stimulus, stance, speculation. It is worth exploring different kinds of stimulus, it is worth adopting a wondering stance rather than an authoritative stance and it is worth developing strategies to promote speculation.

(b) How can I help students make sense of data?

Making sense takes time and involves more than transferring information from data sources to notes. We need to give students opportunities to:

- relate new information to existing knowledge
- select data for themselves so that they become aware of the selective nature of knowledge
- deal with conflicting data
- apply geographical frameworks and concepts to knowledge
- think for themselves about data, to discuss data and to reconstruct information in new ways
- reflect critically on what they have learnt.

References

Allen, J. and Massey, D. (1995) *Geographical Worlds*. Milton Keynes: Open University Press.

Barnes, D. and Todd, F. (1995) *Communication and Learning Revisited*. Portsmouth NH: Boynton Cook Publishers Inc.

Barnes, D., Johnson, G., Jordan, S., Layton, D., Medway, P., and Yeoman, D. (1987) *The TVEI Curriculum 14-16: An interim report based on case studies in twelve schools*. Leeds: University of Leeds.

Bruner, J. (1986) *Actual Minds, Possible Worlds*. Cambridge MA: Harvard University Press.

Bruner, J. (1996) *The Culture of Education*. Cambridge MA: Harvard University Press.

Davidson, G. and Catling, S. (2000) 'Toward the question-led curriculum 5-14' in Fisher, C. and Binns, T. (eds) *Issues in Geography Teaching*. London: Routledge Falmer.

DfEE/QCA (1999a) *The National Curriculum: Handbook for secondary teachers*. London: DfEE/QCA.

DfEE/QCA (1999b) *Geography: The National Curriculum for England*. London: DfEE/QCA.

Leat, D. and Chandler, S. (1996) 'Using concept mapping in geography teaching', *Teaching Geography*, 21, 3, pp. 108-12.

Naish, M., Rawling, E. and Hart, C. (1987) *Geography 16-19: The contribution of a curriculum project to 16-19 education*. Harlow: Longman.

Neighbour, B.M. (1992) 'Enhancing geographical inquiry and learning', *International Research in Geographical and Environmental Education*, 1, 1, pp. 14-23.

Rawling, E. (2001) *Changing the Subject: The impact of national policy on school geography 1980-2000*. Sheffield: Geographical Association.

Roberts, M. (1998) 'The nature of geographical enquiry at key stage 3', *Teaching Geography*, 23, 4, pp. 164-7.

Roberts, M. (2003) *Learning through Enquiry: Making sense of geography in the key stage 3 classroom*. Sheffield: Geographical Association.

Tolley, H. and Reynolds, J.B. (1977) *Geography 14-18: A handbook for school-based curriculum development*. London: Macmillan.

Beveridge, M. (ed) (1995) *Managing the Literacy Curriculum*. London: Routledge.

Wheen, F. (2002) *Hoo-hahs and Passing Frenzies: Collected journalism*. London: Atlantic Books.

Chapter 10

Using ICT to create better Maps

Fred Martin

Before reading this chapter consider the following questions:

■ What does a good map look like and what criteria do you use to assess the quality of maps drawn by students?

■ How does students' use of maps in geography contribute to the development of their visual literacy?

■ How can ICT be used to improve the quality of maps drawn by students and the ways in which they visualise places?

Maps in a time warp

Map drawing in schools can give geography a bad name. At worst, it may be little more than a time-consuming colouring activity. Assessing the quality of a student's map can hinge on individual perceptions of neatness and aesthetics, rather than the application of criteria that identify the student's level of competence to produce a map that is both accurate and technically proficient. There are some occasions in geography when a simple hand-drawn sketch map can be justified. There are even some occasions where a more artistic approach may serve a useful purpose. But on most occasions, the main purpose of drawing maps is to show distributions of data accurately, effectively and with technical competence.

In many schools, the activity of drawing maps seems to be in a pre-computer time warp, sometimes lacking even the most basic technical aids such as mapping nibs and stencil sets (Figure 1). Slarti Bartfast, reputed in *The Hitchhiker's Guide to the Galaxy* (Adams, 1981) to have designed Norway's fjords by hand, would not feel out of place in these schools. Fortunately, this is not universally true. There are schools that have embraced the digital revolution and are taking advantage of the tools that ICT can offer to work in geography, both in general and for mapping in particular. Perhaps what is missing is a shared understanding among members of the geographical community regarding the most basic question of all, i.e. 'What makes a good map?'

Figure 1 |
Good map skills?
Source: National Curriculum
in Action website.

The comment on this map reads 'Good map skills'. The content and choice of mapping techniques may be 'good', but is this the best technical quality one ought to expect from a year 9 student?

Using maps

Map work remains at the heart of work in geography. In its widest sense, map work involves:

- collecting data from primary or secondary sources to form the map's content;
- drawing the map with technical competence using appropriate mapping techniques;
- reading and processing the data from a map to describe what it shows;
- interpreting the map to extract meaning from the patterns.

Of these aspects of map work, the focus in this chapter is on the second, i.e. on drawing a map that reaches the highest technical standards in whatever technique has been chosen to present the data. The other aspects of map work are equally important but lie beyond the present focus. They are aspects of map work that are more in the cognitive domain and have little to do with the practical skills needed to draw a map.

There is little guidance of any real value in either the national curriculum programmes of study for geography or in the subject's level descriptions to show how progression can be achieved in drawing maps, or on which criteria can be used to assess them. This is left to the professional judgement of each teacher, though some elements of guidance are provided as exemplification through the National Curriculum in Action website. Awarding body criteria at both GCSE and post-16 levels include references to the use of ICT and even to the use of geographical information systems (GIS). These references, however, are illustrative and optional, presenting nothing that focuses the minds of either teachers or students on questions of technical competence and on criteria of quality. This lack of guidance means that definitions of quality need to come from within the geography community itself and, in particular, from teachers of geography.

Visual literacy and maps

The development of literacy through the national Key Stage 3 Strategy and in the key skills agenda appears only to focus on skills to read, write and understand text (see Chapter 11). Yet this is a world in which there is an increasing need to develop skills in visual literacy. Images of all types need to be interpreted, both for their obvious meaning and often for the less overt meanings that they aim to present. So in the plethora of statistical data about each student that is currently being used to set targets and identify their 'achievement', the lack of a measure to track achievement in visual literacy is glaring by its omission. In a context in which achievement is defined by figures, there is an inevitable tendency for time and resources to be devoted to what is measured, to the detriment of what is not measured.

The ability to 'read' maps and other images are aspects of visual literacy. Geographers have long been aware of how distributions and patterns can be manipulated in order to convey a message or viewpoint. Different map projections, for example, can be chosen to change perceptions of spatial relationships. Maps in advertisements to attract businesses can make every part of the UK seem to be in a central location. Colours, symbols and other mapping techniques can be chosen to present images that are immediate, whereas text needs to be read and absorbed. These are compelling reasons why students need to be taught about the technical aspects of drawing maps. Geography is the only subject in the school curriculum that does this.

Although learning how to draw maps is important, learning through the use of maps should also be recognised as important in helping many students to access geographical ideas. Theories about multiple-intelligence suggest that many students learn best when accessing data and information that is presented visually. With this in mind, geography teachers should consider how to use maps and other images as part of their repertoire of strategies to support differentiation. This will allow facts and ideas in the subject to be made accessible to the widest number of students.

Geography teachers should also think about how the idea of 'reading age' can be applied to maps. Little research has been done on this in geography, which is surprising given its importance in making the subject accessible to the widest range of students. Unlike text, maps do not allow a simple formula to be applied to lines, colours and patterns. Most students find that small cluttered maps are difficult to use, but there is no generally used index which enables this degree of difficulty to be quantified. Making the map fit for its intended audience is part of the cartographer's craft, so this is an aspect of drawing maps that needs to be taught.

The issue of a map or diagram's 'reading age' is one that publishers of textbooks appear not to understand. The problem becomes manifest in books that aim for different levels, but have a common core of content. Although the text is reduced and edited to make it easier to read, the maps and other images are usually neither enlarged nor simplified to achieve the same effect. One reason for this is that while text is relatively cheap and easy to adapt for different levels, artwork is not.

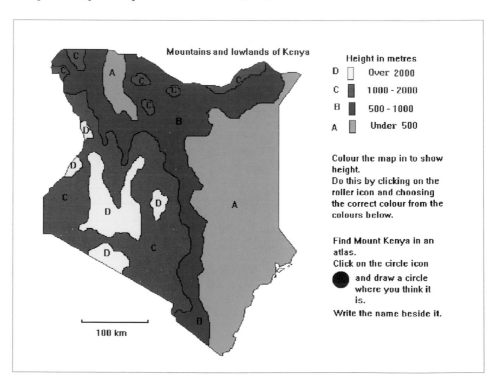

Figure 2 | *Land height (relief) in Kenya: the outline was imported as clip art and the map completed by using the colour infill tool.*

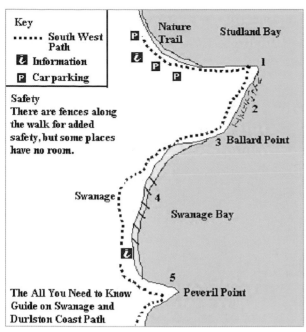

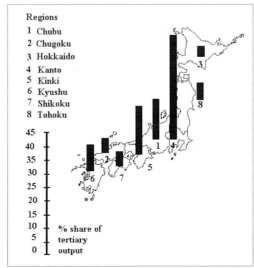

Figure 3 | *The coastal management map redrawn in Paint, using the same content and similar symbols to the hand drawn version in Figure 1.*

Figure 4 | *A map drawn using Paint. Here, the base map is imported as clip art then combined with a graph drawn in Excel, moving the bars to appropriate locations.*

Using ICT to teach the basics and beyond

In the early phases of learning, there is considerable value in teaching students to make calculations without the use of a calculator or to write text without the use of a word processor. In the early phases of work in geography, the same value may be attached to drawing maps by hand using coloured pencils, pens, rulers and tracing paper. However, while colouring by hand can be enjoyable for the many who lack hand-eye co-ordination and/or the patience needed to produce a map of which they can be proud, it can also lead to frustration and lack of motivation. The result is likely to be a lack of interest in the subject. One way of avoiding this is to make appropriate use of ICT, as illustrated in Figures 2-5.

Even simple things such as choosing appropriate colours for a map key can be taught far more effectively and time-efficiently by using ICT. For example, by using a basic drawing package such as *Microsoft Paint*, students can consider colour options for choropleth mapping (Figure 2), taking little more than a few seconds to infill an area with colour and to change the range of colours. A student can thus explore the visual effectiveness of a variety of options in less time than it takes to colour in one map by hand.

There is a case for suggesting that once students have learned to draw their own maps, whether by hand or using ICT, they should no longer need to draw any maps by hand – either partly or completely. After all, teachers have always made use of printed base maps, mainly so that they can reduce the time spent drawing maps in order to make more time available for the more productive activity of mapping the data. Now that clip art, map images and base maps of countries can be downloaded from websites, the need to draw is even less necessary. In addition, highly complex and detailed maps can be obtained in digital form.

Even the most basic drawing packages can save time and improve the quality of the maps that students produce. No longer need time be wasted in printing neat labels for maps, or striving to draw lines that are accurate and of uniform thickness. Now, text tools can be used to print accurate labels and to position them correctly on a map, and editing tools enable improvements to be made (Figure 3). For example, lines drawn on maps using drawing tools in word-processing packages such as *Word* can be re-drawn or edited, and the eraser and cut-out tools in a package such as *Microsoft Paint* enable images to be drawn and/or imported (Figure 4).

Using ICT, such as GIS software (see below), raw data can be mapped to a very high technical standard and with great accuracy by all students, irrespective of their age or ability. Accurate base maps can be imported and areas (polygons), points or lines can be added as separate layers (themes). Once data has been attached to these layers, different mapping techniques can be chosen and used. Neatness and accuracy are handled to perfection by the software, so these aspects of the map are no longer relevant criteria to use for assessment. There are, of course, other elements that can still be assessed, as noted in Figure 5.

There is an argument that drawing and manipulating maps using ICT means that students can no longer express their individuality, and that this is a disadvantage. Indeed, given the nature and universality of the software, there may be no way of knowing which student has drawn which map, unless they add their names. However, nobody would seriously argue that the majority of maps should be drawn by hand to individual and varying technical standards. Also, there are still occasions when personal input is what matters, e.g. for maps which are drawn as part of an advertisement or for a tourist information board.

The case for using GIS

The number of school geography departments that currently make use of GIS software is still small, but growing rapidly. There is a strong case to be made for the use of GIS to become a compulsory part of each student's geographical education (see also Chapter 7). The argument can be made at different levels:

- It is a 'real world' tool that can help bring career relevance to work in geography.
- It is the only ICT application that is specific to work in geography, though it does have uses in some other subjects such as biology and history.
- It offers enormous potential to raise levels of achievement in geography, e.g. by raising the quality of mapping and the ways in which maps can be used to support analysis in geography.
- It provides tools to process raw data, thus making more time available for analysing and making use of the data.

A problem, of course, is that 'achievement' is usually defined by assessment criteria in the national curriculum (level descriptions) and in examination specifications. Until assessment criteria give proper attention to what GIS can do well, it could remain an optional tool. For the purposes of assessment, a definition of 'good geography' that includes the use of GIS software may be what is needed to force the pace of its adoption.

Barriers to the successful use of GIS

Once it is accepted that the use of GIS should be part of each student's geographical education, then the next step is to devise the means of bringing this about. There is no denying that there are some problems:

- the cost of software
- access to ICT facilities may not be easy or available
- teacher training in the use of GIS software may be absent or inadequate
- access to vector based digital maps may not be easy or available
- creating the time needed to teach the techniques to the students.

These problems, however, are more a matter of priorities than insurmountable barriers. Enough schools have already embarked on GIS work to prove that this is true. Cost is relative, and besides, it can be shared with another subject such as science, business studies, or even with ICT itself. Some local authorities (LAs) have had the foresight to

Success criteria	Method: ICT	Method: by hand
Accuracy The position of places and features is accurate and they are drawn to an appropriate scale.	Can be achieved by using on-screen grids and co-ordinates or by importing base maps from the internet and other sources.	Hard to achieve by hand, other than by using tracing paper: map can be drawn on photocopied base map.
Lines Use of a range of line thickness and styles, e.g. continuous, pecked. Lines of each type that are of identical width and clarity.	Use of drawing tools for choice of appropriate styles. Lines drawn with ICT tools have uniform features. Can be difficult to use a mouse to draw curving lines.	Very difficult to achieve uniform effects when drawing lines by hand, though use of a specialist mapping nib can help.
Text Use of different fonts and sizes that appear as entirely standard and with uniform clarity. Positioning of text so as not to obliterate map features.	A wide choice of styles that appear with uniform high quality. The ability to manipulate and edit text to achieve optimum position.	Depends on the standard of handwriting or ability to print. Use of a stencil or Letraset can help, though these are time-consuming and expensive. A trial and error approach that, because labels are added last, often results in poor location.
Shading Use of appropriate colours and/or pattern and tones to illustrate quantitative data or features. The uniform application of colour within areas and to lines. Colours and shading to be contained entirely within boundary lines and occupy all the space within those lines.	The widest choice of colours, patterns and textures. Application of colour in a completely standardised way. Can lack subtlety if this is required for 'artistic' reasons. Perfect results by using colour infill tools.	Choice of colours limited by available coloured pencils and inks: not a major issue. Almost impossible to achieve uniform shading over large areas. The option to add artistic effects, e.g. drawings. Requires considerable time to achieve a perfect colour or shading infill.
Symbols The use of symbols that are appropriate and uniform in appearance for each type. The positioning of symbols in places that relate to features on the map. Accurately drawn and well-positioned quantitative symbols, e.g. located bar graphs.	Each type of symbol is as easy to create as any other with perfect uniformity achieved by copy and paste techniques. Positioning made easy by formatting and other tools. Quantitative symbols created using a spreadsheet then imported, or use of tools in GIS software.	Limitations caused by difficulties in drawing some symbols by hand; very hard to achieve uniformity. Positioning achieved by trial and error, leading to messy editing with an eraser. Some techniques are too complex to attempt, though they may be visually effective.
Interactivity Links to data, e.g. to a choice of quantitative symbols or multimedia resource. Selection of layers to view. Ability to query map data. Statistical analysis of data.	Use of GIS software to link map to recorded data with a choice of quantitative symbols. Select data in GIS software. Database query in GIS software. Tools to measure and process data.	No method of interactivity. Layers can be shown on separate maps or tracing paper layers. No method of automatic data query. Statistical analysis can be cumbersome, e.g. measuring and using formulae.

Figure 5 | *Drawing maps: criteria for assessment, and a comparison between using ICT and hand-drawing methods.*

Principles and techniques for a GIS	Developing GIS principles using ICT techniques in generic software packages (word processing, spreadsheet and drawing)	Sample context for an activity
Record and save data in a spreadsheet. GIS package work Enter raw data into a GIS software package's own data file function.	■ Enter raw data into cells in a spreadsheet, e.g. *Excel*. Use rows in column A for each point, line or area and other columns for the data. (1) ■ Save a file in .csv format as well as in the spreadsheet's default format as some packages only handle .csv format files when imported. (2)	■ Collect and enter data about the size and population for a number of countries. Each country will represent an area. The figures will be data fields. ■ Collect raw data about the number of people who enter different shops in a shopping parade. Each shop represents a point on a map.
Draw or import a base map, either one drawn by hand, scanned, captured or copied, e.g. a map, vertical air photograph or satellite image. Assign map codes for points, lines and areas for which data has been collected. GIS package work ■ Import a base map or image into a GIS package. ■ Use the vector drawing tools in a GIS package to draw a simple map, learning how to choose to show points, lines or areas. ■ Note that GIS packages usually have their own file formats for maps though they are able to import images that have been saved in the common formats.	■ Use the drawing tools in a basic drawing package such as *Paint* to draw a simple map. (3) ■ Use the vector drawing tools in a word processor such as *Word* or in a drawing package such as *Corel Draw*, e.g. to draw a map or line drawing. Codes can be allocated to points, lines or areas by entering a number or letter in a *Text box* and positioning it beside the feature. (4) ■ Capture a map or vertical air photo from a screen and save it as a file, e.g. with the keyboard *Print Screen* tool or by using the *Capture* tool in *Paintshop Pro*. This can be imported as a base map into a drawing package as a raster image. (5) ■ Find out about basic file formats such as bitmaps (.bmp) and compressed formats such as Jpeg and Gif files. (6)	■ Draw a sketch map of a short section of a river. ■ Make a line drawing of a photograph to show its main geographical features. ■ Find a map or vertical air photo for your local area. Do this from a website (e.g. from multimap.com).
Draw multiple layers of data with the ability to look at and work with selected layers. Continue to add map codes to points, lines and areas (as above). GIS package work ■ Use the drawing tools in a GIS package to create different layers of data. Show how each layer can be viewed independently.	■ Use the drawing tools in *Word* to draw three separate maps. Start by drawing one *Rectangle* then copy it twice to give three map frames of the same size. Use the drawing tools to show three layers of data, one to go on each map. Use the *Select Objects* and *Group* tools to group the drawings into their map frames. Then move the three maps over each other so that the three sets of data overlap. You will need the rectangle shading to be set at *No fill* for this to work or the default white infill will block the other maps. You can move each map on or off the base map to simulate layers. (7) ■ Use a CD-Rom such as the *Down to Earth* farming simulation to show how multiple layers of data can be applied to fields.	Draw a map of an area to show different aspects of its topography and other features, e.g. the rivers on one map, roads on another and areas of woodland on another. Look at the maps separately then over each other to see what relationships there might be.
Attach raw data to the map codes for points, lines and areas on the map, i.e. the key step to combining the raw data with the map. GIS package work ■ Set up a spreadsheet either in a generic package or in a GIS package's own data entry function. ■ Draw a map then attach the data to points, lines or areas on the map.	■ Draw a map in a drawing package such as *Paint*. Enter data relating to points, lines or areas in a spreadsheet such as *Excel*. *Copy* and *paste* the data into *Paint*. A variation can be to draw a bar graph of the data and import it to go beside the map. Doing this does not make the automatic attachment of the data to the map that is performed by a GIS software package, but it does make a simple visual link between using a spreadsheet and a map that has been drawn using a drawing package. (8)	■ Show differences in the employment structure for the different regions in Japan. ■ Show the velocity and mean depth readings for a river at selected points along its long profile.

Figure 8 | *The use of generic software packages to develop map-drawing skills.*

Principles and techniques for a GIS	Developing GIS principles using ICT techniques in generic software packages (word processing, spreadsheet and drawing)	Sample context for an activity
	▪ Create hotspots over a map inserted into *Word*. Do this by drawing rectangles over the map at selected points, lines or areas. Set them up as *hyperlinks* to *bookmarked* graphs or data tables. This can be to *bookmarked* points in either the same file or in a different file, e.g. to an *Excel* file. This method will only show one data set at a time, not a completed map showing all the data. (10) ▪ Use a CD-Rom such as the Down to Earth farming simulation to show how quantitative data can be attached to areas (fields).	
Choose different quantitative mapping signs and symbols to illustrate the raw data. GIS package work ▪ Use the mapping tools in the GIS package to create quantitative symbols or shading for raw data on different layers.	▪ Draw a map in *Paint* then use choropleth shading by choosing the *Fill with colour* tool in a basic drawing package or use of standard shapes, e.g. rectangles or circles. Shapes can be kept to standard sizes by drawing one then copying and pasting it. (11) ▪ A set of bands for shading can be worked out by using the *Sort* tool in either *Word* or *Excel*. (12) ▪ Bands of raw data can be identified in *Excel* by using the *Conditional formatting* tool, e.g. to identify data that is equal to, more than, less than or between different amounts. (13) ▪ Use the *Fill colour* tool in *Word* to shade in areas, lines of different thickness and colour and standard symbols. (14)	Carry out an enquiry to find out if there is any relationship between employment patterns and levels of economic wealth as measured by GNP per head in EU countries. Do this visually by drawing and comparing a set of maps with quantitative data shown as shading, located graphs or symbols.
Use tools to measure distance and area. GIS package work ▪ Measure distances and areas by using the GIS package's measuring tools.	Generic software methods ▪ Generic packages such as *Word* and *Excel* do not have measuring tools. Instead, use could be made of CD-Roms such as a route planning package to illustrate how distance can be automatically measured. Some map reading and drawing packages such as *Local Studies* also contain measuring tools. ▪ A cumbersome method of measuring straight-line distances in *Word* or *Excel* could be to draw a horizontal scale line then to use the *Line drawing* tool. A line can be drawn between points, rotated using the *Free rotate* tool to the horizontal, then moved to beneath the scale line to read off a distance.	As part of a decision-taking activity, use measuring tools to work out the optimum location for an economic activity by filling in a distance matrix for a set of locations.
Set up a query to map selected data. GIS package work ▪ Use the *query* tool to select from the raw data. Although data may have been entered in a spreadsheet, the package automatically gives the spreadsheet some functions of a database, e.g. to select and find data.	▪ A basic query to look at selected data can be created by using the *Conditional formatting* tool in *Excel*. This is not, however, automatically able to map the data. ▪ Data can be entered in a database such as *Access* or the more basic *Information Finder* package. While this can find selected data, it cannot automatically map it.	Carry out an enquiry to find out about how air pollution in States of the USA is related to car ownership, clearly identifying the most polluted and the least polluted States.

Figure 8 | *continued*

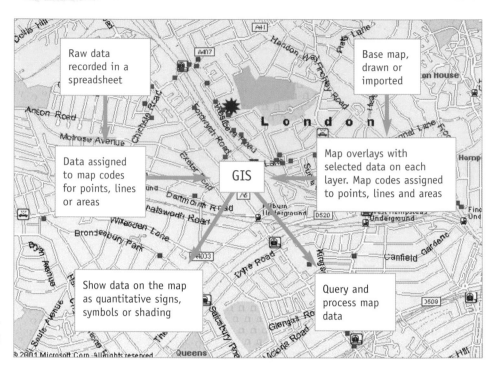

Raw data recorded in a spreadsheet

Base map, drawn or imported

Data assigned to map codes for points, lines or areas

GIS

Map overlays with selected data on each layer. Map codes assigned to points, lines and areas

Show data on the map as quantitative signs, symbols or shading

Query and process map data

Figure 9 | *The elements of GIS software to be included in a teaching programme.*

Even from a relatively early part of key stage 3, most students should be able to work with all of the elements in this list. Some of the individual techniques should even have been taught during key stage 2. Any problems, therefore, are likely to relate to how the package works and the need to put its sequence of operations into the right order (Figure 10). The students will also need to appreciate that using GIS packages cannot be done by the kind of intuition that they often use when playing computer games.

Ideally GIS work should begin as early as possible in key stage 3, the aim being to ensure that by key stage 4 students are able to use GIS software effectively as part of normal lessons or part of their own coursework.

GIS is a powerful tool that can perform many complex functions, so some problems and difficulties are bound to be encountered. To resolve these problems it may be best to adopt a long-term strategy, developing students' ICT techniques in a coherent and consistent way over the longer term, starting in year 7, if not earlier. It is essential to use and re-use the software at regular intervals, thus helping both teacher and students

	Teacher input ⟶ Student input	
Base map	Select and create a base map that is appropriate	
Map basics	Create scale, direction and map key	
Data assembly	Assemble the data before processing and converting to symbols or shading	
Symbols and shading	Devise and apply symbols and/or shading styles for the map	
Text	Write and position text on the map	
Processing map data	Use formulae and tools to process data, e.g. query, measure, sort and make calculations	

Figure 10 | *Progression in drawing maps.*

to consolidate and extend their knowledge of the package. A set of activities can be devised for the key stage 3 years, such those suggested below.

Year 7
- Draw a basic map using the drawing tools to show lines, areas and points
- Give features map codes
- Use prepared maps and data for activities
- Work with websites with basic GIS capability

Year 8
- Import a raster map or vertical air photo to act as a base map
- Add points, lines and areas to set up layers (themes), giving each a map code
- Enter data in a spreadsheet
- Link the data to the map codes
- Map the data, using a variety of options

Year 9
- Import Ordnance Survey digital maps (see Chapter 7)
- Draw layers (themes) on the base map
- Research and enter data, linking it to the map
- Carry out queries, searches and measurements

The result of such a phased programme should be that by year 10, the students are already able to carry out their own research and use the software as part of geographical enquiries. By the time students enter post-16 education they should be competent users of at least one GIS software package and be able to transfer their skills to work with others. Doing all this does mean setting aside an appropriate amount of time in each year's scheme of work. If 'better' geography is the result, it should be time well spent.

An issue that may arise in the early stages of working with GIS software is whether the time is being used productively and whether each individual lesson can be seen as making appropriate use of ICT. For example, it may be quicker to draw a map by hand than to use GIS when handling a limited amount of data and using basic mapping techniques. It is important to recognise that while a GIS lesson in year 7 may appear to bring about limited progress in geographical understanding, it will nevertheless lay the foundations for students to use the skills in the future. This can be, for example, when the students are working with much larger data sets; when they need to use a more varied set of mapping strategies; and when they need to query and process the data.

Maps and other images

As well as maps of many kinds, ICT enables us to gain access to a wide range of other spatial resources, such as vertical air photographs and satellite images. These can be combined with maps to make integrated packages. ICT also makes it possible to link photographs, text, sound and video to maps. Raw data can be isolated and changed to construct maps and it is then possible for students to dynamically link the map to the data. This enables the map to automatically adjust to the new data.

These are dimensions to mapping that are relatively new and which offer exciting opportunities. We can now see maps, satellite images and vertical air photos in 3D, and animate them to zoom in 'fly through' the landscape. The basic but most effective version, Google Earth program, is available on a website as a free download. Virtual landscapes can be created in a way that brings both a more comprehensive visualisation of places and the ability to interact with a place by moving through it to see it from

Figure 11 | *A photograph has been dropped over the 3D virtual landscape using Genesis IV. Source: Geomantics website.*

different perspectives. Changing a landscape is already possible in, for example, computer games such as *Sim City*, though software packages with this kind of processing power have yet to be developed for educational purposes.

The idea of visualising a map can be helped by traditional practical activities such as building 3D landscape models from cardboard or other materials. One cannot feel the landscape on a computer screen, but software exists that can change 2D maps into images with a 3D effect. The *Genesis II* software package has this capability. The starting image can be a digital elevation map, a contour map that has been hand drawn in a basic drawing package, or other options. Once the height data has been entered, the package makes the calculations needed to show the landscape in 3D. It can be viewed from any angle and from any height. But this is just the start. The 3D virtual landscape can then be made to simulate a real landscape by adding colours and surface features. Features that do not currently exist in the landscape, such as wind turbines, can be added so that students can develop a better appreciation of how the landscape might change. It can show the scene at different times of year, with different cloud patterns and with the sun at different angles. Another useful tool to aid with visualisation is the packages facility to drape a vertical air photograph or Ordnance Survey map extract over the 3D image (Figure 11). This is most certainly a powerful aid to developing map skills, perhaps made more enticing by the fact that at the time of writing, a cut down version of the package is available as a free download from the website.

Another development which has become an integral part of modern mapping is the use of global positioning systems (GPS), for which receivers are available at affordable prices from a variety of suppliers. Teaching students about this system should be part of a modern geographical education; the use of GPS can be integrated into GIS work to produce geo-coded maps of high accuracy and, as with GIS itself, it is a tool that brings work in geography into contact with 'real world' applications.

Although vertical air photographs and satellite images are now part of everyday work in school geography, it is probably fair to say that geography teachers have not done much to develop students' understanding of how they are produced and how to interpret them. New courses in geography that have a more 'vocational' emphasis may offer an opportunity to make progress with this kind of work. For example, links could be made to relevant parts of the science curriculum, such as work on the electro-magnetic spectrum; this would help to develop an understanding of how satellite images are obtained. Software is already available which enables images from different wavelengths to be processed, but while this is commonly used on degree courses, it is not yet widely used in schools.

Assessing digital maps

Several references have already been made to the way in which teachers need to think afresh about the criteria for assessment in relation to maps drawn with ICT. One way to approach the assessment of map work is to identify a clear set of headings that can form the criteria. This, for example, could be to assess:

- the map's content
- the choice of mapping technique
- the technical ability to draw the map
- the ability to process map data
- the ability to read and interpret a map.

Assessing the content of a map will be the same for one that has been drawn by hand as for one drawn with the aid of a computer. Likewise with the assessment of choice of mapping techniques, though if a computer is used to create the map, a greater range of techniques can be employed. In terms of technical ability to draw a map, using a computer is bound to result in high technical standards, irrespective of the skill and manual dexterity of the map drawer. A computer-generated map will be neater than one that is hand drawn, and as accurate as the data put into it. Thus it could be argued that there is nothing for which marks should be awarded; the map is either technically perfect or it is not. Looked at one way, the fact that students of almost any age and level of ability can now produce maps to a high technical standard and with great expertise, is something to be celebrated. However, given that one of the key purposes of assessment is to be able to differentiate between students in terms of their level of ability, this poses a problem for teachers. A problem also arises in cases when assessment is being used to identify steps for learning since it is unlikely that qualities such as neatness and accuracy can be improved upon in the case of computer-aided mapping.

Processing map data can be done either by measuring manually or by using the measuring tools provided by computer software. For most operations, using the latter is likely to be both faster and more accurate than measuring by hand. Finally, there is the need to assess a student's ability to 'read' and interpret a map, which because it relates to the cognitive domains, is unaffected by issues of technical ability in relation to map drawing and processing.

Clearly, one issue that has to be addressed is how to mark a map drawn using a computer as compared with one that has been drawn by hand. Not all students have access to a computer at home and access in school may be difficult. Geography teachers now need to decide whether their expectations regarding the standard of map drawing should be artificially lowered to take account of the fact that some students will lack access to ICT, or whether to expect all students to achieve new and higher standards due to the wide availability of ICT. In this respect the use of ICT could be seen as either creating problems for inclusion or, because ICT offers similar tools to all, enabling inclusion to be achieved! Perhaps the assessment of map work will need to focus on the choice of mapping styles, how the map has been designed and on how it is analysed.

Some concluding suggestions

Drawing and using maps is a central and important part of teaching and learning in geography. Maps are far more than graphic tools for the display of raw data. Students need to understand how maps are drawn so that they make use of them for their own enquiries, and understand how they need to be read. They form an aspect of visual literacy that is only partly understood and that, unfortunately, has been largely neglected in the drive to raise national standards of education. Students need to be taught how to draw maps that include relevant content and using appropriate mapping techniques. Their maps should be drawn to the highest technical standards, making full use of ICT as a tool to achieve this. Maps, vertical air photographs and other types of resource should be used in ways that are integrated with raw data in order to produce a comprehensive visualisation of places. Maps have come a long way from colouring in. They have a long way to go.

Implications for practice

(a) **Using maps makes an important contribution to the development of students' skills in visual literacy.**

Visual literacy is an important dimension of every student's education. The use of maps is central to work in geography, as well as playing a part in developing each student's wider skills in visual literacy. It is also important to recognise that maps are not only a tool with which to study spatial distributions and patterns, but also a means by which some learners can be helped to access concepts, data and information in geography. Using ICT can significantly improve the quality of maps produced by students and the way in which they visualise places.

(b) **Plan carefully to develop progression in students' map-drawing skills as well as other aspects of map work.**

A long-term plan for developing map skills is needed in which there is full recognition of the work that students have already done and achieved at each key stage. This will involve ensuring that the different aspects of working with maps are built into schemes of work. This will support progression in the development of these skills, e.g. in the selection and application of mapping techniques to represent spatial data. It is also necessary to take an approach to map work that integrates the use of different types of image, e.g. maps at different scales, globes, vertical air photographs and satellite images.

(c) **Exploit the potential of GIS for enhancing geographical enquiry.**

GIS is a 'real world' tool and an ICT application with specific relevance for geography. Consider the advantages of using GIS software as a tool both for drawing maps and for processing the data they contain. Although using GIS presents some challenges, its use can lead to better quality maps and also provide some useful processing tools for analysing map data. As the technical barriers are overcome and there is improved access to data for schools, the potential of GIS for enhancing students' use of mapping tools will be realised. Students can be introduced to some of the basics of GIS using generic software, such as *Word, Excel, Access* and *Paint* (see Figure 9). A coherent plan is needed for the progressive development of students' understanding and use of the various GIS tools so that by year 10 they are capable, independently, of using these tools to support their own geographical enquiries.

(d) **Assessment of students' abilities to draw maps.**

Maps that are drawn using ICT, whether using a basic drawing package or GIS, may need to be assessed against a different set of criteria than maps drawn by hand. Assessment should be against criteria that are part of a definition of what makes for 'better' geography. By using ICT, students of geography now have the tools to raise their standard of map drawing. It is up to their teachers to ensure that appropriate guidance and opportunities are provided so that the quality of drawn maps can become something that takes pride of place within geography.

Related publication from the Geographical Association:
- Cape Farewell/GA. (2005) *The High Arctic.*
- King, S. (2000) *High-tech Geography: ICT in secondary schools.*
- LFG/GA (2005) *State of the Nation 2005 – Teachers' Notes.*
- Martin, F. (2006) *e-geography (book & CD-Rom).*

References and resources

Print

Adams, D. (1981) *The Hitchhiker's Guide to the Galaxy.* London: BBC Books.

Barnett, M., Kent, A. and Milton, M. (1995) *Images of Earth: A teachers' guide to remote sensing in geography at key stage 3 and GCSE*. Sheffield: Geographical Association.

Barnett, M. and Milton, M. (1995) 'Satellite images and IT capability', *Teaching Geography*, 20, 3, pp. 142-3.

Davis, D. (2003) *GIS for Everyone*. Aylesbury: ESRI Press.

Freeman, D. (2003) 'GIS in secondary geography', *Teaching Geography*, 28, 1, pp. 38-41.

Freeman, D., Green, D., Hassell, D. and Paterson, K. (1993) 'Getting started with GIS', *Teaching Geography*, 18, 2, pp. 57-60.

Hunt, M. and Jebb, J. (2001) 'Differentiation by skills', *Teaching Geography*, 26, 1, pp. 16-21.

Lewis, S. (1991) 'Teaching geography using aerial photographs', *Teaching Geography*, 16, 3, pp. 113-15.

Sheppard, S. (1995) 'Implementing GIS technology in schools', *Teaching Geography*, 20, 1, pp. 17-19.

Williams, A. (2000) 'Teaching and learning with geographical information systems', *Teaching Geography*, 25, 1, pp. 45-7.

Electronic

ER Mapper - www.earthetc.com/

Geocaching - www.geocaching.com/

Geomantics - www.geomantics.org.uk

GIS for Teachers - www.king.ac.uk/geog/gis_for_teachers/

Global Atlas of Infectious Diseases - www.who.int/GlobalAtlas/home.asp (mapping)

Global Positioning System - www.colorado.edu/geography/gcraft/notes/gps/gps_f.html

Google Earth - //earth.google.com

Great Globe Gallery - //main.amu.edu.pl/~zbzw/glob/glob1.htm

Multimap - www.multimap.com (maps and vertical air photos)

MapPoint - //mappoint.msn.com(a2i4dxy3s0f34lfococtgu55)/Home.aspx (finding locations on maps)

National Curriculum in Action - www.ncaction/ (see Investigating the quality of life in Brazil and Coastal management)

NASA - //earthobservatory.nasa.gov/Library/RemoteSensing/ (remote sensing)

NERC Earth Observation Centre - www.neodc.rl.ac.uk/

NOAA - www.goes.noaa.gov/ (satellites and information)

NVIDIA - www.nvidia.com/object/earthviewer.html

Ordnance Survey - www.ordnancesurvey.co.uk/

Royal Geographical Society - www.rgs.org

United States Geological Survey - //edcwww.cr.usgs.gov/earthshots/slow/tableofcontents

GIS software packages

Aegis 3: The Advisory Unit: Computers in Education, 126 Great North Road, Hatfield, Hertfordshire AL9 5JZ. Tel: 01707 266714; Fax: 01707 273684; E-mail: sales@advisory-unit.org.uk; Website: www.advisory-unit.org.uk/

ArcView: ESRI UK Ltd (UK supplier), Prebendal House, Parsons Fee, Aylesbury, Buckinghamshire HP20 2QZ. Tel: 01296 745 500; Fax: 01296 745 544; E-mail: info@esriuk.com; Website: www.esriuk.com/

Digital Worlds International Ltd: Unit 35, Folkestone Enterprise Centre, Shearway Business Park, Folkestone, Kent CT19 4RH. Website: www.digitalworlds.co.uk

IDRISI Kilimanjaro: Clark Labs, 950 Main Street, Worcester, MA 01610-1477 USA. Tel: +1 508 793 7526; Fax: +1 508 793 8842 Website: www.clarklabs.org/

InfoMapper: Tamar Science Park, Derriford, Plymouth PL6 8BX. Website: www.webbased.co.uk/

Local Studies: Soft Teach Educational, Sturgess Farmhouse, Longbridge Deverill, Warminster, Wiltshire BA12 7EA. Website: www.soft-teach.co.uk/

MapInfo: TMS Education Initiatives, websites: www.tms.org/Education/education.html and www.mapinfo.com/

Map Maker Student: MapIT Ltd, 1 Lawrence Road, Ramsay, Huntington, Cambridgeshire PE26 1UY. Tel: 01487 813745; Fax: 01487 813745.

Maps, vertical air photos and CD-Roms

Geopacks: Mastering Mapwork CD-Rom: E-mail: service@geopacks.com

Ordnance Survey Interactive Atlas: Ordnance Survey, Romsey Road, Southampton SO16 4GU. Tel: 08456 050505; Fax: 023 8079 2615; Website: www.ordnancesurvey.co.uk

Window on the World, Window on the UK 2000 and Window on the Universe: The British National Space Centre (free CD resources with vertical air photographs and satellite images that can be used as base maps), 151 Buckingham Palace Road, London SW1W 9SS. Website: www.bnsc.gov.uk/

Chapter 11

Using Literacy productively

Nicholas Hewlett

Before reading this chapter consider the following questions:

■ What role does geography have to play in enhancing literacy standards at key stage 3 and beyond?

■ Why is the promotion of literacy important in actively enhancing the teaching and the learning of geography?

■ What teaching strategies can you use to promote progression in the learning of literacy?

■ How can you apply these teaching strategies to your daily classroom teaching of the geography curriculum?

Literacy (according to the Literacy Strategy)

The Literacy Strategy, as part of the National Key Stage 3 Strategy (now known as the Secondary National Strategy), was introduced in all maintained schools in England from September 2001 (DfES, 2001a). This followed the 'back to basics' movement in the late 1990s that addressed fundamental problems to do with key skills, including literacy. It was noted that weaknesses in literacy held students back in terms of their ability to access and progress in curriculum subjects. Furthermore, after leaving school, students were found to experience difficulties both socially and in their working lives due to literacy problems (Crequer, 1999).

The Literacy Strategy, which is applied to all subject classrooms beyond English, is based on a *'Framework'* of 'word', 'sentence' and 'text' level objectives. 'Word' level development centres on improving spelling and vocabulary whereas 'sentence' level objectives focus on sentence construction and development of the paragraph. 'Text' level objectives are divided between reading, writing, and speaking and listening. The *Framework* uses these objectives to detail progression between years 7, 8 and 9 (Figure 1).

The English department plays a pivotal role in the development of the Strategy within schools. However, although certain aspects of the *Framework* objectives are clearly more the concern of the English teacher, improvement of literacy skills should be considered a cross-curricular priority. Language is at the core of how all children communicate, express themselves and learn across the whole of the curriculum and as such needs to be cultivated as a tool for learning in every subject. Thus all teachers have a vested interest in the implementation of effective literacy.

Applied at	Year 7	Year 8	Year 9
Word level	■ To develop a clear understanding of the spelling of key words – being familiar with subject specific words and those that relate to key concepts as well as words in everyday use.	■ Secure the spelling of key words as well as the more complex, polysyllabic words from a wide range of geographical topics. ■ To understand the precise meaning and context of specialist and complex words.	■ Be able to spell accurately all high order and complex words. ■ Have confidence in their meaning and be able to use these words naturally and appropriately in both speaking and writing.
Sentence level	■ Recognise different ways of starting sentences and paragraphs and how to use initial sentences to orientate the reader.	■ Practise a wide range of ways to open, link and complete paragraphs. ■ Consider different ways of linking sentences to form paragraphs.	■ Be able to work ideas rapidly into coherent and fluid paragraphs. ■ Use a wide range of complex sentences and paragraphs with differing degrees of formality and style designed to suit context and purpose.
Text level – reading	■ Know how to extract relevant information by applying appropriate reading strategies. ■ Identify the main points and ideas in a text and use this information to help solve a question/task.	■ Make notes in different ways. ■ Combine information from different sources into one document. ■ Recognise bias and objectivity and be able to distinguish fact from hypotheses, theories or opinions.	■ Evaluate the relevance, reliability and validity of information. ■ Increase the speed and accuracy of reading and note-making skills. ■ Synthesise information from a wide range of sources and shape material to meet specific requirements.
Text level – writing	■ Be able to plan and draft ideas in a suitable format. ■ Write to inform, explain and describe. ■ Begin to express personal views as well as persuading, arguing or advising.	■ Be able to plan and draft ideas in a range of formats. ■ Be able to persuade, argue and advise and to be able to analyse, review and comment.	■ To have a full understanding of how to plan writing. ■ To be able to integrate a range of information, evidence and opinions into a comprehensive and balanced account. ■ Be able to persuade, argue and advise as well as present counterarguments and offer alternatives.
Text level – Speaking and listening	■ Use talk to clarify ideas giving clear answers and explanations. ■ Work together in a group logically and methodically sharing ideas and solving problems.	■ Ask questions to clarify and refine ideas. ■ Be able to refine comments and questions to a relevant and agreed focus. ■ Use group talk to develop thinking about complex issues and ideas as well as hypothesising, speculating, evaluating and solving problems.	■ Use talk to explain, explore and justify ideas. ■ Identify underlying issues, themes and implications raised in talk. ■ Discuss and evaluate conflicting viewpoints and ideas.

Figure 1 | *The Framework for literacy. Source: DfES, 2001b. Photo: ©Margaret Roberts.*

> *It is in acts of reading, writing (speaking and listening) ... finding the right words, giving shape to an idea articulating what is meant ... that meanings are forged, refined and fixed ... this is where language is synonymous with learning* (DfES, 2001b).

Developing literacy through geography and vice versa

As teachers of geography we have the great advantage of an inherent affinity with literacy. There is little doubt that literacy is an integral part of the subject and lies at the very heart of our teaching.

Geography lends itself well to fulfilling a wide variety of literacy objectives. Its multifaceted nature has long been recognised as one of its greater attributes. It covers a wide range of concepts, subject areas and skills and as such adds to the wider curriculum in diverse and unique ways. It is descriptive, creative, analytical and explorative and it is this diversity that attracts both teachers and students alike. It also enables the subject to address a range of fundamental aspects of literacy development.

The dynamic mix of factual, conceptual and issue-based learning in geography requires a wide range of techniques for channelling classroom expression. Student expression through writing and speaking is very much a part of the geography experience. The geographic vocabulary is as unique and diverse as the subject it supports, containing not only subject-specific words and key terms but words that are part of the everyday language used to express a view, make an argument or clarify meaning. A broad geographic vocabulary lays the foundation for a wide range of writing styles – instruction, recount, explanation and information can aid the learning of case-study material, key concepts, cause and effect. The more open-ended geographic issues provide opportunity for more creative styles of writing such as persuasive, discursive, analytical and evaluative.

The issue-based element of geography, which involves problems, solutions, debate and controversy, lends itself well to expression through speech. Geography is about real-world issues that affect the lives of everybody, including students. Thus they will wish to voice their views and concerns as well as put forward questions to the teacher and the rest of the class. Discussions and debates can help to present a holistic overview of many geographic issues as well as helping individuals to articulate their thoughts, grow in confidence and to speak their mind.

The issues and problems that geography considers may be encountered on television, in newspapers and on the radio, thus they are very real to the students in your classroom and as such lend themselves well to simulation. Simulating board meetings, council debates, public enquiries or even an Earth Summit can help students to engage in the reality of decision making and societal issues as well as improving their ability to communicate and articulate (Chapter 24). Geography is ideally suited to group work such as simulation where they will encounter many variables, viewpoints and possibilities. By working together with their peers, students can begin to discuss, formulate ideas and come to reasoned and informed decisions (Chapter 25).

The fact that students encounter 'geography' on television, radio and in newspapers and other print media such as books of fiction or poetry is a big advantage for the subject in terms of its use as a medium for teaching literacy; it means that every day students are encountering a range of ways of conveying geographical information for different audiences and for different purposes (Chapter 19). We as teachers can make good use of such input and experience to help students to develop their literacy skills. We can also exploit the literacy element in cross-curricular aspects of geography (e.g. ICT, Key Skills (Chapter 35) and citizenship), thus contributing to its wider (i.e. cross-curricular) role as a context for developing literacy skills.

It has long been established that students work best in a classroom characterised by a variety of different teaching strategies – some mainly teacher-led, others student-led. Incorporating a full range of literacy objectives into lesson planning will, inevitably, demand a range of appropriate teaching resources. Strategies for promoting reading, writing, speaking and listening are required in order to cover the content required for teaching the geography curriculum, and also inject variety and diversity into the classroom dynamic. From word play to role-play, from debate to creative writing, the range of literacy strategies that can be used in the teaching and learning of geography is immense. It is this diversity that enables us to use a wide range of learning channels. As a consequence, the role of the teacher becomes more varied, as does the role of the learner.

It is generally accepted that students vary in the ways in which they learn best so it is vital to offer them a variety of styles of teaching and learning in order to provide equal access to and opportunity for learning (Chapter 26). Such variety is inherent in any good geography programme, which by definition will include elements that also belong to the teaching and learning of literacy, such as reading, speaking, acting, creating and reflecting. Literacy has huge potential as a vehicle for learning in geography and it is important for geography teachers to be aware of this and to exploit it fully. New ideas and strategies for teaching literacy are being developed all the time and can be used directly or adapted to suit the needs of the geography curriculum as well as helping to create a more dynamic and exciting learning environment.

Learning geographical words

Figure 2 outlines activities that can help students to learn the spelling of both everyday and subject-specific words, as well as improving their learning and understanding of more complex and unfamiliar words.

Word-walls have become an increasingly popular means of developing the learning of geographic vocabulary and of complex words that are used in everyday situations. Indeed it would seem that being able to visualise words on the classroom wall helps to trigger memory and reinforce both spelling and meaning. However there is a danger that word-

Word-walls and flash cards	
■ Word-walls to be changed with each unit. ■ Teacher to read out a series of five or more 'clues' describing one of the word-wall words. ■ Each student has a blank piece of paper. ■ Students need to write down the word being described after the least number of clues and to hold up their paper for the teacher to see.	*Learning coastal vocabulary (Teacher clues):* ■ *I am a coastal landform.* ■ *I am a coastal landform caused by erosion.* ■ *I start to be formed when waves refract around a headland.* ■ *First the waves undercut the headland from both sides.* ■ *I am not an arch but I start off as one.* ■ *I form when an arch collapses.*
Hot-seating	
■ Select one student to sit on a chair facing the rest of the class with their back against the board. ■ Write a key word relating to a specific topic above student's head on the board. ■ Student has to guess the word by directing yes/no questions at the rest of the class. ■ Student in hot seat can only ask a question to the same person once. ■ Aim is to guess the word in the fewest number of questions.	■ *Can be used for any number of topics where there is a wide range of geographical terminology (weather, coasts, rivers, glaciation, settlement, industry, etc.)* ■ *It is useful to use hot-seating in conjunction with the topic word-wall.* ■ *Can be differentiated by telling students the word will be one of a specific number of word-wall words.*

Photo: ©Steve Banner.

Figure 2 | *Activities for learning geographical words.*

walls can become stagnant and very underused (if used at all). Young people, like adults, quickly become adjusted to their surroundings and daily routine and if certain elements of the daily environment remain *in situ* for very long and without purpose they will inevitably be discarded from the mind. Thus the success of word-walls in their development of geographic vocabulary depends on their being kept dynamic and interactive.

One problem with word-walls is that they can easily become swamped with a mass of words and terms that are unfamiliar and without meaning to the students. This can happen when words for the term or year are posted on the wall at the very beginning of the period of learning. Although intended to serve as an 'objective' to be fulfilled by the end of the year there is a danger that by their sheer number and unfamiliarity word-walls become off-putting and disheartening to the learner. Furthermore, when covering such a wide range of geographic topics and teaching areas, the word-wall is difficult to integrate into classroom teaching.

One possible strategy to overcome this problem is to use the word-wall only in relation to the topic being taught, thus ensuring a change of words every few weeks. Not only is the number of words being taught (and learnt) fewer, and therefore more manageable, but by using a topic word wall, with a title that relates to the period of study, the word-wall becomes more relevant to the moment. When following this method, avoid starting a topic by pinning all the relevant key words on the word-wall. Instead, start the topic with a blank word-wall and introduce the key words gradually. Perhaps at the end of each lesson, after particular words have been covered, a plenary session can be used to review the new vocabulary and write it on the word-wall.

Flash cards can be used very effectively in conjunction with word-walls to provide a simple and quick way of building on student understanding of the meaning of key words (Figure 2). The first activity in Figure 2 is best used as a ten minute starter or plenary. It helps to activate the word-wall as students have to scrutinise all of the words to see which one best fits the description being read out. It also helps the teacher to get a better idea of students' understanding of the meaning of key words as they are forced to reject some and select others. Wrong answers may tell us as much about a student's understanding as do correct ones.

This activity can be differentiated in many ways. As an extension task you may wish to inform the students that you will be describing either a word-wall word or a key word from the last topic of study, thus extending the vocabulary to choose from. For lower achieving groups you might want to narrow the selection of words to just a handful of key words on the wall for selection. There are also several different ways in which this activity can be manipulated. You might consider getting the students themselves to think up a series of clues and use these to test the class on their understanding of the word-wall.

The second activity in Figure 2 works best as a short starter or plenary. Hot-seating is a very useful way of testing understanding of topic key words and is best used in conjunction with the topic word-wall. By getting individual students to try and guess the key word pinned behind them with simple yes/no questioning you are able to evaluate the understanding of both the student in the hot-seat and the rest of the class being asked the questions.

Constructing sentences

The construction of well-crafted sentences is fundamental to securing the fluent and comprehensive writing style needed across the curriculum and in everyday situations, as well as in later life. Geography examinations require a mix of writing styles: causal and descriptive sentences; building more complex paragraphs; discussion of potential

The Sentence Card Challenge	
■ Each student in the class is given a numbered card with a sentence end, sentence beginning or sentence middle written on it relating to a specific topic being studied. ■ Teacher randomly selects a number. ■ The student with that particular numbered card has to construct a sentence (relating to the topic) using only their sentence structure and to speak it to the class. ■ The task can be differentiated so that higher achieving students are given speculative/ hypothetical sentence beginnings.	*Constructing sentences about desertification:* *(ideas for cards)* 1. *And it is in these areas in the world that desertification is most prominent...* 2. *By cutting down trees people...* 3. *Over-grazing causes many problems in the Sahel because...* 4. *Temperatures have been rising over recent years and this...* 5. *I think that if desertification continues...*

Figure 3 | *Constructing geographical sentences.*

solutions; projecting future scenarios and dealing with evaluation and argument. Constructing complex paragraphs requires a sound understanding of a wide range and diversity of sentence styles.

Figure 3 describes an activity designed to help students learn how to structure sentences, to start sentences and paragraphs effectively, and to examine different ways of developing, linking and completing paragraphs and more complex sentences. The activity also develops students' ability to articulate their ideas about sentence construction. This can be done in a number of ways and offers avenues for the teacher to differentiate and adapt the activity. Some individuals may learn best through verbal articulation of the sentence, others may learn better through writing it down. This can be built in to the activity. It is, however, an essential part of the activity that once the students have been given time to write down their sentences students are picked to read them out to the rest of the class. It may be that you, as the teacher, will want to read out examples to the rest of the class, or you might want to get students to read out other students' work. Articulating ideas to the rest of the class and sharing ideas with the other learners is an invaluable way of developing learning at a whole-class level.

There are many ways of differentiating and extending this activity to meet the demands of individual learners. Some sentences are of a higher order and require more advanced skills than others. For example, speculative and hypothetical sentence beginnings demand more of the user than causal and descriptive sentences. These should be given selectively to individual students in the class. It can also be useful and less daunting for some children to work in pairs when thinking up their sentences.

Developing reading

Reading text from a variety of sources and type of geographic material can be an extremely useful way for students to learn about different aspects of a topic. However there is a danger that the reading of text can become little more than a mechanical process, with students failing to acquire any real understanding or the ability to extract key points, issues and concepts.

All reading needs a purpose. Without purpose the learner has no comprehension of what they are looking to extract from the text. All reading is based on priorities. There are elements of the text that are most important and there are elements of the text that are least relevant. It is purpose that distinguishes relevance and without purpose readers are left trying to absorb all the material in front of them. It is the task of the teacher to be very clear about the purpose of the reading. There are many strategies that can help students to read with a clearly defined purpose.

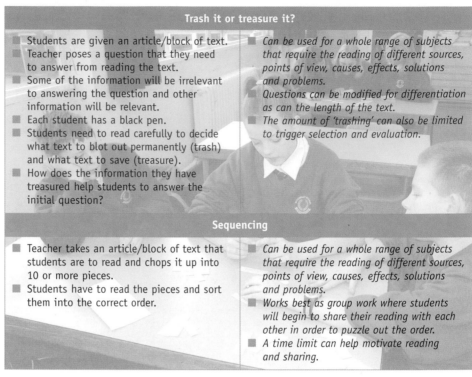

Figure 4 | *Activities for developing reading at key stage 3 and beyond.*

Figure 4 describes activities designed to develop appropriate reading strategies to extract particular information and to develop students ability to analyse and synthesise the material that they read.

'Trash it or treasure it?' works well because the emphasis is placed less on what information is relevant to the purpose and more on what information is irrelevant and needs to be erased. All students should be equipped with a black pen that they can use to blot out all irrelevant text, keeping only that material that helps them to answer a specific question. Getting the students to think about what information is irrelevant to the question means they will inevitably have to read and synthesise the information and, in so doing, will consider which bits of text are relevant to the question. It can help to achieve purposeful reading if the class is told that once they have blotted out text it cannot be uncovered or used in their answering of the question. Clearly the length of text can be altered to cater for the needs of individual students. It can also be helpful to restrict the amount of 'trashing' that can be carried out on the text. You could make the restriction that no more than ten pieces of uninterrupted text are allowed to be erased. In this way you also get the students to start prioritising the importance of the text that needs to be removed, thus adding another dimension to the purpose of the reading.

A large block of writing can be very intimidating to a student. It is far better to break down the text into manageable chunks that can be easily read and their content quickly absorbed. There are lots of ways of breaking down text into formats that are easier to read, all of which can be done on a computer. For example, re-paragraphing a block of text or changing it into a bulleted list can help to separate out the information and make the task of reading and understanding far easier.

'Sequencing' is another way of making text more accessible. Breaking up information into lots of little pieces makes it easier to read, and it instantly seems more manageable and the content more accessible. However, sequencing does far more than this because the chunks of text are completely muddled and out of context. The meaning of the reading can only be found when all the pieces are fitted together. It therefore forces the readers to discuss and explain the content they have read. It is only by working as a team that they can put the individual chunks of text into context to try and work out the original order of the writing and develop the whole picture. This activity forces students to read in detail because it is only if they have a true understanding of what they have read that they will be able to articulate the context of what they have said and uncover the order of the text. This activity can be differentiated in terms of its complexity; the chunks of text can range from little more than sentences to whole paragraphs, and the text can be varied dramatically in terms of length and complexity. For such an activity it is helpful to number the different sections randomly so that you have a checklist of the final correct order.

Information of relevance to geography can be found in a vast array of reading material, written in different styles and with different purposes, from cartoons to magazines and newspapers to journals. One way of maintaining interest in reading is simply to alternate the types of reading matter presented to your students. A variety of writing styles, each presented with a defined purpose, can really help to engage students in their reading and improve their understanding and learning of geography.

Developing writing

Writing for a specific audience and in a specific style is a vital and invaluable skill both in the classroom and in later life. Students should be made aware from very early on that all writing is directed at a specific audience and is to serve a specific purpose. It is therefore essential that before starting a piece of writing all students should reflect on who the writing is for and choose an appropriate style of writing for that particular audience. Varying the styles of writing used not only makes it more interesting for learners, it also helps them to diversify their writing style and enhances the learning of vocabulary. The role of the teacher is therefore to inspire a creativity that is channelled towards a specific style of writing. This creativity is developed through the classroom environment that needs to have a well-focused sense of purpose and place.

Figure 5 describes activities that develop skills for linking and developing paragraphs, learning to write in different styles and for different audiences, and to integrate a range of evidence and opinions into a comprehensive and balanced piece of writing.

The example of 'The Press Office' works particularly well with lower age groups and with topics that involve headline news, such as natural disasters. Setting of the scene is of vital importance. Each student must be very clear as to his or her role for the duration of the lesson: they are all journalists working to a very tight schedule; at the end of the lesson a front page report must be ready for the paper to be sent to print. A good way to start is by discussing how journalists write and what they are trying to achieve through their writing, addressing issues of sensationalism and first paragraph coverage, etc. A discussion on how they might structure the content can also be useful (especially for lower achieving students). Remind them of different writing techniques such as What, Where, When and Why. It is also important that all students have enough information on which to base their articles. Showing a clip of film footage or simply giving them a fact file is important. Providing students with a picture sheet is also good because it helps them to visualise the scene as well as making the whole thing appear that bit more real – the pictures could easily have just been faxed over to you from ...! The designing and

The Press Office	
■ Students split into groups of four. ■ They are told that they are journalists for the lesson. ■ Their Editor (the teacher) needs information fast for a story on ... ■ Using video footage/report/picture sheet, each group has to take notes of all the main facts, causes, effects, issues, etc. ■ Each group has one A3 piece of paper and together they have to create a front page for the morning paper. ■ They only have one lesson to get the paper to the Editor (the teacher). ■ Interrupt the lesson on several occasions with a telephone ringing with 'news fresh in'. ■ Supply students with photos that have come live from location, to fit into headlines, etc.	*Reporting on the Gujarat earthquake:* ■ *Show class video footage of the earthquake as taken in Gujarat with eyewitness accounts and seismologist reports, etc.* ■ *Give each group a set of photos downloaded from the internet, coloured pens, glue, scissors, etc.* ■ *Give each group a fact-file ('faxed over from India!') and a blank A3 sheet.* ■ *Set the time limit. Use phone to pretend you are speaking to a reporter in Gujarat. Tell the class new facts and figures on deaths, injuries, etc.* ■ *You can use your role as Editor to select the best one to go to print – photocopy this one for students as a resource for their books.*
Posters with a Point	
■ Can be used for any number of issues that have a range of viewpoints. ■ Class divided into groups representing different viewpoints on the issue. ■ Each group has to design a poster (or a series of posters) that will persuade an independent observer that their view is right. ■ It is a competition to see which group can display the most convincing argument through pictures and words. ■ They need to think about headlines, content, paragraphing, order of arguments, etc. ■ They have just one lesson to put forward their argument and the independent observer (teacher) will say which viewpoint is the most convincing at the end of the lesson.	*Coastal defences at Sheringham, north Norfolk:* ■ *Proposal by Sheringham Council to spend £1 million on rip-rap and groynes to slow down erosion of an area of rapidly eroding coast by a further 15 years.* *There are four main opinions:* ■ *Local residents don't think it is enough and want a sea wall (at much higher cost) to be built to protect their homes from falling into the sea over the next 100 or more years.* ■ *Coastal experts say that there is no point in constructing sea defences because the building up of sand on this stretch of beach will cause erosion further up the coast.* ■ *Council representatives say that it is the most they can do because other services like the school also need a lot of money.* ■ *Tourists say they don't want anything spent on sea defences because it disrupts wildlife and spoils the views (and tourists bring a lot of money to the town).*

Figure 5 | *Activities for developing writing at key stage 3 and beyond.*

writing of the newspaper article is best done in pairs or in groups to help encourage the exchange of ideas and notes on what has happened. It is important to stay with the students and to remain involved. To add to the momentum you could arrange to have a telephone ringing in the classroom and pretend it is the Editor demanding a first draft – or something similar. Or you could make announcements about fresh information or new pictures just faxed in from source. Maintaining an exciting atmosphere and dynamic pace throughout the activity not only helps to motivate students it also encourages them to write succinctly and with a clear sense of purpose. The activity can be differentiated in various ways, including providing a writing frame which is helpful for lower achieving students.

Posters are often used in geography as a creative way of conveying information. However there is a danger that the design and production process takes precedence over content and geographical learning. One way to try and prevent this is by having a clearly focused context and objective for the poster. 'Posters with a Point' (Figure 5) are best used in a topic that is issue based and involves several viewpoints and opinions. From the very beginning all students must be made aware that the purpose of their poster is to try and convince an independent observer that their view is right and is more important than any other. Spend some time discussing the importance of words and language as a tool for persuasion. The focus on persuasive writing in a competitive environment and with a time restriction means that students tend to concentrate less on the graphic design and production of the poster and more on writing-style, vocabulary and argument.

Geography lends itself well to developing a wide range of different writing styles. Indeed there are many examples that could be used to show the range of writing styles available – formal writing, recounting, explanation, etc. Through learning to write in different styles and for different purposes, students' vocabulary and writing techniques will inevitably be enhanced. Furthermore, working in groups and sharing ideas also enhance learning.

Developing speaking and listening

To be an effective speaker with the confidence to state opinions and convey information is a life-long skill. Once again geography has enormous scope for talk, simulation, discussion and presentation. Using talk to explore, create, question and revise ideas is an extremely effective tool for the learning of geography. As well as bringing variety to the learning environment, the sharing of ideas inevitably heightens understanding and broadens opinions. The task for the teacher is to integrate speaking and listening into the classroom in a well managed and focused way that maintains the desired effect of optimum learning potential. There are many strategies that can be used to develop speaking and listening.

Examples of activities that use talk to question, hypothesise, evaluate, solve problems and develop thinking about complex issues and ideas are shown in Figure 6.

'Read and Recall' is an excellent way of getting students to take in what they are reading to the point where they are able to synthesise that information and articulate it orally to their peers. By giving each student in the group a different piece of information it becomes the responsibility of each individual to understand and remember their particular piece. The competitive atmosphere, whereby each group tries to create the fullest and most accurate account, gives an added purpose for concentrated and close reading. Furthermore, this strategy puts the learning in the hands of the students; they are teaching each other about new information and geographic context. The students will inevitably convey the information in their own language and style which can make it more accessible to listeners as well as reinforcing the speaker's understanding.

Much of the success of this activity depends upon the nature of the information that is given to the students. It should not be a block of prose but rather a well segmented and structured list of points. A bulleted list is often useful. Also, dressing up the content to make it more exciting and appealing means it will be better remembered and, consequently, better narrated. It is usually necessary to write the information yourself or to adapt information to suit your own style.

'Roaming Rainbows' is best used at the beginning of a topic or enquiry project. It will open up a whole field of mini-enquiry questions that need to be answered in order to answer an overarching question for enquiry. It might also be used to ask questions about a picture or image displayed as part of a launch activity at the beginning of a new topic. It can be useful to start by discussing some possibilities for different enquiry questions.

Read and Recall

- Students sit in groups of three.
- Class told that they are going to be given three different pieces of information on each table.
- Each person has to read their piece of information very carefully as they have just three minutes to read and remember as much as they possibly can.
- After the three minutes is up, teacher takes away all information from the students.
- Students take turns to narrate their information as they have remembered it/understood it to the rest of the group.
- The rest of the group takes notes from what the other person is saying.
- After all information has been shared, original pieces of writing are given back and a comparison is made of how well information was remembered/shared.

Learning about the negative impacts of tourism in Cambodia:
- *Three pieces of information are distributed to each table. The information is written as a bulleted list.*
- *The first piece of information is on the problems of soil erosion from deforestation on the banks of the Mekong.*
- *The second piece of information is on the problems of child labour and child smuggling in Phnom Penh.*
- *The third piece of information is on the problems of inadequate services and security at Angkor Wat and subsequent vandalism.*
- *Lots of facts, figures and place names are used to challenge the memory and learning process.*

Roaming Rainbows

- All students to think up an enquiry question to ask about a certain topic.
- All students are then given one of four rainbow colours.
- Teacher then to read out a colour combination – e.g. reds with yellows and blues with violets.
- Students have to move around the room and find someone of the right colour (students only allowed to speak to the same person once).
- Students to share their enquiry questions.
- Process repeated until teacher gets students to sit down and write down the five enquiry questions that they consider the most important.

- *Why did the settlement of London develop where it did and how did it change over time?*
- *Each student is to write a report investigating this enquiry question.*
- *All reports have to be structured around mini-enquiry questions.*
- *Use roaming rainbows to get students thinking about possible lines of enquiry.*
Examples:
- *How important was the River Thames?*
- *Was the land good for farming?*
- *Was the site of London easy to defend against enemies?*
- *Has the use of the River Thames changed?*

Verbal Tennis

- Used in a topic that requires understanding of many different variables (e.g. causes; effects)
- The class is divided into pairs. Each pair has to sit back to back.
- The teacher writes the topic on the board.
- The students have to take turns to name a variable.
- The last one in a pair who is still able to list a variable wins.
- Can be extended to championship whereby two volunteers battle it out in front of the rest of the class.

Revising the causes of rural to urban migration in Tanzania:
- *The main question written on the board is: 'Why are so many people moving from rural Tanzania to the big cities like Dodoma?'*
- *Each pair battles it out to list as many reasons as possible (reasons to include – food shortages, drought, lack of services, no jobs, better quality of life in the cities, etc.)*

Figure 6 | *Activities for developing speaking and listening skills.*

Explain how all questions have to be directed towards better understanding the picture/main enquiry question. To avoid a great deal of confusion as to who is what colour it is best to put a coloured sticker on each student. Getting students to walk around the class and share ideas with each other is an excellent way of starting an activity. It broadens individual ideas and gets students talking and learning with one another. Ideally, the activity should take place in a hall or open space where students can circulate easily.

'Verbal Tennis' is best used at the end of a topic when the students should have a good understanding of the key principles you have covered over the last few weeks. It works particularly well with a topic that involves a large number of variables such as causes and effects. Having got the students to compete in pairs as a whole class it often helps to then give them five minutes to read up on the subject immediately afterwards (by way of giving them a second chance). This invariably gets the students to read voraciously in a last bid attempt to win one back on their neighbour! Once you have repeated the activity ask the class whether anyone considers themselves unbeatable. Bring them to the front and then seek out a challenger for a contest in front of the class. This will encourage the rest of the class to think about different options and thereby learn from the game. The game can be extended by way of adding the rule that at any point you (as teacher) can call on any individual to justify their statement. If they fail to provide a suitable justification then they have to find another choice.

Implications for practice

(a) **Using a range of different forms of 'texts' makes an important contribution towards helping students in their learning to make sense of the real world.**

Geography is a brilliant subject for helping students to address some big issues they will need to face as they grow into adulthood. Using text derived from different sources helps student 'tune in' to different registers and forms of written communication. They can practise writing in different settings and for different audiences too. This helps them engage with the 'real world', as well as the more abstract 'academic' world.

(b) **Geography lessons on controversial issues can help students to understand bias,**

This is a three-stage process:

1. use text from different sources to **detect** bias
2. students rewrite or merge texts from different sources to **correct** bias
3. students are asked to re-present a particular point of view to **create** bias

This three-stage 'understanding bias' strategy could form the basis for developing and expanding argumentation skills in geography, and can be extended through role play, simulations and debate.

Related publications from the Geographical Association:

- Morgan, J. and Lambert, D. (2003) *Theory into Practice: Place, 'race' and teaching geography.*
- Butt, G. (2001) *Theory into Practice: Extending writing skills.*
- McPartland, M. (2001) *Theory into Practice: Moral dilemmas.*
- Biddulph, M. and Bright, G. (2003) *Theory into Practice: Dramatically good geography.*
- Roberts, M. (2003) *Learning through Enquiry: Making sense of geography in the key stage 3 classroom.*

References

Crequer, N. (1999) 'Fifth of 19-year olds struggle to read', *TESNET*, 26 March.

DfES (2001a) *The National Key Stage 3 Strategy.* London: DfES.

DfES (2001b) *Framework for teaching English in Years 7, 8 and 9.* London: DfES (available online www.standards.dfes.gov.uk/keystage3/respub/englishframework/foreword/).

Chapter 12

Cracking the code - numeracy and geography

Clare Brooks

Before reading this chapter consider the following questions:

- What do numbers mean? How do your students respond to numeracy activities?

- What opportunities are there to develop and extend students' numeracy skills within geography?

- How can numeracy be used to enhance students' learning of geography?

- What strategies do you use to support the development of students' numeracy skills?

Using numerical data

1960	89	–
1970	156	–
1980	311	–
1990	519	11
2000	1045	995

At first glance the table is meaningless, but after a second look you were probably able to work out that the first column represented years (in increments of 10) and that the other two columns showed an increasing incidence of something. You may have been able to hazard a guess as to what the phenomena might be. In fact, the second column represents the total number (in millions) of telephone lines. The third column represents the total number (in millions) of cellular phone subscribers worldwide. This example illustrates how, once we are armed with all the information, a table becomes easy to read, but without it the numbers are meaningless.

'I'm no good at maths'

Initiatives such as the National Numeracy Strategy highlighted the importance of teaching numeracy 'across the curriculum', and geography has a clear role to play in this regard, i.e. as a *context* for teaching numeracy skills (DfES, 2000). At the same time, students of geography need numeracy skills in order fully to understand and to analyse geographical phenomena. Thus we as geography teachers have a particular obligation towards our students, especially those from whom the cry 'I'm no good at maths' is often heard. As well as demystifying numbers so that our students can effectively 'crack the code' of what they mean and represent in geography, we must also help them to appreciate the importance of numbers and numerical calculations as essential educational tools.

Take the example of a lesson on indicators of development in which students are asked to calculate the ratio of the number of doctors to population. By doing so, as well as learning how to manipulate numbers in order to calculate the ratio, i.e. learning an essential skill, students will also begin to appreciate why such a simple calculation can be useful for geographers in enhancing their understanding. For example, by making such a calculation students will be encouraged to reflect on the importance of primary health care as a measure of development. The calculation will also highlight the challenges of providing primary health care for a dispersed, or largely rural population, and will raise questions relating to resource deployment and potential inequalities.

In fact, while we may be skilled at reading and interpreting data, we may not be so skilled at breaking down how the calculation, or steps of the calculation, can be performed, or in ways of looking at alternatives and understanding why that calculation is right. As a new teacher I was constantly aware that some of the language of mathematics that I learnt at school was now irrelevant or not used; protractors had become angle indicators. My students were taught to do long-division and to construct pie charts in a very different way. This presented me with a whole new vocabulary and set of techniques that I needed to be familiar with in order to help my students develop their numeracy and to complement the work of my colleagues in the mathematics department. Fortunately, the National Numeracy Strategy made such vocabulary explicit, and enables teachers of all subjects, but particularly geography, to gain access to this world of mathematical literacy. The Strategy has also been very helpful in providing some definitions as well as offering perspectives on what numeracy is and how it can be taught across the whole-school curriculum. (For more detail on the National Numeracy Strategy, see Roberts, 2003, chapter 8.)

As geography teachers it is important that we ask ourselves the following questions:

- How can the development of numeracy skills enhance students' learning in geography?
- What opportunities are there to develop and extend students' numeracy skills within geography?
- What strategies can be used to support the development of students' numeracy skills?

It is not my intention here to promote the argument that geography is merely a useful vehicle for the development of core skills such as those of numeracy. This approach undermines the status and value of geography as an important area of study in its own right. However, it is my view that a skilled geographer needs to have a degree of proficiency in numeracy in order to interpret spatial patterns and processes at a variety of scales.

Developing Numeracy

The National Numeracy Strategy identified the handling of data and the development of map skills (e.g. use of scale, co-ordinates) as important aspects of geography through which numeracy can be developed. But geography can take these numeracy skills further by providing a context for these calculations: working out percentages and ratios is only valuable when performing the calculation has a real purpose. Understanding that purpose and the values of the calculations enables us to select which calculations to perform and to begin to understand the significance of the results. Thus, when such opportunities arise in geography, teachers need to help their students to understand why they are performing the calculations and how different calculations could lead to different results and analyses of the outcomes.

It is my intention here to examine some specific strategies for supporting the development of numeracy skills through geography while still maintaining a focus on geographical understanding. First, it is important to demystify what we mean by numeracy, and then consider how to teach simple calculations. The chapter moves on to consider forms of data handling and the importance of the data-handling cycle within geographical enquiry. Other important numerical skills that geographers use extensively is the reading and interpretation of graphs and charts, and the representation of mathematical phenomena on maps and diagrams, both of which are considered later in the chapter.

The National Numeracy Strategy highlighted geography as a key subject area for the promotion of cross-curricular numeracy skills. It identifies the following priorities for cross-curricular numeracy:

> ■ *To improve accuracy, particularly in calculation, measurement and graphical work*
> ■ *To improve interpretation and presentation of graphs, charts and diagrams*
> ■ *To improve reasoning and problem solving* (DfES, 2000).

These areas have particular relevance for geography, being essential for the development of students' geographical skills and understanding. The National Numeracy Strategy also highlights key areas where geography can make a significant contribution to numeracy. These are used to provide a structure for the remainder of this chapter.

Numbers are merely a way of quantifying phenomena that makes them easy to compare. However they often need a unit of measure of abbreviation to explain their meaning. For example, if you look at two roads and see that one is twice the distance of the other, this is a clear pattern. However, when we are told that one is 37.5km and the other is 18.75km the pattern is less clear. Therefore, our first task is to understand what it is about numeracy that students find difficult, so that they can start to look at the meaning behind the numbers.

What students generally find difficult about ...

■ very large numbers (23,563,956)

■ very small numbers or decimals (2.4007)

■ units that they are not familiar with (27 tonnes per hectare)

■ compound numbers (i.e. numbers that are made up of more than one unit, e.g. 467 people per square kilometre)

■ being asked to perform calculations that they have not covered in mathematics, or doing them differently from the way they do them in mathematics.

Be aware that the *Framework for Teaching Mathematics* (DfES, 2001) does not require students to learn how to construct graphs and scattergraphs until late in key stage 3.

Opportunities for developing numeracy through geography

Adopting an enquiry approach to understanding geographical phenomena often means having to perform simple calculations and to understand numerical data by making predictions about them.

Predictions

The example shown in Figure 1, often referred to as 'intelligent guesswork', is based on

Predictions using life expectancy data

The table shows life expectancy figures for the year 2004 for the following 15 countries:

Afghanistan, Andorra, Bangladesh, Brazil, India, Iraq, Japan, Jordan, Kuwait, Mexico, Peru, Russia, UK, USA, Zambia.

Task

Ask students to 'guess' which countries the data belong to and to offer explanations for why they have made those choices.

Their choices are often made based on assumptions about countries that are not necessarily true or valid. Sharing the actual results (see Figure caption) can lead to further discussion about what the figures mean, what they show and what they hide.

The geographical and numeracy objectives of this activity are to encourage students to think about:

- what the numbers themselves mean (for example, the importance of units and the source of the data);

- what the numbers hide and what they reveal.

Life-expectancy data (2004)
83.5
81.0
78.2
78.0
77.4
76.8
74.9
71.4
69.2
68.2
66.3
63.9
61.7
42.4
35.1

Source: US Census Bureau's International Database website

Figure 1 | *'Intelligent guesswork' on life expectancy. Note: the figures are listed in the following order (highest first): Andorra, Japan, UK, Jordan, USA, Kuwait, Mexico, Brazil, Peru, Iraq, Russia, India, Bangladesh, Afghanistan, Zambia.*

an activity devised by Margaret Roberts (2003). It provides an opportunity for students to think about the meanings of the numbers presented as well as the general pattern that they represent. It also serves some important geographical objectives by encouraging students to question their own conceptions (and misconceptions) of development and their understanding about places.

Using simple calculations

It can often be useful to get students to perform simple calculations (e.g. percentages, averages, ratios) to demonstrate patterns or trends in data. With all these simple calculations, the key to developing numeracy and geographical skills and understandings is to get students to think about what the data represents, and what they mean.

Figure 2 is an activity related to the notion of gross national product (GNP) per capita. It can be incorporated into any part of a lesson and usually takes about 10-15 minutes to complete, depending on the size and age of the group. The activity has two main purposes: to explain what we mean by GNP per capita, and to demonstrate some of the strengths and weaknesses of using averages. The activity can be extended by asking students to calculate the median and the mode, then to compare the results with the mean and the actual distribution of 'wealth' within the group.

The above activity is a short and simple way of demonstrating not only the meaning of GNP, but also the fallibility of averages and what they can hide. The numerical skill of calculating averages is a very small but important part of this activity.

Gross national product

The class should be divided into groups of uneven sizes. This can be done randomly.

1. Ask each individual to count up how much money they have on them at this particular time, and then for the group to count up how much they have as a whole.

2. It is useful to construct a table on the board like the one below, adding in the 'population' of each group or country:

Country or Group	Total population (i.e. number of people in each group)	Total wealth (i.e. total amount of money in each group)	GNP per capita (the mean)
A			
B			
C			

3. Each group reports back to the teacher stating the total of their combined wealth, and this is added to the table.

4. Each group can work out the GNP per capita by dividing the total wealth by the total population (i.e. the mean).

5. The teacher then discusses several points with the group:

   ■ What does GNP per capita mean?

   ■ What relationship does it have to total wealth and to population size? How can these figures affect GNP?

   ■ What does GNP not show? Ask your students to reflect on how much money they had individually, how they contributed to their country's wealth, and what they had compared to the 'average' wealth of the country.

Figure 2 | *Simple calculations using GNP data.*

The data handling cycle

Collecting, analysing and presenting data are activities central to the enquiry process in geography. The data handling cycle, as identified in the National Numeracy Strategy summarises this process (Figure 3).

Although the categories may be structured differently in other forms of enquiry, this cyclical process of handling data is similar to the route followed in geographical enquiry. For the geography teacher concerned with developing geographical understanding as well as developing numeracy skills, this raises a number of issues:

■ In what terms can the 'problem' or 'issue' be specified?
■ What are appropriate data to collect?
■ What are the appropriate ways to process and represent this data?
■ How can the data be interpreted?
■ What conclusions can be drawn?
■ How can the conclusions be evaluated?

This list of questions can be used by teachers when planning a geographical enquiry. It can also be presented to students to enable them to attain higher levels in geography by asking and answering the questions themselves. (For specific examples, see Roberts, 2003.)

Specifying the problem

This is a crucial stage in the cycle as careful specification of the issues drives the selection of data, the type of calculations needed, and the validity of the conclusions to be drawn from them. It is essential that this stage of the enquiry relates to the

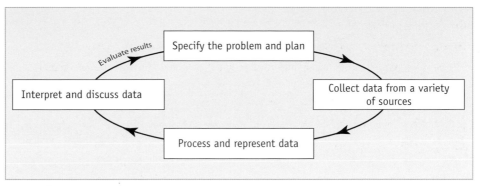

Figure 3 | *The data handling cycle.*

geographical objectives for the topic being studied, and is not driven merely by the data being made available. This may be informed by the national curriculum for geography, examination specifications, or the fieldwork opportunities available. The nature of the topic being investigated needs to drive the selection of data to be used.

Collect data from a variety of sources

Geographers can draw on numerous sources of data – text-based, visual or numerical – some of which may originate from fieldwork. Data sources should be scrutinised for bias and reliability (particularly if collected from the internet), and care taken to ensure that the data are accurate and fit for their intended purpose. The choice of type and form of the data to be collected should be determined by the problem or issue to be studied. Too much data (for example, Census data for a number of wards) can make analysis and interpretation difficult; too little can lead to unreliable conclusions.

Key questions to discuss with students include the following:

■ How much data do we need to answer the question? (scale and scope, and also validity of findings)

■ Are the data we need readily available? If not, are there suitable substitutes (e.g. if information about people's income is not available, socio-economic data could be used instead)? What differences could this make to our analysis?

■ Is there an opportunity to collect primary data from our own fieldwork?

Processing and representing data

This next stage in the data-handling cycle (Figure 3) is crucial to identifying geographical patterns and trends. For the geographer, maps as well as graphs and charts have a central role to play in data-presentation and the analysis of spatial patterns. Again, the over-riding guiding principle should be that of fitness for purpose: how does the processing and representation of the data support the investigation, and how can it help us to 'crack the code' of what the data demonstrate?

Figure 4 demonstrates how ICT can be useful in helping students to decide what is the most appropriate way of presenting data they have collected. By entering data onto a spreadsheet, students can construct a variety of different charts and select the most appropriate to help them answer the question. In this way, students will develop their understanding of the role and function of different graphicacy techniques and how these can be used to support their learning in geography.

The activity illustrated in Figure 4 also shows how the process of identifying a problem, asking questions about the problem and processing information subsequently collected can help students to find out about a place. Using numerical data and other sources of evidence in this way can challenge stereotypes and help students to develop

1. Choose the place (this can be any place for which data are readily available). You might like to choose a clearly defined area in your local area, a small village, housing estate or district.

2. Take students on a tour of the place, preferably a real tour, but if that is not possible then a 'virtual' tour is the next best thing (e.g. using photographs, video footage, newspaper reports, maps, narratives, poems).

3. Encourage students to make predictions about the place they have chosen and visited. You can use questions such as these to prompt them:
   - What are people like?
   - What different groups of people would you expect to find here?
   - What sort of work is in the area? Who does this work? Where do the local people work, and how do they get there?
   - What are the homes like?

4. Now ask the students what types of data (primary and/or secondary) they would need to collect in order to find out if their predictions were correct (see second column of the table below). To do this they will need to have an idea of the types of data that are available. To make this task quicker and easier, you could present students with a range of pre-collected data from which they can make a selection. A table like the one below could be used with students to help them to structure the activity:

My prediction	What data would help me to investigate the accuracy of my prediction?	Where would I find such data? Or, How would I collect the data?	What would be the best way to organise the data?
Mostly young families would live here	Demographic data	Census returns	As a population pyramid
Most people would be working class	Socio-economic data	Census returns	As pie charts
There may be some students living here	Data on the size and composition of households	Census returns	As bar charts
The houses are quite old and may not have many amenities			

Note: The questions posed in the third column can be varied according to the circumstances, e.g. if data is to be collected through fieldwork (see point 5 below).

5. The next step is to collect the data needed (see third column). In the case of fieldwork, this might involve designing a survey of the local area. In the case of secondary data, an activity using Census data is an obvious choice. Decisions also need to be made about the range of data (i.e. which wards to include) and the level of detail needed. Work towards the students being able to make these decisions themselves.

6. Processing the data in a spreadsheet will make it easier for students to decide which techniques they can use to represent their findings to best effect (column four in the table). Selecting an appropriate graph or chart will help them to answer their original predictions or questions.

Figure 4 | *A data manipulation exercise. Note: This activity can also be used effectively to compare quality of life statistics for different places.*

a more in-depth understanding of places. This activity gets students thinking about how data can be used to help them to answer geographical questions, so that data and information becomes a tool at their disposal, and it is up to them to use their geographical skills to decide how to use that data.

The use of ICT can certainly facilitate and enhance the analysis and interpretation of data, but it is vital not to lose sight of the purpose of the activity. The decision about whether to use ICT or not has to be driven by this principle. In the example shown in Figure 4, using a spreadsheet will enable students to construct the graphs and charts quickly and have the opportunity to evaluate them effectively by comparing the different techniques. Students could also consider (or even explore) how long it would take to perform this activity by hand!

Using maps and charts

One of the unique features of geography is its relationship with maps. Maps as a medium help students to understand the significance of numerical data and to identify spatial patterns within the distribution of the data. As with graphs, it is important to choose the type of map best suited to the display of particular trends and patterns. Geographical information systems (GIS) software can support the construction of maps from pre-selected data, examples of which can be found on websites (see Chapters 7 and 11). There are also useful mapping functions in spreadsheets but the parameters of the data sets can often be limiting.

Maps enable students to really interpret data and help to make meaning clear. The 'living graph' strategy used to promote thinking through geography (Leat, 1998) can be easily adapted for use with maps – 'living maps'. This is a great way to get students to think about the data as representing 'living' information. Again, the key principle is that the choice of mapping technique should be appropriate to the data set and the central question or issue being addressed. What pattern or information is revealed by the data? Figure 5 is an isoline map showing the average number of days for which snow fell in winter in each year from 1961 to 1990. (The Meteorological Office website provides isoline maps for several aspects of climate and weather showing actual statistics, including statistics where anomalies exist.) The key to success with activities such as that given in Figure 5 is to choose a map based on data that match the geographical objectives that have been selected for the learning experience.

Figure 5 | *Student activities on the mapped average number of days when snow fell in winter between 1971 and 2000. Map: ©Crown copyright 2005, Published by the Met Office.*

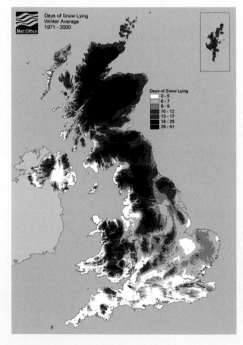

Investigating snowfall in winter

Using the Met Office map showing snowfall in the winter from 1971 to 2000, which areas do you think the following statements describe?

- None of the children in this area have ever experienced a white Christmas.
- Joanne looks forward to winter because she loves to ski and there is a ski resort really close to where she lives.
- Semhar gets really frustrated because even though it snows the snow melts quite quickly and she doesn't get any time off school to enjoy it.
- Sometimes, the Browns get woken up at night by the sound of lorries spreading grit and salt on the road.
- During winter Stephanie often gets snowed in for weeks at a time.

Debriefing the activity

- Ask students where they chose to locate the statements, and why.
- What were the geographical reasons for their decisions and what additional knowledge did they use to make these decisions?
- What additional information would you need to be able to make a more informed choice?

Scale and measurements

When students are using maps to interpret and understand spatial patterns, it is important for them to appreciate how certain characteristics of the map, in particular its scale, affect their perception of what it shows. A simple activity which focuses on this issue can be undertaken using maps of the same place but at different scales (internet-based mapping sites, e.g. Multimap and Get-a-map, can always be used or even global positioning systems). Give different maps to different students then select two places relevant to your study that are close together and ask the students to describe their position in relation to each other. Students then share their descriptions to discover whether the different scales have influenced their perceptions. This simple activity encourages students to think about the importance of scale when understanding and interpreting data.

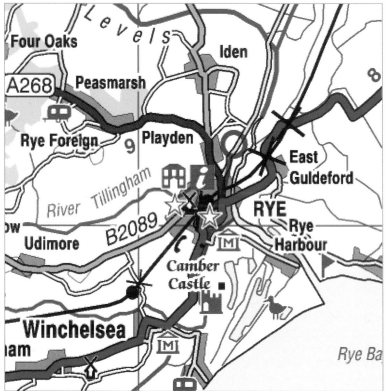

Figure 6 | *Land that has been reclaimed in the Rye district. Reproduced by permission of Ordanance Survey on behalf of HMSO. Crown copyright 2006. All rights reserved. Ordnance Survey Licence number 100017849.*

Using the Ordnance Survey map extract shown in Figure 6, students can perform a number of calculations. If you are focusing on making calculations meaningful, first explain that Rye was once on the coast, then ask the students to use the scale to measure how far Rye now is from the coastline. Using this information, and referring to larger extracts of the map, students can find other areas where more land has been added and go on to discuss land reclamation and coastal processes. Performing the simple calculation thus becomes meaningful, adding real value to the learning experience.

Interpret and discuss data

In this phase of the data-handling cycle (Figure 3) the *meaning* of the data collected becomes clear. This is where we can monitor students' geographical understanding and skills and discover whether they have correctly interpreted the numerical calculations they have made. It is important to refer back to the main issue or problem to identify whether the data collected make it possible to answer the question posed. This logically feeds into the evaluation of the data used, and highlights any inappropriate data. It is also important to identify where assumptions are made that cannot be supported by the data.

Progression

The main focus of this chapter has been on strategies that enable students to crack the code of numbers and what they mean. Students can be supported by ICT when working on several aspects of data handling and manipulation. However, it is also important to

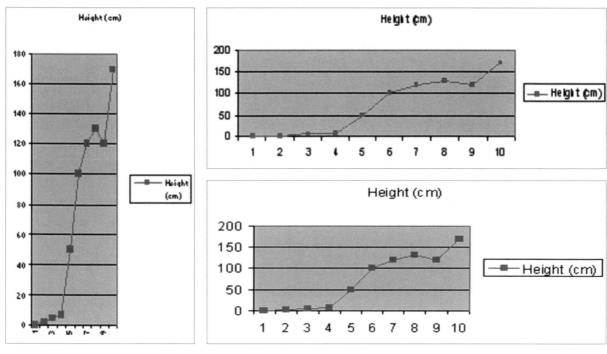

Figure 7 | *Three different ways of presenting beach profile data.*

achieve some progression in the development of students' numeracy skills as well as in their understanding of geography. So what does this progression look like?

Students can progress from simple calculations to more complicated statistical techniques; from calculating the mean to thinking about the differences shown with median and mode before moving towards identifying the standard deviation. To ensure that students create their own interpretation of these calculations, we should encourage them to experiment with the statistical techniques, apply the techniques to different situations and critically examine the outcomes of representing the data in different ways. For example, students can input beach profile data collected from fieldwork into a spreadsheet and change the scales, the axis proportions, and other graphing variables to explore how these changes affect the resulting cross-sections (Figure 7). Once they have determined the scale, orientation, and axis proportions for their cross-section, they can then justify the methodology selected. Deciding on the presentation of the cross-section themselves will enable the students to interpret the outcomes more effectively.

Students achieve progression in the use of numeracy skills by:
- performing simple then gradually more complicated calculations
- choosing their own calculations and statistical tests to perform
- being able to justify the choices they have made in the representation and interpretation of data and the consequent evaluation of results
- being able to make accurate and justified predictions when faced with data sets.

Summary

Geographical phenomena can often be described using numerical data and 'cracking this code' can be the key to achieving greater geographical understanding as well as developing numeracy skills. Students should be encouraged to interrogate the calculations they are performing and recognise the reasons for undertaking them. The use of real data emanating from real geographical issues and questions can ensure that numbers have real meaning for students.

In geography, numerical data are frequently needed and used to aid understanding of geographical phenomena, so an ability to 'crack the code' is essential to a full understanding of the subject, as well as being a significant skill in its own right and one which has application across the curriculum. Students of geography must be encouraged to interrogate the data they use and to consider the calculations they make and their reasons for undertaking them. By using real data relating to real issues in this way, they will be helped to understand that numbers and the skills of numeracy are relevant and meaningful.

Related publications from the Geographical Association:
- LFG/GA (2005) *State of the Nation 2005 – Teachers' notes*
- Roberts, M. (2003) (see below - particularly Chapter 8: 'Focus on numeracy').
- St John, P. and Richardson, D. (1997) *Methods of Presenting Fieldwork Data*
- St John, P. and Richardson, D. (1996) *Statistical Analysis of Fieldwork Data*
- Wright, D. (2000) *Theory Into Practice: Maps with Latitude*

References

Print

DfEE (1999) *Framework for Teaching Mathematics: Years 7, 8 and 9*. London: HMSO.

DfES (2000) *National Numeracy Strategy*. London: DfES.

Leat, D. (ed) (2001) *Thinking Through Geography*. Cambridge: Chris Kington Publishing.

Roberts, M. (2003) *Learning through Enquiry: Making sense of geography in the key stage 3 classroom*. Sheffield: Geographical Association.

Electronic

DfES Mathematics Framework-
     http://www.standards.dfes.gov.uk/keystage3/respub/mathsframework/foreword/

DfES National Numeracy Strategy – www.standards.dfes.gov.uk/numeracy/

Get-a-map – http://www.ordnancesurvey.co.uk/oswebsite/getamap/

Multimap – www.multimap.com

US Census Bureau's International Database – www.census.gov

Implications for practice

(a) **It is vital to adopt strategies for addressing numeracy in geography that fit in with the approaches being developed across the school.**

Check with other departments and with the co-ordinator in your school to find out what strategies are advocated and used for teaching calculations and the construction of graphs. Explore how these approaches can be used and developed within geography. It is helpful to agree about the key vocabulary that will be used in relation to numeracy. Reinforce this vocabulary in your teaching and in displays and resource sheets used with students.

(b) **Numeracy issues should be considered in medium and longer term planning in geography to ensure progression in the development of students' numeracy skills.**

Undertake an audit of where opportunities exist for addressing the development of numeracy across your current geography curriculum. It is perhaps useful to highlight a key aspect of numeracy that will be addressed in each scheme of work. Make the skills identified explicit to students when they are being used in geography and acknowledge their success in performing these skills and in understanding their application (see Chapter 32). Return to these skills whenever possible to reinforce students' understanding of how they can be applied as well as to practise their use of these skills. Try to provide opportunities for students to apply these skills in different situations to support 'bridging' and 'transfer' in the use of such skills (Leat, 1998).

(c) **Identify situations in your geography curriculum where collecting, processing and interpreting data is a key element of the learning process.**

Consider how the data-handling process enhances learning in geography in these areas of the geography curriculum. Review whether students are given opportunities to make predictions about what data may show, and then return to their predictions after performing the calculations. Try to ensure that they can perform alternative calculations so that they can evaluate the methods used. Students should also be given opportunities to decide what data they need to collect from both primary and secondary sources, and have a clear purpose in mind for how the data will be used to answer geographical questions. Always remember to draw attention to the role of numbers as one way of helping us to understand aspects of geography and of the world around us.

Chapter 13

using geography textbooks

John Widdowson and David Lambert

Before reading this chapter consider the following questions:

■ What role should textbooks have in geography lessons?

■ What criteria are used in your school when selecting textbooks for use in geography lessons?

■ How can geography textbooks be used to enhance teaching and learning in geography?

The importance of textbooks in a 'resource ecology'

In the context of the 'information age', how important is the textbook? This is a hard question and is linked to the role textbooks are deemed to play in teaching and learning. The answer depends on who you ask: publishers, authors, teachers, students, parents and awarding bodies – all have a view. How important textbooks are considered to be ultimately depends on what these interested parties actually want from a healthy teaching and learning relationship.

We think it is important to keep an open mind on this issue. It might be a mistake, for example, to indict the textbook as being responsible for boring teaching. Having access to a limited range – or even just a single course-book – does not *necessarily* mean rote learning is the only option: again, it rather depends on what the role of the textbook is thought to be in the educational transaction.

And what about ICT? Is the textbook yesterday's technology for yesterday's schools? We think not. We ask a more sophisticated question – about the place of textbooks in the 'resource ecology' of geography classrooms. Though textbooks seem to be strangely undervalued (or perhaps taken for granted) by teachers, especially in the UK, we will argue that they will remain key, but in fundamentally changing settings, and that their value needs to be reasserted. The fact that state schools are chronically under-resourced with books in comparison with successful private schools, speaks volumes. It is disturbing that students often share books in class, and many schools do not allow them to take books home (often supplying in their place photocopied fragments of the book), in order to fulfill the homework requirement. It is worrying that such a state of affairs seems now to be accepted as normal. Textbooks are relatively cheap, they do not break down and can even work during a power cut! This chapter should help you maximise the benefits of using textbooks in the classroom.

Classrooms as ecosystems

It is now unexceptional to suggest that classrooms can best be understood as 'learning environments'. The analogy is probably especially appealing to geographers! The essence of the ecosystem concept is that any environment can be analysed and understood in terms of how its energy flows through it in a highly organised and structured way. Transferring the concept to classrooms allows us to see them as:

- *Complex* – what you see is not necessarily *all* that is there; e.g. the teacher's preparation, and how the students have been inducted over previous months may be highly significant.
- *Multidimensional* – they have social, psychological, institutional and other dimensions which interact in various ways.
- *Fragile* – they can sometimes be easily upset, maybe by one disruptive element (or person) such as a change in the weather, a news event, an occurrence in the corridor, the network going down ...
- *Different* – subjects, teachers, locations, time of day ... all lead to certain 'givens' or contexts, and different energy flows – compare your year 9s on a Monday morning and a Friday afternoon.
- *Dynamic* – they have an unpredictable quality; change is constant partly because the students always bring their experiences and something new each day to the classroom.

The position and role of the textbook as an element in such dynamic learning environments is poorly understood – or at least confused. They tend to be taken for granted, arguably one of the 'givens' of schooling. In some cases they are understood primarily in managerial rather than educational terms; after all, having a set of textbooks helps a teacher to manage the challenges listed above and stay one step ahead of the students.

Perhaps this is true, but seeing textbooks in such instrumental terms may conceal a number of pertinent educational matters. These can come to the fore if we imagine the textbook as an integral part of the system – the 'biome' – through which there is an energy flow. We do not have to launch a detailed exposition of ecology to make our point, save for an example or two. When we accept that any environment, say a tropical forest or a temperate grassland can be analysed in terms of where its energy is stored, we see that the answer is in the balance between three components:

- in the soil,
- in the dead and decaying leaf and animal matter on the ground, and
- in the living matter itself.

It cannot be anywhere else. However, the precise balance between the three varies considerably.

So where is the 'learning energy' of a classroom stored, and how does it flow through the system? It is not too fanciful to imagine the answer also lying in a balance between three components:

- the students,
- the teacher, and
- the learning resources.

Photo: Banana Stock Ltd.

(We will resist drawing any closer comparison than this, but readers may want to consider the second list in terms of the first, strictly for fun only: Which of the items in the above list is the 'living matter'? Which is the source of sustenance to allow growth, i.e. the soil? Which is the classroom dead and decaying 'leaf litter'?)

If we can begin to analyse classrooms in such terms it may enable us to 'place' textbooks (and other learning resources) in different classroom settings. As with the study of natural ecosystems or biomes, such a study leads us quickly to further questions concerning *function:* thus, in clarifying the role of the textbook in different classroom settings, we can ask (for example):

■ What part do textbooks play in the network of events and relationships that contribute to learning?
■ If textbooks were withdrawn, in what ways would the learning ecosystem be damaged?

The learning ecotone

Our ecological analysis can be developed a little further. Mike Horsley and the Teaching Resources and Textbook Research Unit (TREAT) at the University of Sydney, Australia, have looked at the way textbooks continue to evolve, particularly in the context of the wider resource environment including the digital information explosion. Horsley (2001) has proposed the biological concept of ecotones to help analyse these changes in a way that avoids the erroneous assumption that new computerised technologies will simply replace the old print-based ones. In his own words:

> *Biologists use the term 'ecotone' to describe an area where two adjacent ecosystems overlap – for example, where a forest gradually turns into grassland. The ecotone has an ecology of its own. It can support forms of life not found in either of the adjacent systems. Today, there exists the educational equivalent of an ecotone between traditional learning environments and the emergence of new learning environments designed around student centred interaction and the internet and technology based learning tools* (Horsley, 2001, p. 38).

The underlying point here is that although there have always been different classroom ecologies, as discussed above, they have in fact mostly operated under the same set of educational assumptions. Over the years these have generally governed fundamental classroom relationships within superficially diverse teacher-student-resources learning ecologies. Put another way, differences in traditional classroom appearances may be so superficial that they may be no more than one might expect from within a single ecosystem.

However, there is now burgeoning interest in other possibilities that may result in fundamentally different learning ecosystems. This has been stimulated at least in part by the advent of new technologies, but more importantly by educational philosophies that fully acknowledge the agency of the student in social settings. In short, we are distinguishing here the fundamental differences between traditional knowledge transmission models of education and more progressive constructivist models. We could think of a continuum showing the ecotone lying between the two 'extremes' (Figure 1). The textbook is alive in all environments, but its particular function in the context of wider learning resources and in relation to the energy stores represented by the teacher role and that of the students varies, possibly quite fundamentally.

The left-hand side of Figure 1 captures a traditional learning environment, in which the focus of the curriculum was primarily the identification of worthwhile content and the purpose of teaching was to pass this on to the next generation. The textbook framed the structure of the course in order efficiently to 'deliver' the contents. Textbooks were

Knowledge transmission	Educational ecotone	Knowledge construction
Teacher directed	Transitional	Learner centred
Passive, linear learning	Transitional	Active, question driven
Individual orientation	Transitional	Group and collaborative

Figure 1 | *Two adjacent educational ecosystems and the 'ectotone'.*

authoritative, and sometimes lasted in print for decades. Teachers adopted the role of transmitter, and the students were receivers.

The right-hand side of Figure 1 shows changes in the way the curriculum is understood and which have led to role changes: the collective purpose of teachers, students and resource(s) is to act together to *make meaning*. There is no longer a single, authoritative information source. Teachers facilitate. Students' prior knowledge is valued.

It is likely that at any time many contemporary classroom learning environments lie within the ecotone between (the centre column in the Figure). Both here and on the right-hand side of the continuum the particular role that textbooks play in the learning environment needs clarifying. When clear about the role(s) textbooks can play, teachers can then set about evaluating and selecting those that are best suited to their purpose – and as we go on to show, though many geography textbooks may look fairly similar at first glance, more careful scrutiny reveals significant differences.

In a fascinating piece of research examining the nature of textbooks in geography during the twentieth century, Rex Walford portrayed 'the strange case of the disappearing text' (1995). In the context of our current discussion it is tempting to view this account as one showing the adaptation of textbooks in the ecotone. Walford states that:

> it seems incontrovertible that information text has slowly been disappearing from so-called 'textbooks' over the last seventy years of geography. Some books have better cause to be called 'activity books' or 'work books', given the balance of material within them (1995, p. 5).

His research is inconclusive as to the implications of this, but there is recognition that the loss of extended prose may have been induced by authors and publishers responding to the needs and preferences of students in the information age. Students are said to think 'mosaically' rather than linearly and are used to getting their information more from talking and listening than from reading books. Walford's quote seems to imply that, in his view, it is not just a matter of the days of the textbook being numbered; the traditional 'textbook' may have already died – at least as a single source of authoritative information.

Evaluating and selecting textbooks

We should be clear that we have no doubts that textbooks have a key place in teaching and learning. This is because research evidence (Chambliss and Calfee, 1998; Graves, 2001; Keele University, 1999; Lambert, 1999, 2000; Marsden, 2001) shows that:

- textbooks help teachers,
- textbooks help students, and
- textbooks can lead to healthy curriculum change and renewal.

There is no shortcut method to selecting the best textbooks for your students in your department in relation to the learning environments that you are trying to establish and maintain. It requires considerable thought and discussion. The Geographical Association

Organising initial thinking on textbook resources		
Title		
Author		
Publisher		

Category	Positive	Negative
Claims made by publisher		
How are contents organised and expressed?		
How is text presented and organised?		
How clearly are key concepts, themes or ideas signposted?		
How successfully are photographs and artwork used?		
What forms of exercises and activities have been designed?		
What appears to be the 'ethos' of the book?		
How attractive is the book to young readers?		
Other?		

Figure 2 | *Evaluation of published resources.*

website provides some examples of how to tackle this, and a site where teachers can exchange experiences, templates and approaches. One example of a straightforward template is provided in Figure 2. You will be able to find many others.

Strategies for using textbooks in the classroom

We have now established what criteria to consider when choosing a textbook, so – the next obvious question is: What is the best one for our department to get? Choosing the right textbook is like getting the right car – it depends what you intend to use it for. It is no good buying a small car if you have a family of five to fit in, or a four-wheel drive vehicle if you only ever drive in a city (and it is probably not a good idea to have a car at all if you are concerned about the environment!).

It is the same with textbooks. Bright, glossy covers and lavishly designed pages may convince you that all books are much the same. But more detailed analysis will reveal important differences. Textbooks are written with a range of purposes in mind. There are those that seek to cover the content and reassure the teacher, leaving nothing to chance. These will be used by departments depending heavily on part-time staff or non-specialist teachers. In a similar mould are the increasing number of revision guides and course-books dealing with the nuts and bolts of the curriculum. At the other end of the spectrum are those textbooks that are more innovative in their approaches and attempt to move both the subject, and students' learning, forward. In these books curriculum coverage may have been sacrificed for depth. They will often require greater effort and engagement from the teacher in order for students to get the most from them.

In practice, strategies for using textbooks depend on both the teacher and the nature of the book. On the one hand there is the degree to which the teacher prefers to depend on the textbook, or to be more flexible in its use. On the other hand, the nature of the textbook may be characterised by its approach to geographical enquiry. More of the recently published geography textbooks claim to adopt an enquiry-based approach. The ways in which teacher and textbook may interact to produce varying classroom strategies is summarised in Figure 3. In reality, most teachers would use a range of strategies, and operate along the continua indicated by the arrows across the top and down the side of the Table.

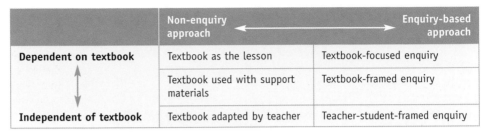

	Non-enquiry approach ←→	Enquiry-based approach
Dependent on textbook	Textbook as the lesson	Textbook-focused enquiry
↕	Textbook used with support materials	Textbook-framed enquiry
Independent of textbook	Textbook adapted by teacher	Teacher-student-framed enquiry

Figure 3 | *The use of textbooks in geographical enquiry.*

We will now describe each of the strategies outlined in Figure 3 in more depth and, in doing so, critically examine how textbooks may be used in the classroom.

Textbook *as* the lesson

We are moving away from teaching and learning that depends totally on a single textbook – and not before time! It is no longer acceptable for teachers to tell students to turn to the next double page in the textbook each time they come into the classroom. Yet, there is still a place for the occasional lesson that is based solely on the textbook and its resources. Textbooks do some things better than many other resources teachers have at their disposal – and they conveniently bring them all together on one (much maligned!) double-page spread. Geography textbooks can help to bring the world alive for students. They provide in-depth case studies about places that would be hard to obtain in such an accessible form from other sources in the limited time available to busy teachers. Large colour photographs and Ordnance Survey map extracts, alone, make textbooks worth having in your classroom. These can often be used as the basis for a whole lesson's work. Some books also contain excellent pieces of artwork, decision-making exercises, games and cartoons which can all provide stimulating activities to engage students with geography.

So, what is the problem with being dependent on textbooks? Meeting the needs of a very diverse student audience is a challenge facing all textbook writers who, understandably, have tended to aim their books at a hypothetical student, somewhere within a perceived range of ability, and aptitude. By playing safe, in order to make their material more accessible to some students, the writer can fail to stimulate or challenge other students. Where the activities in the book are also used as a means of assessing students, there is a danger that students' level of response will be limited. Too many textbook activities involve low-level transformation of information or basic comprehension of the text. Fewer books provide students with open-ended enquiry or decision-making tasks where students can perform at higher levels. This has led to criticism that over-reliance on a single textbook series can limit students' attainment in and experience of geography at key stage 3 (Smith, 1997).

Students learn in a variety of ways and so the strategies we use in the classroom need to reflect this. It is likely that over-reliance on a single resource in the classroom will eventually switch any student off, no matter how good the resource is.

Textbook used with support materials

Most textbook series are now marketed and sold with a teacher's resource book. Such resource books usually provide advice for teachers on how the students' book should be used, advice on issues such as assessment, and photocopiable resource sheets and activities for students to use in the classroom. These materials can be graded for differentiation, allowing teachers to provide extra support for lower-achieving students and more challenge for higher achievers (see also Chapters 26-28). It also enables writers

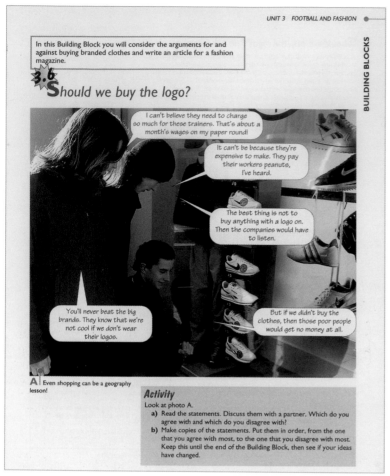

Figure 4 | The students' activity. 'Should we buy the logo? in the students' book. Source: Widdowson, 2002a.

to include other stimulating activities that are restricted by space in the student's book. Some publishers also produce 'foundation' and 'higher' versions of the student's book aimed at students of differing abilities. This development has helped publishers to address the criticism that textbooks are mainly aimed at students in the middle of the ability range. Certainly, the extra materials provided in the teacher's resource book means that textbooks can be used more flexibly in the classroom.

In this example, support material in the teacher's resource book can be used alongside the student's book. Students begin an enquiry into the fashion industry by thinking about the arguments for and against buying branded shoes (Figure 4). They have to read the statements on the photograph in the student's book and place them in order, from the one they most agree with to the one they least agree with. Some students will already have views about this, but others will find it hard to decide without factual information. The extra resource sheet, provided in the teacher's resource book (Figure 5), can be used to help students to make their decision or to refine their initial ideas.

Textbook 'adapted' by teacher

No textbook is likely to match precisely a geography department's own scheme of work. Teachers will always need to think creatively about the best ways in which textbooks can be used. So, it is possible to make use of the things that textbooks do well – bringing the world alive in the geography classroom, in-depth case studies, images and maps, etc. – while improving on what they do less well. Many teachers develop their own tasks and assessment activities based around the resources in the book.

The promotion of activities designed to develop thinking skills through geography (Leat, 1998) has provided more encouragement for teachers to reconsider the ways in which they use textbooks. Traditionally, textbooks aimed to tell students everything that the authors thought they needed to know, and then assess them by finding out if they did! This requires little in the way of active learning or thinking by the students and is the converse of enquiry-based learning where, ideally, students are actively involved in a process of geographical enquiry. Given these limitations it would be tempting to chuck out all the old books that the department has been using for years. Don't be too hasty! There are many ways in which old books can be adapted in a way which encourages students to use the resources provided in more active ways.

Figure 6 shows one example of how a thinking skills' strategy, in this case requiring students to distinguish facts from opinions (Leat, 1998, pp. 98-101), can be used to adapt textbook resources to encourage students to think more actively about the issues covered

FOOTBALL AND FASHION WORKSHEET   PUPIL'S BOOK PAGE 59

3.19

Should we buy the logo?

Name _____

Use this sheet to do the **activity** on **page 59** of the Pupil's Book.

Your task

1 <u>Read</u> the statements below and look at the drawing on the right. <u>Discuss</u> the statements with a partner. Which do you agree with and which do you disagree with?

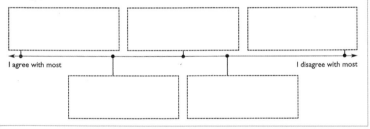

> I can't believe they need to charge so much for these trainers. That's about a month's wages on my paper round!

> You'll never beat the big brands. They know that it's not cool if we don't wear their logos.

> The best thing is not to buy anything with a logo on. Then the companies would have to listen.

> It can't be because they're expensive to make. They pay their workers peanuts, I've heard.

> But if we didn't buy the clothes, then those poor people would get no money at all.

Price £100

The factory gets 12%
Materials   3%
Production costs 2%
(including wages 0.4%)
Profit   2%
Transport and tax 5%

The brandname gets
Research
Advertising   8.5%
Profit   13.5%

The shop gets 50%

Source: www.cleanclothes.org

2 <u>Cut out</u> the statements. Put them in order from the one you agree with most, to the one you disagree with most. <u>Stick</u> them on the line below in the correct order.

Keep this until the end of the *Building Block*, then see if your ideas have changed.

I agree with most   I disagree with most

Figure 5 | *The additional resource sheet in the teacher's resource book. Source: Widdowson, 2002b.*

in these resources. It takes an activity about viewpoints on Antarctica from a much-used key stage 3 textbook and asks students to think a bit more deeply about the issues. The original task required students to read statements about Antarctica from four different interest groups, then to choose the one they most agreed with and another they disagreed with. Using the thinking-skills strategy takes the activity a step further by asking students to evaluate the information provided to identify the facts and opinions in relation to each of the statements. In this way students are encouraged to be more analytical of the views of each interest group. They are thus able to engage in a more challenging learning activity and demonstrate higher levels of understanding than they could through the original task.

Textbook-focused enquiry

It has become quite fashionable – indeed almost obligatory – for publishers to describe their textbooks as being 'enquiry-based'. But what does this actually mean? Is it possible for a textbook to be used for geographical enquiry at all? If so, to what extent should the enquiry depend on the book, or take students beyond the book? Our contention is that textbooks can be enquiry-based, but that this will require considerable rethinking by writers about how their books are put together. It might mean, for example, that textbooks are less driven by content and become more concerned about pedagogy. It also means that teachers will need to reconsider the way that textbooks are used in the classroom.

In some textbooks every double-page spread opens with a question – for example, 'What is a volcano?' – and then proceeds to answer the question for the student. This is not an enquiry! Margaret Roberts (2003) describes a framework for enquiry based on four essential components: creating a need to know, using data, making sense of data, and reflecting on learning (see Figure 6, Chapter 9, page 97). Recent textbooks have started to base their approach to geographical enquiry on this framework. In the example shown in Figure 7, students are asked to consider whether the sinking of the *RMS Titanic* was a natural disaster. They read the story of the *Titanic* (or watch extracts from the film of the same name) and identify possible reasons for the disaster. Some are natural, in other cases human factors are responsible. From the evidence in the story, students are able to decide whether it was a natural disaster or not.

This task has the main components of an enquiry – all on a double-page spread! It can be described as a 'textbook-focused enquiry' since all that is needed for the enquiry is contained in the book. This enquiry comes at the start of a unit about climate change. At the end of the spread students are set an assignment for the rest of the unit, to investigate floods in the UK and drought in Africa, while keeping the story of the *Titanic*

Students working in pairs or threes within groups of five or six were given a copy of the viewpoints sheet shown here. A few class questions are asked to make sure that some key vocabulary was understood. The pairs/threes then look carefully through all the different viewpoints and record them under one or two headings: 'fact' and 'opinion'. They were encouraged to split the statements into parts. After 15 minutes the students were asked to compare their lists with others from their main group and to try to discuss/sort out any differences they might find.

The debriefing aimed to help students understand the processes behind the decisions they made. It included questions such as: 'How did you decide that something was a fact?' and 'How did you decide that something was an opinion?'.

Fact or opinion?
The future of Antarctica

Viewpoints

Task 1

What do people think about the future of Antarctica? Study the four viewpoints below. Choose one view that you support and one view that you disagree with. Explain your choices.

Task 2

Why do different views make conservation more difficult?

Our people have been fishing the Antarctic seas since the early twentieth century. No one owns these waters; they are here for anyone to use. We depend on fishing for our livelihood. What right have people to prevent us from making a living? Our country and our families benefit from our work. Don't stop us fishing; we will control our catches if everyone else does.

(Fishermen)

Antarctica is the last wilderness on Earth. Human activity in Antarctica should be banned, or at least carefully managed. The earth does not need to exploit this area for coal, oil, fish, etc. Antarctica is fragile – spoil it now and it will be lost forever. We must agree on how best to use the region. We support the idea of a World Wilderness Park.

(Environmentalists)

The developed countries want to exploit the resources of Antarctica to keep their superiority over the rest of the world. What rights do they have to ravage the last area of true wilderness? Antarctica belongs to the world and not just to a group of rich and powerful countries. If the resources are to be used, they should benefit the whole world. The use of these resources should be carefully managed to prevent destruction of the Antarctic environment.

(Politicians in the developing world)

(Scientists)

Scientists have been studying Antarctica since 1830. Today, scientists from a number of countries are researching into biology, geology, ice and climate. Many projects are proving to be useful to humanity. Research into climate is helping us to understand the world's changing weather. Pollution studies are providing information on the effects of human activities on climate and new resources are being discovered.

Figure 6 | *Fact or opinion? The future of Antarctica. Source: Leat, 1998. Reproduced with permission of Chris Kington Publishing from Thinking Through Geography (second edition, 2001, ISBN 1899857990).*

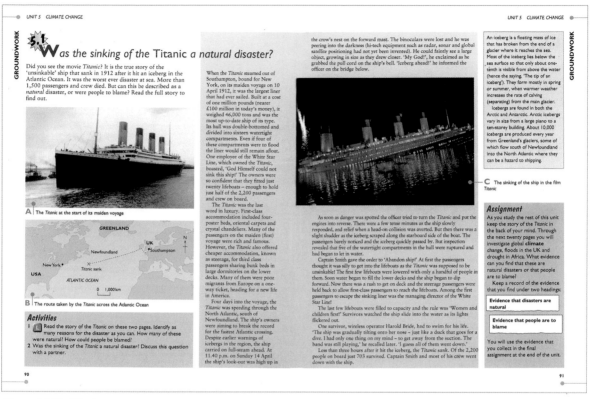

Figure 7 | The Titanic enquiry. Source: Widdowson, 2002u.

at the back of their minds. Following the model of enquiry that has been set up, they now have to find evidence of whether these are natural disasters or whether humans are to blame. They will use the case studies provided in the book, but their enquiry will also take them beyond the textbook to atlases newspapers and websites. At the end of the unit students use the evidence they collected to draw conclusions. This could be described as a 'textbook-framed enquiry'.

Textbook-framed enquiry

One of the features of enquiry in geography, as laid out in the national curriculum, is that students should have opportunities to 'ask geographical questions' (DfEE/QCA, 1999, p. 156). A textbook cannot anticipate all the geographical questions students could ask. But, rather like a good teacher, they can steer students towards the sort of questions that they might want to ask. Certainly (again, like a good teacher), they should stimulate students' curiosity and imagination so that they 'create the need to know' (Roberts, 2003, p. 39). Textbooks can do this by making links between students' every-day experience of the world and geographical concepts, by setting puzzles or mysteries which students want to solve, by introducing controversial statements and issues for students to investigate, by telling an intriguing story that students want to explore further. The possibilities are endless – but what these strategies have in common is that they should encourage students to ask and enquire into geographical questions.

So, a textbook-framed enquiry is one where the book poses questions to which the students will *really* want to know the answer. It will also guide students through the enquiry process while, at the same time, encouraging them to look beyond the book and its resources. It may, for example, suggest fieldwork or surveys for students to collect their own primary data, further research that students could do using an atlas,

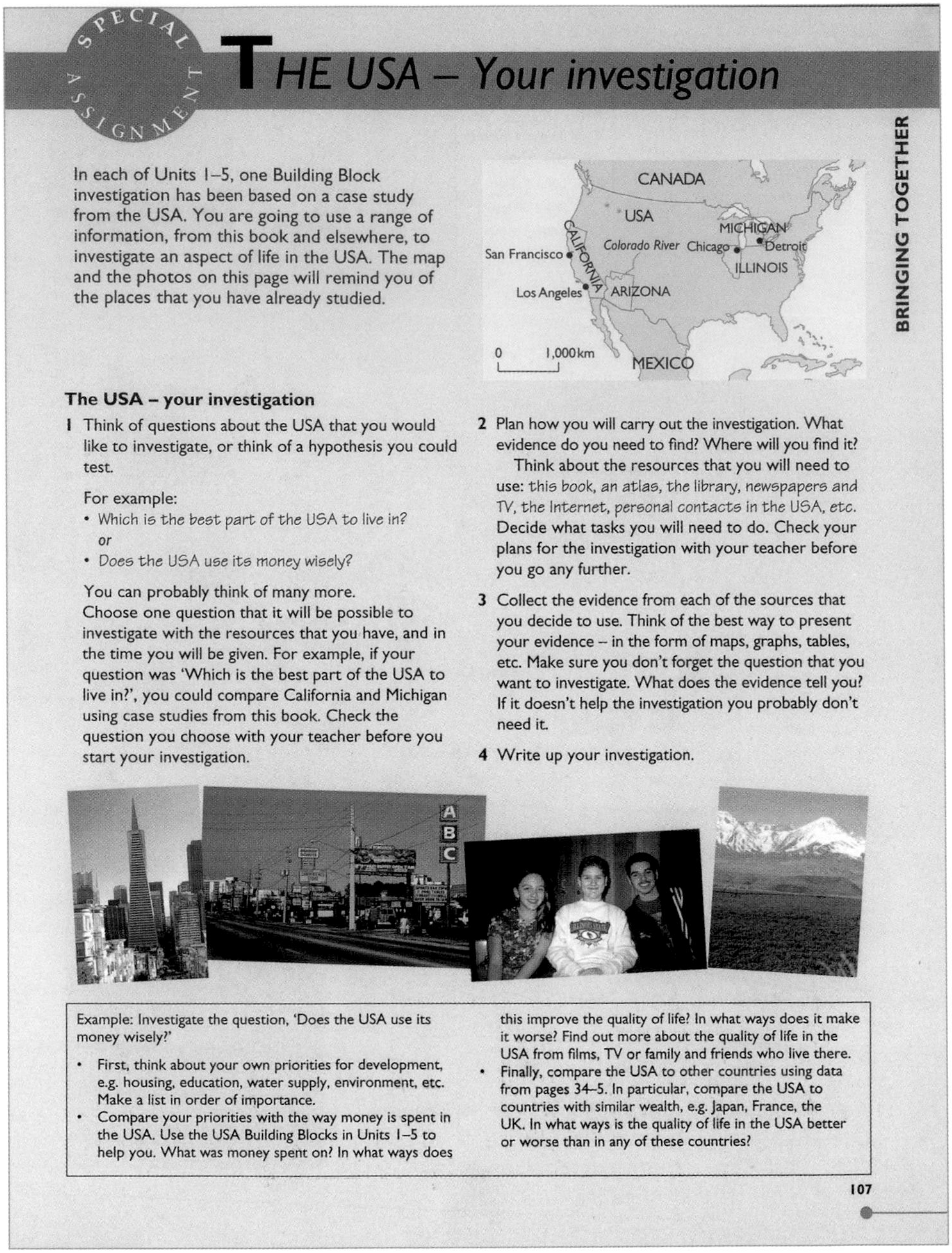

SPECIAL ASSIGNMENT

THE USA – Your investigation

BRINGING TOGETHER

In each of Units 1–5, one Building Block investigation has been based on a case study from the USA. You are going to use a range of information, from this book and elsewhere, to investigate an aspect of life in the USA. The map and the photos on this page will remind you of the places that you have already studied.

CANADA
USA
MICHIGAN
Detroit
Colorado River
Chicago
San Francisco
ILLINOIS
CALIFORNIA
Los Angeles
ARIZONA
0 1,000km
MEXICO

The USA – your investigation

1 Think of questions about the USA that you would like to investigate, or think of a hypothesis you could test.

For example:

- *Which is the best part of the USA to live in?*
  or
- *Does the USA use its money wisely?*

You can probably think of many more.
Choose one question that it will be possible to investigate with the resources that you have, and in the time you will be given. For example, if your question was 'Which is the best part of the USA to live in?', you could compare California and Michigan using case studies from this book. Check the question you choose with your teacher before you start your investigation.

2 Plan how you will carry out the investigation. What evidence do you need to find? Where will you find it?
Think about the resources that you will need to use: *this book, an atlas, the library, newspapers and TV, the Internet, personal contacts in the USA, etc.* Decide what tasks you will need to do. Check your plans for the investigation with your teacher before you go any further.

3 Collect the evidence from each of the sources that you decide to use. Think of the best way to present your evidence – in the form of maps, graphs, tables, etc. Make sure you don't forget the question that you want to investigate. What does the evidence tell you? If it doesn't help the investigation you probably don't need it.

4 Write up your investigation.

Example: Investigate the question, 'Does the USA use its money wisely?'

- First, think about your own priorities for development, e.g. housing, education, water supply, environment, etc. Make a list in order of importance.
- Compare your priorities with the way money is spent in the USA. Use the USA Building Blocks in Units 1–5 to help you. What was money spent on? In what ways does this improve the quality of life? In what ways does it make it worse? Find out more about the quality of life in the USA from films, TV or family and friends who live there.
- Finally, compare the USA to other countries using data from pages 34–5. In particular, compare the USA to countries with similar wealth, e.g. Japan, France, the UK. In what ways is the quality of life in the USA better or worse than in any of these countries?

107

Figure 8 | *A student-framed enquiry. Source: Widdowson, 2000.*

newspapers and websites, or even model enquiries that students could undertake in their own locality. Clearly, though, a textbook can only prepare the ground and suggest the directions in which students could go. It is the strategies and activities selected by the teacher that will make it happen.

Teacher-student-framed enquiry

What happens when enquiry moves beyond the textbook? Do textbooks become redundant, especially now that students can ask their own geographical questions and carry out geographical enquiries online?

It is important to remember that students need to learn the skills of geographical enquiry – they do not just happen! Initially, early in key stage 3, enquiries will be more structured. Textbooks can help to model the structure of and approach to geographical enquiries for students, and this is something that some books have begun to do. As students progress through the key stages, the scale and scope of their enquiries increase and they become more independent learners. They should be able to ask their own questions and suggest appropriate sequences of enquiry. At this point the role of textbooks becomes less obvious. They may simply become another resource in the classroom to which students may refer in their enquiries.

The following example of a student-framed enquiry about the USA uses the textbook as a starting point for their enquiry. It suggests other sources of information that could be researched. Students using the book would have already investigated a number of case studies about the USA. They are now invited to think of geographical questions that they would like to ask about the USA as a whole. One possible question, and the sequence of enquiry that might follow, is modelled for them in Figure 8.

Summary

Textbooks do still have a role in the modern geography classroom, but it is unlikely to be the same role that they have had in the past. Many geography departments have moved beyond dependence on a single textbook for delivering the geography curriculum. There has also been a noticeable increase, in recent years, in the publication of textbooks that claim to be enquiry-based. The degree to which this is a valid claim varies from book to book. However, it does signal recognition from publishers and writers that the books they provide can have an important influence on what happens in the classroom. Teachers need to examine textbooks carefully too, not just for their coverage of the curriculum content, but also for the way they might influence or interact with their own pedagogy to improve learning opportunities.

It has been argued that over-reliance on a single textbook can limit attainment in geography. The question that now needs to be answered is how can textbooks help to raise attainment? Some of the strategies offered here might provide starting points.

Implications for practice

(a) **Geography textbooks have an important role to play in shaping students' experience of the subject; they offer a different potential to empower them through their study of geography.**

Textbooks provide valuable ways of introducing students to other worlds and helping them to make connections between their geographical studies and their life experiences. The resources (including the text) and learning activities provided in textbooks should be used to enhance the quality of students' learning through geography rather than 'becoming the curriculum'.

A goal a teacher may try to accomplish is to design sequences of lessons which successfully create in students an authentic 'need to know', so that textbooks are consulted to 'find out' out of curiosity. Textbooks can act as a deadening influence if lessons are simply designed to take students through the text.

(b) **Criteria for selecting textbooks to use in geography should include pedagogic considerations as well as curriculum coverage and issues related to equal opportunities (gender and ethnocentric bias).**

Visual images are a powerful medium for transmitting ideas and all resources that deal with images of the world bring with them a set of attitudes and assumptions, both explicit and implicit, which are based on broader cultural perspectives. It is vital for geography teachers to give attention to the way in which people and places are represented in textbooks to ensure that issues of gender and ethnocentric bias are addressed (Chapter 30). The style and variety of learning activities in textbooks should provide an appropriate range of challenges and develop a range of learning skills. Tasks that emphasise the low-level transformation of information will have a detrimental impact on students' learning and their experience of geography.

(c) **A wide variety of strategies can be employed to provide students with worthwhile learning experiences and opportunities to develop different learning skills through geography.**

Textbooks provide many opportunities for geography teachers to develop different aspects of students' literacy and use of language. Reading 'around' the class should be avoided but time given to activities which focus students' attention on the structure and meaning of text. Specific literacy strategies (see Chapter 11) can be used to develop students' literacy skills and understanding of geography. Simple games can be adapted to help strengthen students' understanding and use of geographical vocabulary.

Students can use the resources provided in textbooks as a stimulus for creative and extended writing (Chapter 11). They can role-play scenes portrayed in images of present viewpoints about the impacts of human activities or physical processes on landscapes, thereby developing speaking and listening skills (see Chapters 24 and 25). Speculating about future changes in the landscapes shown in photographs can provide opportunities for higher-level reasoning skills to be used or developed.

Textbook resources can be used to create different styles of geographical enquiry including decision-making exercises, games and simulations as well as providing starting points for students' own independent enquiries (Chapter 9). Tasks can be added to textbook activities to extend or to simplify enquiry sequences to provide appropriate challenges for different groups of students. Other resources can be used alongside textbooks to extend the range of information and images available to students enabling them to develop the depth of their geographical understanding as well as using other skills such as those associated with the critical evaluation of sources.

Related publications from the Geographical Association:

■ Roberts, M. (2003) (see below)

The following titles develop specific aspects of the 'resource ecology' of geography classrooms:

■ Butt, G. (2001) *Theory Into Practice: Extending Writing Skills*

■ Wright, D. (2000) *Theory Into Practice: Maps with Latitude.*

■ Morgan, J. and Lambert, D. (2003) *Theory Into Practice: Place, 'Race' and Teaching Geography.*

References

Chambliss, M. and Calfee, R. (1998) *Textbooks for Learning: Nurturing children's minds.* Oxford: Blackwell.

DfEE/QCA (1999) *The National Curriculum: Handbook for secondary teachers in England (KS3&4).* London: DfEE/QCA.

Geographical Association – www.geography.org.uk (see Projects section)

Graves, N. (2001) *School Textbook Research: The case of geography 1800-2000.* London: Institute of Education, University of London.

Horsley, M. (2001) 'Emerging institutions and pressing paradoxes' in Horsley, M. (ed) *The Future of Textbooks? Research about emerging trends.* Sydney: TREAT.

Keele University (1999) *Improving Learning: The use of books in school – a report for the Educational Publishers Council.* Keele: Keele University.

Lambert, D. (1999) 'Exploring the use of textbooks in key stage 3 geography classrooms: a small-scale study', *The Curriculum Journal,* 10, 1, pp. 85-105.

Lambert, D. (2000) 'Textbook pedagogy: issues on the use of textbooks in geography classrooms' in Fisher, C. and Binns, T. (eds) *Issues in Geography Teaching.* London: Routledge Falmer, pp. 108-19.

Leat, D. (ed) (1998) *Thinking through Geography.* Cambridge: Chris Kington Publishing.

Marsden, W. (2001) *The School Textbook: Geography, history and social studies.* London: Woburn Press.

Roberts, M. (2003) *Learning through Enquiry: Making sense of geography in the key stage 3 classroom.* Sheffield: Geographical Association.

Smith, P. (1997) 'Standards achieved: a review of geography in secondary schools in England 1995-96', *Teaching Geography,* 22, 3, pp. 123-4.

Walford, R. (1995) 'Geographical textbooks 1930-90; the strange case of the disappearing text', *Paradigm,* December, 22, pp. 1-11.

Widdowson, J. (2000) *Earthworks 3 Pupil's Book.* London: John Murray.

Widdowson, J. (2002a) *Earthworks Plus Teacher's Book.* London: John Murray.

Widdowson, J. (2002b) *Earthworks Plus Pupil's Book.* London: John Murray.

Chapter 14

understanding 'distant places'

Emma Wellsted

Before reading this chapter consider the following questions:

■ What resources do you use to develop a scheme of work about a 'distant place'?

■ How do you use your personal experiences to enhance learning activities and resources through which students learn about a 'distant place'?

■ How do you ensure that the resources students use to learn about other places are used in active ways to develop their 'sense of place'?

When teaching about 'distant places' we aim to take students on a virtual journey and give them a real 'sense of place'. The national curriculum for geography, and examination specifications, are now such that we as teachers have much more freedom of choice about the places we select for our students to study. There is therefore more likelihood of our being able to select 'distant places' that we have experienced at first-hand, either on holiday, when travelling, or when working abroad. Drawing on our personal experiences enables us to present a more interesting, immediate and well-rounded view of a place to our students, and will mean that we can provide resources obtained at first-hand. However, it may also mean that we have to develop a scheme of work from scratch with few if any supporting textbooks or other published materials.

Why learn about 'distant places'?

Teaching about 'distant places' has always been 'one of the most exciting and challenging aspects of geography' (Binns, 1996, p. 180) as many students are genuinely interested in places that are different from their own. A spectacular increase in air travel has brought the world's people and places much closer together, jetting families to new and increasingly distant locations – hence the concept of a 'global village' (Binns, 1996, p. 177). However, globalisation is not only about the world becoming a 'smaller' place to live in, it is also about the world being brought into our neighbourhoods, i.e. the local becoming global (Joseph, 2000). This has resulted in ethnically and culturally diverse classrooms. In fact, two thirds of UK school children have relatives in at least one other Commonwealth country, presenting 'a multitude of different inheritances, backgrounds, influences, perspectives and experiences' (Brownlie, 2001, p. 11).

In an ideal world, this 'cultural melting pot' would help increase understanding of and respect for difference and diversity, but in reality this is not always the case. Hence the importance of studying different places and cultures in order to promote an open-minded and tolerant attitude towards the differences evident in our society. By studying 'distant places' we as teachers can help to challenge myths and stereotypes and promote a more positive and accurate image of life in a different place. Oxfam, in its (1999) guide to *Global Citizenship*, sees using ideas from a variety of cultures as an excellent way of building positive attitudes towards differences and diversity, and learning about 'distant places' can enable this.

We also cannot ignore the fact that there are staggering global inequalities. There are many examples of significant events bringing into almost daily focus people and places in parts of the world that had previously played a minor role in our lives. We can think of the continuing conflicts in the Middle East as well as the recent conflicts in Sudan, Afghanistan and Iraq. While such events provide opportunities for taking a critical look at why conflicts arise, there is always the danger that stereotypical views about cultures and barriers to conflict resolution will be reinforced. As teachers we must be alert to this and strive to help our students to understand other cultures, and the part played by countries of the global North in global affairs, 'so as to promote national security and prepare our young people for taking part in a multi-ethnic and culturally diverse society' (Tanner, 1998, p. 244).

The challenge for geography teachers, then, is to use the study of 'distant places' meaningfully in order to promote and encourage in our students an interest in learning about places, and to help them to acquire skills of critical thinking so that they can look beyond stereotypes, have respect for other cultures, and be aware of the causes and possible means of resolution of conflicts between peoples.

Selecting resources

Travelling to a new place involves experiencing and learning about that place, ideally with an open mind, and comparing it with our own. We develop a 'sense of place' through using all our senses, we see and touch physical landscapes, eat and smell local foods, listen to music and interact with local people to gain an idea of what life is like in the place. If one of the main aims of teaching about other countries and places is to give students a 'gut' feeling about them (Ranger, 1994, p. 58) then we need to try and take them on a 'virtual journey' so that they can visualise unfamiliar places and gain insight and an understanding of what it might be like to live or work there.

Photo: ©Simon Scoones.

Travel guides, e.g. in the *Lonely Planet* and *Rough Guide* series

Embassies and tourist offices – many provide colour leaflets and brochures free of charge

Language guides and television programmes

Music – there is now a *Rough Guide* series which provides music from almost all areas of the world

Newspapers and magazines

Maps and atlases

Development statistics – obtained from the UN website, NGOs, atlases, etc.

Personal travel journals, stories and knowledge gained

Videos, e.g. *Japan 2000, Brazil 2000* (BBC Education)

Photographs

Literature

Local contacts

The internet, *Microsoft Encarta, googleworld,*

Food

Artefacts and souvenirs

Museums and other educational establishments

School links and pen-pal schemes

Published resources, e.g. photopacks from Development Education Centres, DEA/GA (2004)

Figure 1 | *Resources for teaching about distant places.*

In an increasingly information-rich world it is relatively easy to access information for developing a scheme of work about a 'distant place'. Textbooks are one such source of information but there is a need for students to be critical of their content as they can often present an oversimplified viewpoint, or negative stereotypes of people and countries, as well as 'misconceptions and outdated theories' (Robinson and Serf, 1997, p. 77). Figure 1 suggests some possible resources that could be used instead of, or as supplements to, a textbook (see also Chapter 13).

Figure 1 shows the vast array of resources available to geography teachers to support the study of places. Ideally, a mix of several of these should be used to support the study, including items to excite the senses, such as food, music and artefacts.

Given the comprehensive nature of most good travel guides, these can provide the ideal core resource for a distant-place study. They generally provide a historical perspective, cultural information such as lists of relevant written works by indigenous or travel writers, information about physical geography and conservation areas, travel anecdotes and political comment, as well as useful large- and small-scale maps.

To give an example: an activity based on information in a travel guide was used with some year 9 students during a country study of Japan. It focused on the Tokyo subway map, described by one traveller as an 'action painting by a hyperactive centipede' (Acker, 1988, p. 56), aiming to develop students' 'sense of place' as they empathised with the 'newly-arrived-travellers' negotiating their way from station to station around the city. The value of this exercise was that students were able to imagine the likely frustration that travellers would experience coping with the Japanese language and size of the subway system, as well as gaining some ideas about Tokyo's transport infrastructure.

There are many advantages to choosing to study a place that you, the teacher, have visited or plan to visit: personal experiences can help inject humour and enthusiasm, with narrative accounts being used to personalise the learning process, and may enable the teacher to present a different view of a place from that found in published sources. Items collected during a visit will also help to add interest and substance to the study.

Teachers who have the luxury of visiting a place before devising a scheme of work will have the advantage of being able to plan ahead and to gather information and resources as appropriate. For example, photographs can be taken of specific places, maps drawn or acquired, a journal kept, newspapers gathered, and recordings of music or speech made. With not much effort and an enquiring mind, a wealth of possible teaching activities can be thought up while lying on the beach or strolling around towns. Keeping a journal can help preserve 'gut feelings' about places and information that may be forgotten later, and recalled personal experiences will bring authenticity to the scheme of work. A fellow geography teacher recently said that he would feel uncomfortable about

Photo: ©Simon Scoones.

using his experiences of a holiday in Egypt when teaching about that country as he had 'only been on a two-week sun holiday to Luxor'. Instead, he favoured using a key stage 3 textbook as he felt it would meet all the criteria laid down in the national curriculum programme of study. My contention is that by employing some of the strategies noted above, a 'two-week sun holiday' can offer many opportunities to enhance an existing scheme of work, e.g. when exploring issues such as the impact of tourism on such a place.

Photographs are easy resources to gather when visiting a place and when carefully selected can 'bring it to life' very effectively in the classroom. With a bit of thought and sensitivity (not all people appreciate photographs being taken of them), interesting photographs can be taken which can help to give students a well-rounded 'sense of place' (see Chapter 19 for further ideas about creative strategies when using photographs). However, care is needed when selecting photographs to use in the classroom. Many of us go to a place with an image in our minds about what we expect to see, i.e. a partial and selective image of that place. This is often evident in the photographs we take in that they show what we consider to be typical scenes, e.g. traditional market scenes and mud huts in Africa, llamas and shanty towns in South America. These 'stereotypical' 'simplified' views are often chosen on the grounds that they are less likely to confuse students, but may have the effect of obscuring the complexities of reality. One way of avoiding a one-sided view of a place is to try and take photographs which present 'different' viewpoints such as 'wealthier' and 'poorer' parts or aspects of a city, e.g. tarmaced roads, department stores and large houses, with gardens as well as dirt tracks, shanty houses and communal water pumps.

Recognising that places can have 'multiple identities' is an important consideration when selecting resources for teaching about a 'distant place'. Individuals experience places in several different ways and people's perceptions of places vary greatly. We should not underestimate the influence of the media, parents and peers on students' perceptions and understanding of places. This manifests itself as a complex mix of positive and negative stereotypes, assumptions and generalisations co-existing alongside each other. As teachers we need to ensure that a balanced viewpoint is presented, and to avoid giving only a partial view or 'single identity' of a place.

Ideas for using literature

With many bookshops sporting a wide array of travel literature and guidebooks, it is easy for us to find material about the place being studied. Fiction and poetry provide real insights into life and the environment in other places and cultures and help to bring a human dimension to place studies (Robinson and Serf, 1997). Geography teachers can also create their own texts and narratives about places. Bias is often inherent in written works and need to be made explicit, but using literary sources, including one's own work, is an excellent way of injecting enthusiasm, humour and first-hand experiences into a classroom, all of which help to develop students' 'sense of place' while at the same time addressing the requirements of the key stage 3 national literacy strategy. The challenge for the teacher is to teach students 'how to read a text' and to make sense of it.

One disadvantage of using travel literature and published resources is that while writers may speak with authority, as 'experts', they are often the outsiders to the culture they describe, and may be, presenting patronising or unrealistic views of life in 'distant

Lima is an atrocity. Ankle deep in urine and political graffiti, the old Lima rises from the middle of the largest expanse of wet corrugated iron in the Southern Hemisphere: the new Lima.

Ah! Que lindas las tardes de Lima! ('How lovely those Liman afternoons!') runs the old Spanish song, recalling an elegant past, long faded now. The old Lima died, our hotelier told us, 'when the slum people came'.

Lima's traffic has to be seen to be believed. It is a war between cars and pedestrians in which there are no rules, and many casualties on both sides. Motorists prefer to drive on the right but it is only a tendency. A bare majority of cars have headlights, far fewer have tail-lights, and there is a general amnesty on traffic-lights. No signals at all are used, in any circumstances (Parris, 1990, pp. 2-3).

From the beginning, Lima, the city of Kings and viceroys, was an oasis of culture and elegance in the American Indies. Just a few decades after its foundation, Lima already rivalled Mexico as the most important metropolis in the Spanish-American empire ...

In the 1940s, as growing waves of migrants left the countryside bound for Lima, the capital became a miniature replica of the country itself – a melting pot of people and cultures. Today with a population of 6.5 million, Lima is home to a quarter of the country's population and nearly two-thirds of Peru's economic and industrial activity ...

This alchemy of influences is most clearly seen in the city's innovative cuisine, which gourmets rate as one of the world's finest. UNESCO meanwhile, ranks Lima's architecture as a World Heritage Site, while the city's inhabitants, fun-loving and skillful, have become experts at adapting to change (Peruvian embassy leaflet, 2001).

Figure 2 | *Contrasting texts on Lima, Peru, which could be used as the basis for activities on bias.*

places'. To present a balanced view of a place it is therefore important to include the perspectives of indigenous people. The fundamental question for me when learning and teaching about a 'distant place' is: What is it like to live there? This has been answered to some degree in my own case by observing and experiencing customs, traditions and everyday routines while living and travelling in 'distant places'. However, most of my understanding has come from talking to people who live there or reading accounts written by people who live in or originate from those places. For example, Camara Laye's (1959) account of growing up in Guinea in the 1950s has illuminated for me the customs of rural life, relationships within families and the education system in that country. Similarly, Waris Dirie's (2001) account of growing up as a desert nomad in Somalia provided insight into the role of women and the nomads' relationship with their environment.

One further example that has been used effectively is a book written by Reverend Stuart Lane, which presents a snapshot image of traditional Malawian life (see extract below).

People whose only view and images of Africa come from the media know only of famines, wars, poverty and corrupt Governments and may be surprised that anything good can come out or Africa. People are used to believing that poor people in Africa live lives of desperation and unhappiness. But it's far from true. Of course, Malawians may not have the same access to health, education and protection against natural disasters and wars. But I believe that emotionally, spiritually and socially Malawians are better off than people in North America and Europe and have a very high standard of living despite their poverty. This is true mainly because good relationships with other people are the most important element of society. They are more important than success, development, future plans, contracts of employment, material wealth and personal freedom (Lane, 1995).

The value of this type of opinionated account is that although it presents a 'biased' personal view, it counteracts the negative image often portrayed in the media. A way of using such a text is to discuss with students, before and after reading it, whether they agree or disagree with statements such as 'because Malawi is a less economically-developed country (LEDC), life will be awful there', or questions such as 'Is there anything we can learn from traditional Malawian society?' By reading texts such as Lane's students will tend to review previous impressions and, in this particular case, to compare the traditional view of Malawian life with their own lives in the UK. Discussions can often lead into reflections about whether technological advances, such as the internet, contribute to improvements in people's quality of life.

1. **An enquiry approach.** Encouraging students to come up with their own questions that they want answered about a photograph can be a way of stimulating interest. Answers can be elicited from the students within the class where possible (see also Chapter 9).

2. **Providing key questions or statements.** These can help to focus students' thinking and be used as a springboard for discussion. Using the development compass rose (see also Chapter 28) is a useful way of structuring their responses.

3. **Combining with other resources.** Using photographs together with other media such as maps, atlases, plans, stories and, if possible, visitors who have had first-hand experience of the place being studied can enable students to gain a fuller 'sense of place' (see also Chapter 19).

4. **Writing frames and tables for a structured response.** These can help students to pick out the main ideas from a photograph in a structured way (see also Chapter 26).

5. **Questioning the information presented in the photograph.** Using a 'biased' view can be useful for drawing out students' opinions and perceptions of a place. For example, showing a wealthy area of Sao Paulo can be useful for presenting a less stereotypical view of life in a South American city (see also Chapter 19).

6. **Comparing photographs.** Looking at two or more different photographs showing contrasting views of a place has clear advantages (see also Chapter 19).

Figure 3 | *Active strategies for using photographs.*

As shown above, one approach to using texts is to present students with a 'different' view of that place. Looking at two different texts can be useful to examine 'bias' and help students gain an awareness of places having 'multiple identities'. An example is shown in Figure 2 where two contrasting texts about Lima present very different images of the city. To structure responses to these texts, a table could be provided in which students record 'positive' and 'negative' aspects of the city. Alternatively, to ensure 'reading with a purpose', a question which makes the issue explicit could be posed before reading begins; for example, 'What effect has the migration of people into Lima had on the city?'.

Exploring different perspectives of a place can help students to examine their own perceptions about that place. An example of a commonly studied place is the Amazon rainforest. Often students are presented with romantic views of the rainforest – the medicinal qualities of forest plants, its importance as an ecosystem and the abundance of wildlife there – through television programmes which inspire awe and wonder (e.g. the BBC series *Himalaya*). However, what may be lacking in such depictions is consideration of what it is like to live in or experience the rainforest. Louis de Bernieres, in his book *The War of Don Emmanuel's Nether Parts*, provides some insights into this in an amusing account of the hardships of travelling through a rainforest:

> [He was] obstructed at every step by giant lianas that twisted high into the trees, by swathes of fleshy orchids, by plants that oozed white poison, by plants whose stench caused migraines, by insula ants whose bite made him ill for five days, by scolopendra, whose bites nearly killed him and made him ill for weeks (de Bernieres, 1998, p. 59).

One way of using such a text could be to ask students to underline or highlight the problems encountered by the subject in the story. This gives students a visual way of organising their thoughts which may help to promote the use of more active learning techniques, and lead to discussions about the array of dangers facing unwary travellers in the rainforest. As previously suggested, using 'real' voices of people from places being studied can give a more realistic image of life in that place. In relation to the Amazon rainforest, the *Survival International* pack develops a story about Guiomar, a Yanomami Indian, and her life in the rainforest, through letters that bring to life 'situations with which the students are unfamiliar' (Robinson and Serf, 1997, p. 70). These letters can be used to highlight everyday life, problems encountered, and the influence on the forest of people exploiting its resources.

The examples above show that there are many ways of using texts, with the focus being on 'reading for a purpose'. The challenge for teachers is to identify and select texts which will help to promote critical thinking and provide a well-balanced view of the place being studied.

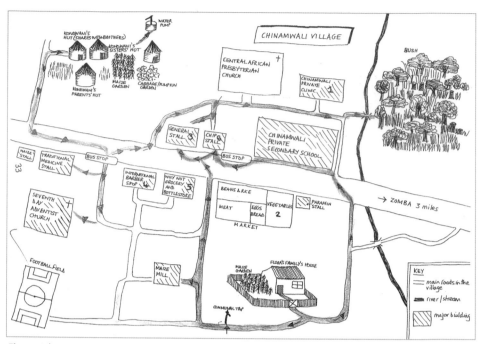

Figure 4 | *Hand-drawn map of Chinamwali village, Malawi, showing the routes that Kondwani and Flora take on their daily journey.*

Ideas for using photographs

Photographs have many advantages as teaching resources: they provide instant visual images, which can help to stimulate students' interest in learning about a place, they are easy to obtain, e.g. from a personal collection gained while travelling, from the internet, or from published resources such as newspapers or magazines; and can easily be duplicated and compared.

In our 'highly visual society, saturated with television, cinema, billboards and magazine articles ... we owe it to students to help them decode the information in those media' (Leat, 1998, p. 135). Thus, using photographs should be viewed in much the same way as using texts, in that skills of 'visual literacy' must be learnt in order for students to use them effectively. Students should be encouraged to look carefully at the image, to go beyond what they can see, to make connections between what is visible and what they already know, and to speculate and hypothesise (Leat, 1998). Figure 3 suggests some strategies for using photographs.

When studying 'distant places', students are sometimes asked to make judgements about what stage of development that place or country may be at. Often, this will be approached through the use of development statistics. Another approach could be to study one aspect of life within the 'distant' country, e.g. education, and to compare it with students' personal experiences in the UK. If students have an awareness of roughly where the UK fits onto the 'development ladder', then such a comparison will help them to decide how developed the 'other place' might be.

An example of such an activity is given below, it is based upon personal experiences of teaching in a Malawian secondary school. Photographs taken of places within the school, such as the library, classroom and playground, formed the basis of the lesson along with a hand-drawn map of the school and a diary account of an average day in the school. The students examined the resources and wrote a list of similarities and

(a)

(b) Write down ten things that this shop sells. How many of the ten products that you wrote down can you buy in the UK?

(b)

(b) Write down ten things that this shop sells. How many of the ten products that you wrote down can you buy in the UK?

Figure 5 | Two of the six photographs and accompanying questions used in conjunction with the map in Figure 4. Photos: ©Emma Wellsted.

differences. To structure the learning, a table was given to the students along with prompt questions to encourage discussion.

At the end of the activity most students had lots of information in the 'differences' column and little in the 'similarities' column – the lists themselves being a visual way of highlighting the inherent differences in the two education systems. Having already studied statistical data and images of what constitutes both LEDCs and more economically-developed countries (MEDCs), the students were able to classify Malawi as an LEDC as a result of this exercise. They were also able to go one stage further, to make comments such as 'it has more than I expected' and 'it's not that poor because they've got quite a few books in the library', thus demonstrating the value of using a combination of visual and other resources rather than development statistics alone.

One obvious drawback with such an activity is that not all teachers will have access to a range of photographs suitable for this type of task. However, setting up a school link or pen-pal scheme can be a way of obtaining similar photographs. Taking some photographs of a British school to exchange for the opportunity to take photographs of a school in a country visited on holiday is another way. This strategy was successful on a recent trip to Ghana where a chance visit to a local school to present a bag of stationery resulted in opportunities to take photographs, chat to the students and teachers, and set up a pen-pal scheme.

Combining photographs with other resources such as maps, diaries and literature is a powerful way of developing a 'sense of place'. An example of a lesson using photographs, maps and diaries, based on personal experience of living in Chinamwali village, Malawi, is described below. The main resource used was a hand-drawn map of the village (Figure 4), drawn from memory of living in the village and teaching in the local school, showing the main buildings and infrastructure within the village. Along with the map, six photographs (Figure 5) of various places within the village were used. One activity required students to mark on the map the position of the six places shown in the photographs, the aim being to help to give students a more 'three-dimensional' view of

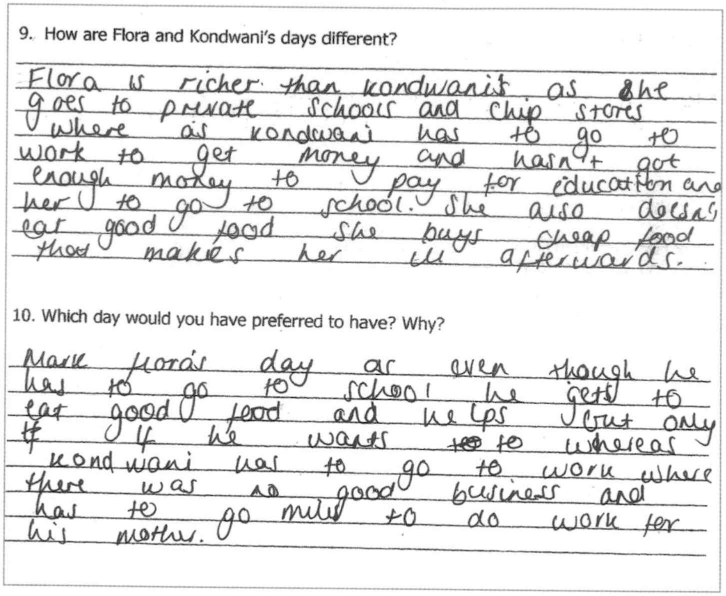

9. How are Flora and Kondwani's days different?

Flora is richer than kondwani's as she goes to private schools and chip stores where as kondwai has to go to work to get money and hasn't got enough money to pay for education and her to go to school. She also doesn't eat good food she buys cheap food that makes her ill afterwards.

10. Which day would you have preferred to have? Why?

Mark Flora's day as even though he has to go to school he gets to eat good food and helps out only if if he wants to to whereas kondwani has to go to work where there was no good business and has to go mules to do work for his mother.

Figure 6 | *Example of a student's work comparing daily lives.*

the village. To ensure that students actively studied the photographs, questions were used to get them to consider what living in the village might actually be like. These open-ended questions encouraged the students to have opinions about what they identified in the photographs and helped to promote further discussion about these opinions.

Extract from Kondwani's diary

'I got up at 5.30 when it got light and went to collect some water from the pump. My family and I went to a service at our church – the Seventh Day Adventist. When we returned I got ready and went off to work. I sell sweets outside Chinamwali market. Most of my trade occurs when the buses arrive in the village.'

The next activity centred on the use of the hand-drawn map (Figure 4) and two diary-style accounts of an 'average day' in the lives of two teenagers living in the village – Flora and Kondwani. Using information from the diaries, students marked on the map the places that Flora and Kondwani visited on an average day. This enabled them to visualise the routes taken and to consider whose day was the hardest and who had to walk furthest. An example of a student's work is shown in Figure 6. Diaries bring in a human dimension to a scheme of work and students expressed real interest when they realised that these accounts had been based on real people known to the teacher. They are also an excellent way of highlighting the fact that in LEDCs there are differences in wealth and opportunity, and that issues that may be thought of as black and white are more likely to be 'shades of grey'.

The activities presented here use personal experiences to help students develop an idea of what it is like to live in Chinamwali village. Teachers who don't have personal resources or experiences from the locality studied could set up a pen-pal link with a school in the area, draw upon the experiences of a colleague or friend, or purchase published photopacks as alternative ways of accessing similar information.

Related publications from the Geographical Association:
- GA/DEA (2003) *Geography: The global dimension.*
- McPartland, M. (2001) *Theory into Practice: Moral dilemmas.*
- Roberts, M. (2003) *Learning through Enquiry: Making sense of geography in the key stage 3 classroom.*
- Save the Children (2005) *Young Lives, Global Goals.*

References

Acker, F. (1988) 'Women and socks' in *The Best of Sunday Times Travel*. Newton Abbot: David and Charles.
BBC Education (2000) *Brazil 2000, Japan 2000*. London: BBC.
BBC (2004) *Himalaya*. London: BBC.
Binns, T. (1996) 'Teaching about distant places' in Bailey, P. and Fox, P. (eds) *Geography Teachers' Handbook*. Sheffield: Geographical Association, pp. 177-85.
Brownlie, A. (2001) *Citizenship Education: The global dimension – guidance for key stages 3 and 4*. London: DEA.

de Bernieres, L. (1998) *The War of Don Emmanuel's Nether Parts*. London: Random House.

Dirie, W. (2001) *Desert Flower*. London: Virago.

Joseph, J. (2000) 'Why a black perspective on development education?', *The Development Education Journal*, 6, 3, pp. 3-6.

Lane, S. (1995) *Learning from Africa*. Malawi: Blantyre.

Laye, C. (1959) *The African Child*. Glasgow: Collins.

Leat, D. (1998) *Thinking through Geography*. Cambridge: Chris Kington Publishing.

Oxfam (1999) *A Curriculum for Global Citizenship*. Oxford: Oxfam DEP.

Parris, M. (1990) *Inca Kola*. London: Orion.

Peruvian Embassy (2001) *The City of Kings and Surrounding Areas* (leaflet). Lima: Peruvian Embassy.

Ranger, G. (1994) 'Teaching about countries', *Teaching Geography*, 19, 2, pp. 58-60.

Robinson, R. and Serf, J. (1997) *Global Geography: Learning through development education at key stage 3*. Sheffield: Geographical Association/DEC (Birmingham).

Rowthorn, C., Ashburne, J., Benson, S. and Florence, M. (2000) *Lonely Planet Japan*. Sydney: Lonely Planet.

Survival International (2000) *We, The World* (accessed via www.survival-international.org).

Implications for practice

(a) **Geography teachers can use a wide variety of different resources to develop students' 'sense of place'.**

There are many ways of using personal experiences of places to aid the learning process, including making use of resources collected 'on location' such as photographs, anecdotes, tape recordings, newspaper articles and souvenirs. Alternatively, travel guides can be used as springboards for accessing information or other resources. A key consideration when selecting resources is to ensure that together they provide a balanced viewpoint and that they convey the 'multiple identity' of the place being studied.

(b) **Literature is a powerful tool for stimulating interest in a place and for portraying different perspectives.**

Finding texts written about a place can be done by using a list of recommended reading in a travel guide, or by visiting a good bookshop, library or internet book-supply service. The challenge when using literature is to focus on 'reading for a purpose', and to ensure that students are given opportunities to make sense of the text.

(c) **The learning experience should be visual, varied and as stimulating as possible.**

Photographic images are generally easy for geography teachers to obtain themselves. Holidays and travelling experiences can be ideal times for collecting photographs of places, but care is needed in their selection. As with texts, active strategies are needed to ensure that students are developing and using interpretative skills – in this case, the skills of visual literacy. Combining resources such as maps, photographs and diaries can be a useful way of providing a 'three-dimensional' view of a place.

Chapter 15

Strategies for approaching values education

Michael McPartland

Before reading this chapter consider the following questions:

- How do you identify the values embedded in a topic or issue being explored by students in geography?

- What strategies do you employ to enable students to explore these values?

- What are the moral dimensions of the issues and topics being studied in geography classrooms?

- How are students being helped to develop moral reasoning through geography?

> *Where is the life we have lost in living?*
> *Where is the wisdom we have lost in knowledge?*
> *Where is the knowledge we have lost in information?*
> (Eliot, 1936, p. 179)

Let us begin with a geographical story. Figure 1 describes a long and complex story both in terms of space and time, with many actors, events and subsidiary stories but a geographical story nevertheless, and one worthy of examination in the geography classroom.

The question is: 'In what ways might we examine this and other stories like it in the classroom, as an exemplar of how we might respond to the challenge of exploring values in geography teaching?'

Beliefs, attitudes and values

The Blue jeans story in Figure 1 has obvious relevance to the geography classroom, dealing as it does with some core geographical ideas and concepts such as the spatial division of labour, the spatial economic and political power of trans-national corporations, globalisation and interdependence.

Implicit in the story are certain beliefs, attitudes and values, and in responding to it readers will of course be influenced by their own. The task of the geography teacher is to explore and interrogate both sets of beliefs, attitudes and values, and the relationship between them, with professional skill, confidence and integrity.

A good place to start then is with some definitions of terms.

This story begins, or ends, in the many clothing outlets in the UK selling blue, stonewashed denim, five-pocket jeans with straight leg and zip fly, made by Lee Cooper. They sell for about £20 a pair. This is the end of a journey which has consumed approximately 64,500km.

The final stage of the journey was by lorry from a large warehouse in Amiens, France, through the Channel Tunnel to the Lee Cooper warehouse at Staples Corner, near the M1, and by road to retail outlets.

A significant part of the journey was from Tunis in Tunisia by boat and train to Amiens. More precisely, from a factory in the small town of Ras Jebel, about one hour's drive north of Tunis, and home to about 3000 people. The factory was opened by Lee Cooper 25 years ago, and there are now others making Lee Cooper products. At the heart of the factory is the hot engine room where about 500 women work hard to make the jeans, earning TND1.31 (Tunisian dinars) (58p) per hour, which is slightly above the legal minimum of TND 1.06 (47p) but below the average for the Tunisian garment industry of TND2.07 (92p) per hour. Workers like Fasedj Siham have to perform three tasks per minute, with bonus payments if they exceed their target. Eight lines of more than 60 people produce 2000 garments a day working from 7.15am until noon, 1pm until 5.45pm with one hour for lunch and a maximum of two 15-minute toilet breaks. There are no safety guards on the machines. The factory cost of these jeans is about TND11.30 (£5).

The hard, dark blue denim from which the jeans are made, Kansas denim, is brought to Ras Jebel by land and sea from Italdenim in Milan, Italy, where it is spun, milled and dyed, and the synthetic indigo used for dying is made in Frankfurt, Germany, and transported to Milan.

In Ras Jebel the denim is cut and sewn and its texture is modified in huge industrial washers, using pumice from an inactive volcano in Turkey, to produce a soft wearable fabric. The dye is washed out in the process and although indigo is benign in its effect, when it enters local streams it can kill plants and fish by reducing the amount of light able to penetrate the water. The excess pumice powder is also a source of pollution at the plant. The pumice stone is quarried in Neveshir, in the heart of Cappadocia, Turkey, and sent to Milan for the industrial process.

The cotton is obtained by Italdenim in Milan, largely from Benin in West Africa, 4350km to the south. Cotton is the main cash crop in Benin, supplying between 50% and 70% of export earnings per year. There is increasing concern about the ecological impact of cotton production: excessive production leads to a serious decline in soil fertility, and there has been an increase in the use of damaging chemical pesticides (endosulfin) and fertilisers. It has also led to the clearance of forests and pastoral land for cotton production, the marginalisation of semi-nomadic pastoralists, and an increase in cattle herds as cotton growers invest in cattle as a source of wealth. Desire Zinkponen, a cotton farmer in central Benin, grows cotton on his 3ha of exhausted land. He is aware of the health dangers of pesticides (37 people died in the 1999-2000 season due to endosulfan poisoning) and concerned about endemic corruption and mismanagement. Associated with cotton production is the issue of child labour and under-education. Drop-out rates are high in Benin schools since most children leave at an early age to work in the fields.

There are many more threads to the story - literally: the sewing thread, made by Coats Viyella in its factory in Lisnaskea, Northern Ireland, is dyed in Spain; the polyester fibre which gives the thread its strength is bought from Japan and manufactured from petroleum products; and the brass used in making rivets and buttons for the jeans is made in Germany, using zinc and copper from mines in Australia and Namibia. In Tsumeb, the centre of the Namibian copper industry, there is great concern about the health effects of copper mining, including lung damage and of the damaging effects of pollutants from the mines.

Websites

The following websites are useful for amplifying the 'Blue jeans story':
New Internationalist - www.newint.org
International Food Policy Research Institute - www.ifpri.org
Get Set Incorporated - www.getipm.com
International Press Services News Agency - www.ipsnews.net/
Pesticides Action Network News Agency - www.panna.org
Pesticide Action Network UK - www.pan-uk.org
Ana Hita Tourism and Travel - www.anahitatravel.com

Figure 1 | *The Blue jeans story: a global issue. Text based on: Abrams and Astill, 2001. Photo:©Bryan Ledgard.*

Beliefs

Simple propositions which a person accepts as being true and about which they may have firm opinions. Beliefs may or not be provable (e.g. Benin is located between Nigeria and Togo in West Africa), are open to challenge (e.g. more sustainable methods of cotton production are needed in Benin), and are often very strongly held or expressed (e.g. Lee Cooper factory workers ought to be paid at least the average for the Tunisian garment industry).

Attitudes

A group of inter-related beliefs. The attitude which a person adopts towards events, issues, etc., will reflect their beliefs. In the context of the Blue jeans story, readers with ecocentric attitudes are likely to assert that what is needed to tackle soil infertility in Benin is ecological cultivation techniques, that indigo should not be discharged into streams, and that ecologically acceptable ways should be found for disposing of the powdered pumice produced by the stonewashing process.

Values

Moral principles or standards by which a person evaluates and judges ideas, opinions, events, behaviour, etc. A person's values are deep-seated and enduring and will be reflected in their attitudes and subsequent actions. In the context of the Blue jeans story, people for whom the principles of equality and human rights are regarded as fundamental will take the view that the garment workers in the Lee Cooper factory in Tunisia are being denied basic human rights, and that action should be taken to improve their circumstances.

Clearly, both teachers and students will bring their own beliefs, attitudes and values to the Blue jeans story which in itself embodies a set of beliefs, attitudes and values. They should bear in mind that it reflects the values of the storyteller as well as the participants in the story – i.e. it is not value free. It is a story about globalisation and the spatial expression of particular social, economic and political values. In using the story as part of geographical education, teachers need to be aware that what and how they teach is inherently permeated with values – values that are expressed in the choice of key ideas and concepts considered relevant and worthwhile, and the modes of enquiry considered to be most appropriate for exploring and understanding them.

Values and population migration

Let us take the topic of population migration in the context of key stage 3 geography and use it to explore values in a little more detail – in particular as reflected in the choice of the topic itself, its constituent ideas and concepts, and the methods used to study it (Figure 2).

At the heart of values education in geography lies the relationship between on the one hand the values the teacher and student bring to the study of any topic and the values embedded in the topic, and on the other hand the pre-eminent value or worth of exploring that relationship within a specific temporal context.

Values

The values which underpin the study of geography are often classified into:
- Social values (e.g. the need to respect human rights)
- Economic values (e.g. the need for wealth creation)
- Environmental values (e.g. the need to maintain biodiversity)
- Aesthetic values (e.g. the need to conserve forested landscapes)

The topic
Values expressed by a consideration of the worth of studying the patterns of movement of people and their interaction, the processes which shape these patterns, and the consequences of such movement, because of the significance of migration in the lives of many people.

The ideas/concepts
Values expressed by a consideration of the worth of using the push and pull concepts as a framework for analysing the causes of migration, the worth of presenting a typology of migration, the worth of using the cost-benefit framework for analysing the consequences of migration, and the worth of using the distance-decay concept as a means of both describing and predicting population migration between places.

The methodologies
Values expressed by a consideration of the worth of using graphical means to illustrate and explain the patterns of population movement, the worth of using stories and imaginative reconstruction through drama and role play to highlight the personal impact of migration, and the worth of using music and poetry to nurture an empathetic response to migration events.

Figure 2 | *Values and population migration.*

- Political values (e.g. the need to participate in the life of the local community)
- Moral values (e.g. the need to act in accordance with a moral code)

In a sense, however, all values, in whatever arena they are located, may take on an ethical dimension and become, therefore, moral values. Social, economic, environmental, aesthetic and political values, related to the study of an issue, may all be subsumed within the category of moral values if one chooses to regard the issue as a moral issue. If I uphold, as an enduring principle, that the human rights of the Tunisian garment worker *ought* to take precedence over wealth creation, that the production process *ought* never to damage biodiversity, and that cotton production *ought* never to threaten the valued forests of Benin, then it is clear that I am adopting a moral stance when faced with the story of the blue jeans.

In examining the costs and benefits of population migration both for the host and the donor countries and for the families and individuals involved in the process of migration, how might one justify the assertion that it may be regarded as a moral issue? To the extent that:

1. it springs from deep inequalities in human welfare, a clear consequence of disparities in resource availability, production and consumption, in economic opportunities, in social amenities and political power for which migration might be regarded as a corrective response,
2. its existence often reflects a lack of concern for human rights and it challenges us to respect and care for others based on an empathetic understanding of their situation, and
3. it invites all of us, including students, to make reasoned judgements on the causes and consequences of migration; judgements which may have wider applicability than a specific migration event.

On these grounds, then it is possible to argue that population migration embodies moral considerations. This, for the same reasons, may equally apply to other topics in geography.

Summary of key propositions

- That it is worth examining the relationship between the values which the student and teacher bring to the study of a topic, and the values embedded in the topic.
- That this relationship often gives rise to a whole range of conflicting issues which need to be addressed in the geography classroom.
- That this relationship may assume a moral dimension if, during the study of the topic, we express the view, drawing upon such principles as respect for human rights or equal opportunities, that certain situations and events are right or wrong and that this judgement ought to apply to similar situations and events.
- That geography is permeated by moral values and geography teachers need to consider ways of teasing out the moral stances adopted by students in the classroom.

Approach	Description
Values inculcation	Designed to instil a set of pre-determined values as part of the process of character formation
Values analysis	Designed to analyse logically the values contained within the evidence presented by the topic as a prelude to further discussion
Values clarification	Designed to assist students to become aware of their own value orientation in relation to the topic
Moral reasoning	Designed to encourage a process of moral reasoning in the student as a means of developing their moral awareness
Action learning	Designed to encourage students to act upon the moral choices which they have made in relation to a defined geographical issue

Figure 3 | *Summary of approaches to values education in geography.*
Source: Lambert and Balderstone, 2000.

Approaches to values education

A number of approaches to values education in geography have been proposed in recent years, five of which are summarised in Figure 3.

Whatever approach to values education is adopted, and for whatever reason, the following should be taken into account:

1. the central importance of ***moral reasoning*** in whatever approach is adopted, given that all values may be considered from a moral perspective;
2. the central importance of ***discussion***, both between teacher and students and between students;
3. the central importance of defining the ***professional role and responsibility*** of the geography teacher in orchestrating such discussions about important moral issues where the development of moral reasoning is a central objective.

Moral reasoning

Students in geography classrooms need to:

- develop the capacity to make reasoned judgements about geographical issues, informed by the available evidence;
- reflect upon those judgements;
- evaluate them critically;
- think about the consequences of acting on such judgements, for all parties involved in a given situation;
- appreciate and respect alternative judgements if based on sound evidence;
- be open minded in the face of any fresh evidence which might challenge their judgements.

If these issues are considered to incorporate a moral dimension then the need to nurture this capacity for reasoning becomes of paramount importance. It implies our reasoning ought to be based on the notion that human beings have certain intrinsic rights, that these rights are universal, and that we ought to empathise with anyone whose rights are being infringed and seek ways to support them. In short, to base our reasoning on such principles as respect for others, fairness of treatment and a sensitive consideration of their interests. To do unto others what you would have them do unto you (Haydon, 2000).

One way of helping students to develop their moral reasoning is to construct and invite them to consider a story, rich in contextual detail, at the heart of which lies a moral dilemma (see e.g. Figure 1).

Nestor is a graduate student living in England, studying for an MSc in chemistry at an English university. He is from Benin. He came to the university on a scholarship financed by the Benin government. His father, Desire, is a cotton farmer in the Borgou province in the north of Benin.

Desire is trying to earn a living from his 3ha of land. The cotton he produces is exported to Italy to make jeans. The lack of urban centres, the undeveloped infrastructure and high transport costs in Benin combine to make it difficult to grow and sell crops.

Cotton is the main cash crop in Benin, but is degrading the soil. Cotton cultivation robs the soil of nutrients, and neither crop rotation nor fallow periods are used to help to prevent soil degradation; so to improve yields, artificial chemical pesticides and fertilisers are used. There is some concern that the use of pesticides is having a negative impact on river quality, biodiversity and the health of workers in the ginning mills (in which the cotton is separated from its seeds). Last year, one of Nestor's cousins became seriously ill after eating corn which was growing near his father's cotton field.

Nestor is in the final stages of his MSc. He is an excellent student, hard working and committed to his research. Last week, a well-known international French chemical company offered him a well-paid job based in Paris. Nestor is fluent in French, the official language of Benin. His job will be to help to develop a new range of pesticides.

He has to make a decision by next week.

What are the moral reasons and, therefore, moral requirements underpinning Nestor's decision: to take or not to take the job? How finely balanced are they?

Figure 4 | *An example moral dilemma.*

What is a moral dilemma?

A person is faced with a moral dilemma when they are obliged to make a choice between different courses of action, and that for each course of action there exists moral arguments which might oblige one to choose that course of action (i.e. a moral requirement). The essence of a moral dilemma is, however, that the moral arguments supporting each course of action are finely balanced or equally weighted and that, unfortunately, both courses of action cannot be adopted at the same time, but has to choose one of them (McPartland, 2001).

We may construct a moral dilemma based on Nestor, an imaginary character, linked to the story of the blue jeans (see Figure 4).

The value of narrative as a medium

Using the narrative form to convey ideas and provoke discussion has several advantages: a story can incorporate both cognitive (What does this mean?) and affective (How do I feel about this?) aspects, and readers can be invited to reflect on the (moral) points it contains. The story must be plausible and factually accurate, otherwise there is a danger that students will make superficial, uninformed and morally careless judgements.

Creating a moral dilemma

Seven aspects must be taken into account when creating a moral dilemma, each one is related here to the Blue jeans story.

■ **Identify** the issue (e.g. the manufacture of blue jeans).
■ **Relate** it to the scheme of work (e.g. global issues and interconnections).
■ **Locate** additional relevant, up-to-date and varied resources (e.g. the websites listed at the end of Figure 1).
■ **Identify** the key moral decision which has to be made, as well as when it has to be made, in the context of the unfolding story (e.g. to buy or not buy a pair of jeans, to work or not to work for a company implicated in the production process, to take action or not to take action in support of a local pressure group), and the moral requirements linked to that decision. Figure 5 indicates reasons why Nestor should or should not take the job.
■ **Enrich** the biographical details of those actors in the story faced with the need to make a moral decision and those facing the consequences of that decision (e.g. Nestor, Desire and his family).
■ **Provide** a context for the story, rich in accurate and plausible detail, to help to inform the decision and to act as a vehicle for examining key ideas and concepts. In relation to Benin this might include:

Why Nestor should take the job	Why Nestor should not take the job
■ Worked hard to gain his educational qualifications ■ Take advantage of his qualifications in chemistry ■ Acquire a secure, well-paid job ■ Able to send money back home to support his family ■ Might influence the company to develop more ecologically sensitive forms of pest control, etc.	■ Environmental damage being done by pesticides and chemical fertilisers, produced by chemical companies, in his home country ■ Indirectly supporting an over-reliance on cotton production in Benin and over-dependence on trans-national chemical companies ■ Need to show solidarity with his family ■ Could take another job which uses his scientific knowledge, e.g. to research organic cotton growing

Figure 5 | Issues related to Nestor's decision.

■ Landscape and climate (flat, undulating terrain, tropical climate with hot, humid south and semi-arid north)
■ Environmental issues (drought, deforestation, desertification and impact of cash crop farming)
■ Population characteristics of Benin (age structure, fertility and mortality trends, migration, impact of HIV/AIDS)
■ Economy (e.g. reliance on agriculture)
    The story can be enriched with photographs (of Benin), diagrams (of cotton production, changing yields), maps (location of Benin and the Borgou province), etc.
■ **Revise** the story, after evaluating it in the classroom, and incorporate into it the geography scheme of work.

The content of the blue jeans story is such that it could be used to study a range of different moral dilemmas.

The role and value of discussion

Discussion plays a crucial role in values education in general, and in considering moral dilemmas in particular, so careful thought must be given to the nature and quality of discussion, and the kinds of teaching activities designed to promote it in the geography classroom (see Figure 6 for examples).

The teacher's role and responsibility

In reflecting on the moral decision made and the justifications for reaching it, the teacher will be involved in orchestrating class discussions, especially when debriefing the learning that has taken place through these discussions in plenary sessions, for example. An effective plenary session, conducted by the teacher, is likely to incorporate the following characteristics (Leat and Kinninment, 2000):
■ Open rather than closed questions inviting a range of extended responses.
■ Higher-order rather than lower-order questions, promoting connected thinking and speculation.
■ Student talk rather than teacher talk emphasising the importance of self-evaluation, peer evaluation and evaluative feedback from the teacher.
■ Focus on the ideas and concepts central to the topic, rather than the factual detail.

1. *Role play:* in which students take on the roles of various actors in a story (e.g. Nestor or Desire) and re-enact the events leading up to the point where the moral dilemma has to be faced and a decision made. The role play may also involve actors having to justify decisions they make, perhaps in the context of a public meeting.

2. *Court of enquiry:* in which Nestor has to defend his decision in a 'court' in which other students act as judge, defence and prosecution lawyers, witnesses and jury.

3. *Hot seating:* in which students, in groups, assume the role of a particular group of people or organisation (e.g. Benin cotton farmers, environmental pressure group, chemical company) and subject themselves (take the hot seat in a circle of chairs) to interrogation by other groups about the decision Nestor must make.

4. *Badge of allegiance:* in which students wear a badge which represents the degree of agreement or disagreement they feel (five degrees ranging from strongly agree to strongly disagree) towards Nestor's decision. Students circulate and discuss their view with other students whose view is at variance with their own, starting with those whose view is similar and moving towards those whose view is least like their own. Students can change badges at the end of the discussion period.

5. *Concentric circles:* in which the students are arranged in two equal groups on an inner and outer circle of chairs. Everybody sits facing a partner. The students are given Nestor's decision for discussion. They discuss their response to the decision with their partner opposite. After two minutes, students in the outer circle move one position to the left and discuss the same decision with their new partner.

6. *Grouping and ranking:* in which students making a similar moral decision are paired and asked to select the two most important moral requirements underpinning that decision; then two pairs of students making a similar moral decision are grouped to select, now in fours, the four most important moral requirements linked to that decision, and so on.

Figure 6 | Suggestions for activities involving or leading to discussion, in the context of the Benin story. (See also Chapter 24).

■ Paying attention not only to the product of the moral reasoning (the moral decision made) but also the process of moral reasoning leading up to that decision, and inviting students to explain and justify that process.
■ Linking the learning to other contexts as a means of encouraging its transfer.
■ Being genuinely interested in what the student thinks, the quality of reasoning used by the student, and the significance of the moral decision made.
■ Integrating insights gleaned from previous small-group discussion as a means of extending the discussion.

In orchestrating discussions, the teacher can take one of several stances in relation to the process of moral reasoning, as well as the product of that reasoning. Four possible stances which the teacher might take in relation the treatment of controversial issues have been identified (Stradling *et al.*, 1984) and are equally applicable to the treatment of moral issues within the context of moral dilemmas since they too embody conflicts in belief, attitudes and values (Figure 7). These four stances are: *procedural neutrality, stated commitment, balanced approach* and *devil's advocacy.*

A potential strength	Stance and behaviour	A potential weakness
Minimises undue influence of teachers' own bias	**Procedural neutrality** Teacher as impartial chairperson	Artificial
Students know where the teacher stands on the issue	**Stated commitment** Teacher makes explicit his or her views during discussion	Can stifle class discussion
Useful where there is much conflicting information	**Balanced approach** Teacher presents students with a wide range of views	Is there such a thing as a balanced range of opinions?
Effective in stimulating discussion	**Devil's advocate strategy** Teacher deliberately takes up opposing positions	May reinforce student's prejudices

Figure 7 | *Four approaches for dealing with controversial issues in the classroom. Source: Stradling, 1984, pp. 111-12.*

It might be argued that procedural neutrality is the only defensible stance in a plural and diverse society in which there is a professional ethic that the teacher subscribes to. In respecting this stance, the teacher merely invites students to elaborate and/or speculate and evaluate the viewpoint of others, then clarifies responses, draws attention to the available evidence, redirects questions, summarises positions taken and ensures the rules of discussion are maintained. The teacher would not express agreement or disagreement with the views expressed, provide no positive or negative feedback, and would resist the temptation to articulate their views about the issue under discussion. There is evidence that the stance of procedural neutrality increases speculative confidence in students, encourages critical thinking and promotes oral skills (Harwood, 1998).

But is the stance of procedural neutrality feasible and justifiable? Is it not inevitable that teachers will reveal in their choice of words and body language their response to the issue? How can a teacher advocate the worth of revealing, clarifying and analysing issues in the classroom but decline to subject his or her own views to the same critical scrutiny? Is it not more credible and justifiable for the teacher fully to participate in the discussion while submitting themselves to the same procedural guidelines as the student? It is important for teachers to recognise that:

■ their view of the moral dilemma must be supported by evidence, and that evidence linked to the moral requirements of the alternative decisions is available;
■ their views might be flawed;
■ they must be prepared to change their minds in the light of classroom discussion or additional evidence.

Above all, teachers need to create a positive atmosphere in the classroom where students are not inhibited from challenging the views of the teacher, feel comfortable when expressing their own views and are free from ridicule. Students should also be able to accept that the teacher has a right to hold and communicate a view about issues of moral concern because by not doing so they abdicate moral responsibility in the face of some of the most urgent moral issues of our time.

Related publications from the Geographical Association:
■ Biddulph, M. and Bright, G. (2003) *Theory into Practice: Dramatically Good Geography*.
■ McPartland, M. (2001) *(see below)*.
■ Roberts, M. (2003) *Learning through enquiry: Making sense of geography in the key stage 3 classroom*.

Implications for practice

(a) **The relationship between the values students and teachers bring to the study of a topic in geography and the values embedded in it is worth exploring.**

This relationship lies at the heart of values education in geography. A whole range of conflicting issues may emerge from this relationship and these issues need to be addressed skilfully in geography lessons. The values permeating topics studied in geography and their links to the constituent ideas and concepts in these topics need to be identified and appropriate modes of enquiry planned. There are a variety of different approaches to values education depending on whether the purpose is to explore specific values or to help students in analysing or clarifying values as part of a process of making decisions.

(b) **Geography is permeated by moral values and geography teachers need to ensure there is a more explicit focus on the moral dimensions of the issues explored through the subject.**

Geography can make a significant contribution to the moral education of young people. 'If ethics can be defined as the systematic reflection on moral questions or specific moral concerns, within geographical contexts, then all geography teachers are engaged in an ethical endeavour' (McPartland, 2001, p. 8). Moral dilemmas provide a useful device for exploring these dimensions because they combine both specific geographical content and a process of reasoning deployed in an attempt to resolve them. In this way geography teachers can involve young people in a process of moral reasoning.

(c) **The nature and quality of classroom discussion and the activities designed to promote discussion is of crucial importance in values education.**

A whole range of strategies can be employed to promote values education depending on the objectives of the enquiry. Locating moral dilemmas within a narrative structure provides detailed and realistic geographical contexts within which the dilemma can be explored so that the process of moral reasoning can be informed by the geographical ideas and concepts. Discussion enables students to articulate and understand the values underpinning their reasoning and judgements as well as their attitudes towards people, places and issues. Effective debriefing is a vital element in this process (see Chapter 16) and the stance adopted by the teacher also needs to be addressed.

References and further reading

Abrams, F. and Astill, J. (2001) 'The story of the blues', *The Guardian* – G2, 29 May, pp. 2-4 (available online: http://www.guardian.co.uk/g2/story/0,,497788,00.html).

Development Education Centre (1992) *Developing Geography*, Birmingham: DEC.

Eliot, T.S. (1936) 'Choruses from "The Rock"', *Collected Poems, 1909-1935*. New York: Harcourt Brace.

Harwood, D. (1998) 'The teacher's role in democratic pedagogies' in Holden, C. and Clough, N. (eds) *Children as Citizens: Education for participation*. London: Jessica Kingsley Publishers, pp. 154-63.

Haydon, G. (2003) 'Teaching moral reasoning' in Gardner, G., Cairns, J. and Lawton, D. (eds) *Education for Values*. London: Kogan Page, pp. 27-37.

Lambert, D. and Balderstone, D. (2000) *Learning to Teach Geography in the Secondary School*. London: Routledge Falmer.

Leat, D. and Kinninment, D. (2000) 'Learn to debrief' in Fisher, C and Binns, T. (eds) *Issues in Geography Teaching*. London: Routledge, pp. 152-72.

McPartland, M. (2001) *Theory into Practice: Moral Dilemmas*. Sheffield: Geographical Association.

Pike, P. and Selby, D. (1988) *Global Teacher, Global Learner*. London: Hodder & Stoughton.

Stradling, R., Noctor, M. and Baines, B. (1984) *Teaching Controversial Issues (Teaching Matters Series)*. London: Hodder & Stoughton Educational.

Chapter 16

Thinking skills and the rôle of debriefing

Adam Nichols

Before reading this chapter consider the following questions:

- How does students' learning in geography benefit from debriefing?

- How do you help students to make sense of their learning in geography (the learning that has taken place)?

- What strategies do you use to debrief students' learning?

This chapter explores the relationship between thinking skills, thinking-skills strategies and teaching thinking, and argues the case for debriefing: the difference that makes the difference. It is fair to say that the full potential of the strategies to support the development of thinking skills in most classrooms has yet to be realised.

Teacher: *Why don't you think, boy?*
Young Nichols: *I don't know how to, Sir. Nobody's told me.*
Teacher: *Well work it out for yourself!*

Why teach thinking skills?

For many teachers, teaching students to think effectively is considered an exciting challenge, but there is still a minority in the profession who do not believe that students can be taught to think. When asked, they would not deny that the vast majority of their students are better thinkers – that is to say they are capable of higher levels of cognition – at the end of their school careers than they were at the start. Such teachers acknowledge that something happens to develop students' thinking abilities, but if it was not systematic and planned it must have been happening accidentally by induction and osmosis, or perhaps outside the school environment altogether. Generally, however, there is an increasingly healthy dialogue among teachers about effective teaching and learning, informed by what is now known about how young people learn. This has been stimulated in many schools recently through engagement with the Key Stage 3 Strategy (now known as the Secondary National Strategy) and related school improvement initiatives with a teaching and learning focus, including teaching thinking. With what is now known about how young people learn, geography has much to gain from embracing a rôle in the teaching of thinking skills because:

■ it can enhance, enrich and lead to more effective learning in the subject;
■ the subject is tailor-made for providing a wide range of opportunities to use and develop thinking skills;
■ it can increase enjoyment and motivation in lessons both for students and for teachers.

The popularity of and levels of attainment in geography at GCSE in schools where geography departments have injected thinking skills lessons into schemes of work, especially at key stage 3, provide clear evidence of the value of such an approach. Research undertaken by a teacher involved in a masters course with the Thinking Through Geography team at Newcastle University indicated a gain of almost 0.8 of a GCSE grade over groups that had not been taught using thinking-skills approaches (Chapman, 2000).

There is also the national curriculum statutory requirement (DfEE, 1999) which states that thinking skills 'are embedded in the national curriculum'. And so they may be, but there is a long way to go before they are embedded in every unit of work, and even further to go for them to be systematically planned for progression.

So what can be identified as belonging to those skills known as thinking skills?

■ Information processing
■ Reasoning
■ Enquiry
■ Creativity
■ Evaluation

The skills listed above represent the ones that we use and develop most often through the study of geography. They are generic and transferable between subjects (like

Context
This activity was carried out with a mixed ability year 7 class during a lesson early in the autumn term. The teacher was consciously seeking to provide positive experiences of both geography and thinking-skills lessons.

Preparation
Before the lesson, a poster was put up to replace a wall map of Europe, but a satellite image of Europe was left in place so that students could make use of it to, for example, identify coastlines and recognise or interpret upland areas – features that were clearly visible from across the classroom.

Two copies of a map of Europe were placed on a central table and an A4 photocopy of the same map was given to each group. The nearest river and main settlement to the school had been marked on the map. (It is important not to add too much information in case the map becomes overcrowded.) The room was arranged for groups with three or four students in each, and the groups were given a sheet of plain A4 paper, a pencil and an eraser.

Launching
Once the class arrived and had been settled into groups they were told that the lesson would involve memory, drawing skills and teamwork. The lesson began with a few quick-fire questions about facts of the kind found in the *Guinness Book of Records*, such as 'Which are Europe's highest mountains ... longest rivers ... biggest cities?' (Other ideas can be found in the national curriculum geography key stage 3 requirements (DfES/QCA, 1999).)

Instructions
The groups were asked to allocate a number (1-3 or 4) to each member, and for members of each group to come out in number order to look carefully at a map for 20-30 seconds, then return to their group and, for two minutes, draw what they could remember. The remaining students would then, in turn, add to what those before them had drawn. They were allowed to alter their group's map if they wished to make it more accurate.

The groups were encouraged to discuss how they were going to attempt the activity, and were told that if they could work out an effective way to do it, they could use it again in other lessons. Approaches varied – some groups decided to start on the coastline, one group's strategy was to wait and see the maps first, and another group looked carefully at the satellite image. (Listening to the students' discussions provides useful material for the debriefing phase later on – see Figure 4.)

Managing the activity
During the activity the teacher hid the map from view. This raised some complaints from students but they quickly returned to their tables and referred instead to the satellite image. Some students shouted instructions to one another, argued, or tried to grab the pencil from its rightful user. The teacher had to introduce an 'official drawer only' rule, which calmed them down.

After all of the students had taken part once, they were asked to nominate one person to have one other go. One group's enthusiasm led to a squabble, suggesting that in future the 'rule' should be explained at the start, in order to avoid confrontation later. When it became clear that the groups were making adjustments, rather than additions to their maps, the activity was stopped.

Debriefing
The debriefing for this lesson is described in detail later in Figure 4.

Figure 1 | *'Maps from Memory' in action. Adapted from: Nichols with Kinninment, 2001, pp. 27-8.*

geography) and wider contexts. However, within these broad categories of skills lie many more specific thinking processes that can inform both the planning and the debriefing process.

It might be useful at this point to consider a specific example of a classroom activity designed as a thinking-skills strategy, and to try to identify which of the above thinking skills are introduced and developed by it (see below and Chapter 40).

Applying thinking skills to a classroom mapping activity

The 'Maps from Memory' thinking-skills strategy (see also Chapter 40) was one of those included in *More Thinking Through Geography* (Nichols with Kinninment, 2001). Under the name 'Collective memory', the strategy also features in the National Strategy thinking-skills whole school initiative 'Leading in learning'. It is accessible and relatively easy to implement in the classroom, and is popular in many subjects besides geography.

According to Nichols with Kinninment, the process of making use of maps and diagrams involves three steps:

1. *identifying the component parts by detecting one kind of symbolic representation from another (e.g. lines, points and areas)*
2. *recognising what the symbols represent*
3. *interpreting the spatial distribution of the symbols* (2001, p. 22).

The same authors also claim that 'Maps from Memory' stimulates these processes ... being able to draw [maps and diagrams] from memory can be a key to unlocking the understanding associated with them' (Nichols with Kinninment, 2001, p. 22) (Figure 1).

Statutory requirements are rather blunt instruments for encouraging development in pedagogy but any teacher with a commitment to raising the level of achievement of all students through improving the quality of their teaching and students' learning will be interested in helping their students to be better thinkers. Apprehension is only natural if this is a new dimension to a teacher's practice and, for a few, the pedagogy of teaching thinking may conflict with long-held models of teaching (see Chapter 40). We have to be convinced by a rationale before taking risks with new approaches, and it may be a bumpy ride. Students, too, have mental constructs of learning and they have been known to show reluctance to being challenged to think as well as do.

Fortunately, in addition to the developmental work of the Thinking Through Geography team, which was described in *Thinking Through Geography* (Leat, 1998) and *More Thinking Through Geography* (Nichols with Kinninment, 2001), support is available and (at the time of writing) funded by DfES through the Teaching and Learning in the Foundation Subjects strand of the Secondary National Strategy. This provides an infrastructure for professional development, consultant support and container loads of training materials, many of which, while generic in nature, have been written by well-known geography educators, so are riddled with exemplars from geography contexts (see websites listed at the end of this chapter). Modules in the *Training Materials for the Foundation Subjects* (DfES, 2003a) grouped under the sub-heading *Knowing and learning* are of particular interest in establishing a clear rationale for teaching thinking through collaborative learning and reflection. Even more exciting is the *Leading in Learning: Developing thinking skills at KS3* pack (DfES, 2005) which provides guidance for teachers to develop their teaching-thinking skills and relevance. In short, there is both the expectation and the know-how for all teachers in the maintained sector to engage with the pedagogy of teaching thinking.

Photo: ©Adam Nichols.

What is special about a thinking – skills lesson?

A thinking-skills activity in a lesson may be an episode; a phase of the lesson that contributes to the achievement of the learning objectives of the lesson as a whole. However, the activity itself should have three parts: launching, doing the activity, and debriefing (Lofthouse, 2002).

Skills lessons in isolation are of questionable value, as are lessons in map skills that are then left unused for months on end, as seems often to happen at the start of year 7. In fact, a thinking-skills lesson is one in which the subject-learning objectives and the teaching-thinking objectives are intertwined and symbiotic. If the thinking skills do not enhance geographical learning, what are they doing in a geography lesson?

Developing specific geographical learning can be the main objective of activities that promote thinking. Teaching strategies that make students think through appropriately challenging problems or issues, and solving or resolving these challenges involves mental effort. This is 'cognitive conflict'. Such strategies have a sound basis in educational theory, e.g. Vygotskian, where the learner's knowledge and understanding are acquired through social interaction. Co-operative learning involves students discussing and explaining their reasoning to each other, which helps them to achieve higher levels of understanding. A key feature of such a thinking-skills lesson, then, is the prominent role and time given to student talk while they wrestle with problems and challenges by speculating, reasoning and engaging critically with each other's ideas. This 'exploratory talk', in effect audible thinking, is relatively rare in most classrooms, but is a major feature in thinking-skills lessons – or, at least, the emphasis is on 'students talk more; teachers talk less'.

Students working and learning together not just in pairs and groups (as individuals) but as groups on a common task (operating collaboratively – see Chapter 25) is a strong dimension of a thinking-skills lesson which can be highly effective and motivating and one which students will support. A random sample of students in year 8 at Farringdon School, Sunderland, were asked for their views on various teaching approaches used in the school. A video presentation of them expressing their views was used in whole-school in-service training and made a big impact on the staff. With respect to discussing and working collaboratively with peers, these comments were typical of the whole group:

> ■ *Really good because it's more fun and you can get help from your friends who might put it in an easier way.*
> ■ *Friends can explain things better than the teachers can. You don't mind asking them.*
> ■ *You can express yourself how you want.*
> ■ *You learn more by listening to other people's opinions.*
> ■ *It makes the work seem easier. You learn more.*

Working together helps to build student confidence and removes many of the barriers to taking risks. While it is possible for students to undertake many of the thinking-skills strategies individually, to do so completely misses the point.

Learning activities promoting thinking

A thinking-skills lesson will provide a variety of debriefing opportunities where students can reflect upon and evaluate the ways they went about the tasks. Through this, the process of learning (*how* students learn) is accorded a status on a par with the subject content (*what* students learn). Awareness of, and thinking about thinking, is called metacognition and is a vital stepping stone to students becoming autonomous, self-regulating, independent and effective learners. These are overarching aims of the (largely subject-based) school curriculum we all have a responsibility to promote, and students become better learners if we do (DfES, 2003b). This gap between lofty ideals and the narrower focus of subject teaching can be plugged partly by teaching thinking.

When am I teaching thinking?

Imagine this scenario: a young person attends a job interview armed with a letter of application that says geography was one of their favourite subjects because it involved lots of thinking skills in class.

Interviewer [with eyebrows raised]: *That's very interesting. Tell me something about the thinking skills that you are good at.*
Interviewee: *I'm really good at 'Mysteries'.*
Interviewer [with furrowed brow, perplexed]: *Er ... Go on. Tell me more.*
Interviewee [enthusiastically]: *And 'Most Likely to ...'*
Interviewer [bamboozled]: *You do what?*
Interviewee: *Yes I do, but 'What' is only one of the '5Ws'. I can do them all. And then there's 'Living graphs' [on a roll now], oh, and 'Mind movies' as well, and....*
Interviewer [now gobsmacked] interrupts: *But I'm not sure that we have a call for those sorts of things in this vacancy. It really needs someone whose strengths lie in sorting, classifying and seeing patterns in a wide variety of data, interpreting and drawing conclusions from the data, comparing and contrasting, hypothesis testing, reasoning, predicting and making judgements [etc.].*
Interviewee [with broad grin]: *I'm the person you are looking for, then. I can do all those, and more!*
Interviewer: *Well why on Earth didn't you say so?*

This vignette makes two serious points. Our interviewee is able to recall some learning strategies that were engaging and enjoyable, but needed prompting to recognise that a whole range of mental processes are embedded within them. A question to ask of *any* task we set our students is 'What kinds of thinking are involved in this activity?' The second point is that the value of the skills developed in the geography (or other) classroom is severely limited if the learner perceives them to be bounded by the context in which they met them. Transfer and application of a strategy to another context, sometimes called 'bridging', multiplies the value of the skill in the learner's toolkit. There is evidence from student interviews that this can occur instinctively with some, but in the main it is our job to help them make links with other contexts within the subject, across the curriculum and with the outside world. This is precisely what the *Leading in Learning* materials (DfES, 2005q.v.) seek to encourage and facilitate.

Teaching thinking helps us leave behind the low levels of cognitive demand and repetitive nature of many geography lessons that can turn students off and hamper progress, as was highlighted by Ofsted in its subject reports, especially at key stage 3:

> *There continues to be more unsatisfactory teaching in geography than in most other subjects. Common weaknesses include a narrow range of teaching approaches and an over-reliance on a single text book or inappropriate photocopied worksheets ... Teachers' expectations are insufficiently high [students] are often denied access to higher levels of the geography curriculum by the nature of the tasks set* (Ofsted, 2001).

Thinking-skills strategies aim to accelerate learning and increase motivation by introducing higher levels of challenge, in terms of complexity and the nature of problems to solve, that require the use and development of 'higher order' thinking skills. For this we need to do the following:

1. Be aware of specific thinking skills involved in the activities. The checklist (Figure 2) can help you identify them. (Here is a second opportunity to refer to the 'Maps from Memory' strategy to identify the specific thinking skills that underpin the 'big thinking skills'.)
2. Develop in the learners a language with which to discuss thinking and learning processes. In time learners will instinctively apply particular strategies when thinking about a task.
3. Provide time for the learners to reflect on and evaluate how they tackled a task.
4. Establish links between this and other learning strategies that use the same skills, and with which students are familiar, so that they can apply these skills.
5. Revisit and reuse the thinking skills in a different or more challenging context.

adapt to adjust to
adopt to choose to accept
amalgamate to combine or blend into one
(give an) analogy to clarify by comparing a new idea with a similar, familiar one
analyse to examine something methodically in detail
apply to put to a relevant use
assess to evaluate or estimate the value of something
assume to accept as true without proof

challenge to question the truth of something
characterise to describe using the distinctive features of
check to examine something for its accuracy
chunk to group ideas or information into manageable bundles
classify to put data into groups (classes) according to their shared characteristics
combine to join together or unite
compare to look for similarities
compromise to reach agreement by each side making concessions
contrast to look for differences
convert to change the form of

decide to settle an issue in your mind
decipher to discover the meaning of something, perhaps written in a code
decode to find the meaning of something in a code
deconstruct to take apart to expose how something works
deduce to arrive at a conclusion by reasoning
define to describe something by its qualities and circumstances
develop to evolve from a simple to a more advanced state
differentiate to identify difference or make different
discriminate to observe distinctions
distinguish to tell apart

employ to use or set to work
evaluate to judge the value of
examine to investigate, to consider critically, to weigh and sift arguments
explain to say how and why
extrapolate to project from given data

forecast to predict, foresee or calculate beforehand
formulate to set out in a methodical way

generalise to apply ideas widely, based on frequently occurring features of case studies

hypothesise to float an idea or propose a limited explanation as a basis for investigation

identify to recognise something by studying its characteristics
imagine to suppose, to form an idea or image in the mind
implement to put into effect
infer to deduce by reasoning
interpolate to insert into a series
interpret to explain the meaning of
inter-relate to find the connections between two or more things

judge to examine evidence and form an opinion; to hear a case and reach a verdict
justify to give good reasons for
juxtapose to place one thing alongside another

link to make connections between ideas or data

manipulate to move things about with skill
model to create a description that exemplifies how something happens

negotiate to discuss in order to reach a deal or agreement

order to arrange things methodically
organise to arrange parts into a 'living whole'

paraphrase to restate in a new way to make something clearer
plan to make preparations for
predict to say what will happen in the future
present to show or offer for consideration
prioritise to organise tasks in order of importance

rank to arrange things in order of importance
recall to remember
recognise to recall the identity of something or somebody
reconstruct to rebuild or reassemble
refine to make minor changes to improve something
reflect to think deeply about past events, actions or thoughts
reorganise to arrange parts differently into a 'living whole'
respond to reply or react to something
restructure to create a new framework for; to put together again in a different way
reword to put into other words

scan to examine closely to identify information
sequence to organise into a logical order
skim to look at something quickly to identify the main points
specify to identify clearly and definitely
structure to create a framework for; to put together
summarise to make a brief version of something; to sum up
symbolise to use something to represent meaning
synthesise to combine into a complex whole

test to verify by experiment
transfer to move something from one location or context to another
transform to change the way in which something is presented
translate to interpret or express in clearer terms
trigger to cause something to happen

validate to confirm
visualise to see in your mind's eye

Figure 2 | *Thinking-skills vocabulary and definitions.*

Level	Level of use by teacher(s)	Level of use by student	Benchmark criteria
1	Using an example as you find it for an interesting, challenging lesson.	I know I can use this here and now. ('off the peg')	The thinking-skills strategy helps with this particular piece of new learning.
2	Adapting the example or applying the strategy in another syllabus context for use with other age or ability groups for even more interesting and challenging lessons.	I can see how to use this particular thinking skill on other occasions in this subject (a 'routine expert').	'Near transfer' of the skill, which is a step in the right direction.
3	Debriefing the use of the strategy to focus on the learning processes and big concepts that students can transfer to other contexts.	I understand how this thinking skill 'works' and how to use it more effectively (metacognition established) in other contexts.	The critical level for making the most of thinking skills in any subject and across the curriculum: debriefing.
4	School policy extends and integrates thinking skills into a curriculum, bursting at the seams with interesting and challenging lessons.	I have added this thinking skill to my toolkit which I can choose to use on any appropriate occasion any time, anywhere (an 'adaptive expert').	With this 'distant transfer' the school's aims for the student are more likely to be realised.

Figure 3 | *Enhancing the thinking-skills toolkit for teachers and learners.*

Consider this analogy: a group of students are told the rules of football, given a football once a week and sent out to play. Apart from the goalkeeper, they pursue the ball all over the pitch like a swarm of wasps. Some students will be more likely to pick up some skills intuitively over time than others, but it is likely to be a lousy game. Then along comes the coach who introduces specific skill development, roles and responsibilities of positions, and the tactics of the game. Now the players are in a better position to reflect upon, discuss and improve their own game and that of the team next time they play.

Teaching thinking, then, is rather more than the occasional use of a thinking-skills strategy in class. We have a rôle in helping students not only to *use* a skill but to *develop* it for more effective learning in different contexts. Black and Dockrell (1980) refer to this kind of intended learning outcome as 'background learning'.

Why is debriefing important?

Activities for developing thinking skills and the strategies for debriefing the resulting learning can be employed at different levels, as shown in Figure 3, which also provides benchmark criteria for assessing students' thinking skills.

Consider the following discussion (somewhere between level 1 and level 2 in Figure 3) during an in-service training session on thinking skills.

Teacher: *Venn diagrams? Don't tell me they're back again. We used those years ago.*
Teaching and learning consultant: *Why did you stop?*
Teacher [Indistinct response along the lines of]**:** *Why are you picking on me ... You don't know what it's like working here ... I've got 25 years of experience ...*
Teaching and learning consultant [thinking to him/herself]**:** *More likely to be one year of experience repeated 25 times.*

Level 4, originally something of a pipedream for the Thinking Through Geography team, is fast becoming a reality in many schools. Embedded thinking skills are now mainstream and feature in many school improvement plans, encouraged by the national curriculum, and the DfES teaching and learning agenda and the availability of *Leading in Learning* as

Maps from Memory 1

(See Figure 1 for details of the 'Maps from Memory' activity.) This fell into two related phases: assessment, and reflection on how the students performed. I had originally planned to pin the students' maps on the wall for judging, but realised that viewing the maps properly would pose classroom management problems. Instead, they were asked to consider three aspects of their maps that they ought to be judged by. (With higher-achievers the term 'assessment criteria' could be used.) Their first response was 'neatness' (tends to indicate a strong consciousness about this aspect of students' work among those from particular feeder primary schools). 'Whether it's right or not' and 'If it's all there', so it was agreed that accuracy, detail and neatness would be fine.

After handing out the A4 photocopies of the Europe maps, the groups were asked to score themselves out of five for each criterion and suggest ways in which they could have achieved a higher score. One common point to emerge was that the students needed to spend more time looking at the map to appreciate, interpret and establish the inter-relationships between its components. They also needed time to associate the meanings of the labels and key with those of the marked features. This is a really valid point. In the rationale of the 'Maps from Memory' activity, Nichols with Kinninment (2001) make it clear that teachers should try to encourage these very things if the activity is to achieve more than simply memorising of patterns and points, and that students need to be given enough time to enable them to do a task meaningfully and effectively. Another interesting point made by a higher-achieving student was that 'Neatness isn't worth much if it's wrong'. Scores for accuracy and detail seem to relate to how hurriedly they had drawn the map – another argument against the competitive dimension. (This also encompasses national curriculum key skills: evaluation, and improving own learning and performance.)

Most groups thought that if you did not get the coastline 'right' then you could not possibly position other features accurately. A further problem for them was the size of their handwriting for labels, compared with the printed version. Large lettering caused a bit of confusion and some felt that their labels prevented them adding any other features in that area of the map. (Students have to decide what is important. An appreciation of the process of map making grows out of this.)

This led into the second phase of the **debriefing**. As an outcome of the previous discussion, the students suggested that next time they would make an effort to draw the coastline (or whatever form the 'base map' might be) as well as possible first and to leave the words until last. Was this a sign of real understanding of what maps are about?

Maps from Memory 2

Debriefing is not always very easy, partly because while you may be sure what strategies work for you, you may not be able to approach the situation from, say, a year 7's perspective. They tend to want firm solutions and answers, while you may want them to be thinking freely, speculating and testing ideas and ways of doing things, and feeling confident enough to take risks. This is one reason for letting students evaluate their own maps rather than expose them to public comparison. They know what a 'perfect' map looks like anyway. This viewpoint is, of course, at variance with the occasional use of competition as a spur to effort. As *thinking-skills* practitioners frequently say, there isn't one correct solution. It's a matter of professional judgement!

Figure 4 | *Teachers' experiences of debriefing Maps from Mercury activities. Source: Nichols with Kinninment, 2001, pp. 28, 30-1.*

Classroom activity (inc. content)	Concept of skills focused on		Date: Time: Class info:	
Focus: Whole group/small group/pairs/individual **Debriefing objects:** *For students* *For self*	**Briefing** *Key features of task/launching*	*Analogies/examples to be used*	**Students' comments overheard**	**Used**
Context: *Previous attempts* *Class-related factors*	Debriefing *Debriefing questions:* Outcome: O Interpersonal: I	*Transfer contexts to be suggested*		
Key words/terms/vocabulary	Mental: M	**Follow up tasks/homework**		

Figure 5 | *Planning for debriefing. Source: Leat and Kinninment, 2000.*

a whole school initiative for school improvement. Debriefing a thinking-skills activity is far from easy and you may often feel that it leads nowhere, but how else are students to 'go meta' and begin to exercise control over their thinking processes?

In a brief, then, reflecting on and becoming aware of the learning process has the following advantages:

- Students become more independent by developing the ability to monitor and regulate (make choices about) their learning.
- Understanding the learning process helps to de-mystify it. Students can then approach it with more confidence.
- Reflection helps students to generalise about learning processes and outcomes.
- This in turn enables them to undertake near and distant transfer of learning. It connects knowledge in its widest sense.

What does a debriefing episode look like?

There is no standard script for debriefing. Figure 4 shows two teachers' reflections on debriefing 'Maps from Memory' activities (see above and Chapter 40). The aim of debriefing is always to draw out and make explicit the various approaches used by the students in a task, to consider how to do it better and how and where else to use these approaches. There is inevitably an element of explanation needed for students to justify their approaches. Making them aware at the start of the activity that they will be asked to account for the way they tackled the task helps to prepare the ground. The precise leading questions you may ask to tease out the learning depends on the particular strategy being used. While many textbooks nowadays incorporate suggestions for a range of thinking-skills strategies, they tend to skip the debriefing process because of the challenge of scripting it effectively. The advent of teachers' guides to thinking-skills strategies, giving clear directions and alternative ways of running the debriefing phase, is to be heartily welcomed. For example, a 'Maps from Memory' activity involving a global population patterns map in *It's a World Thing: Thinking skills* (Lofthouse, 2002) suggests a large range of debriefing questions designed to tease out both the learning processes and the subject-specific content:

Number	Typical question-and-answer episode	Debriefing episode
1	Most questions are closed – demanding 'right' answers	Most questions are open – inviting a range of responses
2	Emphasis on 'low order' questions demanding recall of facts or simple ideas	Emphasis on 'higher order' questions[a] demanding linking of ideas, reasoning, speculating, justifying
3	The teacher aims to find out if students have understood what is in the teacher's mind	The teacher is interested in what is in the students' minds and how it got there
4	The teacher dominates the talk	Student talk dominates
5	Students' contributions are brief, often one word	Extended student responses, developing ideas
6	Emphasis on what has been learned	Emphasis on both what was learnt and how it was learnt, drawing on what the teacher has heard and seen during the activity
7	The teacher asks questions	Teacher asks questions, invites responses, makes statements and probes reasoning
8	The teacher judges the answers	Responses are used and offered to the class to enhance and develop discussion
9	Wrong answers corrected by teacher or other student	Teacher encourages student to explore reasoning behind response, uncovers misconceptions
10	Knowledge tends to be 'situated' in the context of the lesson	Teachers and students explore links to other contexts and subjects, often using analogies (bridging or transfer)

Figure 6 | *Characteristics of talk in question-and-answer and debriefing episodes compared. Adapted from: Roberts, 2003. Note: a. See Bloom's Taxonomy in Unit 4 Questioning, Training materials for the Foundation Subjects, DfES 2002.*

What strategies did you have for remembering parts of the map? Was this the same for everyone? What did you talk about in your groups? How did this help? How might these help in other situations? How would you do it differently? ... What features does this map have that you would expect to find on other maps? How does the map suggest that population patterns are related to wealth or development? The bar graphs [for Malawi and Germany] are very different. What might this mean for the authorities in each country? (Lofthouse, 2002, pp. 49-50).

Where such guides do not exist, teachers must initiate debriefing for themselves.

The second teacher in Figure 4 would, perhaps, have benefited from using the planning for debriefing sheet shown in Figure 5.

Figure 6 indicates how debriefing as a discursive episode has a number of features that distinguish it from typical question-and-answer plenaries.

Debriefing in practice

The extracts shown in Figure 7 are taken from the transcript of a lesson at Knottingly School, Wakefield, and illustrate many of the characteristics of an effective debriefing episode which is, of course, a form of plenary (DfES, 2003a). Before the class began a

'Maps from Memory' activity, which involved drawing an outline map of Rome to show the main features, groups were given the opportunity to think about the nature of the task and to devise a plan for tackling it. The teacher drew their attention to the fact that the groups had been considering other strategies encountered in other lessons and were going to adapt them (Figure 7). This bridging indicates a key step towards learner autonomy. The transcript shown in Figure 7 can be used during a departmental meeting.

It is evident from this debriefing episode that learning thinking skills was the objective of the lesson. At present it is rare to find such objectives being explicitly shared with students even if debriefing is a feature of the lesson, so it must mystify some students to find a process focus to the end of the lesson. This class, though, is experienced in using thinking-skills strategies. Through debriefing thinking skills are given a higher profile, a status on a par with the subject specific content. A balance of the two is needed.

As Figure 7 indicates the students do their best to describe and explain how they have tackled the task. At times the teacher introduces an appropriate 'thinking word' to indicate the thinking they are describing. Would they have been able to express themselves more fully and accurately if they were able to draw upon a wider thinking-skills vocabulary (e.g. Figure 2)? You should be able to find ten or more useful words describing 'thinking' that fit what they are trying to say. Students' confident and appropriate use of such words is a good indicator of progression in metacognition.

How do students learn from the debriefing process?

Students readily perceive some aspects of learning; others are more abstract. Figure 8 shows distillations from interviews by Leat and Kinninment (2000) and some the author's own. The value of what students learn through debriefing can be deduced by some of their comments.

Finally, debriefing helps students to understand, and teachers to focus on the two-fold purposes of lessons: What and how new learning has taken place.

Reflections

Debriefing is not easy, needs practice and may not work well every time. There are pitfalls. This should not deter us: the same could be said of many question-and-answer sessions and other aspects of pedagogy. Debriefing succeeds best where it relates to really thought provoking tasks without a self-evident or algorithmic solution. Make sure the activity is worth reflecting upon before trying to debrief it. (To test this idea, try finding any thinking skills in Figure 2 that are involved in a word search and consider how you might meaningfully debrief it.)

To support successful debriefing, consider the following pitfalls and related pitprops:

- **It's time consuming:** How long is a piece of string? Debriefing can be as long or short as befits the complexity of the strategy. 'Taboo' needs far less debriefing time than a 'Mystery' does. In the early days it can seem a bit laboured but as familiarity with the process and language of debriefing grows, it speeds up. On revisiting a thinking skill, you can kick off with a question like 'How did you do it differently or *better* than last time?'

- **Pace:** Plenaries can seem to go on forever, dragging every last thought out of each group. Enough contributions to reveal the variety of ways the task was tackled will suffice. Move on to evaluating them and discussing improvements. This phase should be as upbeat and engaging as the rest of the lesson.

- **Running out of time:** Students don't concentrate during a hurried debrief any more

Activity

On a copy of this transcript identify the key features of debriefing.

Teacher	Now, excellent. We've used a variety of strategies, a variety of techniques. Some people have changed them, adapted them as you did in the tasks. What I want to know now is how did you do it?	
Eleanor	We divided the top bits all into different sections.	
Teacher	Divide the map into sections. Any other strategies we used? Aidan?	
Aidan	We went up, looked at five and just kept remembering it all in our heads so we don't forget them and when we got back we just wrote the five down 'cos we kept saying it over and over so we didn't forget it.	
Teacher	Two things there. Collect only five pieces of information and repeat in your head, repeat over and over again. Aidan felt he can only remember five pieces of information and he repeated them over and over again in his head to make sure they were secure in his head. Good, let's have Aaron.	
Aaron	I went to look for landmarks; Christine went to look for roads and shapes and Kim went to look for names and Zin went to look for names as well.	
Teacher	Good. So we had different features didn't we? Okay, so we split it into three according to the features not according to the map itself. So landmarks, shapes, names – good. What about the shapes? What shapes did people get on their maps? Jamie?	
Jamie	A river.	
Teacher	And how did that river help you?	
Jamie	'Cos it split it up into half and then we split it again in the middle. One did top corner, we split the top into two up and someone did them and bottom two and someone did them.	
Teacher	How else was the river useful? John?	
John	It were like River Thames in England, it's like a divide.	
Teacher	And it's a familiar shape isn't it? Okay, meanders we know, we watch Eastenders; we know what it looks like; we use it as something to hang on our information. When we did our plan of attack we were planning our different strategies and whilst we were doing it, okay, we were testing it weren't we? Testing our ideas, experimenting, checking. Aidan's group were checking that he got the right information. He knew when he came up he wasn't looking at anywhere else other than the bottom right-hand corner 'cos he knew when he got back they were going to check, and they did. How do you think doing an activity like this would help you, if you arrived at Rome with your travel guide. How would it help you get around? What might you look out for? How would you use the map? Peter?	
Peter	You get used to the map and where things are.	
Teacher	Okay, you get used to it. Have you got used to this map Peter?	
Peter	Memorising it.	
Teacher	Okay, so what would you look out for when you're in Rome walking around with your map? What kinds of thing would you look out for?	
Peter	Famous landmarks.	
Teacher	Can you pinpoint why they would be helpful.	

Figure 7 | *Transcript from debriefing a 'Maps from Memory' activity.*

Peter	*'Cos then you'll be able to pinpoint where other things are.*
Teacher	*You could almost orientate yourself, we say, okay, work out where other places are. What else might you look out for?*
Peter	*River.*
Teacher	*Why would a river help you?*
Peter	*Then you know if you might be on right side.*
Teacher	*Excellent. You might know whether I'm on the right bank, as they say. Which side of the river? Am I totally lost? Okay. But which side of the river am I on? Excellent.* *There's a pattern emerging of the strategies we've used, isn't there? We started off looking at shapes and outlines. So we got down an outline of a map, either by using the river or by using the railway line, okay, some of you marked down the different districts, some of you even mentioned colour, it was David who spotted this colour that you could use. What did we start adding to our map when we'd got the outline? Keeley?*
Keeley	*Miss, we put roads in because once we put the roads in then we can split it up into smaller sections and each of us can find words out of sections.*
Teacher	*Good, so we've got the main outline, then we divide into sections, either using roads or maybe perhaps minor railways if there are any. Then what do we add? Then what are we beginning to add? Joleen?*
Joleen	*Like all pictures and that.*
Teacher	*It's the place names, isn't it? The different places and the pictures. So we're then adding in the detail. You've seen the whole picture first, okay, and then we're going to add in the parts. Just like, remember if you were writing an essay, if you were planning an essay, you might want to know exactly what you're going to put into it and then you need to think about it – well how am I going to structure it so it makes sense? So it's a skill you could use in other areas, not just in geography.* *You've been planning your strategies, testing them and checking them. Making sure that they work, checking with each other, sharing ideas.* *There are different strategies but because you've worked as a team what have you discovered? Jason?*
Jason	*More information about landmarks and more, like, names, and we discovered that more strategies work better.*
Teacher	*And we've found out, well, other groups have completely different things that may be suitable for something you were trying to do, okay. Last point, John?*
John	*Miss, it's easier to work in a group than by yourself 'cos there's more brains included and it's like more easier.*
Teacher	*Why is it easier?*
John	*'Cos it's not as hard. Helping each other out.*
Teacher	*Just to finish off, a little sheet here entitled 'Going on holiday', okay. I want you to think about how you would make sense of a map of a strange place. Think about what we've done today, any ideas that are on the board. And I've put 'What skills might you need to pack?' Instead of just packing your clothes, what thinking skills you're going to have to take with you as well?*

Aspect of learning	Students' comments
Identifying and evaluating thinking skills	*I've learnt how to group things effectively, how to discover important causes and less important causes.*
Collating ideas: alternative strategies and ideas are made public, available for all to consider	*You find out more ways of doing it; things you hadn't thought of.*
Valuing group talk: students have a growing and critical awareness of group dynamics and responsibilities. The debrief draws all the threads together coherently.	*There's only more brains if everyone uses them ... and some people don't listen so they're not much help. The teacher, like, sums it all up at the end.*
Promoting self-esteem through teacher support: attention and reference to what students said in discussion values students' efforts and thinking. This builds a trusting rapport with the class.	*X makes you feel more confident about answering questions. Anything you say is right as long as you can explain it.*
Providing feedback: Debriefing is the epitome of *Assessment for Learning* and reflects its key characteristics (DfES, 2004). It provides immediate diagnostic and formative feedback to help students identify their 'next steps' and the teacher hers/his.	*You can see how we could have done it better.*
Developing and justifying their reasoning: with encouragement, students clarify their thinking and enrich their responses. Explaining takes practice. We often want them to do it in writing and we can model the process orally with prompts like 'Can you add anything to help me understand a bit better?' or simply 'Go on ...'	*You have to keep going 'til you've put what you thought into words. In the end you either know you know it or you know you don't.*
Transfer: making connections between the learning in question and everyday life, other subjects and other knowledge wherever it came from helps understanding and memory. Analogies are particularly valuable for linking the same idea to another, familiar context.	*This is like life; you learn how to handle information.*
Solving problems and representing understanding in different ways: other thinking-skills techniques can be used to help organise and connect understanding, for example using concept maps, diagrams and classification.	*You can keep those in your head – see what's in the boxes*

Figure 8 | *Aspects of learning and students' comments on thinking-skills strategies.*

than they take in your homework instructions. Plan your time slot and stick to it. Let them know in advance that debriefing will occur and what you will be expecting of them. This also helps prevent their premature stampede for the door when the activity stops and you clear up 10 minutes before the bell goes.

■ **Skill development:** The learning cycle is as relevant to teaching thinking as any other form of learning. Debriefing is the necessary reflective stage before applying the learning gained. If students cannot try it again, having reflected on it, how can they improve their thinking? Plan to revisit the *skills* which may or may not be through using the same thinking-skill strategy. Classification, as one of the 'big' geographical skills, is, for example, embedded in numerous strategies such as 'Most likely to ...', 'Mysteries', and 'Odd One Out'. The process of classifying itself involves identification, differentiation, specification, generalisation, testing and validation – among others. Progression can be achieved through increasing the complexity of the context (often the number of variables involved) or of the conceptual level involved. For example, classification of cutlery in the kitchen drawer is less challenging than classifying vehicles in a car park.

- **An optimum solution:** You are faced with a dilemma. Giving the students a best solution goes right against the grain as it is students' thinking processes that are being shared – but perhaps their thinking strategies are all ineffective. You can suggest other approaches that other classes have tried and collectively compare and evaluate them against criteria. They can be reminded of the discussion before they try using the strategy again.

- **Imbalanced use of strategies:** A general survey in some Sunderland schools indicates a strong preference for the quick and easy to prepare strategies such as 'Maps from Memory', 'Odd One Out', 'Mind Movies' and '5Ws'. There is a danger that by over-working a limited repertoire of strategies, a limited range of skills will be addressed and perhaps even not advanced. Debriefing could become monotonous and the potential for promoting transfer of a learning strategy to other contexts (e.g. other thinking-skills strategies) is inhibited. Identify a range of thinking skills to include in each scheme of work. Share the preparation of more demanding strategies with colleagues. It is crucial to integrate into a scheme a range of strategies that promote and develop thinking skills.

- **Transfer:** Making connections within our own subject is not a major problem, but we often ask questions like 'Where else might you be able to use a strategy like this?' How aware are we of what goes on inside classrooms where subjects other than geography are taught, and of the thinking skills that students need or use to learn in them? The probable answer is not aware enough to enable optimum transfer of skills, knowledge and understanding across the curriculum. For this to happen effectively, cross-curricular whole-school dialogue is essential.

Conclusion

A key stage 3 consultant demonstrated a lesson involving a 'Mystery' to a year 8 class. The teacher observing this was surprised: 'I never would have dreamed they were capable of thinking like that ... but perhaps I've never let them'. Changing the climate of the classroom to enable effective debriefing is vital. The classroom becomes a learning community in which collective knowledge is shared and learners are less afraid of challenge because working with peers and the teacher scaffold their learning. Debriefing is a crucial part of that scaffolding; by promoting metacognition it enhances the value of lessons for learning thinking skills. It is the difference that makes the difference.

Implications for practice

(a) We need to understand the nature of progression in thinking skills as well as the subject.

So what does 'better thinking' look and sound like in the classroom? The debriefing process should provide much of the evidence and if you find that it ceases to reveal anything new, consider whether the learners need more scaffolding or more challenge to move them on. The *Leading in Learning* materials (DfES, 2005) are particularly helpful here.

(b) Teaching thinking enhances the learning process and needs to be planned, not bolted-on.

There is a curricular entitlement for all students to be taught thinking skills which complement the other tools for learning: the key skills of communication, working with others, improving own learning and performance, and problem solving – all frequently called upon by pedagogic strategies. Collectively, these are what we want all our students to employ in order to learn our subject better. As with subject-specific content, we must consciously plan for teaching thinking by designing opportunities for thinking skills to be developed by students in all schemes of work.

(c) How well does our current practice in assessing student achievement reflect the range of ways in which, individually or collectively, they are making progress?

If one of our objectives is to teach thinking, we need to know if we are succeeding. Debriefing of thinking-skills activities has a central role in identifying which skills students are developing and how they are using them. This is a vital component in assessment for learning (see also Chapter 32). What kinds of thinking do our existing assessment activities tap into? If they do not involve higher order thinking, how is it possible for students to demonstrate what they are genuinely capable of achieving?

(d) How conducive to open discussion is the climate of the classroom?

Students need to feel comfortable about discussing how they work, both with their peers and the teacher. Where teacher questioning borders on interrogation and where most questions are closed or pseudo-open, attempts at debriefing can be somewhat frustrating. However, the more students become accustomed to thinking-skills strategies, which by their nature tend to give students the freedom to tackle things in a variety of ways and to produce a range of possible outcomes, the easier it becomes to debrief them. Teacher questioning needs to be an unthreatening experience for students, which invites rather than demands an insight into their thinking. The nature of classroom dialogue is in large measure the product of our questioning technique, which can make or break our efforts to improve students' learning (DfES, 2005).

Related publications from the Geographical Association:
- Leat, D. and Nichols, A. (1999) *Theory Into Practice: Mysteries Make You Think.*
- McPartland, M. (2001) *Theory Into Practice: Moral Dilemmas.*

References

Assessment Reform Group (1999) *Assessment for Learning: Beyond the black box*. London: ARG.

Chapman, N. (2000) *Does Thinking Through Geography Add Value to Geography GCSE Pupils?* Unpublished MA dissertation, University of Newcastle Upon Tyne.

DfEE/QCA (1999) *The National Curriculum Handbook for Secondary Teachers in England (KS3&4)*. London: DfEE/QCA.

DfES (2002) *Making Good Use of the Plenary*. London: DfES.

DfES (2003a) *Key Stage 3 Training Materials for the Foundation Subjects (DVD DfES 0283/2003 Module 8: Plenaries)*. London: DfES.

DfES (2003b) *Teaching and Learning in Secondary Schools Unit 8: Developing effective learners*. London: DfES.

DfES (2004) *Assessment for Learning, Unit 1*. London: DfES.

DfES (2005) *Leading in Learning: Developing thinking skills – a KS3 pack*. London: DfES.

DfES Standards site – www.standards.dfes.gov.uk/keystage3/strands/?strand=TLF&publication=1

Leat, D. (ed) (1998) *Thinking Through Geography*. Cambridge: Chris Kington Publishing.

Leat, D. and Kinninment, D. (2000) 'Learning to debrief' in Fisher, C. and Binns, T. (eds) *Issues in Geography Teaching*. London: Routledge Falmer.

Leat, D. and Lin, M. (2003) 'Developing a pedagagy of metacognition and transfer', *British Education Research Journal*, 29, 3, pp. 385-7.

Lofthouse, R. (2002) *It's a World Thing – Thinking skills*. Oxford: Oxford University Press.

Mercer, N. (2000) *Words and Minds: How we use language to think together*. London: Routledge.

Nichols, A. with Kinninment, D. (2001) *More Thinking Through Geography*. Cambridge: Chris Kington Publishing.

Ofsted (2001) *Secondary Subject Report 2000/01: Geography* (HMI 374) (available online: www.ofsted.gov.uk).

Roberts, M. (2003) *Learning through Enquiry: Making sense of geography in the key stage 3 classroom*. Sheffield: Geographical Association.

Chapter 17

Using ICT to enhance Learning in geography

Sheila King and Liz Taylor

Before reading this chapter consider the following questions:

- ■ In what ways do you use ICT to enhance geographical enquiry in your lessons?

- ■ What is the geographical focus of these learning activities?

- ■ What factors make it difficult for you to use ICT effectively in geography?

- ■ What role does ICT play in your professional development as a geography teacher?

At Riverwoods School, Ms Jones enters the geography suite to find year 10 already at work. In one corner a group is analysing discharge measurements collected from a data logger in a local river, as part of their project to model the impact of flooding. In another area of the room a group is working on their laptops, linked by a wireless network, putting the finishing touches to their research project on the Mississippi floods, which they intend to present to the rest of the class next lesson. Their slides and notes will then be put on the class bulletin board for other groups to use to answer a practice examination question. Ms Jones meets up with a group of students who signed up, again on the bulletin board, for a revision session on factors affecting river discharge. To illustrate her explanation she has downloaded some digital video footage taken on the previous year's fieldwork in the Peak District. The students will use the electronic whiteboard to annotate stills from this footage to apply what they have learned.

This is an imaginary scenario, but all of the technology involved is relatively mainstream. In the Apple Classrooms of Tomorrow (ACOT) project, in the USA, researchers found that in classrooms where a rich variety of ICT was readily available, there was a move towards student-centred, collaborative, active learning, though not without much angst on the part of teachers over their role in the learning process (Dwyer *et al.*, 1990). For geography teachers in some schools, access to technology is still a major issue, though UK secondary schools are comparatively well resourced with ICT hardware compared to other European countries (RM, 2000).

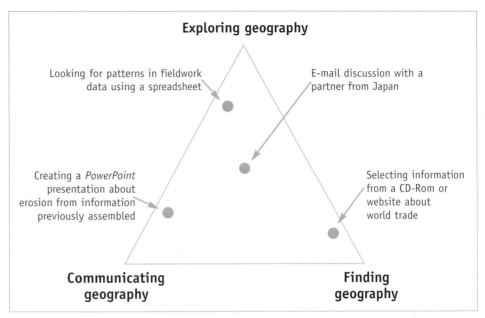

Exploring geography

Looking for patterns in fieldwork data using a spreadsheet

E-mail discussion with a partner from Japan

Creating a *PowerPoint* presentation about erosion from information previously assembled

Selecting information from a CD-Rom or website about world trade

Communicating geography

Finding geography

Figure 1 | The exploring, communicating and finding geography through ICT triangle. Source: Taylor, 2001.

Many sources (see, for example, Freeman, 1997; Hassell, 2000; Taylor, 2001) detail the potential for the use of ICT in geographical learning, but provision and accessibility alone will not guarantee effective use of ICT. As with other learning strategies it is easy to fall into the trap of superficiality – students may well be using ICT, but is their geographical learning deep, stimulating and worthwhile?

It is interesting that teachers taking part in the ACOT project seemed to pass through a series of stages in their use of ICT with their classes, from 'Entry' (where the primary concern is dealing with the equipment) through to 'Appropriation' (which involves major change in the organisation of teaching and learning). Most teachers in the UK are in the earlier stages of this model, where ICT is incorporated into existing ways of working, so this chapter will focus on good practice at this level, just hinting at some other possibilities.

A good starting point for planning stimulating and effective learning activities using ICT is to determine the focus of geographical learning. This, in turn, will help in the selection of appropriate ICT. One way of thinking about the geographical learning process is to divide it into three strands: *finding* geography, *exploring* geography and *communicating* geography. As each of these strands is likely to be present, to a greater or lesser degree, in every piece of geographical learning, the relative emphases can be represented diagrammatically (Figure 1).

Knowing the focus of the geographical learning enables us to select types of ICT which support that focus, and also to reflect this emphasis in our allocation of learning time.

Photo: ©David Livingstone.

Finding geography

The use of ICT dramatically expands the range of primary and secondary data available for geographical learning. In addition, digital data storage makes it much easier to develop and add to collections of information customised to the needs of the geography department. Some schools have taken advantage of these possibilities by building up files of digital photographs, digital video panoramas and files from data loggers on fieldtrips, so that classes can share one another's data and see patterns of change over time (Fox, 2003). Websites also provide a massive source of secondary data including text, images, datasets and sound files. So, availability of information is not an issue. Instead, the challenges for teachers are, first, to set up stimulating and focused opportunities for geographical learning and, second, to equip students with the necessary information-handling skills so that they can be independent and critically aware in their learning.

To address the first issue, some geography teachers are moving beyond the superficial learning associated with simple transfer of information from website to worksheet by setting up engaging enquiry questions which involve manipulation and application of the information accessed (Roberts, 2003). This minimises the possibility of students copying information without thinking. Such tasks do not have to involve advanced computer skills, or even online use by students. For example, a trainee teacher at The Perse School, Cambridge, accessed aerial photographs, maps and information through the internet to set up a role play on whether a quarry in the Peak District National Park should have its licence renewed. One of the reasons that the level of geographical thought and learning was so high was the quality of the stimulus material that the teacher had accessed about a real-life situation.

A starting point with the second issue is for geography departments to identify the information-handling skills which they think students will need and then plan for the development of these skills in their medium – and longer – term planning. For example, if we want students to be able to select, analyse and argue using information from secondary sources *without assistance* in their GCSE coursework, then we need to be providing explicit opportunities for them to develop and practise their skills of skim reading, selecting, critically assessing and writing up findings during key stage 3.

Exploring geography

In the earlier example, the trainee teacher had prepared effectively using the internet as a resource to find geographical information so that her class could focus on exploring and communicating. It is important to identify and prioritise the aspect of the enquiry process which we feel is most important at a particular time. For instance, how many classes have spent most of the lesson inputting data to a spreadsheet and drawing one graph, only to rush through a discussion of results, just before the bell goes? This is fine if a main purpose of the lesson is to learn how to input data, perhaps building up towards more independent enquiry later in the term, but often the learning objectives in such a lesson are to analyse and understand the information – exploring geography – and this gets squeezed out. So, sometimes we need to use ICT to speed up specific aspects of the enquiry process (perhaps by students accessing a spreadsheet set up by the teacher with some graphs already drawn) so that we have more time available for other aspects, such as analysing the trends shown on the graph and watching what happens to the graphs if we change some of the data points (see also Chapter 12).

Exploring geography often involves analysing large amounts of data to identify patterns and model effects, and it also involves thinking about change and hypothesising about the future. Two attributes of ICT – capacity (i.e. the ability to cope with large amounts of data/information) and provisionality (ease of change) – can aid significantly

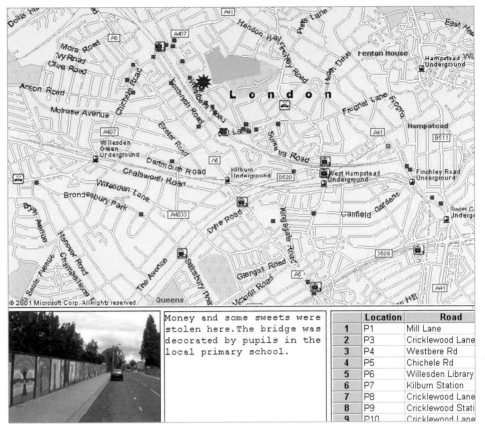

	Location	Road
1	P1	Mill Lane
2	P3	Cricklewood Lane
3	P4	Westbere Rd
4	P5	Chichele Rd
5	P6	Willesden Library
6	P7	Kilburn Station
7	P8	Cricklewood Lane
8	P9	Cricklewood Stati
9	P10	Cricklewood Lane

Money and some sweets were stolen here. The bridge was decorated by pupils in the local primary school.

Figure 2 | *The end product on a standalone computer.*

our explorations. Many geography departments are experimenting with spreadsheets to analyse statistical data, but much geographical data is also spatial, and while some spreadsheets have a mapping facility, a dedicated geographical information systems (GIS) package gives a wider range of options. Green (2001) presents a number of useful GIS case studies (for further examples see Chapters 7 and 10).

Noel Jenkins, Hampstead School, London, used *MapPoint 2000* to plot data from a spreadsheet onto a map (Figure 2). Year 9 students mapped crime data onto a map of London boroughs to display different murder rates. As it took less than half an hour to input the data and print out a map, students could spend time analysing the results. Although not genuine GIS, this product provides a useful and easily used introduction.

In addition, graphics packages can be used to manipulate photographs – perhaps to show the impact of a new supermarket on a greenfield site or to 'fast-forward' the effects of erosion on a waterfall. One trainee teacher at Arthur Mellows Village College, Peterborough, used this technique with a class to demonstrate cliff erosion on a coastal headland. Further ideas on image manipulation can be found in Taylor (2004).

Communicating geography

The attribute of provisionality is also powerful when we are helping students to develop their skills in communicating geography. It is so easy to change material produced using a word processing, GIS or graphics package that we can afford to give more emphasis to the process of planning, drafting, proof reading and presenting high quality geographical argument than we were able to do in the past (see Hassell and Taylor, 2003 for more ideas).

There are also new possibilities for developing our practice in formative feedback. Students can be asked to improve their *current* work rather than their *next* piece so that they see the role of such feedback in extending the level of their work. Some schools are experimenting with e-mailing draft work to peers or teachers for comment. For example, in a collaborative project on tourism with year 8, classes at King Edward VI Grammar School, Chelmsford, posted *PowerPoint* slides onto a bulletin board for review and online feedback as part of the development of their presentation. This use of ICT also meant that the material was available out of school hours and could be shared between geography groups (see Taylor, 2004).

Collaborative work of this kind does not need to be just within the school – many schools have experimented with e-mail links or video conferencing with schools in different localities or countries (Ashmead, 2004). Such opportunities give a real purpose and audience for the communication. In the European YoungNet project, students aged 8-14 in 50 schools made presentations online about their local area. They then read each other's presentations and used e-mail and the message board to ask each other questions about their local area; how it was similar to or different from their own. The use and manipulation of digital images has attracted the interest of many teachers. At Charles Edward Brook School in Lambeth, London, students used their skills with digital imagery software to 'clean up' digital photographs showing graffiti and litter for a brochure to encourage tourists into their local area.

Teacher planning and intervention

Whether the purpose of learning is finding, exploring or communicating geography, two aspects of the teacher's role are vital: effective medium-term planning and effective teacher interventions during the learning activity. Effective medium-term plans follow from long-term plans where careful thought has been given to progression in geographical learning, and the structured development of ICT and data-handling skills. Then, within the medium term enquiry sequence, each lesson should play its part in building the learning 'plot', so that the choice to use ICT in certain lessons is strategic – to make a purposeful contribution to this sequence. In schools where access to ICT equipment is subject to considerable timetabling constraints, this aim may be hard to realise, but we need to work towards it.

The second consideration, effective teacher intervention, reminds us to think about the quality and nature of our verbal interaction with students, particularly when teaching in a computer room. If we believe that verbal interaction with a more experienced peer or teacher is crucial for new learning to be constructed and internalised, then it is not appropriate for our normal practices of whole-class discussion and teacher-student conversations about geographical learning to disappear just because we are in a computer room. This means that sometimes we will need students to move from their workstations so that we can discuss a point of interest with them as a class. It may also mean that we need to plan whole-class or one-to-one interventions about geographical learning, not just about instructions for the use of hardware and software. The questions and discussions we use to evaluate, challenge and move on students' learning are just as important in the computer room as in a standard classroom. It is also helpful to use previously completed student work to demonstrate learning outcomes and encourage good quality work from current students.

Using ICT beyond the computer room

A DfES statistical survey indicates a 5.4:1 student:computer ratio in secondary schools and states that in England '90% of secondary schools are now connected to the internet via broadband' (Ofsted, 2004, p. 5). This gives us an idea of technology provision at that time, although such optimistic figures can mask less than ideal conditions in some schools. For example, many geography departments still have restricted access to networked rooms or clusters of computers and some do not have fast and reliable broadband internet connections. Where teachers do have access to equipment and resources there is much that can be done within the subject and suitable activities have been described by other authors (Freeman, 1997; Fisher, 2000; Hassell, 2000; Watson, 2001; Walton and Roberts, 2004).

Increasingly many geography teachers are making effective use of resources beyond the dedicated networked school computer rooms and as the technology continues to develop they are becoming more selective in the purchase and use of resources within their department.

Figure 3 | Creative ways of developing the interactive use of ICT using a single computer.

Photo: Bananastock Ltd.

Mrs Abey demonstrates map scales using a web-based mapping site (e.g. Multimap.com) on a large-scale monitor linked to a computer with internet access. A student enters the school's postcode and calls up first a 1:10,000 street map; then larger-scale maps, before reversing the process and considering different information available on each *(Cardinal Wiseman RC High School, Ealing).*

Mr Hussain borrows a school portable computer and sets up a spreadsheet for the input of his class's AS-level field data on environmental quality. In the first part of the lesson the data is input by students and saved to disc. One student then transfers it to a computer with a printer and prints off both data and graphs. Having manipulated the data quickly and effectively the students spend the bulk of the lesson analysing the printed information and drawing their conclusions *(The Green School, Hounslow).*

To introduce year 7 students to satellite images Ms Parmar has downloaded images from the school internet onto her laptop. She connects this to a portable data projector set up in the classroom and presents her lesson as an interactive quiz, explaining each image as the class examines it *(Newstead Wood School, Bromley).*

Year 10 students who are working on hydrology are first shown a computer-based Ordnance Survey image on a large screen and then images of the river both in flood and under normal conditions. All images had been collected from the internet at home and transferred onto the computer for use in the lesson *(Windsor Boys' School, Windsor).*

Introducing year 8 to the new topic, Japan, Mr Steele uses a computer with internet access and a large screen monitor to present a slide show of images of Japan. He has downloaded some images earlier to save time and in case of technology failure! However at the end of the lesson he successfully 'goes live' to a webcam ... but it's just a black image. It takes students some time to realise that what they are looking at is the Japanese countryside at night! Later images show the contrast with Tokyo's neon lights *(Denefield School, Reading).*

For whole-class teaching, a single computer linked to a data projector or interactive whiteboard and preferably with an internet connection can really help to make geography up to date, real and fun. A number of examples of how this equipment can facilitate knowledge, and concept and skill acquisition, are given in Figure 3.

Many departments now have portable computers and hand-held data-logging equipment for use in the field. Using this equipment, data can be transferred straight into spreadsheets and these can be linked to graphs that grow as data are added. The changing vegetation along a sand dune transect or the amount and type of graffiti along an urban transect can be viewed onscreen straight away, enabling students to begin their analysis while the work is in progress. Software is now available with files pre-set to enable students to operate either in the field or back in the classroom, but for most teachers their own versions will be adequate.

Another important ICT aid for use in fieldwork is the digital camera. It allows images to be manipulated and incorporated into coursework and to provide evidence of the work done on field trips which can be brought back to the classroom for all to see (see Chapters 6, 18 and 35). Maps and other images can also be retrieved from the internet and similarly incorporated (see Chapters 7 and 10). Teachers therefore need to demonstrate how such images should be manipulated and annotated. Although these skills are in many ways similar to those used with conventional photographs and maps, students working on computers often spend too much time on presentation and insufficient time on bringing out the geographical elements. Teachers must therefore emphasise the geographical aspect with students.

Research by Becta found that in England '88% of over 2000 pupils at key stage 4 have access to home computers and that 64% have internet access' (2001, p. 12). Few geography departments take account of this high level of ownership and incorporate opportunities while planning the curriculum. Teachers have been reluctant to invite students to complete homework using computers. With the relatively small amount of time students can spend at a computer within school time it makes sense for teachers to use home access for extended pieces of work. This does, of course, raise the question of equity but students without home access can be given priority access or even loaned portables for short periods of time. A growing number of departments encourage e-mailing of work and communicate to the home via bulletin boards and websites and no doubt more will do so in future.

In one project with a year 9 class, students were asked to work in pairs to produce a three-minute presentation on one aspect of globalisation. The teacher gave clear guidance about topics, research and criteria upon which the presentations would be judged. Having been told that a portable computer, projector and screen could be used for the presentations, two students spent the weekend experimenting with both the geography and *PowerPoint* to make their presentation. Other students chose to use overhead transparencies or visual artefacts. Afterwards, on their evaluation forms, the two students pointed out that their own presentation was not as good as some of those that had not used ICT and that the teacher had discussed the advantages and disadvantages of each method of presentation!

ICT to support management and assessment

The use of ICT within the geography department can facilitate communication, production and sharing of resources and monitoring students' progress. However, it is important not to add unnecessary burdens, so in developing any new initiative the department should make sure that it is responding to a real need and that the ICT is fit for its purpose. Quality and accessibility of ICT resources is also an issue; for example, there is no point in moving much departmental business onto a bulletin board if some

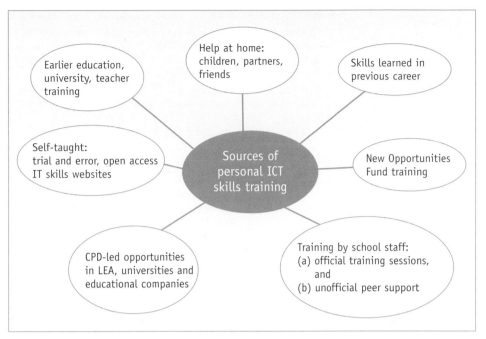

Figure 4 | *Developing your own ICT skills as a geography teacher.*

teachers have restricted access to computers.

However, where resources are good and departmental staff have a culture of ICT use, systems such as e-mail and bulletin boards can improve communication. For example, some schools involved in teacher training use e-mail to disseminate their trainees' teaching targets for the week, helping whole departments to take an active role in training. Similarly, when developing new departmental policies it is possible to circulate them electronically for comment, making use of the facility to highlight changes provided by some word processing packages. This ensures that all members of the department have a chance to comment, without generating unnecessary paperwork, and helps the originator of the document quickly to review and respond to suggestions.

Many schools now use ICT to collate and analyse student assessment data, and some staff use an electronic mark book on a daily basis (see also Chapters 32-34). The success of the latter strategy again depends on easy access in the classroom – preferably by a laptop computer. In setting up such systems it is also important to think through whether ways of transferring data to other systems in the school and to make provision for written comments, as these are often more revealing than a simple list of grades.

Teachers' professional development

Most geography teachers recognise that personal competence in ICT and using ICT with students are important for teaching and learning in their subject. Ofsted writes that the £240 million New Opportunities Fund (NOF) money spent on training teachers to use ICT in their subject areas has been 'unsatisfactory in its overall effect' and that NOF training materials have often been of 'little value' and 'failed to excite teachers' (Ofsted, 2002). However, NOF training was effective in some cases in that it became the catalyst needed to encourage teachers to develop their work with ICT; the end result is now a body of teachers willing to embrace new technology and use it as one of many tools to improve their way of working. The challenge now is to harness new skills and develop the pedagogical understanding of what ICT can do for students' learning in geography. For example, students often add images into their work but under-utilise features that enable them to annotate and enhance their work.

Anecdotal evidence gathered during school visits and work with a number of geography departments suggests that the following (see also Figure 4) have been important in improving teachers' ICT skills:

- support from friends and family; often from teenage children or partners in other jobs;
- purchase of own computer equipment, as few geography teachers have qualified for government schemes;
- peer support, particularly where the head of department has a good skill base;
- the proficiency of new teachers in encouraging and supporting others.

There is much evidence from independent research and from Ofsted secondary school reports of the wide variation in the effective use of ICT between schools, between geography teachers and between key stages (Stevenson, 1997; Watson, 2001; Ofsted, 2002). Ofsted reports that 'for all subjects the gap between the best and worst ICT provision is unacceptably wide and increasing. In the most outstanding examples, ICT is starting to have a pervasive impact on the way teachers teach and young people learn!' (2004).

Some geography teachers remain disillusioned or frustrated with using ICT. As recently trained teachers, more confident in using ICT, move into the profession, and as equipment, such as interactive whiteboards (Figure 5), become more available and reliable, the situation is improving. However there will always be new software and new ideas that require further training as well as further demands on departmental expenditure. Geography departments are likely to be fighting their corner for the foreseeable future.

It is crucial that geography departments ensure that ICT can enhance their geography curriculum by developing students' understanding of geographical concepts rather than being used simply for word processing or as a search tool. Clear strategies showing when and where ICT can be effectively used and promoted should be developed.

- A simple first step is to use the whiteboard tools to annotate a digital image (e.g. of a U-shaped valley) from within a familiar program such as a word-processing package.

- Then try using the interactive whiteboard tools to demonstrate a geography ICT exercise to your class. For example, how to calculate average stream velocity using a spreadsheet package.

- Next, get to know your interactive whiteboard's dedicated software package (use the on-screen tutorial). Experiment with tools such as spotlights or pre-set backgrounds and clipart (good for country quizzes). Use these to design an interactive lesson starter.

Figure 5 | Getting started with interactive whiteboards.

This can be achieved by building ICT into schemes of work, sharing the learning outcomes through wall displays and presentations and involving students in homework activities so that parents can see what is being achieved. It is also important for the subject leader for geography to be seen to be proactive in promoting their subject in terms of the contribution it can make to the delivery of whole-school, cross-curricular objectives for the use of ICT, and thus to the development of students' key skills in this area.

The following questions should be addressed when planning this contribution:

- What is the school ICT scheme of work? When is each ICT skill introduced to students?
- In what ways can geography make a significant contribution to the ICT curriculum so that students' geographical skills can be built on, or worked on simultaneously, alongside the development of their ICT skills?
- Is there a school policy for giving priority to students with no home computers or access to the internet, to ensure they have access to school machines so that effective homework tasks using ICT can be set?
- Where ICT skills are demonstrated through geography-related tasks, can the teacher assessment taking place in geography at key stage 3 be utilised to provide evidence for the assessment of students' ICT skills for formative and summative assessment in ICT at key stage 3?

Crucially, geography departments must ensure that they discuss how ICT will have a positive impact on teaching and learning in geography. They must be clear about what ICT does and does not bring to their work; in other words, what students learn and do not learn using ICT in geography. They must then be able to articulate this to students, parents and their own school managers.

Related publications from the Geographical Association:

- Broad, J. (2001) *A-Z Advancing Geography: Key skills*
- Donert, K. (1999) *A Geographer's Guide to the Internet*
- Fisher, T. (2002) *Theory into Practice: Webquests in geography*
- Martin, F. (2006) *e-geography* (book and CD-Rom)

References

Print

Ashmead, M. (2004) 'The Gemini project', *Teaching Geography*, 29, 3, pp. 155-7.

Becta (2002) 'ImpaCT2 – emerging findings from the evaluation of the impact of information and communications technologies on student attainment', p.12 (available online: www.becta.org.uk/impact2/ngflseries_impact2.pdf).

Dwyer, D., Ringstaff, C. and Sandholtz, J. (1990) *Teacher Beliefs and Practices, Parts 1 and 2, ACOT Report #8 and #9*. Apple Computer Inc (available online: www.apple.com/education/k12/leadership/acot/library.html).

Fisher, T. (2000) 'Developing the educational use of information and communications technology: implications for the education of geography teachers' in Fisher, C. and Binns, T. (eds) *Issues in Geography Teaching*. London: Routledge Falmer, pp. 50-67.

Fox, P. (2003) 'Putting you in the picture', *Teaching Geography*, 29, 3, pp. 128-33.

Freeman, D. (1997) 'Using information technology and new technologies in geography' in Tilbury, D. and Williams, M. (eds) *Teaching and Learning Geography*. London: Routledge Falmer, pp. 286-97.

Green, D. (2001) *GIS: A sourcebook for schools*. London: Taylor and Francis.

Hassell, D.(2000) 'Issues in ICT and geography' in Fisher, C. and Binns, T (eds) *Issues in Geography Teaching*. London: Routledge Falmer, pp. 80-93.

Hassell, D. and Taylor, L. (2002) 'Linking ICT to thinking and literacy skills', *Teaching Geography*, 27, 1, pp. 44-5.

Ofsted (2002) *ICT in Schools: The effect of government initiatives. A progress report*. London: Ofsted (available online: www.ofsted.gov.uk).

Ofsted (2004) *ICT in Schools: The effect of government initiatives*. London: Ofsted (available online: www.ofsted.gov.uk).

RM (2000) *The RM G7 (8) Report 2000: Comparing ICT provision in schools*. London: RM plc.

Roberts, M. (2003) *Learning through Enquiry: Making sense of geography in the key stage 3 classroom*. Sheffield: Geographical Association.

Stevenson, D. (ed) (1997) *The Future of Information Technology in UK Schools*. London: McKinsey and Company.

Taylor, L. (2001) *ICT in Geography*. Cambridge: Pearson Publishing.

Taylor, L. (2004) *Re-presenting Geography*. Cambridge: Chris Kington Publishing.

Walton, M. and Roberts, R. (2004) 'Creating 3D virtual landscapes from OS maps', *Teaching Geography*, 29, 3, pp. 120-3.

Watson, D. (2001) 'Information and communication technologies: researching the realities of use' in Kent, W.A. (ed) *Reflective Practice in the Teaching of Geography*. London: Chapman pp. 219-27.

Electronic

European YoungNet Project – www.youngnet.at

Implications for practice

(a) Knowing the focus of the intended geographical learning is an essential starting point when planning learning activities using ICT in geography.

Being clear about how we hope students' geographical learning will be enhanced through the use of ICT will help us to select appropriate applications of ICT to support this focus and to plan for an appropriate allocation of learning time. A useful way of thinking about the purpose of this geographical learning is to consider whether the students will be *finding, exploring* or *communicating* geography.

Using ICT expands the range of primary and secondary data available for geographical learning (*finding geography*). Identifying appropriate enquiry questions and carefully planning how students' information-handling skills will be developed are vital if data are to be used effectively to enhance geographical learning. Thorough preparation is needed if large amounts of data need to be analysed to enable students to study geographical patterns and processes (*exploring geography*) otherwise valuable learning time can be wasted on low-level tasks such as inputting data. ICT can also make a valuable contribution to the development of students' skills in *communicating* their knowledge and understanding of geography, and support formative assessment processes such as peer assessment.

(b) There are creative ways of overcoming problems with access to ICT facilities.

Linking a single computer to a data projector or interactive whiteboard can promote more interactive use of ICT with students, e.g. for collating and sharing data, interrogating images, or for a quiz. The development of digital technology provides a growing range of opportunities for more stimulating student-centred and flexible methods of data collection, particularly in geographical fieldwork. Home access to computers and to the internet is increasing among students so geography teachers can exploit the opportunities to develop a greater range of geographical enquiries, particularly more independent forms of enquiry learning.

(c) The need to use ICT effectively to enhance students' geographical learning places additional demands on geography teachers' professional learning.

Geography teachers need to continue to develop their own personal ICT skills as well as their pedagogical understanding of how ICT can be used to enhance teaching and learning in geography. Training is available from a range of sources, but often peer support and coaching can be one of the most effective forms of professional learning in this area. Reading the software reviews, practical ideas and considered viewpoints in *Teaching Geography*, is one of the best ways geography teachers can keep up to date with developments in the use of ICT in teaching and learning in geography.

Chapter 18

Planning geographical fieldwork

David Holmes and Mark Walker

Before reading this chapter consider the following questions:

- What principles lie behind the development and planning of the fieldwork provision in your school or college?
- What would an 'audit' of the fieldwork experiences in our geography courses reveal about the strengths and weaknesses in this provision?
- How do you introduce students to sampling issues and develop their understanding of how to use sampling techniques in appropriate ways?
- Are there aspects of your fieldwork provision that are looking 'tired' and would benefit from 'freshening up' with more stimulating approaches?

First-hand experiences outside the classroom are normally referred to as fieldwork studies. Fieldwork can be defined as activities that take students to learn outside the classroom, or where learning can take place via first-hand experience outside the constraints of the classroom setting.

The importance of fieldwork in geography is continually asserted, and it remains a key element of geography education at all levels of secondary education (Rynne, 1998). Indeed many teachers regard fieldwork as one of the most valuable learning experiences for students in geography and it is often the highlight of an academic programme especially when it takes the form of a residential course. These opportunities offer a highly intensive educational experience (QAA, 2000). Fieldwork is also common in the world of academic geography and there is little doubt that it provides a valuable learning experience for students in higher education (Clark, 1996). Yet the very soul of fieldwork is under pressure. Internal and external demands on the school timetable, pressure of preparation, reluctance from students to give up their time, and increased anxiety in terms of health and safety have unquestionably led to the squeezing of fieldwork. Familiar comments and questions like, 'Do we have to go?', 'How much will it cost?', or 'I am busy on that weekend' always seem to accompany the out-of-classroom experience.

Fieldwork is central to the ethos, culture and pedagogy of geography. This chapter aims to give geography teachers some support in planning successful fieldwork experiences for students. It presents a variety of ideas and approaches for improving the quality of school fieldwork, together with practical advice on how to integrate fieldwork within a whole scheme of work. Figure 1 shows a model for planning fieldwork experiences. We will draw upon this rich seam of approaches (qualitative, quantitative, creative and exploratory) and provide inspiration for some fresh strategies to invigorate and add value to this vital aspect of geography.

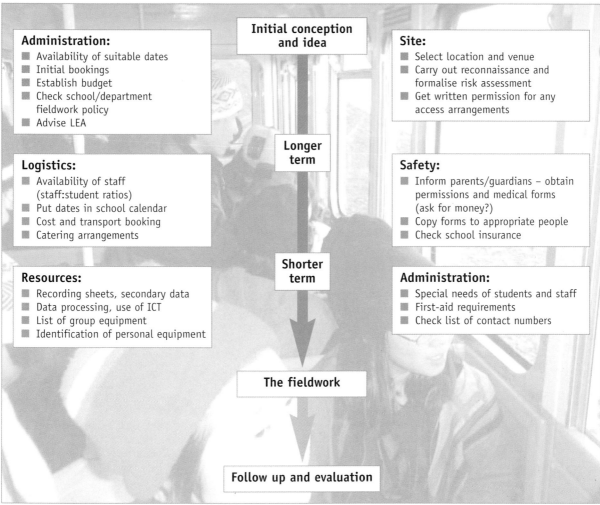

Figure 1 | *Planning the out-of-classroom activities – some considerations. Photo: ©David Holmes.*

The diagram in Figure 1 contains the following boxes:

Central flow (top to bottom): **Initial conception and idea** → **Longer term** → **Shorter term** → **The fieldwork** → **Follow up and evaluation**

Administration:
- Availability of suitable dates
- Initial bookings
- Establish budget
- Check school/department fieldwork policy
- Advise LEA

Site:
- Select location and venue
- Carry out reconnaissance and formalise risk assessment
- Get written permission for any access arrangements

Logistics:
- Availability of staff (staff:student ratios)
- Put dates in school calendar
- Cost and transport booking
- Catering arrangements

Safety:
- Inform parents/guardians – obtain permissions and medical forms (ask for money?)
- Copy forms to appropriate people
- Check school insurance

Resources:
- Recording sheets, secondary data
- Data processing, use of ICT
- List of group equipment
- Identification of personal equipment

Administration:
- Special needs of students and staff
- First-aid requirements
- Check list of contact numbers

Planning fieldwork (including 'fieldwork audits')

The planning, delivery and administration of any out-of-classroom activity can be a daunting task. If fieldwork is being started from scratch, then there are certain key ideas to consider (see Figure 1).

Often the use of a checklist to document activities will be necessary. In this way the planning processes can be approached in a logical order and the main tasks given priority. Figure 2 shows an extract from such a checklist.

More usually, however, the starting point for the fieldwork activity is the provision and implementation of an internal field-course audit. This will refocus attention on the logistics and learning outcomes, as well as providing support and background information for any new members of department staff.

A logical start point is the evaluation of existing fieldwork:

1. When do you go? (reasons for this)
2. Where? (reasons, including resource investment)
3. What type of fieldwork? (reasons for this)
4. Residential or day trips? (self-led versus buying in from a fieldwork provider)

The organisational and planning procedures for an out-of-classroom visit	People responsible	Task completed
1. Area identified for visits and suggestions for site visits		
2. Discussions with colleagues and year leaders/co-ordinators on feasibility. Potential/need identified		
3. Availability of secondary data and site information/context		
4. Preliminary visit – made by group leader(s), teachers, adult helpers, etc.		
5. Details of: ■ Parking availability and restrictions ■ Access rights and site services, e.g. toilets ■ Safety regulations in place and recommendations ■ Wet weather facilities/shelter ■ Eating provision and locations ■ Availability of first aid ■ Nearest land-line/mobile phone reception		
6. Educational aims, objectives and outcomes Attainment targets identified		
7. Briefing and discussion with adult participants Explanation of task, behaviour of students and philosophy		

Figure 2 | *Extract from guidance for organisation (planning checklist).*

There are a number of factors which may force change within the existing fieldwork framework, i.e. the demands of a new specification, change in school off-site policy, diminishing motivation of students, reluctance of staff to give up time within certain periods of the school year. It may also be an opportunity to consider whether there are advantages to 'buying-in' (i.e. using centre-based provision) or 'going it alone' (i.e. leading your own fieldwork) (Figure 3).

Risk assessment

The formalisation of any out-of-classroom activity requires a detailed and documented risk assessment to be undertaken. Remember that fieldwork is generally a very safe activity, but any out-of-classroom activity carries some element of danger or risk. The function of risk assessment is to anticipate, minimise and manage possible risks, both for the group leaders and throughout the fieldwork. Initial site assessments and appraisals must be carried out in an advance recce; any costs incurred, e.g. travel expenses, can be legitimately added to the total price that students will pay. In making a risk assessment, a list should be drawn up under the following headings:
■ Potential risks to those taking part
■ Points of contact (land-lines, shops, residential properties, etc.)
■ What will happen in an emergency?

Risk assessment will need to take account of:
■ Hazards particular to the location (i.e. urban versus rural)
■ Weather conditions likely to be encountered
■ The age and experience of the group and its leaders
■ Students with special needs (e.g. mobility impairment, asthma, visual impairment)
(adapted from Bland *et al.*, 1996).

Type of course	Advantages	Disadvantages
Teacher-led (school-based)	■ Fieldwork focus on specific school and students' needs ■ Tends to be cheaper ■ Leaders have a good understanding of students' ability and have already established a relationship ■ Allows progressive building of support during lessons ■ Resources can be re-used on subsequent trips and during normal school contact time	■ Administration, preparation and logistics are potentially complex and time consuming ■ Appropriate staff:student ratios may be problematic during a busy school year ■ Leaders may be unaware of risks in unusual fieldwork context ■ Fatigue due to teaching, driving and supervision ■ Lack of range and number of fieldwork resources available in school
Provider (centre-based)	■ Can be delivered as an intense, focused, compact and self-contained course; tutors are local 'experts' ■ The unfamiliar learning environment may stimulate student learning and participation ■ Access to secondary data, resources and case study material ■ Reduction in teacher stress (safety and logistics handled externally) ■ Visiting staff primarily take on a supporting/supervisory role; opportunity to observe students at work	■ Sometimes prohibitive cost (both in terms of course and travel) ■ Fieldwork days can be over-used causing sterile teaching ■ Poor tutoring can result in crucial 'missed opportunities' for attending students ■ Lack of control over course structure ■ Alien environment may act as a barrier to effective learning ■ Frequent lack of post-fieldwork support

Figure 3 | Pros and cons of teacher-led (school-based) versus provider-based fieldwork courses.

It is almost certain that all schools and their respective departments have systems and procedures in place for the assessment and documentation of risks. Advice can also be sought from LA Advisors, particularly for any activities which may be regarded as especially hazardous such as canoeing and abseiling. Figure 4 shows a risk assessment for a walk in the Berwyn Mountains, North Wales.

Once the audit of current provision has been carried out, attention can be given to the mechanisms that may be enhance the fieldwork experience:

1. How will the fieldwork experiences and outcomes be used after the trip – e.g. group findings and research, case studies, basis for issues analysis?
2. How will other useful skills be developed through the fieldwork, e.g. working in groups, problem solving, use of numbers, ICT?
3. What resources need to be provided to support the fieldwork, e.g. quality measuring equipment, laptop, digital camera, video equipment? The library (or school intranet) with access to selected secondary data and extracts from past projects can also be developed to support the fieldwork activity and analysis of its outcomes.

Increasing pressures on school fieldwork mean that it has to represent good value. That is good value not only for the students, but also for staff, colleagues and parents/guardians. With this in mind fieldwork audits should be viewed not as a luxury but as a necessity, to maintain standards, motivation and interest in the subject from all concerned.

Geography field study: risk assessment

Approach	Description	
Nature of activity	Guided walk to Llyn Lluncaws, Berwyn Mountains, North Wales	
Location	Tan-y-Pistyll/Pistyll Rhaeadr car park SJ073295 (OS Landranger Sheet 125)	
Date of assessment	November 2002	**Assessment led by** David Holmes

What are the hazards?

1. Fast-flowing stream close to footpath
2. Slippery nature of boulders on and adjacent to footpath, especially near waterfall at start of walk
3. Steep and slippery grass banks and slopes
4. Weather conditions can change rapidly – risk of hypothermia and/or sunburn
5. Exposed location at altitude (up to 600m)
6. Boggy conditions off the footpath, particularly in the upper stretches of the walk
7. Loose rocks on walls
8. Old walls can present a risk in terms of their stability

Who might be affected by them?

■ Any member of the party could be affected by the above hazards

What safety measures need to be in place to manage the risks?

■ All group leaders and accompanying staff should be briefed and aware of hazards

■ A detailed weather report will be sought immediately prior to the visit

■ All members of the party will be verbally warned of potential hazards during the visit; students will be shown the risk assessment prior to the visit

■ Regular assessment of the weather conditions will be made by the group leader

■ At least one adult in the group will be a qualified first-aider (and have with them a suitable first-aid kit)

■ Headteacher and school secretary informed of route, nature of visit and timings

■ The group leader will check that the land-line at Tan-y-Pistyll is working

Can the group leader put all the safety measure in place?

■ All can be put in place, with assistance from accompanying staff

What steps will be taken in an emergency?

■ The situation will be assessed, all members of the group made safe and first aid administered if required

■ Appropriate emergency services/support will be contacted by phone and assistance sought

■ A member of staff will return to the car park (Tan-y-Pistyll) to relay advice to the emergency services; other staff will stay with rest of the group

■ The rest of the group will return to the car park at the earliest possible time

■ Senior staff at the school will be notified – this will allow any documentation regarding the incident to be completed

Figure 4 | Risk assessment for a walk in the Berwyn Mountains, North Wales. Framework recommended by Shropshire County Council.

Getting back to basics – sampling

Sampling issues need to feature in any discussion about fieldwork. Rigorous and effective sampling lies at the heart of successful fieldwork activities. Without a reliable sample, the conclusions drawn can be worthless and certainly incomplete. This applies as much to the collection of dust particles around a hard-rock quarry, as to the identification of visitor 'hot-spots' at a local beach.

A sample is a small part or fragment of a whole and is taken to represent what the whole picture is really like. Sampling is an accepted short-cut where there is simply not enough time, energy, money or equipment to record every element in a population. Figure 5 suggests as possible 'route' for planning sampling procedures.

Once the study area has been defined, a decision is needed regarding the specific type of sampling. An awareness of this is critical, as the value and quality of data collected is directly dependent on the selection of an appropriate sampling technique.

Figure 6 provides an alternative way of approaching the selection of an appropriate sampling strategy. For GCE A-level students it is also a popular line of assessment within the simulated fieldwork examinations. Recent questions have included:

■ 'Describe and justify the sampling technique used to collect one type of primary data'
■ 'Describe an appropriate sampling procedure that could be used to collect data'
■ 'Identify the primary data you would collect and explain the sampling procedures you would use'

So sampling can be both complex and time consuming – yet for so many fieldwork investigations it remains central to the value of the outcomes. Teaching about sampling is never easy but success can be achieved if different approaches to sampling are exemplified through a range of investigations of different environments. Some practitioners have even developed their own sampling 'game'.

New ideas for old hands

Given the pressures from other subject areas, fieldwork can present a daunting prospect for many students. When asked to develop their own fieldwork investigation, students often ask 'What project can I do which is original?'. The reality is that there is very little that can be achieved at school level which is genuinely original. However that should not stop practitioners thinking about fieldwork which is re-worked, has a fresher flavour and is more imaginative, in other words, the development of fieldwork which is both imaginative and fit for purpose.

Strategies for freshening up fieldwork

■ Use familiar and popular themes but get the students to think of ways in which they can personally inject something individual, lively and even thoughtful. This can be approached using a photo-stimulus activity (see Figure 7).
■ Collect 'standard' data as a group activity, for example in an urban area, and then ask the students to refocus group ideas into a more individual route to enquiry. This is very much along the lines of the 'discovery' fieldwork methodology with a 'heuristic student-centred' approach, where the teacher acts as guide for the students (see Figure 8).

STEP 5: Decide on the support and equipment that will be required. Allow the students to get to know how the equipment works (together with its limitations) before it is used. Also decide if a pilot survey is appropriate.

STEP 4: Decide on repeat sampling at some or all of the survey points, if appropriate. This allows for temporal variation, e.g. vehicle counts at several different times of the day/week from the same location.

STEP 3: Decide upon the sample size (or number of sampling points) and express this as a sampling percentage if possible, e.g. a blood donor weighing 10 stone will have about 10 pints of blood in their body – 1 pint = a 10% sample.

STEP 2: Decide on your sampling strategy: point, line or area sampling on a random, systematic or stratified basis. This allows for spatial variation.

STEP 1: Define the study area and delimit it on a base map, *e.g. a town centre, a rural parish, a beach, a woodland, an upland area above 400m, a sub-catchment of a stream*. Note that some study areas are far easier to delimit than others. Get the students to justify their defined study area. It may be appropriate to grid the study area, to allow easy reference and for the use of random numbers.

Figure 5 | *Recommended route to sampling. Source: Holmes and Farbrother, 2000.*

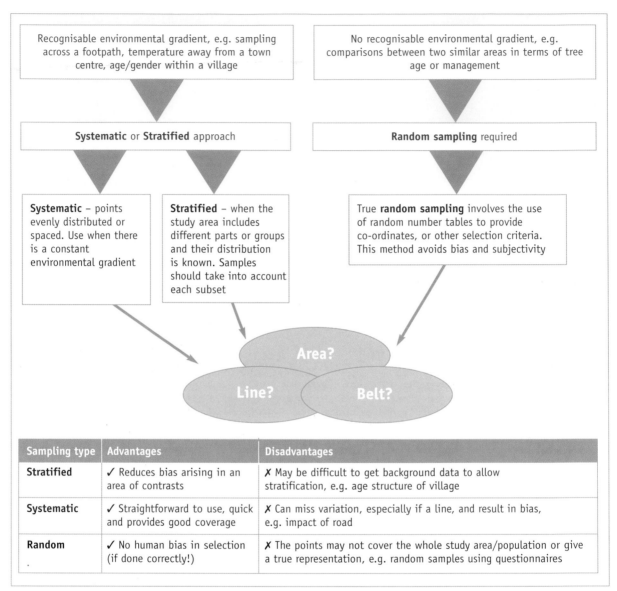

Sampling type	Advantages	Disadvantages
Stratified	✓ Reduces bias arising in an area of contrasts	✗ May be difficult to get background data to allow stratification, e.g. age structure of village
Systematic	✓ Straightforward to use, quick and provides good coverage	✗ Can miss variation, especially if a line, and result in bias, e.g. impact of road
Random	✓ No human bias in selection (if done correctly!)	✗ The points may not cover the whole study area/population or give a true representation, e.g. random samples using questionnaires

Figure 6 | *Different types of sampling strategy or frame. Adapted from: Fletcher, 1997.*

■ Generate imaginative enquiry titles that are small-scale and manageable. This often means that new ideas will come to light, even in a relatively localised environment. Many can be based on more topical issues such as citizenship and sustainability. Here is a list of some ideas that have been used successfully:

- ■ To investigate the effectiveness of a turf roof at reducing storm-runoff
- ■ An assessment of three alternative sites for the relocation of football ground X
- ■ A study of the distribution and usage patterns of allotments in town X
- ■ Production of a soil-risk map and management plan for farm X
- ■ To what extent does town X provide access for disabled visitors?
- ■ How important are mental maps for navigating round shopping centre X?
- ■ Has bus deregulation in village X improved the quality of access and service?
- ■ An assessment of playground provision and usage in wards X and Y

High-density tower blocks offer a lower standard of living compared with single-storey accommodation

Develop a management plan to improve the architecture

Work out the sphere of influence of shoppers, and nature of journey, i.e. shopping or visiting

Traffic counts to establish the peak flows and traffic hot-spots

The incorporation of a bus lane improves access and reduces journey time to the town centre

An identification of factors which would allow delimitation of the CBD

Zone of urban land use, showing some retail, residential and transport functions. At the time the photograph was taken there were relatively low traffic flows and low pedestrian densities, suggesting the image was taken either away from the core CBD area, or at a time (e.g. early morning) when there were few people around. The residential dwellings are typical of 1960s upwards build (tower blocks) enabling high density housing in areas of high bid-rent. Nowadays, this type of accommodation is often viewed as less desirable and is sometimes associated with a higher than average incidence of crime. The retail outlets look to be of a similar age, perhaps 1970, with a typical mix of concrete and blockwork giving a utilitarian landscape. There is evidence of modernisation in the scene with the addition of flags and other coloured steelwork, together with more recent facia boards.

Figure 7 | Using photographs as a stimulus for generating ideas, issues and connections with an environment. Comments were supplied by a group of year 11 students. The panel shows the written commentary that was also developed as a group activity.

- Developing an index of 'burglarability' – how does it relate to perceived fear of crime?
- Exploring the feasibility and potential impact of wind power generation in community X
- An assessment of the reliability of qualitative and quantitative techniques for the determination of air pollution along transect X
- A study of the need for (and people's attitudes towards) recycling in community X
- A management strategy outlining the development and need for energy conservation measures in school X
- Why does beach X have Blue Flag status and beach Y not?
- Investigating the impact and significance of air pollution on people's health in an area

Being creative with fieldwork

These days fieldwork is mostly 'product orientated', that is the purpose and process of the fieldwork activity are driven by the need to achieve a particular outcome. This usually takes the form of a piece of written work, or for post-16 students it may mean a simulated fieldwork experience which is examined. Sometimes this leads to the

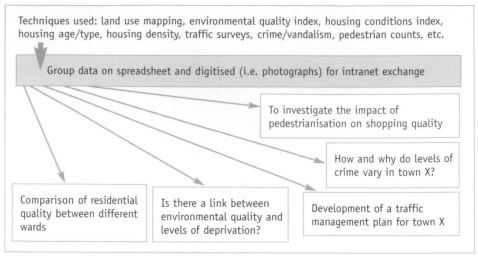

Figure 8 | *What to do with the standard 'urban fieldwork' day.*

suffocation of originality and a reluctance to allow fieldwork which is more student-centred and less product-based.

However, if you are prepared to be bold, and willing to use fieldwork more as a tool to enrich learning, then there are some significant advantages. First, the logistics of fieldwork become more manageable as the drive to collect data becomes less significant when the real purpose of the fieldwork is to establish a connection to and appreciation of the environment and its role within the community. Second, students who are involved in more open-ended enquiry-based learning tend to be more positive about the experience – this is particularly useful for motivation (Chapter 9). A third advantage is that the outcomes of such an experience can be diverse, imaginative and often insightful. Ideas that are worth trying include (see also Chapter 6):

- **Geographers as artisans:** Design a fieldwork activity which appeals to students who have strong artistic and visual tendencies. Take a physical geography theme and incorporate creative responses to the environmental processes. This might involve ideas using poetry, drama, sculpture, song or dance.

- **Making connections – linking local to global:** A fieldwork experience which explores interconnections between people and places at a range of scales. For instance, collect a series of images to illustrate how the area studied links with other parts of the world. What are the implications of such linkages and how do they influence other people's quality of life?

- **Web-designers:** Use a web storyboard as a mechanism for learning about a place. Encourage students to carry out internet research to construct a virtual field course that could be used prior to the real excursion. How would they design navigation around their site? What would people like to know? This activity will engage and connect the students to the location while forming an important part of the pre-course preparation.

- **Tricky trails:** Ask the students to design two short trails around a local town. The first is a route which shows the best elements, high quality of life, best sights, etc. The other trail is an 'eyesore' route, which takes in the worst parts. Explore how the use of photographs and captions could illustrate these contrasts in such a small geographical area. This activity could be extended to introduce the more complex idea of bias and selectivity – how do these affect our views about both people and landscapes.

Progressing fieldwork

When framing a departmental fieldwork policy, a key consideration must be the provision of opportunities for students to progress in relation to:

- Skills and techniques utilised
- The nature and difficulty of the tasks involved
- The degree of supervision (and the mode of delivery, i.e. teacher-led versus student-centered)
- Place and theme of studies undertaken
- Context of ideas and conceptual difficulty

(adapted from Bland *et al.*, 1996).

In terms of building progression between phases and year groups, it might be expected that older students will use more sophisticated methods of collecting data, and collect data from a larger spatial area. It might also be expected that they will be able to demonstrate a greater range of skills in the reporting back of such data, and need less support in the analysis and interpretation of their findings.

Figure 9 shows an approach to developing progression in fieldwork using one environmental theme. This approach was developed by PGCE student teachers during a training event at Flatford Mill field centre in Suffolk. It could be further developed to include a more detailed section on observations, analysis and interpretation, such as that outlined in Figure 10.

Progression is not only important for the reasons outlined above, it is also vital to maintain motivation as students progress from one year group to the next. Imagine that the students undertake an investigation of a river in year 8. If they then use river environments for their GCSE coursework, and also for AS/A2, without carefully planning in terms of differentiated activities and learning outcomes, there are unlikely to be any significant learning gains for the students and they could feel that the experience is just the same. 'We have done rivers before', would be the most likley outcome from a departmental strategy that has not addressed progression in its fieldwork provision.

ICT and fieldwork

There is growing use of ICT in schools and universities to enhance geographical fieldwork. Web-based enquiries for instance are now a common feature in many geography courses, with the internet providing an ideal storage solution facilitating resource-rich information delivery and exchange. ICT can support fieldwork in a number of ways, including:

- Development of spreadsheets to process data (see Figure 11).
- Use of the internet to obtain secondary data to support a range of enquiries – there are now many opportunities to use online digital resources to enable students to make the most of field courses.
- E-mail 'experts' in cyberspace to ask them a specific question.
- Use digital and electronic monitoring equipment to help in the data collection process.
- Use digital projectors to show photographs and site information before and after the field visit.

One of the most exciting and imaginative ICT developments that has relevance for the future of fieldwork experiences is the virtual field course. So far there has been relatively little research into the ways that fieldwork investigations can use digital technologies to enhance students' learning (Taylor, 2005). Some teachers may struggle to integrate 'cyberspace' into their classroom environments through such trips of discovery. Perhaps

	Key stage 3	Key stage 4	Post-16
Preparation	Conduct virtual fieldwork prior to visit, e.g. support with photographs of location, basic sketch map, fact cards about green energy sources	Provide 1:10,000 OS map of study areas. ICT investigations by students on the nature and purpose of the field centre at Flatford. Newspaper articles about green energy	Range of map scales and land use maps to contextualise area. Recent reports/articles which show the government's attitude towards green issues
Fieldwork:			
Content	Basic terminology, e.g. renewable and recycling. Location of Flatford (set scene). Discuss processes involved in basic assessment of environmental impact	Idea of site and situation (using data to support ideas). More detailed examination of the processes involved with environmetal impact and waste. Table to outline advantages and disadvantages of these	Role of Rio 1992 and local to global links (e.g. LA21). Rights and responsibilities of individuals, importance of communities. Suggest mechanisms for carrying out an energy and waste audit
Key questions	■ What is a green energy source? ■ Why do we want green energy sources?	■ What is sustainability? ■ What is an ecological footprint? ■ How do we begin to assess an ecological footprint?	■ An assessment of the methods to quantify energy use ■ Government policy towards waste disposal and energy production and use ■ How can energy use and waste disposal be better managed?
Activities	Basic energy-use questionnaire to a limited number of people. Assessment of the pros and cons of hydro-electric power (HEP). Field sketch based on pre-drawn template. Recording with photographs	Energy audit of the centre (individual rooms) to calculate energy usage. Recce of site to identify possible locations for alternative energy systems, e.g. hydro-electric power (HEP), wind farm. Use of photographs to support ideas	Selection of suitable site for HEP (following evaluation of other options). Calculation of discharge and energy potential; or examination of the sites potential for wind energy – site selection, etc.
Outcomes:			
Skills and follow-up	Processing of questionnaire data – simple graphs to represent views. Use of photographs to produce group presentations (ICT/*PowerPoint*) about the green possibilities at Flatford Mill	Coloured base maps showing energy use hot-spots. Annotated photographs showing reasons for choices. Design a noticeboard display about sustainability to inform visitors. Produce a simple plan (in groups) so that energy can be minimised from hot-spots and waste managed	Mapping, analysis of past questionnaire data. Use river flow data to calculate output per year. Develop a management plan to reduce the ecological footprint of Flatford Mill; strategies for informing visitors about green issues (leaflets). Potential for the development of an issues analysis exercise
Links	Citizenship, role of community, sustainability, globalisation (local versus global), ecological stewardship; also ICT, number and writing		

Figure 9 | *Progression in an investigation of the 'ecological footprint' found at Flatford Mill Field Study Centre.*

developing an electronic field trip for use in the classroom should form part of a geography teacher's professional development to advance the use of this technology? Virtual fieldwork has its roots in the ideal of providing a variety of resources about local, regional and more distant places through background information, photographs, virtual tours, clickable maps, activities and tests (see Figure 12 for example). There is likely to be an increasing number of examples of such virtual fieldwork resources in the coming years.

Basic ◄──────────────────────────────────────► Complex	
Observations:	
■ Small number of descriptive terms, e.g. big/small and high/low ■ Qualitative assessments, e.g. basic justification ■ Simple instrumentation, e.g. ruler, tape	■ Larger number of differentiated terms, e.g noisy, deserted, active, peaceful ■ Qualitative and quantitative assessments, including basic number manipulation ■ Range of more sophisticated instrumentation, e.g. clinometer, digital thermometer
Presentation, analysis and interpretation:	
■ Dominance of bar charts and pie charts (not always appropriate or applicable to the data collected) ■ Limited understanding of averages and basic comparisons only ■ Simplistic data analysis, e.g. good/bad and high/low; mostly descriptive ■ Limitations are restricted to equipment and operator errors	■ Greater range and breadth of techniques, e.g. scattergraphs, histograms, which are used *appropriately* ■ More complex analysis, including measures of central tendancy and dispersion; also the use of statistics to inform decisions ■ Recognition that results may be only partial or tentative, based on the limited data collection programme

Figure 10 | *Examples of more detailed observations, analysis and interpretation during fieldwork.*

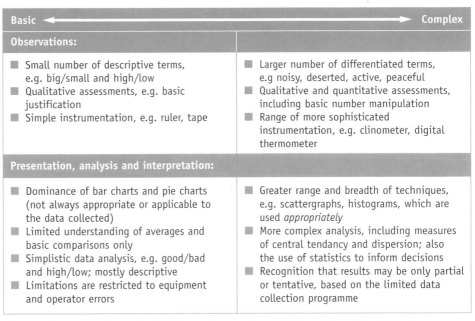

All the other cells in the workbook are locked and protected. This prevents students from tampering with the spreadsheet and it can only be unlocked with a password. Cells are protected under the 'Format' menu. If the protection check box remains un-checked for a particular cell then data can be written into it.

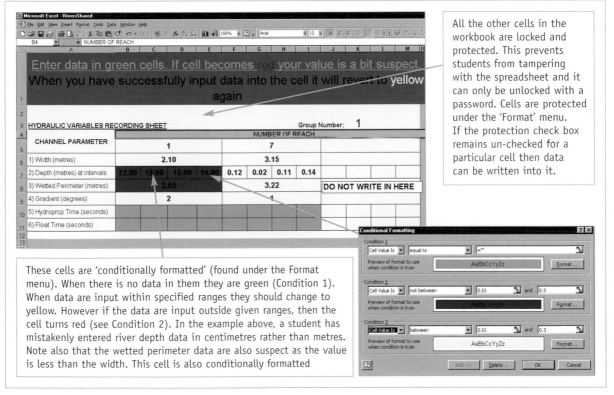

These cells are 'conditionally formatted' (found under the Format menu). When there is no data in them they are green (Condition 1). When data are input within specified ranges they should change to yellow. However if the data are input outside given ranges, then the cell turns red (see Condition 2). In the example above, a student has mistakenly entered river depth data in centimetres rather than metres. Note also that the wetted perimeter data are also suspect as the value is less than the width. This cell is also conditionally formatted

Figure 11 | *Activating the conditional formatting command within Excel and using cell protection.*

Figure 12 | *A virtual field course at Cwm Idwal, North Wales. Note: the red dots indicate clickable hotspots. Source: Virtual Montana website.*

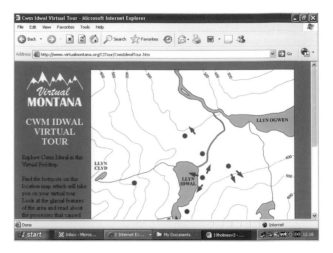

These tags indicate that the 'Autofilter' has been activated (go to Data, then Filter and select 'Autofilter')

This is a large spreadsheet of 8444 records (the whole of England and Wales down to ward level)

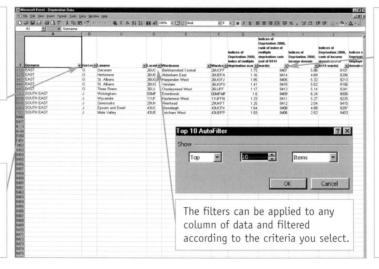

The filters can be applied to any column of data and filtered according to the criteria you select.

This tag is active (it has changed to blue). Do this by simply clicking on it. You are then presented with a series of options to select specific data in rows. In this instance the 10 least deprived wards have been selected. Simply select the top 10. The spreadsheet will then instantly filter the top 10 items in this column.

Using Census data in support of fieldwork activities:

■ **Quality of life index**

Secondary Census data can be combined with primary data (housing conditions, house prices, incidence of burglar alarms, size of gardens, availability of open space, etc.) to develop a quality of life index based also on primary research.

■ **Distribution of housing tenure and ethnicity**

A research-based enquiry which maps the spatial distribution and concentration of particular groups of people, e.g. single parents, the elderly. Are there any links to housing tenure type or age?

■ **Crime and criminal activity**

Mapping and accounting for the deprivation/affluence in two comparative urban wards. This can be linked to primary research on the incidence of graffiti and vandalism and street quality. It might also be feasible to link these data with health statistics and school catchment areas.

■ **Morbidity and mortality**

Surveys examining the geography of health. A comparison of two wards or enumeration districts, looking at income/employment levels and health statistics.

■ **Consumer surveys**

Linking postcodes and Census data to see whether there are any patterns in where people come from (socio-economic background) and their shopping preferences/habits.

Figure 13 | *Using Excel to filter deprivation data. (Note: this data can be downloaded free from the UK neighbourhood statistics website).*

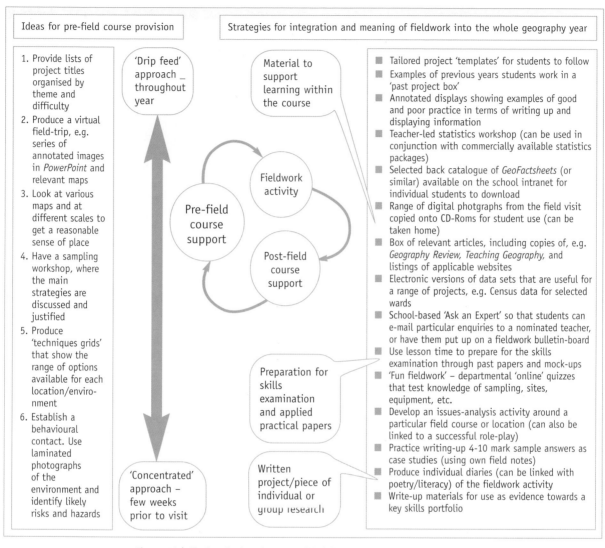

Figure 14 | *Closing the loop in geographical fieldwork.*

As fieldwork is a resource-expensive feature of the school year, making the best use of the time in the field is critical. Virtual fieldwork can support this by increasing the amount of effective preparation and follow-up time available. Virtual fieldwork should also provide more interactive learning opportunities for students in the future by facilitating participation, exploration, analysis and the learning and testing of skills.

ICT can also be an invaluable tool for enhancing data presentation and the rapid processing of group data. Figure 13, for example, shows how 'filters' can be applied to a large *Excel* spreadsheet. In this instance the data become more manageable once the 'Autofilter' sequence is applied to selected columns. Spreadsheets can also be utilised to aid data entry. The 'sharing' facility in *Excel*, for example, allows for multiple access and for students to 'write-to' the same spreadsheet. This is a useful tool, supporting the rapid entry of data via a suite of networked machines.

Developing the whole package: pre- and post-fieldwork support

The notion of 'closing the loop' is an important consideration in any fieldwork activity. Rather than the out-of-classroom activity being seen as an isolated, one-off 'day out', it needs to fit into the wider scheme of work in a geography course. In this way students are better prepared for the field visit (they have expectations of what is required from them, an idea of place and of the resources they will be presented with to undertake and complete the task). The post-fieldwork support will be determined by the learning outcomes required from the course, i.e. coursework/project, skills for an examination's practical paper, or the desire to build on theories and ideas developed in the classroom. Figure 14 provides practical strategies for 'closing the loop' and thereby maximising the learning outcomes from geographical fieldwork.

Related publications from the Geographical Association:
- GA/FSC (2005) *Managing Safe, Successful Fieldwork.*
- Holmes, D. and Farbrother, D. (2000) (see below)
- Job, D., Day, C. and Smyth, T. (1999) *Beyond the Bikesheds: Fresh approaches to fieldwork in the school locality.*

References

Print

Bland, K., Chambers, B., Donert, K. and Thomas, T. (1996) 'Fieldwork' in Bailey, P. and Fox, P. (eds) *Geography Teachers' Handbook.* Sheffield: Geographical Association, pp. 165-75.

Clark, D. (1996) 'The changing national context of fieldwork in geography', *Journal of Geography in Higher Education*, 20, pp. 385-91.

Fletcher, T. (1997) 'Practical geography', *Geography Review*, 10, 5, pp. 7-9.

Holmes, D. and Farbrother, D. (2000) *A-Z Advancing Geography: Fieldwork.* Sheffield: Geographical Association

QAA (Quality Assurance Agency) (2000) *Benchmark Statement for Geography.* Gloucester: QAA (available as a download from: http://www.qaa.ac.uk/benchmark/geography.pdf).

Rynne, E. (1998) 'Utilitairian approaches to fieldwork', *Geography*, 83, 3, pp. 205-13.

Electronic

Virtual Montana – www.virtualmontana.org/virtualmontana/ and www.virtualmontana.org/CITour/CwmIdwalTour.htm

UK neighbourhood statistics – www.neighbourhood.statistics.gov.uk/Statistics_By_Subject.asp

Implications for practice

(a) **Geographical fieldwork provides students with experiences that are intrinsically valuable, but detailed planning can ensure they maximise the wide-ranging educational benefits from such activities.**

The planning and preparation of fieldwork experiences needs to be of the highest standard possible, not least to ensure that teachers' legal responsibilities and obligations, particularly in relation to health and safety, are met. The Geographical Association and the Field Studies' Council provide guidelines for geographical work outside the classroom based on current good practice. School or college and local education authority policies must be followed rigorously. Rather than becoming a burden, this should be viewed as an enabling process giving teachers confidence in the standards of their fieldwork provision. Fieldwork audits are an essential element of this planning process giving attention to the full range of issues including administration, organisation, resourcing, fieldwork styles and strategies, the desired learning outcomes and how these will be utilised to enhance students' learning through geography.

(b) **Effective sampling is crucial to the success of fieldwork investigations.**

Students need to be introduced to sampling issues as a key element of any fieldwork investigation so that they can develop their understanding of how to apply appropriate techniques and of the importance of such techniques in determining the reliability of fieldwork outcomes. This can be done in a practical way by devising fieldwork activities that enable students to apply and then evaluate the use of different sampling techniques for collecting data. It can also be achieved by making explicit the sampling techniques being used for particular investigations and the reasons for their selection. Another approach is to use classroom-based activities where students have to apply their understanding of different sampling strategies to fieldwork situations presented in images or even simple games. In each case, it is important to ask students to explain their evaluation and justify their selection of these techniques.

(c) **Trying out some more imaginative approaches and strategies can produce more stimulating fieldwork experiences for students, thereby improving their levels of motivation as well as enhancing the learning gains.**

It is possible to freshen up the fieldwork experience by looking for more stimulating geographical ideas and issues to investigate. Alternatively, similar themes, such as land use, environmental quality and impacts of recreational activity can be investigated using more creative techniques. This could be achieved by harnessing the use of new technologies (e.g. digital still and video cameras, environmental sensors). One of the benefits of using such technology is that it can put the student at the centre of the fieldwork experience giving them more autonomy over the selection of data to be collected as well as helping them to project the sense they make of the places and issues being investigated.

ICT can enhance data processing and support the analysis of data collected through fieldwork. Finding creative ways of using the outcomes from fieldwork can also provide stimulating learning experiences as well as enabling students to utilise and develop a greater range of skills.

Chapter 19

Media Literacy and geographical imaginations

Chris Durbin

Before reading this chapter consider the following questions:

- Do you think school geography is concerned mainly with teaching the 'authorised facts' (the given, the official, codified in official documents and textbooks) or should geography be engaged with what has been called 'unauthorised knowledges' (the personal, the unofficial, informal, local, diverse)?

- School geography is often perceived to be concerned mainly with the mimetic representation of the world ... describing the world accurately 'as it is'. Do you think this is possible?

- Is school geography in fact a particularly interesting branch of media studies?

Is geography only the study of the world around us? Or is it better described as the study of the way people perceive the world around them? The geographies that people experience are developed from thoughts about the places they encounter. While each person demonstrates preferences towards the environment in which they live; it has been shaped by the experience of family and community. The media they experience also determines their geography. This chapter discusses how, in our global information society, thoughts, attitudes and values are shaped by the values that are spread throughout the media and how geography teachers can make use of these sources in exploring and developing students' geographical imaginations.

What shapes our views of the world?

When young people study geography they are in fact studying many geographies – of rich and poor, young and old, rural and urban, and so on. They are also studying the world as it is perceived and experienced – both by themselves directly, and indirectly through various media. Thoughts, attitudes and values do not develop in isolation. In the modern world they are shaped and profoundly influenced by the images and messages we receive from the media. This is why media literacy is such an important part of geographical education and why, as geography teachers, we must ensure that our students are fully aware of these influences, and can examine them critically.

It could be assumed that as young people have become more and more 'connected' to the world around them, through mobile communications, the media, travel and so on, that their experience and understanding of the world must have increased. Running

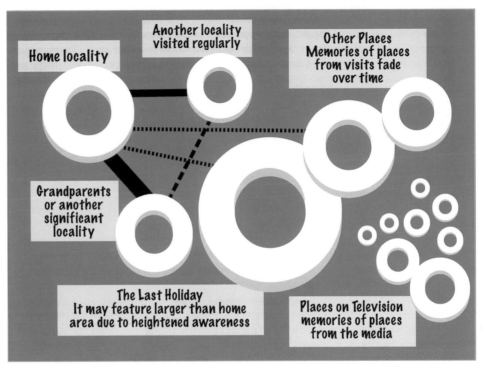

Figure 1 | *A model of a key stage 2 pupil's experience of the world.*

counter to this, however, is the increasing constraint on direct experience of the environment around us. Not only are young people increasingly experiencing the world in a 'virtual', constructed way, they are also increasingly constrained from exploring their own and wider environments independently.

Much research has been done with regard to the latter (Spencer, 1995; Holloway and Valentine, 2000); namely that children up to the age of 11 have far less direct experience of their own locality than was the case 20-30 years ago. We know from research that children are now less likely to walk alone, or to play and roam in their local streets. This is in part due to (adult) fears about safety, relating to crime and increased traffic, and in part to changing trends such as the increasingly institutionalised nature of leisure (clubs and classes, etc.), and the wider availability of electronic entertainment (hyper/virtual reality).

Indirect experience of the wider world, once confined to books, radio, pictures and conversations with other people, is now available through the internet, and as media companies are now able to reach places once thought of as 'remote', so we can 'virtually experience' environments and ways of life that were previously unknown. Even our direct experience of distant places is manipulated and filtered to a greater or lesser degree – consider theme parks, usually detached from the local environment, and tourist resorts.

How young people experience the world

On the basis of observation and assumption it is possible to construct a model of how 7 to 11 year-olds perceive the world around them. Figure 1 shows such a model. The 'polo mints' represent the children's 'experience' of their world – the size of the mint varying in part according to how powerfully that experience is felt. Thus, while the home locality is the most familiar, it may have less impact on children's senses (at least in the short term) than a more distant place which may be associated with adventure and pleasure (albeit only temporarily).

Clearly, no one model fits all. Some 7-11 year olds rarely if ever move beyond their home area while others travel widely and often. The model shown in Figure 1 can only capture a particular moment, and will change radically over time. For example:

- The memory of a trip to a distant place will fade over time, so the mints which represent this sphere of experience will reduce in size.
- The mints may merge as children make connections between different areas of experience.
- The mints may disappear completely as circumstances change (e.g. grandparents move or die).
- The number of mints may increase over a wider area of the world as children travel further.
- The mints which represent 'places on television' will constantly change in size as 'current' experiences fade and are replaced by others of more immediate interest.

Then there are the holes in the middle of the mints. These can be taken to represent 'gaps' in spatial awareness and will gradually fill in as children gain wider knowledge and understanding. And this of course is where we as geography teachers have a role to play, but we must first try to get into the heads of our students in order to understand their 'geographical imaginations' (see also Chapter 4) – to see how the model looks for each individual and to try to shape their learning accordingly.

Take the following example of a dialogue between three students and a school Inspector, following a field trip from their urban school to Dove Dale in Derbyshire:

Lovers Leap, Dovedale: Photo: ©Diane Wright.

Inspector: 'So you have been to Dove Dale; can you tell me what you saw.'
Jade: 'There was nothing there.'
[Two other students (Ella and Daniel) nod in agreement.]
Inspector: 'What do you mean, nothing there, are you sure?'
Jade: 'Yep, sure; no shops, no people and nothing to do.'
Inspector: 'Yes, but what about the stepping stones over the beautiful River Dove, and the lovely pyramid-shaped viewpoint [Thorpe Cloud] over the steep limestone valley? Not to mention the sheer cliff of "Lover's Leap"?'
[Shrug of shoulders and a look of disbelief on Ella's face and a look of 'so what' on Daniel's.]

In this example, the students' 'blindness' to what seems so obvious to the Inspector may seem shocking to us, and may be seen simply as the result of a lack of interest and motivation, which in part it probably is. But we need to remember that these are students conditioned by an urban environment; for them, 'nothing there' means nothing to which they can relate. They measure 'something' in terms of human activity. In other words, their 'geographical imagination' is limited by their experience. To help to enlarge that experience, we as teachers must help our students to understand themselves, to be aware of what influences their perceptions of the world, and to give them the skills to become independent learners.

But first we must understand the forces, influences and trends that shape their understanding of the peoples and places they encounter – directly and indirectly (Durbin, 2000a). The next section explores some of these, starting with television.

The role of the media

Because so many of our geographical source material is derived from television, it is vital that in a secondary school geography curriculum we take account of the distortions that can result from this particular source of images and ideas. Many television genres are constructions of reality and can bias our views, albeit unintentionally. These include:

- **News** items tend to emphasise the 'negative' in the world, so that if a person only encounters a place through news then a negative perception will tend to ensue. Wars, famines and natural disasters dominate.
- **Holiday** programmes tend to emphasise the 'positive' in the world. The emphasis is often on coastal places, spectacular scenery and people having a good time. The corollary may be that issues are ignored.
- **Wildlife** programmes tend to emphasise the natural, the wild, or cruel people involved in destruction. If a person only encounters a place through this route they may get the feeling of an absence of people or that the people there are ignorant and cruel.
- **Charity** appeals tend to illustrate poor people. If this is all a person sees about a country in this form of media, it may encourage patronising attitudes and a notion that the people are ignorant and dependent. Depending on their own outlook, a young person may feel sadness, and generosity too.
- **Travel/exploration** programmes tend to feature a personality presenter and these tend to leave you with a sense of the tourist's view rather than local people's ways of interpreting the place. Sometimes this interpretation helps, but at other times it hinders.

Photo: ©Steve Banner.

A person's description of a place can tell us as much about the person as it does about the place (Durbin, 1995). Geographical description is not value-free. David Attenborough, in describing the rainforest, clearly portrays his lifelong passion for ecology, nature and biodiversity (BBC series *The Living Planet*). Some of us are convinced by the passion and feel the beauty, and agree with him and support the preservation of these special places. Some of us remain unmoved, unconcerned or disconnected from remote environments. The reaction of Lenny Henry, the comedian, when camping in the Amazon rainforest portrayed his origins from the UK's urban Midlands. He was clearly scared by the biodiversity, the 'creepy-crawlies', and was hoping to get out of the 'jungle' and back home; back to clean crisp sheets. A Brazilian farmer who is trying to eke out a living for his family may see the forest as an enemy. In essence, one person's exhilarating wilderness is another person's terrifyingly lonely place. Taken together all these insights, or geographical imaginations, help us get a more rounded view of the places we are studying.

As geography teachers, it is important for us to help young people to understand how media constructs reality so that they can be critical watchers, and aware of what is absent as well as what is present. We could add the way newspapers bias sources too. In some, international news is non-existent; indeed news about places is non-existent. Articles on Europe often focus on anti-European Union attitudes rather than people, and reports on the USA are more common than ones on Asia. The USA features in many aspects of a newspaper but coverage of countries in Africa may appear only in the news section. However, it may be churlish to place all the blame on the media organisations themselves as young people partly self-select their own media and therefore bias their experience of the world in a way that is unique to themselves. Teachers need to respond to this by selecting a range of newspaper sources (including supplements and adverts) for scrutiny as well as encouraging students to construct articles for themselves.

The arrival and growth in scope of the internet may seem to improve our access to places worldwide, and indeed it does on the surface. However, when using it as a source of information we need to be aware of how it influences the geographies inside our heads. We need media literacy and, thus, to consider the following:

- Anyone can publish anything on the internet, so questions of purpose and quality arise.
- When searching the internet there is a tendency for 'English language' sources to dominate with the result that non-English language places and voices may remain unheard.
- The poorer countries of the world have less access to modern technology and so many sources about them sit within the richer world.
- When searching for information on issues, pro or anti groups may dominate our sources. There is a need to ask whether different opinions are represented, what other opinions there are, and who else we might ask.

Given, too, the nature of the modern information superhighway (Negroponte, 1995) or information overload society, it is the most stimulating messages that get seen. The media uses emotions like fear, shock and sadness to engage our interest (Reeves and Nass, 1996). 'Spin' is rife – not only among politicians but also business people, journalists, advertisers and environmentalists. We are constantly bombarded with bold or dominant images, assertions, persuasive texts, rhetoric, and contradictory views. It is not surprising that this media merry-go-round makes some people jaded and confused. However, getting inside the minds of spin-doctors and marketing executives can make us better geographers.

Geographies in teachers' heads

> The real act of discovery is not discovering new lands but seeing them with new eyes (Marcel Proust).

What Proust is suggesting here is that life is a journey of self-discovery that involves transforming the way we see things. As geography teachers our own education has taught us to see the patterns in landscapes that reflect the theories that we have been taught. Models and theories are constructions of reality which reflect an understanding at a point in time. Given this, and the multiplicity of variables involved, our models and theories may be of little use in helping students to make sense of the world. Indeed, there is a danger that these constructs may become reality in students' minds.

Take the example of a water-cycle diagram; if we take this literally, it only seems to rain on hills. This is a relatively harmless example, but it does exemplify how the model can limit learning. Other messages may be more harmful. For example, young people may come to believe that inner cities are dreadful crime-ridden places to live in, and which become associated with ethnic minorities (Moore, 2001, 2003). To avoid unwitting institutional racism it is crucial to question the hidden messages that result from geographical education.

" *It is better to communicate good information than to offer misinformation in the name of good communication* (Alistair Fraser, n.d.).

In saying this, Fraser is alerting us to the dangers of simplifications. A simple classification of a river into upper, middle and lower course works for many rivers, e.g. the River Tees, but when applied to the Great Ouse the model may begin to slip a little in credibility. Sometimes this approach puts a lid on the learning that can take place. Plate tectonic theory provides a reasonably good explanation of the pattern of volcanic eruptions, but not all. Hawaii is the most volcanic place on Earth but this cannot be accounted for by plate tectonics. The following exchange illustrates what can happen if geography teachers unconsciously or deliberately make errors as a consequence of simplification.

> The morning after the 'Dudley earthquake' of 22 September 2002, this conversation took place in a class within a few kilometres of the epicentre:
> **Ahmed:** 'Miss, you told us yesterday that earthquakes didn't happen in England and that they only happened near plate boundaries.'
> **Teacher:** 'I am sorry, but I was doing it so as not confuse you. I should have said that they are less likely to happen in England.'
> **Nazeem:** 'Miss, our chimney pot fell off and I woke up. Did you hear it?'
> **Teacher:** 'No, I didn't wake up. Now we must go back to the textbook to see if you have understood plate tectonics.'

We live in a dynamic world where places that we might once have cited as perfect examples of particular phenomena may no longer be so. Thus, we may regret having to abandon what was once the ideal case study: inner cities that are attracting people back; a favela which is no longer on the edge of the city; and a country that we studied as a less economically-developed country is now the eighth largest economy in the world. It is vital, therefore, that we make sure our students are aware of the 'unreality' of models and theories, and that we ask them to criticise them, noting the ways in which they are inadequate (see also Chapter 1). This is 'good scientific method', and good education.

Teaching media literacy

What follows are suggestions for ways good use can be made of various media as sources of information and stimuli for learning. These teaching approaches involve both developing critical literacy about media sources and getting students involved in creativity. While the internet makes sourcing the activities much easier; it also enables teachers to encourage students to become aware of the limitations as well as the value of such sources, and what it is that shapes their perceptions of places and processes.

1. Make sources a mystery

Mystery pictures tend to be scrutinised more closely than ones of 'known' places and by being asked about them students have to consider what shapes and informs their perceptions of unfamiliar places. 'Japan or not' is a simple image sorting activity. Taking ten very different images of Japan (including Figure 2), students could be asked which scenes they think are in Japan and which are not, with reasons. It may surprise them to discover that there are poor homeless people in Japan, as well as wild and empty places, and that it is not all high-tech heaven. In a similar activity involving images of Italy, one could be included which shows a local pizza restaurant in the UK.

Figure 2 | *Conditions at this tropical atoll is Ishigaki, Japan (latitude 26 degrees north) contrast strongly with those around Hokkaido where the sea is frozen in winter and temperatures may drop below −10°.*
Photo: ©Yasuyuki Ozeki.

2. Put them in the picture more

Make every lesson a virtual experience; a journey of the geographical imagination. Ask students to 'sense' the place – e.g. You are standing on the cliff top:

- How far down is it?
- What are your gut feelings?
- What is under your feet?
- What is on the horizon?
- What sounds do you hear?
- What can you smell?

By placing students in the role of eyewitness, rather than dispassionate onlooker, they are helped to develop a sense of place and, in the context of landscapes, a sense of scale. You can do this activity with a 'guided reality' (Durbin, 1995) or a 'mind movie' (Leat, 1998), or using a big image or images. The variety of image sources available to us has multiplied a million-fold in recent years, and digital projectors and interactive whiteboards have overtaken the slide show as the main means of presentation.

3. Ask students to *be* the people they are studying in photographs or videos

Using Figure 3 of a favela in Rio de Janeiro, Brazil, you could suggest the following scenario to students: 'You are the boy in the favela running down the street' or 'You are the girl who is looking after her little sister':

- What have you just been doing?
- What are you going to be doing?
- What are your worries?
- What are your hopes and fears?
- What would you say in answer to the questions 'What is good about the place where you live?' and 'What can be improved?'

This will encourage empathy both in relation to the people and the place being studied. A video extract can be used effectively for a similar activity. Pause the programme at a particular moment, pose some questions, then continue with the video and compare the 'reality' with the students' own observations (see also Durbin, 2000b).

4. Never use less than two sources

Whenever possible, use diagrams of varying types, quality and complexity to illustrate geographical processes. For example a number of different ways of depicting the water cycle can be sourced from the internet (using a search engine, e.g. Google). Students can

Figure 3 | *Vigaro Real – a favela in Rio de Janeiro, Brazil. Photo: ©Chris Durbin.*

be asked which one they think is 'best' and which is 'worst', and why. Drawing attention to the fact that some diagrams are better than others helps students to be more thoughtful and critical, especially when working autonomously with the internet, for example, designing simple animations of longshore drift or coastal erosion.

5. Research and present a variety of opinions

Rarely do people's opinions about places, events, etc., coincide, and students need to be aware of this, and the reasons why views differ according to individual perspective (including their own of course). Rather than presenting stereotypes of various stakeholders, look for authentic sources, and for the views of both interested and disinterested parties. For example, consult urban as well as rural dwellers when considering views on the siting of a new wind farm or a mobile phone mast in the countryside; use two or more video clips about a rainforest, each illustrating a different perspective.

Polarised opinions can be juxtaposed and debated. For example, a critical commentary on climate change (such as that by Professor Philip Stott, see Anti-Eco-hype and Envirospin websites) could be compared with the views of environmentalists (e.g. Greenpeace or Friends of the Earth).

Young people should be encouraged to consider arguments from different sides and to explore the values that underpin them. More and more pressure groups put their case to students via the internet and at first-hand so they must be well-equipped critically to evaluate what they are told. Web-based enquiries (see e.g. Staffordshire Learning Net geography pages; Fisher, 2002) have added to our portfolio of possibilities for this approach.

6. Spot 'dodgy data'

Deliberately embedding 'wrong' or contradictory data/opinions in a resource given to students is a very powerful way of getting them to think more deeply about both the meaning of the data and the reasons why errors can occur. Climate graphs and development and population data can be used in this way. Figure 4 illustrates one such example. The same activity can be extended to spotting rogue interpretations. Fact or opinion activities (Leat, 1998) support this and are used in the development of critical literacy (see also Chapter 12).

Figure 4 | *Rogue and accurate development data. Source: UN Cyber Schools Bus.*

7. Deliberately manipulate pictures

The intention here is to ensure that students understand that images of places are

Country	Population Under 15 (Number of people, 1995)	Growth Rate of Population (%/annum, 1950-2030)	Infant Mortality Rate (per 1,000 births, 1995)	Total Fertility Rate (births per man, 1995)
Brazil	0.00	1.44	47.00	2.44
USA	22.10	10.00	9.00	2.05
Ethiopia	46.20	3.17	119.00	17.00
India	35.00	1.76	78.00	3.39
Japan	16.20	0.25	4.00	1.48
UK	19.30	1.00	70.00	1.78

Country	Population Under 15 (%, 1995)	Growth Rate of Population (%/annum, 1950-2030)	Infant Mortality Rate (per 1,000 births, 1995)	Total Fertility Rate (births per woman, 1995)
Brazil	31.70	1.44	47.00	2.44
USA	22.10	1.00	9.00	2.05
Ethiopia	46.20	3.17	119.00	7.00
India	35.00	1.76	78.00	3.39
Japan	16.20	0.25	4.00	1.48
UK	19.30	1.00	7.00	1.78

Figure 5 | *Different messages from one image of Kumasi, Ghana. Photo: ©Simon Scoones.*

partial, and are snapshots in time. Partiality can be for benign reasons, i.e. there is only a certain number of images that an author, publisher or producer can choose (see Chapter 13). On the other hand, it might be deliberate – for commercial or political reasons. In manipulating students' thinking about a place, it is possible to show them how pictures can be selected, cropped and altered to confirm a message. Through a debriefing activity, you can explore what that place is really like. Figure 5 challenges students to describe a city in Ghana and then, when the other half of the picture is revealed, to reappraise their opinions.

8. Apply critical appreciation to sources

This is really about provenance. When dealing with a particular issue, students may be exposed to different genres of text. It may be persuasive, stating an opinion or arguing a case. Research into its use has highlighted different approaches to the critical appreciation of video (e.g. Roberts, 1987; Butt, 1991; Durbin, 1995). In this case a framework of questions enables students to go beyond what is in the source in order to deconstruct underlying possible explanations. Questions that are designed to challenge include:

- ▪ What are their opinions?
- ▪ Why might they think the way they do?
- ▪ What is their evidence?
- ▪ How credible is it?
- ▪ What are they not telling you?

Figure 6 shows an extract from a worksheet that allows students to deconstruct sources critically.

9. Put students in the role of producers

Ask students to create storyboards for media representations of geographical phenomena. Examples are news reports on events such as floods, pollution incidents or urban developments. Designing scripts for the in-depth analysis of earthquakes or migration for the BBC's *Newsnight* programme, rather than a descriptive account. The storyboard in Figure 7 illustrates the use of script writing with still pictures to develop geographical understanding of a current event.

10. Put pupils in the role of spin-doctors

Create an activity that involves students in representing places from a particular point of view. For example, get pairs

An interest group from Rimside Moor, Northumberland www.wind-farms.co.uk/	For, Against or Balanced	Type of interest group
What do they argue?		
Why they argue as they do		
Local BBC News report from Norfolk www.bbc.co.uk/norfolk/news/042001/05/wind2.shtml		
What do they argue?		
Why they argue as they do		
The British Wind Energy Association www.bwea.com/index.html		
What do they argue?		
Why they argue as they do		
Country Guardian www.countryguardian.net/case.htm		
What do they argue?		
Why they argue as they do		
A report from The Guardian www.guardian.co.uk/uk_news/story/0,3604,605968,00.html		
What do they argue?		
Why they argue as they do		
Skye Windfarm Action Group SWAG www.sw-ag.org/		

Figure 6 | *Critically deconstructing web sources. Source: Staffordshire Learning Net geography enquiry pages.*

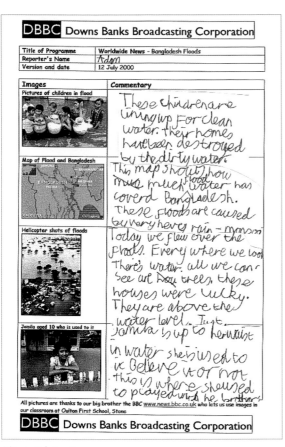

Figure 7 | *Two lower achievers' storyboard for a series of images showing flooding in Bangladesh.*

or groups of students to choose a role within which they then create a *PowerPoint* presentation or a poster about a favela. Their role might be:

■ a member of a community association making a case to the city council for some improvements,
■ a member of the police force, making the case for more resources to reduce crime,
■ a tourist operator wishing to persuade someone that a 'favela experience' for visitors is a good idea, or
■ a member of staff in a development agency looking to increase its funding in the area.

11. Be creative in your enquiries

Many of the above activities can be set in the context of creative geographical enquiries (Durbin, 2003a,b; Roberts, 2003). Creativity and criticism are two watchwords for the geography teacher. In defining creativity, *All Our Futures* (DfES, 1999), the report of the National Advisory Committee on Creativity, Culture and Education, recognised four characteristics of the creative process:

■ it involves thinking or behaving imaginatively,
■ the overall imaginative activity is purposeful, i.e. it aims to achieve an objective,
■ it generates something original,
■ the outcome must be of value in relation to the objective.

Figure 8 illustrates this process as a wheel, because it is possible to start from any point. It suggests a sequence of lessons based around maps in order to apply this type of creative thinking. One way to use the creativity wheel is to start with 'judging value', as illustrated in Figure 9. First, look at outcomes (in this case examining cartoon maps drawn by previous students, see Dudley Cartoon web) to help students begin to understand the importance of 'quality' in relation to achieving the objective. Second, engage students in thinking about the purpose for the map, with questions such as: 'About which issue do you wish to provoke debate?' and 'Why is it important to do this?'. Third, imagine what might be a creative cartoon map, and how to make it original, creative and capable of provoking discussion. In understanding this creative process, young people will become better geographers, creating better outcomes, in visual or textual form.

Geography is a tentative enquiry

In summary, school geography should be about the development of the geography that is inside students' heads; their geographical imaginations, shaped by their experiences of places in and out of school, by the media and by the attitudes and values of the people around them. To help students to become more analytical, critical and reasoned it is important to expose them to different perceptions through the attitudes and values of the teacher, the attitudes and values of textbook authors, and

Figure 8 | *The creativity wheel and mapping. Source: Durbin, 2003a.*

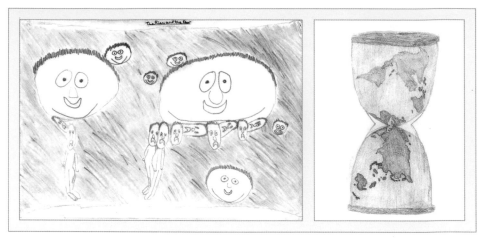

Figure 9 | *'Judging value': students' creative world maps from Madeley High School, Staffordshire.*

the attitudes and values inherent in other resources to which they are exposed.

As geography teachers we have a particular responsibility because our subject is full of partial truths, is in many ways an uncertain science, and involves issues in which there are many vested interests and about which there are varying opinions. None of this is divorced from a national curriculum. Through approaching the development of geographical knowledge and understanding as a tentative enquiry we can reach higher standards because uncertainty, complexity and multiple causality involve higher-order thinking, analysis, synthesis and evaluative skills. This philosophy of geographical education is reflected in the expression 'the more you know, the more you know there is to know'.

Related publications from the Geographical Association:
- Cape Farewell/GA (2004) *The High Arctic*.
- DEA/GA (2004) *Geography: The global dimension (Ks3)*.
- Fisher, T. (2002) (see below)
- LFG/GA (2005) *State of the Nation 2005–Teachers' Notes*.
- Roberts, M. (2003) (see below)
- Save the Children (2005) *Young Lives, Global Goals*.

References

Print

Butt, G (1991) 'Have we got a video today?', *Teaching Geography*, 16, 2, pp. 51-5.

DfES (1999) *All Our Futures*. London: DfES.

Durbin, C. (1995) 'Using televisual resources in geography', *Teaching Geography*, 20, 3, pp. 118-21.

Durbin, C. (2000a) 'Access all areas', *Primary Geographer*, 42, pp. 18-20.

Durbin, C. (2000b) 'Moving images in geography' in BfI *Moving Images in the Classroom*. London: British Film Institute.

Durbin, C. (2003a) 'Creativity – criticism and challenge in geography', *Teaching Geography*, 28, 2, pp. 64-9.

Durbin, C. (2003b) 'Seven by seven ways to be creative in geography', *Teaching Geography*, 28, 3, p. 113 (and A1 poster).

Fisher, T. (2002) *Theory into Practice: WebQuests in Geography*. Sheffield: Geographical Association.

Holloway, S.L. and Valentine, G. (eds) (2000) *Children's Geographies: Playing, living, learning*. London: Routledge Falmer.

Leat, D. (ed) (1998) *Thinking through Geography*. Cambridge: Chris Kington Publishing.

Negroponte, N. (1995) *Being Digital*. London: Hodder and Stoughton.

Reeves, B. and Nass, C. (1996) *The Media Equation: How people treat computers, television and new media like real people and places*. Cambridge: Cambridge University Press

Roberts, M. (1987) 'Using video cassettes', *Teaching Geography*, 12, 3, pp. 114-17.

Roberts, M. (2003) *Learning through Enquiry: Making sense of geography in the key stage 3 classroom*. Sheffield: Geographical Association.

Spencer, C. (ed) (1995) *The Child's Environment (Readings in Environmental Psychology Series)*. London: Academic Press.

Electronic

Anti-Ecohype – www.probiotech.fsnet.co.uk/forest.html

Cartoon web – www.cartoon.web

Envirospin – http://greenspin.blogspot.com

Fraser, A. (n.d.) Bad meteorology – www.ems.psu.edu/~fraser/BadMeteorology.html

Friends of the Earth – www.foe.org.uk

Google – www.google.co.uk

Greenpeace – www.greenpeace.org.uk

Staffordshire Learning Net – www.sln.org.uk/geography

UN Cyber School Bus – www.un.org/Pubs/CyberSchoolBus/

Implications for practice

(a) Think about investigating the media in geography. Consider the mutable nature of geography as a subject.

What this chapter helps to illustrate is that there are times when geographical learning is akin to 'natural science' (e.g. weather, meteorology, erosion), close to 'social sciences' (e.g. migration, economic change, cities as communities), 'artistic' (e.g. recording personal to responses places or events), 'psychological' (e.g. investigating people's perceptions and personal responses) ... and a lot more besides. It is important to be clear to your students about what forms of enquiry to emphasise during certain units. Think further about the ways that critical media skills outlined in this chapter require a consciously different approach from other forms of geography.

(b) Employ the techniques and strategies of media geography.

Work with colleagues to consider how the techniques and strategies described in this chapter can enable you to 'reach out' to students by challenging and extending their perceptions, experience and knowledge at the same time as their broadening their horizons broaden and deepening their understanding of specific issues.

(c) Embrace uncertainty.

Learning about the world requires circumspection, caution and a significant level of uncertainty. Teaching about it requires imaginative and confident teaching. In a 'shrinking', globalised world, with all its interdependence and diversity, consider how you can develop and further refine the approaches described here.

Chapter 20

Geography's contribution to vocational courses

Alan Marvell and Bob Holland with Keith Shuff

Before reading this chapter consider the following questions:

- What opportunities does geography provide for teaching vocational courses at key stage 4?

- What styles of learning activity are appropriate for you to provide students with vocational experiences through geography?

- How different are vocational qualifications from GCSE Geography?

- What are your experiences of teaching on these courses?

- What resources are available for you?

Opportunities at key stage 4

In terms of their attitude towards vocational courses, geography teachers tend to fall into one of two groups: those who embrace the idea of new opportunities and diversification, and those who regard the development of vocational courses as a threat to the status of geography. Where there is much competition for space on the school timetable any new subject offerings are likely to be met with some opposition as they upset the status quo. National statistics reveal a steady decline in the number of students opting for GCSE Geography from 303,858 in 1996 to 251,778 in 2000 and 227,832 in 2004 (Joint Council for Qualifications). The decline cannot be attributed entirely to the growth of vocational courses, whatever their cause, but falling numbers have meant that geography departments have become increasingly aware of their position and relative status compared to other departments and courses (Rawling, 1997; Tomlinson, 2004).

Within the school curriculum there is the potential to offer three pathways: academic, applied and vocational courses. The difference between these pathways has become less distinct as 'traditional' subject areas such as geography have promoted themselves in terms of providing opportunities for work-related situations, while vocational courses proclaim their academic comparability. As Rawling (2001) suggests, both sides have much to learn from each other in terms of their delivery of the curriculum. Recent developments in the OCR Pilot GCSE Geography use terminology such as 'predominantly vocational' and 'applied' (see Pilot GCSE webpages). Although a clear definition is not offered in the specification, using the term 'applied' is a conscious attempt to distance the qualification from the 'vocational'. 'Applied' suggests that some subject-specialist skills and techniques are being adapted to specific roles found within the workplace. In the GCSE Geography Pilot, applied options include Urban Transport for Sustainability, and Geographical Information Systems. 'Vocational' tends to be regarded as work-related, particularly to a career or occupation, and as encompassing a wider range of non-academic skills. Although the Pilot GCSE Geography has vocational options, such as GIS and Travel and Tourism Destinations, it differs in emphasis from vocational qualifications. The Pilot GCSE equivalent of a vocational unit on Travel and Tourism, for example, is more concerned with geographical impacts and global processes than with work-based operations such as ticketing and sales (Westaway and Rawling, 2003; Wood, 2004).

It is estimated that 60% of schools provide vocational GCSE courses (Goulbourne, 2004) and many geography departments are involved in their delivery. The results of a survey by the Geographical Association's Secondary Education Section Committee of 496 schools in 2001 suggests that 23% of geography departments contribute to the teaching of vocational courses, compared with 16% in 1995. The most popular subjects (88% of total respondents) for geographers teaching vocational courses are leisure, travel and tourism (Thompson *et al.*, 2002). However, not all geographers are comfortable teaching leisure and tourism as many have little experience of the industry (Ofsted, 2004).

The term 'vocational qualifications' is generally associated with National Vocational Qualifications (NVQs) and General National Vocational Qualifications (GNVQs). GNVQs were launched in 1992 to provide a general education within a vocational context. They were designed to deliver underpinning knowledge and skills relevant to a range of occupations and were mainly taught in colleges and sixth forms. At Intermediate and Foundation levels they were the equivalent of attaining four GCSEs. The GNVQ Part One was more suited to key stage 4 and was the equivalent of attaining two GCSEs. GNVQs received mixed reviews: some applauded the competence-based assessment, even though it was cumbersome, and the contemporary approach was seen as a distinctive alternative to the academic curriculum; others have pointed to the apparent lack of intellectual depth of GNVQs and a superficial focus on business and management issues (Rawling, 2001).

GCSEs in vocational subjects were launched in 2002 and were designed to replace the Part-One GNVQ, both being equivalent to two GCSEs and requiring 20% of curriculum time. The move towards GCSE was to encourage parity between key stage 4 qualifications within the National Qualifications Framework.

Vocational GCSEs are best taught using an investigative approach and with reference to topical case studies, to ensure topicality and relevance. Visits to places outside the school are integral to vocational qualifications, just as fieldwork is an essential part of geographical learning. As Marvell *et al.* (2000) point out, vocational courses can benefit from taking a geographical perspective, just as vocational courses can offer opportunities for geographers.

Figure 1 | *Suggested activities and skills relevant to vocational GCSEs. Source: DfES, 2003.*

GCSEs in vocational subjects encourage practical and work-related rather than theoretical learning. While the aim of vocational GCSEs is similar to traditional GCSEs, i.e. to increase knowledge and understanding and develop skills, the emphasis is more on learning within a vocational context, as the following list of ways of learning demonstrates:

- visits to placements in industry and/or business to gain some practical experience of the skills used;

- project work undertaken jointly with groups of students to develop self confidence and to increase awareness of the values and attitudes relevant to work;

- using the internet to find out about an industry or a particular organisation;

- use of case studies and business-based materials;

- role play and workplace simulations;

- finding out about what people do at work, and the qualifications and training they have;

- engaging in mini enterprise, perhaps with expert help from industry.

Photo: ©Simon Scoones.

The eight vocational GCSE subjects launched in 2002 are as follows (and more titles may be added in future):
1. Information and Communication Technology
2. Science
3. Engineering
4. Manufacturing
5. Art and Design
6. Business
7. Health and Social Care
8. Leisure and Tourism

There are striking similarities between vocational GCSE Leisure and Tourism and Part One GNVQ Leisure and Tourism. Both are based around three units: 'Unit 1 Investigating Leisure and Tourism', 'Unit 2 Marketing in Leisure and Tourism', and 'Unit 3 Customer Service in Leisure and Tourism'. The main aims of GCSE Leisure and Tourism are to:

- provide a broad background of understanding and core knowledge of the leisure and tourism industries in the UK;
- encourage a student-centred approach to learning together with the opportunity to forge links with leisure and tourism businesses;
- foster cross-sector themes and approaches so that students can gain an insight into related sectors, such as business, retail and distribution, and hospitality and catering;
- provide opportunities for progression into employment in the leisure and tourism industries or higher level vocational qualifications in these or related sectors.

There is some dispute about how far the new vocational GCSEs are truly vocational and some contend that the emphasis on knowledge and understanding means they have moved too far away from their forerunners, the GNVQs (Marvell and Holland, 2002). This in turn has led to the criticism that vocational GCSEs are too academic in approach (Henry, 2002; Curtis, 2004).

Planning appropriate learning activities

Vocational courses have had a great impact on teaching and learning styles. Students are encouraged to take more responsibility for their own learning through investigation and enquiry. 'Underpinning knowledge' of the curriculum is essential in establishing the foundations on which to build deeper understanding and greater autonomy of learning. The approach may vary but often groups are taught as a whole class in order to establish a community of understanding. Student-centred activities usually follow to enable students, either in groups or individually, to research, reflect and report on their findings. An active and investigative approach is just one of the distinctive features of vocational education.

Learning activities are best placed within a vocational setting, either through a scenario or using materials that are appropriate to the travel and tourism industry. The teacher needs to be able to relate to the needs of the curriculum but also be aware of the wider issues of the demands of the travel and tourism industry in terms of both knowledge and skills. For example, 'travel geography', knowledge of key destinations and travel routes, is an essential element of the industry but one that new employees often lack. The travel and tourism industry is largely 'people-orientated' so staff need to have good communication skills, an awareness of the needs of other people, an understanding of ICT and also be able to demonstrate numeracy skills. So activities need to provide opportunities for students to develop and apply these skills as well as to reflect on them.

Tourist towns, cities and routes

Tourist organisations have to provide information to visitors before they arrive at a destination.

Imagine that you have received the e-mails below and have to respond to them. What information could you provide to the visitor? You may need to use road atlases and a range of websites to find the information.

From: J Gilbert, Washington DC, USA

I am arriving at Heathrow Airport and my plane is scheduled to land at 0830. What is the best way to get to Canary Wharf in Docklands and how long will it take me?

From: Shane Rawlings, Sydney, Australia

I am due to visit my aunt who lives in Bournemouth. I've never been to the UK before and want to know what there is to do in Bournemouth for younger people?

From: Mireille Leschamps, Paris

I am driving to Oxford from Paris. I have a ferry to Dover and I arrive there at 11 o'clock in the morning. Please could you tell me the quickest way to get to Oxford and how long the journey should take?

From: Jim McGuire, Ontario, Canada

I'm flying Air Canada from Toronto to Manchester Airport. I need to get to Blackpool. Please could you tell me the best way to make the journey?

Figure 2 | *Example of student activity set in a vocational context. Source: Tourism Educational Consultancy, 2004.*

Figure 2 provides an example of a student activity that consolidates students' knowledge of the principal functions and attractions of tourist towns, cities and routes. The activity is set in a vocational context with students being required to respond to questions asked by tourists. Students are encouraged to use websites and other sources to research information which will help them to reply to the questions asked.

For teachers, an awareness of the needs of the travel and tourism business is essential for preparing appropriate activities for students. Thus, it is important to establish links and partnerships between education and industry. Students can be introduced to the 'real world' of the industry in a number of ways, e.g. by inviting guest speakers to the school, and by arranging for students to visit local businesses connected to the travel, tourism and leisure industry. Most year 10 students take part in some form of work experience and this provides another opportunity to gather data or investigate potential career routes.

The business world expects high standards, and not all areas of work are highly paid or necessarily stimulating. Learning activities should reflect this reality while also being appropriate for the learning styles of the class and meeting the requirements of the awarding bodies' specification. As teachers, the question we are frequently required to address is: 'How do I convey the ideas of the curriculum in a stimulating, fun and accessible way to a mixed ability group of tourism students in 50 minutes, ensuring that key ideas stay embedded?' By reinforcing key ideas, using a range of case studies and examples that the students identify with. Tasks should be clearly structured that lead to further investigation of more complex issues.

To ensure that learning activities are contemporary and relevant it is important to keep up to date with developments. However, time and resources are required to organise these activities, to meet and brief guest speakers, and to visit potential industry hosts. Senior managers within school should be made aware of the demands that this, and the need to access relevant resources, can place on a teacher's time.

When a new vocational course is being established there may be an expectation within the school that it will offer business links, placements, day visits and residential field visits from day one. This is clearly unrealistic: it is best to begin gradually, start locally, establish contacts and become familiar with the demands of the specification and assessment and to build from success. Other subjects are likely to have a long tradition within the school and are therefore well-established in terms of procedure, expectation and resources. However, approaches that can be adapted from existing courses, such as the transfer of enquiry-based learning from geography to the vocational curriculum, should be exploited where possible. Similarly, opportunities should be taken to use geographical resources, fieldwork and skills learned in geography.

A recent report by Ofsted has revealed that there is a need to provide appropriate learning opportunities for students and that weaknesses are evident in this regard:

> The majority of teachers have little or no experience of teaching leisure and tourism. A large number are geography teachers who struggle to teach this very different subject. This constrains the range and quality of students' experiences. Even in the minority of schools where teachers have taught GNVQ leisure and tourism, their subject knowledge tends to be very theoretical. Most teachers lack first-hand and up-to-date experience of the leisure and tourism industries and so cannot provide practical examples to enliven teaching, or good, relevant resources. Additionally, they often have few links, if any, with local employers or organisations which can support practical work-related experiences. In a majority of schools, leisure and tourism is being taught as an academic subject with an over-reliance placed on secondary sources such as textbooks. The practical and vocational elements are weak (Ofsted, 2004, p. 20).

Establishing an active learning environment with a mixed ability group in a limited timeframe is certainly a challenge, but it can also be rewarding. When planning for vocational education the school should try wherever possible to allow sufficient blocks of time for students to engage with the subject material. Visits and contact with relevant businesses is essential and classes should be allowed the time to pursue these opportunities. They are as important to vocational education as fieldwork is to geography.

When planning learning activities it is important to consider the learning outcomes. These should relate directly to the relevant awarding body specification and be appropriate to the topic of study.

Learning outcomes and assessment

There is a difference between the way that vocational and 'traditional' GCSE qualifications are assessed, with two-thirds assessed by coursework in the case of the former (Figure 3).

GCSE Leisure and Tourism includes a 'What you need to learn' section which is equivalent to the subject content in non-vocational GCSEs. In addition there is an assessment grid for the two centre-assessed units and one for the externally assessed unit. This grid outlines what is to be assessed across three grade boundaries. Not all of the unit content is represented within this section, so although these assessment grids form an important aspect of curriculum planning, the 'What you need to learn' section cannot be ignored.

Students need to be aware of how to prepare for the externally assessed unit and use pre-release material, if required by the assessment. Any pre-release material demands thorough preparation.

Students should be well prepared in terms of meeting the expectations of the higher level demands and not just on meeting the demands of the lowest level of competency. Questions such as 'suggest reasons why ...' and 'account for ...' require critical thought and assimilation of ideas. Using a wide variety of resources to stimulate responses and engage the students with the subject will enhance this process of enquiry (see Chapters 9 and 20).

Resources

Compared to Leisure and Tourism, very few subject areas offer such a stimulating range of materials from which resources can be developed. A vast array of brochures, leaflets

For assessment objective (proportion of final mark for coursework)	Students are expected to...
A01 (25%)	Show knowledge and understanding of the specified content in a range of vocationally related situations
A02 (25%)	Show knowledge, skills and understanding specified in the subject content in a range of vocationally related situations
A03 (50%)	Plan and carry out investigations and tasks in which they examine vocationally related issues and problems; gather, record and analyse relevant information and evidence; and evaluate evidence, make reasoned judgements and present conclusions.

Figure 3 | *The assessment objectives and associated learning outcomes for GCSE Leisure and Tourism.*

and other information is available from different organisations, and marketing strategies for local authority Country Parks and visitor numbers for tourist areas are comparatively easy to obtain. Many teachers of tourism tend to return from holidays with a bag full of information leaflets from attractions and destinations they have visited. The challenge is to find time to develop these into accessible resources and learning activities for students.

Publishers have realised that there is a market for leisure, travel and tourism resources and a wide range of textbooks is now available. Many of the most recent ones closely follow the existing specifications and provide excellent support for both teachers and students. However, examiners and moderators are beginning to use phrases such as 'over-reliance on a single text' to indicate to centres that they are able to recognise where a student has perhaps made too much use of a particular textbook in producing the portfolio evidence for certain criteria (see also Chapter 13).

It could be argued that the delivery of 'vocational' courses should not rely too heavily on published texts. Information obtained directly from businesses is of equal value, particularly because the aim of such courses is to enable students to apply their skills to real situations. Similarly, centres should attempt to obtain information which is of relevance to the local area. Very few schools have joined their appropriate regional tourist boards but those who have tend to gain access to an interesting range of information.

Figure 4 | *Websites for tourist attractions, such as Chessington World of Adventure, often include downloadable school resources.*

Over the last decade, tourist attractions in the UK have responded to the demands of vocational students in a number of ways. Some have devised substantial 'educational packs' with a variety of information on customer service, marketing and so on. Although of some value, there is a danger that some of these will become dated as both the educational and industrial worlds move on. Some of these materials are available online – Chessington World of Adventures, for example, provides material for download in its education section (Figure 4). Similarly, organisations such as English Heritage and the National Trust have devised a range of reliable resource packs and videos, and have educational websites especially for use in schools.

Some schools subscribe to trade journals, e.g. *Travel Weekly, Travel Trade Gazette* and *Leisure Weekly*. While much of the content may be of little interest or relevance, e.g. the arguments between airlines and travel agents over commission payments, such magazines are a good source of stimulus material, e.g. job advertisements and sections on mystery shoppers.

When researching destinations outside of the UK, organisations such as the World Travel & Tourism Council and the World Tourism Organisation are worth investigating. In terms of the volume of information available, few publications can match the *World Travel Guide* – if you want to know what times the banks open in Tahiti, it's there. The *Michelin Guides, Rough Guides* and *Fodor's* Guides are also very useful. For statistics relating to tourism in the UK, Star UK is of particular value, and local authority websites usually have a lot to offer.

What did we do before the internet was available? Often too many students attempt to include too much information from websites – downloaded directly into their portfolios. Students should be aware of the origin of websites to check for bias (i.e. whether it exists, the extent to which it exists and why it exists), and need to be taught how to develop relevant information skills, e.g. identifying appropriate sources. This is part of the wider theme of questioning sources within geography. There is no shortage of source material – the real challenge is finding the time to develop resources that meet the needs of a particular group of students and help to bring the subject to life.

Teaching vocational courses

This section considers the experiences of geographers teaching vocational courses in two different centres. Both centres have been teaching vocational courses for over ten years with their initial expectations and fears resulting in a steep learning curve that has had an impact on their approach to teaching.

Case study 1: Delivering Leisure and Tourism courses

Several years ago Leigh City Technology College, Dartford, Kent, decided that it would place an emphasis on vocational education by changing its curriculum model for the upper school, with all year 10 and 11 students being required to take a vocational subject. There was a wide range of subjects on offer to the students and the humanities department was given the task of delivering GNVQ Leisure and Tourism. None of the staff in the department had any background in the subject and it was felt that the geographers in the team might find it easier to adapt than others. In later years history and religious education teachers were to get involved.

There was little in the actual content of the course that was familiar; the exception being the unit entitled Investigating Leisure and Tourism, which involved locating the various facilities within the industry in a specific location. Concepts such as marketing and customer service were a complete mystery to us all, and it is true to say that the initial learning curve was pretty steep.

From day one it has been obvious that my geographical skills have been of assistance in developing my teaching of Leisure and Tourism. Most of our geography curriculum is based around enquiry and I had many years of experience of setting up fieldwork-based investigations, particularly at GCSE and A-level. The way in which I designed coursework tasks became a model for our vocational assignments, i.e. structured tasks based around the collection of primary data, supplemented by secondary data.

Today we have refined the delivery of Leisure and Tourism into a well-established format. We start each unit by teaching the basic concepts. We use a variety of techniques including role-play, internet research and videos. The purpose of these lessons is two-fold: (a) to prepare the students for what they need to learn, and (b) to provide them with the necessary background knowledge that will be applied in their assignment.

After this initial training we then start the assignment itself. All assignments begin with a visit to a leisure or tourism company where students collect the basic data that they will require over the coming weeks. They then continue with their assignment which contains a number of structured tasks. Where necessary they collect additional research material – most well-established leisure and tourism companies now have useful websites.

Vocational assignments have precise requirements which must be met if the students are to pass with a high grade. If a student does not meet all the assessment criteria laid out in the specification they are not likely to succeed, so careful guidance is essential. Geographers who have experience of designing coursework are familiar with this approach.

Case study 2: Introducing GCSE Travel and Tourism

GCSE Travel and Tourism was introduced at Wyvern Community School, Hampshire, in order to extend opportunities for students at key stage 4. In the first year of the course it was offered as an option for those less likely to be successful at academic subjects. After the first year it became apparent that, compared with GNVQs and NVQs, GCSE Travel and Tourism was not a 'true' vocational course, instead it required similar demand as other GCSE subjects. Since then the course has been offered as an option to all key stage 4 students.

Travel and Tourism has been a popular course as many students already work in the travel and tourism industry or anticipate working in it in the future. Others see the subject as a stepping-stone towards further education. Within the school, GCSE Travel and Tourism is promoted as a subject which looks at the travel and tourism industry. Some students expect the course to be two years of watching television travel programmes, e.g. *Club Reps, Airport,* and looking through holiday brochures. In reality, the subject draws upon geography and business studies and a lot of issues are covered in depth.

A positive aspect of the course is the requirement to be familiar with the use of geographical case studies and examples of travel and tourism destinations are an important feature. As a result there are plenty of resources that can be used to support the course, from texts to local businesses and promotional material from holiday companies, tourist destinations and visitor attractions. However a lot of travel and tourism resources are aimed at old GNVQ specifications, although many have now been adapted for GCSE Leisure and Tourism.

The negative aspects are that there are as many, if not more, links with business studies than geography. There is a danger that these links may not be fully explored if teaching is undertaken solely from a geographical perspective. Getting away from a geographical approach can be difficult although there are clear benefits in adopting an enquiry-based approach where it is appropriate to do so.

The main drawback is that there are few resources which are entirely dedicated to the subject. Those that exist are often aimed at older students, are not suited to students with lower reading ages, and many assume that students will have a command of business language – which is not often the case.

The subject suffers from being viewed as non-academic and therefore more suited to lower achievers. Despite efforts to convince both members of staff and students otherwise, this reputation still exists as part of the culture of many schools. Students who join the school in the middle of key stage 4 are almost always placed into GCSE Travel and Tourism. It is thought by senior managers that they can easily catch up in this subject, despite never having studied it before. They invariably cannot.

The opportunities do outweigh the challenges however. Students regard travel and tourism as being relevant to their lives and having potential for future careers. There are lots of opportunities for practical work including:

- Work experience
- Field visits
- Guest speakers
- Presentations
- Organising actual events as work simulations

Students have the opportunity to make good use of key skills such as ICT through report writing, investigations and data handling. Students have also entered local competitions based around travel and tourism, as the tasks have been relevant to the course requirements.

Final thoughts

Geographers have an important role to play in the teaching of vocational courses. Their expertise in providing enquiry and investigative-based learning is essential in ensuring that students engage in practical exercises relating to the vocational context in which they are studying: 'Often there are few practical opportunities to visit vocational settings or engage in simulation and role play' (Ofsted, 2004, p. 19). There are also lots of possible cross-curricular links that can be explored between leisure and tourism, geography, business studies, ICT, art and design and religious studies. At the time of writing (2005) it is far from clear what opportunities may arise in the new 14-19 curriculum arrangements.

Acknowledgements

The authors wish to thank Amanda Connell and Matthew Ford, formerly teachers of geography at Wyvern Community School, Hampshire, for their contribution to this chapter.

Related publications from the Geographical Association:
- Broad, J. (2001) *A-Z Advancing Geography: Key Skills.*
- Marvell, A. and Watkins, C. (2005) *Changing Geography: Sustainable tourism.*

References

Print

Curtis, P. (2004) 'Vocational GCSEs too academic', *The Guardian* (www.guardian.co.uk/uk_news/story/0,3604,1264797,00.html), 20 July.

DfES (2003) *GCSEs in Vocational Subjects: A general guide and overview of the qualifications* (second edition). London: DfES.

Joint Council for Qualifications (2004) *National Provisional GCSE (Full Course) Results – June 2004 (All UK Candidates)* (www.jcq.co.uk/), accessed 31 August.

Goulbourne, A. (2004) *GCSE and Work Related Learning Team, DfES* (www.semta.org.uk/NTOPubImages.nsf/vGraphics/dfes/$file/dfes.ppt), accessed 20 July.

Henry, J. (2002) 'Ministers' "British disease" cure at last', *Times Educational Supplement*, 12 July, p. 3.

Holland, B. (2004) *Assessment Exercises for GCSE Leisure and Tourism*. Reading: Tourism Education Consultancy.

Marvell, A. and Holland, B. (2002) 'AVCE Travel and Tourism: an overview', *Teaching Geography*, 27, 2, pp. 65-7.

Marvell, A., Smith, J. and Shuff, K. (2000) 'Opportunities of a changing curriculum', *Teaching Geography*, 25, 4, pp. 170-4.

Ofsted (2004) *Developing New Vocational Pathways: Final report on the introduction of new GCSEs*. London: Ofsted.

OCR (2004) *GCSE in Geography (Pilot)*. Cambridge: OCR (see also Pilot GCSE webpages).

Rawling, E. (1997) 'Geography and vocationalism – opportunity or threat?', *Geography*, 82, 2, pp. 163-78.

Rawling, E. (2001) *Changing the Subject: The impact of national policy on school geography 1980-2000*. Sheffield: Geographical Association.

Thompson, L., Lodge, R. and Day, C. (2002) 'The state of geography in secondary schools: six years on', *Teaching Geography*, 27, 2, pp. 56-60.

Tomlinson, M. (2004) 14-19 *Curriculum and Qualifications Reform: Final report of the working group on 14-19 reform*. London: DfES.

Westaway, J. and Rawling, E. (2003) 'A new look GCSE Geography?', *Teaching Geography*, 28, 2, pp. 60-3.

Wood, P. (2004) 'The new Pilot GCSE – a progress report', *Teaching Geography*, 29, 2, pp. 98-9.

Electronic

Chessington World of Adventures – www.chessington.co.uk
English Heritage – www.english-heritage.org.uk
Fodor's Guides – www.fodors.com
Michelin Guides – www.viamichelin.co.uk
National Trust – www.nationaltrust.org.uk
Pilot GCSE – www.geography.org.uk/pilotgcse
Rough Guides – www.roughguides.com
Star UK – www.staruk.org
Tourism Education Consultancy – www.bobholland.org (Tourism Education Consultancy, 19 Rothwell Gardens, Woodley, Reading, RG5 4TJ; e-mail: bob@bobholland.org)
Travel and Tourism Programme – www.springboarduk.org.uk/ttp (Springboard UK, Enterprise House, Cardiff Bay, Cardiff, CF10 5LE; e-mail: ttp@springboarduk.org.uk)
World Tourism Organization – www.world-tourism.org
World Travel and Tourism Council – www.wttc.org
World Travel Guide – www.columbusguides.com

Implications for practice

(a) Vocational subjects require rigorous planning and organisation.

Vocational subjects need a dedicated person to lead the delivery of the subject area who has the time and responsibility to make the most of the many opportunities on offer.

(b) Collaboration is important.

Make links with other schools and share ideas, good practice and resources. Some local authorities organise teacher networks or 'clusters' in order to bring teachers of subject areas together.

(c) Make best use of available support.

Support is available from the Travel and Tourism Programme and the Tourism Education Consultancy, which provides resources, ideas, and can assist with enquiries. There are also many internet resources available (see the websites listed at the end of this chapter).

(d) Base learning activities around projects and investigations.

Students prefer to get involved and gain ownership of tasks rather than work in a didactic way. Consider what tasks would be required of them in business and try to establish simulations within the classroom to reflect these. A study of a local leisure, travel and tourism employer can lead to a range of curriculum projects and activities.

(e) Enlist the support of local businesses.

Try to arrange speakers from and visits to the local authority, Business Link, local tourist office, and major leisure, travel and tourism employers. If a visit is not possible, guest speakers can be just as effective and they often bring materials with them which can be added to the resources within the classroom.

Chapter 21

Homework and independent study

Denise Freeman and Simon Miller

Before reading this chapter consider the following questions:

Think of the five most recent homework tasks you have set:

- What purpose did you have in mind for each of these tasks?

- What contribution did the homework make to longer term learning objectives in geography?

- Were the tasks accessible for all students?

- How engaging and motivating did the students find each of these homework tasks?

Most teachers set homework. Most teachers feel that it is something that a 'good' teacher should do. Yet how often do we stop to question why we are setting homework and actually reflect upon the value of it? As practitioners, are we able to justify the homework that we set and can we be certain that it is meaningful? Taking time out to reflect upon these questions is important but it does not end there. For teachers, there is also the challenge of how to engage and motivate students through homework. How can students be encouraged to learn away from the classroom and how can this learning be fed back into lessons in an effective and valuable way? Our aim is to provide a fresh look at homework and explore how it can be used to enhance teaching and learning in geography.

Homework

Homework can be defined as 'work set by teachers that students are expected to complete out of school hours' (Sharpe, 2001, p. 7). Although it is usually the teacher who decides upon the nature of a homework task, it is the student who tends to be in control of the learning process and determines the outcome of the work. However, this is a very simplified picture of homework and in reality the responsibility for it is often shared among parents, teachers, peers and a growing network of support via the internet.

During the 1990s the Government and Ofsted published research findings and reports in support of the view that homework is an 'essential part of a good education' (Ofsted, 1999, p. 7). With this in mind they encouraged schools to develop policies for the setting, monitoring and management of homework. Today Ofsted provides clear guidelines

- Homework can promote independent learning skills, that can be usefully applied to GCSE Geography coursework.

- Post-16 geography coursework gives students the opportunity to research an area of personal interest within the curriculum.

- Students can be given the opportunity to enhance their research skills and use ICT equipment not always available to them in the classroom (Grimwade and Martin, 1997).

- Setting homework in geography allows students to make use of and become aware of community resources, e.g. local libraries, interviewing local residents, exploring the environment around them.

- Homework gives students the opportunity to involve parents/carers and other adults in their work (Grimwade and Martin, 1997).

- Homework can help teachers and students to overcome the problem of time constraints on the curriculum. For example, at post-16 level students can complete their own case studies and reading at home, thereby 'freeing up' lesson time to explore important concepts or ideas.

- Homework can enable students to develop links between work done in class and their experiences and interests outside of school. Students can bring these experiences to the classroom in future lessons.

Figure 1 | *The potential benefits of using homework in geography. Photo:©Graham Butt.*

regarding the amount and type of homework that should be set for students, and homework is used as an important indicator for measuring standards in schools. According to Ofsted (1999), an effective homework programme helps to raise achievement, improve standards in education, and enhance student motivation. It is also argued that homework can be an effective way of involving parents/carers in their children's education, and strengthening links between home, school, and the wider community. Figure 1 outlines some of the potential benefits of setting homework in geography.

However, the value of homework is a contested issue. Some researchers report evidence of homework becoming a source of family tension, exhaustion and anxiety (Hallam, 2004), and studies have shown that homework can often be counterproductive and have a detrimental effect on student motivation (MacBeath and Turner, 1990). For teachers, the setting, collection and assessment of homework can be a daunting task and its recurring nature a burden.

Moreover, like many other aspects of education, homework is often used as a political football. Changing political and educational ideologies can influence the degree of emphasis that schools place upon homework (Freely, 2000). For example, when people become concerned about falling standards in schools, the amount of homework being set increases. As student workloads rise, people begin to air concerns about the pressures being placed upon young people and the amount of homework being set starts to decrease. When commentators report that standards in schools are beginning to slip again, the amount of homework being set in schools increases once more. While this may be a simplified version of reality, the fact is that students, parents/carers and teachers are confused about the role and importance of homework.

Homework is an issue full of contradictions. It is unpopular yet expected. Most parents/carers expect homework to be set and the majority of students and teachers believe it to be an important part of teaching and learning (Balderstone and Lambert, 1999). As a result homework continues to occupy a prominent role in contemporary education. In light of this, the debate over homework needs to be opened up beyond simply discussing the pros and cons (MacBeath and Turner, 1990). If teachers are going to continue to set homework, then its purpose and contribution to learning need to be explored. Practitioners should be given the opportunity to reflect upon why they are setting homework and how it can be used effectively to support learning. Homework needs to be meaningful and well planned; if it is not maybe it should not be set, echoing the familiar notion 'do it properly or not at all'. The following discussion aims to provide a framework for beginning to question and evaluate the place of homework in geography and suggests ways in which homework can be used to enhance learning.

Why set homework?

Teachers, students and parents generally expect homework to be set and most students believe that homework is important in helping them to do well at school. However, there needs to be a good reason for setting homework. As with effective teaching and learning in the classroom, homework should have a clear purpose that is understood by both students and teachers. When the aims and objectives of a homework task are clearly specified and shared among all involved (including parents/carers) students are able to see what they have to do and how to improve upon the outcomes of previous work (Balderstone and Lambert, 1999). The following questions should be considered when reflecting on the purpose of homework:

- Why do I set homework?
- Why am I setting this particular piece of homework?
- What is the purpose of this particular piece of homework?
- What are the intended learning objectives?
- Have these been shared with all involved?
- What are the intended learning outcomes?
- Are there any alternative strategies that could be used to achieve these outcomes?

Figure 2 outlines some of the reasons why teachers may set homework in geography. A recurring question surrounds the value of asking students to finish off classwork at home. 'Finishing off' can be useful as it allows full coverage of the curriculum and enables students to see a clear relationship between what is studied at home and in school (MacBeath and Turner, 1990). However, this can lead to inequalities in the amount of homework expected of different students. For some higher achieving students, 'finishing off' can mean no homework, while for others there will be a great deal of work still to do. It is those in the latter group who are most likely to struggle with the homework, meaning that it is often left incomplete. Yet 'finishing off' is often considered a necessity, particularly when there is extensive curriculum content to be covered.

What is 'good' homework?

Much of the research and writing on homework, both now and in the past, has tended to focus upon four key areas:

1. Exploring the link between homework and attainment.
2. Exploring the link between homework and the development of independent study skills.
3. Exploring the impact of homework (upon students, teachers and families).
4. Exploring the attitudes of students, teachers and parents/carers towards homework.

There has been limited discussion about what constitutes 'good' homework. In an attempt to refresh the debate it is important to generate a framework that will enable us to start thinking about what 'good' homework may look like in geography. Figure 3 draws together some of the qualities that can be seen as desirable features of 'good' homework. What evolves is a list of criteria. But the list should not be viewed as an essential 'shopping list' that must be adhered to every time homework is set. Instead it should be seen as a starting point for consideration, critique and reflection. It could be argued, however, that the more criteria we meet the more effective homework becomes.

What is the purpose of setting the homework	In what instances may this type of homework be used?	What questions should be considered before setting this homework?
To finish off	To finish work started in class, or while in the field, e.g. presenting fieldwork results using graphical techniques.	■ Does the work need to be finished? ■ Do students have access to suitable resources? ■ Can the students do it without teacher support? ■ Can all students complete this task? ■ Will this task challenge all students? ■ Has the task been differentiated?
To extend	Adding to a case study started in class. The students may have compiled a case study during lesson time and be asked to investigate or expand upon a certain aspect of it, e.g. what has been done to prevent or prepare for future flooding in Mozambique, since the floods of 2000? Such a task may be designed to coincide with the showing of a television documentary or film, which the students can use to add to and update their notes.	■ What guidelines/structure have been provided for the activity? ■ How will this activity add value to the work already completed in class? ■ Has the task been differentiated? ■ How will the outcomes of this task be assessed? ■ Will the outcomes of the task be fed back into class work? Do they need to be?
To apply learning	Making use of knowledge, skills and understanding learnt in class, e.g. designing a party invitation that gives accurate directions to an event, making use of compass points and map symbols.	■ Have all the learning objectives been achieved during the lesson? ■ What provisions can be made for students who have not understood the task? ■ Can the outcomes of this homework task be used in future lessons?
To gather data/ To research	For coursework. As part of a geographical enquiry, e.g. e-mailing students in a school abroad (as part of a school link programme) to ask about their locality. To collect survey data, e.g. surveying students at the school to find out what brands of sports clothes they wear and why.	■ Do all students have access to the relevant information and technology to complete the task? ■ Are the students working in small groups for this task? ■ How will the groups be selected, organised and managed? ■ How will the outcome be assessed?
To review/ To consolidate	Revising a topic before an assessment. Preparation for external examinations, e.g. completing practice examination questions. Producing a glossary of key terms following the completion of a topic.	■ Are there any significant 'gaps' in the students' knowledge? ■ How can these be identified and addressed? ■ How will this work be assessed? ■ How will the outcome of this task be used to plan future classwork?

Figure 2 | *Why teachers set homework.*

Homework for learning

The subject of homework is very often discussed alongside the issue of assessment. Indeed the two do have strong links; students do homework, teachers mark it (Balderstone and Lambert, 1999). However, it could be argued that the two are becoming increasingly disconnected. The development of the assessment for learning guidance has refocused interest on assessment issues. However, homework has not been subject to the same scrutiny or debate. Like assessment, homework can and should be used to support the classroom learning and help students to achieve. In fact, many of the principles developed by the Assessment Reform Group (2002) (see Figure 3, Chapter 32, page 419)

Is the homework inclusive?
☐ Can all of the students take part in the homework?
☐ Can all of the students gain from the homework?
☐ Do all students have access to the resources they need to complete the task?
☐ Do individual students have something different or unique to bring to this task, e.g. drawing on their cultural background?
☐ Has the work been differentiated? Does it need to be?

Is the homework meaningful?
☐ Is the homework relevant to the work the students are doing in school?
☐ Does the homework have a clear purpose?
☐ Are the students clear about the purpose of the work?
☐ Is it clear where this task is heading?
☐ Does the work have any relevance to the lives of the students? Is this possible?

Is the homework motivating for both teachers and students?
☐ Do the students want to do this homework?
☐ Does the homework encourage students to be involved in geography?
☐ Does this task encourage students to achieve in geography?
☐ Does the homework make the students want to find out more?
☐ Will the outcome of the homework be interesting from the teacher's point of view?

Is the homework engaging?
☐ Does this task engage the students?
☐ Does this task capture their imagination?
☐ Does this homework encourage students to explore new places, ideas or activities?

Is the homework planned?
☐ Has the homework been planned for as part of a scheme of work?
☐ How will the outcomes be used to help teaching and learning in the classroom?
☐ Will the students be given an opportunity to reflect upon the homework they have undertaken?
☐ Will the students refer to their homework in class?
☐ Should all homework be planned for? Who should plan it?
☐ Is it possible to develop homework tasks that arise as a direct response to ideas or issues that students have raised during a lesson?

Is the homework manageable?
☐ Have the students been given all the resources that they need to do this piece of work?
☐ Have the students been given enough time to do this piece of work?
☐ Do the students know where or to whom they can go to get support with this piece of work?
☐ How will the work be marked and assessed? Should it be marked?
☐ Does the homework encourage the students to use and develop geographical skills?
☐ Does the task encourage students to practise their existing geographical skills or learn new skills?
☐ Does the homework allow the students to use skills that they cannot always use in the classroom?
☐ Does the homework encourage creativity and innovation in geographical thinking?

Figure 3 | *A checklist of criteria for setting good homework in geography.*

are very relevant and in some cases directly transferable to the principles of effective homework. Is it time to widen the debate on assessment in order to begin talking about 'homework for learning'?

Setting good homework in geography

In geography, the opportunities for homework are rich and varied; however this can be a double-edged sword. The diverse nature of the subject and the wealth of resources available to geographers can make it quite difficult to plan and resource manageable homework tasks. Furthermore, the conceptual nature of geography and the different ways in which students understand the subject can make setting homework a challenge. Addressing this challenge should form an important part of any critical reflection about the role and value of homework in geography (Figure 4).

Examples

The second half of this chapter uses three examples, to illustrate how homework can be used effectively in geography to support and enhance teaching and learning. The first example looks at how homework can be used creatively to engage and motivate students. The second looks at how homework can be planned for and integrated into schemes of work. The example introduces students to the links between place and crime. The final section looks at the use of a log book in which students can present the outcomes of their homework.

Example 1: Colourful landscapes

The homework task described here is intended to be **motivating and engaging** for both students and teachers, as well as **manageable** for both parties. The task is one that can be adapted to many different topics and issues and is particularly useful for introducing a topic. The work is based around the use of household paint colour charts, which can be obtained from local DIY (do-it-yourself) stores. It shows how homework can be:

Issue	Questions
Access to resources	Is there a way of enabling students to have access to classroom resources outside of lesson time?
	What resources do the students have access to in school, out of lesson time?
	What resources do the students have access to at home?
	What resources and information do the students have access to within the wider community, e.g. library or community centre?
	How can students be encouraged to reflect upon the resources that they have used in a lesson and refer to these in their homework?
ICT access	Would it be valuable to audit the students' access to ICT facilities both in school and at home?
Student skills	Do the students know how to gain access to the resources around them, within school and within the wider community?
	Do the students know how to gather information effectively from sources such as the internet, the library or local information centres?
	How can we help them to develop these skills?
Completion of homework	What strategies could be used to help the students complete homework tasks based upon their experiences in the classroom?
Differentiation	How can homework tasks be differentiated to enable students to explore their own individual interpretations and experiences of the world around them?

Figure 4 | *Reflecting upon the challenge of resourcing and managing homework in geography.*

- **manageable and inclusive** because it does not generate marking and the resources (which are free) are given to all of the students,
- **inclusive** because it involves only a small amount of writing and encourages the students to be creative and think independently about geography and what it means to them, and
- **meaningful** because it is clearly linked to what the students are doing in later lessons.

The task

The students are given a single colour strip from a household paint colour chart (from a DIY store). They can staple this into their homework diaries or planners. The students are then asked to find an object that matches that colour and to bring it to the next lesson.

The task is directed by the nature of the topic being studied in class. For example, students may be asked to find an object from the following sources:

- The natural landscape – this could be used to introduce environmental geography topics or help students with work on natural landscapes, e.g. rivers, geology or tectonics.
- The human landscape – this could be used to introduce work on urban or rural geographies or help students with work on how humans shape landscapes, e.g. pollution, environmental degradation or even enhancement.
- The school locality – this could be used to introduce work on what the school locality is like and what activities take place there.
- Related to consumerism – this could be used to introduce GCSE or post-16 level topics on globalisation, trans-national corporations or economic geography.

The next lesson

Back in the classroom, the objects brought in by the students can be used to create themed collages/wall displays and to stimulate creative writing and oral presentations and/or discussions (Figure 5).

The work produced by the students provides a wealth of opportunities for exploring local places and developing geographical skills. Themes that could be explored through the outcomes of this homework task include:

- The idea of community (what is community?)
- Health and fitness services in the area (what are attitudes to health and fitness in the local area?)
- Roads and transport
- Mapping features of our local area
- A sense of local identity (mapping and understanding street names)
- Local businesses
- Scale (what do the students see as local?) (where are each of these places in relation to each other?)
- Young people's knowledge of the area (how do the students view this area?)

It is useful to take time to evaluate the outcomes of homework, and respond to these outcomes through future lesson planning. Key questions for consideration include:

- How can homework shape future classwork?
- How can the outcomes of a homework task be integrated into future classwork?
- Should this always be the done? (Is this always desirable or appropriate?)

Example 2: Exploring perceptions of place and crime

This example highlights the way in which homework can be **planned for** as an essential part of a scheme of work. The task is based around work on the geography of crime. An annotated lesson plan (Figure 6) indicates how the homework task has been planned for and how the task plays a key part in the work that the students are doing in class. This example also shows how the homework can:

- **be manageable** because it does not directly generate marking or assessment and all of the students are given the resources that they need to complete the task;
- **encourage students to use and develop geographical skills** – the students use survey skills and then present their findings later using a variety of graphical techniques;
- **be meaningful** because it is intrinsically linked to what the students are doing in lessons and the outcome of the task should interest both students and teachers.

The task

The students are asked to complete a small survey in which they show people a photograph of a place within the school locality. The students then ask each respondent what words they would associate with that place and if they would feel safe being there during different times of the day. The students are provided with a recording sheet for their findings.

Images of three different places are featured in the survey. Copies of the three images are handed out randomly among the students, each receiving one photograph.

The task is differentiated in the sense that the students can decide for themselves the number of respondents that they wish to take part in their survey. The minimum number of responses allowed is one and students are encouraged to survey at least one student from the school. This makes the task very accessible for all of the students and therefore as inclusive as possible.

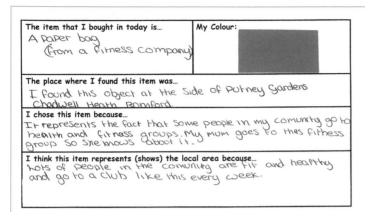

The item that I bought in today is...	My Colour:
A paper bag (from a fitness company)	

The place where I found this item was...
I found this object at the side of Putney Gardens Chadwell Heath Romford.

I chose this item because...
It represents the fact that some people in my comunity go to health and fitness groups. My mum goes to this fitness group so she knows about it.

I think this item represents (shows) the local area because...
Lots of people in the comunity are fit and healthy and go to a club like this every week.

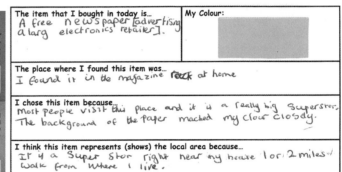

The item that I bought in today is...	My Colour:
A free newspaper [advertising a large electronics retailer].	

The place where I found this item was...
I found it in the magazine rack at home

I chose this item because...
Most people visit this place and it is a really big Superstore. The background of the paper matched my colour closely.

I think this item represents (shows) the local area because...
It is a Super Stor right near my house 1 or 2 miles walk from where I live.

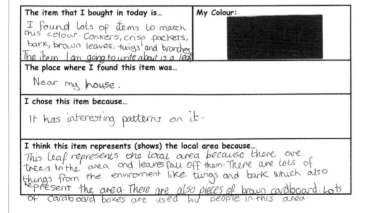

The item that I bought in today is...	My Colour:
I found lots of items to match this colour. Conkers, crisp packets, bark, brown leaves, twigs and branches. The item I am going to write about is a leaf.	

The place where I found this item was...
Near my house.

I chose this item because...
It has interesting patterns on it.

I think this item represents (shows) the local area because...
This leaf represents the local area because there are trees in the area and leaves fall off them. There are lots of things from the enviroment like twigs and bark which also represent the area. There are also pieces of brown cardboard. Lots of cardboard boxes are used by people in this area.

Figure 5 | *Examples of follow-up classwork based on colour chart homework task.*

The context

The outcome of this homework task forms an essential part of a lesson investigating the geography of fear and perceptions of crime and place. The lesson, outlined in Figure 6, is the second in a series of lessons on crime. During the first lesson the students explore the possible links between crime and geography. They have already explored perceptions of place in an earlier unit of work.

Lesson plan Topic: The place of crime: Exploring perceptions of crime and place		Year 7	

Objectives
- To recap the idea that people have different 'perceptions' of places.
- To introduce the idea that people have different perceptions about the risk and nature of crime in a particular place.
- To begin to look for reasons for such perceptions.
- To develop students' survey skills.

Key terms
- Perception
- Place
- Risk
- Crime
- Fear

Resources
- Survey findings – completed as a homework task.
- Photographs of places
- Sugar paper
- Large marker pens
- Local OS maps
- Outline tables

> The homework forms an important part of the planning and preparation for this lesson.

How have the students prepared for the lesson?
Last lesson the students were each given a photograph of a place within the school locality. They were asked to show the photograph to people and ask them what words they would associate with the place shown in the picture and whether they would feel safe being there. The students were given a survey sheet on which to record their ideas (Figure 7).

> The homework task is referred to in the opening section of the lesson. It is clear to the students that the homework is linked to their class work.

Stimulus/remember
- The students are given large copies of the three photographs featured in the homework task.
- Each photograph displays a grid reference and the students use local OS maps to locate each of the places. The students place small stickers on their map to highlight the location of each place.

Time 5 mins

Model
The students work as a class to collate the responses that they gathered from their homework. These could be collated on the board in a table showing the percentage of people who would safe in each area and the percentage that would not. Alternatively the results could be collated in an *Excel* spreadsheet, where graphs grow as data are added to the screen (Figure 8). The graphs could then be displayed using a data projector.

Time 10 mins

> The outcome of the homework task is intrinsically linked to the learning taking place in the lesson.

Try
- The students are given a piece of sugar paper. They stick the large photographs onto the sugar paper and annotate them with the describing words that people came up with during the homework survey.
- The students then discuss possible reasons for the responses that were given.
- The students display their findings around the classroom.

Time 15 mins

Apply
- Working as a class the students use their displays and the graphs to discuss their survey findings.
- They then consider the question: 'How can we begin to explain our findings?'
- The students gather evidence from local OS maps and the annotated photographs to begin to put together a series of reasons why some places are perceived as safer than others. They record their thoughts in a table.

Time 20 mins

> The homework completed by the students is not a closed task, it raises questions that still need to be considered.

Secure/plenary
The students work as a class to discuss their explanations and come up with a series of questions that remain unanswered through this activity, e.g. is there a known record of high crime in any of the areas? Are any of the areas supported by a good neighbourhood watch scheme?

Time 10 mins

Differentiation Through teacher and peer support	**Follow-up homework to be set this week** Students collect evidence of crime in the local area. Could be in the form of photographs (digital pictures taken by students at lunchtime with supervision), newspaper articles, personal accounts, quotes, interviews, etc. Presentation of findings could include production of a large display or collage.

> The homework needs to be contrasting in nature to the previous task *but* it needs to build upon the interest that has developed during the lesson. How can we continue to engage the students and create a 'need to know' (see Figure 9)?

Figure 6 | *The 'Exploring perceptions of crime and place' lesson plan.*

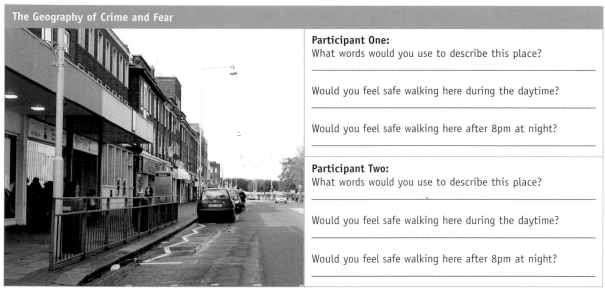

Figure 7 | *A photograph and the mini survey sheet on the geography of crime and fear to be completed for homework. Photo: ©Denise Freeman.*

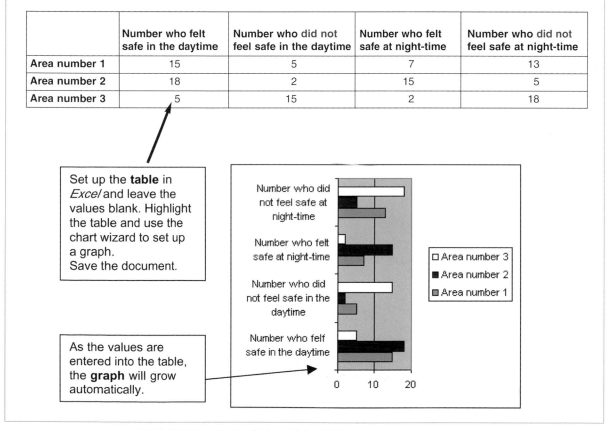

	Number who felt safe in the daytime	Number who **did not** feel safe in the daytime	Number who felt safe at night-time	Number who **did not** feel safe at night-time
Area number 1	15	5	7	13
Area number 2	18	2	15	5
Area number 3	5	15	2	18

Set up the **table** in *Excel* and leave the values blank. Highlight the table and use the chart wizard to set up a graph.
Save the document.

As the values are entered into the table, the **graph** will grow automatically.

Figure 8 | *Presenting the findings of the mini survey.*

Generating a 'Need to know'

Effective homework practice (Figure 3) helps to motivate and engage students in geography and in the work that they are doing. Motivating and engaging students through homework can enhance learning in the classroom and raise achievement. In her work on geographical enquiry, Roberts (2003) discusses the way in which students have a 'need to know'. Homework can play an important role in helping to generate or foster this need to discover more about the world. This is one of the aims of the crime homework example. It is intended that the work will 'grab' the interest of the students and that the homework will offer opportunities for them to go out and satisfy and broaden this interest.

Having engaged the students, one way of maintaining their interest and enthusiasm is to place them at the centre of their learning by putting them in control of their homework. The following questions may help to structure a lesson plenary and allow students to tap into their sense of curiosity and their need to know:

■ How could we continue working on this topic?

■ What could we do in the next lesson?

■ What preparations do we need to make?

■ What would be an appropriate homework task?
   (Students can be encouraged to set their own homework and their own targets for their homework.)

Figure 9 | Creating a 'need to know'. Adapted from: Cowley, 2004. Photo: ©Denise Freeman.

Using a homework book

The presentation and collation of homework can be a challenge for teachers. Where will the students present the outcomes of their homework? What if they lose their exercise book when they take it home to do their homework? Will the homework be appropriately presented or will it be handed in on a scrap of paper? If homework is to prove valuable and add value to learning then the outcome needs to be worthwhile and the students need to feel that this is the case. One solution can be the use of homework books. Such books are take a variety of different forms, that will also prove a useful way of helping to identify a clear place for homework within teaching and learning. Homework books can be designed to follow a certain theme, e.g. recording geography in the news, and provide an opportunity for students to be creative and take more control over their learning. There are many ways in which homework books may be used in geography, these include scrapbooks and independent study books.

Scrapbooks

Plain 'scrapbooks' (larger than standard exercise books) are ideal for enabling students to keep a record of geographical themes and ideas that are covered in the news or on the internet. They can be used during a specific unit of work when students are asked to research a particular issue or comment on a specific news story, to speak to local people and record their comments, or when undertaking work that involves reflecting on their culture, lifestyle or experiences. Enabling students to assume ownership over the work they complete can motivate students and heighten their interest in geography. A scrapbook carves a particular 'niche' for homework and gives it a clear place within the geography curriculum. It may also enable the students to become engaged in contemporary issues or events. The outcomes can be multiple and thus allow for inclusion on as many different levels as possible.

Independent study books

At GCSE and A-level students can be given a separate exercise book for independent study and in which they complete homework tasks. Such books allow them to organise work in their own way and encourages them to think independently about what activities may support their classwork. For example, students may collect relevant newspaper articles and annotate them, develop and organise revision notes, research case studies, make notes on television programmes or practise past examination questions. An independent study book also enables students to develop areas of geographical interest away from the constraints of the examination specification. In order to foster notions of responsibility and independence the students could be asked to set their own homework tasks, appropriate to the work that they have been doing in class. For example, students can be encouraged to stick in newspaper clippings that they find interesting and relevant to geography. To this end, class time is spent on how to collect and where to look for information for their scrapbook. It is, essentially, a place for homework that may be assessed, but extra personalised work may either simply be checked or be referred to by the teacher as a lesson starter in a 'show and tell style', e.g. tell us about a programme you watched and made some notes on this week.

However, the effective use of a homework book does depend on students being skilled at studying independently. Many of them fail to undertake research effectively; for example, when using the internet they may simply print out page after page of text that they have barely read or understood. It is important, therefore, to make time and find ways for developing students' study skills. The following list of questions may provide a focus for such work:

- Where can we find sources of information on geographical themes or issues? The students may be given a tour of the school library or asked to complete a teacher-led research project which enables them to become familiar with accessing the resources available.
- How can we identify useful websites? The students may be asked to complete an activity involving evaluating and rating the usefulness of particular websites (and search engines).
- How can we read and begin to understand text from a website or a newspaper article? Students could be asked to highlight different aspects of texts using different coloured pens, then summarise their findings.
- How can we extract relevant information from a piece of text? The students may be encouraged to develop a proforma for collating information.

Figure 10 | *Curriculum development at year 9 – using a 'travel log book'.*

Taking a Year Out

This scheme of work is designed to engage and motivate key stage 3 geography students. Before they begin their GCSEs students spend the whole of year 9 on an imaginary gap year. During their gap year they 'travel' around the world through their work. The students visit a number of countries, including India, Sri Lanka, Australia, New Zealand, Brazil, Antarctica and South Africa, working through the themes and concepts of the curriculum while visiting each country. They record their travel experiences and store copies of the letters and e-mails they have sent 'home' during their time away in their logbooks. This logbook is also their homework book.

The notion of a round the world trips helps avoid the problem of lengthy periods of time spent on a small number of case studies. It enables the students to study a course that is relevant to them; many of the students travel with their families to or have family connections with the places they 'visit'. Popular cultural texts are used to create a sense of place, as are films, magazines, music, clothes and television. While some may comment that this type of work simply exposes students to a 'travel log' geography, in which they view life through the lens of a tourist, the fact that they are 'tourists' gives teachers an opportunity to unpack the way in which places are represented to foreign onlookers, and provides an opportunity to develop critical thinking skills among students.

Travel logbooks

Figure 10 outlines a geography course for year 9 based around the idea of a 'round the world' trip. The students keep a log of their trip throughout the year in their homework book; this provides them with a clear and meaningful purpose for their homework. The 'logbook' provides an example of a way in which homework can be used to support a scheme of work and enables students to be creative and take ownership of their work. It is something that the students can take pride in and should enable them to see clear links between their homework and work done in class.

Extracts from two log books (Figure 11) illustrate how homework tasks can fuel students' imaginations and encourage them to refer to their own personal experiences of places. This can help motivate students and allow them to see links between the geography and their own lives.

Dear Diary, I'm just going to bed after a hard day's voyage. It is an experience that I will never forget! As you know this is my first stop on my gap year and today, to begin the year, I have come to New Delhi. I came off the plane at about 1 o'clock Indian time. When I got outside the airport, a taxi driver named Rashid was waiting to take me to my accommodation. It took about 50 minutes, travel to my hotel but I didn't notice the time go by because I was so intrigued by my surroundings. The streets that we drove in were rather narrow, closed-in spaces, filled with people, stalls and products. Some of the stalls were filled with fruits, vegetables, herbs, spices and more. Major stores sold clothes, food and music. Some of the women were wearing Punjabi suits, but mainly they wore saris. Most of the men wore shirts and trousers. Even though I was in a car, I could smell the wonderful aroma of Indian food such as vegetable curry. From my knowledge I know that most people are Hindu and that they don't really eat meat. All of the writing on the signs was in several different languages as well as English. Perhaps the other languages were Gujarati or Punjabi. I asked Rashid to stop (luckily he spoke English) so that I could have a quick look around the stalls ... I just couldn't stop thinking about how different the streets were to where I live. In England the roads are smoother. Another difference is definitely the work. The women, I noticed, were hand washing clothes in huge tin bowls. That doesn't happen much in London. Lastly there is more technology in London. There are some similarities between India and England or London and New Delhi, which include the subjects we have in school, although they finish at 2pm. Also they have TV but only if they have good wages.

(Ayesha's first diary entry).

In 'FANtastic' I bought a really nice fan. I bought it in case the air conditioning breaks when I am out there, as it will be hot'.

'W.A. Smiths' is where I bought my very vital sun cream. Above Australia there is a thin ozone layer, this causes the sun's rays to shine down hard and can cause skin cancer if you don't wear sun cream. I also bought a hat. This is to keep my neck and head protected from the sun.

From 'Cameraland' I bought a camera. It is very small with digital facililites. The camera is so I can capture all the wonderful moments and the sights. I can capture the scenery and landscape and show my friends back home.

As I was walking to 'New Delhi Deli' I saw 'Water Sports World'. This reminded me that I had to buy a Jet Ski. A Jet Ski would come in handy for cruising down the east coast don't you think?

After eating at 'New Delhi Deli' I looked for a map of Australia to take with me. I couldn't find one, I even asked a German tourist travelling to Zimbabwe whether he had seen a map shop. After an hour of looking I found a map in a hiking shop. I wanted the map so that I could plan my trip and discover geographical features.

(Scott's diary entry on shopping at New Delhi Airport for items to take to Australia.)

Figure 11 | *Beal High School students' homework diary entries for their travel-logs.*

Students' work can be assessed by the teacher simply marking the book (as with other homework), or it may be peer marked – with students looking at each other's work and assessing it against given criteria. Alternatively, if it is a more personal piece of work, the teacher will allocate time in lessons to discussing homework books with individual students and set targets for enhancing their work.

Figure 12 | Example cards showing tasks and the ways in which parents/carers can help students with homework. Photo: ©Denise Freeman

Putting parents/carers in the picture

Parents and carers often feel uncertain about what exactly their child is expected to do for their homework, how long should be spent on it, and what role they, as a parent, should play in its completion (Freely, 2000). Communication with parents about homework is vital (although it is important not to swamp them with information about

Your task	How parents/carers can help
Interviewing a family member about changes to the local area Using the interview techniques you have learnt in class you must conduct an interview with a family member who has lived in the area for some time. You must ask them: ■ What the area used to be like ■ How it has changed ■ What they think about these changes Remember to record their responses on the record sheet provided. Date due: **14 December**	Your child needs to interview you (or another member of your family who has lived in the local area for some years) about how the area has changed. They have learnt about interview techniques and should conduct this as an 'official interview'. It would be very helpful to show them any old pictures or maps you may have available. *Thanks for your assistance!*
Producing a profile of a place you visit over the holiday period For a day trip or holiday destination find out the following information: ■ The location of the place ■ Why you think tourists go there ■ What facilities are available ■ What transport links are available You must then write a short review (no more than 300 words) of your family day out/holiday destination, explaining how successful the place was in catering for the needs of your family. Date due: **7 September (first lesson back!)**	As part of a family day out or holiday you child must collect information for a profile of that destination. Please encourage your child to pick up any information brochures or leaflets that you come across, as these will provide a useful resource. If possible, tell them about why you chose this destination, and try to get them thinking about how you travelled there, who seems to be holidaying there and what is on offer. *Thanks for your assistance!*
Collecting data from a shopping trip Accompany your parents on their next trip to a supermarket or shop and record the following information: ■ What items were bought ■ How much they cost ■ Where they were produced Write this information down in rough while at the shops/supermarket and then copy it up in neat onto the recording sheet provided. Date due: **8 March**	Your child must collect and record data from your weekly shopping trip. They should accompany you around the supermarket or shops finding out what is bought, how much it costs and what country it is from. You may also want to give them the receipt from your trip to help them. If it is not possible to carry out this activity then old receipts and groceries at home should allow them to complete the task. *Thanks for your assistance!*

school and departmental policies or information about the expectations of individual teachers). A small printed sheet stuck in an exercise book or homework diary can provide both parents and students with clear guidelines for a particular piece of homework and help parents to understand the purpose and intended outcome of the task. Information about how the work is going to be assessed can also be provided. In addition, a leaflet can be produced for parents which details key texts and resources that may help students to complete homework in geography, along with the school contact details for individual members of the department. These could be given out at parent evenings or open days.

The rich and varied nature of the geography curriculum provides plenty of opportunities for parents/carers to go beyond just supporting the completion of homework and enables them to become actively involved in the subject. One way of getting parents involved is to develop homework cards that explain the homework task, along with suggestions for ways in which parents can help. The cards are addressed to both students and parents (Figure 12).

Implications for practice

(a) Reflect on and critically evaluate the role of homework in the geography curriculum.

The place of homework in the curriculum needs to be discussed and reflected upon. Homework is often regarded as an 'add on' rather than as a valuable ingredient of the learning process. When used effectively homework can help to engage students in geography and allow them to explore areas of personal interest to them. This motivation can help students to achieve in the classroom. However, to enjoy these benefits, homework must be shifted from the fringes of curriculum development to a more central position. Teachers may benefit from beginning to think about why they set homework and what they hope to gain from setting homework.

(b) Homework needs to be worthwhile and contribute to students' learning.

Fitness for purpose should be kept in mind when setting homework: what do we hope students will gain from doing this homework? Not all homework is good homework and not all homework will help students to learn. In order for homework to add value to classroom learning it must be planned for and its aims made clear to students, teachers and parents. Students should be able to see a clear link between the work that they are doing in class and the work they have been asked to do at home. Students also need to understand how they can achieve through their homework and where the work is heading.

(c) Developments in ICT may provide opportunities for enhancing homework practice in schools.

The potential for enhancing learning in geography through the use of ICT continues to develop. One growth area is the use of ICT to support homework and independent study, resources for which can be accessed via a local intranet or school website. At a wider scale, the number of interactive learning tools available through the internet is expanding. However, these developments cannot be seen simply as the answer to the homework dilemma. Rather, ICT needs to be used in a useful, inclusive and effective way to support homework practice.

Related publication from the Geographical Association:
- Grimwade, K. and Martin, F. (1997) (see below).
- Roberts, M. (2003) (see below).

References and further reading

Assessment Reform Group (2002) *Ten Principles of Assessment for Learning* (available online: http://www.assessment-reform-group.org.uk).

Balderstone, D. and Lambert, D. (1999) 'Sunday evening at the kitchen table', *Teaching Geography*, 24, 2, pp. 89-91.

Cowan, R. and Hallam, S. (1999) 'What do we know about homework?', *Viewpoint No. 9*. London: Institute of Education.

Cowley, S. (2004) *Getting the Buggers to Behave*. London: Continuum.

Freely, M. (2000) 'Home alone', *The Guardian*, 14 November.

Gee, N. (2001) 'Fieldwork focus: a study of crime', *Wideworld*, 13, 2.

Grimwade, K. and Martin, F. (1997) *Homework in Geography*. Sheffield: Geographical Association.

Hallam, S. (2004) 'Homework: the evidence', *Bedford Way Paper 21*. London: Institute of Education

Lambert, D. and Balderstone, D. (2000) *Learning to Teach Geography in the Secondary School*. London: Routledge Falmer.

MacBeath, J. and Turner, M. (1990) *Learning Out of the School: Homework policy and practice*. A research study commissioned by the Scottish Education Department. Glasgow: Jordanhill College.

Ofsted (1999) *Homework: Learning from practice*. London: HMSO.

Pain, R. (1999) 'The geography of fear', *Geography Review*, 12, 5, pp. 22-5.

Roberts, M. (2003) *Learning through Enquiry: Making sense of geography in the key stage 3 classroom*. Sheffield: Geographical Association.

Sharpe, C., Sharp, C., Keys, W. and Benefield, P. (2001) *Homework: A review of recent research*. Slough: National Foundation for Educational Research.

Chapter 22

Let's get physical

Tom Inman

> **Before reading this chapter consider the following questions:**
>
> ■ What are the main challenges that your students experience when learning about physical geography?
>
> ■ What different strategies do you use to develop students' understanding about process and pattern in physical geography?
>
> ■ How do you assess students' conceptual understanding in physical geography?

This chapter considers how we teach about process and pattern in physical geography. It aims to raise awareness of how we develop appropriate approaches to learning about physical geography in order to promote both understanding and motivation.

Where are we coming from?

> *The current drift toward concentrating attention on human geography in the school curriculum shows signs of leading to a potentially damaging neglect of the physical environment* (Mottershead, 1987, p. 80).

Though written more than 18 years ago, the above quote continues to ring true. While aspects of the academic discipline of physical geography have enjoyed significant development and attention in recent years, this is not the case with *teaching and learning* in physical geography in schools. When, in the late 1990s, attention was focused on thinking skills, physical geography tended to be neglected and the thinking-skills agenda has had less impact on the way we approach the teaching of physical processes and patterns than on other aspects of our subject.

This neglect of the pedagogic side of the subject is perhaps surprising given that pattern and process, and the inextricable links between them, continue to feature in GCSE and A-level specifications. It is also a cause for concern: there is evidence of poor understanding and a lack confidence as well as motivation among students with regard to physical geography – a problem that may be compounded by the fact that they are offered a wide choice in written examinations, so can steer clear of questions that deal with purely physical aspects of the subject.

One consequence of this neglect is that students do not have the foundation they need to build on when they move on to higher education. Indeed concerns have been expressed by academic geographers about the apparent lack of depth in school geography, and the fact that an increasing amount of time is needed in the first year of undergraduate courses to bring students 'up to speed'. As Davidson and Mottershead observed when referring to the interface between school and university, in relation to physical geography, '[it] is probably under greater strain at present than at any other time in recent history' (Davidson and Mottershead, 1996, p. 278).

The nature of the challenge

A good deal of physical geography is taught and learnt within the confines of the school classroom. Given the nature and scale – both in time and space – of many physical processes, even when students are taken into the field they cannot witness processes at work, only the landforms or patterns that they produce (see Chapters 5-6). Thus, it may be argued that field visits are of little value in terms of helping students to grasp underlying concepts, and this may have significant implications for the popularity of physical geography in schools.

It may be assumed that these 'constraints' in terms of teaching about physical processes will come to light through assessment. In order to analyse this we need to consider the standards expected of students in external examinations, as well as the way in which the assessment of the concepts is carried out. The assessment 'norm' is a written response by students for consideration by either a teacher or external examiner. But does this format adequately assess understanding of the concepts involved? Written responses may be based on rote learning which may mask confusion and misconceptions. The true depth of a student's understanding can only be probed and revealed by using other means – in particular, conversation and demonstration. Taking the example of glacial landforms, a typical 'key question' for a lesson might be: 'How are landscapes of glacial erosion formed?' While such a question may stimulate students to discover the ways in which spectacular features of the environment came to be, it does not invite them to construct their own understanding.

One of the consequences of the peculiar problems associated with physical geography is that classroom teaching tends to be more teacher-led than is the case with other areas of the subject. This means that students have fewer opportunities to enquire and speculate about how physical processes work, or how and why the processes result in particular patterns. The fact is that it is all too easy to teach without thinking about how students' conceptual understanding develops; and there is an added problem in the case of physical processes, which is that they stay the same. Given the changing nature of other aspects of geography and how we teach them, it is therefore easy to see why physical processes receive relatively little attention, and so sit low down on the priority list in terms of development of teaching and learning.

Photo: ©Steve Banner, Wildlife and Wilderness.

Figure 1 | *Using a home-made wave tank to model coastal processes. Photo: ©Paul Cornish.*

Searching for answers

Clearly, the nature of the challenges we face in teaching about physical processes and patterns are more diverse and complex than there is space to consider here. They are influenced by the inter-relationship between the process (or pattern) being studied, the learning styles of all those involved (both teacher and students), their past experiences, and the environment and resources available.

The purpose of this chapter is to start asking questions about how we teach about physical process and pattern, and thus to raise standards in geographical learning. Obviously, the routes that we take in finding answers will vary, but there is a common thread which binds the following discussion together: namely, that learning is most effectively achieved through a constructivist paradigm, where students are 'at the helm' of their own learning experiences, through geographical enquiry (see Roberts, 2003). This is not a new concept, particularly in the realm of physical geography. Indeed it has been recognised as a fundamental part of education for some time. Bruner's first principle was 'to initiate and develop in young people a process of question-posing' (from his 1966 project 'Man: a course of study') and this was reflected in a shift in teaching style towards more activity-based learning. In terms of the possible gains of the enquiry and activity-based approach, Raths observed that 'All other things being equal, one activity is more worthwhile than another if it asks the student to engage in inquiry into ideas' (1997, p. 67).

However, while this approach inherently suits the nature of our subject, in relation to physical geography it does not appear to have been translated into classroom practice. Perhaps this is due to the nature of such a teaching approach, where a degree of uncertainty is expected in terms of outcomes.

1. 'Outside-in': bringing the processes into the classroom

In many school subjects, illustrations are useful accessories; in geography they are essential components of the teaching/learning situation (Warwick, 1987, p. 118).

There is a need to engage critically with, and to scrutinise the ways in which we facilitate concept acquisition in physical geography. We can begin by thinking about how students 'see something' and how to 'paint appropriate pictures' in their minds. If learning occurs through seeing the process 'visually', then students' visual representations should tell us a lot about what they have learnt.

Visual representation can take a number of forms, both static and dynamic, and in two or three dimensions. The majority of resources are static (e.g. annotated sketches, diagrams, slides, photographs, cartoons) but as well as videos, computer animations are increasingly used as the relevant technology becomes more available and accessible. While they have obvious benefits, static illustrations cannot easily indicate the gradual impact of physical processes unless a number are used in a series to illustrate different points in time. With moving images, the facility to speed up, slow down or pause the image is very helpful for exploring these gradual processes and the ways in which they produce particular forms and patterns. Animation, in particular, allows the key elements of the process to be illustrated in the absence of background 'noise', much as a field sketch concentrates on the geographical phenomena under investigation.

To view processes in operation in three-dimensions generally involves making small-scale physical models. An example often found in the geography classroom is a home-made wave tank (Figure 1), used for investigating coastal processes and the impact of coastal management. Simulations of this kind allow the collapsing of timescales from thousands of years into minutes or seconds, thus enabling students to conceptualise mechanisms that link form and process, and scaling down the spatial dimension to allow a holistic perspective of landscape where linkages between subsystems can be appreciated (Job and Buck, 1994).

When using models of this kind it is important to make sure that students are aware of their shortcomings; in particular that such simulations represent closed systems with 'defined boundaries' and so differ markedly from and lack the complexity of open systems in the real world. Nevertheless, they are very useful tools for developing understanding of physical processes and how they determine form or pattern.

The challenge for us as teachers is to be able to design ways in which processes can easily be simulated or described within the classroom environment. This may involve the adoption of one of two different approaches, as described below.

(a) Here is the pattern. What processes may have been responsible for this and how do they work? (pattern → process)

This approach starts with the end-result of the processes, i.e. using a landform as the stimulus for asking questions about its formation. A number of critical decisions need to be taken regarding the extent and nature of the support given by the teacher, which may be provided informally (such as through whole-class discussion) or formally.

One such technique used for this is sequencing (Roberts, 2003), which involves considering the formation of particular landscapes in a number of stages, placed in order of occurrence. This requires students to understand how the operation of certain processes explains the differences between each stage. An example of such a sequence is shown below. It was used in the context of the question: 'How was the East African Rift Valley formed?' (Figure 2).

Students are provided with a number of both textual and visual 'clues' to support the development of their understanding. Text and diagrams first need to be paired, then placed into the correct sequence.

(a)

Molten rock rises up through the cracks to form volcanoes along the edges of the Rift Valley

Two of the biggest faults were parallel to one another. The land between them collapsed

Around 70 million years ago the land in this area was fairly flat

Water draining down into the Rift Valley became trapped and caused the lakes

The faults or cracks were caused by two plates colliding

(b)

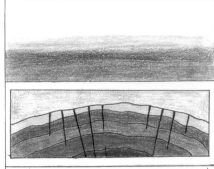

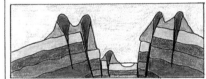

Around 70 million years ago the land in this area was fairly flat.

A series of collisions with neighbouring plates created a system of faults or cracks in the African plate.

Two of the largest faults were parallel to one another. The land between them collapsed as sections of the crust began to move apart.

Magma from below the surface forced its way up through the cracks to form lines of volcanoes along the edges of the rift valley.

Water draining down into the rift valley became trapped and formed a series of lakes. The same process caused smaller cones to form on the valley floor.

Figure 2 | *The formation of the East African Rift Valley: (a) sequencing cards, and (b) one student's explanation. Source: Roberts, 2003.*

	Technique	Description	Support
1.	Illustrations and descriptions (pre-matched)	The illustration of the pattern is given with an explanation of the description of the process that has resulted in its formation.	**HIGH**
2.	Illustrations and descriptions (dominos style)	In this case an illustration is matched with the description that matches the subsequent 'stage'.	
3.	Illustrations and descriptions (not matched)	Both illustrations and explanations are provided, but need matching prior to sequencing.	
4.	Illustrations only	Students are required to create their own description of the process to match each illustration, as well as ordering.	
5.	Descriptions only	Similar to the above task, but students illustrate the pattern created by the process that has been described.	
6.	Incomplete descriptions/illustrations	Each stage is represented either by a description or an illustration – students complete missing descriptions and illustrations. Some stages may be omitted entirely.	**LOW**

Figure 3 | *Varying the level of support for sequencing activities.*

(a)

Powerful waves attack the chalk rock.	The cliffs of the South Dorset coast are composed of resistant chalk.
The pressure created by the process of hydraulic action forces the rock to break open.	Vertical weaknesses (joints) in the rock are particularly vulnerable to erosion.
Continued action by waves increased the size of the joint to form a small cave.	The size of the cave expands as more weaknesses are exposed.
As the arch continues to widen, the roof is less supported and more vulnerable.	Eventually the cave reaches to the other side of the headland, opening up to form an arch.
The roof eventually collapses under its own weight, creating a stack.	The water is forced into the joints in the cliff.

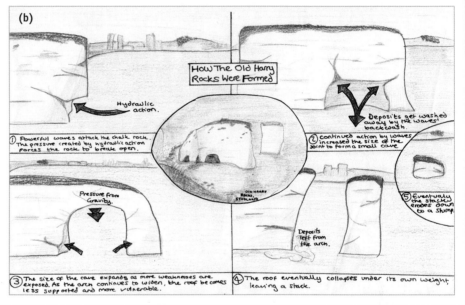

Figure 4 | *The 'How was Old Harry formed?' activity: (a) cards, and (b) student's completed sketches.*

This strategy can be adapted to a range of situations where students have varying degrees of familiarity with the process. Differentiation can be achieved by providing students with more than one of level of support (Figure 3). Furthermore, the task can be designed specifically so that an increasing level of support can be provided when required.

Example: How might 'Old Harry' have been formed?

When this activity was used with year 12 students, a photograph of Old Harry Rocks, Dorset, was used as the stimulus, together with the question: 'How might Old Harry have been formed?' Since the illustration of Old Harry's formation was diagrammatic, it presented an opportunity to discuss the role of field sketching. This created a link to the series of staged diagrams that students were asked to create. They were provided with a number of cards (see Figure 4a), each of which described a stage in the process of Old Harry's formation. This enabled them to create a series of, annotated illustrations. The

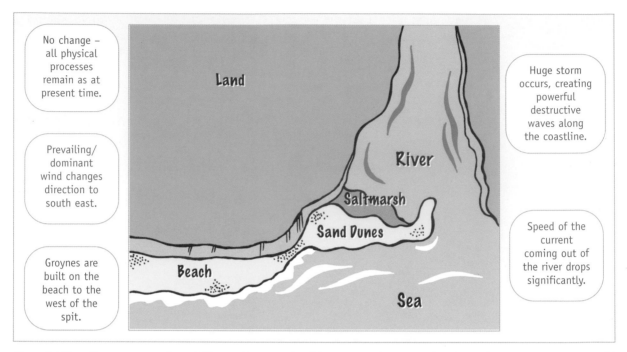

No change – all physical processes remain as at present time.

Prevailing/ dominant wind changes direction to south east.

Groynes are built on the beach to the west of the spit.

Land

River

Saltmarsh

Sand Dunes

Beach

Sea

Huge storm occurs, creating powerful destructive waves along the coastline.

Speed of the current coming out of the river drops significantly.

Figure 5 | *The spit formation diagram and scenario cards.*

number of illustrations was in this case pre-determined at four, though the number could be left to the discretion of the students (Figure 4b).

An alternative approach is to use 'play dough' to model the changes in the landscape. This helps students to visualise the impact of the processes in a kinaesthetic way. Also, by 'manipulating' the landscape they can replicate gradual change over time, which is closer to reality than a series of static 'stages' which tend to suggest that changes to a landscape occur suddenly, rather than gradually over time, which is more often the case.

(b) These are the processes at work. What pattern might they create? (process → pattern)

A logical extension to the above activity is to ask students what they think the landscape will look like at some point in the future, i.e. to use their knowledge of processes to speculate about how landscapes may change in times to come. This strategy provides an opportunity for students to apply their understanding to a new situation. For example, using ICT students can use *Paintbrush* tools to manipulate an image (using an airbrushing technique) to show how a particular landscape may change in appearance over a period of time. (The Staffordshire Learning Net website includes an example of coastal erosion on the island of Zakynthos, Greece, using this technique.) Clearly, such a facility has massive potential for students to 'create' images of their own (Taylor, 2004).

In reality, the processes that will determine landscapes of the future cannot all be known about, or predicted, so such activities have their limitations. However, by making students aware of this unpredictability, activities can be used as opportunities for them to consider different interpretations and a wide range of possible outcomes. This encourages independence of thought and speculation, promoting high-level discussion and debate as to likely future outcomes. It also has potential for differentiation, by creating a number of 'What if ...' scenarios, perhaps involving human intervention in physical processes, or uncertainty regarding the nature and rate of the processes involved. This lends itself easily to group work where students 'forecast' future patterns from 'scenario cards' that are given to them. Each group presents their predictions to other groups using a variety of media. A strong sense of ownership can be achieved by encouraging students to ask speculative questions themselves.

Example: Spit formation and change

This activity considers a range of factors that influence spit development and morphology. Students have to work out how the coastline may change as a result of the circumstances described on given scenario cards. They are given a diagram showing spit formation which they can manipulate and annotate to show changes and the reasons for them (Figure 5).

2. 'Classroom fieldwork': promoting the enquiry approach

'Finding out' in physical geography involves what is essentially scientific methodology, involving the creation and testing of hypotheses by observation and explanation (Parsons and Knight, 1991). In geography, as in other disciplines, teaching about methods of finding out is an essential part of any course.

Fieldwork provides an opportunity to use a problem-solving approach in school geography; it helps students to link process and form in different landscapes, once the processes have been understood. However, as noted earlier, it falls short when it comes to promoting conceptual understanding since few physical processes can be observed in action (Job and Buck, 1994). So how do we create conditions which enable us to meet our goals?

One thing we can do is to create an atmosphere of speculation in the classroom. The key here is to set up activities which have the potential for a range of outcomes, and which allow students to speculate and use their theoretical understanding to hypothesise, observe, record, analyse and evaluate physical processes. The debriefing process is particularly important in this context, and regardless of outcomes has the potential to generate the most learning. A 'successful' outcome (i.e. one that 'fits' the physical process being represented/simulated) allows parallels to be drawn and understanding to be acquired. However, an unsuccessful outcome may be just as valuable, actually supporting a deeper examination of processes and patterns.

Using models as part of 'classroom fieldwork' is usually very effective in grabbing students' attention. At the most basic level, models can support a descriptive approach to the study of physical processes, but they can (and should) be used to encourage a rigorous and scientific approach to enquiry. Things that can be achieved include:

- discussion of what models are and why they are used
- establishment of the similarities and differences between the model and reality
- development of multiple hypotheses
- establishment of appropriate methodologies
- description and analysis of the outcome
- discussion of the limitations of the model in representing a given physical process (particularly in the case of outcomes that do not match hypotheses).

The following example demonstrates such an approach using the idea of a blancmange glacier (Lambert and Balderstone, 2000) to investigate the nature of glacier movement.

Example: The blancmange glacier

In this instance the blancmange glacier 'experiment' was used with year 9 students who were studying the process of glacier movement and its role in landscape evolution. Emphasis was placed on the procedure of creating and testing hypotheses. After the 'model' was explained, students were given time to write down an expected outcome, with the opportunity to discuss it with a partner if they so chose. Examples of their comments are shown in Figure 6.

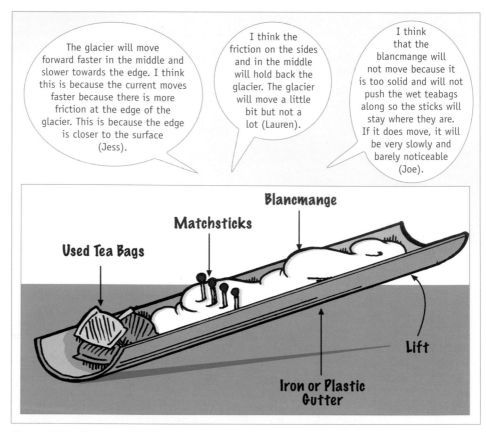

Figure 6 | *The blancmange glacier and students' thoughts on its expected behaviour.*

When analysing the responses of the students to this or similar experiments, it is useful to consider their levels of understanding in terms of two 'domains'. The 'base domain' refers to basic understanding of the model or analogy that is being used to represent a particular physical process that occurs in the real world (the 'target domain'). 'Success' can be assessed according to the extent to which a student's understanding is successfully transferred from the base domain to the target domain.

Joe's response exhibited understanding at the level of the 'base domain', being limited to the concrete confines of the model itself. This raises an important issue relating to the use of models in this way: that the 'realism' and strong visual quality of the model itself may inhibit students' ability to transfer their understanding from base to target domain. Care must be taken to avoid this happening.

The responses of the other two students, Lauren and Jess, show that they were not inhibited in the same way as Joe, since each of them described the movement of 'the glacier' (target domain), showing that they understood the model as simulation of reality. Jess's response in particular shows a clear understanding of the role of differential friction and its impact on glacier movement. This suggests a 'successful outcome' in terms of using the model, as he showed a clear understanding of the real-world processes that it was designed to demonstrate.

Dealing with uncertainty in outcome

It is perfectly possible, and in some cases likely, that the desired outcome for a particular activity does not actually occur, and knowing this is so is one reason why some teachers are reluctant to use models of the kind described above. While such inhibition is understandable, it is well worth trying to overcome it because what might in one sense be regarded as 'a failure' may in fact be an ideal opportunity for extending learning. For example, in the case of the glacier experiment, when the blancmange glacier failed to move in the ways expected this led to an informative and high-level discussion about the reasons for why this was so. Students were able to consider the relative properties of ice and blancmange, the nature and morphology of the 'valley floor' (the guttering), and the absence of meltwater to lubricate the base. There was even some discussion about alternative and more effective ways of 'representing' glacial processes.

3. Models of the mind: the use of analogies

A note on terminology

The terms 'analogy', 'metaphor' and 'comparison' are often used interchangeably. However, there are some important differences. Analogies are 'non-literal comparisons between superficially dissimilar knowledge domains' (Zook, quoted in Iding, 1997, pp. 234-5). In other words, they are about comparisons between the structure rather than the content of different domains. An example of this is the explanation of the human eye as a camera, where, for example, the retina records information in the same way as the film in a camera. The true meaning of a metaphor is significantly different from an analogy: 'Taken as literal, a metaphorical statement appears to be perversely asserting something to be what it is plainly not, such as calling a teacher "the captain of the ship"' (Black, 1979, p. 21).

The use of analogies to aid 'visualisation' and learning relates to the fundamental idea that 'students cannot learn more than their own experiences permit' (Hantula, 1975, p. 326). What this underlines is the importance of students being able to relate ideas to what they can see or have observed. This is particularly important in relation to processes of landscape formation.

Possible uses of analogies include:

- *To develop understanding* – structuring our teaching about a physical process around a 'real-world' analogy. There is considerable scope for grabbing the attention of students, and involving them in demonstration. For example, the idea of erosion, transport and deposition could be introduced to year 7s through 'Bob the Builder' in his truck, picking up, moving and unloading soil!
- *To confirm understanding* – having taught a physical concept (either with or without the use of an analogy), you could ask the students to think of appropriate analogies to represent the processes involved. You might even get them to bring in 'props' for a class demonstration – it will certainly lead to some interesting results!
- *To assess understanding* – e.g. for a named process, students select one from a number of analogies that best represents the process in question. Alternatively, students can be asked about how different features of the analogy represent different features of the process being considered.

Example: Using analogies to confirm understanding

The use of analogies to enhance and confirm understanding of erosional processes was undertaken with year 8 students. The students were provided with two sets of information: definitions of the processes themselves, and a 'menu' of objects from which they had to select items that enabled them to demonstrate each process using an appropriate analogy (Figure 7). Differentiation was achieved between groups of different abilities by choosing to include a number of 'dummy' items. While largely successful,

Process with description	Analogy	Illustration
Hydraulic action The pressure created by the force of water and air in cracks in rocks splits the rock apart.	Popping a bag of crisps: the force of the hands on the air (within a confined space) leads to increased air pressure, causing the bag to split open.	 *Photo: ©Diane Wright.*
Abrasion The wearing down of a surface through the friction created by the movement of particles across it.	The action of sandpaper against a block of wood: the coarse grains of the sandpaper create friction as it rubs against the surface of the wood, leading to wearing down of the wood surface.	 *Photo: ©Tim Lawson.*
Attrition The wearing away and breaking up of particles as a result of the force created by their collision with other materials.	The collision of blocks of Lego bricks: the force of the collision on a number of weaknesses within the blocks causes them to fail.	 *Photo: ©Liz Lewis.*

Figure 7 | *Using analogies to illustrate processes.*

what became clear was that it is vital to ensure full understanding of the analogy (the 'base domain') at the outset. This requires the teacher to spend precious time taking prior knowledge into consideration and, if required, providing explanations. In the absence of such groundwork, there is the risk that misunderstandings will be transferred to the physical process being represented. The importance of using appropriate analogies is also self-evident.

When devising strategies for enhancing understanding of physical processes it is vital to consider the metacognitive aspect of learning. Failure to do so will soon expose the fact that there are many potential pitfalls. However, given proper preparation, the benefits of such strategies can be considerable. As stated in the thinking-skills literature, it is often in discussion and reflection that real gains are made, which is why it is so important for teachers to create the conditions that will allow this to happen.

Related publications from the Geographical Association:
■ Titles in the *Classic Landforms of ...* series
■ Knight, P. (2005) *Changing Geography: Glaciers and glacial landscapes.*
■ Roberts, M. (2003) (see below)

References

Print

Adamczyk, P., Binns, T., Brown, A., Cross, S. and Magson, Y. (1994) 'The geography-science interface: a focus for collaboration', *Teaching Geography*, 19, 1, pp. 11-14.

Balderstone, D. (1996) 'An evaluation of the impact of a range of learning experiences on concept acquisition in physical geography' in Slater, F. (ed) *Reporting Research in Geography Education*, Monograph No. 4. London: Institute of Education, pp. 33-54.

Black, M (1979) 'More about metaphor? in Ortney, A. (ed) *Metaphor and Thought*. Cambridge: Cambridge University Press, pp. 19-43.

Bruner, J. (1966) *Toward a Theory of Instruction*. New York: WW Norton & Co.

Davidson, J. and Mottershead, D. (1996) 'The experience of physical geography in schools and higher education' in Rawling, E.M. and Daugherty, R.A. (eds) *Geography into the Twenty-First Century*. Chichester: Wiley, pp. 277-88.

Hantula, J. (1975) 'Use of analogy as curriculum tool', *Journal of Geography*, September, pp. 326-8.

Iding, M.K. (1997) 'How analogies foster learning from science texts', *Instructional Science,* 25, 4, pp.233-53.

Lambert, D. and Balderstone, D. (2000) *Learning to Teach Geography in the Secondary School*. London: Routledge Falmer.

Mottershead, D. (1987) 'Physical geography ... the debate continues', *Teaching Geography*, 12, 2, pp. 80-1.

Nelson, F. (1975) 'Use of analogy as a learning-teaching tool', *Journal of Geography*, February, pp. 83-6.

Parsons, T. and Knight, P. (1991) 'Finding out in physical geography: a question of science?', *Teaching Geography*, 16, 1, pp. 15-17.

Raths, J. (1997) 'Identifying activities that seem to have inherent worth', *Prospero*, 3, 2, pp. 67-8.

Roberts, M. (2003) *Learning through Enquiry: Making sense of geography in the key stage 3 classroom*. Sheffield: Geographical Association.

Taylor, L. (2004) *Re-presenting Geography*. Cambridge: Chris Kington Publishing.

Warwick, P. (1987) 'How do children "see" geographical pictures?', *Teaching Geography*, 12, 3, pp. 118-19.

Electronic

Earth Science Learning Centre at the Institute of Education – www.ioe.ac.uk/index.htm

Staffordshire Learning Net – www.sln.org.uk/geography

Implications for practice

(a) Consider a variety of ways of simulating physical processes inside the classroom.

While fieldwork is a vital part of physical geography, a field visit can only provide a brief snapshot of physical processes at work. There are increasingly varied and accessible ways of demonstrating how physical processes work, ranging from traditional sketches, photographs, etc., to moving images, including computer animations, and three-dimensional models. The advantage of models and moving images is that they can show change over time, and can illustrate how changes tend to occur gradually, rather than in a series of static steps or stages.

An alternative to using models is to use analogies or metaphors. The risk here is that if misunderstandings occur they can be carried over to the 'real world' processes and patterns, so careful preparation is needed.

(b) Use different approaches to teaching and learning about patterns and processes.

There are two main approaches: one where the pattern which results from a process is known and can be used as a starting-point for learning, and one where the pattern is inferred from an understanding of the process.

(c) Devise ways to encourage a scientific, enquiry approach to learning.

It is important to develop and adopt a scientific approach to enquiry through hypothesis testing. This facilitates speculative enquiry, where outcomes are not necessarily known beforehand, and leads to depth and structure in the analysis of outcomes.

Chapter 23

Teaching geography for a sustainable future

Alun Morgan

> **Before reading this chapter consider the following questions:**
>
> - If the rest of your life will be spent in the future and the future starts today, what kind of future do you want: (a) as an individual? (b) as a member of society? (c) as a geography teacher?
>
> - How does your teaching of geography help your students to clarify their visions for a more sustainable future?
>
> - Why is so little attention given to the future in education?

.Geography is the subject that holds the key to our future (Michael Palin).

Sustainable development is concerned with improving the quality of people's lives, both their economic security and their social well being, without destroying the systems on which future generations depend. Sustainability is the main outcome. It is future oriented.

Justifying a 'futures dimension' in geography

The 'future' – preparing young people for adult life – is arguably what all education is for, yet remarkably little attention is paid to it overtly through the curriculum in classrooms and schools. This chapter argues that not only is attention to the future in geography education desirable, it is positively essential, and young people have an entitlement to explore *their* futures across a number of geographical and temporal scales.

The following assumptions underlie what follows in this chapter:

- The world of the present could and should be a better place; and the achievement of a better world in the future is possible and desirable. This is a goal-directed activity. That goal is sustainable development (see 'Facets of the world...' below)
- The students of today will play an active role in making that better future
- Geography teachers have a significant role to play in equipping students with the requisite knowledge, skills and values for creating a better future
- Attention to the future *now* is the fundamental starting point in the process of working towards a better future.

Even if not everyone agrees with these assumptions, the justifications for attention to the future, or more correctly, alternative futures, are compelling when considered from the perspectives described below.

Looking at the future through a 'geographical lens'

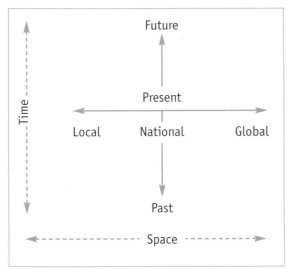

Figure 1 | *The spatial and temporal dimensions. Source: Hicks, 2001.*

Geography is most usually characterised as a distinctive domain of human knowledge by its focus on place and space. Yet these are dynamic categories which cannot be understood without the temporal dimension. Thus, geographers must grapple with the complexity, interconnectedness and dynamism of place and space across temporal and spatial scales (Figure 1). This could also be taken as a definition of being human since we must all engage with this process of exploration in order to make sense of the world so that we are able to function in it.

This insight provides a strong justification for the continued existence of geography in the curriculum; in its most holistic and eclectic forms, geography can come nearest to providing a consummate 'worldview'. It does this by providing a number of 'lenses' through which to investigate the world, each of which will bring into sharp focus one or more facets of that world by varying the emphasis on place, space and/or scale (see 'Facets of the world...'). Taken in isolation, each perspective represents only a partial representation of a reality that is inextricably spatio-temporal; to obtain a truly comprehensive understanding requires attention to several if not all of these perspectives. While it goes without saying that a geographical study that pays no regard to the spatial dimension is almost meaningless, it is true to say the same of one which pays no regard to the temporal dimension.

Facets of the world revealed through the geographical 'lenses' of place, space and scale:

■ the integration in place both of physical, biological and social phenomena (*spatial dimension*); and the past, present and future (*temporal dimension*)

■ the interdependencies between places brought about through the flows of people, materials and ideas through space (*spatial dimension*); and over time (*temporal dimension*)

■ the interdependencies among scales from the local to the global (*spatial scale*); and from the recent to the distant past or future (*temporal scale*).

■ Human-environment dynamics – the reciprocal impacts of people and environments (*both spatial and temporal dimensions*)

■ Environmental dynamics – including biogeography, climatology and geomorphology (*both spatial and temporal dimensions*)

■ Human-societal dynamics – the inter-relationships between economic, social, political, and cultural processes (*both spatial and temporal dimensions*)

A useful analogy might be the geographer as cinematographer. One of the first decisions for either is how much to have in the field of view. For the cinematographer it is a matter of selecting a macro or wide-angle lens, while for the geographer it is about selecting what spatial scale, from the local through the regional to the global, is appropriate for the focus of the enquiry (see also Chapter 4). And just as it is much more versatile for a photographer to have a zoom lens to change quickly between close-up and distant images, the ability to shift the focus from local to global and back again is an important skill which needs to be developed by the geographer. Another choice involves what timescale to work in. For the cinematographer this can range from the extremely short scale (usually involving 'freeze-frame' and time-lapse technology) through 'real-time' (e.g. the recent *24* drama series starring Kiefer Sutherland, or the Johnny Depp vehicle *Nick of Time* (Badham, 1995)), to the long timescale (e.g. over several years, an individual's lifespan, or even several generations). The geographer can work with, and across, a number of timescales, and within a range from the atomic to the geological! But the geographer has a considerable advantage over the cinematographer (perhaps with the exception of those working in the genre of science-fiction) in that they can point their metaphorical lens into the *future*. In particular, this ability to speculate and forecast both near and far into the future based on a sound understanding of geographical processes and phenomena represents one of the greatest contributions made by geography as an applied discipline. In the current precarious epoch this is imperative as we work towards a sustainable future (see below).

Sustainable development

Sustainable development refers to the process of working towards a better world simultaneously at the local and global levels through enhancing the environment, society and economy in a balanced and reciprocal fashion. Essentially, it is a process that is directed towards the achievement of a balance between the human and natural life-support systems.

Major efforts have been under way to work towards realising a sustainable future since the Rio Earth Summit in 1992, although only limited impact has been recorded to date. The Rio +10 Earth Summit took place in Johannesburg in September 2002, but for many this too has not resulted in enough progress. It is only in 2005 that the USA, for example, has accepted that global warming is happening and human behaviour may be a contributory cause. But even now there is little appetite to risk economic damage by putting any real limit on fossil fuel burning. Sustainable development is a fiercely difficult issue.

While providing a precise definition of the term is problematic (about 200 are in current usage), sustainable development is by its very nature future-orientated since this is where a sustainable world will exist, and since consideration of the extended future (i.e. at least several generations) is a fundamental cornerstone. This is encapsulated in notions such as stewardship, intergenerational equity, and the 'precautionary principle'.

The educational purpose

Curriculum

The national curriculum requires schools to equip students 'for their future lives as workers and citizens [and] secure their commitment to sustainable development at the local, national, regional and global levels' (DfEE/QCA, 1999, p. 11). It is impossible to see how these goals can be achieved without a futures dimension to their learning. This need for a futures perspective is reinforced in the Sustainable Development Education Panel's reference to the needs of future generations (SDEP, 1999). It provides geography teachers with phrases that clearly demonstrate how sustainable development relates to the geography curriculum:

" *Education for sustainable development is about the learning needed to maintain and improve our quality of life and the quality of life of generations to come. It is about equipping individuals, communities, groups, businesses and government to live and act sustainably; as well as giving them an understanding of the environmental, social and economic issues involved. It is about preparing for the world in which we will live in the next century, and making sure that we are not found wanting* (SDEP, 1999, p. 30).

Pedagogy

There is currently an emphasis on pedagogy and learning theory, reflected in educational programmes seeking to promote 'thinking skills', 'creativity', and 'accelerated learning'. These have partly emerged from a recognition that the 'banking' model of education, in which existing knowledge is passed on to the next generation, is no longer satisfactory in a rapidly changing and unpredictable world where much of this knowledge soon becomes obsolete. Thus, students need to be prepared for the challenges of living and working in a future society by equipping them with a number of skills which will allow them to adapt to change and uncertainty. In addition, many educationists have recognised that learning is best achieved if students are able to construct their own knowledge, and reflect on their learning (so-called 'metacognition', see Chapter 16) either individually or collaboratively. Futures education is well-placed both to prepare students for an uncertain future and to enhance their cognitive development in the here and now (thereby raising achievement) since it addresses a number of inter-related skills and dimensions:

- anticipating change
- critical thinking
- clarifying values
- decision making
- creative imagination
- visioning
- recognising patterns and processes through time
- cross-generational empathy.

Student motivation

A major educational justification is that futures education is more relevant to the needs of young people (see below) and consequently is likely to be more engaging, thereby raising achievement through enhanced motivation.

a. Geography education – putting the two together

Obviously, the geographical and educational justifications coincide strongly in education for sustainable development. The need to incorporate a futures dimension has been a recurring theme in a variety of initiatives established by the Geographical Association (GeoVisions) and the Qualifications and Curriculum Authority (Futures Forum website) among others. This is echoed in a report to QCA on the future for *Geographical Education in the 21st Century*, which cogently argues for a curriculum that has at its heart a focus on sustainable development and attention to the temporal dimension, including the future (Butt and Foskett, 2001). Strategies aiming to promote thinking through geography such as 'Mysteries' and 'Mind movies' can also be used to address the futures dimension in a creative way (Leat, 1998, and see Chapters 16 and 40).

Another justification is that a futures dimension in geographical teaching can only serve to make the subject itself a more attractive option since it will mean it relates more clearly to the needs of students. Anything that makes the subject more relevant and attractive to students should be welcomed in these times of uncertainty in terms of the subject's continued position in the curriculum.

Focus	Age 11	Age 14	Age 18
Personal	Fear of violence Hope for good education, good job, material well-being	Desire for happiness Fear of unemployment and ill-health	Most interested in their personal future Hope for material success, good education, good job Happiness *per se* Fear of unemployment, poor health, money worries Positive that things will be better than now
Local	Keen to see the local area improved (less pollution, more recycling, less traffic; more facilities for the homeless, disabled and children) Sometimes confuse local and global affairs	Fear of crime Fear that local area will become too developed and/or rundown New technology and immigration blamed for unemployment Television blamed for increasing crime	Least positive age group about conditions improving locally Fear of crime and unemployment Hope for increased prosperity Feel strongly that there will be less racism and greater gender equality Hope for increased environmental awareness Skeptical of the influence they can have Aware of systems 'out there' that control things but don't feel part of the process Aware of political dimension but feel powerless
Global	Fear of increasing poverty and increasing pollution	Hope for eradication of global poverty and pollution Key areas of concern include global warming, ozone depletion, deforestation, nuclear war	Least positive age group about conditions improving globally – but this age group desires it the most
Visions	Commitment to improving the environment and to learning about global issues highest at this age	Less optimistic than 11-year-olds about world conditions improving and ambivalent about whether they can do anything themselves to help make the world a better place	Aware of systems 'out there' that control things but don't feel part of the process – skeptical of the influence they can have

Figure 2 | The hopes and fears of 11-, 14- and 18-year-olds in England. After: Hicks and Holden, 1995.

b. Geography education and the needs of students

Research undertaken by David Hicks and Catherine Holden (1995), into the hopes and fears for the future expressed by secondary-age students, reveal some startling observations (summarised in Figure 2). Their research shows that all age groups in the secondary phase have a real interest in the future at the personal, local and global levels, but that they all feel that they receive insufficient education about either global issues or their own future. Clearly, secondary school students have a yearning to explore these dimensions and would find lessons that address them engaging. Perhaps most worrying is the apparent decline in optimism among students through the secondary phase, both in terms of their expectation that a better future for the local and global environment will be achieved, and their role in bringing about positive change. Unless opportunities to counteract this trend are taken in education, this disempowerment could increase levels of disaffection among students (see also Chapter 31).

c. Geography education and the needs of society

Futures education will bring benefits to wider society through the nurturing of flexible and creative decision makers who are able to anticipate and accommodate change. Students' moral development should be as important as their cognitive development. It is imperative that we nurture a society which is committed to achieving a better world through responsible citizenship. This is a major focus of futures education, global citizenship education, and education for sustainable development. This moral imperative is perhaps the most contentious justification given its utilitarian, if not overtly political rationale. Yet as geographers know, a general consensus is emerging that the 'globalised' world is currently on a dangerous trajectory that could lead to the exacerbation of existing societal inequalities and even the destruction of the life support system of several million species, including our own. Young people are aware of several threats and challenges to their own well-being, as indicated in the concerns outlined in Figure 2. Thus, things must change if we are to achieve a better world in the short, medium and long term. Futures education will be a significant force in this process of working towards sustainable development (see above). No one presently has all the answers but 'successfully structuring a sustainable society requires that we have some vision of what it would look like' (Brown, cited in Hicks, 1994a). This will be impossible unless a futures dimension is incorporated into students' education, and as geography has the pre-eminent role in teaching about sustainable development, the subject must address the future in its teaching.

Integrating a futures dimension into geography education

There is no better starting place for a consideration of teaching materials and techniques for integrating the futures dimension in teaching than the influential work of David Hicks, who started out his professional life in geography education. In particular, his teachers' handbooks contain a wealth of teaching ideas, which can be highly recommended (see 'References and resources'). What follows are some suggestions for bringing the future to life in the geography classroom and they are heavily reliant on David Hicks' ideas.

Getting into a new time-frame

This section provides a range of strategies designed to help students to conceptualise timescales different from those that they are familiar with.

Strategy 1: Using sequences of film

Students can be shown a short video sequence that covers an extended period of time. For example, time-lapse photography of a flower opening, a woodland changing with the seasons, a dead rodent decomposing (a particular favourite with some students), a crowd arriving or dispersing from a concert, or a building being constructed. Such material is often to be found in educational or natural history programmes. Alternatively, video tapes of time-lapse sequences can be obtained from Computerised Time-Lapse Cinematography.

A number of Hollywood films can be used in the same way. For example, the opening credits of the film *Waterworld* (Reynolds, 1995) shows the fictional melting of the ice caps and the subsequent inundation of the land. *The Time Machine* (Pal, 1960; Wells, 2002) provides a particularly interesting starting point for discussion because it involves a story set initially in Victorian times, filmed with the sensibilities and knowledge of the contemporary world (the 1960s and the beginning of the twentieth century, respectively), with a vision set well into the future. The time-travel sequences show an extended period from one vantage point that experiences wars, redevelopments and changing land use. The 2002 version includes a sequence showing the onset of a new Ice Age which could be used against the melting ice-cap sequence of *Waterworld* with discussion focusing on very different but related views of the future. The 2004 film *The Day after Tomorrow* (Emmerich, 2004) can also be used to stir debate about possible and

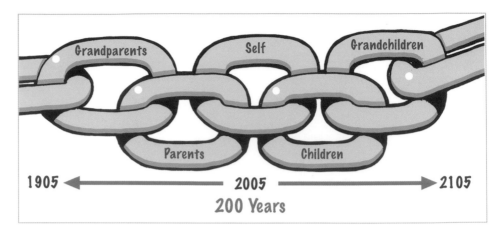

Figure 3 | *The extended present: a family chain. Source: Hicks, 2001.*

probable futures, and to stimulate enquiry into the scientific evidence about the likelihood of particular future scenarios.

Strategy 2: The extended present

This simple device (Figure 3) allows students to make the connection in a very personal way between the past, present and future over a period spanning approximately 200 years. They consider how far into the past they are directly connected through people they know (i.e. parents and grandparents) and how far into the future they are likely to have a connection to the people yet to come (i.e. their children and grandchildren).

Strategy 3: Using the geological or planetary timescale

A number of simple tricks have been used to enable people to relate the almost inconceivable geological timescales to their own lives, e.g. using a 24-hour clock, conceptualising the Earth as a 47-year-old human. At the time of writing two Earth Galleries at the Natural History Museum, London, are good for playing with timescale and the future: 'From the beginning' (Gallery 63 – and associated publication) deals with the geological history of the Earth to the present, while 'Earth today and tomorrow' (Gallery 65) addresses the future implications of current resource use and abuse.

A short walk away (and therefore easily manageable as a combined visit) is the Science Museum, in which the 'Making the modern world' exhibition also has an interesting take on time. The exhibition ends with a prototype of the 'Clock of the long now', which will ultimately be built in Great Basin National Park in Nevada, USA. Figure 4 shows the clock, which will chime every thousand years, ticking once every year, and is intended to keep time for the next 10,000 years (see Long Now Foundation website for further information and other interesting time-perspectives).

Another resource which plays with the relationship between the geological and human timescales is the *Geology of Biology* mural by Jason Middlebrook. Commissioned by the Wellcome Trust (see website) and inspired by the human genome project, this mural uses art to relate the human body to geological structures and can provide an interesting starting point for a discussion of different timescales.

Strategy 4: Time capsule and future pen-friend

An activity made popular by the BBC children's programme *Blue Peter* is to create and bury a time-capsule. The class could work collaboratively to determine the contents of the capsule (real or imaginary), intended to convey to people in the future how they lead their lives. As a follow-up, students could then imagine themselves discovering the capsule in the future and write a 'letter from the future' outlining the impressions and questions raised on 'opening' the capsule. Exchanging the letters between class members helps to set up temporal 'pen-friendships'.

Strategy 5: Suspended animation

A person from the present in suspended animation and who is re-animated far into the future is a popular science-fiction device, which should be familiar to students who watch *Futurama* or *Red Dwarf*. Students could be asked to imagine that they have been reanimated in their home locality or another familiar place some considerable time in the future, and asked to recount their experiences through, for example, drama (see Chapter 24). It will be interesting to evaluate the extent to which their stories are sensational or more prosaic, and the degree of commonality among the class. For example, are there differences associated with gender?

Strategy 6: A treasure from the past

This time the students are asked to step aside from their own perspective and imagine instead that they are someone from the future – an explorer in a flooded world who can dive down to the present school locality to find a *treasure with a twist*, e.g. something that we would consider relatively useless but is considered extremely valuable to their explorer from the future. The sequence in *Waterworld* (Reynolds, 1995) where 'the mariner' (Kevin Costner) swims down to the flooded New York would provide a suitable stimulus for this imaginative activity, the outcome for which could be a piece of creative writing.

Figure 4 | *Clock of the long now.*

Strategy 7: Images of the future

Science-fiction books, films, comics and electronic games provide a wealth of material for exploring images of the future. Students should be encouraged to reflect critically on these visions of the future. For example, much science fiction is predicated on a *dystopian* future, i.e. one in which the future is extremely undesirable and threatening, often having arisen from some local or global catastrophe which is often human in origin (the ubiquitous post-apocalyptic vision). Questions for discussion include: Why is this? What does it say about our current society and its fears for the future? Or is it simply that a *utopian* future is less exciting? Are there gender differences in terms of the attractiveness of different futures portrayed? To what extent are these futures reflecting students' ideas about the future, or shaping and constraining them? There is a wealth of geography in these sources. For example, the comic *2000AD* often uses maps of 'Mega-cities' and 'The Cursed Earth' to reveal that these thrilling and strange adventures are actually taking place in familiar geographical settings (for example, Mega-city 1 is on the eastern seaboard of the present-day USA – see Figure 5).

Envisioning the future

Strategy 1: Probable and preferable futures

A very simple device to help students to think about their own images of the future is the 'probable/preferable futures timeline'. Students are asked to consider an issue. It may be one that relates to them personally (e.g. their personal ambitions) or to people collectively (i.e. affect the community), and can operate over any spatial scale from the local (e.g. employment, traffic issues) to the global (e.g. global climate change). They then draw a single time-line outlining crucial events relating to the issue up to the present, their time-line then forks into two branches. The *probable* (usually the lower

GUIDE TO SPECIAL SYMBOLS

POPULATION CENTRES
SITES OF SPECIAL INTEREST
CITIES DESTROYED DURING JUDGEMENT DAY

ICE DESERTS
OTHER DESERTS
NUCLEAR DESERTS / Mutant Population
MUTAGENS IN ENVIRONMENT off limits to humans

LIMITS OF HIGHER OCEAN POLLUTION
EXTREME VOLCANIC ACTIVITY
WHIRLPOOL outer limit of navigation

Figure 5 | *The location of imaginary places in 2000AD. Map Copyright© 2006 Rebellion A/S. All rights reserved. www.2000ADonline.com.*

limb) is labelled with the likely events that would occur, given the existing trajectory. The *preferable* (upper limb) is labelled with the events that the student(s) would like to see happen. The timescale can range from the relatively short (e.g. to the end of the school phase) to the longer term (e.g. 50-100 years), depending on the nature of the issue or the ability of the students to think more abstractly as they peer into the future.

This activity could be extended by asking students to describe in words or pictures the scenarios for each of the two futures. A particularly engaging way of achieving this is to get students to create maps to demonstrate the contrasts. A base map of the locality under consideration can be drawn and then separate transparent overlays (e.g. tracing paper or acetate) used to map the consequences of the two futures. Each transparency can then be overlain on the base map to demonstrate the potential geography of each future. (Chapter 7 demonstrates how, increasingly, technology enables students to carry out this type of activity using ICT.)

Scenarios of possible futures can be presented to students in various forms, e.g. maps, sketches, short stories, and used to capture their imagination by highlighting different aspects of the chosen future (Hicks, 1998). The Yorkshire Dales National Park (1989) used scenarios in its leaflet *Landscapes for Tomorrow* which was designed to research the views of the public on different futures for the landscapes of the National Park (see Figure 6). The leaflet included sketches of different future landscapes which were accompanied by a brief explanation of what decisions in the present would bring about each one. The questions in the leaflet can be used as the basis of an activity aimed at exploring students' views about possible futures for such landscapes. Alternatively, the leaflet can provide the stimulus for students to design ways for their peers to investigate possible futures for other environments. The outcomes could be used to assess individuals' understanding of some of the geographical processes influencing such environments.

Strategy 2: Thinking through the future

The 'Mind movies' strategy (Leat, 1998; see also Chapter 40) is inherently concerned with getting students to consider 'what happens next', i.e. the future based on the trajectory set out in a stimulus story. The examples given in Leat (1998) are relatively short term (e.g. an earthquake, a nuclear disaster) but the strategy could be adapted to stimulate the visioning much further into the future. It would be interesting to get students to evaluate the extent to which their stories differ, in order to demonstrate the variety of futures available to us.

Choosing the future

Having got students to appreciate that there are potentially many possible futures, some more preferable than others, it might be helpful to ask them to investigate commonly held 'worldviews' of the future. David Hicks has provided an accessible approach to this by presenting four future scenarios ('More of the same', 'Technological fix', 'Edge of disaster' and 'Sustainable development') with worksheets to unpack them. These cartoon-like drawings are packed with information, but are necessarily simplistic and rather stereotypical – therefore likely to stimulate much debate as students unpick them.

Once students have had a chance to work with alternative 'worldviews' or perspectives on the future, they should then be encouraged to clarify their own value positions. This is obviously where the futures dimension in geographical education explicitly enters the realm of attitudes and values clarification and therefore can contribute to citizenship education and moral development (see also Chapter 15).

The BBC *If ...?* series (March 2004-June 2005) speculated, using a mixture of 'docudrama' and expert perspectives, about possible dystopian (negative) futures. The series took a scenarios approach, i.e. dramatically highlighted a particular issue. Each scenario provides a suitable starting point for some real geographical thinking and discussion about the future of the students' own local and national context, including:

- *If ... the lights go out:* catastrophic power cuts
- *If ... things don't get better:* the widening gap between rich and poor and the creation of 'gated communities'
- *If ... the generations fall out:* an ageing population and the consequent financial drain on the younger generation
- *If ... women ruled the world:* changing gender roles and the effect on traditional societal structures
- *If ... we don't stop eating:* the geographical/socioeconomic concentration of ill health in deprived inner-city areas.

As part of the series, a discussion was held about the medium used. It was focused on *If ... we stop giving aid to Africa* and examined the role of aid in the development of countries. The approach was one that could be applied to a whole range of issues relating to development and global citizenship.

Exploring the connectedness of places

In contrast to earlier examples, which explore how different decisions in the present will lead to different future landscapes, this activity highlights the 'connectedness' of places. It is drawn from an issue of *Global Eye* and uses materials from the United Nations' Sustainable Cities Programme (see websites).

First, students are provided with a copy of Figure 7a, or directed to the sustainable cities page on the Global Eye website. Next, descriptions of two cities of the future are handed out and, for each one, students must think about these questions:

- In what ways is the city... sustainable?... not sustainable?
- What improvements would make the city more sustainable?
- Who has made the decisions about planning the city?
- Who should decide what the city of the future should be like?
- Which city would you prefer to live in?

These questions could form the basis of an enquiry into how sustainable different cities are or different future city scenarios might be (Figure 7b).

A sustainable future – the choice is ours

As stated earlier, this chapter takes as a basic assumption that it is desirable for geography education to promote the notion that sustainable development is highly desirable. Indeed, the national curriculum directs teachers to 'secure [students'] commitment to sustainable development at the local, national, regional and global levels' (DfEE/QCA, 1999, p. 11). Thus the challenge facing us as geography teachers is to adopt a pedagogy that promotes critical thinking and raises awareness of the ways in which

How to play

1. Up to four people can play. You will need red, blue, yellow and black pens, a dice and counters.
2. Follow the marked route, watching out for any points which send you backwards or forwards. If you read the information as you go along, it may help you when you get to the large question marks.
3. When you get to one of the six large question marks you should pause and make your choices about the landscape. Refer to the options printed in the choices table and mark the colour of your choice into the code boxes provided.
4. At the end of the game, look through the colour code for each painting to try to find one that matches yours. If none match very closely, see if you can work out which pictures could be mixed together to make your future landscape.

Choice questions

Answer each question in turn as you pause at the large question marks. Mark your colour code in the box provided.

1. **What sort of walls would you like to see?**
   Blue – many modern fences, few dry-stone walls
   Red   – many dry-stone walls, few modern fences
   Black – few or no walls or fences
   Yellow – some modern fences, some dry-stone walls

2. **What sort of meadows would you like to see?**
   Black – few or no hay or silage meadows
   Blue   – many silage meadows, few hay meadows
   Red   – many hay meadows, few silage meadows
   Yellow – some hay meadows and some silage meadows

3. **What sort of barns would you like to see?**
   Blue   – many modern sheds, few stone barns
   Red   – many stone barns, few modern sheds
   Yellow – some modern sheds, some stone barns
   Black – few or no barns or sheds

4. **What sort of trees would you like to see?**
   Yellow – some broad-leaves, some conifers
   Blue   – many conifers, few broad-leaves
   Red   – many broad-leaves, few conifers
   Black – few or no trees

5. **What sort of woods would you like to see?**
   Blue – very large woods
   Red   – large woods
   Black – small or no woods

6. **What sort of heather moors would you like to see?**
   Black – small or no heather moors
   Red   – very large heather moors
   Blue – large heather moors

	Player 1	Player 2	Player 3	Player 4
Walls				
Meadows				
Barns				
Trees				
Woods				
Moors				

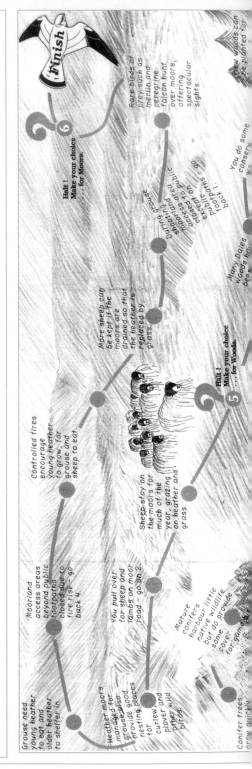

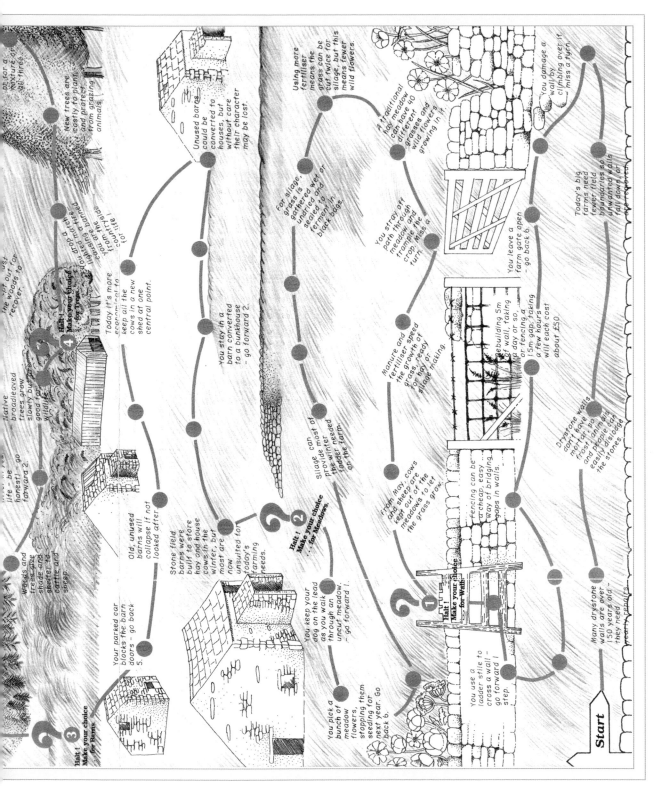

Figure 6 | *(a) The playing board and instructions for* The Choices Game. *Source:* Landscapes for Tomorrow, *Yorkshire Dales National Park Committee, reproduced by permission (see over for Figure 6b).*

Today's landscape

This typical Dales scene supports a community earning a living from farming or tourism. It is the product of an agricultural system that was, until recently, supported by subsidies intended to increase food production and maintain a healthy rural economy. Some meadows are cut for hay, while others are used for silage production. Some walls and field barns remain in good order, but many derelict ones are replaced by fences or modern sheds. Many broad-leaved woodlands are being damaged by stock and some heather moorland is deteriorating due to over-grazing.

Landscape A

In this landscape future farming subsidies have been taken away, leaving upland farmers to compete with better farms in the lowlands. In this situation, many owner-farmers would sell-up, while tenanted farms would be taken back into estates and their buildings used for alternative purposes. The few remaining farmers would keep smaller flocks on improved land, but outlying meadows and pastures would be abandoned. With no money to maintain field barns, walls and woodlands, they would decay and become derelict. To survive some farmers would turn to farm-based tourism or forestry.

Landscape B

In another 50 year or so the Dales might look like this if governments continue to subsidise livestock farming in the way they did until recently. Some farms would become very intensive, others would merely tick over with few stock. Most meadows would be intensified and some moors would suffer from over-grazing. Old woodlands would be uncared for and die, while conifer plantations would provide an additional income. Many walls and field barns would become derelict, to be replaced by fences and large modern sheds.

Landscape C

This landscape, geared to food production, is supported by no public money. With access to the latest technology and breeding techniques, larger farmers could still make a profit by buying out the smaller farmers to create big livestock ranches. The flowering meadows would be intensified and the grass taken mainly from silage. Large sheds and wire fences would replace walls and field barns. Broad-leaved woodlands would die as a result of stock damage and extensive conifer woodlands would be planted. Some heather moorland would convert to grassland due to over-grazing.

Landscape D

In this landscape there would be greater control exercised by countryside management authorities. Using their own finances, or by taking advantage of conservation grants, farmers would be encouraged to maintain their best landscape features, whilst tidying-up any dereliction. Many flowery meadows would remain and more heather moorland would be created for sheep, grouse and wildlife. There would also be more care in the planting of new conifer woods and the sitting of new farm buildings.

Landscape E

Here more public money would be available to enable farmers to continue to farm livestock, whilst also maintaining traditional landscape features. Farmers would be helped by grants from conservation agencies and would have access to a pool of labour to help with landcape maintenance work. Farmers could also supplement their income from farm-based tourism. There would be more heather moorland and flower meadows than today. Broad-leaved woodlands, walls and field barns would be well looked after.

Landscape F

If farming subsidies are withdrawn the traditional estate may become the dominant economic unit, with game shooting and leisure providing more income than farming. Some livestock rearing would still be carried out by tenant farmers, although many owner-farmers would have sold up. Tenants would be encouraged to improve habitats, such as moorland, broad-leaved woodlands and meadows, for game and wildlife. Some barns would be converted to new uses and estate owners would diversify into local industries and tourist activities, like nature trails or riding.

Landscape G

If a whole dale was deliberately taken out of private ownership and set aside, or if farm support was withdrawn and much land was abandoned, a wild, forested landscape would develop. Since there would be no farming, visitors could wander where they wished, except in special wildlife reserves. The ecological balance of the area would need to be managed by an appropriate authority. In time even the barns and farm buildings would become overgrown. A few people would find employment providing outdoor recreation.

Figure 6 | *(b) The future scenarios for* The Choices Game. *Source:* Landscapes for Tomorrow, *Yorkshire Dales National Park Committee, reproduced by permission.*

(a) What makes a sustainable city?

S – Sharing decision making with local communities

U – Using renewable energy to fuel houses, factories and transport

S – Space is used in the best way possible to benefit everybody

T – Treating waste as a resource to recycle

A – A diversity of people where everyone is treated with respect

I – Inventing ways to use resources more wisely to cut down on waste

N – Neighbourhoods, where people look out for each other, are important

A – Air quality is clean

B – Building technology that improves lifestyles

L – Lively, fun and enjoyable places to live

E – Environments that are safe and healthy

(b) Local community involvement

The best ideas for managing a city often come from local neighbourhoods within the city, where people are likely to know best what their locality needs, and how to make the most of local resources. In Phnom Penh, the capital of Cambodia, recycling and re-use among poorer communities is standard practice. In cities like Phnom Penh, the throwaway rate is approximately 10% of that in cities in richer countries. Students could investigate other community-based initiatives online, for example:

■ The Living Streets website includes information on a campaign to reconnect and revitalise neighbourhoods in UK cities.

■ Find out from the MSL website about Malaysia's plans to develop the world's first sustainable cyber city.

■ For examples of success stories in sustainable cities visit the Best Practices website

■ Visit Global Eye website to find out about projects that focus on community self-help in the favelas of Rio de Janeiro, Brazil.

■ For a list of weblinks to networks and projects for sustainable cities around the world visit the LSX online resource centre.

Figure 7 | *Ideas for teaching about sustainable cities: (a) What makes a sustainable city?, and (b) 'Recycling Cambodia' and an activity aimed at finding out about other similar initiatives. Source: Global Eye – Simon Scoones.*

individuals and groups of people can engage in appropriate action to promote a sustainable future.

The global scale

Dealing with the bigger picture can be more challenging because the issues and processes are often more abstract, and more remote from young people's everyday experience and lives. However, young people are clearly aware of the major global issues relating to the environment, poverty and hunger, war and peace (Figure 2). Hicks suggests that we might respond to students' concerns by asking them:

> ■ *What are some of the events going on in the wider world that they are aware of? How do they feel about these?*
> ■ *To list individually three fears that they have in relation to the future of the world.*
> ■ *Finally, to list individually three hopes that they have for the future of the world* (1998, p. 168).

Examining how the environment has been changed in the past, how human activity might be changing it now, and how it might be changed in the future will provide opportunities to address many of the students' concerns and help them to think more critically and creatively about the future. When we do not have direct experience of or images of events or places, it is in our imagination that we hold images of geographical features, places, and probable and preferable futures (see also Chapter 4). Envisioning is a process that enables students to make use of their imagination to clarify their preferred visions of the future. According to Hicks, 'visions of the future can only exist in the human imagination' (2001, p. 59). Figure 8, drawn from *Global Eye*, uses an imagined future to help students to consider possible futures resulting from climate change. It could be used with a short video sequence from a film that provides an extreme view of what the future might be like as a result of climate change, e.g. *The Day after Tomorrow* (Emmerich, 2004).

The attainment of a sustainable future

The notion that in making choices today we should consider the implications for a time well into the future is not new – a traditional English agricultural saying is 'Live like you will die tomorrow; and farm like you will live forever'. Inspirational stories about individuals who had a vision beyond their own lifetime can be used to develop literacy in geography lessons, e.g. Johnny Appleseed, and The Man Who Planted Trees (see end of chapter). Students would also benefit from learning – perhaps as a supported self-study enquiry – about the Iroquois Confederacy that once existed in present-day upper New York State in the USA. The Confederacy incorporated a simple planning principle into its decision-making process – the Doctrine of the Seventh Generation. Each council meeting would start with one member saying: 'In our every deliberation we must consider the impact of our decisions on the next seven generations'. Another council member would then represent and vote on behalf of those who would live about 150 years into the future. Given the short-termist decision-making practice common in much of the western world, this is an apt and powerful message. How very different our world might be if this simple doctrine had been adopted as a guiding principle when Europeans first contacted the Confederacy approximately 400 years ago. Students could model this approach to decision making either though role-play or in actual decision-making situations. They might also approach the local parish, district or county council and offer to represent future generations in this way.

The potential educational benefits for geography students in exploring what planning for sustainability requires are immense. A number of ideas are outlined below.

Strategy 1: Games in geography

SimCity (latest version – *SimCity III*) is a simulation game requiring 'gamers' to change an area of countryside into a sprawling metropolis with associated utilities, land-use zones (including industrial and residential) and services for the population. This is managed using a perspective map of the area with a zoom capability (allowing you to see cars and people milling around). Choices made by the 'gamer' set in train a sequence of events which take some time to unfold and often have unforeseen consequences. An accompanying website outlines how *SimCity III* can be used in lessons (see websites below). Who thought geography lessons could be this much fun?

Strategy 2: Geographical information systems (GIS)

As well as contributing significantly to the purposeful integration of ICT into the geography curriculum, GIS technology enables students to, for example, explore a parcel of land in terms of different management choices. The more powerful GIS packages can be used to create 3D landscapes and drape different land use cover over an area to facilitate enquiry into different management regimes (e.g. *VistaPro, ArcView*; see also Chapter 7). The animation potential of more powerful GIS packages permits students to 'fly-through' landscapes and run time-series sequences to recognise existing trends that can be extrapolated into the future, or predict the consequences of hypothetical decisions.

Strategy 3: Fieldwork in the imagination

David Hicks (2001) presents a fieldwork activity for envisioning the future that can be worked through with students to help them to use a process of visualisation to explore what their preferred future might look like (Figure 9). 'At its most basic this involves students making a simple journey using the inner eye to "visit" their preferred future, led by the teacher' (Hicks, 2000, p. 59).

Strategy 4: Sustainability checklist

Increasingly organisations are using 'Sustainability checklists' to establish whether or not

Following a technical problem with our Mars transmitter there is no virtual news service today. We apologise for the inconvenience – the service will be resumed as soon as possible. Click on your console if you want to print out today's news.

Bringing you the latest news from around the world from BBC Dot Com. Here is the main story for today:

The United Nations High Commissioner for Refugees (UNHCR) reports a growing crisis in the number of 'environmental' refugees. The UNHCR claims that over 150 million people are currently on the move following a series of climatic catastrophes. In Bangladesh alone, 15 million people have lost their homes after 1m sea level rises have reduced the size of the country by a fifth. Unlike 'political' refugees, 'environmental' refugees have no rights under the 2030 Geneva Convention II, and most are finding refuge in poorer countries that are already under pressure.

Egypt is struggling to cope with 7 million 'environmental' refugees following the inundation of large parts of the Nile delta.

Meanwhile, in New Zealand millions of people originally from the South Pacific continue to live in makeshift camps. The former leader of Tuvalu, the first country to be inundated, is arguing the case in the UN for Tuvalu islanders to become the first 'citizens of the world'.

The UN is also preparing for a new battle between the West and the powerful coalition of Brazil, India and South Africa that is defending the interests of the newly-industrialised countries. The Brazilian government is facing increasing unrest at home following last month's Hurricane George. Riots have broken out in São Paulo after favelas were buried under mountains of mud and debris following two huge landslides. The Indian government is also under pressure after the worst flooding in living memory in Orissa State. Since the floods, millions have caught a strain of malaria that is resistant to the hypo-sprays currently available.

In Europe, deaths have become commonplace during severe heatwaves and forest fires in recent summers. In the USA, farming in the former 'breadbasket' has dwindled as large swathes of farmland have turned it into a dustbowl. But this is little comfort to the 50 countries, mostly in Africa, that now live with severe food and water shortages brought on by prolonged drought. US President Justin

Timberlake has pointed out that recent bumper harvests in Siberia, New Zealand and Canada will help re-stock the granaries of the UN World Food Programme.

On a lighter note, the World Tourism Organization has announced new frontiers for tourism. Next summer, routes for cruise liners across the Arctic Ocean – once frozen over by ice and home to the now extinct polar bear – will open up. Here in London, the mayor is soon to announce the opening of the city's latest tourist attraction, the underwater viewpod for the Thames Flood Barrier.

Global temperatures have risen by 30°C since 2005. Back then, people still drove cars that ran on fossil fuels. And oil – who had it and who used it – was still a major source of conflict. In the Arctic melting permafrost is adding to the problem as thawing peat bogs release more carbon dioxide and methane. The biggest concern is over the shrinking Greenland ice sheet. If the ice sheet disappeared altogether, sea levels could rise by another 6m, affecting the lives of billions and making the current 'environmental' refugee problem a drop in the ocean.

The scenario described in this news report has not happened, but some think it could ...

- ◼ Read through the article carefully and try to sort out the predicted impacts of climate change using your own categories.
- ◼ According to this forecast, who is most likely to be affected by climate change in the future?
- ◼ How would you answer the question at the end of the article, 'Where did it all go so wrong?'
- ◼ What changes need to take place now in order to right these wrongs? And whose responsibility is it to make these changes?

Figure 8 | *The 'Climate change tomorrow?' scenario. Source: Global Eye.*

This activity should only be used after the following steps have been taken within the study of a particular locality or geographical issue:

1. clarification of the current problems to be resolved;
2. identification, by individual students, of three differences they would most want to see in their preferred future for this situation;
3. a brief introduction to use of the creative imagination.

Note: When reading this text allow sufficient pauses for students to focus on their own images.

Since the future has not yet happened, it exists only in your imagination, awaiting its invention. If we do not clarify our choice of preferred future then we are likely to get somebody else's. We are going to use the creative imagination now to 'visit' your preferred future (for ...) in 2026. Remember this is not about trying to predict the future but about exploring your most optimistic vision. You will need to get comfortable, relax and close your eyes – as if you were going to daydream for example – but in this case it is for a particular purpose. Just let images arise in the mind's eye, allowing your imagination to act as a source of inspiration to you.

Imagine yourself following me out of the building where, instead of the usual scene, you are confronted by a high hedge stretching as far as you can see in either direction. Look at it in detail. What sort of hedge is it? How does it look, feel and smell? Set in the hedge you see there is a closed door. What does it look like? Look at the detail. On the other side lies your preferred future of 2026.

Hold your previously identified hopes for the future in the mind's eye and see where you find yourself as you step through the door. Are you inside or outside, in a town or in the country? A variety of images may come to mind, don't start judging them just note them. Remember this is not an exercise in forecasting. Maybe you are in a place you knew back in 2006. If so, how has it changed?

In what ways is life in 2026 different from today? What is it that indicates that your desired future has actually come about? Be as specific as you can. How have things changed? How is life different? What are people doing differently in this place? What are they saying that is different? What are the words, feelings, colours and sounds? What do people say to you? Which of the images or ideas that come to you feels the most interesting? Focus on it and make it as concrete as possible.

How is this society or place different? How do you know that your preferred future has come about? What is the specific evidence? Look for details – for central images or themes. Search for the compelling, that which you can't let go of, which feels like the future speaking to you. Look for the detail which makes you say 'Yes, this is how it should be!'

Remembering these details turn back to look at the hedge and follow me again through the door returning to this room in the year 2006. Without speaking to anyone else describe in an annotated sketch the main features of your preferred future.

Figure 9 | Visualising the future. Source: Hicks, 2001.

their current practice or project proposals are likely to contribute towards sustainable development. Two government-recommended checklists are available on the internet (see 'References and resources'). Most local authorities have produced their own checklists (see e.g. Worcestershire County Council) which students can use as a tool for assessing real or imaginary organisations (including the school) or in projects, e.g. a decision-making exercise.

A more sophisticated method of establishing the sustainability of a project prior to implementation is to undertake an 'environmental and social impact assessment' (ESIA). This differs from the traditional environmental impact assessment in that the social and cultural impacts of the proposal are integrated into the assessment. Unfortunately, the procedure is quite complicated and time consuming and it may be impractical to do more than simply introduce the general concept in the classroom. Nevertheless, outlines of ESIAs in practice can be found on the internet, e.g. the URS Europe website.

Working with real planners and making real decisions

Finally, there can be no better resource than real planners working in the students' home locality. The Royal Town Planning Institute (RTPI) now has an education for sustainable development network, and may well be able to support learning through its local branches. The RTPI also supports Planning Aid – a charity providing planning advice and support to individuals and community groups (including schools). Being even more ambitious, you might try to persuade the planning department of the local council to work in partnership with students on a planning issue which will benefit both their citizenship education and their geographical education. The Commission for Architecture and the Built Environment (CABE) has also developed interactive online resources for investigating futures dimensions in the design and development of the built environment. For example, the 'Making better places' (see websites) programme incorporates a range of activities to inspire students' interest in influencing the future of places where they will live, work and play, culminating in a project to design an area of a town.

An engaging future-orientated national initiative called 'Futuretown' operated in the mid-1990s. It involved secondary students working with town centre managers and high street chains (including Boots and Marks & Spencer). The rationale was for these groups to work together to protect and enhance town centres by planning for their future. The initiative, co-ordinated by School Curriculum Industry Partnership based at Warwick University, provided teachers with a resource pack and was supported locally by Education Business Partnership (EBP) or local education authority education-industry liaison officers. While the national initiative no longer operates, it could provide a model for EBP links.

Summary

This chapter demonstrates the need for a futures dimension in geographical education and provides some ideas for integrating such a dimension into the geography curriculum in schools. One of the chapter's main objectives has been to encourage you to explore ways in which you can help your students to think more critically and creatively about the future. The challenge for us as geography educators is appropriately summarised by Rex Walford:

> *In urging that we teach a geography of the future, I do not mean to say that we should give up teaching the geography of the past: but we should make the past the servant of the future. If the future is unavoidable, let us at least not walk backwards into it* (1984, p. 207).

Related publications from the Geographical Association:
- *Teaching Geography* (2001) Focus on: teaching and learning about citizenship and sustainable development', Vol 26, No 2.
- *Teaching Geography* (2003) One section devoted to: Focus on sustainable futures, Vol 28, No 4.

References and resources

Print and film

Badham, J. (director) (1995) *Nick of Time*. Paramount.

Butt, G. and Foskett, N. (2001) *Geography in the 21st Century – A review and perspective on geography in the curriculum*. London: QCA.

Emmerich, R. (director) (2004) *The Day After Tomorrow*. Fox Home Entertainment.

Fien, J. and Gerber, R. (eds) (1988) *Teaching Geography for a Better World*. Edinburgh: Oliver & Boyd.

Gough, N. (1988) 'Alternative futures in geographical education' in Fien, J. and Gerber, R. (eds) *Teaching Geography for a Better World*. Edinburgh: Oliver & Boyd.

Hicks, D. (1994a) *Educating for the Future: A practical classroom guide*. Godalming: Worldwide Fund for Nature.

Hicks, D. (ed) (1994b) *Preparing for the Future: Notes & queries for concerned educators*. Godalming: Adamantine Press Ltd/WWF.

Hicks, D. (1998) 'A geography for the future', *Teaching Geography*, 23, 4, pp. 168-73.

Hicks, D. (2001) *Citizenship for the Future: A practical classroom guide*. Godalming: WWF-UK.

Hicks, D. and Holden, C. (1995) *Visions of the Future: Why we need to teach for tomorrow*. Trentham Books.

Pal, G. (director) (1960) *The Time Machine* (time travel sequences). Warner Studios.

Reynolds, K. (director) (1995) *Waterworld*. Universal Studios.
SDEP (1999) *SDEP: First Annual Report*. London: DETR.
Walford, R. (1984) 'Geography and the future', *Geography*, 69, 3, pp. 193-208.
Wells, S. (director) (2002) *The Time Machine*. Universal Studios.
Yorkshire Dales National Park (1989) *Landscapes for Tomorrow* (leaflet). Skipton: YDNP.

Electronic

2000AD – www.2000adonline.com/
Best Practices – //bestpractices.org/bpbriefs/Urban_Development.html
DLTR – www.regeneration.dtlr.gov.uk/sustainable/guide/22.htm
Education Business Partnerships – www.nebpn.org/ (full list of local partnerships)
Geology of Biology – www.wellcome.ac.uk/en/1/awtconloc215.html
Global Eye – www.globaleye.org.uk/secondary_summer2002/eyeon/improve.html
Johnny Appleseed – www.ccmr.cornell.edu/~weeds/SchoolPages/Appleseed/welcome.html
Living Streets – www.livingstreets.org.uk
Long Now Foundation – www.longnow.org/index.html
LSX – www.lsx.org.uk/resourcecentre/suscities_page263.aspx
Multi-media Super Corridor – www.mdc.com.my
Royal Town Planning Institute – www.rtpi.org.uk/ (and Planning Aid)
The Man Who Planted Trees – www.kav.cas.cz/asc/~buble/text/en/TheManWhoPlantedTrees.html
UNESCO – www.unesco.org/education/tlsf/theme_a/mod03/uncom03bod.htm
URS Europe – www.urseurope.com/services/environmental_consulting/env_consult-impact_ass.htm
Voices from the field – www.lab.brown.edu/public/voices/4qrt1999/almost.shtml
Worcestershire County Council – www.worcestershire.gov.uk/home/index/cs-index/cs-chief-exec/cs-chief-exec-bvm-appendix4.htm

Implications for practice

(a) Arguably all school learning should be 'future oriented'.

However for much of the time this orientation is implicit. One of the significant realisations from this chapter is that geography has considerable scope and potential for 'delivering' education for sustainable development – which has an explicit concern for the future.

(b) Futures education is by definition different from 'teaching the best of what is known'.

To be sure, knowledge of the world is vital, but projecting to the future requires the teaching and the learning to engage with uncertainty. School geography may be characterised by arguing that is, at least some of the time, open-ended and tentative. Indeed teaching students how to be comfortable with uncertainty may be a significant contribution of geography.

(c) Don't be bashful about the technical teaching skills required to operate successfully with futures.

This chapter summarises some of the strategies available to you – and offers links to other sources of support for developing such teaching skills.

(d) Occasionally, geography in school is criticised in the press for becoming little more than 'green washing'.

Richard D North has a website which energetically promotes environmental scepticism – which is a useful 'test'. If 'teaching geography for a sustainable future' is reduced to unquestioning assumptions and straightforward solutions then perhaps it deserves severe criticism. However, the real point is that we need to be clear about the difference between *education* and *propaganda*. Geography classrooms should focus on the former wherever possible – through a questioning approach.

Chapter 24

Theatrical geography

Mary Biddulph and Jo Clarke

Before reading this chapter consider the following questions:

- In what ways do you enable students to explore the 'affective' dimensions of geography?

- What value might drama have in helping students to discover 'new understandings' of geography for themselves?

- What factors might encourage or inhibit you from using drama more often in your teaching of geography?

As geography teachers we like to think that geography is dynamic; ever-changing, inherently interesting and 'all around us'. As a curriculum subject it is content-rich, visually impressive and provides a tremendous vehicle for students and teachers to explore new realms together. To tap into all that geography has to offer it is essential that we think beyond its contribution to 'the cognitive' and that we look for opportunities to explore the 'affective' dimensions of geography. Our aim is to encourage you to consider how drama can enable teachers and students to do just this. We discuss the 'How?' and 'Why?' of drama in the geography classroom through some practical suggestions and discussion of factors influencing the effective use of such strategies.

The drama–geography interface

Drama as a teaching methodology conveys many different meanings, and for the geography-turned-drama teacher there can be much confusion about what actually constitutes 'drama'. Neelands (1992) identifies drama as being:
- a practical activity
- a form of shared cultural identity
- a vehicle for exploring human nature and experience
- taking on roles and adopting different viewpoints in 'real' experiences
- generating vocal and active responses to fictional situations (what he defines as a 'unique form of literacy')
- developing the imagination's ability to 'make believe'.

So how does this world of the imagination relate to a subject such as geography, where emphasis is placed on the study of real people, places and situations and issues? Drama methods of teaching have much to offer a geographical education that involves students in:

"
- *Provoking and answering questions*
- *Using different scales of enquiry*
- *Developing knowledge of places and environments*
- *Using a range of investigative and problem-solving skills*
- *Understanding and resolving issues about the environment and sustainable development*
- *Encountering different societies and cultures*
- *Thinking about their own place in the world, their values, their rights and their responsibilities to other people and the environment*

(DfEE, 1999, p. 14).

Drama can provide teachers with strategies which enable students to engage with less tangible aspects of geography and to begin to consider how they feel about key geographical and environmental issues, and it is through this engagement of 'feelings' that students 'make lateral moves outside their established framework of thought so as to generate fresh insights and perspectives' (MaCleod, 1992, p. 12). (See also Chapters 4 and 15.)

Opportunities for learning geography through drama

To facilitate such engagement geography teachers must first consider it worthwhile; that it is an important part of geographical learning that students empathise with the lives, predicaments and values of others and that they have the opportunity to critically evaluate their own perspectives. If this is a given then there are myriad opportunities that drama can provide.

Students can learn by using appropriate drama methodologies. For example, the process of planning a dramatic exploration of the location of a new landfill site, where different points of view need to be known, understood, explained, exemplified and argued, will require students to engage with the hallmarks of what Resnick describes as high quality thinking:

Photo: ©Peter Fox.

> ■ **Uncertainty** – where would an appropriate location be?
> ■ **Complexity** – different individuals/groups have different perspectives on the best location, others may question whether or not landfill sites are the best solution to waste disposal at all.
> ■ **Multiple solutions to problems** – some sites may have advantages over others but these will not usually be clear-cut. Other potential solutions may also emerge in discussion.
> ■ **Nuanced judgement and interpretations** – the notion of a 'best site' will be contentious and perspectives will be influenced by individual and group bias.
> ■ **The application of multiple and conflicting criteria** – a final decision about location could rest on obvious criteria such as transport links and/or impact on the local natural environment. However, less obvious criteria may also emerge, such as noise pollution, changing (as opposed to damaging) the local natural environment, the creation of a health hazard, and so on (cited in McGuinness, 1999, p. 6).

Figure 1 | A model for planning lessons using drama. Neelands 1992.

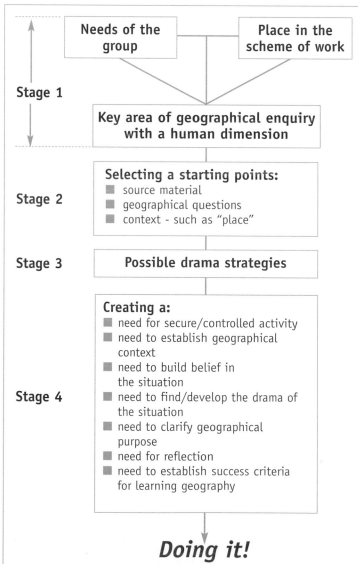

And to undertake an activity such as that described above with any degree of success students need the opportunity to communicate; to talk to each other and to the teacher; to listen, to each other and the teacher; to interrogate any resources such as photographs, maps, graphical data; to be creative through such means as the creation of visual aids to demonstrate a particular point or to illustrate a particular message, and to use their imaginations, to imagine themselves in a particular place, at a particular time, considering a particular issue. To participate in such varied forms of communication affords students the opportunity to consider and reconsider geographical knowledge and concepts at a range of levels, and in doing so:

> young people are realising and extending their ability to imagine new futures and alternatives, new problems and solutions, a world beyond the street corner (Neelands, 1992, p. 7).

The 'roles' of the teacher in drama lessons

The creation of the type of learning described above is dependent upon the teacher. Teachers will often take on many different roles during a geography–drama lesson. These roles will be overlapping, at times conflicting, and will sometimes require the teacher to take on more than one role at a time! The main difference with geography–drama lessons is that as well as being a teacher the teacher may also be required to be the local news reporter, the local Councillor, or whatever.

The following is an attempt to contextualise the key roles a teacher might expect to adopt if using drama as a teaching method.

The teacher as planner

For any geography lesson, high quality planning and preparation is essential. Planning lessons using drama methods can be much the same as for other lessons where students need to appreciate the geographical questions underpinning their learning and understand the structure and routines of a particular lesson. What is different however, is the role of learning outcomes in the planning process. In drama-led lessons, tightly prescribed learning outcomes detract from the role of the students in their own learning and prevent students from exploring complex geographical issues for themselves in a detailed and thoughtful way. Students need to be able to (and be trusted to) 'participate' if the deeper thinking we want from them is to develop.

Figure 1 provides a framework for thinking about planning a lesson using drama methods. The framework is dependent upon the teacher being prepared to allow open-ended learning to take place, but within a secure and well-managed environment. For the geography teacher the main challenges will be:

- identifying suitable themes in which to use drama teaching;
- using geographical source material in such a way as to support students in 'getting into' the drama; creating the right atmosphere, generating a climate of high expectations and insisting on commitment to the task from students;
- selecting the drama methodology which will best meet the needs of the group and the learning of the subject.

However, the success of such lessons also depends upon the teacher as subject expert, in that geography teachers use their subject knowledge to support the learning process. Timely interventions, the use of appropriate questioning, effective management of groups and the whole class are no less crucial to a drama–geography lesson than to any other form of geography lesson.

The teacher as resource provider

When using drama the teacher's role in providing stimuli to spark the geographical imagination can be very effective in engendering students' interest in a topic. The right stimulus can bring a distant place closer to the students and make it seem more real. As with any teaching resource, enabling the students to 'get underneath' the means of presentation is important. To establish a dramatic approach students can be invited to respond to the stimulus and also develop their visual literacy skills. For example, questions about a photograph could involve:

- Where is it set?
- Who took it?
- Why did they take it?
- When did they take it?
- What is the subject of the photograph?
- What is happening in the background?
- What might be happening beyond the photograph?
- What headline/caption might be associated with the photograph?
- What sequence of events might have taken place before the photograph was taken?
- What sequence of events is likely to have occurred after the photograph had been taken?
- How do I feel about what I see in the photograph? How would I like to change the photograph?

Other stimuli could include a piece of clothing, an artefact, either from the place being studied – e.g. a piece of volcanic rock or a Panama hat – or something that is symbolic

Photo: ©Steve Banner,

of the theme – e.g. a teddy bear – when dealing with the issue of refugee children. It can be verbal, e.g. a taped conversation, an answerphone message; it can be text, e.g. a newspaper cutting, a letter, a diary entry, a secret code or a travelogue.

Maps and graphs are obvious sources and can be used to reinforce students' use of these essential geographical skills as well as being used to stimulate discussion to inform a piece of drama. A graph of the falling output of a steel plant coupled with information on unemployment in the region, or a map showing routes taken by certain commodities such as cocoa, or by migrants, can provide sufficient information about a situation while simultaneously encouraging the desire to find out more.

The teacher as manager

When managing students' behaviour in drama lessons, what has to be accepted is that a balance needs to be struck between effective class management, enabling learning to take place, and the need to allow students to learn for themselves in an open and supported way. In order to be effective the teacher needs to select the drama conventions (see pages 301-305) that are appropriate to the needs of the class. The teacher has the opportunity at the planning stage to choose a convention that ensures that students are comfortable with and can handle the amount of freedom given to them. In the first instance, and until the teacher is comfortable with using drama methods, he/she may select more manageable conventions such as freeze-frames or hot-seating, or conventions in which students are in role by choice, such as swapping hot-seats or in 'conscience alley'. Observing a drama teacher can help to identify management strategies that students are already familiar with and which can be applied to geography lessons.

The teacher as assessor

The assessment of geographical learning through drama is an issue that needs careful consideration. Follow-up work may serve as evidence that drama has enhanced geographical understanding.

Written work such as diaries, letters or journals written in role can be used to show opinions and attitudes or highlight conflict, and written descriptions or pictorial representations of the drama 'story' can show understanding of processes and how these lead to changes: students step into the role of the media in order to report on the issue or thematic areas that they have explored. Newspaper articles, web pages, radio or television news broadcasts can show geographical understanding in addition to a range of values and attitudes. Annotated photographs taken as part of a drama, e.g. freeze-frames, could illustrate processes or patterns.

Summative assessment with clear criteria is as important in the drama context as it is for any other learning situation and drama can provide the geography teacher with a range of evidence of attainment. However, if we want students to understand their own learning they need to understand their learning processes. So a more important role for the teacher in drama lessons is perhaps to support reflection.

The teacher as reflector

Reflecting on learning can be as important as the learning itself. This is especially significant when using drama as a teaching strategy, to ensure that the geographical knowledge and understanding is not relegated to second place. The purpose of students' reflecting on the drama is twofold:
- to consider the geography they have learnt
- to appreciate the use of the drama itself.

In order to achieve the former, students can be asked to summarise the drama, either verbally, visually or in written form. An innovative approach would be for students in a

freeze-frame to give a piece of information or opinion on the thematic topic. The latter can be effectively fulfilled using a pre-prepared set of debriefing questions focusing on what went well/badly, what can be improved upon, and the extent to which the students feel the drama helped to improve their understanding of the thematic topic (see also Chapter 16).

Reflection need not be exclusively evaluative or come solely at the end of a drama session. Somers (1994) identifies ongoing reflection as important in deepening students involvement in the process of learning as well as having the potential to sharpen their understanding. This suggests that frequent reflective activities should be planned and that reflection can be effectively used within learning activities to promote student appreciation of the motives, values and attitudes of the drama character. Nixon (1982) suggests that the following questions can help to support this process of 'reflection-in-action':

- What might happen next?
- What would you do if ...?
- What other arguments may be used here?

'Conscience alley' is a method encouraging reflection in a 'dramatic' way and it can be used effectively at the end of a sequence of dramatic processes in order to realise a final decision. A small number of students are chosen to walk down an alley that is formed by the rest of the students standing in two lines. As they walk very slowly down the alley the other students voice thoughts, advice, warnings, quotes or arguments about the situation that has been previously explored during the drama process. When the group reaches the end of the alley they either improvise the final part of the drama sequence or they speak aloud their final decision about the situation. The issue identified about the location of a new landfill site could conclude with such an approach. When the arguments have been made, the points of view expressed and the complexity of the final decision identified, all students could come together to make their final contribution in the 'alley' and await the final decision from a group of their peers.

Reflection is necessary for teachers as well as students. For the teacher considering his/her own learning – about geography, about individual students, about their skills as a teacher – reflection is essential if he/she is to gain from the experience.

Drama conventions and their uses in geography teaching

As identified, a key issue to be faced by geography teachers is how to select and use appropriately the range of drama methods available. When considering this it is important to remember that the purpose of using drama in geography is not to produce a polished production for show, but rather to expand students' geographical knowledge and understanding. The following sections introduce a number of dramatic conventions, with a justification for their use, a description of how to use them, and an illustration of their application in geography teaching.

Setting up the dramatic process – short pieces of drama

The conventions outlined here can be used in two main ways:

1. As scene-setters to longer pieces of drama work. These conventions enable students to establish the role that they are playing, i.e. understanding their character's physical and emotional make-up, and specifically from a geographical context their values, attitudes and subsequent motivations for and reactions to change. The conventions will also establish the location of the dramas such as the community and/or environment in which the drama is set.
2. To introduce or summarise geographical knowledge and understanding and as pieces of drama in their own right.

Convention 1 – Freeze-framing

Freeze-framing involves students in creating still images, using themselves and available props. One practical advantage of freeze framing is that it is relatively easy to manage students' behaviour and it is a good tool for encouraging reflection. The teacher can explore students' thoughts and feelings about a particular scenario through 'thought-tracking'. Students establish their still image (or can be stopped part way through an improvisation or prepared play) and, when tapped on the shoulder, they have to reveal what their character is thinking or feeling at that moment. Thought-tracking, via questioning students in role, can be used to ensure that they develop a deeper understanding of the situation they are illustrating; this can also be a useful management device for refocusing students' thinking.

Migration is one possible theme in which to use this convention (see programmes of study: 6fii, DfEE/QCA, 1999, p. 158). Students could be asked to set up the equivalent of a photo album where they:

1. develop a freeze-frame showing why a group of people have left a place, then ...
2. a second freeze-frame showing what the migrants' imagine their destination to be like, and then ...
3. a third freeze-frame showing the reality of the destination.

Thought-tracking the students as migrants can encourage them to think carefully about the hopes and fears of economic or political migrants, and begin to develop what Slater refers to as 'concerned insights into the situation, feelings, anxieties and intentions of other people' (1982, p. 85), in other words – empathy.

Freeze-frames and 'photo albums' are good for exploring human characters and behaviour. This may be either the ultimate aim of the drama or may be used to establish characters for use in a subsequent drama.

Convention 2 – Soundtracking

In conjunction with freeze-frames students can create a soundtrack that can be used to accompany action or to describe an environment. The stimulus for developing a soundtrack could be a photograph, a story or an environment of which the students already have an understanding; this convention relies heavily on the students' knowledge of the environment that they are soundtracking. A soundtrack could be created involving the use of spoken words (which may focus on the motivations or opinions of the people involved in the action, such as tourists and locals on a beach) which can represent an environment through spoken descriptions or through sounds associated with an environment, e.g. a busy street. The noises and sounds can be produced using the students' voices, props in the classroom or actual musical instruments or they may also be pre-recorded and students' voices superimposed over them.

Narrative conventions and developing dramatic sequences – longer episodes of drama

Students usually feel comfortable working in narrative (story telling) conventions as they are familiar with them from reading fiction and from watching television programmes and films. We often investigate change in geography, and 'story telling' can be a powerful way of exploring aspects of change. The success of such a method relies less on the quality of the final 'performance' and more on the time spent planning, preparing and reflecting on the processes involved.

Careful context setting is essential, i.e. the teacher needs to work with the students to ensure that they have a good understanding of the geographical concepts which underpin the drama. Without this students will feel divorced from the characters with the likely result that they will lack empathy and miss opportunities for learning. Another advantage of this context setting is that it establishes a set of norms for behaviour; for example, if the action is set in a courtroom or takes the form of a public enquiry then students must behave accordingly. However, such contexts are likely to be alien to students' direct experience and so behaviour norms will have to be explained and justified.

Convention 1 – Teacher-in-role

Teacher-in-role is effective for providing links within a drama. The teacher adopts a role and then develops the knowledge and understanding of the students from within that role. Teacher-in-role can encourage participation and also change the dynamics of the drama as the teacher brings in new characters and involves different students. He/she can create new opportunities for interaction by setting up new situations between different sets of students. The teacher can assume a number of different roles during the dramatic process each of which demands a different response from the students. Teacher-in-role is effective because it excites interest among students and can also establish different learning and power relationships between students and the teacher.

In one year 9 class where the teacher-in-role convention was used successfully, the students were in role as travelling performers and had prepared plays aimed at informing villagers in rural India about why and how to reduce the birth rate. The teacher was the village elder and had the task of introducing each travelling group and leading the discussion that followed. The teacher was able to guide the students' learning towards issues concerning family size and birth rates in LEDCs via careful questioning and subsequent discussions. In addition the teacher was able to establish classroom control by varying voice tone to introduce tension into the proceedings, thus capturing the students' attention.

Convention 2 – Meetings

Meetings are good for initiating or summarising a dramatic sequence. They have the advantage of being very structured and the teacher can retain control in his/her role as the chair, which may or may not require him/her to be 'in role'.

The range of meetings that can be 'called' is enormous. Secret meetings such as 'gang' meetings or protest meetings can be especially effective in building interest and tension and therefore encouraging participation. More formal meetings such as public enquiries, parliament and hustings are good for hearing and articulating different points of view. They enable students to get to grips with the range of viewpoints impinging upon a particular issue and they provide students with the opportunity to develop, express, justify and question and defend a particular position.

Following some teaching about the process of suburbanisation, the meetings convention was effectively used with a year 7 group to consider the issue of 'Changing villages'. The context for the meeting was a 'typical' village' where the local Council was

proposing a development of 50 new houses, a new road, a new bus service and a post office. In addition the 'villagers' had to consider how best to spend £500,000. In small groups the students created their own villager, taking account of characteristics such as age, gender and occupation (references to the ITV television series *Emmerdale* were useful here!). Following some discussion students then integrated into village groups and set up a freeze-frame of the village.

The subsequent lesson involved the students reassembling into character groups and discussing their character's reactions to the changes proposed by the Council. They then attended a public meeting, chaired by the teacher acting in role, to discuss the Council's proposed development. Students were successfully able to respond to the proposed developments 'in role' and therefore appreciated that the different characters had different views and different priorities concerning change within a rural community.

Convention 3 – Hot-seating

Hot-seating is an excellent strategy for developing students' questioning skills. Students have the opportunity to 'quiz' the teacher or each other, in or out of role, as a mechanism for exploring issues and to clarify understanding. The types of questions asked can reveal a great deal about students' level of understanding, and the responses given – by the teacher or other students in role – can contribute to learning, reveal misconceptions and clarify thinking. Hot-seating can be used very flexibly, for example during the creation of a freeze-frame where an individual student can be 'unfrozen' so that the teacher and other students can question them, thus requiring the individual to draw on their geographical knowledge and understanding to explain and justify the events they are presenting.

Teachers and students can also swap roles as students can opt to take their place in the hot-seat at a time that they think is appropriate. For example, if the teacher is hot-seated as the town planner then a student, in the role of the developer, may feel that there is an appropriate point at which he/she would like to be in the hot-seat.

Convention 4 – Interviews and interrogations

Interviews and interrogations are an adaptation of the hot-seating convention but normally form an entity in themselves. They can develop students' questioning skills as such strategies demand the use of appropriate questioning from the students. The advantage of interviews and interrogations is that they clearly reveal motives and attitudes as students ask probing questions.

This convention can involve the teacher taking on a number of different roles; for example as a business owner who wants to open a business in new premises in a developing country. Students interview the teacher to find out what their business is like, what the wages will be, what its labour laws are, what jobs local people will get, etc. They may also question the business owner's ethics, and motivation for establishing premises in an LEDC. The students can then use the information and evidence they have, as well as their wider geographical knowledge, to decide to which business to lease the premises and why. The technique was used effectively with a group of year 7 students who were investigating the impact of a skiing development in a village. Students' interest was sustained by bringing in a teacher to act as the representative of a neighbouring village. The students asked the villager numerous questions such as:

- What have you gained from developing skiing in your village?
- What jobs have been created and who has benefited from these?
- What has happened to the wildlife in the hills?
- The roads are all very narrow – how do you manage all of the extra cars?
- This is a very beautiful area – how do you ensure that the skiers don't spoil it with their 'touristy' ways?

For homework students were asked to write about how they thought their village would change if skiing were to be developed there.

Convention 5 – Small-group play-making

This is a common way in which drama has been used in geography. Students are put into small groups and asked to 'make up a play' about an issue that has been studied. This can be useful for reinforcing and clarifying prior learning, but if it used independently of any other dramatic conventions it can result in rather shallow analysis and be more of a repetition exercise than a process exploring empathy, motives, values and attitudes. This has obvious implications for behaviour management.

The technique was used to explore the human response to a volcanic eruption in the Congo in 2002 with a year 8 group. While some geographical learning did occur, the shortfalls of this technique were also clear. The stimulus for the drama was a video of a television news broadcast, focusing on the refugees from the crisis. A short time was spent developing the characters of the refugees using the context building conventions described above. Students then put together a play that was supposed to show the refugees fleeing from the hazard and to highlight the physical and emotional anguish of their flight. However, the plays simply involved a lot of screaming, wailing and running around and the consequence was a rather shallow understanding of the feelings of the individual characters. The geographical learning was limited as students did not use any specific geographical vocabulary, demonstrate any knowledge of place or environment, or illustrate their appreciation of the impact of a natural hazard and people's response to it.

A more productive approach might have been to focus on the issues facing local people, and also to draw on 'expert' knowledge to inform the dramatic process. Some students could have taken on what, in drama, is defined as 'the mantle of the expert'. By taking on roles such as a vulcanologist, the representative of an agency which supports refugees, or a spokesperson for the refugees, they could have drawn on their subject knowledge to inform the drama and thus added some depth to the final product.

Some concluding thoughts

Students understand that the world is a dynamic place consisting of myriad complex and intricate issues for which it is not always possible (nor desirable) to provide neat and simple solutions. So for teachers and students to explore this complexity together, to consider geographical issues in a more holistic way, as well as developing and challenging together their (teachers and students) underlying values and attitudes, seems infinitely desirable.

Many students enjoy drama because:
- it provides them with the opportunity to share ideas,
- it enables then to develop and express their point of view,
- it enables them to appreciate the views of others in an interesting way,
- it provides a vehicle for developing questions and seeking answers,
- it is very visual,
- it is fun.

Within the context of geography all of the above are essential if students are to feel enthusiastic about their learning (and therefore will want to learn) and if they are to develop a range of geographical skills and understandings. Drama can provide students with the opportunity to explore the lives, identities, cultures and values of 'others' via authentic experiences of what it means to live and be in different places, different environments and different societies. But it also creates other opportunities: for students to reflect upon their own values and attitudes and to place these in a wider context, and for students (and teachers) to display different qualities that other approaches to learning do not necessarily permit.

Related publications from the Geographical Association:
- Biddulph, M. and Bright, G. (2003) *Theory into Practice: Dramatically good geography.*
- McPartland, M. (2001) *Theory into Practice: Moral dilemmas.*
- Roberts, M. (2003) *Learning through Enquiry: Making sense of geography in the key stage 3 classroom.*

References

DfEE/QCA (1999) *Geography in the National Curriculum (England)*. London: HMSO.

McCleod, H. (1992) *Teaching for Ecologically Sustainable Development*. Queensland, Australia: Department of Education.

McGuinness, C. (1999) *From Thinking Skills to Thinking Classrooms: A review and evaluation of approaches for developing pupils' thinking* (Research Report RR115). London: DfEE.

Neelands, J. (1991) *Structuring Drama Work. A handbook of available forms in theatre and drama*. Cambridge: Cambridge University Press.

Neelands, J. (1992) *Learning Through Imagined Experience: The role of drama in the national curriculum*. London: Hodder and Stoughton.

Nixon, J. (ed) (1982) *Drama and the Whole Curriculum*. London: Hutchinson.

Slater, F. (1982) *Learning Through Geography*. London: Heinemann Educational.

Somers, J. (1994) *Drama in the Curriculum*. London: Cassells Educational.

Implications for practice

(a) Geography can contribute to students' 'affective' development.

With so much emphasis on the development of students' knowledge, skills and understanding, the need to develop students' emotional qualities tends to get neglected. Developing students' affective qualities requires us to recognise that geography can and should make a contribution in this and that the teaching strategies used in the geography classroom need to provide opportunities for students to explore their own feelings and perspectives in order to be better able to understand the feelings and perspectives of others. Drama can provide geography teachers with appropriate strategies to enable them to engage students with these affective dimensions of geographical enquiry and to develop high quality thinking.

(b) Open-ended learning is the key to successful geography–drama lessons.

By this we mean that much more responsibility for the development of geographical understanding needs to be placed in the hands of the students. Teachers need to be prepared to provide structured support, guidance and subject expertise, but students need to have the responsibility to develop their own understanding and take responsibility for their learning. The role of the teacher in geography–drama lessons is much more that of facilitator, with high expectations and a clear sense of purpose.

(c) Not all aspects of geography 'lend' themselves to geography–drama lessons.

Neelands' (1991) definition of drama, and the national curriculum for geography (DfEE/QCA, 1999), together indicate that drama is appropriate for geographical enquiry where students need to engage with complex issues. These issues often require students to consider different perspectives, to understand different cultural or social values and be able to participate in conversations that require them to synthesise the opinions of others. It is important to identify where students will encounter such complexity in their geographical work and then to consider how particular drama conventions (freeze-framing, soundtracking, teacher-in-role, meetings, hot-seating, interviews and interrogations, or small-group play-making) might be used to help them to explore this complexity effectively.

(d) Reflection is an essential part of geography–drama lessons.

By encouraging students to reflect on their learning at different stages of the geography–drama process it is more likely that they will be able understand both the way in which they have been learning and what they have learned. Both are crucial if geography–drama lessons are to have purpose: one without the other can result in lessons that lack focus and direction. Opportunity for reflection must therefore be built into geography–drama learning experiences otherwise the geographical knowledge and understanding we want students to develop may be lost. Certain drama strategies, such as 'conscience alley', can in themselves encourage reflection.

Chapter 25

Collaboration, collaboration, collaboration

Denise Freeman and Caroline Hare

Before reading this chapter consider the following questions:

- What are the benefits for your students of learning geography through collaboration?

- What are the characteristics of successful collaborative learning in geography?

- What strategies and resources can you use to support collaborative learning in your geography?

Collaborative learning is learning together. As teachers we can sometimes be unaware of the extent to which collaboration permeates the everyday teaching and learning that goes on in our classroom. When completing a task, students often look to each other for support and ask each other questions about their work. There is a danger that teachers can overlook this collaboration; instead we tend to 'home in' on the students that appear to be 'just chatting' and are off task. Students can be observed learning collaboratively in a variety of ways during lessons. This collaborative learning is often initiated by the student's themselves, and is not the direct result of an instruction from the teacher. Furthermore, the nature of the collaboration is determined by the needs of individual students. This chapter recognises the value and role of students learning together in a variety of situations, and aims to help teachers to understand the processes involved in facilitating collaborative learning in the geography classroom.

What is collaborative learning?

Collaborative learning helps to achieve a number of important goals – student-centred learning, active participation, greater engagement, responsibility for own learning and that of others (Lambert and Balderstone, 2000). Working together also helps students to develop their academic as well as their social skills (Hopkins and Harris, 2000). Furthermore, collaborative learning strategies can play an important part in making geography 'more relevant'.

Curriculum development initiatives such as the Thinking Through Geography project (Leat, 1998) and Valuing Places (see GA website) have provided teachers with a range of strategies and resources designed to engage students and foster an atmosphere of collaboration. One of the biggest contributions to this area of learning have come from key charities and organisations involved in development education. Resources published by these groups provide opportunities for students to gain an understanding of development issues through collaboration and active learning. For example, the game *Trade Rules!* (Christian Aid, 2002), aimed at post-16 students, encourages them to consider how the World Trade Organization and the world's wealthiest countries control the flow of goods and raw materials between countries. Students are assigned roles and work collaboratively in small groups.

The process of collaborative learning

Collaborative learning can be viewed as a process. This process needs to be unpacked and understood in order to add to and enhance teaching and learning in the geography classroom. We have already acknowledged that collaboration takes place each day at a variety of scales and in a variety of ways, yet teachers and students stand to gain further from learning more about the processes involved in working together.

Collaborative learning is a complex process, often involving a range of variables. To draw a model to show how collaboration in geography works would be an impossible task as every classroom situation and every school day is different. However, it is possible to identify six key features of the collaboration process (Figure 1). The process often begins with the *planning* and *preparation* of a proposed collaborative activity or project. This is followed by the *launch*, and subsequent *management* of the collaborative task. The *outcomes* of the activity are then presented. During the final stages of the process the participants engage in *evaluating* and *reflecting* upon the task, which will help to inform future practice. Both students and teachers may be involved in all of these stages, e.g. older students may design and launch their own group work activity. The ways in which different people are involved in the collaboration process are outlined in Figure 1 along with details and explanations of the six components of the process. The coverage is not exhaustive; rather it provides a starting point for thinking about the processes involved in collaborative learning.

It has been suggested by various commentators that both students and teachers stand to gain a great deal from participating in the processes of collaborative learning. A summary of the benefits to be gained is presented in Figure 2.

Photo: ©Margaret Roberts.

Student | **Teacher**

1. Planning and preparation

Participants (students or teacher) decide to use collaborative strategies and develop plans and resources. May refer to previous experiences with this or other teaching groups.

1. Planning and preparation
What idea/concept/topic is being taught? What previous learning has taken place?
What learning strategies could be used here? Is group work appropriate? What will collaboration add to the learning experience? What information do I need? What resources do I need? What support do I need?

2. Launch

The participants introduce the idea of collaboration (to begin with) and explain the nature of the task and outline expectations (for behaviour, conduct and final outcomes).

2. Launch
Is everything I need ready and set up for launch?
Have I talked to support staff and other helpers about what we are doing?
How will I introduce the task? What form will instructions take?
Does everyone know what they are going to do and what they need to achieve?
Do the participants know what is expected of them?

3. Manage

This can be the most daunting and complex part of the process but one where participants will learn the most. This section sees the participants interacting with one another using pre-prepared resources. There are lots of variables to be managed, e.g. time, performance, learning, group dynamics.

3. Manage
Who will manage the activities?
Are rules needed? Who will write these rules?
Who will ensure these rules are kept?
How will groups be formed?
How will groups be managed?
How will movement around the room be managed?
How will discussion be managed? Who will manage time?
Who will manage the debrief? How will everyone's ideas be heard?

4. Presentation of outcome

The outcomes of group work go beyond just the work produced or the ideas discussed, they also include the skills developed and the process of learning together.

4. Presentation of outcome
What do you expect the students to produce from the collaborative activity?
What do you expect the students to gain from the collaborative process?
How will the outcomes be assessed?
(Are the students aware of this?)
How will the outcomes be presented?

5. Evaluate

Evaluation is an essential part of the collaborative process and should be undertaken by all participants. Evaluation can be used to feed forward into future collaborative opportunities.

5. Evaluate (these questions should be asked of both teachers and students)
How was the task introduced?
Did the groups work effectively?
Did working collaboratively enhance geographical learning?
Did working collaboratively enhance geographical skills?
What did the students learn about working collaboratively?
What did the students gain from working collaboratively?
Were the learning objectives and outcomes met?
How can the students build upon their experiences in future collaborative work?

6. Reflect

Reflection can be a long-term process, as it occurs immediately after the activity, and when returning to the same or other collaborative activities.

6. Reflect
A SWOT (strengths, weaknesses, opportunities and threats) analysis could be completed here by all participants.
What lessons can be learnt for future collaboration in classrooms at all levels?

Figure 1 | The six key features of collaborative learning.

Knowledge and understanding	Skills	Student inclusion and support	Student achievement and attainment
It is suggested that students gain a better long-term understanding through group-based discussion than solely teacher-led activities or tasks (Stimpson, 1994).	Collaborative learning promotes the development of many skills, including:	Students of all abilities are motivated and encouraged to participate in learning. Furthermore they may also feel supported in the learning process by their peers (Slavin, 1995).	Collaborative learning enhances achievement among lower achieving students of minority groups (Slavin, 1995; Panitz, 2002).
Collaborative strategies motivate students to learn and increase enjoyment of the learning process (Lambert and Balderstone, 2000).	▪ Problem solving ▪ Communication ▪ Those associated with social interaction, e.g. interpersonal skills ▪ Questioning ▪ Debating	Some may argue that working with others increases student confidence and security and therefore they are more likely to participate in lessons.	As students are encouraged to discuss ideas in groups, levels of understanding tend to rise resulting in improved achievement and attainment.
Students are encouraged to think about and question geographical information. The enquiry process allows them to follow their own routes of interest within a topic area.	▪ Thinking ▪ Enquiry ▪ Research ▪ Groupwork ▪ Teamwork ▪ Leadership ▪ Presentation ▪ Reflection and evaluation	Improves cross-cultural understanding and ethnic relations (Slavin, 1995). Helps students to understand and appreciate the values of others.	Collaborative learning strategies reward more than just knowledge and understanding. Skills-based assessments can be made. Students are encouraged to evaluate their own progress and that of their group.
Enquiry learning skills are developed.		Students are encouraged to talk about and discuss their views and experiences, which helps to develop empathy and understanding among students.	Reflecting and feeding back upon collaborative work can allow students to gain an insight into the learning process (Panitz, 2002).
Provides opportunities for evaluation of and reflection on learning, enhances knowledge and understanding.		Promotes a spirit of co-operation and mutual respect among students (Whitaker, quoted in Lambert and Balderstone, 2000).	Students and teachers are able to set targets and address areas for future development.

Figure 2 | *The benefits of collaborative learning.*

Types of collaborative learning

Collaborative learning is not new but it is only in recent decades that educational practitioners have begun to develop specific collaborative learning strategies and, more importantly, evaluate their effectiveness (Slavin, 1995). Lambert and Balderstone (2000) suggest that it is possible to identify two main forms of collaborative learning. The first of these involves students working as a group to complete a structured task (usually set by the teacher). Each member of the group has a specific and essential role to play in order to achieve the final group outcome. The second form of collaborative learning could be regarded as less structured and open to more student negotiation. Students are given an open-ended task, such as an investigation or decision-making exercise, which they work through as a group by sharing knowledge and ideas (Lambert and Balderstone, 2000). This latter form of student collaboration often requires the students to take a lead role in the learning process; thus flexibility and a certain organic quality are central to its success.

The range of collaborative learning strategies available for use and development by geography teachers is immense and it would be impossible to document them all. Figure 3 provides an insight into some of the ways in which collaborative learning may be implemented in the classroom. The suggestions range from quick lesson starters to activities that may be extended to form a series of lessons.

	Possible purpose/ reason for collaboration	Suggested learning activities/strategies	Examples	What next? Development opportunities
Pairs	■ Launch new topic or issue ■ Share ideas ■ Recap/recall/revisit previous learning ■ To develop IT skills and learn through ICT	■ Back to back (see example) ■ Card sorting ■ Matching ■ Listing ■ Concept mapping ■ Odd one out (Leat, 1998) ■ Geographical games, e.g. Taboo. ■ Model building	**Back to back:** Students work in pairs and are told to sit back to back. One of the students is given an image, the other student asks geographical questions about the image, and builds up an accurate mental picture of it. The activity may be timed. The students then switch roles with a new image. They may then produce a piece of extended writing about the place they have been enquiring about, or replicate a sketch of the image from their notes.	This task develops many geographical skills, particularly enquiry skills. Students must ask well-thought-out questions: Is there evidence that the beach has been managed? Has material built up against the groyne and if so on which side? How many storeys is the hotel building? They must also use geographical vocabulary accurately, e.g. in relation to compass points, scale, names of landscape features and place names. These are all skills that can be referred to and used in other tasks or activities, particularly those involving maps or images.
Small group	■ Launch new topic or issue ■ Share ideas ■ Present ideas, including orally ■ Skills development, analytical, e.g. problem solving, and evaluative skills ■ Fieldwork ■ Enquiry ■ Research ■ To develop IT skills and learn through ICT	■ Mysteries (Leat, 1998) ■ Team participation in geographical games, e.g. *The Trading Game* ■ Card sorting ■ Problem solving ■ Decision making ■ Role plays ■ Presentations (*PowerPoint*, short videos, audio tapes) ■ Model building	**Map recall work:** Students work in small groups. They will be shown a map for a limited time, which they will be expected to reproduce from memory. The team will send one member at a time to look at the map for approximately 30 seconds each and then as a team they will work together to reproduce the map on a large piece of paper. Before beginning the task the group is given approximately 5 minutes to plan how to tackle the task and to develop a plan, e.g. one student will memorise the roads and another settlements. Adapted from the Key Stage 3 Strategy Foundation subjects video 'Plenaries'.	This task reinforces student's map skills and can be revisited as an activity more than once. Over time the students will develop clear strategies for approaching the task and establish a well-planned groupwork approach, with clear roles for each member. The collaborative skills developed from this task can then be transferred to other groupwork activities, e.g. working with others to carry out a geographical enquiry or fieldwork activity.
Large group	■ Share ideas ■ Explore new concepts ■ Debate/discuss ideas ■ Enquiry	■ Role play ■ Conference ■ Discussion/debate ■ Concept mapping	**Conference:** The conference debated whether or not a large supermarket chain should increase its range of Fair Trade products, to include a new line of teas from Sri Lanka. Students adopted roles according to different interest groups involved in Fair Trade. The conference was divided into two large groups; those opposed to the expansion and those for it. A variety of Fair Trade products including the teas under debate were offered to students to taste.	Students organise their own conference. They report on the conference through a piece of extended writing or ICT work, e.g. a video presentation.

Figure 3

	Possible purpose/ reason for collaboration	Suggested learning activities/strategies	Examples	What next? Development opportunities
Whole class	■ Launch new topic or issue ■ Share ideas ■ Recap/recall/revisit previous learning ■ Explore new concepts ■ Debate/discuss ■ Fieldwork	■ Map orienteering ■ Geographical games, e.g. map skills bingo ■ Concept mapping ■ Conference/debate	**Matching geographical pairs:** Each student is given the name of a place, name of a geographical feature or a geographical term printed on a piece of paper and attached to their back. They have not seen this name/word. They must move around the room and ask other students questions, to which they can only answer using the words yes or no. Students must find their matching partner to make a pair, e.g. the name of a country and its capital city or the name of a country and its GNP.	This activity develops the students' team-/group-work skills as well as their geographical enquiry skills. The students must ask appropriate, well-thought-out questions using accurate geographical vocabulary. The activity can be 'snowballed' so that the students have to form larger groups, e.g. grouping together all the people in the room that belong to a particular continent, or grouping together all the countries that are prone to earthquakes or volcanoes.
Wider collaboration	■ To foster collaboration with other schools and other institutions, both nationally and internationally ■ Fieldwork ■ Researching contrasting or distant places ■ Place based or issue-based enquiry ■ Develop IT skills and learn through ICT	■ Research via e-mail or video conferencing ■ Attending conferences to help GCSE or post-16 students ■ Collaborative fieldwork ■ Coursework data collection	**Key stage 3 local area enquiry:** This work aims to compare two contrasting school locations. Students collect data on their own school locality through classwork and fieldwork. They then share this with students from another place. The data are sent to the other school via e-mail, digital images, video, the internet and by post. The teachers from each school may visit the partner school and talk to the class as a 'guest speaker'.	This work may be developed further to include joint fieldwork between the two schools. The students may visit each other's school locality or even work together on other fieldwork ventures. The collaboration could develop into a school 'twinning' system, like our twinned towns! Further collaboration can be sought on other projects and in other subjects. Furthermore, teachers can collaborate on areas of curriculum design.

Figure 3 continued | Ways in which collaborative work can be instigated in the classroom with different sized groups.

Facilitating collaboration

A framework for considering the process of collaborative learning was outlined in Figure 1. However, some aspects of this process require further examination, particularly with regard to forming groups and the management of group work.

Forming groups

Forming groups is a key part of the collaborative process yet in many ways it can actually be an obstacle to successful collaboration. There can be difficulties with poor group dynamics or dealing with a situation where a few students in the group do all the work while the others are just carried along by the group. Furthermore, forming groups can be time consuming and stressful for both students and teachers. It is essential therefore to form a plan before the lesson so that groups are formed quickly and the learning begins promptly. There are several ways in which groups may be formed. Ginnis (2002) provides teachers with a clear set of questions to ask before choosing how to establish groups; these are outlined below. Considering the individual nature of each class is vital to the decision-making process.

> ■ *What group-forming method shall I choose?*
> ■ *Which method will work best for this activity?*
> ■ *Which method will work best given the current state of the class?*
> ■ *Which method will move them on socially?*
> ■ *Which method haven't we used for a while?*
> (Ginnis, 2002, p. 207).

Ginnis suggests that there are at least eight types of groups: Random, Friendship, Interest, Skill, Mixed skills, Learning style, Support, and Performance groups.

Effective groups

Simply organising students into groups and asking them to work together does not always translate into effective collaborative learning. To encourage them to co-operate with each other students generally need a shared interest or common goal (Johnson and Johnson, 2000). Developing a shared agenda will form an important part of preparing for and introducing a collaborative task. Furthermore, like businesses, schools can also benefit from investing time in team building and group motivational work. This may begin with whole-class strategies to promote co-operation, e.g. displaying students' ideas and views around the classroom, to team building activities at the start or end of the lesson. Evaluating classroom layout and design can also be the key to developing a collaborative environment and learning ethos. Students can be encouraged to rotate tables regularly and work with different peers. Some primary schools designate tables or areas of the room as colour zones and pupils are assigned to work with others, in a particular zone, on a given task. Students can be encouraged to co-operate with each other and share ideas through written work (e.g. a class log book or comment book) as well as oral presentations.

Ginnis identifies the following features of successful group work:

> ■ **Seating:** *The group sits so that each group member can hear and see all the others easily.*
> ■ **Speaking:** *One person at a time speaks during the discussion.*
> ■ **Listening:** *Everyone turns to face the person who is speaking.*
> ■ **Expectations:** *Individual group members remind others if they break group rules. And any member at any time is able to explain: what they are doing, how this contributes to the overall group task, what other group members are doing and why, and what the next step will be.*
> ■ **Group planning:** *The group always works to agreed and explicit deadlines – each member should be able to answer the question: 'When will this be finished?'*
> ■ **Teamwork:** *A group member who finishes a task early offers to help others, or negotiates the next step with the group manager.*
> ■ **Responsibility:** *Everyone contributes equally to looking after resources, to clearing up and to moving furniture* (2002, p. 218).

Inevitably, during the process of learning to work effectively with others, issues or problems may arise. Teachers and students need to address these through self-evaluation and reflection. However, teachers can adopt specific strategies in order to increase the chances of success. Teachers could, for example:

1. circulate around the room without spending too much time with one particular group or individual;
2. give students a clear and constant idea of the time frame in which they have to work;
3. make sure that students are clear about rules and roles, both as a whole class and within their groups;
4. refer all participants back to what was learnt during previous collaborative activities and consider how this can be applied to today's work;
5. have a back-up plan in case things go wrong.

Evaluating collaborative learning

As already stated, evaluation is an essential part of the collaborative process. In order to feed back and to inform future learning, evaluations should be made by both students and teachers. By evaluating group work, students can improve their understanding of the collaborative process and how groups function. They can also gain an important insight into what the teacher had planned to achieve through the activity and how their work may be assessed. By evaluating group work, *teachers* can consider the role of group work; assess how it has contributed to student learning in geography and how it may be used in future. There are four key evaluative questions that can be asked by teachers following a piece of collaborative learning:

- Did working collaboratively enhance students' geographical knowledge, skills and understanding?
- What did the students learn about working collaboratively?
- How did collaboration help to achieve the desired learning outcomes?
- How can the students build upon their experiences in future collaborative work?

These can be supplemented by the teacher's own questions and students' self-evaluation sheets (Figure 5).

Group name:
Names of group members:
Was there a group leader? If so how was he or she chosen and what did they do during the activity/lesson?
What role did each group member play during the lesson? Name of member and role: Name of member and role: Name of member and role: Name of member and role:
How did you share out the work within the group? How were decisions about this made?
Were rules established during the lesson? If so, how and when were these set up?
Do you think your group worked effectively (i.e. you worked well and managed to meet your aims)? Explain your answer.
List five things you learnt in this lesson:
How did working as a group help you to learn during this lesson (if it didn't explain why)?

Figure 5 | *Students' self evaluation sheet for collaborative learning activities.*

Using ICT

The fast changing world of ICT and multimedia provides teachers with a variety of opportunities for supporting student collaboration and active learning (Figure 6). Furthermore, collaboration is no longer confined to the classroom or computer room; the internet and other telecommunications technology now enable teachers and students to collaborate over great distances, through e-mail, video conferencing and live web chats.

Example 1: Studying counterurbanisation

In this example, GCSE students at Beal High School in Ilford, worked collaboratively to explore the phenomenon of counterurbanisation. Counterurbanisation and rural

Possible collaborative learning strategies using ICT in geography	
Group presentations: Groups of students can use *PowerPoint* and a projector to give presentations. Where appropriate students may use the internet for their research and/or incorporate digital images.	**Role play:** Students work in groups to prepare role plays and record their work using a digital video camera (Fox, 2002). The process of making the video aids student-centred learning and the edited video provides teachers with a stimulating teaching resource for future years.
Asking enquiry questions: Students may work in groups to develop a series of enquiry questions about a place or issue. They may then e-mail these to someone living in the relevant place and collaborate via the internet. Students could also conduct an enquiry using video conferencing.	**Newsroom simulation:** In a newsroom simulation students are asked to respond to breaking news. They work in news teams to research and present the story. The internet, CD-Roms and video footage can be used for research. They can present their news using *PowerPoint, Publisher* or digital video.

Figure 6 | *Opportunities for collaboration in geography using ICT and multimedia technology.*

settlement in MEDCs are topics that appear on many GCSE and A-level specifications. Although the lessons outlined here were aimed at year 10, the ideas can be adapted and developed for older students. The work took place over three lessons and involved collaboration at a variety of levels, both in the classroom and in a computer room. ICT was an important learning, communication and research tool throughout.

The stimulus for this collaborative learning came from a dedicated GCSE course textbook (Finders, 2001). The village of Cutnall Green is used as a case study of counterurbanisation. It is situated close to the city of Birmingham and other business centres (e.g. Kidderminster). Good transport links and an attractive rural setting have made Cutnall Green an ideal location for counterurbanisation. Most of the students involved in this case study have lived in a urban area all their lives. They have a poor understanding of rural issues and the rural way of life and of why someone may want to move to the countryside. Many of the students know little about life outside Greater London. Thus, the work had three aims:

1. To help the students develop a 'real' sense of place for a rural area of England otherwise unfamiliar to them.
2. To allow students to understand why counterurbanisation is taking place in many MEDCs and what the impacts are of this phenomenon.
3. To enable the students to explore the issue of counterurbanisation and rural settlement through active participation, role play and collaboration.

Figure 7 | *The four main stages of the counterurbanisation collaborative work.*

Stage 1: Students work in pairs to complete a short mystery (card-sorting activity) exploring the concept/phenomena of counterurbanisation.

Stage 2: Acting in role, students attend a meeting in which they discuss the issues facing the people of North Worcestershire, including those relating to counterurbanisation. After initial guidance students develop their roles.

Stage 3: Students break down into smaller groups according to which settlement in North Worcestershire their role play character comes from. Greater discussion takes place on the issues facing that particular settlement.

Stage 4: Students work in pairs or threes to produce a webpage design for their settlement, presenting a discussion about relevant local issues, particularly those relating to counterurbanisation.

Why is Miss Freeman in Cutnall Green?

Miss Freeman lives in a large house. It has a big old fashioned fireplace and a huge garden.	Sometimes people stop and give Miss Freeman a lift home in their car.	It can be dark in the winter after school but Miss Freeman never feels afraid of walking home on her own. Just a little cold!
This is Miss Freeman's dream home. She is even happier as the house was bought at a very affordable price.	At the weekends Alfred plays football for the local team. Meanwhile, Miss Freeman looks after horses at the local sanctuary. She loves animals.	She had an unlucky year last year. Her old house was broken into and someone tried to snatch her purse while she was shopping.
She lives with her boyfriend Alfred. He works in the city for a large bank.	Miss Freeman was once a show jumper, but had to stop after a nasty fall.	It takes Alfred about an hour to get to work.
They met each other at a music club where they both play the clarinet.	Miss Freeman used to live in an old terraced house. It had a small garden and it wasn't big enough for all of Miss Freeman's pot plants. It took Miss Freeman and Alfred ages to save the money to move to a bigger house.	
Every morning at 7am, Alfred goes to work. He takes the train as he can't stand lots of traffic and hates being late.	Miss Freeman loves her new life. She only gets stressed occasionally when Ofsted visit.	Miss Freeman and Alfred are thinking about having children soon. The area seems perfect for starting a family.
Miss Freeman walks to school where she works. It is only 10 minutes from her house and she loves taking in the fresh clean air.	Miss Freeman's best friend Katie has also moved to the area. She works from home writing GCSE revision books. Miss Freeman loves popping round to visit Katie for tea.	Miss Freeman and Alfred used all of their savings to buy their first house but they thought that it was worth it because it was so close to all the shops and entertainment facilities that they needed.

Figure 8 | *The cards for the counterurbanisation mystery: 'Why is Miss Freeman in Cutnall Green?'. Written by Ron Spicer during a teaching practice at Beal High School.*

The work involved collaboration at a variety of levels and in groups of varying sizes – sometimes using a 'reverse snowballing' effect (i.e. reducing from larger to smaller groups). Figure 7 indicates the four main stages to their work, which ran over of 3-4 lessons.

The collaboration process in action

This case study is explained by working through the six stages of collaboration, from the planning and *preparation* through to the *evaluation* stage (Figure 1). A discussion of management issues takes place towards the end, once the case study has been fully explained.

Planning and preparation

Before launching the main activity several steps were taken in order to *plan* and *prepare* for the *launch* of the central activity. Although in this case study this part of the process was teacher led, with a greater amount of time and futher planning, students could have completed many of the tasks shown below.

■ **Teacher-led research:** Research carried out using the course-based textbook (good for facts, figures and statistics), a county-based ('This is Worcestershire') and the local government websites.
■ **Developing resources:** Maps of Cutnall Green, local bus timetable and other service information, and property information (including pictures) were sourced from the internet.

Meeting agenda

Chair: Miss Freeman
Settlements represented: Kidderminster, Droitwich, Birmingham and Cutnall Green
1. Welcome and aims
2. Kidderminster Extra Police Campaign
3. Droitwich shops' Christmas sales figures
4. House prices in Cutnall Green
5. Bus service in Cutnall Green
6. Young Farmers' Association – meeting in Cutnall Green – Wednesday 15 January
7. Transport congestion
8. Birmingham - new M6 toll road development
9. Birmingham NEC events
10. Birmingham University open days
11. Any other business

Figure 9 | *The agenda for the meeting of 'The People of North Worcestershire'.*

About You

Name:
Age:
Occupation (job):
Where do you live? (Name of town or village)
How long have you lived here?
Where do you work?
Do you usually attend village/town council meetings?
Do you own a car?
Do you use public transport (e.g. bus or train)?
Where do you do your weekly shopping?
What type of music do you listen to?
What type of books do you read?
What do you do in your leisure time?

Figure 10 | *The survey given to students to help them develop their role.*

- **Background learning:** Students introduced to the idea of counterurbanisation using a geographical mystery (Figure 8). Key concepts fully explored using the debrief session. Centring the mystery on the class teacher engaged the students – particularly as some of the comments were very far fetched!
- **Locational knowledge:** Students develop a sense of place for North Worcestershire through map work and images. Students label a map of the region, showing the key factors that have encouraged counterurbanisation in the area, e.g. good transport links, ease of commute, 'ideal' rural village location, proximity to urban business and services.
- **Gathering support:** Trainee teacher approached to take part in the conference intended to launch the main collaborative activity.
- **Possible options for further preparation:** Contact details could be found for established community groups and community leaders. These people could be e-mailed to help teachers gather case study information and students could be encouraged to do this too.

The launch

The meeting of 'The People of North Worcestershire' was launched as detailed below. It formed one of the main activities in this series of lessons, but the students were unaware of the format so they were not expecting anything 'different'. During the previous lesson they had completed the counterurbanisation mystery and explored the ideas relating to urban-rural migration.
- **Room preparation:** The room was set up in a conference format and an agenda (Figure 9) for the meeting was left on each student's chair along with a personal profile/survey (Figure 10) to be filled in on arrival.
- **Support staff:** The trainee teacher, working with the class, was briefed about what to expect and his role in the conference was discussed. He was a 'guest speaker', who could liven up the discussion if it began to decline.
- **Introducing the work:**
  - The students were ushered into the room and welcomed to the meeting of 'The People of North Worcestershire'.

Bank manager, aged 47, works in a bank in Birmingham, lives in Cutnall Green at weekends, reads books on economics, owns a sports car, does not attend village meetings as he is a busy man.

Television presenter, aged 32, lives in Cutnall Green in a very large house, works in Birmingham, listens to opera and classical music, reads Dickens and autobiographies (including my own). Spare time spent walking, reading, watching television and taking the kids out, as well as attending salsa and pilates classes.

Writer, aged 44, lives in Cutnall Green in a very large home, owns a large car, doesn't use public transport, enjoys jogging, gardening and listening to classical music. Wants her voice heard at village meetings.

IT consultant, aged 27, lives in Kidderminster, been married just six months, attend town meetings, shops at out of town shopping centres, does use a bus occasionally. Likes jazz music.

Travel agent, aged 22, has lived in Kidderminster for six months, doesn't own a car, uses buses, visits out of town shopping centres, likes going shopping and visiting the pub.

Figure 11 | Students' development of their roles during the Council meeting.

- The students were given a card as they entered the room. On it was written age and occupation, e.g. 'You are 26 and work as a nurse'. Students were given no further information about their role.
- The teacher acted as Chair from the outset, introducing the meeting and urging students to read their agendas and complete their personal profile/survey.
- The students were expected to complete their personal profile by thinking about work covered in the previous lesson and the possible characteristics of a person living in their given role. The most important part of the survey was for students to decide where in North Worcestershire their person was likely to live. Questions such as 'Would a young nurse (key worker) live in a village where house prices are rising dramatically due to counterurbanisation, or would they live in a large town?' were raised.
- The meeting format was used to get students thinking about the issues that may be raised at such an event. The teacher talked through the agenda items, taking questions from the students in role and asking the 'guest speaker' for comments on each item.
- **Group-forming:** The students worked as a class during the main meeting, which lasted 20-25 minutes. They were then asked to find and group together with other people living in the settlement that they had chosen. This meant that the groups were mixed, random and linked closely to the work. The students were too busy locating other 'residents' to worry about who was working with who.
- **Making tasks clear:**
  - From the start of the lesson the teacher, acting in role, gave all instructions. As Chair of the meeting they and the guest speaker guided the students through the formalities. The written agenda and survey helped students to engage actively with what was going on.

- When the students broke off into smaller groups they were given written instructions, explaining what was expected of them. They were asked to discuss the issues facing that particular settlement. The groups were expected to compose an agenda (with notes) for a hypothetical local Council meeting in their own town or village. As their detailed agenda was the expected outcome, questions such as 'What issues would appear on their agenda?' provided stimulus. They were not expected to actually hold the meeting.

■ **Possible options for further development:** Post-16 students may plan, research, prepare and chair their own local Council meetings, including inviting guest speakers (real or imagined).

The sample of student responses to the personal profile in Figure 11 show a good understanding of the places and issues being studied. The students' roles were an important part of the group-forming process.

Presenting the final outcome

During the next lesson the students were asked to work in pairs or threes to produce a webpage design (or community newsletter) for their settlement. They were required to present a discussion about relevant local issues, particularly those relating to counterurbanisation. The aim was to provide the students with a modern, relevant and stimulating form of communication. When putting together their webpage the students were encouraged to use the internet to research current 'real' events and issues, relating to their settlement. This enabled them to consider the way in which information is presented on the internet and the way in which language is used. They were encouraged

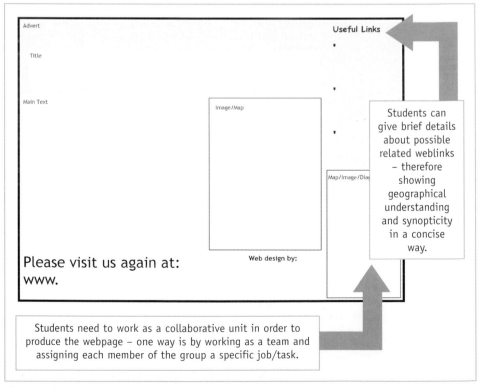

Figure 12 | *The webpage template. Note: This was produced using Publisher.*

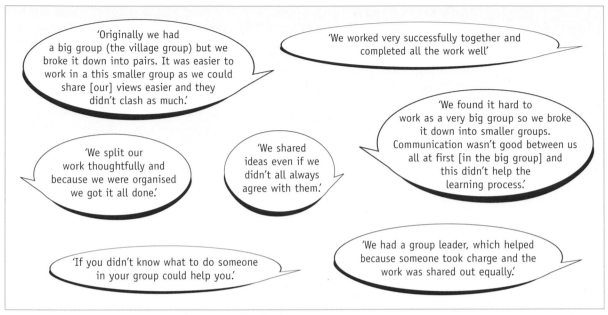

Figure 13 | *Student self-evaluation comments.*

to use digital pictures in their work. It was essential that the students worked as a team and delegated tasks, e.g. research, presentation, creating images, identifying links and constructing graphics, in order to put together their work. A webpage outline was provided by the teacher so that the students could simply add their own information in the relevant places (Figure 12).

Management

Because the counterurbanisation work involved a variety of tasks, to be carried out over a number of lessons, it raised a range of management issues, including:

- What happens if groups are developed randomly but appear unbalanced in terms of knowledge or skills? Should the teacher intervene by altering groupings?
- Should a teacher intervene with groups experiencing difficulties with group dynamics and if so how?
- When students are working in groups using ICT how can the access to the equipment be fairly shared out?
- When groups are working in the computer room, is every individual being given the opportunity to access the equipment and develop their IT skills? (In some cases the IT work may be completed by 'someone who is good at it'.)

Evaluation

After they had completed their final task (produced their webpages) students were asked to complete an evaluation form. Some of their comments are shown in Figure 13. A common theme is that of communication between group members. Many of the students viewed communication as a vital component of effective group work. These students had taken part in just one collaborative activity at this stage in their GCSE Geography course (a group presentation task). However, that they understood how groups function effectively and what aspects of group work supported the learning process is evident in the language used on their evaluation forms. This may suggest the transfer of evaluative skills from another subject area within the school curriculum. An important finding was that students viewed completing their work as a significant indicator of effective group work. This may be an area for future development in order that the students learn more about the process of collaboration.

A teacher-based evaluation of the activity was also undertaken. This raised a series of questions about the organisation, management and feedback of collaborative work. One issue in particular was to what extent groups should be 'left' to explore the process of learning as a group and learning to work in a group (i.e. without teacher intervention). In relation to specific learning objectives, such as the development of knowledge and understanding, this work highlighted the potential for learning through collaboration in geography. Collaboration enhanced the learning process by allowing the students actively to engage with the concept of counterurbanisation through the role play. They were also able to take responsibility for their learning by developing their roles, determining the local meeting agenda and deciding what information to present on their webpage.

Figure 14 | *The series of activities for the HIV/AIDS lesson.*

Example 2: HIV/AIDS in southern Africa

Stage 1: Students work in pairs to discuss ideas about Nkosi Johnson (see Figure 15) and his role within South Africa's HIV/AIDS programme. These ideas were then shared in small group and full class discussion.

Stage 2: Working in pairs students made use of a series of resources and their analytical skills to identify the long-term economic and social impacts of HIV/AIDS in southern Africa. Students had key geographical terms to work into their written responses.

Stage 3: Students next worked on a focus case study looking at Botswana - how the country is now and how HIV/AIDS may change it.

Stage 4: Students work individually to prepare a promotional advertisement for Hope HIV (a charity). Students work was based on the ideas and themes discussed during the lesson.

Stage 5: Students worked in role and attended a meeting of Hope HIV Advert Editors in which they decided upon the criteria for selecting the best advertisement. Students assessed their own work and set marking criteria in order to complete this task. Student collaborative skills were also assessed in this lesson.

Context and background

Year 9 students worked collaboratively on an investigation of the geographical impacts of HIV/AIDS across southern Africa as part of scheme of work based around local/global issues. The work, which took up two lessons, was designed for use near the end of their key stage 3 studies. Similar activities based on these lessons have been adapted to the needs of both older and younger students with good results, and could the use of ICT and other media.

The emphasis was on the students identifying geographical issues considered to be of both interest and importance to them; thus, the original ideas for the lessons came from the students. As part of the local/global issues studies in year 9, students are encouraged to identify current geographical issues at a range of scales (local, regional, national, global). The lessons focused on HIV/AIDS as a geographical issue and, specifically, on its impacts in southern Africa. A benefit of this type of scheme of work is that it enables geography to contribute to citizenship education. The aims were for students to:

- understand the impacts of HIV/AIDs across a range of southern African nations (a part of the world with which they are largely unfamiliar);

care for us and accept us
we are all human beings
we are normal

we have hands, we have feet
we can walk
we can talk,
we have needs just like everyone else
don't be afraid of us
- we are the same

- Nkosi Johnson

donate now

Nkosi Johnson Aids victim, age 12 years. Born 1988, died Friday 1st June 2001.
 * Who was Nkosi Johnson?
 * Why are his words so important??
 * Why does this image have such an impact?
 * Why was he chosen as South Africa's public face of HIV/ADIS?

Figure 15 | The Nkosi Johnson introductory stimulus.

■ identify the long-term social and economic impacts of HIV/AIDS in southern Africa;
■ design an advertisement proposal for a charitable organisation;
■ work through a collaborative decision-making process to select the best advertisement proposal.

The lessons involved collaboration at a variety of levels and in groups of varying sizes, through which the sharing of ideas and information took place (Figure 14).

The collaboration process

Using the information on Nkosi Johnson and other resources, the students completed the tasks as follows:

■ **Teacher-led research:** Research carried out using UN Population website, *Global Eye* magazine and accompanying web pages and teacher's notes.
■ **Developing resources:** Obtain and print – images of Nkosi Johnson as stimuli for discussion, lesson worksheets (Figure 15), storyboard outline for Hope HIV advertisement proposal, and Hope HIV Advert Editors' meeting resource.
■ **Background learning:** Students introduced to the issue of the geographical impact of HIV/AIDS through independent research in preparation for lesson. Students given opportunity to discuss ideas.
■ **Locational knowledge:** Students identify study area through teacher-led atlas-based studies.
■ **Possible options for further preparation:** Contact details could be found for established community groups and community leaders. To gather case study information, the teacher or the students could e-mail these people.

The launch

The points below show the way in which the issue of HIV/AIDS in southern Africa was launched. The students were aware that they would be investigating this issue as they had selected the ideas for the local/global issues scheme of work. As shown above

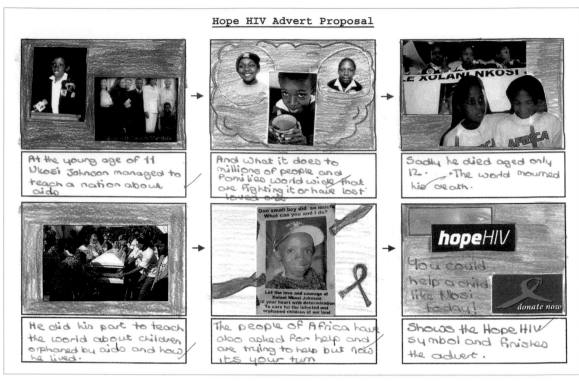

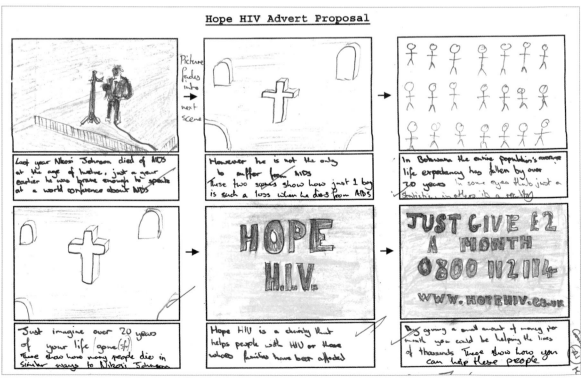

Figure 16 | Lauren's and Luke's complete Hope HIV advert proposal storyboards.

Hope HIV Directors – Advert Editors Meeting

Location: Directors Boardroom, Hope HIV Headquarters

TASK: In today's lesson you are taking on the role of the board of directors and will be deciding which advert proposal is to be chosen to launch your new campaign, which aims to raise awareness and money for your cause.

1. Before looking at the advert proposals   select a set of criteria on which you can judge the quality of each advert. Put the criteria in the table below:

Out of 5.

Ranking Criteria	Proposal 1	Proposal 2	Proposal 3	Proposal 4
Best looking.	2	4	4	4
Most effective.	4	4	3	4
Most Informative.	4	4	2	3
Most memorable.	4	5	4	4
Most touching.	3	5	4	4
Most colourful.	0	3	5	4
	17	(25)	22	23

2. Put the advert proposals in a rank order.

3. Using the criteria carefully look at each advert and judge it.

4. Do the criteria you have used to judge with and your chosen ranking order match? (YES) / NO

5. If you answered NO to the above question explain how you are going to decide which advert proposal to choose.

_____

_____

_____

_____

6. Which advert proposal have you selected? Proposal 2

7. Why did you make this choice? Explain your answer in detail in the space below (consider the message the advert gives, information about the problems of HIV in Southern Africa, does this advert consider the implications this could have for the world?)

We made this choice because it's informative, memorable and touching; so it scored the highest in our criteria above. It sends a touching and simple message to the viewer that does not leave much to the imagination, It gives prices and phone numbers.

Figure 17 | *Robert's completed evaluation sheet for his group from the Advert Editors' meeting.*

(background learning), students had undertaken independent research to develop their background knowledge of the issues and this was used as a starting point for discussion.

■ **Room preparation:** The room was set up with the tables organised into groups of six. Seating arrangements were checked to ensure that all students would be able to see the front of the class and the whiteboard.

- **Introducing the work:**
  - After being welcomed into the room, students were told they could select their own working groups of up to six members and were advised to select people they knew they were able to work with.
  - Students were asked to look at the image of Nkosi Johnson that had been placed on their group tables and consider why his face was chosen for an HIV/AIDS poster.
  - They were asked to put forward some of the research they had undertaken prior to the lesson. Their ideas were discussed and written on the board and the geographical links were identified and explained.
  - The aims, outline and purpose of the two lessons were also explained.
  - The students completed some introductory work based upon the image of Nkosi Johnson and settled into their groups. The students were encouraged to share their ideas and develop their responses from this.
  - The groups of students continued to work through a series of resource-based tasks which encouraged them to analyse the information provided in preparation for the Hope HIV advertisement proposal.
- **Group-forming:** During this stage the students collaborated on ideas within their groups, and some whole-class discussion also took place.
- **Making tasks clear:**
  - The teacher gave all instructions throughout, but students were encouraged to discuss responses and question each other's ideas within a mutually respectful environment.
  - The initial task was laid out on the group tables so that students could settle straight down to it, ensuring a smooth start to the lesson. This is especially important when students are arriving from different parts of a school.
  - Possible options for further development: an ICT-based task would allow students to access HIV/AIDS information for a range of different countries, either around the world or within a specific region, in order to build up a profile of the geographical spread and impact of HIV/AIDS.

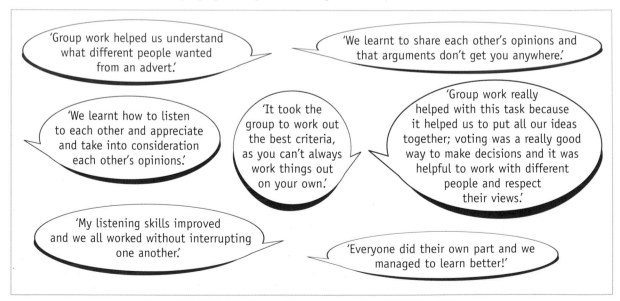

Figure 18 | *Students' self-evaluation comments on the HIV/AIDS activities.*

Presenting the final outcome

Following the initial enquiry-based activities in groups, which focused on southern Africa and then specifically upon Botswana, students began developing ideas. Each student was tasked with producing a storyboard for their Hope HIV advertisement proposal (Figure 16). The advertisements were to be designed for a charity that helps people living with HIV and supports children who have been orphaned by AIDS. The students were briefed that the charity was planning an advertising campaign in time for the first anniversary of Nkosi Johnson's death (this could be adapted by identifying other people or events in the news). The advertisement was to target viewers in western Europe with the aim of raising both money for and awareness of the charity. The students were to use the knowledge gained during the first part of the enquiry as the basis for this piece of work. They were given time to discuss ideas in their groups and were encouraged to question one another to clarify their geographical knowledge and understanding about the issues.

On completion of the proposals students in the class were invited to an editorial meeting for the Advert Editors of Hope HIV. Students were asked to work in role for the lesson and were set into groups of approximately six in order to select the best advertisement. They were effectively marking and assessing their own work. This was carefully structured with students setting ranking criteria for marking each proposal. Students made decisions on how they would assess, i.e. number scales, work scales, rank order, and were given the opportunity to work collaboratively in order to solve a problem and reach a decision (Figure 17). On completion of this activity they were asked to evaluate their collaboration skills and, most importantly, to understand how they could improve upon and transfer these skills into geography lessons in the future.

Management

Where the advertisement proposals were to be completed during lesson time, the work could be extended to three lessons. This series of tasks raised a number of issues relating to the management, including:

- What happens if not all students are prepared for the second lesson? How best should a teacher deal with this, bearing in mind that most students have produced the work?
- During the meeting of Advert Editors, to what extent should the teacher support and direct the process of setting ranking criteria for groups finding it hard 'to get started'?

Other, more general, management issues arose and have already been noted in relation to Example 1 (page 321).

Evaluation

At the end of the second lesson, once the collaborative decision-making exercise had been completed students were asked to evaluate the success of their work. Their comments on the benefits of collaborative learning are shown in Figure 18. Specifically, students focused upon the importance of communication skills, in particular having the opportunity to have their own voice, and developing skills in listening to others. They also identified the importance of being able to put all their ideas together in order to achieve what was perceived by them to be an improved, stronger and more geographically sound outcome. This was certainly observed to be the case for most groups. Another theme that emerged was that of trust. Although tasks were carefully structured, room was left for students to set their own decision-making criteria and to reach a final decision. Students valued the trust placed in them to carry this through. As with the previous case study, collaboration enhanced the learning process by allowing the students to engage actively with the issue of HIV/AIDS through enquiry-based tasks.

References

Print

Christian Aid (2002) *Trade Rules!* London: Christian Aid.

Flinders, K. (ed) (2001) *A New Introduction to Geography for OCR GCSE specification A*. London: Hodder and Stoughton.

Ginnis, P. (2002) *The Teacher's Toolkit*. Carmarthen: Crown House Publishing.

Hopkins, D. and Harris, A. (with Singleton, C. and Watts, R.) (2000) *Creating the Conditions for Teaching and Learning: A handbook of staff development activities*. London: David Fulton Publishers.

Kim-Eng Lee, C. (1996) 'Using co-operative learning with computers in geography classrooms' in Van der Schee *et al.* (eds) Innovation in Geographical Education. Netherlands Geographical Studies 208, Utrecht/Amsterdam.

Lambert, D. and Balderstone, D. (2000) *Learning to Teach Geography in the Secondary School*. London: Routledge Falmer.

Leat, D. (ed) (1998) *Thinking Through Geography*. Cambridge: Chris Kington Publishing.

Norton, A., Hendy, W. and Adams, G. (1998) 'More geographical games and puzzles', *Teaching Geography*, 23, 4, pp. 190-3.

Norton, A. (1999) 'On the cards', *Teaching Geography*, 24, 1, pp. 25-9.

Rogers, J. (2002) 'Trade rules!', *Teaching Geography*, 27, 4, pp. 173-5.

Slavin, E. (1995) *Co-operative Learning*. Needham Height MA: Allyn and Becon.

Taylor, E. (2001) 'Using presentation packages for collaborative work', *Teaching Geography*, 24, 1, pp. 43-5.

Electronic

Global Eye - www.globaleye.org.uk/

GeoVisions - www.geography.org.uk/projects/geovisions.asp

Hope HIV - www.hopehiv.org/

Johnson, T. and Johnson, W. (2002) 'An overview of cooperative learning', *The Cooperative Learning Center at the University of Minnesota Homepage* (www.clcrc.com).

Panitz, T. (2002) *Ted's Co-operative Learning e-book* (www.home.capecod.net /~tpanitz/).

This is Worcestershire - www.thisisworcestershire.co.uk

Implications for practice

(a) **Collaborative learning can be viewed as a process and it can be developed at a variety of scales.**

Collaborative learning can take place in groups of varying sizes (see Figure 3) and within one or a series of lessons a number of different-sized groups may be operating at one time. The size of the group(s) can be adapted to suit the need of individuals within a class, and to suit the learning context. Students recognised that 'working with different people' can be highly productive, leading to successful learning outcomes. Giving them opportunities to initiate and explore their own routes of enquiry through collaboration will enable them to develop independent learning skills.

(b) **Careful planning for each stage of a collaborative activity will ensure that the benefits for students' learning are maximised.**

There should be a clear purpose for students having to work together to produce the desired learning outcomes. It is essential to have strategies for launching activities and for building each stage progressively. Explicit instructions about what students need to do and how this will help them to achieve the desired learning goals are essential. Resources used should be stimulating and enable students to employ specific learning skills to complete the collaborative tasks. It is also important to establish an appropriate learning environment for collaboration, physically (classroom layout), emotionally and psychologically.

(c) **Self-evaluation helps students to reflect on the development of their collaborative skills.**

Student self-evaluation is a vital part of the collaboration process. Students should be encouraged to identify and reflect on the range of transferable skills they use and develop through the collaborative elements of geographical enquiry. They should evaluate the role of these skills in bringing about successful learning outcomes for their group.

दु. नम्बर 1 आमेर
हमारे यहाँ हर चीज़ बाज़ार भाव
मिलती है।

Section three
Geography for all

Photo: ©Bryan Ledgard.

Section three:

Geography for all

> Good teaching is by its nature inclusive, because it is based on a knowledge of students and an understanding of the learning process. Teachers need to be able to unravel the way in which students learn and reassemble this process to provide access and the greatest chance of success for all (from Travers, P. and Higgs, L. (2004) 'Beyond the naming of parts' in Travers, P. and Klein, ??? (eds) *Equal Measures*. Stoke on Trent: Trentham Books, p. 44).

> Understanding how geography disables people, then, is as much about understanding how the environment conveys messages of belonging and exclusion as it is about understanding the organisation and structure of places (from Kitchin, R. (2000) *Disability, Space and Society*, Sheffield: GA, ???).

> When considering how to 'stretch' your more able students, it is worth thinking in terms of challenging their ability and enriching or enhancing their learning. It is essential that the approach you adopt does not encourage these students to be passive receivers of information. Activities should challenge them to analyse, interpret and evaluate information, to search for meaning and derive theories and generalisations (from Lambert, D. and Balderstone, D. (2000) *Learning to Teach Geography in the Secondary School*. London: Routledge Falmer, p. 193).

> Students need to be firmly theoretically grounded, to develop the concepts they need to analyse a complex social process such as racism. The more important theoretical challenge is to uncover deeply rooted essentialist notions of race, and to clarify the ways in which racialisation occurs through social construction. In addition, students need facts, both as a basis for knowledge and to empower them in their antiracist actions. They need to understand the history of racism in our society, and they need to be able to fix racism in terms of the concrete circumstances of life for racialised people (from Kobayashi, A. (1999) '"Race" and racism in the classroom: some thoughts on unexpected moments', *Journal of Geography*, 98, pp. 176-8.)

Chapter 26

Inclusive geography

Lynda Evans and Deborah Smith

Before reading this chapter consider the following questions:

- How can you create an environment in your classroom that will encourage all students to learn?

- How do you know what the individual needs of all your students are? And how do you set suitable learning challenges?

- What strategies can you use to ensure that geography is made accessible to all students?

- What strategies can you use for students with very specific learning needs?

Greater inclusion of students with special educational needs within mainstream schools and in the general curriculum is a strategic aim of both the Special Educational Needs and Disability Act 2001 and the policy to counteract social exclusion from school (DfES, 2003a). The quest for developing a more inclusive curriculum is furthermore reflected in the government's drive away from 'mass production' educational principles to those of 'personalised learning' (DfES, 2004):

> ... *building the organisation of schooling around the needs, interests and aptitudes of individual students; it means shaping teaching around the way different youngsters learn; it means taking care to nurture the unique talents of every student* (Milliband, 2004).

The National Curriculum 2000 sets out three principles that are essential to developing a more inclusive curriculum:

> 1. *Setting suitable learning challenges*
> 2. *Responding to students' diverse learning needs*
> 3. *Overcoming potential barriers to learning and assessment for individuals and groups of students* (DfEE/QCA, 1999, p. 32).

Figure 1 indicates how, when drawn as a Venn diagram, inclusion can be conceptualised as falling in the overlap of these three principles.

So how can geographers put these principles into practice?

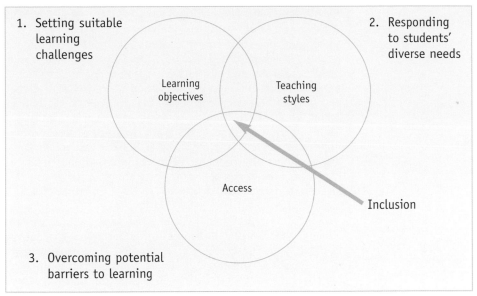

1. Setting suitable learning challenges

2. Responding to students' diverse needs

Learning objectives

Teaching styles

Access

Inclusion

3. Overcoming potential barriers to learning

Figure 1 | *The circles of inclusion. Source: DfES. 2002.*

Creating an appropriate learning environment

If geography is to be truly inclusive, we must create, in our individual classrooms, a learning environment in which students feel comfortable and confident in their ability as geographers. This can be achieved in a variety of ways:

- Get to know your students as quickly as possible as individuals, both as learners and as people. This will help you to differentiate by the support you give them individually
- Use a wide variety of teaching and learning strategies that encourage all students actively to participate, regardless of their needs. Geographers need to ensure that teaching styles and resources are varied so that they appeal to visual, kinaesthetic and verbal/auditory learners
- 'Celebrate' the work of all students through the use of display and a reward system which recognises the achievement of individuals at their own level
- Adopt an 'enquiry' approach to teaching, encouraging students to ask questions and think geographically about the world. For example, use holiday photographs for display and as the basis for geographical discussions, as appropriate
- Think about what you consider the key 'big' concepts in geography and have these on display in your classroom. I (Lynda Evans) have 15, each with an appropriate illustration, placed around my whiteboard. By constantly referring to these I hope I am helping my students to become familiar with geography as a subject
- Think carefully about how you group students in your classes. In a mixed ability situation, try to ensure that students are grouped so that they can support one another (see also Chapter 25). Also, effective deployment of classroom assistants will ensure that groups and individual students can stay focused and will provide them with another support network
- Encourage oracy and listening skills. Not everything needs to be written down! Remember, even assessment opportunities can be developed to ensure that students can demonstrate their learning through talk or practical demonstration.

Identifying individual student's learning needs and setting challenges

It can be quite daunting, when faced with a new group of 26+ students, to get to know them, find out their strengths and weaknesses and decide how this will affect their learning in geography. Remember, a lot of the work will have been done for you; you just need to find out who has the information and what it means. For example, I (one of the authors) teach in a high school, so our intake is year 9, from three main feeder schools and many others who send one or two students for various reasons. One feeder middle school sends information on students' key stage 3 level (e.g. 4a, 5b, 6c) and also what their target was for year 8. While any awarding of levels before the end of key stage 3 is quite arbitrary in many ways, the fact that I can see how each individual compares to his/her target gives me a useful insight into their motivation as well as ability. I will also know, from the very first lesson, which students are working at a much lower (or higher!) level than they should be and so can begin to think of adapting my existing resources accordingly.

Once the new term has begun, I can expect to receive more specific information on students with learning difficulties in the form of individual education plans (IEPs) and I can look more closely at how this will affect their geography. A student who has practical difficulties with writing, for example, will need me to produce some quite sophisticated writing frames or perhaps see if he/she can have access to a laptop or classroom computer. It is important that I know which students are dyslexic as it might not be appropriate to ask them to read. Similarly, if I know that another student has attention deficit hyperactive disorder (ADHD) I will be able to think about appropriate ways of handling his/her behaviour and discuss this with support staff or the special educational needs co-ordinator (SENCO) if necessary. Figure 2 shows extracts from an example IEP.

GAP reading scores can also provide the teacher with greater insight into the individual. Teachers can then adapt resources so that they are pitched at a suitable reading age to enable students to access them with a greater degree of independence. CAT test data provide another valuable insight into an individual's capabilities as, in our experience, several students with low literacy and/or numeracy scores have demonstrated high levels of non-verbal reasoning. In terms of geography, this means that such students may relish thinking-skills activities such as 'living graphs' or 'mysteries' that rely heavily on oracy. This links back to careful consideration of groupings and seating within the classroom, so that all students can collaborate effectively and assist one another in accessing the task set.

Conducting an audit of preferred learning styles is also a useful way of getting to know your students. Asking them to complete an 'I learn best when ...' ranking activity can also allow you to plan to capitalise on their preferred learning styles. Hay McBer's 'Kolbs Learning Style Inventory' provides an example of a multiple intelligence questionnaire that can be used with students to establish their preferred learning styles. Current research (e.g. Goleman, 1996) into emotional intelligence develops this further still by attempting to assess students' concentration span; confidence; ability to control emotions; motivation; leadership qualities. Spending time at the start of the year to find out about students in this way makes them feel at ease and able to succeed and can only help to make my life easier in the long run.

Most students with special educational needs, with appropriate access strategies and teaching styles, will be able to work on the same learning objectives as the rest of the class. However, if students have difficulties in cognition and learning, then the teacher may need to 'track back' objectives and possibly refer to the QCA Geography P scales. These have been designed by QCA for those students who are not yet working at national curriculum level 1 in order to enable them to progress. Figure 3 provides an example of the geography support material available for these students from QCA. For example, if the class are graphing fieldwork data and are constructing flow lines or proportional circles,

Individual Education Plan

Stage: School Action (LD/BD)   **Name:** James*   **Form:**

Nature of student's difficulties

CAT (October 2002)	Absent all tests
NfER group reading test (May 2004)	6.11
Skills percentage (May 2004)	58

James has reading and comprehension difficulties that will cause problems for him throughout the curriculum. He will need individual help to read and interpret worksheets and to record answers.

Reading

James's reading accuracy is weak although letter recognition, blending and phonic skills are quite good.
He is not a fluent reader and misses the ends of words.
He is not willing to read aloud.

Speaking

He speaks clearly with fairly good vocabulary but weak expressive skills. Oral communication is poor and is limited by his vocabulary and he is unwilling to join in classroom discussions. He is not confident orally and does not initiate conversation.

Listening

He has quite poor listening skills and does not always pay attention to instructions. He is able to understand simple verbal instructions but needs them broken down into small steps and repeated regularly in a variety of ways. He has a short attention span and has difficulty retaining information. His reasoning and thinking skills are limited.

Writing

James does not produce enough written work and the content quality is poor. The presentation of his written work is poor although his handwriting is joined up. Spelling is quite poor and punctuation is limited. He is unable to spell many of the words on the checklist. He is not able to write in complete sentences and his use of capital letters is poor. He uses upper and lower case letters indiscriminately.

Classroom conduct

James's classroom conduct is poor. He seldom settles to work without encouragement and seldom stays on task. Tasks are rarely completed and he does not always do as he should be doing. He is easily and often distracted by other students and sometimes he causes distraction. He does not make the best use of his ability.

Social and personal

He is always late to lessons and seldom has the correct equipment. His manner is aggressive and he resents criticism. He has many friends and tends to mix with older, troublesome students. He resents authority. He is awkward about accepting support and ignores help.

Recommendations

- Regular reading practice with a sympathetic adult
- Instructions broken down into manageable steps
- Regular repetition of instructions in a variety of ways
- Regular handwriting practice
- Short, achievable tasks
- Clear guidelines consistently upheld

- Judicious seating
- Help to read and record subject-specific vocabulary
- Regular reminders to stay on task
- Praise for completed work
- Praise for good behaviour

Action:

SEN provision

- In-class support in English, mathematics and French
- Teaching in smaller groups with students of similar ability
- One session a week in learning support with a specialist teacher to develop reading skills and independent learning strategies
- Regular reviews to monitor progress

Staff involved

Student support manager
Deputy SENCO
Specialist learning support teacher
Learning support assistants
All subject staff
External specialists:
None at this stage

Specific programmes: A structured reading programme to improve reading and comprehension skills; a class reader and short plays to develop reading fluency and expression; a structured reasoning skills programme; oral comprehension to develop listening and expressive skills and to increase vocabulary; short tasks to increase attention span; a phonic spelling programme; handwriting and punctuation instruction; a basic numeracy programme.

*Figure 2 | Extracts from an IEP (the full plan, which includes information on specific activities and resources, parental support, pastoral/medical arrangements and monitoring and assessment may be downloaded from the GA's Secondary Handbook webpage). *Pseudonym.*

Objectives	Learning outcomes	The big picture
Whole class – *Be able to:* ■ look at differences between floods in the UK and Bangladesh ■ find out how floods affect people and their lives in those countries **Group 1:** (working between P4 and P6) – *Be able to:* ■ Make a flood to see what happens to a river when it rains heavily and overflows its banks ■ Use at least two key words to describe the effects of flooding, e.g. 'houses wet' **Group 2:** (working between P7 and P8) – *Be able to:* ■ Recognise maps of the UK and Bangladesh ■ Describe some of the effects of flooding in each country ■ Identify some differences between flooding in Bangladesh and the UK **Group 3:** (working between NC levels 1 and 2) – *Be able to:* ■ Understand some effects of flooding on people and places ■ Understand some differences between the effects of flooding in Bangladesh and the UK ■ Use appropriate geographical vocabulary about flooding	**Group 1 – the students** ■ Create a flood in the sand tank ■ Use words like 'dry' and 'wet' to describe the effects of flooding in the sand tank **Group 2 – the students:** ■ Describe the effects of flooding shown in photographs of the UK and Bangladesh ■ Sort the photographs into 'the UK' and 'Bangladesh' and provide reasons when prompted (orally) **Group 3 – the students:** ■ Explain the effects of flooding shown in photographs of the UK and Bangladesh using geographical vocabulary ■ Write simple sentences, using a writing frame, explaining how Bangladesh could reduce the effects of flooding	We have already learned about the causes and effects of flooding in York. We have looked at the impact of flooding on people and the buildings in York. We are now going to think about how flooding in Bangladesh is the same as or different from flooding in York (the UK). In the next lesson we will decide if Bangladesh could use the same ways of stopping the effects of flooding as they did in York and if not, why not.

Starter	Development	Plenary
Focus students on geography and flooding by listening to a piece of music about rainfall and spraying 'rain' water. Learning objectives shared with students and understanding clarified. Key vocabulary (not shown here) revisited. Recap on previous learning about flooding in York. **Questions** Knowledge 1. What does this music remind us of? 2. What have you been doing? 3. Which country have we already looked at? 4. Can you remember which city it was? Comprehension 1. What effects did flooding have on York? 2. What causes flooding? 3. Why does flooding happen if there is too much rain?	Introduce flooding in Bangladesh to the whole class. Use a world map to locate Bangladesh. Students move to their groups. **Group 1: Practical activity (teaching assistant)** Simulate rainfall and flooding in a practical activity using the sand tank. Students observe the effects of flooding. ■ What is this? (point to the 'river channel') – *knowledge* ■ Is the soil/carpet wet or dry? – *comprehension* ■ How did the soil get wet? – *comprehension* ■ What has happened to the animals/houses? – *comprehension* **Group 2: (teaching assistant)** Describe the effects of flooding in the UK and Bangladesh shown in the photographs. Sort the photographs into those of the UK and those showing Bangladesh. ■ Which map is the UK and which is Bangladesh? – *knowledge* ■ What causes flooding? – *comprehension* ■ What could be done to stop the river flooding? – *comprehension* ■ Which country does this photograph show? – *analysis* ■ How do you know? – justify, *synthesis* **Group 3: (class teacher)** Discuss why effects and solutions to flooding differ between more and less developed countries. Complete an explanatory writing frame on the effects of and solutions to flooding in Bangladesh. ■ What effects in Bangladesh are shown in the photographs? – *comprehension* ■ How could Bangladesh reduce flooding if it had more money to spend? – *synthesis* ■ What things are the same in both countries … and what things are different? – *analysis* ■ Where will most damage have been done – the UK or Bangladesh? – *evaluation* ■ In which country will the flooding have killed more people? – *evaluation/synthesis* ■ Which country will need more money to repair the damage? – *evaluation/synthesis*	Play 'fact or fiction'. Give out statements about flooding on cards. Students decide whether it is true or false and put the cards onto a board under correct heading. Ask Group 3 students to explain why they think they are true or false. Review the whole-class objectives. Discuss whether they have been achieved.

Figure 3 | *Extracts from 'Planning lessons using QCA P levels – Sample Lesson F'. Source: DfES, 2003b.*

but some students do not yet understand how to draw a simple bar graph, there would be a clear case for tracking back to an earlier objective for those concerned. Lateral or maintenance progression targets (i.e. where students consolidate their understanding) may be more appropriate than vertical progression (i.e. where students develop increasingly complex knowledge, skills and understanding) for some students. However, the plenary session can be used to draw in the student's learning alongside that of his or her peers.

Examples of strategies to promote inclusion

1. 'Simple experts'

'Simple experts' also forms part of the Key Stage 3 Strategy to develop oracy in Teaching and Learning Foundation strand. It is a useful technique to use if there is a topic to study which naturally breaks into different sections, e.g. land use zones (central business district (CBD), twilight zone, old inner city, inner city redevelopment, private suburbs, out-of-town council estates). Arrange students in mixed ability groups of six and give each student a number between 1 and 6. Set the task, e.g. each group will produce an A3 display of the six different zones in a city. Explain to them that before they can complete this task, they must become 'experts' in one of the six zones. Allocate each student a zone: 1 = CBD, 2 = twilight zone, etc., and then rearrange the class into their 'expert' groups, i.e. all number 1s together to find out about the CBD and so on.

Some advance planning is needed to make appropriate groups and provide a variety of different resources which will enable all students to take part in some research, e.g. textbooks, photographs, simple diagrams, a short video clip, a taped description, depending on the needs of your students. The idea is that in their 'expert groups' students find out and agree on the key points about land use in their allocated zone so that they each take the same amount of information back to their original group at a later stage. Support given during the expert stage will depend on how the groups have been organised – if there are several students with learning difficulties they could be in the same expert group and work with you or, if available, a support assistant. Alternatively they could be spread around the expert groups and be supported by their peers – you will know which method is best suited to your own class. The research stage probably needs a full 50-60 minute lesson and the agreed points will need to be written (or drawn) by each student. This gives them the information they need to complete the A3 display summary for the next lesson when they are back in their original groups. Students should first be encouraged to discuss their findings with the rest of their group and decide how best to complete the task.

2. Maps from memory

The use of this thinking-skills activity is documented in *More Thinking Through Geography* (Nichols with Kinninment, 2001, see also Chapters 16 and 40). Here it is explained as a strategy to get all students involved. One of my year 12 students recently told me this was her favourite activity and, when I used it with a mixed year 11 class for the first time, the results were pleasing, especially when Martin, a dyslexic student who had showed very little interest in anything, absolutely shone and thoroughly enjoyed the activity! Again, students need to be in groups, but this time four is probably more appropriate. You need to find or make one or two large copies of a diagram students need to know – this could be an annotated map, e.g. of the chemical industry on Teeside, or a theoretical diagram, e.g. of the shopping hierarchy or a land use model. The aim of this activity is that each group must produce an exact replica (words, colours, etc.) of your diagram but they have to do it from memory. Number students in the group – explain

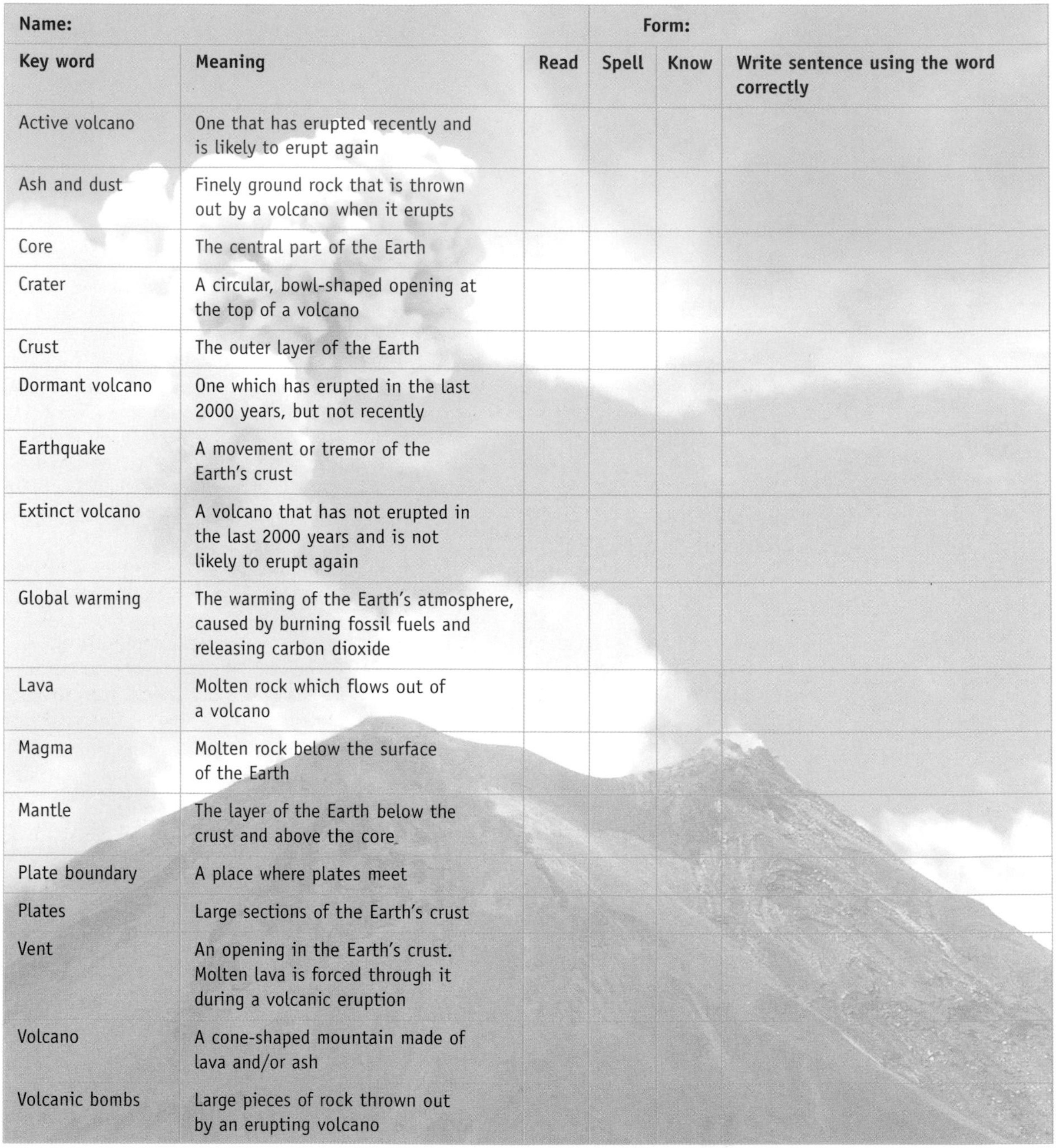

Name:					Form:
Key word	Meaning	Read	Spell	Know	Write sentence using the word correctly
Active volcano	One that has erupted recently and is likely to erupt again				
Ash and dust	Finely ground rock that is thrown out by a volcano when it erupts				
Core	The central part of the Earth				
Crater	A circular, bowl-shaped opening at the top of a volcano				
Crust	The outer layer of the Earth				
Dormant volcano	One which has erupted in the last 2000 years, but not recently				
Earthquake	A movement or tremor of the Earth's crust				
Extinct volcano	A volcano that has not erupted in the last 2000 years and is not likely to erupt again				
Global warming	The warming of the Earth's atmosphere, caused by burning fossil fuels and releasing carbon dioxide				
Lava	Molten rock which flows out of a volcano				
Magma	Molten rock below the surface of the Earth				
Mantle	The layer of the Earth below the crust and above the core				
Plate boundary	A place where plates meet				
Plates	Large sections of the Earth's crust				
Vent	An opening in the Earth's crust. Molten lava is forced through it during a volcanic eruption				
Volcano	A cone-shaped mountain made of lava and/or ash				
Volcanic bombs	Large pieces of rock thrown out by an erupting volcano				

Figure 4 | *An example of a key stage 3 'Read, spell, know' vocabulary sheet. Photo: ©Simon Scoones.*

they will be called out and given 30 seconds to study the diagram before returning to their group to begin to draw their copy. You can support weaker students by suggesting they focus on a particular aspect – colour for example. Continue calling out numbers until most groups have completed the task. What I like to do then is give them a copy of the original to compare with theirs. Afterwards I 'pretend' to judge finished products, but usually say it is impossible to decide, so that the whole class gets a reward.

3. Taboo

'Taboo' is another thinking-skills activity, also in *More Thinking Through Geography* (Nichols with Kinniment, 2001), that is excellent for helping students to learn geographical terms. It is like the card game of the same name where one person has to try and explain something, e.g. precipitation, without using certain 'banned' words, e.g. rain, snow, water, evaporation. You can devise your own set of 'taboo cards' for whole-class or small-group use, or try a more complex strategy in which students are given the key words and have to decide in groups what the 'banned' words might be. They can then test their taboo cards on each other. Returning to this activity as a starter or plenary provides excellent reinforcement and the opportunity for all students to participate.

4. Literacy related strategies

To help students to learn the geographical vocabulary for each topic, you could consider devising 'read, spell, know' sheets (see Figure 4).

Research through the University of the First Age has also shown that students tend to focus on the left-hand side of the room, so displaying the words prominently in this area helps students to 'absorb' the vocabulary. Directed activities related to texts (DART) are specifically designed to aid the comprehension of the written word and support literacy and can be adapted for use in the geography classroom. Cloze procedure, sorting sentences, paragraphs or short texts and matching heads and tails, are all valid ways of ensuring that students can access the curriculum. Writing frames can be developed to allow students to construct simple sentences, and matching labels to parts of a diagram or pictures can help them to consolidate knowledge and demonstrate their understanding.

For students with literacy difficulties, poetry writing about a geographical topic has marked advantages. Teachers can provide students with simple formats and structures on which to model their own attempts. Geographical vocabulary can be reinforced through the medium of poetry, along with allowing students to empathise with others. Poetry with a geographical theme can ignite the imagination of many, particularly at key stage

---

Walker School Geography Department

National Curriculum Key Stage 3

Name _____ Form___ Mark 10 — PAC 2

Climate; Mean Temperature

WOW excellent

The difference between the heat of the day and the cool of the night is known as the **RANGE OF TEMPERATURE**. When we need to describe a day's temperature we have to remember that it changes at different times of the day. The only way to decide which temperature to use is to make an **AVERAGE** or **MEAN**.

To do this, the highest or **MAXIMUM** (e.g. 30°C) and the lowest or **MINIMUM** (e.g. 10°C) of the day are measured using a thermometer; they are added together (30 + 10 = 40) and divided by 2; (40 ÷ 2 = 20°C) An average or `mean temperature is always used in books which means that although the temperature may have been hotter in the sun and colder at night, at was approximately 20°C that day.

For the 10 days on the right work out the AVERAGE or MEAN temperature

Day	Maximum temperature	Minimum temperature		Average temperature
Day 1	28°C	12°C	=	20°C
Day 2	31°C	13°C	=	22°C
Day 3	32°C	16°C	=	24°C
Day 4	29°C	21°C	=	25°C
Day 5	27°C	17°C	=	22°C
Day 6	32°C	14°C	=	23°C
Day 7	29°C	15°C	=	22°C
Day 8	24°C	14°C	=	19°C
Day 9	26°C	12°C	=	19°C
Day 10	27°C	12°C	=	19.5°

Figure 5 | *One student's completed 'Calculating temperature averages' worksheet.*

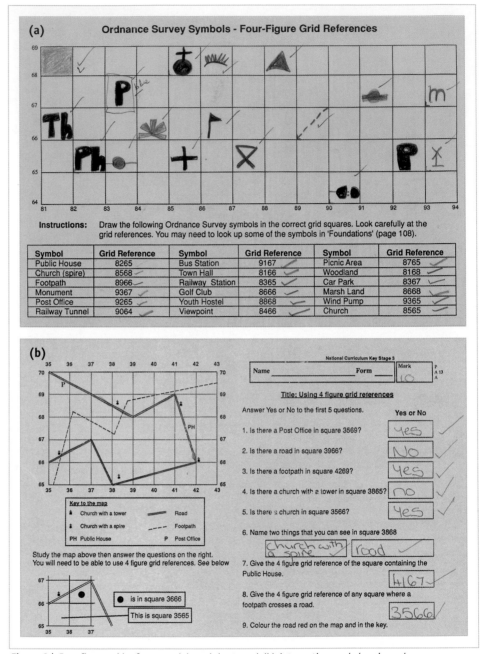

Figure 6 | *Four-figure grid references: (a) worksheet, and (b) interpreting symbols using a key.*

3. Students also enjoy writing up the poems in the shape of the object under study, e.g. in a spiral if it is about a tornado, so that it becomes more visual.

Poetry models to consider include the following:

■ Onomatopoeic poems that can be written to describe the sounds of a place or an event, such as a forest fire

■ Octopoems that describe a topic through an eight-line formula, with the teacher stating what the theme for each line should be. For example, if students have just

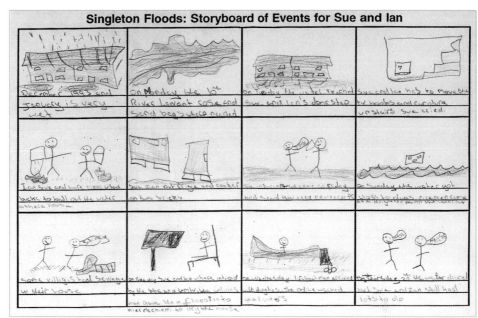

Figure 7 | *Student's storyboard of the Chichester floods. (Student profile: Cat Test V: 1, Q: 2, NV: 2.) After: Newcastle University's Thinking Through Geography Group materials.*

completed a study of Japan, line 1 could be about the climate, line 2 about the industry, etc.

■ Acrostic poems where a key geographical word or topic is chosen and the letters are written vertically and words are selected to describe the topic in question

■ Sense poems that explore human emotions in response to a geographical event. Each line takes a theme, such as line 1: colour, line 2: taste, line 3: smell, line 4: appearance, line 5: sound, and line 6: feelings.

5. Numeracy related strategies

Geography provides a wealth of opportunities to develop students' numeracy. Opportunities should be provided for students to develop their ability to handle data, use calculation strategies, to develop a sense of space and measures, and to reinforce their knowledge of numbers. Apart from the examples shown in Figures 5 and 6, students enjoy decision-making activities (e.g. making animals) where they have to spend a budget and have a choice of what to buy. This combines numeracy with planning and makes it more 'real'. Again, students should be paired carefully so that they have the opportunity to work with a 'buddy' who can help them with calculations.

6. Use of images and photographs

This is a powerful way of ensuring that students can access the geography curriculum and of inspiring curiosity and motivation. Students can make posters and use images and storyboards to demonstrate learning (Figure 7). Students can show learning by labelling photographs to highlight certain features. Video footage of such things as natural hazards, can also allow students with learning difficulties to access the curriculum and can engage immediate interest.

PowerPoint presentations can aid students' understanding if images are used to accompany text. English as an additional language (EAL) students and those with low literacy levels can access the tasks set through the visual images. The example shown in Figure 8 is of an oracy task where groups of year 9 students had to decide what five things they would take with them to the desert and then say why. These all actively

Imagine you are planning a
journey by truck to the desert

A Spare Water

B Spade

C Radio Transmitter

D Strong boots

E Spare parts for the truck

F Extra fuel

G Spare Tyres

H Umbrella

I Extra food

J Sun-screen

Figure 8 | *Excerpt from PowerPoint used in a year 9 topic on deserts. Note: This presentation was designed to complement a worksheet from Nelson Thornes, 1998.*

contributed to the group and class discussion.

The use of images in *PowerPoint* presentations has proved to be a very effective GCSE revision tool (Figure 9), and feedback from those students with special educational needs was extremely positive. Students were shown images such as those below in structured revision lessons leading up to the examination. The *PowerPoint* presentations were also on the school network so students could access them in 'Study Option' time. Those interviewed afterwards said they had remembered the pictures and this had significantly helped them to answer their GCSE examination papers; a few also said they believed that this helped them to secure a pass. When differentiated further, this is an effective way of preparing all students for examinations.

Animated images are also invaluable resources that enable students to visualise geographical processes. A year 13 student with dyspraxia who was struggling with weather and climate, began to understand it much better after being shown an animation of the tri-cellular model and the stages of a depression (see Staffordshire Learning Net geography website for excellent animations).

Students' questioning ability can be developed when presented with an image. This strategy is discussed in depth in *Thinking Through Geography* (Leat, 1988). Using an image of women collecting water in Kenya, students are encouraged to think of three questions (in pairs) to try and get as much information as possible about what the image shows. Emotions can be explored, which can develop students' ability to empathise with others. They can provide a good stimulus to creative writing where students, using a writing frame if appropriate, can write about what they think happened next. Alternatively, role play or drama can be used for students to explore the events leading up to the situation shown in a photograph or those that happened after it was taken.

Students with special educational needs can become highly challenged yet motivated by Mysteries (see Leat, 1988; Leat and Nichols, 1999). The Mystery 'What happened to the Singh family and why?' shown below was used with a mixed ability year 7 class that contained 27 students in total, among whom:
- one had a statement for autism and emotional and behavioural difficulties,
- three were at school action plus level (one student with behavioural difficulties combined with specific learning difficulties, associated with reading and comprehension, one with emotional and behavioural difficulties, and another with learning difficulties), and
- three were at school action level for learning difficulties.

Students were grouped in either pairs or threes in such a way as to allow those with low literacy levels or poor comprehension to be supported by stronger readers. Those with potential behavioural problems were seated with peers with whom they had worked well in the past. Students had studied river basins in advance, and the reasons why rivers flood. As a class we read through the Mystery statements (Figure 10a) to allow clarification of any difficult words. Following an explanation of the task, students began to classify the 'clues' to help solve the mystery. To make the task less daunting, the main question was subdivided into several smaller questions (Figure 10b); reinforcing the concepts of 'cause' and 'effect'. As many students feel that there is only one correct

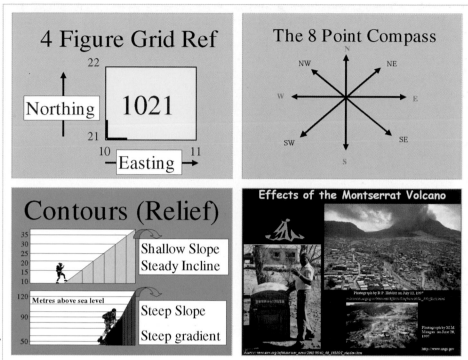

Figure 9 | *Excerpts from a revision PowerPoint used by GCSE students.*

answer, the fact that they would come up with different theories was stressed, and was acceptable as long as they could say why they thought this had happened.

One 50-minute lesson was spent discussing the clues and trying to sort them to answer the questions. A learning support assistant worked with the student with autism and I (Deborah Smith) adopted a facilitator role. The plenary session involved students reporting back what they had solved 'so far', and revealed that many recognised the need to link clues together in order for them to make sense. The discussion was extremely animated and all students were eager to contribute, including the student with autism, who can be withdrawn at times.

The following lesson involved students finishing off the discussion and then writing up what they had learnt. The literacy objectives were to write in full sentences (for those with learning difficulties) and to start to write in coherent paragraphs (for those for whom it was deemed appropriate in the class). Before the written activity, students were shown two excerpts of extended writing by 'fictitious' students and asked to comment on which was better and why. This helped students to understand the concept of a paragraph and how to write coherently. Although a writing frame was provided for some students, most were keen to try without it. They were given a word bank of geographical terminology that they could try to include in the written work, and those who opted not to use the writing frame were provided with a 'sentence starters and connectives' sheet as a literacy aid. In fact, due to the volume of 'student talk' in pairs and as a class, the understanding of what had happened and why had seemingly been 'internalised' by all students, regardless of ability. Even very reluctant writers were keen to try to write up the Mystery.

As this was part of classroom-based research, a sample of students was interviewed about the lesson afterwards. They said that they enjoyed the collaborative nature of the

(a)

Many trees in the Himalayas had been chopped down for fuel	Mrs Singh was at home, preparing dinner	Mr and Mrs Singh live in a village called Pabna; near the place where the River Ganges meets the Brahmaputra River
Mr and Mrs Singh have one son who is called Mohammed	At 3.50pm the boat overturned	There is no high ground near Pabna
Sewage pipes quickly overflowed into the water supply	A neighbour who survived last saw Mrs Singh clinging to a piece of wood	Grandmother lives in Saidpur in north-west Bangladesh
Mohammed and his grandmother wept when they heard the news. Mohammed was unable to reach his village for one month	Bangladesh is 1m above sea level and is very flat	Mr Singh held on for 12 hours until he was rescued
The monsoon rains lasted longer than usual	The rivers started to rise rapidly on 4 January	On 4 January, Mr Singh went fishing in his boat early in the morning
Mohammed went to visit his grandmother on 2 January	A warning was broadcast on the radio at 3pm	The populations of Nepal and Bangladesh are growing at an alarming rate
The Singh's house was built of corrugated iron and wood	Mr and Mrs Singh were saving up to buy a radio	The beds of the River Ganges and the Brahmaputra river have been rising steadily over the years
Twelve of the villagers who survived died within a month	The nearest hospital was six hours' walk away	

(b)

First paragraph: ■ What event happened? ■ Where did it happen? ■ When did it happen?	**Second paragraph:** ■ What caused this event to happen: ■ Human causes? ■ Physical causes?
Third paragraph: ■ What happened to Mohammed Singh? ■ Why do you think this?	**Fourth paragraph:** ■ What happened to Mrs Singh? ■ Why do you think this?
Fifth paragraph: ■ What happened to Mr Singh? ■ Why do you think this?	**Sixth paragraph:** Imagine the same event happened in Great Britain: ■ Do you think the effects would have been different? ■ In what ways would they have been different? ■ Why do you think this?

Figure 10 | Resources for the 'What happened to the Singh family and why?' Mystery: (a) statements, and (b) writing support sheet. Note: You may wish to offer the sixth paragraph as an 'extension task' for higher achieving students only.

'thinking', and when asked to complete a log about what they had learnt, it was clear that the learning was immense and not just confined to 'content'. Those with special educational needs identified other learning outcomes such as 'I learnt to listen to other people's opinions', 'I learnt what classification means', 'I learnt to work with a new person' and 'I learnt to work things out for myself'. The power of student talk also became apparent when, several weeks later, it was clear that they had retained a lot of knowledge about flooding in Bangladesh.

In another year 7 class, there was one student who found it hard to recognise the alphabet so it would be more appropriate for him to be video-taped than assessed in a

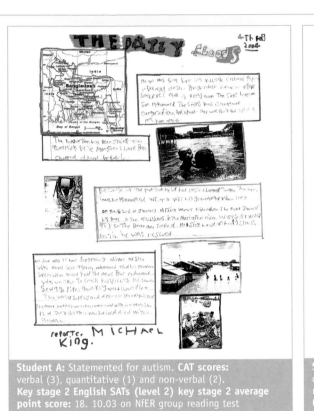

Student A: Statemented for autism. CAT scores: verbal (3), quantitative (1) and non-verbal (2). **Key stage 2 English SATs (level 2) key stage 2 average point score: 18.** 10.03 on NfER group reading test

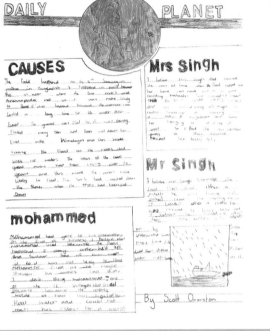

Student B: School action plus for learning and behavioural difficulties. CAT scores: verbal (1), quantitative (1) and non-verbal (1). **Key stage 2 English SATs (level 2). Gap:** 8.09, Neale reading age: 8.09 and Comprehension: 7.07

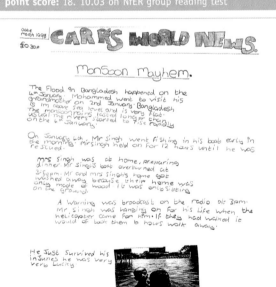

Student C: School action plus for behavioural difficulties and specific learning difficulties. CAT scores: verbal (1), quantitative (Abs) and non-verbal (2). Key stage 2 English SATs (level N). **Key stage 2 average point score: 21.** 7.08 on NfER group reading test

Student D: School action for visual impairment. CAT scores: verbal (1), quantitative (1) and non-verbal (1). Key stage 2 English SATs (3). **Key stage 2 average point score: 21.** 10.06 on NfER group reading test

Figure 11 | *Students' work resulting from the 'Bangladesh flooding' Mystery.*

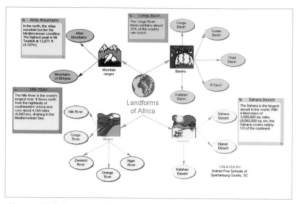

Figure 12 | *Example of using the Inspiration package to construct a Mind Map. Source: Inspiration website.*

written format. Another student, who was dyslexic, was helped by a classroom assistant who acted as a scribe.

Overall, students were clearly very proud of the work they had produced (Figure 11) and many asked to show it to their parents at open evening or came along to receive the work at IEP review meetings.

8. Mind mapping

Mind mapping is widely recognised as a very powerful learning tool for students of all ability levels. I (Lynda Evans) currently have a year 13 student with dyslexia and dyspraxia who finds it very difficult to write sequentially. At the moment he is preparing for a challenging written essay paper. He has used the first half term to make mind maps of each of the topics studied and, as essay practice is introduced in the second half term, will use these mind maps to help him plan a structured answer. Later his mind maps will become his revision tools and he will use the extra time he is allocated in the examination to produce a rough topic mind map and use this to plan his answer. Mind mapping software (see e.g. Figure 12) is available, which may also improve access to the curriculum for students with dyslexia and dyspraxia (*OpenMind* and *Inspiration* software).

9. Venn diagrams and concept maps

Simple Venn diagrams can be made for students with learning difficulties. Teachers can supply a variety of sentence cards and students can place these into the correct part of the diagram. Simple concept map 'link sentences' can also be supplied for a blank concept map (Figure 13a). Students can then read the statements and decide what concepts they are linking. They can then stick or write these along the link line they have chosen. After completing a concept map or Venn diagram, teachers can supply students with a writing frame to write up a summary about what they have learnt (Figure 13b).

10. ICT opportunities

As the use of ICT within our department has increased, it has become clear that it is a great 'leveller', both in terms of the quality and quantity of work produced and in terms of the behaviour of students. Most enjoy the opportunity to learn in a different way, and more and more software and web-based resources are available, many of which can now be purchased with e-learning credits at no cost to the school or department! Our network, like most, has a 'shared area' where staff can put work they have produced for their students and I (Deborah Smith) find this an excellent, unobtrusive way of giving students differentiated tasks.

11. Games

Most students love the challenge of playing a game, especially if it involves teams – boys versus girls, one table versus another, the class versus the teacher, and so on; and quizzes and other games make excellent starters, plenaries and revision tools. Figure 14 shows an 'Odd one out' game about coasts. You just need excellent classroom control, lots of prizes or rewards, loads of imagination, and to be able to make sure that, over the course of a couple of lessons, everyone has had a chance to win!

Along the lines of the University of the First Age (see website) 'brain gym' principles, a good way to organise games for younger students who are seated in groups is to insist that after a question has been asked, everyone lifts up off their chairs to lean forward into the middle of the table to discuss the answer. Not only can you instantly check that

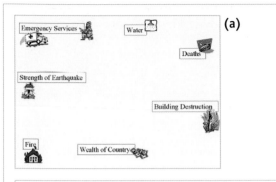

(a)

(b) Concept map about Earthquakes

Use your concept map to do some written work. Try to paragraph your ideas using the following writing frame.

The strength of an earthquake affects _____

This is because when an earthquake is strong

_____ whereas when an earthquake

is weak _____

The wealth of a country is important. If a country is rich, the emergency services would be _____

_____ This would mean that _____

_____ If a country is poor the effect

can be bad because _____

The number of deaths depends upon _____

_____ and

This is because _____

Overall I have learnt that the effects of an earthquake

depend upon _____

Figure 13 | Investigating earthquarks: (a) concept map, and (b) writing frame.

everyone is involved, but students will automatically sit down after discussion, so you can see when to move on to the next question. It also satisfies the needs of kinaesthetic learners and ADHD students to move about, and removes the pressure from individuals with learning difficulties to 'get it right' as they are operating as part of a group.

Visually impaired students

My (Lynda Evans) school includes a unit for visually impaired students, thus all staff are expected to be able to adapt their materials and teaching strategies if a student from the unit is in one of their classes. Ninety per cent of the time a student with a severe impairment will have one-to-one support in geography lessons, but there are occasions, such as during last year, when a visually impaired student's (Michael) assistant was unavailable, when the lesson has to be adapted at short notice. Specific strategies for visually impaired students will depend on each individual, but below are some general ideas that can be used and adapted:

■ Specific products can be purchased, such as globes and maps with raised surfaces.

■ Our visual impairment (VI) unit has the facility to produce Braille copies of worksheets for students to use so they can, with a support assistant, work alongside other students in their class. This is important because being part of the entire lesson, listening to explanations and participating in starters, plenaries and question and answer sessions is vital if students are to understand the geography involved. A word of advice, however: Michael completed 'Brailled' activities much faster than the sighted students and I needed to make sure he had enough to do. Michael also had a Braille machine that he could type work into and staff could print off, enabling me to assess accurately his geography understanding and monitor his progress. This machine also proved extremely useful on occasions when Michael appeared in lessons without support – I could talk to him about the topic, ask him questions, and he could Braille his answers while I helped the other students in the class.

■ For less severely visually impaired students, we enlarge worksheets and the VI unit enlarge and bind copies of the most important textbooks we use. Arrangements can also be made with awarding bodies for examination papers to be enlarged as necessary. Other students also use a special magnifying glass and for those with impairments that are much less severe, sitting close to the board, or having printed information if handwriting is poor, may be all that is required (see also Snowdon, 2003).

■ Specific individual support, when available, means that VI students need not miss out on activities such as fieldwork. Many will have a good spatial awareness and having somebody to describe what they can see geographically can be extremely

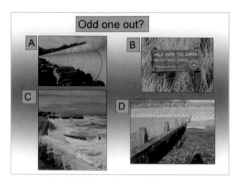

Figure 14 | *'Odd one out' coasts using visual images (for interactive whiteboard use)*
Source: David Mitchell on SLN website.

important in helping them build up an image of the world around them. Braille maps and diagrams can be prepared before and during fieldwork. Verbal input by the teacher prior to the fieldwork can help prepare students, so that they can get as much as possible out of the experience and have sufficient knowledge to question the site. First-hand experience in handling and exploring geographical concepts is invaluable to help to develop students' understanding of processes that they cannot observe. Ideally, choose a site suitable for tactile fieldwork, e.g. a pebble beach, as this also aids understanding.

- For lessons involving map work, ensure support staff know in advance of the lesson where partially sighted students should be looking, so that they can help them to access the task. Access can be further improved through the preparation of a base map, perhaps showing simple contours and features such as rivers, which can then be built up using a series of overlays on acetate that show only features that are relevant to the topic under study. Tactile maps can be developed but teachers must ensure that a map does not exceed the size of a hand-span.

- Understanding of scale and features can be strengthened for partially sighted students through the use of photographs, particularly where a known object is in the photograph as a scale reference.

- In advance of GCSEs, familiarise students with Ordnance Survey map symbols designed for use with blind and partially sighted students, as modifiers of geography examination papers use them.

Hearing-impaired students

Students with hearing impairment will rely heavily on visual clues or lip reading. To support these students in the classroom, teachers must be aware of the following:

- Students with hearing impairments cannot read an overhead projector and watch the teacher's mouth at the same time. Students should be provided with handouts, and given time to read them before the teacher speaks.

- Teachers must not talk while writing on the board or while walking around the room as students need to see the speaker's mouth at all times.

- It a student lip-reads it can be difficult to watch videos with a commentary 'over the top'. In such situations, ask the student to watch the video and then supply them with a written handout of the key points of the commentary afterwards.

- When managing class discussion, ask all students to raise a hand when speaking as this will help hearing-impaired students to locate the sound source.

Many students in mainstream education have some degree of hearing impairment and providing such strategies and sympathetic seating arrangements are put into place, this should not affect their ability as geographers to access the curriculum.

Specific learning difficulties

Dyslexia

Students with dyslexia may:
- have a marked and persistent difficulty in learning to read, write and spell;
- have poor reading comprehension, handwriting and punctuation;
- have difficulties in concentration and organisation and in remembering sequences of words and events;
- mispronounce common words or reverse letters and sounds in words.

It is highly likely that in an 'average' mixed ability class in an 'average' comprehensive school, there will be one or two students with some degree of dyslexia. This does not need to and indeed should not have any impact on their ability as geographers. In fact, candidates with quite severe dyslexia have written some of the best geographical answers. A wide range of teaching and learning aspects need to be addressed in order to help these students reach their full potential and not become disaffected by the amount of written work they are often expected to complete in secondary schools:
- Boardwork/overhead projectors/*PowerPoint* presentations: if different colours are used this helps students to follow a presentation or find their place when copying from the board or overhead projector.
- When some students are told to just write a few important words of a sentence or answer they are much more likely to attempt written work. If help is available, e.g. a classroom assistant or time in study support sessions, more detailed work can be written or typed up if necessary.
- Homework should be given on printed sheets so that students can listen to the instructions, rather than worry about recording it correctly.
- Coursework, worth 25% of the marks in most GCSE Geography specifications, is often an extremely daunting task for dyslexic students (as well as those with other learning difficulties and those who lack motivation or are disaffected, see Chapter 31). I have had considerable success this year with Mark (a fan of 'Maps from memory' (see Chapters 16 and 40) who previously would make little attempt to start work and showed no motivation whatsoever. However, by using writing frames (Figure 15) Mark has found the task much more straightforward to complete: he can see in advance how much he needs to write and each section is clearly structured for him with headings, sentence beginnings and, where appropriate, table layouts already in place.

Dyspraxia

Dyspraxia is associated with problems of perception, language and thought. According to the Dyspraxia Foundation, the most common difficulties experienced by students with dyspraxia are:
- **Gross motor co-ordination skills** – poor balance, posture, hand-eye co-ordination and clumsiness
- **Fine motor co-ordination skills** – lack of manual dexterity, poor manipulative skills, difficulty with dressing
- **Speech and language** – talk continuously, repeat themselves, unclear speech, uncontrolled pitch, volume and rate
- **Eye movements** – poor tracking movements, poor relocating
- **Perception** – poor visual perception, over-sensitive to noise, lack awareness of spatial relationships, poor sense of time, speed, distance and direction
- **Learning, thought and memory** – poor memory, poor organisation skills, accuracy problems, difficulties following instructions, poor concentration, slow to finish a task
- **Emotion and behaviour** – difficulty with non-verbal cues, tendency to take things literally, impulsive.

Introduction	How has Gateshead grown?
What is the broad purpose of the investigation? To study the urban environment of Gateshead. An urban environment is [space left here for response] **Where is Gateshead?** [space would be left here for a map to be drawn]	**Date** **Event** [the student would be expected to complete this section as a table] **Main aim of the investigation** The main aim of this investigation is to answer the question 'How does the urban environment of Gateshead change along a transect from the centre to the Allerdene Estate on the outskirts?' I think I will find out that [space left here for response]

Sequence of investigation
Before we started the investigation we studied
[space left here for response]
I completed a pilot survey of my street
[space left here for response]
On .... We went to Gateshead and
[space left here for response]
Now I need to present and analyse my results in order to answer my main aim.

Data collection writing frame
To find out how the environment changes along a transect from the centre of Gateshead to the outskirts Allerdene we needed to collect a variety of primary and secondary data

Primary data collected [space left here for response]
Why this was needed [space left here for response]

Secondary data collected [space left here for response]
Why this was needed [space left here for response]

Data collected and how	Advantages of data	Disadvantages of data
Observation notes		
HAQI survey		
Photographs		
Handouts from teacher		
Internet research, e.g. into urban models		
House prices		

Analysis of results
Changes in the housing from the centre of Gateshead to the outskirts
What are the differences? [space left here for response]
Why are they like this? [space left here for response]

How does Gateshead compare with the urban land use models I have studied?

	Similarities	Differences
Reasons		
Burgess		
Hoyt		
Multiple nuclei		

Figure 15 | *Writing frame for GCSE coursework prepared for a dyslexic student. Source: Gosforth High School Geography Department.*

Clearly effective classroom strategies need to be adopted to allow these students to access the geography curriculum. Such students will need:

- more time to complete tasks
- clear, easy-to-follow short instructions in a written format
- help in setting out work, for example a page layout frame
- partially completed diagrams.

Many dyspraxic students have performed outstandingly well in geography up to A2-level. Students will require support during fieldwork when, for example, mapping out land use or environmental features. Poor visual perception and spatial awareness often manifests as an inability to link the 'real' to the map, and students should be placed with peers who can provide support. Animations, for example of the formation of a spit, can also improve perception and understanding of processes.

Autistic spectrum disorders

When planning work for autistic students, it is important to minimise the need for independent decision-making. When setting tasks, limit the number of choices that the autistic students are faced with. Many will struggle with the concept of independent problem solving because this involves making choices and decisions (Humphrey, 2003, p. 1).

Lessons that are noisy and involve lots of movement may be distressing for autistic students. Always communicate to students in advance if you are intending to do such a lesson. In a recent noisy 'Maps from memory' lesson, an autistic student was warned in advance of the lesson and asked if he'd like to take part. He declined and opted to work in a quiet area with his support teacher and one other student, doing a similar activity, as an alternative. This is a valid strategy to employ, as the student would have been very anxious if he had remained in the room.

Careful consideration needs to be given to group work and the sharing of equipment. One student chose to sit alone with his support assistant at first and was reluctant to socialise with others. Over time he was gradually introduced to social interaction as other students, who are aware of and sympathetic to his difficulties, have been invited into his space, and he is now quite happy to work in a group of four. As this group has remained stable, he will now offer contributions to small-group discussions and is willing to read to others. Remember it is still possible to assess the progress of students in geography with carefully structured questions.

Concluding comments

Inclusion is much more than just having students with special educational needs physically present in the mainstream classroom. Due to the dynamic nature of the subject and innovative teaching strategies, geography provides many opportunities to adopt successful inclusive practices that will engage students in a positive creative manner and will ensure that learning is taking place and progress is being made. In the long run this can benefit all students in the class.

Acknowledgments

Very special thanks are due to Lynda Wafer for her invaluable advice when working as SENCO at Walker Technology College and in her current role as School Improvement Advisor for Newcastle City LEA. Also many thanks to Anne Leck, SENCO at Walker Technology College.

Related publication from the Geographical Association:
■ Swift, D. (2005) *Meeting SEN in Geography*. David Fulton/GA/Valuing Places.

References

Print

British Dyslexia Association (2000) *Dyslexia-friendly Schools Pack*. Reading: BDA.

Cooper, P. and Ideus, K. (1997) *Attention Deficit/Hyperactive Disorder: A practical guide for teachers*. London: David Fulton Publishers.

DfEE/QCA (1999) *The National Curriculum: Handbook for secondary teachers (KS3&4)*. London: DfEE/QCA.

DfES (2001a) *Inclusive Schooling: Children with special educational needs* (ref: 0774/2001). London: DfES.

DfES (2001b) *Special Education Needs Code of Practice* (ref: DfES 0581/2001). London: DfES.

DfES (2002) *The National Literacy and Numeracy Strategies – Including all children in the literacy hour and daily mathematics lessons* (ref: DfES 11/2002 and 0465/2002). London: DfES.

DfES (2003a) *Social Inclusion: Student support – Every child matters* (Circular 10/99). London: DfES.

DfES (2003b) *SEN: Training material for the foundation subjects*. London: DfES.

DfES (2004) *Every Child Matters: Change for children*. London: DfES.

Goleman, D. (1996) *Emotional Intelligence*. London: Bloomsbury.

Humphrey, G. (2003) 'Managing autistic students in mainstream schools', *Croner Teacher's Briefing*. 113, 13 June.

Leat, D. (ed) (1998) *Thinking Through Geography*. Cambridge: Chris Kington Publishing.

Leat, D. and Nichols, A. (1999) *Theory into Practice: Mysteries make you think*. Sheffield: Geographical Association.

Kolb, D.A. (1999) *Kolbs Learning Style Inventory*. Boston: Hay Resources Direct.

McManus, J. and Whitehead, A (2002) 'Children who have difficulty understanding', November, Newcastle City LEA: SENTASS Speech and Language Teachers.

Medeva Pharma Limited (2000) 'An equal opportunity for children with ADHD – This is for my teacher' (leaflet). Leatherhead: Medeva Pharma Ltd.

Milliband, D. (2004) 'Choice and voice in personalised learning'. Speech at DfES Innovation Unit, 18 May (available online at: www.dfes.gov.uk/speeches).

NCET (1993) *Differentiation: A practical handbook of classroom strategies*. Coventry: NCET.

Newcastle City Council and Northumberland County Council (1999) *Inclusion: Geography and history guide. Access to the curriculum for the student, with visual impairment* (leaflet). Newcastle upon Tyne: SENTASS SensoryTeam, Visual.

Newcastle upon Tyne Hospitals NHS Trust (2002) *Developmental Co-ordination Disorder (DCD) Information Booklet*. Newcastle upon Tyne: Secondary Child Health Department.

Nichols, A. with Kinninment, D. (2001) *More Thinking Through Geography*. Cambridge: Chris Kington Publishing.

QCA (2001) *Planning, Teaching and Assessing the Curriculum for Students with Learning Difficulties: Geography*. London: QCA.

Snowdon, S. (2003) *'Teaching geography to students with a visual impairment', Teaching Geography*, 28, 1, pp. 20-4.

Wafer, L. (2004) 'Inclusion: providing effective learning opportunities for all students', unpublished *PowerPoint* presentation delivered during Newcastle upon Tyne's Springfield Centre as part of Inclusion Day, 1 April.

Electronic

BBC News – www.fire.org.uk/BBC_News/News2002/January/bbc300102e.htm (refugee photograph)

Dyspraxia Foundation – www.dyspraxiafoundation.org.uk

Inspiration –
www.inspiration.com/productinfo/inspiration/using_insp/index.cfm?fuseaction=socialstudies (mind mapping software)

Images of Monserrat were sourced from:
www.unv.org/infobase/unv_news/2003/95/03_08_18MOT_shadow.html,
www.volcanoes.usgs.gov/Hazards/Effects/SoufriereHills_PFeffects.html and www.usgs.gov.

National Curriculum (2003) – www.nc.uk.net/inclusion.html (Inclusion: Providing effective learning opportunities for all students)

Ofsted (2000) – www.ofsted.gov.uk (Evaluating Educational Inclusion: Handbook for inspecting secondary schools)

Staffordshire Learning Net: geography – www.sln.org.uk/geography and animations

Implications for practice

(a) Teachers are expected to be addressing the specific needs of individuals.

How can the requirements of the SEN Code and Ofsted (DfES, 2001b) be achieved in your school? What are the implications of the *Every Child Matters* (DfES, 2004) framework for your department? Can you make use of the QCA Geography P scales or the Staffordshire Expanding Geography Scheme Level descriptors (see SLN website), which show progression between levels 1 and 2? These may help 'pitch' geography at an appropriate level for those with specific learning difficulties and profound and multiple learning difficulties to help them to 'enjoy and achieve' (DfES, 2004). QCA is asking schools to use P levels for target setting, reporting and assessment purposes from September 2005 for those students who operate under level 1.

Do remember that you may have needs as well – you may need guidance from your SENCO team on how to adapt resources for students with specific learning difficulties or EAL. Identify these and be pro-active in seeking help and training as necessary. Could your department co-operate with a local special school or EAL unit to utilise the expertise of colleagues?

(b) Peer pressure is often a barrier to learning.

Think about the ways that you and your department try to address this issue. It is important to create a classroom environment in which achievement at any level is rewarded and low-level bad behaviour is ignored, as far as possible, until students realise they will get attention and praise only for good behaviour. Judicious seating arrangements are another factor to consider.

Producing resources that are effectively differentiated and yet challenging, and delivering lessons that appeal to visual, auditory and kinaesthetic learners will help make geography 'fun' for all. Students very quickly pick up the idea that attention and their own success are closely linked and can become motivated to learn for its own sake.

Think about how you deploy your teaching assistant? Some students feel stigmatised by being 'singled out' for in-class support. If students can work with some degree of independence at times during lessons, can you direct your teaching assistant to facilitate others of varying ability levels?

(c) Getting to know students.

How do you really get to know your students as quickly as possible? What information is made available? Have you considered just getting to know them as young people by finding our their interests as this can be linked into what is being taught? How do you find out about individual learning styles? Devising a simple questionnaire for students to discuss and complete with a teaching assistant may provide you with an invaluable insight into what motivates students. To find out about your students at the beginning of the year takes a little bit of time but the pay off comes throughout the year when you are able to address their individual needs through careful, targeted planning of resources and activities. You will also be in a very good position to identify any additional support your students may need. This knowledge will also enable you to quickly build a rapport with students; always a good idea to do quickly with the potentially difficult ones – a personalised greeting or a query about one of their interests can easily be made at the start of a lesson.

(d) Developing your own confidence in using different strategies.

Don't be afraid of failure! Ask for any help, e.g. from ASTs, classroom assistants, SENCOs, parents and the students themselves. Don't try and reinvent the wheel – there are lots of good resources available and sharing good practice with colleagues, both within the department and within and between LEA subject networks, is essential.

Chapter 27

Geography and students with EAL

David Balderstone, Marielle Dow and Vicky Henn

Before reading this chapter consider the following questions:

■ Which aspects of learning geography (vocabulary, concepts and processes) are most challenging for bilingual students?

■ In what ways do you use the cultural background and first languages of bilingual students in geography?

■ What strategies and resources do you already use successfully to support students' language development (whether or not they are learning English as an additional language)?

If a man does not keep pace with his [sic] companions, perhaps it is because he hears a different drummer. Let him step to the music which he hears, however measured or far away (Henry David Thoreau).

In Britain, while the number of school students for whom English is an additional language (EAL students) is greatest in urban schools, linguistic diversity is now a common feature in many British classrooms. In some urban schools, over 90% of the students may be bilingual, that is 'they have access to or need to use two or more languages at home and at school' (London Borough of Tower Hamlets, 1992), and at different stages of English language development.

This chapter considers some of the challenges that face bilingual students in geography, and provides guidance for ways of working with them to help raise their achievement in the subject. It draws upon the experience of teachers who work with EAL students in geography on a daily basis, as well as on the growing body of evidence about how these students learn.

Identifying and meeting students' needs

An important first step is to recognise and make a distinction between second-language barriers to learning, and learning difficulties which may account for bilingual students struggling to make progress. As was stated in the 1981 Education Act:

A child is not to be taken as having a learning difficulty solely because the language (or form of language) in which he [sic] is, or will be, taught is different from a language (or form of language) which has at any time been spoken in his home.

Stage 1: Beginner Bilingual
Beginner bilingual learners of English will have minimal or no literacy skills in English. They are likely to have only been living in England for a very short period of time. They may well remain completely silent in the classroom or use just a little (supported) English because their speaking and listening skills will be at a very early stage of development. However, they will be competent and fluent speakers of their first language. They may engage in learning activities, in groups, using their mother tongue but will need considerable support to do so in English.

Stage 2: Developing Bilingual – becoming familiar with English
Students at this stage will often have increased their fluency in spoken English and will be able to understand instructions and conversations. They can participate in learning activities where the context is clear. Although they may be able to express themselves orally in English quite successfully, their reading and writing will require considerable support. Their 'social talk' may suggest that they are more competent with oral language, but the development of English for academic purposes can take much longer and needs to be planned for, explicitly taught and learning reinforced in meaningful contexts.

Stage 3: Developing Bilingual – growing in confidence as users of English
Bilingual students whose oral and written English is developing well, enabling them to engage successfully in all learning activities. They will need continuing support to develop their reading and writing skills. Their written English will tend to lack complexity and show evidence of structures and errors associated with the student's level of language acquisition. Errors in writing often result from the different syntaxes of English and their first language. Help is needed particularly with extended writing about academic and abstract concepts.

Stage 4: Fluently Bilingual
These students will be competent and fluent users of English, as well as other languages, in most social contexts and learning activities. They write as native speakers and do not make errors that are influenced by their mother tongue. Being literate in other languages, they will understand how more than one language is structured. They will often be high attainers capable of being very successful learners in geography.

Figure 1 | Stages of English learning in the secondary phase indicating students' prior experience of learning English.

The Standards for Qualified Teacher Status require us to be able to identify the levels of attainment of EAL students, to analyse the language demands of learning activities, and to provide support to help them to meet the cognitive challenges of these activities.

For EAL students to acquire sufficient linguistic competence to enable them to understand concepts and processes in geography, they will need support to extend their speaking and writing repertoires and to practise using new words and phrases in relevant contexts (Figure 1). Giang Vo, a Vietnamese refugee who now teaches in an inner-city school, illustrates how geography can provide a stimulating context and motivation for developing linguistic competency:

> The desire to answer questions and understand the work about glaciers in geography ... pushed me to use and extend my vocabulary. These classes were the perfect incubators for my language development (Giang Vo, 2004, p. 5).

It is wrong of course to assume that students with English as an additional language are a homogenous group. Some of them will have been born in the UK and have had all of their education here. Others may have arrived more recently and will be in the early stages of learning English. In some of the schools we have worked with in London – and the same is true in other cities across the UK – over 30 languages are represented.

As Lynda Evans and Deborah Smith state in Chapter 26, the establishment of a supportive, inclusive learning environment is of crucial importance when trying to help students with particular learning needs to make progress. Some students for whom English is an additional language may also be refugees (Figure 3) and as a result may well have experienced stressful events, both in their country of origin and upon arrival in the

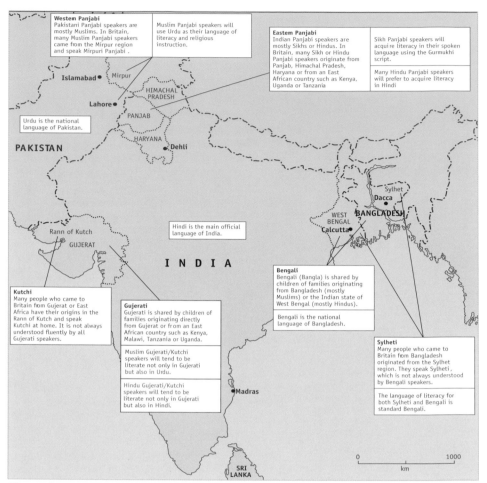

Western Panjabi
Pakistani Panjabi speakers are mostly Muslims. In Britain, many Muslim Panjabi speakers came from the Mirpur region and speak Mirpuri Panjabi .

Muslim Panjabi speakers will use Urdu as their language of literacy and religious instruction.

Eastern Panjabi
Indian Panjabi speakers are mostly Sikhs or Hindus. In Britain, many Sikh or Hindu Panjabi speakers originate from Panjab, Himachal Pradesh, Haryana or from an East African country such as Kenya, Uganda or Tanzania

Sikh Panjabi speakers will acquire literacy in their spoken language using the Gurmukhi script.

Many Hindu Panjabi speakers will prefer to acquire literacy in Hindi

Urdu is the national language of Pakistan.

Hindi is the main official language of India.

Kutchi
Many people who came to Britain from Gujerat or East Africa have their origins in the Rann of Kutch and speak Kutchi at home. It is not always understood fluently by all Gujerati speakers.

Gujerati
Gujerati is shared by children of families originating directly from Gujerat or from an East African country such as Kenya, Malawi, Tanzania or Uganda.

Muslim Gujerati/Kutchi speakers will tend to be literate not only in Gujerati but also in Urdu.

Hindu Gujerati/Kutchi speakers will tend to be literate not only in Gujerati but also in Hindi.

Bengali
Bengali (Bangla) is shared by children of families originating from Bangladesh (mostly Muslims) or the Indian state of West Bengal (mostly Hindus).

Bengali is the national language of Bangladesh.

Sylheti
Many people who came to Britain from Bangladesh originated from the Sylhet region. They speak Sylheti , which is not always understood by Bengali speakers.

The language of literacy for both Sylheti and Bengali is standard Bengali.

Figure 2 | *Origins of the South Asian languages of Britain. Source: London Borough of Tower Hamlets, 1992.*

UK. Although some will have attended school before coming to the UK, their education may have been disrupted.

The loss of close family members, homes and possessions; traumatic experiences such as violence, war, separation from family and hostility encountered in the UK; as well as material deprivation, changes in social status, cultural differences and the challenge of learning a new language, are all examples of stresses faced by refugee students. Their families are often given temporary accommodation and may have to move at short notice. Most refugee students seem to be able to cope with such stresses but others remain psychologically vulnerable. As teachers, we need to be aware of the effect these challenges can have on their learning. It is always important to seek the support of specialists either within your school or, where appropriate, from your local authority Refugee Education team. Emotional support can include autobiographical writing to help students explore their feelings, and homework clubs, which can help them cope with the demands of the curriculum. Talking and listening are very important aspects of support for refugee students and bilingual learners.

The need to acquire a language motivates bilingual learners as they need the language in order to survive and to achieve. However, feelings of anxiety and rejection can hinder second language acquisition. Bilingual learners will learn more quickly and easily in a supportive environment where their language and culture is valued. This helps to build confidence and self-esteem. If they feel valued and accepted by the wider community, and that they can participate in the language of that community, bilingual learners will acquire that language more easily and effectively.

> *When people talk about refugees and immigrants they often focus on the problems they bring. No one concentrates on how we can best use the talents and experience these people bring. Few people think about the need to explain ourselves* (Giang Vo, 2004, p. 8).

What the research tells us

- It takes up to two years to develop basic interpersonal communication skills but five to seven years to acquire the full range of literary skills needed to cope with the literacy demands of GCSE.
- A silent (receptive) period is natural in the learning of a second language.
- Teachers/schools should have information available about the language backgrounds of their bilingual students.
- Bilingualism can be educationally enriching and has a positive effect on intellectual performance.
- Appropriate use of students' first languages (mother tongue) can be of crucial importance in their learning and attainment. Bilingual students' progress can be impeded if their first language is not supported in appropriate ways.
- Students learn roughly the same regardless of their first language as there are development features common to both native and second language acquisition.

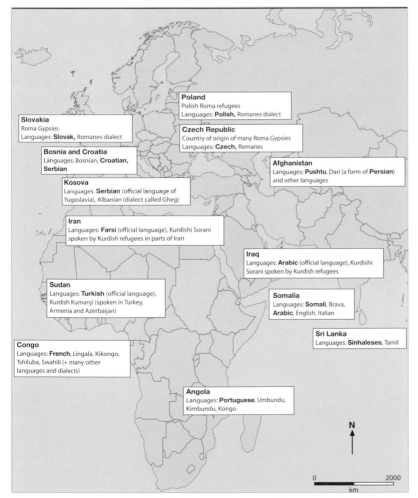

Figure 3 | *The main languages of refugee groups.*

Using first languages

Encouraging the use of their first language helps students' language development, particularly in the early stages of learning English. It is helpful for them to use their first language when tackling tasks which involve critical thinking and problem solving, both of which are challenging in a second language. It helps if concepts can be explained in the first language and then consolidated through English appropriate to the bilingual learner's stage of English development. Trying out ideas in the first language is particularly useful before writing in English or responding to text or other source material. Students who are literate in their first language should be encouraged to use bilingual dictionaries to support their work in geography (though important geographical vocabulary may be missing in some of these).

However, bilingual students do need opportunities to discuss and articulate their ideas and understanding in English in order to improve their fluency and to prepare for written tasks. When preparing for examinations, they will need opportunities to practise expressing their ideas quickly in English. Taking risks in their use of spoken English will help them to develop their confidence. As students' acquisition of English develops, it is important to be sensitive to the way in which their first language can be a resource to support learning, while at the same time providing adequate opportunities for them to articulate their understanding in English.

Oracy and the need for listening time

Talk is vital for language acquisition. Barnes and Duncan (1992) aptly described the role of talk in classrooms as a means of 'working on understanding'. Students develop their understanding of ideas and experiences through speaking and listening. Speech is also important for developing skills for thinking and arguing a case.

In the early stages of learning English, students need time to listen and absorb the language before they are ready to speak it. This 'silent period' can last from weeks to months. It is important not to push students into speaking before they are ready; too many direct questions can lead to anxiety. Often bilingual learners will use the English they have learnt in peer group activities, but teacher-student communication may take longer to develop.

Active and collaborative learning

Language learning needs to take place in appropriate contexts which, for bilingual learners, is with their English-speaking peers in mainstream classes. They need meaningful interaction with competent English speakers to develop the full range of language use, from the informal to the curriculum-specific language used in geography. Active and collaborative learning is of great benefit to second-language learners (Hall, 1995). Working together in small groups, they can share skills and support one another. Such strategies encourage oral work, which helps students to explore ideas and to develop understanding. The need to communicate also provides students with a strong motivation to learn.

Peer groups provide a wide range of models of language use and are therefore a powerful learning resource. It is important to take into account the languages and literacies prevalent in these peer groups. In some inner-city schools, the majority of students share a common language and cultural identity other than English. In this situation, students find it helpful to use their first language in the early stages of learning English and, for them, the teacher becomes the main role model of spoken English. Clear expectations need to be established for the use of English as the target

Thought showers (Brainstorming)

Pairs, a large group or even the whole class contribute words, thoughts or ideas related to a particular subject, question or problem. All contributions are listed and then students use the list to select tasks or classify the ideas etc.

Twos to fours

Students first work on a question or problem in pairs. They then join another pair to explain what they have achieved and compare this work with that of the other pair. This provides valuable opportunities to express understanding and respond to the ideas and views of others in a more supportive context than whole class feedback.

Jigsaw

This is an extremely effective form of collaborative learning. Topics, questions or problems are sub-divided into different areas. Groups are formed and each member is given one of these areas in which to become an 'expert'. Each member leaves the home group and forms an 'expert' group. Each expert group works on its allocated area then members return to their home groups to report back and share in putting what they have discovered together. This process can go on over one or more lessons. Jigsawing gives each student a key role to play in the work of the group and the division of labour provides opportunities for differentiation.

Envoys

If a group needs to obtain some information or check something, one of the group can be sent as an envoy to another group (or other information source such as the library or a computer) and report back. Alternatively, an envoy can be sent to other groups to report, explain or obtain responses and bring them back to the group. The use of envoys helps students find help and support without necessarily having recourse to the teacher.

Rainbow groups

Each member of a group is given a number or a colour. After working together in their group, they form new groups of the same number or colour. This is a way of ensuring students experience working alongside others.

Listening triads

Working in groups of three, students take on the roles of speaker, questioner and recorder. The speaker explains or comments; the questioner seeks clarification and prompts; the recorder takes notes and summarises the conversation at the end. The roles are then changed in subsequent activities encouraging students to practise different roles and skills.

Critical friends

A member of the group uses a simple list of prompts to observe how the group works. The observations are reported back and discussed by the group. Students can devise their own observation prompts. This strategy helps students to reflect on their collaborative skills and develop skills of evaluation.

Figure 4 | *Collaborative grouping strategies. Source: National Oracy Project.*

language and for oral rehearsal in this language.

Where there are just a few students sharing a common language, they may be able to support each other's understanding, exploring ideas in their first language before moving into the use of English. Where there is a range of languages and cultural groups, teachers can encourage students to use their knowledge of how different languages work and compare them in developing their use of English. Where a student is the only learner of English as an additional language in a class, he or she is totally immersed in the English-speaking environment but may feel excluded (Hall, 1995). It may take such 'isolated learners' more time to develop the confidence to try to say anything in English.

Students in the early stages of learning English should be grouped with supportive peers, particularly those with a shared language (see Figure 4, Chapter 25, and Ginnis 2002). However, it is not helpful to group all 'mother tongue' speakers together in groups as they need to work with students who can provide good models of English speaking.

Partnership teaching

The provision of support for geography teachers working with EAL students varies from school to school and between local authorities (LAs). This can include support from an Ethnic Minority Achievement (EMA)-funded specialist EAL teacher who can take on specific teaching responsibilities, helping with planning, resource development, teaching, assessment and evaluation. Where support is provided by an EMA-funded classroom assistant, their role mainly involves supporting and assessing the students' learning needs (Figure 5). In either situation, it is important to plan lessons collaboratively so that each person's role is clearly defined and understood. Sometimes

Siddiqur is 12 years old. He came to England from Sylhet in Bangladesh in July 2003. His family moved here in search of a better education for their children and for improved employment opportunities. They moved to Tower Hamlets in London where they already had family friends. Siddiqur attends Sir John Cass Foundation School in Stepney, East London.

> *When I came to England, I found it very weird with the different culture, but I was very happy when I started school. Although nervous, my first experiences of school were good. I found the school to be nice and it was easy because Mrs Choudhury (Teaching Assistant) helped a lot, explaining how things work, such as how to use the library.*

Before coming to England, Siddiqur had studied English at school in Bangladesh but could only speak and write a limited amount of English. Learning geography in Bangladesh was very different, involving using textbooks all the time, reading text and answering questions. Geography lessons were mainly about Bangladesh, and only a few other countries. Siddiqur remembers learning about weather and climate.

The main focus of Siddiqur's early work at Sir John Cass Foundation School was on literacy, with the aim being to increase his vocabulary and establish the foundations for second language development. This involved using a wide variety of resources, particularly images, to establish key words and match them to words in Bengali. Understanding the meaning of key words helped him to decode text and questions. Writing frames including key words and phrases were used to develop his understanding and use of basic sentence structures. Siddiqur quickly grasped the structures used for comparing places and for writing explanations.

In geography, Siddiqur feels that he is usually able to tackle all of the tasks presented to him. He finds using a bilingual dictionary and exploring ideas in Bengali (his first language) particularly helpful in developing his understanding. Becoming confident about asking for help has been an important factor influencing his progress. Two years on, Siddiqur is writing basic sentences using capital letters and basic punctuation. He can check spellings with a dictionary and knows how to use an atlas.

Siddiqur is beginning to identify and explain processes in geography and he can make comparisons between places. Although at first he found numeracy work difficult, he can now draw graphs and is confident about interpreting them. The most challenging aspect of learning in geography for Siddiqur has been the amount of subject-specific vocabulary he has had to learn, particularly when studying weather and climate. As his use of English has improved, the emphasis has been on developing his ability to write in full sentences and progressively to reduce his use of translated materials.

Figure 5 | *Siddiqur's progress in geography.*

support may come from someone who speaks the students' first language and who can provide useful advice about what students know and can do in that language. In other situations, support from EAL teachers and advisers with planning and resource development may be infrequent. Even so, this support can be particularly helpful when planning for inclusion and can significantly enhance students' learning through geography as well as improving geography teachers' knowledge and understanding of strategies for supporting second language acquisition.

Strategies for supporting EAL students

The rest of this chapter introduces specific strategies that have proved to be successful when working with EAL students in geography. They focus on particular aspects of language development in order to maximise EAL students' inclusion in learning activities in geography. This focus is based on the assumption that EAL students will not achieve their potential in geography without planned intervention in and support for their English language development. The ways in which these strategies are applied will be influenced by factors such as your knowledge of these students' prior experiences of learning (formal schooling) and of learning English, the composition of collaborative and peer groupings, and the availability of classroom support, as discussed earlier.

Speaking and listening

Opportunities for talk are a crucial part of the process of learning a language. EAL students need to practise their use of English orally and exploratory talk helps them to develop understanding through the metacognitive process of 'thinking out loud' (DfES, 2002). During collaborative activities students can practise using different language structures for explaining, questioning, comparing, predicting and presenting an argument. In each case, the teacher should model these language structures in appropriate geographical contexts before students attempt to use them. The purpose and main features of these language structures should also be explained.

For example, when watching a video, EAL students should be given an 'active watching strategy' and provided with a 'listening frame' to help them to pick out the main points and key words used in the video programme. When introducing the task, it is important for the teacher to identify and explain the features or processes covered and how the frame should be used to complete the task. Student groupings should include fluent English speakers to support the EAL students and enable them to discuss their ideas.

It is important to provide adequate listening time for EAL students and when asking questions wait for at least 15 seconds for them to answer. Giving them an opportunity to practise an answer with a partner can also be helpful, with full responses being encouraged rather than one-word answers. Sometimes they can be encouraged to practise answers in their first language before moving into English.

Reading

Students often read a variety of texts to obtain information when learning in geography. As children develop as readers, their knowledge, experience and understanding of texts grows and they need to experience a wide range of texts to achieve critical literacy (Hall, 1995). When working with EAL students, it is helpful to observe the reading strategies they use, so that any support provided can be focused on the nature of the task. When reading for information, students need to be able to focus on the specific information required to complete the task (DfES, 2002). EAL students will often need support to access meaning and to use the information provided in the texts in their learning of geography.

EAL students can experience a variety of challenges when using texts in English, depending on their previous experiences of reading (DfES, 2002). Confusion can arise as a result of cultural differences, for example when reference is made to aspects of life in the UK with which they may be unfamiliar. The use of metaphors, imagery and the passive voice in geography textbooks can also be a source of confusion. As noted in Siddiqur's story (Figure 5), geography has a large amount of subject-specific vocabulary and some words can have different meanings in certain contexts than the students have encountered elsewhere (e.g. depression). At a more general level, confusion can arise

(a)

DARTs are strategies that help to structure reading for students so that they can understand the meaning of text and also help them to understand the ways in which texts are structured for different purposes.

Reconstruction DARTs alter the text in some way (e.g. cutting it up into segments) so that it has to be reconstructed by students.

Analysis and Reconstruction DARTs present the text as a whole and require students to analyse its component parts and then reconstruct these component parts into a simpler form.

Examples of DARTs

Sequencing – copies of text are cut into segments to be organised into an order to focus attention on the structure of the text.

Diagram completion – students present information visually in flow charts, tables and diagrams to focus attention on relationships between information or to reassemble ideas. Alternatively, students can use the diagrams to help them to write or complete a text.

Deletion/filling in gaps – single words that are in some way critical to the meaning of a text are removed. In pairs, students agree on suitable replacements for the missing words.

Prioritising – students read statements which focus attention on important information in a text. They identify true or false or the most important statements. This leads to discussion, justification of decisions and clarification of understanding.

Marking the text – students mark or highlight the text that deals with issues or categories identified by the teacher. Students underline or highlight relevant information before reconstructing this information in another form, e.g. in flow diagrams, tables or concept maps.

Matching photographs or pictures to text – students select photographs to match information or paragraphs in a text.

Matching terms and definitions or matching cause and effect – students use the information in a text to find the meaning of important terms or to identify cause and effect relationships.

Planning frames – students use information in a text to complete tables or comparison grids, e.g. comparing features or places. These frames provide a structure for a task to prepare for discussion or writing.

(b)

Figure 6 | *Directed activities related to text (DARTs): (a) different approaches, and (b) an example of a DART.*

when understanding is developed through more complex sentences in texts.

As with all aspects of language development, it is very important to make the purpose of reading clear and to model the strategies to be used for these different purposes (scanning, skimming, and reading for meaning, etc.). This will help EAL students to engage more effectively with the texts and to relate what they are reading to the geographical objectives for the learning activity. They will also benefit from structured support and active tasks that will help them to access the information they need, for example through 'directed activities related to text' (DARTs) (see also Chapter 11). DARTs can be used as part of guided reading in pairs or small groups, or in interactive whole-class teaching. Figure 6a outlines a variety of DARTs that can help to structure reading for EAL students, and Figure 6b shows an example of a DART.

Writing

Students learning English as an additional language often experience their greatest challenges with their writing. It is possible (easy) to be misled about their progress if their oral use of language appears to be relatively fluent. As with reading and speaking, EAL students need support to develop the skills required to produce extended writing in geography (Figure 7). Opportunities for discussion in pairs and small groups before writing begins can generate ideas and familiarise EAL students with the content and vocabulary of a writing task. Vocabulary can be established, sentences practised and understanding of sentence structures developed.

The National Literacy Strategy (2001) (see also Chapter 11) emphasises the importance of modelling extended writing styles so that students can see how writing is structured at word and sentence levels. EAL students need to see examples of the type of writing they are required to produce. Comparing and analysing different examples helps them to see what constitutes a good piece of writing.

Writing frames with sentence starters and connectives can support EAL students in developing the skills and understanding needed for independent writing (Figure 8). They are particularly useful for students working at Stages 2 and 3 of learning English (i.e. those 'becoming familiar with English' and those 'growing in confidence as users of English'). A writing frame provides them with beginnings of sentences in key paragraphs and also helps them to link their ideas together in a coherent way using connective words. It is important to monitor how EAL students' extended writing develops and progressively to reduce their dependence on 'scaffolding' using these frames, removing them when no longer necessary.

There is also a wide variety of strategies that require students to complete sentences or short paragraphs where the missing words may be provided elsewhere, where the first letter of the missing words is given, or where the words have to be supplied from memory. Substitution tables can be used to help EAL students who are learning how to construct sentences (Figure 9). Sequencing given sentences to form a short, continuous piece of writing can help EAL students to develop their understanding of how to structure paragraphs.

Assessment and monitoring is a crucial element in the process of developing EAL students' writing skills. Diagnostic marking enables geography teachers to identify common errors in writing and in understanding so that misconceptions can be addressed and the next stages in the development of students' writing established. Encouraging EAL students to share their writing with others in their peer group and in other groupings provides opportunities to share approaches to writing as well as thinking critically about their own and others' writing.

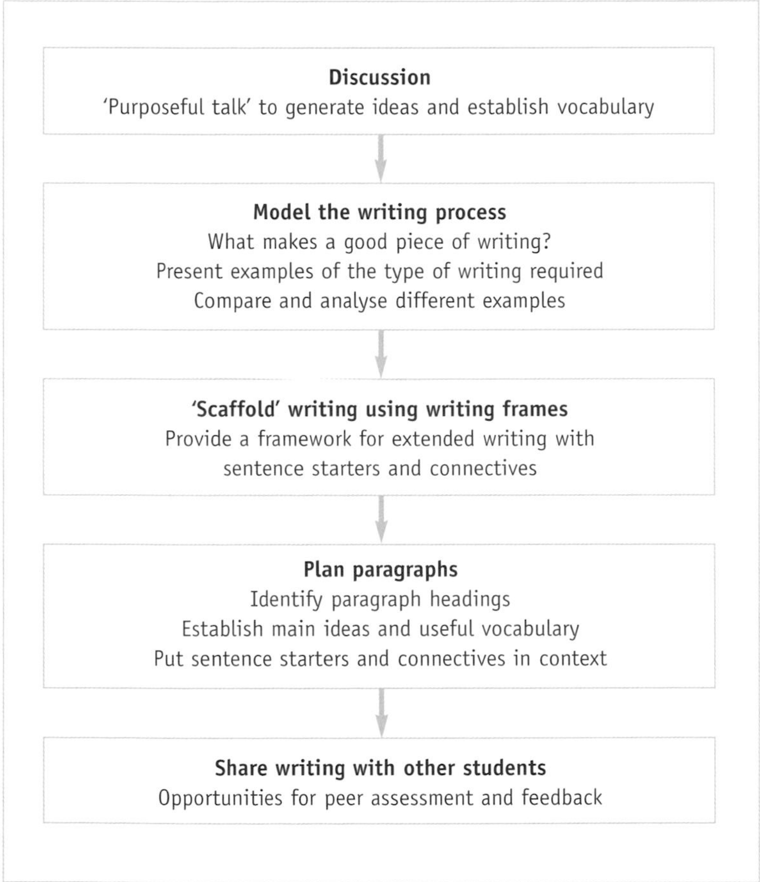

Discussion
'Purposeful talk' to generate ideas and establish vocabulary

↓

Model the writing process
What makes a good piece of writing?
Present examples of the type of writing required
Compare and analyse different examples

↓

'Scaffold' writing using writing frames
Provide a framework for extended writing with sentence starters and connectives

↓

Plan paragraphs
Identify paragraph headings
Establish main ideas and useful vocabulary
Put sentence starters and connectives in context

↓

Share writing with other students
Opportunities for peer assessment and feedback

Figure 7 |
Supporting EAL students' extended writing.

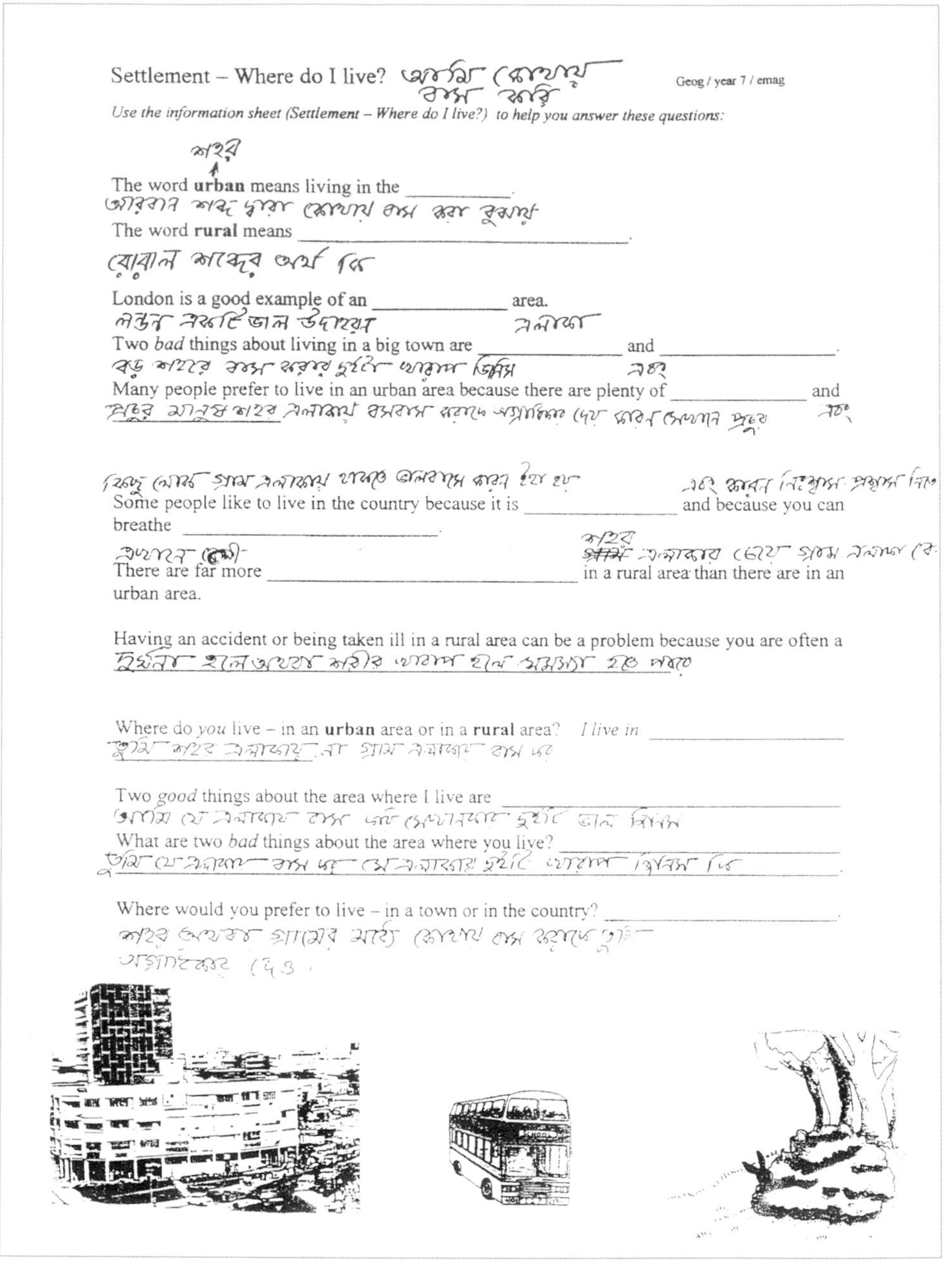

Settlement – Where do I live? [handwritten Bengali text]   Geog / year 7 / emag

Use the information sheet (Settlement – Where do I live?) to help you answer these questions:

[handwritten Bengali text]

The word **urban** means living in the _____.

[handwritten Bengali text]

The word **rural** means _____

[handwritten Bengali text]

London is a good example of an _____ area.

[handwritten Bengali text]

Two *bad* things about living in a big town are _____ and _____.

[handwritten Bengali text]

Many people prefer to live in an urban area because there are plenty of _____ and

[handwritten Bengali text]

[handwritten Bengali text]

Some people like to live in the country because it is _____ and because you can breathe _____.

[handwritten Bengali text]

There are far more _____ in a rural area than there are in an urban area.

[handwritten Bengali text]

Having an accident or being taken ill in a rural area can be a problem because you are often a

[handwritten Bengali text]

Where do *you* live – in an **urban** area or in a **rural** area? *I live in* _____

[handwritten Bengali text]

Two *good* things about the area where I live are _____

[handwritten Bengali text]

What are two *bad* things about the area where you live? _____

[handwritten Bengali text]

Where would you prefer to live – in a town or in the country? _____

[handwritten Bengali text]

Figure 8 | *Example of a writing frame used with EAL students.*

Resource development

A geography curriculum that is rich in its use of visual resources supported by well-structured tasks provides the most effective way of helping EAL students to learn successfully through geography, as well as providing opportunities for them to develop their use of English. There are many simple ways of producing effective resources that can help EAL students to engage with geography. Compiling a picture glossary using photographs and other illustrations can help them to develop their knowledge,

Italy Nigeria India Bangladesh Kenya	is a country in	Asia Africa Europe

Figure 9 | *An example substitution table.*

understanding and use of geographical vocabulary through cutting and sticking photographs, maps and diagrams into work books and labelling them with words, phrases and short sentences. Activities can be linked with the glossary to help students to learn spellings and practise using the alphabet. First languages can also be added for students who are in the early stages of learning English. The next logical step is to relate definitions to specific geographical terms, and the glossary can also be referred to when preparing for more extended writing.

If appropriate EAL support is available, existing resource materials can gradually be adapted for use with EAL students. Writing some of the key words and phrases on resource sheets in the first languages of EAL students can provide those in the early stages of learning English with access to many of the learning activities in geography lessons. 'Word mats' (see Staffordshire Learning Net website) can gradually be produced in first languages for different aspects of geography using bilingual dictionaries, websites and the help of first-language speakers in a school.

Conclusion

Providing access to the geography curriculum for learners with English as an additional language might feel like an overwhelming challenge, particularly if we just focus (reflect) on our own lack of familiarity with the first languages in which they live. The intention of this chapter is not to establish a list of unrealistic expectations for geography teachers working with EAL students, rather to provide suggestions about realistic ways of working that can enhance these students' achievements and learning through geography. Being multilingual is an advantage, so enabling students to draw upon their own cultural background and language can be particularly effective in the early stages of learning English. Using first languages can enhance the conceptualisation of complex ideas. Encouraging skills in speaking and listening is vital for developing understanding. Thinking out loud and talking through ideas are essential parts of the learning process. As an Ofsted survey of educational support for ethnic minority students noted, some of the most effective lessons for these students 'included the use of specifically prepared materials to match the pupils' levels of English and tasks which enabled them to work purposefully with their peers and encouraged them to become increasingly independent of support' (Ofsted, 1994).

Implications for practice

(a) **Establishing a supportive, inclusive environment is a crucial factor influencing the progress and achievement of bilingual students.**

Bilingual students are motivated by the need to learn a language in order to survive and to achieve. They will acquire this language more easily and effectively if they feel valued and accepted by the wider community. This encourages them to take risks in their use of spoken English which is an important part of learning the language. Feelings of anxiety and rejection can hinder second language development. Feeling valued and accepted is particularly important for refugee students who may have experienced stressful events in their country of origin or upon arrival in the UK.

(b) **Bilingual students' first languages should be used in appropriate ways, particularly with students in the early stages of learning English.**

Tasks that require critical thinking and problem-solving are more demanding in a second language. Encourage students to explore more complex ideas in their first language before consolidating them through English appropriate to their stage of English development. It is helpful for those in the early stages of learning English to try out ideas and answers in their first language before writing in English or responding to questions or texts. Adapting existing resource materials by adding some of the key words and phrases in their first language can help bilingual learners to engage more successfully with activities and resources in geography.

(c) **Planning should take account of bilingual students' prior experiences of schooling, learning English and the particular demands of the geography curriculum they will be experiencing.**

Students in the early stages of learning English need time to listen and absorb the language before they are ready to speak. Talk is vital to language acquisition and EAL students need meaningful interaction with competent English speakers to develop their use of the language. Active and collaborative learning is of great benefit to second language learners. Whenever specialist support is available, EAL teachers, assistants and first-language speakers should be involved in the planning and evaluation of resources and activities for EAL students in geography.

(d) **EAL students will not achieve their potential in geography without planned intervention in and support for their English language development.**

Whether speaking, reading or writing in geography, it is helpful for teachers to explain the purpose and model the language structures and strategies to be used by EAL students. Bilingual learners benefit from having opportunities to practise answers with a partner and they need structured support (listening and watching frames, DARTs and writing frames) when preparing for oral work, reading and extended writing. Diagnostic assessment can help us to identify common errors in bilingual students' use of English and to monitor their understanding of geography.

References and further reading

Barnes, T. and Duncan, J. (1992) *Writing Worlds*. London: Routledge.

Cummins, J. (1984) *Bilingualism and Special Education*. Avon: Multilingual Matters.

DfES (2002) *Access and Engagement in Geography: Teaching pupils for whom English is an additional language*. London: DfES.

Giang Vo (2004) 'Speaking from experience' in Travers, P. and Klein, G. (eds) *Equal Measures: Ethnic minority and bilingual pupils in secondary schools*. Stoke-on-Trent: Trentham Books, pp. 5-8.

Ginnis, P. (2002) *The Teacher's Toolkit*. Carmarthen: Crown House Publishing.

Hall, D. (1995) *Assessing the Needs of Bilingual Pupils*. London: David Fulton.

National Oracy Project (1993) *Learning Together Through Talk at KS3 and 4*. London: Hodder and Stoughton.

Ofsted (1994) *Educational Support for Minority Ethnic Communities*. London: HMSO.

Ofsted (2001) *Managing Support for the Attainment of Pupils from Minority Ethnic Groups*. London: HMSO.

London Borough of Tower Hamlets (1992) *Policy statement*.

Travers, P. and Klein, G. (eds) (2004) *Equal Measures: Ethnic minority and bilingual pupils in secondary schools*. Stoke-on-Trent: Trentham Books.

Electronic

Enchanted Learning - www.enchantedlearning.com/geography

Linguanet - www.linguanet.org.uk

NGFL Inclusion pages - www.inclusion.ngfl.gov.uk

Refugee Council - www.refugeecouncil.org.uk

Staffordshire Learning Net – www.sln.org.uk/geography

Your Dictionary - www.yourdictionary.com

Chapter 28

Gifted young geographers

Neil Enright, Anne Flook and Catherine Habgood

> **Before reading this chapter consider the following questions:**
>
> ■ Is it possible to identify students as being gifted in geography?
>
> ■ How do you know when you have a gifted student in your classroom?
>
> ■ In what ways should you challenge gifted students?
>
> ■ Above all, how do you plan lessons that keep the gifted challenged while ensuring that all students in your classes make maximum progress and enjoy learning?

Good teachers want to provide a suitable level of challenge for every student in their classroom. To ensure full inclusion it is necessary to extend and motivate the brightest students. Being a high achiever presents a form of special educational need (SEN), yet is at the opposite end of the spectrum from where SEN work is traditionally applied. Educational policy has, for a number of years, concentrated on preventing students from sinking, rather than providing assistance to the already able swimmers. However, attention has been given to the gifted and talented more recently, particularly as a result of the work of Excellence in Cities (EiC). Nevertheless, it remains a thorny issue in many staff rooms, being readily dismissed as élitist.

Geography teachers are blessed with a subject that in terms of content and presentation is accessible at all levels; it has more potential than most to excite and stretch. As a result, we geography teachers are challenged to be open minded practitioners, capable of devising learning experiences for the highest achievers, which raise their thinking to new levels rather than lowering it to the class average. This chapter examines practical ways of focusing on their needs and providing an environment in which they can reach their full potential.

What does 'gifted and talented' mean?

This question has been the subject of intense and protracted debate. Terms such as 'exceptional', 'very able', 'most able' and 'gifted' are variously defined and disputed, but remain awkward. All of our students have their own gifts and talents. The meanings have moved on from being single-dimensional (related to having a high intelligence quotient) to recognising multiple abilities and intelligences. EiC have settled upon the following:

- 'Gifted' students are those who have high levels of ability or potential in one or more of the national curriculum subject areas (other than art, design, music and PE, but usually including RE).
- 'Talented' students are those who have high levels of ability or potential in art and design, music, PE, performing arts.

EiC works on the basis that the top 5-10% of students in any school should be targeted as gifted and talented, regardless of that school's ability profile. Many educational authorities and schools outside EiC have adopted the same criteria, while others prefer to use benchmarks. EiC's inclusive approach ensures that no school misses out, but inevitably the result has been that the programme has captured varying abilities. Within departmental schemes, it is better to choose an objective basis for inclusion.

Identification in geography

Before we can deliver an appropriately challenging curriculum in geography, we must first identify the gifted. The curriculum cannot be divorced from identification since it facilitates detection in addition to delivery, and detection takes place through the medium of subjects. Geography has a particular role to play here as there are more opportunities than in most other subjects to provide for all of Howard Gardner's (1993) intelligences: linguistic (e.g. e-mailing an explanation to someone), logical-mathematical (e.g. constructing a diagram), visual-spatial (e.g. a concept map), bodily-kinaesthetic (e.g. role play), musical (e.g. composing a jingle or rap), interpersonal (a discussion) and intra-personal (e.g. planning). Whatever their preferred learning style, gifted students are usually switched on to geography (see also Ferretti, 2005).

As in most subject areas, checklists for helping with identification are problematic, although they can be a starting point. So, while acknowledging that gifted students are not a group of like individuals, it is possible to begin to characterise high levels of ability or potential in geography as being associated with those aspects shown in Figure 1.

Most geography teachers will rightly look to objective data to support teacher nominations and aid identification. This has become easier as schools have become more data-rich with CAT scores (cognitive ability tests), MidYIS (middle years information system) and of course SATs (standard assessment tasks). Which information sources are chosen, or how they are weighted, is a matter for individual policy but research indicates that whatever teachers prioritise as the chief behavioural criteria, it is 'always in combination with good school grades' (Freeman and Josepsson, 2002). Attainment data must be used intelligently and put carefully into context if it is not to be misleading. Registers or lists of gifted students must be regularly reviewed and we must be prepared to move additional students on (late developers) and other students off in cases where there has been misidentification, but not when those gifted students are underachieving.

What should be clear is that a gifted student is not necessarily a perfect student who works hard and gets the top grades. Recognition of this is vital to avoid making mistakes in identification. Some of the gifted are lively, curious, well motivated and eager to please. Others withdraw or display 'acting out behaviour': 'the class clown is frequently the ablest of all' (Pimeoff, 1995). These students may have what Leyden has termed the 'handicap of exceptional ability' (1985, p. 68). Being gifted in geography may not be a student's only educational need and unfortunately this, along with other emotional and physical obstacles, can prevent identification.

Photo: ©Simon Scoones.

Possible aspects	Possible student responses
Curiosity	Students will seek information and understanding beyond that which is immediately presented to them. They raise questions and are motivated to find the answers.
Scope of general knowledge	Students will want to discuss topical issues relating them to the work being covered in class. They will have a wide range of interests and an excellent memory for detail.
Conceptual understanding and application	Students quickly and easily grasp new ideas and theories and are able to apply them to real situations. It will sometimes feel as though full explanations from the teacher are unnecessary.
Perceptiveness	Students appreciate the complexity of the world around them. They can identify and justify other people's viewpoints. They have acute observation skills.
Well developed thinking skills	Students demonstrate originality and divergent thinking when they approach problems. They can see many different routes for getting to the same end point. They are capable of metacognition (thinking about thinking) and can help to raise the roof off the classroom.
High levels of geographical literacy	They are accomplished at matching style of communication (whether oral or written) to the task and audience. They are also likely to have an advanced vocabulary. They will be excited by and sensitive to the fact that geography has its own language for learning and will enjoy technical terms and precise definitions.
High levels of geographical numeracy	Students very quickly pick up on sequences and patterns. They are confident in applying mathematical principles such as area and shape. They enjoy looking for spatial patterns in map work tasks and will be excited by learning situations involving statistical testing or geographical information systems.
Attitude towards less formal learning experiences	Some students will come into their own in situations where they are asked to take part in a role play or simulation. They will display innate confidence and adopt a leadership role. They will tend to be very enthusiastic about fieldwork and relish the challenge of setting and testing hypotheses.
Interaction with peers	Gifted students have no consistent manner of interaction with their peers. Some may display a preference to work alone or with older students. Others will relate very well with their peers and be keen to help those who are not as quick to grasp new ideas. Some will look to hide their ability from the rest of their classmates.
Teacher perceptions	This list does not profess to be exhaustive but students may be considered to be one or more of the following: aloof, arrogant, eccentric, impatient, insensitive, intolerant, intuitive, lazy, non-conformist, obstinate, opinionated, perfectionist, persistent, precocious, preoccupied, rude, sensitive, underachieving, withdrawn.

Figure 1 | *The characteristics of high levels of ability in students.*

Furthermore, the negative impact on some students of being labelled in categories such as 'gifted' or 'exceptionally able' is not to be underestimated. Generally they do not like it, finding 'the label to be a detriment both socially and emotionally' (Parke, 1989, p. 6). The labelling can be difficult for teachers too. Such students can be testing as they can be as frustrated by their situation as any other child with a special educational need. We must be careful not to behave negatively towards them; humour can be mistaken as a 'put down', and it is all too easy to find ourselves challenging them, even implicitly, to 'prove to me that you are as gifted as you think you are' (Buescher, 1989).

Provision

Some argue that the 'cream always rises to the top' (Rader, 1976, p. 36). According to them, special support for the gifted involves providing help where none is needed and siphoning off resources which could be put to better use with more deserving groups whom nature has placed at a disadvantage (McLeod and Cropley, 1989). This is emphatically not the case; departments should grasp opportunities to produce differentiated materials for those with a real aptitude for geography. As with any innovation, there is the added benefit that teachers will be reinvigorated by the opportunity to look at and adapt their practice.

The learning journey for the gifted student is just as difficult as for any other; they make mistakes and need close attention if they are to stay on course. Gifted learners are discerning and we need to work hard to keep them engaged: 'Able students need clear structures and routines, but they also need to be surprised' (Coultas, 2003). Three modes of provision exist: acceleration (tackling study material earlier), enrichment (increasing breadth of study) and extension (increasing depth of study).

There are different forms of acceleration. The most obvious and least bureaucratically disruptive is to move gifted students up a year, but this generates the problem of missing work and alienates students from their own age group. In some schools there is a tradition of some subject areas, mathematics for example, moving students through the curriculum (particularly for examination classes) in less time than might be expected for most. This is one option for geography departments, although it only really works if it is continuous, with early university entrance, or if undergraduate-level work can be brought into schools in a meaningful way. Without this, you run the risk of setting up gifted students for a period in school when they stand still and become bored. At the moment co-ordination and agreement between schools and higher education institutions is not coherent enough to enable curriculum exchange, although EiC is an attempt to do so.

Enrichment and extension are about doing more that gives added value above and beyond the standard curriculum. At face value they can seem relatively straightforward to manage. They involve self-study, or small group work with comparable peers, the use of information and communciations technology (ICT), libraries and resource rooms; teachers and students can also draw on other resources in the community such as local museums, environmental education centres and groups such as Local Agenda 21. With enrichment and extension also come great difficulties. First, they demand a great deal from teachers as they often require specialist assistance. Sometimes, with imagination and negotiation, others can provide this support, including undergraduate 'Ambassadors' which some universities now organise to be made available to schools. Second, additional work, after the end of the school day, at lunchtime or during holidays, while ensuring valid enrichment and extension, can seem like a punishment. It is also easy for extra tasks not to enrich or extend at all. For example, students may be encouraged to do more reading on the same level or look at something else, which everyone else will do shortly.

Again, as geography teachers we are fortunate in that our subject provides a suitable medium for a wide range of challenging experiences beyond the classroom. Some of these are listed below.

- **Summer schools and masterclasses** – EiC funding may well be available for this in your school or local education authority. However, there is an inclusion issue to be resolved in that some students may not be able to participate if they take place in the evenings, at weekends or during the holidays.
- **Fieldtrips and visits** – A whole host of opportunities exists to suit most time and financial budgets.
- **Lecture programmes** – Invite outside speakers to school. Share expertise with geography departments in other schools. Enable your gifted geographers to meet students of similar ability levels from other schools in your area.
- **Geographical Association's Worldwise** – Enter a team for this, and ensure that your students enter other national competitions such as the Royal Geographical Society's 'Young geographer of the year'.

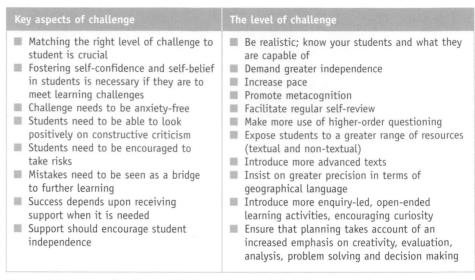

Key aspects of challenge	The level of challenge
■ Matching the right level of challenge to student is crucial ■ Fostering self-confidence and self-belief in students is necessary if they are to meet learning challenges ■ Challenge needs to be anxiety-free ■ Students need to be able to look positively on constructive criticism ■ Students need to be encouraged to take risks ■ Mistakes need to be seen as a bridge to further learning ■ Success depends upon receiving support when it is needed ■ Support should encourage student independence	■ Be realistic; know your students and what they are capable of ■ Demand greater independence ■ Increase pace ■ Promote metacognition ■ Facilitate regular self-review ■ Make more use of higher-order questioning ■ Expose students to a greater range of resources (textual and non-textual) ■ Introduce more advanced texts ■ Insist on greater precision in terms of geographical language ■ Introduce more enquiry-led, open-ended learning activities, encouraging curiosity ■ Ensure that planning takes account of an increased emphasis on creativity, evaluation, analysis, problem solving and decision making

Figure 2 | *Key aspects of challenge and raising the level of challenge in the geography classroom.*

The list could go further. Nonetheless, it has to be accepted that enrichment and extension beyond the normal curriculum is insufficient on its own. It is not acceptable for students to be bored in their normal timetabled lessons.

Challenge in the classroom

It will come as no surprise that while extra-curricular provision is vital, getting the classroom teaching right is key to the best provision. At the heart of this is the concept of challenge (see Figure 2).

The organisation of classroom provision is approached in different ways. Some schools and departments favour setting so that high achievers learn together; others aim for proximal seating for identified gifted students within a mixed ability class, so that they can be set different or additional tasks. There are many approaches and none is perfect. Some are impossible in schools but it is worth experimenting before deciding what works best in your context.

Benefits for all

Teaching and learning strategies that you incorporate into your planning for gifted students will certainly benefit all students. For example, being paired or placed in a small group with one of the highest achievers in the class can help a lower achieving student or one with English as an additional language to go further with a task than they would have done otherwise. Providing it is managed sensitively these students get to share in the overall success of the pair or group upon the completion of the activity, which boosts their confidence and self-esteem. Be assured that by incorporating provision in your planning for the gifted you are not doing a disservice to the rest of the class. The best approach is to be creative; using your imagination and being original makes lessons fun and adds most value to student progression. Games and simulations, for example, cross the ability boundaries because the decision making can take place at different levels with different groups of students, thereby providing appropriate levels of challenge for all.

As has already been stated, the definition of gifted and talented geographers should no longer refer to a simple single dimension but instead incorporate multiple abilities and intelligences. In this regard, teaching and learning strategies will be exemplified (see below) by identifying activities that develop speaking and listening or reading and writing skills in geography. The Key Stage 3 Strategy (now known as the Secondary National Strategy) has encouraged the effective use of starters and plenaries in lessons. However, the four-part lesson structure (starter, introduction, development and plenary) can be effectively implemented at all key stages as a method of organising and focusing student learning. The exemplars that follow provide a few ideas on how challenge can be introduced into teaching and learning activities in the geography classroom at key stage 3 and above. The overall message is that we should strive for demanding objectives for all, rather than simply bolting on extension activities for higher achievers.

Speaking and listening activities

Starters and plenaries

Starter and plenary activities provide a purposeful beginning and end to lessons. The aim of a starter activity is to engage and motivate students from the outset, creating an expectation that thinking and participation will be required throughout the lesson. The plenary activity is designed to summarise the learning that has taken place, allow students to identify the progress they have made in terms of geographical knowledge, understanding and skills, and provide an opportunity for informal teacher assessment. With regard to challenging gifted and talented students, they therefore allow teachers to identify students who may excel within that lesson. An effective starter challenges by encouraging students to build independently on their prior knowledge, and a plenary can extend learning of the highest achievers by requiring them to synthesise and critically evaluate their learning.

1. The tableau

A tableau is a silent 'freeze-frame' image portrayed by students of a pre-determined situation linked to a specific geographical issue (see also Chapter 24). The students involved in the tableau take on different roles within the situation and express non-verbally their values and attitudes towards the given issue or event. On observing the tableau the class then deconstruct the 'freeze-frame' through questioning the body language and expression of individuals and predicting their thoughts and feelings regarding the issue. For example, when studying the sensitive and contentious issue of migration and refugees, students could be given the following situation:

'Ahmed joined your class a year ago and has settled in to school life very well. His family has just received a letter from the Government stating that their claim for asylum has been rejected. They must return to Iraq. Ahmed has just told you this news. Develop a tableau to express the reactions of the following people: Ahmed, his closest friend, a member of the form who has been bullying Ahmed, and the teacher.'

The tableau enables challenge of the geographically gifted and talented by encouraging students to empathise with the values, attitudes and emotions of others and learn to express these understandings in non-written or verbal ways. The deconstruction activity requires students to justify their understanding of the views of others by questioning and explaining what might be informing these attitudes.

Brazil	UK	China	Pakistan
Birth rate 26/1000 Death rate 8/1000 Infant mortality 32/1000 Life expectancy 66 People per doctor 1080 GNP per capita 2680 Adult literacy 86% Primary sector jobs 23%	Birth rate 14/1000 Death rate 12/1000 Infant mortality 5/1000 Life expectancy 71 People per doctor 620 GNP per capita 1670 Adult literacy 99% Primary sector jobs 1%	Birth rate 21/1000 Death rate 7/1000 Infant mortality 25/1000 Life expectancy 71 People per doctor 1000 GNP per capita 370 Adult literacy 86% Primary sector jobs 50%	Birth rate 42/1000 Death rate 11/1000 Infant mortality 76/1000 Life expectancy 59 People per doctor 2910 GNP per capita 380 Adult literacy 45% Primary sector jobs 44%
USA	**Paraguay**	**Tanzania**	**Australia**
Birth rate 14/1000 Death rate 9/1000 Infant mortality 7/1000 Life expectancy 76 People per doctor 470 GNP per capita 21,700 Adult literacy 97% Primary sector jobs 2%	Birth rate 33/1000 Death rate 6/1000 Infant mortality 27/1000 Life expectancy 67 People per doctor 1460 GNP per capita 1100 Adult literacy 95% Primary sector jobs 2%	Birth rate 50/1000 Death rate 13/1000 Infant mortality 104/1000 Life expectancy 55 People per doctor 26,200 GNP per capita 120 Adult literacy 78% Primary sector jobs 48%	Birth rate 14/1000 Death rate 8/1000 Infant mortality 5/1000 Life expectancy 77 People per doctor 440 GNP per capita 17,080 Adult literacy 100% Primary sector jobs 3%

Figure 3 | *Examples of Top Trumps development profile cards.*

2. The video commentary

Following the viewing of a short video clip revealing the formation of a geographical landform, e.g. a waterfall, students develop a verbal commentary to explain what is happening in the clip. The activity challenges students as it requires a sound understanding of the geographical processes, an ability to extract the salient points and a need to express these in a verbally clear and concise manner using geographical vocabulary. The skill of précis is an essential development in the gifted and talented geographer. Students could then be encouraged to self- and peer-assess the commentary in terms of understanding and presentation and develop constructive targets for improvement.

3. 'Top Trumps'

A set of top trump cards can be produced for various countries revealing their development profile statistically through different indicators, such as gross national product, birth rate, population per doctor, etc. Pairs of students are given a set of cards and divide them equally (e.g. Figure 3). One student starts play by calling out an indicator of development from the first card. For instance, the birth rate on Claire's first card is 11/1000 and she believes this indicates a more developed country than Sadia's. Claire calls it out; if it is higher Claire wins the card. If it is not, Sadia has 'Top Trump' and wins the card. Sadia then takes control of the game, moving her won Trump cards to the bottom of her pile. The winner is the person with the most cards at the end of the time limit.

This activity promotes high-level geographical learning as it requires a sound understanding of how different indicators reveal levels of development. In debriefing the activity, teacher questioning should encourage student metacognition – they must explain and justify the strategies and decisions made during the game. The following questions can be used:
- Which countries were winning countries? Why?
- Which countries were difficult to play with? Why?
- How did you approach the game?

4. Peer teaching

As we all know, teaching requires full knowledge and understanding of the subject content! Therefore, by encouraging students to investigate an issue and develop a mini-lesson for their peers, including verbal exposition, key notes and resources, students must synthesise information and present it to a target audience in a coherent and logical manner. This has been successfully developed with an A2-level physical geography class studying the formation of landforms of coastal deposition. In examinations at this level, students are required to be concise and focused in explaining landform development, referring to the essential conditions, features and processes in their answers in order to achieve the highest level of response. The peer teaching activity provides an opportunity for this to happen. In debriefing individual presentations, class members should be encouraged to develop questions to clarify points and extend their peers – a role normally carried out by the teacher. Examination mark schemes could also be used to peer assess the teaching and suggest improvement targets.

Development activities

1. Decision-making exercises

Decision-making exercises can be developed in the context of a wide range of geographical topics, highlighting for students the fundamental link between geography and real-world issues. Titles could include:

- Where should the dam be built on River A?
- Which coastal management strategy should be implemented at B?
- Where should the new housing development be built in town C?
- Should country D's debt be cancelled?

Decision-making exercises engage high-level thinking skills – information synthesis, evaluation of advantages and disadvantages, appreciation of the values and attitudes of different interest groups, critical analysis of evidence and the development of conclusions consistent with evidence. Furthermore, a fundamental part of decision making involves effective team work. Geographical extension is encouraged in these situations through peer interaction – students 'bounce' ideas off each other and challenge their team members' thinking. Different team work organisational strategies can be implemented during decision-making exercises. The following could be assigned to students:

- Real-life roles of people who may be involved in the decision making or who may have different views and attitudes about the problem, e.g. in considering debt cancellation these might be: the leader of the country involved, a World Bank representative, a citizen of the country and a representative from a development charity such as Christian Aid.
- Personality traits to adopt during team discussion and debate, e.g. leader, diplomat, antagonist, distracter (Figure 4). These roles encourage students to think about the skills essential to effective group work discussion and debate. The exercise also allows metacognition – thinking about the way in which they present themselves and respond to others. Debriefing questions that could be used include:
  - How did you recognise the roles that others were playing?
  - Did you learn anything about yourself in this activity?
  - Did you have a helpful or an unhelpful role?
  - Are there other helpful or unhelpful roles in group work?

2. The seminar

The seminar is an effective method of bringing university-style learning into the geography classroom. It is therefore a particularly effective strategy at A-level but with careful planning and management could also be effectively implemented to challenge

Mebo's Father

Viewpoint information
Your three-month-old daughter, Mebo, has just died from malaria. This could have been prevented if there was sufficient funding.

Key questions to think about when writing your viewpoint:
■ How did Zambia's debt cause the death of Mebo?
■ Is Zambia's debt your fault?
■ How would this death be viewed in an MEDC such as the UK?
■ Why do you think the World Bank and EU won't want to cancel their debt?
■ What arguments do you expect the World Bank and EU representatives to make? What responses will you have?

Personality/character information
You take up an **extreme position** with respect to the subject under discussion. You:
■ Put forward one view as the explanation for everything
■ Come back continually to one idea
■ Express yourself in extreme terms
■ Refuse to compromise

President of Zambia

Viewpoint information
You were elected president of Zambia in 2001 and one of your election promises to your people was to solve your country's debt problem to help reduce poverty. If you don't manage this you may not get re-elected.

Key questions to think about when writing your viewpoint:
■ Why did Zambia get into debt?
■ Was it Zambia's fault?
■ How has the debt affected the country's education, health and employment?
■ Is trade helping Zambia get out of debt?
■ Why do you think the World Bank and EU won't want to cancel their debt?
■ What would you be prepared to do to solve the debt problem?
■ What arguments do you expect the World Bank and EU representatives to make? What responses will you give?

Personality/character information
You are an **organiser.** You get the discussion started and try to stop the group straying off the subject. You encourage everybody to get the job done.

You are likely to say:
■ 'don't forget what we're supposed to be discussing'
■ 'come on everyone, don't let's waste time'
■ 'let's keep to the point'

EU Representative

Viewpoint information
You hold a senior post in the European Union and you represent all governments of countries of the EU that have lent money to Zambia. The governments want their money back, but they are also under growing pressure from the people of Europe to help poorer countries like Zambia where possible.

Key questions to think about when writing your viewpoint:
■ Is it fair for the EU countries to lose all this money?
■ What has Zambia done with the money it has borrowed?
■ Is Zambia doing enough to help itself get out of debt?
■ Under what conditions would you consider cancelling the debt? (don't forget the pressure from the people of Europe!)
■ What arguments do you expect Zambia's President and Mebo's father to make? What responses will you give?

Personality/character information
You are an **idea seeker.** You ask others to express their ideas and opinions.

You are likely to say:
■ 'I would like to know what Arjun's views are'
■ 'Sam, what do you think?'
■ 'We can't decide until we've heard everybody's opinion'
■ 'How do you feel about that?'

World Bank Representative

Viewpoint information
You hold a senior position in the World Bank and have been working there (in New York) for over ten years. The World Bank is one of the organisations that have lent a lot of money to Zambia.

Key questions to think about when writing your viewpoint:
■ Is it fair for the World Bank to lose all this money?
■ What has Zambia done with all the money you have lent it?
■ Is Zambia doing enough to help itself get out of debt?
■ What arguments do you expect Zambia's President and Mebo's father to make? What responses will you give?

Personality/character information
You are a **show off.** You try to show how clever you are by:
■ Mentioning books and writers that nobody else has heard of
■ Using long words whenever possible
■ Dropping names of important thinkers into conversation
■ Suggesting to people that they should read so they understand the subject better

Figure 4 | *Example 'Personality' cards for the seminar on Zambia and debt.*

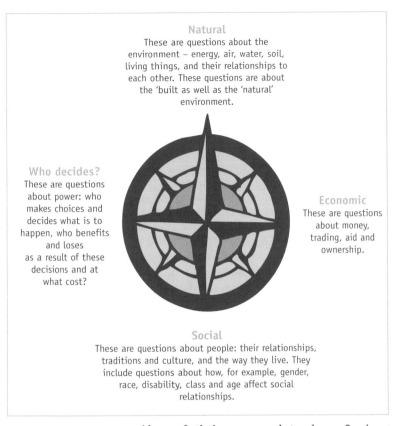

Natural
These are questions about the environment – energy, air, water, soil, living things, and their relationships to each other. These questions are about the 'built as well as the 'natural' environment.

Who decides?
These are questions about power: who makes choices and decides what is to happen, who benefits and loses as a result of these decisions and at what cost?

Economic
These are questions about money, trading, aid and ownership.

Social
These are questions about people: their relationships, traditions and culture, and the way they live. They include questions about how, for example, gender, race, disability, class and age affect social relationships.

Figure 5 | The Development Compass Rose. Source: Birmingham DEC, 1995.

younger gifted and talented students. Students are provided with a pack of reading materials, perhaps including information from textbooks, and newspaper and academic articles. The pack may also include some focus or stimulus questions to direct thinking before the seminar. Students should also be encouraged to think 'outside the box' by developing their own notes, ideas and questions for discussion. The role of the teacher is to facilitate discussion and learning. The final product of the seminar could be an essay. Seminars are particularly effective when studying contentious contemporary geographical issues such as global warming, de-industrialisation and immigration.

The seminar is a powerful tool in developing the gifted and talented geographer. It necessitates the ability to discuss issues in depth, often leading participants beyond the comfort zone of their existing understanding. Furthermore, they develop the confidence and ability to challenge the conventional wisdom relating to the issue and the ideas of their peers and teachers. Seminars can also be used to prepare budding undergraduate geographers for interviews and university study, Oxbridge applicants in particular.

Reading and writing skills in geography

Starters and plenaries

The development compass rose

The development compass rose (Figure 5) can be applied to a variety of situations – interpretation of a photograph, analysis of the impact of a human activity upon an area, geographical description or the structuring of an essay.

In the context of starter and plenary activities, the compass rose has been successfully used to develop students' ability to write geographical descriptions from photographic stimuli. At the start of the lesson, individuals write a geographical description of a photograph. During the course of the lesson the compass rose is introduced, along with descriptive geographical vocabulary. The plenary activity involves students re-writing their starter descriptions using the compass rose structure. In addition to developing their photographic interpretation, students are also able to see the progression they have made during the lesson. Once students are familiar with the compass rose it can be used to frame and structure high level analysis of visual stimuli during a starter/plenary activity. For example, a photograph of a tourist resort to analyse the impact of tourism on the area.

geography classrooms, notes that differential attainment and performance does not relate only to simple divisions of sex and is briefly reported upon later in this chapter.

The main assessment issues

Reports and updates published by Ofsted (2000) and QCA (2003, 2004) highlight the range of standards achieved by students at key stage 3, GCSE and A-level. These clearly establish that in nearly all subjects, and at almost all levels, boys consistently perform less well than girls in formal assessments. This finding is not new – indeed since the mid 1990s concern has been expressed about the under-achievement of boys, both generally and within the context of geography education (Butt and Smith, 1998). Examination statistics reveal that in fact *both* boys *and* girls have improved their attainment over recent years, but that girls' assessed performance has improved *faster* than boys. A similar trend can be seen in other developed countries – giving rise to debates about boys' under-achievement either in terms of them being 'failed' by the education system, or about the effects on their schooling of the innate characteristics of their sex (Epstein *et al.*, 1998).

In addition, huge differences in levels of performance still occur between schools whose students come from different socio-economic backgrounds. Indeed these usually represent the more significant and enduring variables with respect to attainment. The variation in performance between the sexes is just one element in a wider and more complex set of assessment issues – for example, there are also notable differences in reported attainment between ethnic groups and in relation to parental levels of education.

Research questions and differential attainment

Within the small action research projects conducted by AEWG members, three key questions were identified:
1. Does girls' comparatively better performance in geography in English and Welsh schools tell us more about the assessment methods used than about inherent differences in ability?
2. Do assessors themselves have an influence on patterns of student performance?
3. Are differences in the attainment of boys and girls related to preferred learning styles in geography rather than to any innate differences in their ability to learn geographical concepts and ideas?

Research which simply looks at the differences in achievement and attainment in geography on the basis of sex alone (that is, the mere differences in performance of boys and girls) is limited in its usefulness. Account needs to be taken of the factors which contribute to these differences. Researching possible relationships between assessment outcomes and gender may be more complicated but will ultimately yield more meaningful results.

However, let us at least start from the baseline of comparative levels of performance by considering the evidence of boys' and girls' attainment in geography at key stage 3, GCSE and A-level in 2003 and 2004 (Figure 1).

Here we see that girls out-perform boys in geography at each of the formal assessment points in secondary education. It is worth noting that such results include both teacher assessments (in key stage 3) and external assessments (in GCSE and A-level). Within Figure 1 history is used for comparison purposes at key stage 3 and reveals similar variations in girls' and boys' performance to those seen in geography. (Girls also perform above the level of boys at key stage 3 in design and technology, information technology, modern foreign languages, art and music.)

(a) Percentages reaching expected levels (5 and above) in geography at the end of key stage 3 in 2003. (data for 2002 included for comparison purposes).

Subject	Boys		Girls		All students	
	2003	2002	2003	2002	2003	2002
Geography	63	61	73	71	68	66
History	62	60	73	71	67	65

(b) Cumulative percentages of GCSE Geography results by grade, 2004

	A*	A	B	C	D	E	F	G	U
Male	6.3	18.8	35.0	**59.4**	75.8	86.7	93.9	96.9	100.0
Female	10.0	25.8	43.2	**66.8**	80.6	89.6	94.8	97.7	100.0
Total	8.0	21.9	38.6	**62.7**	77.9	88.0	94.0	97.3	100.0

(c) Cumulative percentages of A-level Geography results by grade, 2004

	A	B	C	D	E	U	Total entry
Male	19.9	45.5	**70.8**	89.1	97.6	100.0	18,762
Female	29.0	57.6	**80.0**	93.2	98.7	100.0	15,453
Total	24.0	51.0	**75.0**	91.0	98.2	100.0	34,215

Figure 1 | *Geography assessment and examination results by sex, 2003 and 2004. Note the variation in the 'gender gap' at level 5 in key stage 3 (10%), at level C in GCSE (7.4%) and at level C at A-level (9.2%). Source: QCA, 2004.*

Age and level	English		Mathematics		Science	
	Girls	Boys	Girls	Boys	Girls	Boys
Age 11, level 4 and above	73	57	58	59	69	70
Age 14, level 5 and above	72	55	62	62	55	55
Age 14, level 6 and above	35	20	37	38	24	24

Figure 2 | *Percentage of girls and boys reaching expected levels at age 11 and 14 in 1999 in English, mathematics and science. Source: Ofsted, 2000.*

Interestingly, when similar data for the core subjects are considered we find that the large variations in performance between the sexes seen in most non-core subjects at key stage 3 occur only in relation to English (Figure 2). In mathematics and science boys' and girls' performance is almost identical (that is, within a percentage point of each other). It might be reasonable to suggest that the differences in attainment between the sexes in geography and history at key stage 3 has something to do with both subjects being more 'literary' than 'scientific/mathematical' in their content, approach and means of assessment. It can be argued that geography *should* have a reasonably strong 'scientific/mathematical' element within it (which might draw girls' and boys' performances closer together), but this is not apparent from the differential attainment of the sexes in geography at this level. We might therefore assume that because girls perform better than boys in 'literary' subjects – as suggested by the data in Figures 1 and 2 – geography is perhaps being taught, and, more importantly, assessed, as a 'literary' subject at key stage 3.

Wood (2002) has carried out research to pursue the question of whether the dominance of 'literary' assessment in geography favours girls rather than boys. Drawing upon evidence collected across all subjects and age groups within his secondary school Wood discovered that girls and boys in his school followed national trends in their overall pattern of assessed performance in geography (the data included both teacher assessments (see Chapter 34) and external examination results and the results of a questionnaire survey of students' attitudes towards learning geography). Importantly, Wood concluded that:

> *in those assessments which are focused on longer, prose styles and on investigative work in years 7 and 9 – where there is less direct structure both to lessons and the nature of the work produced – girls do substantially better than the boys* (Wood, 2002, p. 42).

However, this 'gap' in the performance of the sexes had narrowed by the time students reached the age of 16.

Drawing on evidence from questionnaires completed by students within the school, Wood also discovered that:

> - *at key stage 3, boys do not enjoy writing about geography as much as girls. However, by GCSE they are equally likely to enjoy this aspect of the subject,*
> - *whilst not enjoying writing about geography, boys appear to think they are better at it than girls, although again this is so only at key stage 3, showing no gender difference at GCSE,*
> - *boys appear to enjoy using computers and discussing geography much more than writing about it, especially at key stage 3. Girls generally enjoy these aspects more than they do writing about the subject, but are not as enthusiastic as the boys,*
> - *once again, boys feel more confident than girls about their use of computers and their ability to discuss the subject, and*
> - *interestingly, while boys tend to take note of teacher comments nearly as assiduously as girls at key stage 3, this is not the case at GCSE* (Wood, 2002, p. 43).

When conducting interviews, Wood found that boys often said that they preferred assessment feedback to be in a verbal rather than a written form as they were able and willing to take immediate note of any main points from assessments and make use of them in subsequent work. Girls, on the other hand, were found to prefer written comments, arguing that these allowed them more time to reflect on, and make use of, the feedback. In the light of these observations it is clearly important for teachers to consider multiple formats when feeding back to students on the work they have completed.

Bradley-Smith (2002) shifted the focus of research away from the under-achievement of boys compared to the generally higher achievement of girls – towards the 'invisibility' of significant numbers of girls who may also under-perform in geography. She characterises these girls, found across different ability and gender groupings within schools, as:

> *always quiet and compliant; they demand little and contribute little. They draw so little attention to themselves that it is often difficult to recall whether or not they were actually present in a particular lesson* (Bradley-Smith, 2002, p. 143).

Bradley-Smith identified three major action research questions:

1. How do certain girls manage to achieve 'invisibility'?

Photo: Margaret Roberts.

2. Are they under-achievers?
3. What are the implications for my teaching?

Underpinning these questions were several others:
-   Do such girls behave the same in *all* lessons?
-   How do they cope with groupwork or practical sessions?
-   Is 'invisibility' a condition they have chosen to adopt?
-   Are such girls being isolated by the system, their teachers and their peers?
-   And, significantly, if 'invisible' girls are found not to be underachievers, does their silence and apparent lack of engagement actually matter?

Research was conducted with a group of year 9 girls through structured lesson observation, interviews and an analysis of subject reports. Those 'invisible' girls studied tended to conform to Bradley-Smith's original view – they were 'quiet and compliant', neither 'demanding nor contributing'. They did, however, engage in a great deal of 'horizontal' interaction with their peers and were generally happy to talk to, and get help from, other members of the class. When interviewed these girls said they were not afraid of talking to the teacher, nor worried about getting answers wrong, but that they preferred the support of their peers – an approach they had adopted since primary school. The girls all said that their teachers did not really know them, but that this was not really a concern. All claimed that groupwork was the best type of learning activity, that friendship bonds were important and that they either 'liked' or 'quite liked' school. In practical lessons these girls might be 'covered' by other girls; 'invisible' girls would also avoid attention being drawn to them from the teacher by ensuring that classwork was completed, although not always to their highest standards. Bradley-Smith concludes that:

> *The invisible girls seemed to have found a 'comfort zone' within the school system whereby they have removed themselves from the possibility of any personal challenge or pressure* (2002, p. 146).

Evaluations of reports written on these girls confirmed that very few teachers really 'knew' them, and often teachers' comments were phrased in a non-committal manner.

Figure 1 | *Sara Hakeem's reflections on images of Luton.*
Photos: ©Sara Hakeem, Denbigh High School, London.

Scenes such as these, epitomise the idea of a 'diverse Britain' - exotic, colourful and cultural. A Britain where various communities from different ethnic and religious backgrounds come together to form a thriving and vibrant multi-cultural Britain.

But is it? Bury Park like many other inner city areas across Britain can be seen as zones of bounded culture rather than multi-culture - these areas are specifically for and lived in by the 'Asian community'. We could say that places like Bury Park lack multi-culture and cultural intermingling and instead are bounded segregated spaces.

Do these scenes indicate a positive intermingling of people and multi-culture? Or, are they representative of mono-cultural areas in which White, Asian and Black communities are polarised and segregated? When people and places such as these are thought of as exotic, colourful and cultural ... do we actually mean different, separate and 'other'?

Perhaps we need to think of ways to encourage better understanding and intermingling between communities through creating a positive sense of belonging to Britain by celebrating similarities as well as difference.

reason why geography teachers today may find it so difficult to contribute to the anti-racist project; the content of the curriculum mitigates against it. For example, if migration is taught as a series of models and 'laws' based on notions of 'rational economic man [sic]', or rural areas are studied as networks of settlements obeying Christaller's assumptions about an 'isotropic plain', it is difficult to see how questions of race and the complex geographies of power can be made the focus of school geography lessons. As an aside, it is worth noting that there was some work in the tradition of 'spatial science' that studied 'race' as part of a welfare tradition. However, this work suffered from the fact that it conceptualised space as an explanatory factor rather than understand the social processes that underpinned the observed distributions.

This is why, despite the declared commitment to 'diverse cultures' and 'cultural heritages', the revised geography national curriculum introduced in 2000 reflects only minimal change (DfEE/QCA, 1999). Although there is a commitment to inclusion and anti-racism in the document, there are few clues as to how the themes of the curriculum might be interpreted to support anti-racist teaching. The same is true, I would argue, of the schemes of work published by QCA (1999) to support the teaching of the curriculum. Further, the same 'absence' is evident in the textbooks designed to support the geography national curriculum, and which largely reflect the geographical approaches developed in the 1960s and 1970s.

This point is well made by Sara Hakeem in Figure 1. She notes that photographs of her home town – Luton – may, on the surface, appear to highlight the cultural diversity of the town and thus be of value in providing students with 'positive images'. However, there is a danger that such an approach glosses over some of the real challenges and difficulties encountered by those who live in multicultural cities. Sara's point is an important one, not least because there may be a tendency for geography teachers to avoid controversy in lessons.

There are, of course, exceptions to the trends and approaches outlined above. For example there were some geography teachers in the 1970s who sought to draw upon critical perspectives in the discipline to develop a geography curriculum that was relevant to the situations of the students they taught. Most notably, in large urban centres, geography teachers joined their colleagues in the development of anti-racist education (Gill, 1982, 1999). They developed accounts of racism that focused on the political forces of imperialism and colonialism. These 'radical' or 'anti-racist' perspectives were positioned against multicultural education which was accused of celebrating difference at the expense of explaining the structural causes of racism. Walford (1993) refers to this as a time of crisis in school geography. The debates around anti-racism received quite a lot of media coverage, but became marginalised by the arguments about and eventual implementation of the national curriculum. Despite comments about the need to teach a multicultural geography, the first version of the national curriculum (1991) reinstated a traditional view of the subject, and teachers had to work hard to interpret the document in such a way as to incorporate anti-racist perspectives throughout the curriculum.

The implication of this analysis is that if geography is to contribute to the realisation of anti-racist teaching, as discussed by Gillborn (1995), we need to take a critical look at the way the geography curriculum is constructed. While school geography has moved on from a reliance on environmental determinism to a commitment to the scientific method, it has tended to ignore new ways of thinking about race in geography. In the rest of this chapter, I will suggest ways that may be more fruitful in developing anti-racist geography teaching.

Different approaches

Bonnett (1996) suggests that there have been three main approaches to 'race' in geographical studies since the issue was 'rediscovered' in the 1960s:
- The first approach assumed the existence of empirically-defined categories of 'race' that geographers could 'plot' and 'map'. In other words, it assumed that 'race' has a geography that can be studied empirically. Geographers set about mapping the distribution of non-white immigrant settlement and developing indices of segregation. However, the danger with this approach is that the degree of sophistication in explanation of these patterns does not always match that of the tools for description. For example, we can map the distribution of Bangladeshis in London but what does this tell about the processes of settlement and what it means to be a Bangladeshi in London?
- The second approach is concerned with the geography of race relations, and draws upon sociological ideas in order to go beyond simple description to explain observed patterns. Thus, housing patterns might be explained in terms of concepts such as accommodation, resistance, or avoidance. A recent textbook, for example, offers the following explanations for the 'tendency for the black and Asian communities to

Chapter 31

Inspiring disaffected students

Jeff Battersby with Neil Hornby

Before reading this chapter consider the following questions:

- Recollect a time when your learning was rapid and effective (e.g. on the birth of a child, during your teacher training) and consider the conditions that can cause learning to go off the chart.

- We have all experienced the situation of 'being present in body but absent in mind'. What are the conditions that explain a lack of engagement or disconnection with learning?

- In your geography lessons, how is creating a need to know or find out among the students achieved?

As teachers we are concerned with students' learning, their levels of achievement and the progress they are making. However, there is a real danger that we can be so pre-occupied with creating optimum strategies and opportunities to deliver assessment targets that we sometimes sacrifice an enjoyment of the subject and reduce satisfaction in learning at the expense of achievement. Teachers often feel they exist in a highly regulated and highly accountable environment, which can result in their seeking a low-risk approach to lesson planning and curriculum development. A too-rigid structure to lessons, to learning and to assessment can reduce levels of interest, motivation and ultimately achievement for our students.

Student disaffection and underachievement are inextricably linked and are issues which continue to tax teachers, schools, parents and successive governments. Students express their disaffection with the school curriculum through their disruptive behaviour, disengagement from the learning process and through underachievement in their work. Students do not have to be engaged in learning activities in order to carry them out. They may appear to be involved in learning and, as Sayer (1987) suggests, demonstrate a 'pathology of presence', going through the motions of engaging with tasks presented to them in lessons, but not learning through them or from them. Given that the majority of students are in school, in body if not always in mind, then how can geography switch students on to learning? Can geography in fact reduce disaffection and raise levels of achievement?

Kinder (1990), Ruddock *et al.* (1996), among others (quoted in Battersby, 1999), claim that there is considerable disaffection with the school curriculum which is related to the nature of the national curriculum and the subject content of the core and foundation subjects as well as the strategies and approaches to learning. Students show low levels of engagement with learning in many of their lessons due to the perceived irrelevance of the learning experiences, tasks and content which makes little connection between work in school and the world outside, certainly the world they inhabit. They have little control over what they learn or the way in which they learn, both of which are decided for them by their teachers, the geography Orders or the examination specification. Equally, they are given few, if any, opportunities to experience learning in or through real situations. If a lack of purposeful engagement in learning represents disaffection then it is likely to manifest itself in the form of underachievement and irregular attendance as well as in inappropriate behaviour in the classroom (Battersby, 1999).

A great opportunity

As the new century unfolds, human actions are affecting the environment in ways that are unprecedented, unsustainable, undesirable and unpredictable – a situation which presumably cannot be divorced from current practice in education. According to many mainstream scientists, the global environment has deteriorated to such an extent that the great life-supporting systems of the planet's biosphere are being threatened. Changes in the Earth's climate, the accumulation of waste products, soil exhaustion, deforestation and the destruction of ecosystems are all too apparent in our world today. Decisions which are made about the environment affect the quality of life of everyone on the planet from a local to the global scale. As consumers and producers our use and abuse of the environment has wide-ranging effects on other people, other living things, communities and environments. There is a need for all of us to at least be aware of *'sustainable development'* and the need to integrate rational environmental and economic considerations by our actions and through our decisions. Where is geography if not here, engaging with these issues? Surely, with these contexts geography provides the resource for designing relevant, worthwhile and enjoyable learning for even the most reluctant student?

Though there has never been a greater need for young people to be aware of the necessity to look after the environment, and for them to understand their roles as the custodians of the planet, responsible for the world in which, in turn, their own children will grow up, it is crucial to avoid what could become preaching moralistic messages. Fortunately, there is ample evidence to support the notion that the environment matters to young people. Many appear genuinely concerned to safeguard it and to understand the problems that face society in deciding how to balance different competing needs. Many can see the environment as something they are able to influence in small ways themselves and, through the media, have been able to form their own feelings and opinions on local, national and global issues.

Photo: ©Neil Hornby.

Schools, particularly through the geography curriculum, can help students to develop the knowledge, understanding and skills they need to make informed judgements about the world and, in later life, to make a valued contribution to decisions, whether in their own immediate locality or more widely. It is apparent from observations of the curriculum in action that teachers can engage their students in environmental discussions and ask them for their ideas about improvements to their immediate and other environments (Battersby, 1999). The point here is to tune into students' interests and prior learning.

Often students can be alarmed when environmental problems are emphasised without any reference to possible solutions. It can lead to apathy in relation to problems which might appear too great to solve as far as the students are concerned. Helping students to adopt a positive approach to the environment should be central to any engagement or coverage of these issues. This would manifest itself in encouraging students to develop an awareness and curiosity about the environment, leading to an informed concern for, and an active participation in, resolving environmental problems; not an insignificant challenge to schools and the curriculum. Students should be encouraged to examine and interpret the environment from a variety of perspectives: the physical, geographical, biological, sociological, economic, political, technological, historical, aesthetic, ethical and spiritual. This is, of course, one of the main strengths of geography – enabling us to take a holistic perspective.

'Real world' learning

The national curriculum in the UK and other countries takes into account that children and young people today need to work with real-life situations (DfEE/QCA, 1999). They need to be given concrete and real tasks. The curriculum is based on the idea that knowledge is more than facts and skills. Students are taught to know about different alternatives for action and should be able to describe such alternatives. They should be able to carry through such actions, to develop and use specific skills. They should be able to make a connection between the intention of the action and the action itself, to reflect on the results and justify their actions. 'Real world' learning – by which learning *in* and *through* the environment is usually the meaning (i.e. fieldwork) – is a central tenet of geography education.

Photo: ©Neil Hornby.

Inspiring disaffected students on field trips

On a recent trip to the Malvern Hills with a group of year 9 students it was a surprise to find that less than half had been to the hills before, even though the students all lived within walking distance of them. For disaffected students, who have often not been given the experience of visiting places outside their immediate environment, the trip must at the very least be enjoyable, and if possible inspiring and perhaps sufficiently motivating to encourage them to go to similar places in their own time. For a disaffected class, geographical 'content' should, perhaps in the short-term, be nearer the bottom of the learning objectives than the opportunity to bond, which will reap a huge benefit in terms of a more focused class in future.

Here are some comments and ideas on how you can help disaffected students enjoy a field trip:

- Do students always need to fill in a worksheet or take notes? This is perhaps often done as a controlling tool or out of concern that they are not learning otherwise. However, it can take away the enjoyment if a student struggles with literacy, embarrass them to be seen asking for help in a public place, and distract them from developing an aesthetic and/or spiritual appreciation of a beautiful landscape (see Chapter 5).
- Perhaps you could write a class poem or piece of prose – students coming up with thoughts and feelings which you the teacher jot down for later use in class. This could also serve as a way of showing them how much they have learnt and answering questions raised.
- Show the students your wider interest in and appreciation of the landscape – talk about the architecture, history, wildlife or an interest you have, such as hill walking. Many disaffected students might not know how to appreciate or enjoy a place, or see its value other than as a venue for geography fieldtrips.
- Take a football or rounders bat for a short game after a lunch break; this could also be a great control tool on the trip, inspiring students to work towards it.
- They will not enjoy a fieldtrip if they are wet through or their new trainers are ruined. If it is wet, postpone it.
- Provide a treat on the trip; you could drop into a coffee shop or café on the way home. This can do more to turn around an unmotivated class than the most 'inspiring' lesson.

The geography curriculum has a distinct advantage in that it legitimately engages with environmental issues which invariably demand a response from the students; they are required to make a choice about a course of action, about alternatives. They become involved in the ethics of decision making and embroiled in the discussion of alternative courses of action and of the relative merits of different proposals or strategies to solve perceived problems. They are asked to consider who might gain and who might miss out when certain decisions are made, such as in the relocation of a hospital, the siting of a new superstore, or controls over the dumping of waste in a local river. They appear to relish the challenge of putting theory into practice as well as wrestling with the complexity of decision making.

Environmental projects

Practical environmental projects can be hugely motivating for students, giving them the feeling that they can make a difference in relation to their school and a global issue. They offer the teacher a great opportunity to build a sense of team within a disaffected class and inspire a level of motivation throughout the year that more than justifies the curriculum time spent. At key stage 4, the projects outlined below have been used on various occasions as coursework elements for Entry Level Qualifications or for the environment section of the ASDAN Youth Award Scheme.

- We have set up recycling bins at two or three points around the school. Their use has been promoted in assemblies and tutor time to encourage the whole school to feel a sense of ownership and to inform students how to use the bins correctly. It also needed good relations with a friendly caretaker. Although many councils now have a 'green rubbish' collection service, check they will collect from your school, and be aware that they may class the school as a business and try to charge for collections.

Photo: ©Neil Hornby.

- Following lessons on development education, students have researched a charity that they want to find out more about and raise money for. Projects like building a well or providing a village goat have been the most successful as the students have had a real-life target and more of a sense of ownership than they would with a non-specific donation. Discuss this kind of response to development in the context of work on values education.

- We have built a pond in the school grounds with a budget of less than £100. All you need is some hard digging, and a pond liner. Pond plants will come in by the bucketload if you put a plea in the school newsletter. As with the recycling bins above, it is important to consider how it will be maintained and who will take responsibility if you move on.

- Growing seeds in the classroom is something that is cheap and easy and makes little demand on curriculum time. Choose plants that are representative of a location being studied or even grow cress seeds as a visual representation of population density. If they can be consumed at the end of term even better.

Practical projects are often taken up by the local newspaper. If their interest can be secured beforehand, there are often local businesses who are willing to contribute resources or sponsor a project. In addition the young people get a real buzz from brokering this kind of deal. (See Eco Schools website for further ideas.)

Research carried out by one of the authors (Battersby, 1999) has shown that students often felt that they adopted a more positive attitude to learning when they were learning about the environment: 'I am more interested in the environment so I become more interested (in learning) and pay more attention (in class)'. Some students claim that they produce 'better quality work' and gain 'better marks' because they are 'better motivated'. This virtuous circle of positive achievement lies at the heart of strategies to build up students' self-esteem, raise their levels of attainment and reduce their disaffection and underachievement at school.

Into the geography classroom – the role of questions

While the preceding discussion might provide a convincing argument for the inclusion of specific issues in geography lessons which engage students, what particular strategies can be employed in the lessons themselves? How are students enabled and encouraged to learn? What are the positive experiences which engage the students to develop their knowledge and understanding as well as explore their values and attitudes to issues that concern them?

Throughout most lessons we are preoccupied with questions, either asking them or answering those asked of us by students. It is through questions that we gauge the levels of knowledge, understanding and skills of the individual or a group of students as a whole. We are constantly assessing our students, following their response to these questions before asking subsequent questions which reinforce our judgement of their ability. But why ask questions? Some of the reasons are to:

- encourage students to talk constructively;
- signal an interest in hearing what students feel and think;
- stimulate interest and awaken curiosity;
- encourage a problem-solving approach to thinking and learning;
- help students to externalise and verbalise knowledge;
- encourage 'thinking aloud' and exploratory approaches to tasks – the 'intuitive leap';
- help students to learn from each other and to respect and evaluate each other's contributions;
- monitor the students' learning – its extent, level and deficiencies;
- deepen students' thinking levels and improve their ability to conceptualise.

Answers to questions generate knowledge which is shared and, ideally, owned by the class group as a whole. The knowledge generated by an individual student can trigger a demonstration of additional knowledge from others in the group, with or without an acknowledgement of the initial input. How far does the learning demonstrated by one student owe itself to that of another? What if the original owner of the knowledge does not demonstrate a level of knowledge and understanding of subsequent contributors because they are denied any opportunity to do so? Our attitude to and management of the knowledge input, transfer and ownership can have either a positive or negative effect on the individual student. How do we ensure that all students are enabled rather than disabled by the opportunities within our classroom to demonstrate their capability? Do *you* claim ownership by repeating, rephrasing or putting a different emphasis on the input from a student or do you accept that input for what it is, however expressed? How aware and sensitive are we as teachers to the de-motivating possibilities that exist in this context? Do we facilitate learning by providing *time* for students to think? How quickly do *you* fill any silence that follows a question? Do we provide strategies to help students to think? Answers to these will have an impact on the motivation, engagement and achievement of our students.

The geography curriculum encourages us all to enquire, investigate, and to ask questions. The following have become standard and very useful prompts for geographical enquiry:

- What is it?
- What is it like?
- How and why is it changing?
- Who benefits and who loses?
- Where is it?
- How did it get like this?
- What are the implications of this?

This series of questions allows and encourages students to engage in a range of increasingly demanding thought processes which mirror Bloom's taxonomy of thinking by asking questions which:

- draw on knowledge
- require application
- invite synthesis
- test comprehension
- encourage analysis
- promote evaluation.

An analysis of tasks and activities found in many of our popular textbooks reveals an emphasis on 'lower order' objectives with limited opportunities for students to engage in the 'big task', the higher level thinking skills required of questions which demand evaluation of alternatives (see also Chapter 13). This limitation is exacerbated each lesson when tackling the 'double page spread' on a topic we ask the students to 'answer question 1, then question 2', usually asking for comprehension, before they progress, if

The concept of 'action competence' has in recent years played a central role in the pedagogical discussion of environmental education, especially in European countries. To develop the students' action competence means developing their ability and will to take part in democratic processes concerning people's exploitation of and dependence on natural resources in a critical way (see Jensen and Schnack (1997) and Breiting and Mogensen (1999)). In Denmark, for example, the overall objective for environmental education is seen as the development of students' action competence. This is different from mainstream environmental education in that its goal is to improve and to save the environment here and now through behaviour modification of the students. It is also the intention that, in the long run, the students will be better qualified to handle environmental problems. However, teaching in schools is first and foremost aimed at the far-sighted goal of action competence with the immediate goal of how to live with environmental issues as a part of young people's daily lives.

Concluding thoughts

There is an agenda of challenges facing all teachers involved in the construction of a relevant, workable and enjoyable school curriculum that can address disaffection and underachievement. These can be addressed through a number of key questions which include:

- How are the complex relationships between human beings and their environment best represented and explored through the curriculum and how can students' own experiences be brought into this formulation?
- How can environmental education through geography become part of mainstream curriculum provision which is accessible to all students?
- How can we foster in students an active engagement in understanding and improving the environmental conditions in which they live their lives?
- What pedagogical processes can be developed for handling the value issues raised by attempts to involve students in action to improve the environment?
- What pedagogical process can be developed that links locally defined environmental concerns with global issues?
- What content or evidence generated by the environmental sciences should be selected to inform student enquiry into local problems?
- In what ways should teachers be involved in finding answers to these questions through a process of collaborative action research in their schools?

Responses to these questions will inform and shape our curriculum for our students. This is why the Geographical Association has successfully engaged in CPD-led curriculum development projects such as 'Valuing Places'. The products of these projects are available in print form or from the Association's website.

A curriculum which emphasises, encourages and enables students to engage in learning has the potential to reduce disaffection with it and with school in general, as well as contributing to the reduction in underachievement by students. Such a curriculum may succeed in reversing the findings of Barber's (1994) survey of 10,000 students in schools in England which revealed that up to half of all secondary school students lacked motivation, 70% of students counted the minutes left until the end of the lesson and 30-40% would rather not go to school.

A major challenge to teachers, to schools, and to curriculum planners in particular, is to entice, interest and motivate the disappeared, disruptive, disappointed and uninterested students, to raise their self-esteem and achievements and perhaps reduce significantly their disaffection with their school experiences (Tattum, 1986). This is where geography has achieved success in many schools.

Notes
1. The latest thinking in the Bloom tradition, for example, Krathwohl, 2002, is useful background reading.
2. Christian Aid also produce other inexpensive games including 'The Chocolate Trade Game', 'The Dept Game', 'Trade Rules' and 'The Paper Bag Game'.

Related publications available from the Geographical Association:
- The Red Cross (2005) *Global Lines – Teaching resource*. London: The Red Cross.
- Save the Children (2005) *Young Lives, Global Goals*. London: Save the Children.
- Swift, D. (2005) *Meeting SEN in Geography*. David Fulton/Geographical Association/Valuing Places.

References

Print

Barber, M. (1994) writing in *The Guardian,* 23 August.
Battersby, J. (1999) 'Does environmental education have street credibility and the potential to reduce student disaffection within and beyond their school curriculum?', *Cambridge Journal of Education*, 29, 3, pp. 447-57.
Breiting, S. and Mogensen, F. (1999) 'Action competence and environmental education', *Cambridge Journal of Education*, 29, 3, pp. 349-53.
Christian Aid – www.christian-aid.org.uk
DfEE/QCA (1999) *Geography: The national curriculum for England (KS1-3)*. London: DfEE/QCA.
Eco schools – www.eco-schools.org.uk
Jensen, B.B. and Schnack, K. (1997) 'The action competence approach in environmental education', *Environmental Education Research*, 3, pp. 163-78.
Kinder, K. (1990) 'Causes of disaffection: the views of students and education professionals', *EERA Bulletin*, 3, 1, pp. 3-11.
Krathwohl, D. (2002) 'A revision of Bloom's Taxonomy: an overview on theory into practice', *Theory Into Practice*, 41, 4, pp. 212-18.
Ruddock, J., Chaplin, R. and Wallace, G. (1996) *School Improvement: What can students tell us?* London: David Fulton.
Sayer, J. (1987) 'Why have you come to school today? A pathology of presence' in Reid, K. (ed) *Combating School Absenteeism*. London: Hodder and Stoughton.
Tattum, D. (ed) (1986) *Management of Disruptive Student Behaviour in Schools* (chapter 3). Chichester: Wiley.

Implications for practice

(a) Consider revising your schemes of work to make them more engaging for disaffected students.

If the evidence shows – or your instinct tells you – that your geography scheme of work is not sparking interest in certain groups of your students, how can you change this in order to re-engage them? Think about the principles that would guide your content selection, as well as those that would influence your organisation of the content and pedagogy.

(b) Account needs to be taken of the resources used.

In order to re-engage students, special care is needed in the choice of the resources used in learning. For instance, ICT can help bring colourful, moving images to the classroom, images that the students themselves may be able to manipulate (see Chapter 19).

(c) Practical usefulness.

Consider ways in which your geography lessons can be shown to be 'practically useful' to students who may have a record of low achievement, short concentration spans or low levels of determination or ambition.

Section Four
Assessment

Section four:
Assessment

> Assessment has always been an integral part of teaching and learning. We would all accept that the 'educational purpose' of teacher assessment is to help young people to progress in their learning in geography (from Balderstone, D. (2000) 'Beyond testing? Issues for teacher assessment in geography' in Hopkin, J., Telfer, S. and Butt, G. (eds) *Assessment in Practice*. Sheffield: GA, p. 9).

> Teacher assessment is fundamental to good teaching. By making assessments during the key stage, you will build up your knowledge of individual students' strengths and weaknesses, which will help you plan your teaching (Dearing, 1996, p. i)

> Much of the most valuable information about students' achievements comes from day-to-day observation, questioning and discussion as they work. This form of assessment is mainly informal and intuitive, but it has the potential to make most impact on students' progress. It helps to answer the question 'what next?', and is, therefore, at the heart of formative assessment (from Hopkin, J. (2000) 'Day-to-day assessment' in Hopkin, J., Telfer, S. and Butt, G. (eds) *Assessment in Practice*. Sheffield: GA, p. 37).

> Self-assessment has an essential role to play in formative practice. Teachers can create wonderful lessons by facilitating debates on ideas and providing guidance on the next learning steps but it is only the learner who can do the learning; it cannot be done for them by the teacher. In other words, students need to be able to self-assess (from Weeden, P. and Lambert, D. (forthcoming) *Geography Inside the Black Box*. NFER/Nelson

Chapter 32

Assessment for Learning in geography

Paul Weeden and John Hopkin

Before reading this chapter consider the following questions:

■ How is assessment used to support your students' learning in geography?

■ To what extent do your students understand how they are learning geography? (What opportunities might exist for improving this understanding?)

■ What are the main features of the feedback you provide to students about their learning in geography?

> *Formative assessment is ... assessment undertaken by teachers, and by their students in assessing themselves, which provides information to be used as feedback. [This] becomes formative assessment when the evidence is actually used to adapt teaching work to meet the [students'] needs* (Black and Wiliam, 1998b, p. 2).

Assessment: measurement or learning?

Assessment is rightly a key concern of geography teachers, and an aspect of practice that presents particular challenges to all teachers in secondary schools. A succession of reports on secondary education has asserted that assessment remains one of the weakest features of teaching in most subjects, especially at key stage 3.

The last 15 years have seen major changes in the way schools and teachers approach assessment (Rawling, 2002, see also Chapter 8). Government has seen assessment as an important 'lever' to raise 'standards'. They have tried to specify educational standards, often indirectly through other bodies such as the Qualifications and Curriculum Authority (QCA) or awarding bodies, and then expected teachers to achieve them. Assessment has thus become increasingly 'high-stakes' because measurement of 'performance' is now central to the many new initiatives introduced by successive governments. The belief underlying this policy is that testing improves performance. National curriculum assessment, GCSE and A-level scores, target setting and rigorous inspection are all used for monitoring and accountability purposes to judge schools and teachers. As a result the summative purposes of assessment have tended to dominate the agenda for many teachers.

The attempts to specify 'standards' more closely have caused problems for teachers.

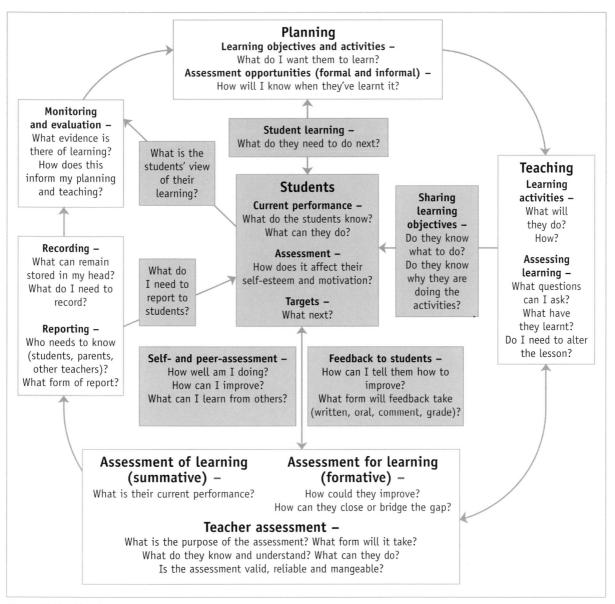

Planning
Learning objectives and activities –
What do I want them to learn?
Assessment opportunities (formal and informal) –
How will I know when they've learnt it?

Monitoring and evaluation –
What evidence is there of learning? How does this inform my planning and teaching?

What is the students' view of their learning?

Student learning –
What do they need to do next?

Teaching
Learning activities –
What will they do? How?

Assessing learning –
What questions can I ask? What have they learnt? Do I need to alter the lesson?

Recording –
What can remain stored in my head? What do I need to record?

Reporting –
Who needs to know (students, parents, other teachers)? What form of report?

What do I need to report to students?

Students
Current performance –
What do the students know? What can they do?

Assessment –
How does it affect their self-esteem and motivation?

Targets –
What next?

Sharing learning objectives –
Do they know what to do? Do they know why they are doing the activities?

Self- and peer-assessment –
How well am I doing? How can I improve? What can I learn from others?

Feedback to students –
How can I tell them how to improve? What form will feedback take (written, oral, comment, grade)?

Assessment of learning (summative) –
What is their current performance?

Assessment for learning (formative) –
How could they improve? How can they close or bridge the gap?

Teacher assessment –
What is the purpose of the assessment? What form will it take?
What do they know and understand? What can they do?
Is the assessment valid, reliable and mangeable?

Figure 1 | *Teaching, learning and assessment. Source: Weeden et al., 2002.*

Educational standards are not fixed or immutable – they are 'established by professionals within a particular field to define levels of performance and/or quality' (Butt, 2002, p. 5). The issue for teachers is whether they can use their 'professional' judgement to define levels of performance, or are they now just 'technicians' implementing imprecisely defined quality-control procedures (level descriptions)? This question is still unresolved and as a result many teachers feel disempowered and confused about assessment in the classroom.

The belief that testing improves performance is contested. Another view proposed by the Assessment Reform Group (ARG) is that testing is only motivating for those who anticipate success. Even then students are often only motivated to perform better, not to learn better. For less successful students, repeated tests lower self-esteem and reduce effort. This increases the gap between high- and low-achieving students (ARG, 2002b). How can students and their learning become more central to the assessment process? Figure 1 shows how the different purposes and functions of teaching, learning and assessment overlap and are interconnected. It also indicates some of the questions that teachers and students can ask during the assessment process. The person being assessed is at the centre of the assessment process with the information collected being used to aid learning through 'feedback' and 'feed-forward'. Research suggests performance improves when formative assessment is central to teaching and learning in the classroom and there is active dialogue between student and teacher about progress.

The rest of this chapter considers how formative assessment can be used to promote learning.

We suggest a number of strategies that teachers have used and found successful in different situations. However, a note of caution is needed at this point: formative assessment is not an instant solution in relation to performance. It involves both teachers and students in reconsidering their approaches and may involve significant changes in teaching and learning.

What are the purposes of assessment?

Assessment has a wide range of purposes and functions, and it is easy to confuse them. Among other purposes we use assessment in the ways described in Figure 2.

The distinction between formative and summative assessment is important. It is helpful to recognise that these terms do not relate to the assessments themselves as any assessment could be used for both formative and summative purposes:

- If used **formatively** assessment helps students understand their strengths and weaknesses, is done at an appropriate time as part of the teaching and learning process and involves feedback that helps the student 'close the gap' between current and expected performance (Sadler, 1989; Stobart and Gipps, 1997).
- Whereas, according to Stobart and Gipps, 'to be **summative** the assessment would be used to record the overall achievement of the student in a systematic way. Thus a level score from a key stage test is a summative assessment' (1997, p. 19).

Governments have spent a lot of money promoting summative assessment and appear to believe that formative assessment is not a problem because it goes on in classrooms all the time. To some extent this is true, as Black and Wiliam suggest:

> *Whatever the labels that are used to describe it, formative assessment itself is, of course, nothing new. Almost all successful teaching ... relies heavily on adapting the teaching in the light of evidence about the success of previous episodes* (quoted in Stobart and Gipps, 1997, pp. 19-20).

However, in an important review of research, Black and Wiliam (1998b) found substantial evidence that day-to-day formative assessment could be improved. They identified three areas of difficulty: that the assessments used did not encourage effective learning; that assessment had a negative impact on the motivation and self-esteem of many students; and that much assessment was for managerial and social purposes rather than educational purposes.

More recently a research review by the Assessment Reform Group (ARG, 2002b) found that tests do have a significant negative impact on motivation and learning. Tests 'narrow the curriculum' with teachers 'teaching to the test'. Performance can appear to rise as teaching strategies such as frequent test practice and tips on answering specific questions are used, but real learning may not be taking place. Allowing students to judge their work in terms of grades or marks can affect motivation, especially if they are

- help teachers better to understand students' progress in learning
- guide teachers' responses to students' learning, e.g. decide on the next steps
- help raise students' achievement
- help give students feedback on their learning
- monitor standards of students' work
- evaluate the effectiveness of planning and teaching

- make judgements about progress or attainment in relation to levels or grades
- inform other teachers about students' achievements
- inform parents about students' progress
- help teachers and schools to address accountability
- inform evaluation and development planning

Formative / Summative

Figure 2 | *Formative and summative assessment.*

compared with others. Test anxiety can impair some students' performance, especially girls and lower-achieving students. Reliance on test scores as an 'objective' measure of 'ability' can lead to teachers underestimating potential.

The rest of this discussion will therefore look at formative assessment, with the following two provisos:

> - *Summative assessment does have a place in education, mainly in the form of end-of-course tests and external examinations but*
> - *it should be kept in its place, because it can exert influence that is not always educational* (Lambert, 2002, p. 123).

Why is formative assessment important?

While summative assessment focuses on attainment at a specific point and tends to look back to what has been achieved, formative assessment looks forward to support progress and future learning. The link between the two is that formative assessment supports teaching and learning, leading students to their best possible level of achievement in the next summative assessment. So formative assessment is important because, as Ofsted point out, 'overall, the purpose of assessment is to improve standards, not merely to measure them' (1998, section 5.6).

Black and Wiliam's review (ARG, 1999) suggests that formative assessment can be one of the most powerful ways of promoting effective learning, particularly for low achievers. They found evidence that a sustained focus on formative assessment would help raise attainment by between one and two GCSE grades across the board.

The key features of formative assessment are:
- it supports teaching and learning by providing information and feedback to students and teachers by:
  - helping teachers to plan, and to identify the next steps in students' learning
  - helping students to improve their work, for example by showing them the qualities to aim for;
- it helps answer the question 'What next?' and so is at the heart of good teaching and learning.

The Assessment Reform Group who commissioned the Black and Wiliam study have further developed these key features and published Ten Principles of Assessment for Learning (2002) (see Figure 3). These principles provide an underpinning theoretical framework for assessment for learning from which teachers can develop procedures that work in the classroom.

Central to these principles is the idea that assessment for learning is a key professional skill that needs to be developed and practised. This is supported by Ofsted reports on English schools where improving formative assessment is seen as a priority:

> *Assessment and its application to teaching and learning remain comparatively weak areas... I welcome the work that is going on nationally under the heading of 'assessment for learning'. In this work lies the potential to make progress on the aspect of teaching that successive reports have emphasised as a weakness: the failure of assessment to make enough difference to teaching and learning* (Ofsted, 2004, p. 3).

What does formative assessment look like?

> *Assessment for learning is the process of seeking and interpreting evidence for use by learners and their teachers to decide where the learners are in their learning, where they need to go and how best to get there* (ARG, 2002a).

For teachers working in an educational culture that is strongly focused on measurement and formal, data-based evidence, an increased emphasis on formative assessment might seem to be an unnecessary extra burden. However it is useful to remember that 'the pig doesn't get fatter just by being weighed'. Assessment that merely 'measures performance' will not magically raise standards by itself; there needs to be some associated action, by someone – teacher and/or learner – to improve learning. Ideally assessment information will be the basis for a dialogue between student and teacher.

Formative and summative assessment have always gone together, but one area of dispute among authors is whether the methods used for formative assessment could be the same as those used for summative assessment. The important concept here is that of 'fitness for purpose'. In reality, while some assessments will be better for one purpose, many assessments will be used for both.

An assessment that is informal, intuitive and based on professional judgements may be better as a formative assessment tool because the data may be more open to question and more difficult to commit to paper, but it could also provide useful summative data in the right context. Similarly useful formative information can arise from more formal assessment situations (examinations or tests) if the data are analysed by both teacher and student and if the result is a constructive dialogue about how the work can be improved.

What is important in formative assessment is that the data are not just recorded as fixed judgements of performance (for example a mark, level or grade) but are analysed more carefully and used to improve performance. Initially this may be time consuming, but if students take more responsibility for their learning and teachers are selective in what they assess in this way, using formative assessment can become a more effective method of teaching and learning.

As noted above, the research suggests that the learners who will get the most benefit from this process are the lower achievers. While most higher achievers appear to understand what the assessor is looking for (they 'know the rules of the game'), many low achievers need to be taught in a variety of ways so that their learning is reinforced.

Recognising the characteristics and value of formative assessment is an important aspect of professional development. For this reason assessment for learning is one focus of the Teaching and Learning in Foundation Subjects Strand of the Key Stage 3 Strategy (DfES, 2002; now known as the Secondary National Strategy).

Assessment for learning...

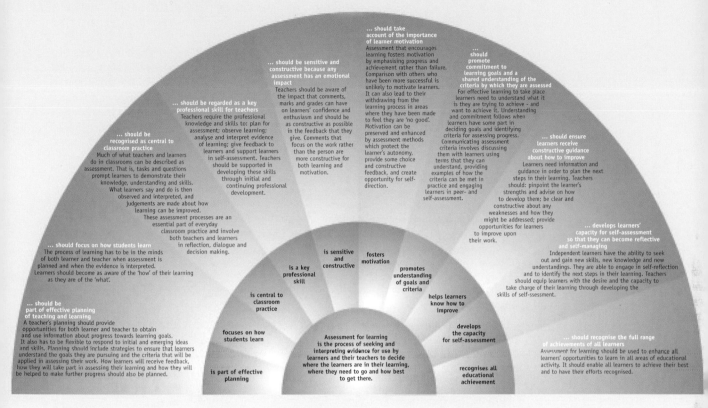

Figure 3 | *The ARG's Ten Principles for Formative Assessment. Source: ARG, 2002a.*

Support from the Secondary National Strategy

Assessment for learning is being actively promoted as part of the Secondary National Strategy, through a series of training materials (DfES, 2002, 2004),. The training materials are designed to support self-review and school-based professional development, although they can also be used for centralised training, for example within a local education authority. Although they are primarily intended to raise achievement at key stage 3, the ideas they contain are just as applicable in GCSE or post-16 courses. Many schools have identified assessment for learning as a whole school development area.

These training materials consist of useful exercises that promote discussion about using assessment for learning in everyday classroom situations, the formative use of summative assessment, oral feedback, marking and self- and peer-assessment. The supporting video/DVD materials illustrate assessment for learning in different contexts, with geography lessons being well represented in the clips. For example, the footage of a geography teacher (AfL module 4) encouraging students to use criteria to develop their descriptions and explanations shows how this teacher has used oral feedback and self- and peer-assessment to improve students' work.

The support material for the Foundation Subjects module 1 ('Assessment for Learning in everyday lessons') includes a really useful checklist for observation, based on Black and Wiliam (1998b). Geographers can use this for self-review within the department, or for observing each other's lessons. While much of the support material is based on Black and Wiliam's work, some of the more controversial issues, such as potential conflicts between grading and improvement are under-emphasised. Geography specific assessment for learning materials have also been developed to expand and illustrate many of the ideas.

Although the first two modules of the Foundation Subjects materials have most to say about assessment, several others are directly relevant to assessment for learning, and as they are focused on classroom practice may be more attractive starting points. Particularly relevant are modules on starters and plenaries, questioning, explaining, thinking and learning objectives; and geography lessons are well represented in the video clips for these modules. These strategies support assessment in an informal way, based on professional judgement, so it is less easy to produce lots of paperwork about them, but probably as useful and more enjoyable to put into practice.

Where is formative assessment used?

We can look for formative assessment in practice in planning documentation, in action in the classroom, and in assessing students' work. You can use the checklists below to self-evaluate your own practice, or to observe others, remembering that you would be unlikely to find all these aspects going on at once.

Planning

In planning documentation, 'Where are we now?', 'What do I want them to learn?', 'How will I know when they've learnt it?' and 'What next?' decisions in the teacher's mind might be shown by:
- identifying previous learning or points carried forward from previous lessons,
- being clear about learning outcomes – not just 'what' but also 'how' and 'why',
- identifying assessment opportunities,

and annotations indicating:
- a change of pace,
- additions, supplementary/extension work,
- work planned but not covered,
- assessment information about individual/group successes and problems,
- evaluative comments, aspects needing development: where next?

Figure 4 indicates one way in which some of these aspects of the teacher's thinking can be recorded for future reference.

Action in the classroom

In the classroom the teacher starts by ensuring that students know 'what they have to do' and 'why they are doing it'. They will be making continuous assessments of learning by asking questions, discussing progress, giving feedback and identifying the next steps. Teaching, learning and assessment are therefore combined by a mixture of the following:
- sharing lesson objectives with students at start of the lesson
- sharing and exemplifying standards with students
- reflection on lesson objectives during and/or at the end of the lesson
- helping students understand 'how' they are learning
- intervention in students' learning to provide 'on the spot' teaching
- interventions or change of pace for the whole class
- feedback to individuals, groups, or the whole class, about aspects needing attention
- target setting for individuals, groups
- use of open/probing questions

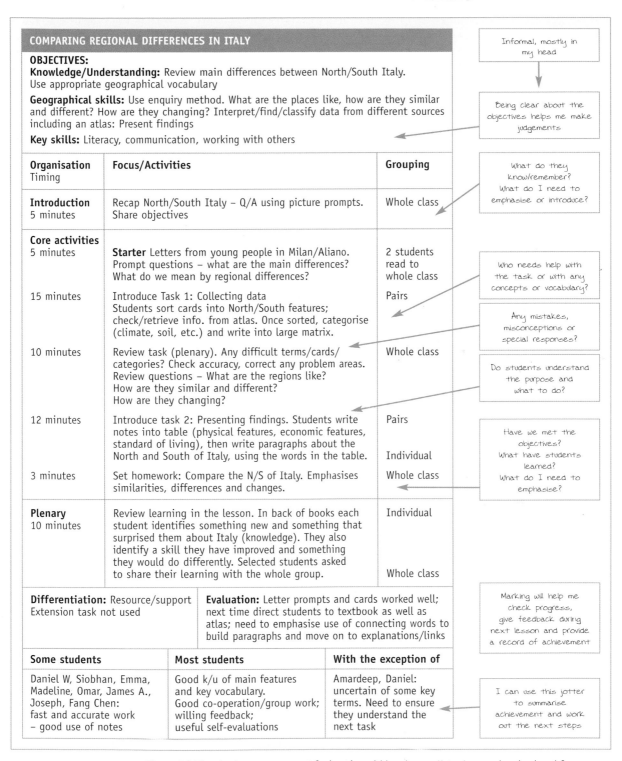

COMPARING REGIONAL DIFFERENCES IN ITALY

OBJECTIVES:
Knowledge/Understanding: Review main differences between North/South Italy. Use appropriate geographical vocabulary

Geographical skills: Use enquiry method. What are the places like, how are they similar and different? How are they changing? Interpret/find/classify data from different sources including an atlas: Present findings

Key skills: Literacy, communication, working with others

Organisation Timing	Focus/Activities	Grouping
Introduction 5 minutes	Recap North/South Italy – Q/A using picture prompts. Share objectives	Whole class
Core activities 5 minutes	**Starter** Letters from young people in Milan/Aliano. Prompt questions – what are the main differences? What do we mean by regional differences?	2 students read to whole class
15 minutes	Introduce Task 1: Collecting data Students sort cards into North/South features; check/retrieve info. from atlas. Once sorted, categorise (climate, soil, etc.) and write into large matrix.	Pairs
10 minutes	Review task (plenary). Any difficult terms/cards/ categories? Check accuracy, correct any problem areas. Review questions – What are the regions like? How are they similar and different? How are they changing?	Whole class
12 minutes	Introduce task 2: Presenting findings. Students write notes into table (physical features, economic features, standard of living), then write paragraphs about the North and South of Italy, using the words in the table.	Pairs Individual
3 minutes	Set homework: Compare the N/S of Italy. Emphasises similarities, differences and changes.	Whole class
Plenary 10 minutes	Review learning in the lesson. In back of books each student identifies something new and something that surprised them about Italy (knowledge). They also identify a skill they have improved and something they would do differently. Selected students asked to share their learning with the whole group.	Individual Whole class

Differentiation: Resource/support Extension task not used	**Evaluation:** Letter prompts and cards worked well; next time direct students to textbook as well as atlas; need to emphasise use of connecting words to build paragraphs and move on to explanations/links

Some students	Most students	With the exception of
Daniel W, Siobhan, Emma, Madeline, Omar, James A., Joseph, Fang Chen: fast and accurate work – good use of notes	Good k/u of main features and key vocabulary. Good co-operation/group work; willing feedback; useful self-evaluations	Amardeep, Daniel: uncertain of some key terms. Need to ensure they understand the next task

Handwritten notes (right margin):
- Informal, mostly in my head
- Being clear about the objectives helps me make judgements
- What do they know/remember? What do I need to emphasise or introduce?
- Who needs help with the task or with any concepts or vocabulary?
- Any mistakes, misconceptions or special responses?
- Do students understand the purpose and what to do?
- Have we met the objectives? What have students learned? What do I need to emphasise?
- Marking will help me check progress, give feedback during next lesson and provide a record of achievement
- I can use this jotter to summarise achievement and work out the next steps

Figure 4 | *Planning to use assessment for learning within a lesson. Note: Lesson plan developed from an original idea by Lucy Kirkham.*

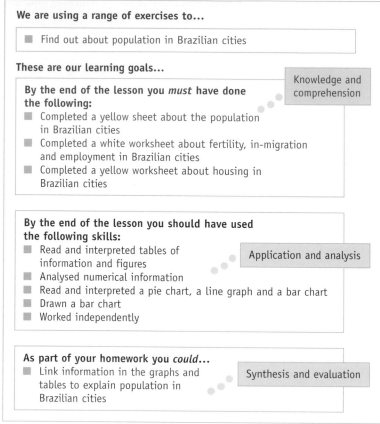

We are using a range of exercises to...

■ Find out about population in Brazilian cities

These are our learning goals...

By the end of the lesson you *must* have done the following:
■ Completed a yellow sheet about the population in Brazilian cities
■ Completed a white worksheet about fertility, in-migration and employment in Brazilian cities
■ Completed a yellow worksheet about housing in Brazilian cities

Knowledge and comprehension

By the end of the lesson you should have used the following skills:
■ Read and interpreted tables of information and figures
■ Analysed numerical information
■ Read and interpreted a pie chart, a line graph and a bar chart
■ Drawn a bar chart
■ Worked independently

Application and analysis

As part of your homework you *could*...
■ Link information in the graphs and tables to explain population in Brazilian cities

Synthesis and evaluation

Figure 5 | *Brazil – the 'big picture': learning briefing sheet. Source: Arber, 2003.*

■ provision of extension activities
■ using a variety of approaches to differentiation, thus providing access to activities
■ actively involving the students in the assessment process
■ involving students in self- and peer-assessment
■ teachers believing that all students can improve.

Sharing learning objectives with students

For effective learning to take place, learners need to understand what it is they are trying to achieve – and want to achieve it. Teachers can:
■ share learning objectives at the beginning of the lesson, and where appropriate during the lesson, in language that students can understand;
■ use these objectives as the basis for questioning and feedback during the plenary;
■ evaluate this feedback in relation to achievement of the objectives to inform next stages of planning.

Teachers frequently do this in their lessons, for example, by writing objectives on the board and referring to them throughout the lesson. Nicola Arber (Head of Sixth Form at Bournville School, Birmingham) regularly uses learning briefing sheets to inform students about a task and these are referred to during the lesson and reflected on at the end. In Figure 5 Nicola describes how they used to give students the 'big picture' in a research exercise she undertook as part of a Best Practice Research Scholarship (BPRS) (Arber, 2003).

Help students to recognise the standards

If work is to be assessed it is helpful to ensure that students know the expected standards. Andy Tsintas, a novice teacher, reflected, in an assignment on assessment for learning, on the importance of knowing the assessment criteria:

> *This was well demonstrated during a whole-school issues lecture at the beginning of the course where people were assessed on their ability to clap their hands. Some had been told the assessment criteria and scored much higher than those who had not* (Andy Tsintas' response to a PGCE assignment, University of Birmingham, 2002).

To make students aware of the expected standards a number of strategies can be used:
■ Show students work that has met criteria, with explanations of why
■ Give students clear success criteria that relate to the learning objectives
■ Model what your expectations should look like. For example, exemplify good standards of graphicacy on the board
■ Ensure that there are clear, shared expectations about the presentation of work

■ Provide displays of students' work that show processes as well as finished products.

Another novice teacher, Julia Sparkes, commented on the benefits and problems of 'front-ending' or sharing learning objectives and criteria with students:

> *A year 9 class were creating a tourist information brochure about the Mount Pinatubo eruption in 1991 as a levelled piece of work at the end of the topic. I went through what was expected of them, showed them some brochures from previous years and together we made a checklist of things that had to be included in the brochure. The outcomes were lower than I expected and, I felt, a poor reflection of their potential.*
>
> **Why were the outcomes disappointing?**
> *The brochures themselves were mostly well thought out and presented, with most of the criteria on the checklist included. However on analysing the results it became clear that they were all being let down by a section where they had to write an account of what happened before, during and after the eruption. The explanations were generally poor and on reflection I realised that I hadn't gone through how to achieve the highest scores sufficiently and given them a clear enough idea of what to aim for* (Julia Sparkes' response to a PGCE assignment, University of Birmingham, 2002).

Helping students to understand how they learn

A group of teachers, supported by the BPRS scheme, has investigated gender and achievement in geography (Wood, 2002; Bradley-Smith, 2002) (see Chapter 29). One area investigated was students' preferred learning styles (Gardner, 1999). It was found that students had a wide range of preferred learning styles, and that the process of identifying learning styles and discussing them with the students was beneficial in a number of ways. Teachers were encouraged to incorporate a wider variety of learning styles into their lessons and students had a chance to think more carefully about the process of learning, not just about completing the task. Perhaps most important was the dialogue between teacher and student about learning.

Nicola Arber uses a number of different ways to help students think about their learning and continues to explore ways of improving teaching, learning and assessment (Arber, 2003). For example, to help the students in a year 9 class to create a newspaper article about the future of industry in Japan she encouraged Julia Buckley, a novice teacher, to use the Progress Based Learning Model. This model involves the following prompts, which students and teacher use to review progress:

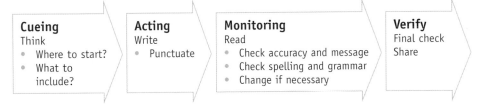

Cueing
Think
• Where to start?
• What to include?

Acting
Write
• Punctuate

Monitoring
Read
• Check accuracy and message
• Check spelling and grammar
• Change if necessary

Verify
Final check
Share

Julia commented on the value of using this model for supporting students' learning:

> *The model helped me plan the lesson. The students and I had a structure to follow and the lesson could then be divided into manageable sections. I could also plan 'sharing' time into the lesson.*
>
> *Students were therefore constantly assessing their own work and were given opportunities to read others' work. They were informing each other and diagnosing how they could improve their own and each other's work. Evidence of improvement could be seen when I compared their original plans (cueing) to the final outcomes* (Julia Buckley, response to a PGCE assignment, University of Birmingham, 2002).

The year 9 students Julia refers to had a clear framework within which their learning was taking place. The identification of the learning process was a major part of the planning for this piece of work and was emphasised throughout. Students were being 'taught' about their own learning and were given a language and skills that most of them used effectively. The overall quality of their work was also improved.

Provide feedback

Feedback is a complex and often sensitive issue as it can be seen as a comment on the individual not on their performance in a task. We have all experienced unintended effects of feedback which can result in a number of different responses. Four types of responses have been identified for when students are told there is a gap between their current performance and what is expected. Some students are motivated and attempt to reach the expected standard, while others are de-motivated and give up trying to improve. A third response is to change the standard (either up or down) to make it more achievable, and a final response is to deny there is a gap at all, so they just carry on as before.

Clearly it is helpful if students adopt the first approach as standards should be made achievable. Black and Wiliam (1998b) found that low-achieving students could make the greatest improvements if given appropriate help. Many students in the LEARN project expressed their preference for oral feedback (Weeden and Winter, 1999). It is certainly worth finding ways of providing oral as well as written feedback whenever possible.

Black and Wiliam also report that giving grades and comments can be less effective in improving performance than giving comments by themselves. What is important here is that, to be formative, comments need to focus on performance in learning and how to improve, not merely give students praise ('good work') or criticism ('try harder'), neither of which give any guidance about how to change.

Nazan Helvaci, a novice teacher, reflected on the use of feedback as follows:

> When I marked the summative tests I used five different methods to feedback to the students:
>
> 1. I gave them a mark out of the total, so they could see where they had lost marks for each question and the total number of marks they had got right
> 2. I gave them a grade A/B/C according to their percentage. I did this because some students relate better to an 'A' than they do to 70% as they know 'A' is good even if they don't know what a percentage is
> 3. I had to give them a National Curriculum level
> 4. I wrote a comment that stated how pleased I was with their work and where they could have improved so that they have it to refer back to and so know how I had marked them
> 5. Finally I gave the whole class oral feedback on the overall strengths and weaknesses of the test results and I gave them about ten minutes to look at their papers and confer with me if they had any issues to raise (Nazan Helvaci, response to a PGCE assignment, University of Birmingham, 2002).

What it is important to recognise here is that types of feedback 1, 2 and 3 are essentially summative in nature and do not help students to improve. Their purpose is as a record of performance on this particular assignment. Indeed they might well get in the way of improvement if the students focus on them rather than the feedback in 4 and 5. In fact, it is bad practice to use national curriculum levels for individual pieces of work. They do not give precise criteria for judgements. They are intended for use at the end of the key stage as 'best fit' statements that reflect students, overall performance. Unfortunately many schools are using them in totally inappropriate ways. It is not possible to subdivide them into part levels accurately enough to record performance every half term or term.

In contrast, 4 and 5 are formative and should help students in the future. This is because there is the beginning of a dialogue about current performance and how to improve. The key to effective feedback is that it is constructive rather than simply positive, identifying what the student has done well, what needs to be done to improve, and how to do it. Howes and Hopkin illustrate how written *comments on each student's work* can provide appropriate guidance. They suggest that 'these [written comments] are an essential part of formative assessment and should describe the strengths and weaknesses of the work and offer suggestions for future improvement (which could be in the form of target setting)' (Howes and Hopkin, 2000, p. 148). They go on to give some exemplar comments from a key stage 3 investigation for students working at level 5/6:

> ■ *You have made good use of wide-ranging specific examples of volcanoes*
> ■ *You should aim to make more use of informative labelled diagrams in future*
> ■ *You have described the features and causes of volcanoes but you needed to say more about the hazard which they present to people*
> ■ *You have made good use of ICT and your work shows promising written language skills*
> (Howes and Hopkin, 2000, p. 148).

Clarke (2000) suggests that for teachers to be able to give effective feedback they need to be clear about intentions for learning. These must be shared with students and can then form the basis of written feedback by highlighting sections of work that meet the intention. Clarke's work with younger students suggests that three correct intentions and one improvement, identified by an arrow, is sufficient at any one time. The arrow should have a 'closing the gap' comment by it. This strategy is exemplified for a student's

Figure 6 | Marking work using 'Closing the gap' comments. Adapted from Clarke, 2000.

The **Learning intentions** were shared with the students beforehand. They emphasised:

■ use of data (numbers should be used)

■ correct description and explanation of patterns

■ comparison statements using linking words

The prompts are linked to the learning intentions.

1. Reminder prompt
Use percentages to give a more precise answer, rather than 'lots more' or 'most'

2. Scaffolded prompt
Can you describe the differences in the population patterns in Senegal and France? What shape are the population pyramids?

Compare Senegal and France under the following headings:
■ Population structure
■ Employment structure

In Senegal there seems to be lots more kids than there is adults because they don't have protection from pregnancies and there is a low life span so there isn't many old people. Most of the jobs are primary like farming or mining but in France it is more evened out as to the population with people living until they are 70+ most people in France have a tertiary job in a service because there is a lot of people.

Positive comments
You have shown you can read the data and have used your knowledge to give reasons for the patterns.

You have explained and justified your statements using words such as 'because' and 'so'.

You have started to compare the countries by using the word 'but'.

3. Example prompt
You could make the comparison clearer by using linking words and by not mixing up population or economic structure in the same sentence.

In Senegal there are ... people over 50 whereas in France there are ...

In France ... % work in ... industries while in Senegal most (...%) jobs are ... such as ...

response to a GCSE question (Figure 6). Teachers of older students will need to identify the optimum number of comments on a piece of work, but it is probably better to keep it small. One important feature of this method of feedback is that students have to respond to the comments. It is probably best if this is done within class, so time will need to be set aside.

Clarke goes on to suggest that spelling should be corrected only after the geography has been worked on. If grades need to be given, record them in a mark book, not on the work, although it is possible to give them to students after the work has been discussed. This method of written comments removes the need for long comments at the end of work.

The group of teachers working with Clarke found that they used three types of 'closing the gap' prompts:

1. Reminder prompt (often enough for higher attainers)
    * What is the purpose of congestion charges?
2. Scaffolded prompt
    * What effect will congestion charges have on traffic?
3. Example prompt
    Choose a phrase:
    * congestion charges will reduce traffic because ...
    * congestion charges will increase traffic because ...
    * congestion charges will have no effect on traffic because ...

They suggest that example prompts were the most successful with younger students (apart from the highest achievers). 'One of the outcomes ... was that children often decided on their own word or phrase if given some examples. The modelling of examples appears to encourage children to think of their own improvement more easily' (Clarke, 2000, p. 42).

Improving questioning

An area that Black and Wiliam (1998b) identified as one that needed improvement in many classrooms was questioning. There is no doubt that skilled questioning is one characteristic of good teaching.

One common way of categorising questions is closed versus open; closed questions requiring a single answer, and open questions eliciting a range of possible answers. Closed questions are often thought to be 'bad' and open 'good', yet there is clearly a place for both so some people prefer the terms 'narrow' and 'broad'. Whichever terms you use, asking a range of different types of question is good practice, including some that demand thought as well as those that test observation or recall. Skilled questioners also sometimes allow time for students to respond, especially for 'thought' questions, ask follow-up questions and distribute questions around the class.

Try these top ten questioning tactics to support your formative assessment:

1. Ask broad as well as narrow questions (open as well as closed).
2. Develop a range of stock open/broad question stems, e.g. What have you come up with?, How did you do it?, Are there any other solutions/answers?
3. Sometimes ask supplementary/follow-up questions.
4. Develop a range of stock supplementary questions, e.g. Go on ..., Say a bit more ..., Why ...?, Can you explain ...?
5. Target questions to make sure that students of all abilities are involved and contribute, or find other ways such as working in pairs.
6. Allow some thinking time for students before they respond.
7. Plan to ask some thought questions; plan some specific questions in advance.

Photo: Bananastock Ltd.

8. Try to increase the level of demand of your questions through the session/lesson.
9. Use questions to help structure students' investigations, e.g. the six W's (Who, What, Where, Why, When, hoW).
10. Try some question games, e.g. 'Work out the questions which match these answers' for review work.

Sheila King (1999) provides further guidance on types of questions and questioning strategies.

Asking questions has a clear link with geography's enquiry focus. The level descriptions explicitly refer to questioning, so geography teachers have an obligation to develop students' own questioning skills, particularly if they are to access higher levels of attainment.

Elizabeth Rynne (2000) has described how she involved her students in the design of their own fieldwork. She argues that by participating in this way their understanding of the enquiry process increases and more is achieved than just enabling them to be successful in carrying out the mechanics of data collection and analysis. She also encouraged them to use self- and peer-assessment as part of the process, thus utilising one of the strategies that Black and Wiliam (1998a) found was most effective in raising performance.

Involving students in self- and peer-assessment

In those cases where formative assessment was used effectively, Black and Wiliam found gains in attainment that were accompanied by changes in classroom management and teaching. The gains were also dependent on a philosophy of students accepting some responsibility for improving their own learning (Hamson and Sutton, 2000, p. 8).

Several different strategies can be used to involve students in self- and peer-assessment, such as:

- Giving students opportunities to talk about what they have learned, and what they have found difficult, using the learning objectives as a focus
- Encouraging students to work/discuss together, focusing upon how to improve
- Asking students to explain the steps in their thinking (How did you get that answer?)
- Giving opportunities for students to reflect upon their learning and to identify where they still have difficulties
- Identifying, with students, the next steps in learning.

A group of BPRS teachers in Staffordshire have developed a framework that helps students understand how to improve their work by giving better descriptions and explanations (Figure 7). The teachers described how they used it with groups of higher achievers and subsequently adapted it for use with low achievers (George *et al.*, 2002; Clarke *et al.*, 2003).

The process helps students to clarify expected standards, as their comments reveal. Before the process a student described a best piece of work as follows: 'It's long, it's neat and it is coloured nicely', while a piece they weren't satisfied with was 'not neatly written and … not spelt very well'. Afterwards the comments reflected better understanding: 'I now understand how I can get better and better'; and 'I now know the difference between an explanation and a description'.

Hamson and Sutton (2000) describe how teachers at The Garendon High School have developed a range of assessment tasks that involve students in self-assessment:

> At the end of each assessment task students are required to set one geography-specific and usually one generic target for the next assessment task. The process of self-assessment and target setting is assisted by record sheets which are made available to students at the beginning of a particular assessment. Significantly, as a result of ongoing formative evaluation, the format of the record sheet has evolved and this has made the process of self-assessment and target setting more manageable for teachers (Hamson and Sutton, 2000, p. 9).

Hamson and Sutton continue by describing how the scheme helps students to become more responsible for their own learning:

> In each assessment task, students are made aware of the basis on which they will be assessed. These criteria are based on the level descriptions but written in student friendly language. This means that for each assessment, as well as the specific target previously identified for that student, all students are given the targets or criteria from which they can achieve the highest levels. As they work, these criteria allow them to assess their own work accurately and identify their specific target(s) for future assessments. Students use phrases like 'I can describe patterns', 'I can explain processes', 'I need to substantiate my conclusions', and use and understand these when they make comments on their reports for their parents (Hamson and Sutton, 2000, p. 11).

The BPRS teachers suggest a series of steps for using the model with students (George *et al.*, 2002):

1. Set a task which has both description and explanation in its writing.
2. Mark the work, giving it a stage of the model, but keep it to yourself for the moment.
3. With the group, discuss what makes a good piece of writing, then ask them to record what you have discussed.
4. Relate the model of students' writing to the discussion and then let them have a go at marking their own work.
5. Select four pieces of work from the class, one for each stage and encourage the students to identify which stage they are at and why.
6. Ask the students to once again set a stage for their own writing.
7. Ask the students to set targets for the next piece of work.
8. Set another piece of work.
9. Mark the work, and/or get the students to mark each other's work (peer assessment). Identify (or get the students to) the stage and choose four examples of improved work to show how the model can help their writing.
10. Set targets (you and/or the students) for the next piece of work.

The approach shown above is one way that is appropriate for use in the context of the Garendon High School – as the example of the Progress Learning Model described earlier was appropriate for Bournville School. What is important in both contexts is that the teachers are involving the students in a dialogue about their learning.

A practical way of helping students to start using self-assessment effectively in the classroom is to use the concept of traffic lights (red, amber and green) (Black *et al.*, 2002). The students are asked to identify when they have not understood something (red), have partially understood it (amber), and have understood it clearly (green). The next steps in learning can then be identified for each of these different groups with the students themselves providing peer support for others' learning.

Teachers believing that students can improve

If performance is to be raised teachers have to believe that their students can improve. There is an unfortunate legacy in England, perhaps supported by the culture of

	Better explanation			Better description
	Explaining that one feature is caused by another (e.g. a settlement began in the place because there was a bridge over a river; a place is hot throughout the year because it is close to the Equator; the beach was polluted because of sewage from the coastal resort)	Stage 1	Extremes 	Using accurate place names to identify locations and using extremes like hard/soft; hilly/flat; wet/dry; rich/poor to describe features and places
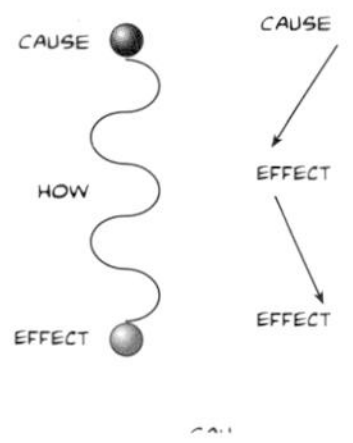	Explaining how one feature is caused by another or how one feature causes another (e.g. a settlement began because businesses were set up to serve the trade using the bridge over the river)	Stage 2	Different types 	Recognising different types of places using words like warm, cool, freezing and very hot as well as hot and cold; using terms like semi-detached, detached, and terraced and flats to describe different dwellings
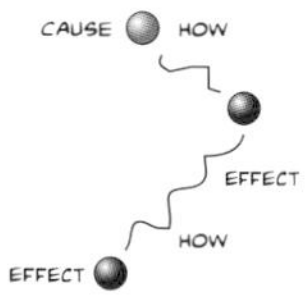	Explaining how one feature causes another and then how that feature causes another (e.g. an increase in the number of tourists to the resort led to a big increase in waste including sewage and this was released into the sea because it was cheaper than treating it)	Stage 3	Comparisons 	Using numbers to compare features (e.g. twice as many people, half the range of temperature) and places and describing the differences within places
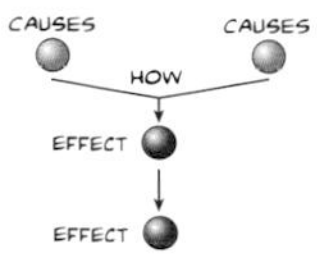	Explaining how two causes work together to create one feature which then causes another (e.g. the Sun's rays are more concentrated when the Sun is overhead at the Equator and as the Sun moves round the Earth the position of the Sun in the sky does not change very much, so it is very hot throughout the year)	Stage 4	Ratios and patterns 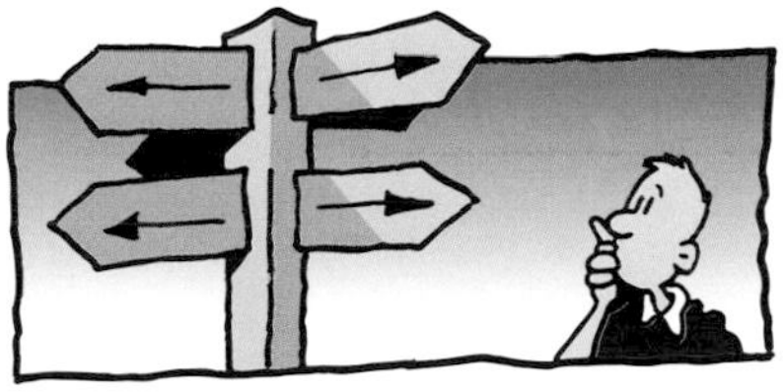	Grouping descriptions to give a sense of a whole place and using terms that combine ideas like population density, converge and diverge, and humidity to describe features and places

Figure 7 | *A model for evaluating students' writing. Source: George et al., 2002.*

'measurement', that intelligence is fixed. Teachers talk about high- and low-achievers without always recognising that context and labelling can affect self-esteem and performance.

David Leat and Julie McGrane (2000), in describing how they set about trying to assess students' thinking in geography, demonstrate their belief in student improvement by emphasising the importance of finding effective ways to 'close the gap between currnt and desirable performance'.

> *This is what target setting has to be about. However it only works if you can begin to translate the desire for better grades into achievable steps for students. The teacher must be able to recognise what interventions will encourage improvements in students' performance, whilst creating an environment in which students value this process and understand its purpose ... The argument that we have been stressing here has three elements. First, activities which promote thinking tend to make students' thinking more visible and explicit. Second, once you have drawn students' thinking out, you can assess its quality in terms of levels and individual performance. Third, you can use this information to help close the gap between current performance and potential performance. This is an immensely powerful notion around which to build your assessment practice, arguably a good theory* (Leat and McGrane, 2000, pp. 6-7).

There are many ways that geography teachers can help students to learn more successfully. Being clear that every student can improve and learn and communicating this to them is a crucial starting point that establishes a culture for success in the classroom. Identify small steps in learning to enable students to see and monitor their own progress, thus building confidence and self-esteem. Providing opportunities and encouragement for students to explain their thinking and reasoning within a secure classroom ethos helps them to understand their own learning and thus develop the ability to apply this learning to different situations in the future.

Some final thoughts

Black and Wiliam's research provides a helpful summary of the key features that support formative assessment; it is not difficult to see that they fit in closely with what we know about good practice in teaching and learning, especially the active involvement of students:

> *Improving learning through assessment depends on five, deceptively simple, key factors:*
>
> 1. *giving effective feedback to students;*
> 2. *the active involvement of students in their own learning;*
> 3. *adjusting teaching to take account of the results of assessment;*
> 4. *recognising the influence assessment has on the motivation and self-esteem of students, both of which are crucial influences on learning;*
> 5. *enabling students to be able to assess themselves and understand how to improve* (Assessment Reform Group, 1999, pp. 4-5).

Related publications from the Geographical Association:
- Hopkin, J., Telfer, S. and Butt, G. (eds) (2000) (see below)
- 'Assessment Matters' – a regular feature in the GA's secondary journal *Teaching Geography*.
- Rawling, E. (2002) (see below)

Implications for practice

This chapter provides a number of suggestions about ways of improving formative assessment. Suggestions for practical strategies that can be used in your classroom and department to take assessment for learning forward are as follows:

		For example
In your planning	Clarify learning objectives ■ for the unit of work (e.g. like QCA Schemes of Work) ■ for the lesson (very specific objectives)	■ To know about ... ■ To understand ... ■ To be able to ... ■ To express an opinion about ...
Start of lessons	Share learning objective(s) with students Get learning objectives written up Try to keep the learning objective and the task separate Share success criteria to explain what students are aiming for	■ What I want you to learn ... ■ So by the end of the lesson ... ■ What I'm looking for is ... ■ For example you'll need to ... ■ This is because ...
During lessons	Use a range of questions Show students what the criteria look like Show students what good work looks like Revisit the learning objectives during the lesson, e.g. through discussion/questioning Try to focus on a group or a few students for feedback in more depth	■ Plan some questions ■ Go for a range of questions: include some more open questions, follow-up/probing questions for individuals, groups ■ Give students time to answer
End of lessons	Reflect back on learning objectives: What did we learn? Feedback: How well? Next time ...	■ Reflect back: What were the main things we learned? Which were the difficult bits? How did we tackle it? What helped us to learn? How can we improve ■ As whole class, or as groups, or as pairs: evaluation – thinking skills – key skills
Marking (during or after)	Focus on the learning objective Focus on strengths/areas for development: the qualities of the work Feedback information: comments which show how to 'close the gap' with targets, make improvements Extended comments more helpful than marks and grades only	■ Give specific/focused praise and highlight areas for improvement ('I like the way you ...' 'Next time, you need to ...') ■ Show how improvements could be made ■ Concentrate on learning in geography, rather than in literacy or ICT, for example
As co-ordinator	Jointly plan a key assessment opportunity for each unit or work Get year groups to use these to reflect on students' progress over each unit Ask each year group to collect a sample of students' work which identifies their (subject) attainments Relate your students' work to standards of attainment	■ Collect this information to help you monitor students' progress in geography over the key stage, and evaluate the effectiveness of your planning and teaching ■ Use examples of students' work from the QCA website
Policy	Make clear the purposes of assessment in the short and longer term	■ Consider separating formative and summative purposes in the policy ■ Consider developing student self-assessment
Training	What does assessment look like?	■ Plan together if possible ■ Observe each other's lessons ■ In-service training

References

Print

Arber, N. (2003) 'Assessment for Learning', *Teaching Geography*, 28, 1, pp. 42-6.

Assessment Reform Group (1999) *Assessment for Learning: Beyond the black box*. Cambridge: University of Cambridge School of Education.

Assessment Reform Group (2002a) *Ten Principles of Assessment for Learning* (available online: www.assessment-reform-group.org.uk).

Assessment Reform Group (2002b) *Testing, Learning and Motivation*. Cambridge: University of Cambridge School of Education.

Black, P. and Wiliam, D. (1998a) 'Assessment and classroom learning', *Assessment in Education* 5, 1, pp. 7-74.

Black, P. and Wiliam, D. (1998b) *Inside the Black Box: Raising standards through classroom assessment*. London: School of Education, Kings College.

Black, P., Harrison, C., Lee, C., Marshall, B. and Wiliam, D. (2002) *Working Inside the Black Box: Assessment for learning in the classroom*. London: School of Education, Kings College.

Black, P., Harrison, C., Lee, C., Marshall, B. and Wiliam, D. (2003) *Assessment for Learning: Putting it into Practice*. Maidenhead: Open University Press.

Bradley-Smith, P. (2002) 'Closing the gender gap in geography: update 2 – "invisible girls"', *Teaching Geography*, 27, 3, pp. 143-6.

Butt, G. (2002) *Reflective Teaching of Geography 11-18*. London: Continuum.

Butt, G., Lambert, D. and Telfer, S. (1995) *Assessment Works: Approaches to assessment in geography at key stages 1, 2 and 3*. Sheffield: Geographical Association.

Clarke, S. (1998) *Targeting Assessment in the Primary Classroom*. London: Hodder and Stoughton. (Includes excellent general advice, especially on sharing objectives, giving feedback and setting targets.)

Clarke, S. (2000) 'Getting it right – distance marking as accessible and effective feedback in the primary classroom' in Askew, S. (ed) *Feedback for Learning*. London: Routledge Falmer, pp. 32-45.

Clarke, S. (2001) *Unlocking Formative Assessment*. London: Hodder and Stoughton.

DfES (2002) *Key Stage 3 Strategy: Training materials for the Foundation Subjects*. London: HMSO.

DfES (2004) *Key Stage 3 Strategy: Assessment for Learning, whole-school training materials*. London: HMSO.

Gardner, H. (1999) *Intelligence Reframed: Multiple intelligences for the 21st century*. New York: Basic Books.

George, J., Clarke, J., Davies, P. and Durbin, C. (2002) 'Helping students to get better at geographical writing', *Teaching Geography*, 27, 4, pp. 156-60.

Hamson, R. and Sutton, A. (2000) 'Target setting at key stage 3', *Teaching Geography*, 25, 1, pp. 8-11.

Hopkin, J. (2000) 'Assessment for learning in geography', *Teaching Geography*, 25, 1, pp. 42-3.

Hopkin, J., Telfer, S. and Butt, G. (eds) (2000) *Assessment in Practice: Raising standards in secondary geography*. Sheffield: Geographical Association.

Howes, N. and Hopkin, J. (2000) 'Improving formative assessment in geography', *Teaching Geography*, 25, 3, pp. 147-9.

King, M. (1998) *The Diagnostic Value of Self-assessment in Geography at Key Stage 4*, (available online: www.gtce.org.uk/research/standcasestud.asp).

King, S. (1999) 'Using questions to promote learning', *Teaching Geography*, 24, 4, pp. 169-72.

Lambert, D. (2002) 'Using assessment to support learning' in Smith, M. (ed) *Teaching Geography in Secondary Schools*. London: Routledge Falmer, pp. 123-33.

Lambert, D. and Balderstone, D. (2000) *Learning to Teach Geography in Secondary Schools*. London: Routledge Falmer.

Lambert, D. and Lines, D. (2000) *Understanding Assessment: Purposes, perceptions, practices*. London: Routledge Falmer.

Leat, D. and McGrane, J. (2000) 'Diagnostic and formative assessment of students' thinking', *Teaching Geography*, 25, 1, pp. 4-7.

Ofsted (1998) *Secondary Education in England 1993-1997*. London: Ofsted.

Ofsted (2004) *Standards and Quality 2002/03. The annual report of Her Majesty's Chief Inspector of Schools.* London: Ofsted.

Rawling, E. (2002) *Changing the Subject: The impact of national policy on school geography 1980-2000.* Sheffield: Geographical Association.

Rynne, E. (2000) 'Year 9 students design fieldwork', *Teaching Geography*, 25, 2, pp. 61-5.

Sadler, D. R. (1989) 'Formative assessment and the design of instructional systems', *Instructional Science* 18, pp. 119-44.

Stobart, G. and Gipps, C. (1997) *Assessment: A teacher's guide to the issues* (third edition). London: Hodder and Stoughton.

Weeden, P. and Winter, J. (1999) *The LEARN Project: Report for QCA.* London: QCA (available online: www.qca.org.uk/ca/5-14/afl).

Weeden, P., Winter, J. and Broadfoot, P. (2002) *Assessment: What's in it for schools?* London: Routledge Falmer.

Wood, P. (2002) 'Closing the gender gap in geography: update 1', *Teaching Geography*, 27, 1, pp. 41-3.

Electronic

Assessment Reform Group – www.assessment-reform-group.org.uk/

The Association for Achievement and Improvement though Assessment (AAIA) – www.aaia.org.uk

General Teaching Council for England (for case studies) – www.gtce.org.uk/

DfES Key Stage 3 Strategy – www.standards.dfes.gov.uk/keystage3/

DfES – Schemes of Work for KS3 – www.standards.dfes.gov.uk/schemes/

National Curriculum Online – www.nc.uk.net/

National Curriculum in Action (QCA exemplification) – www.ncaction.org.uk/

Qualifications and Curriculum Authority – www.qca.org.uk/

Chapter 33

Target setting and target getting in geography

Linda Thompson

Before reading this chapter consider the following questions:

■ How does your department go about setting individual student and cohort targets in key stages 3 and 4?

■ What school, local authority and national data do you use in your department to inform target setting?

■ How does your department go about translating its numerical targets into curricular targets which can have a positive impact on teaching and learning?

When anyone is trying to learn, feedback about the effort has three elements: recognition of the **desired goal***, evidence about* **present position***, and some understanding of a* **way to close** *the* gap *between the two. All three must be understood to some degree by anyone before he or she can take action to improve learning* (Sadler cited in Black *et al.*, 2003).

The setting of targets is something from which there is no escape in the modern world. If students, and teachers, are to reach their 'desired goals' then it is essential for them to determine their 'present position' and to understand ways in which they might 'close the gap' between the two. This chapter explores the processes of target setting and target getting in secondary school geography, for both teachers and their students. To do this it will cover both the setting of numerical targets, and even more importantly, curricular targets, and the strategies that can be used to help students achieve them.

There is no doubt that many teachers find the process of target setting daunting. Similarly many feel threatened by thoughts that numerical target setting data may be misused or interpreted out of context or without consultation. Despite these misgivings the setting of individual student and cohort targets, when used to inform assessment for learning processes, and developed and utilised within a culture that is positive, supportive and consultative, can be of great benefit to both teachers and students.

National statutory requirements for school targets

Statutory target setting was introduced to schools in England and Wales in 1998 (for key stages 2 and 4) and in 2001 for key stage 3. The government sees national, local authority (LA) and school numerical targets as an essential part of its commitment to

raising educational standards for all children. The government states that target setting establishes specific measurable goals for improved student performance with the intention that schools should use assessment and other performance data to:
- predict student potential
- focus effort on raising attainment
- support school improvement initiatives.

Schools must currently set and publish the following statutory numerical targets:
- **Key stage 3**
  - the proportion of students expecting to achieve level 5+ in English, mathematics, science and ICT by the end of the key stage
- **Key stage 4**
  - the proportion of 15-year-olds expected to achieve five or more A*-C GCSEs or equivalent
    - an average points score.

A school's governing body is required to report statutory targets to the LA in December each year (for the year 8 and year 10 cohorts) thus allowing the school five terms for action.

As far as statutory targets are concerned, only key stage 4 GCSE/GNVQ geography results contribute to the proportion of students achieving five or more A*-C GCSEs or equivalent and the average points score. No discrete geography targets are required. At key stage 3 only the core subjects must set targets.

Increasingly though, schools generate internal targets for all subjects at key stages 3 and 4. In both instances performance data from core subject statutory tests can prove very useful in informing the setting of such targets.

What data are available to inform target setting in geography?

There is now a wealth of national, local (e.g. LA) and internal information available to schools, and to individual subject areas, which provides performance data for their students. These data are generated from statutory end-of-key-stage assessments, external examinations and a range of school-based assessments. It is important that leaders and teachers of geography are fully aware of the data available to support target setting and how they can be put to good use.

Data that can usefully inform target setting in geography departments include:
- The Autumn Package (Figure 1)
- The Performance and Asssessment (PANDA) reports which includes subject difference or 'residual' data for GCSEs
- End-of-key-stage 2 and key stage 3 statutory test results in English, mathematics and science
- Fischer Family Trust analyses which use a database of historical performance data (covering all key stages) and match this to the PLASC (Pupil Level Annual School Census) data collected from schools. Data is available to schools in LAs which belong to the project, and provides student level indicators for GCSE Geography.
- Commercial forecasting packages such as MIDYIS (years 7, 8 or 9) and YELLIS (year 11)
- NFER CAT tests scores (often carried out in the year of entry)
- Teacher assessments in geography (see Chapter 34)
- Departmental historical data.

National summary of results for all subjects at key stages 3 and 4 which enables departments to compare their own performance with the most recent national results and national results for previous years.

National Value-added Lines compare students' results from one key stage to the next. These are available for geography at key stage 4 and can be used by teachers to evaluate progress made by previous cohorts, and help establish expectations about what current students might achieve at the end of year 11. Only core subject information is available at key stage 3.

Benchmark tables allow schools to make comparisons of their performance with similar schools, on the basis of similar free school meals eligibility and prior attainment. PANDA reports also contain benchmark information specific to each school.

Progress charts (see below) are based on the same matched student data as the value-added lines relating performance in one key stage to a later key stage. However, they represent the relationship in a different way, showing the range of outcomes achieved by students with similar scores at the end of the previous key stage. Although retrospective, they are a useful aid in establishing future expectations for individual students.

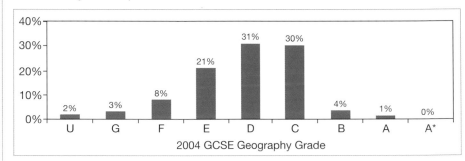

The distribution of performance in geography at GCSE in 2004 for students achieving an average points score of more than 31 and less than 33.

The **Pupil Achievement Tracker** software (from the DfES) allows schools to analyse their own student performance data against national performance data published in the Autumn Package.

Figure 1 | *Building a picture of performance with the Autumn Package. Note: A booklet explaining how to get the most out of the Autumn Package, and information about it and the Student Achievement Tracker is available from the Standards website.*

How might a geography department set targets?

By using the data available to it, a geography department can arrive at challenging but realistic targets for individual students at key stages 3 and 4. It can be advantageous to set up a tracking document, ideally as part of the school management information system but alternatively using a spreadsheet, to record student data as it accumulates and to allow it to be processed and graphed.

The extract shown in Figure 2 is from a year 11 GCSE group spreadsheet. This shows some of the data a geography department might use to set targets and includes:

- the key stage 3 teacher assessment in geography;
- forecasts based on end-of-key-stage 3 statutory tests, Fischer Family Trust data and a commercial package;
- a teacher-predicted grade;
- grades generated from student assessments over the course of key stage 4.

Figure 3, taken from a year 9 class spreadsheet, shows student attributes, for example English as an additional language; key stage 2 core subject test data; key stage 3 English and geography test data; and department-generated targets for each student and progress made towards these when compared with key stage 2 average points scores.

Forename	KS3 geography level	KS3 core subject test average	Fischer Family Trust forecast	GCSE target set Autumn 03	Y10 exam grade June 04	Y11 exam grade Jan 05	Coursework grade (25%)
Kharoun	6	6.00	B	A	C	B	A
Shane	5	5.33	C	B	C	C	B
Noah	6	5.33	C	B	D	C	C
Jake	4	5.67	B	B	C	B	C
Ismail Ali	5	5.00	D	C	D	D	C
Thomas	6	5.33	C	B	C	C	C
Aiden	5	5.33	C	B	C	B	B

Figure 2 | *Spreadsheet showing a range of predicted and forecasted GCSE grades for individual students.*

Surname	Forename	EAL	FSM	KS2 Rd Level	KS2 Wr Level	KS2 En Level	KS2 Ma Level	KS2 Sc Level	KS2 APS	Y8 Gg TA	Y8 Gg points	Y8 En test	KS3 Gg forecast	KS3 Gg target	Progress
Dear	Aaron	N	Y	5	4	4	4	4	27	5	33	5	5	5	6
Dixon	Connor	N	N	4	3	4	5	4	29	4	27	4	5	5	-2
Eggleton	Luke	N	N	5	5	5	4	5	31	5	33	6	5	6	2
Evans	Laura	N	N	4	4	4	4	4	27	5	33	4	5	5	6
Gambrill	Brad	N	N	5	5	5	4	4	29	5	33	5	5	5	4
Goodwin	Leisha	N	Y	3	3	3	4	5	27	4	27	4	5	5	0
Groh	Naria	Y	N	4	4	4	4	4	27	5	33	5	5	6	6
Groves	Kelly	N	N	4	3	4	3	4	25	5	33	5	5	5	8

Figure 3 | *Spreadsheet showing individual student data for a year 9 geography class.*

The individual targets from this process can then be aggregated to arrive at an indication of overall targets for a department and for individual teachers within departments. Figure 4 shows a spreadsheet extract containing a range of aggregated data from which targets can be derived. This was calculated using individual student GCSE spreadsheet information like that shown in Figure 2 together with historical data for this department. It is clear that, in this department's case, the key stage 2 and YELLIS forecasts for A*-C (columns 3 and 7) do not provide challenging targets as the Fischer Family Trust forecasts and departmental historical data (columns 5 and 8) are much higher at 73% and 76%. A realistic but challenging cohort target for this department, based on aggregated individual student targets, has been set at 80% (column 11).

It is important that cohort targets are created through the aggregation of individual targets and not the other way around, i.e. individual targets should not be an artificial dis-aggregation of a cohort target. However, if geography teachers are genuinely to engage in cycles of improvement it is also valuable for them to compare their own department's performance with other similar schools. This can lead to a significant re-think of cohort targets and challenge teachers about the targets they are setting for the individuals which make up the cohort if it becomes apparent that their expectations of students could be higher. This is explored further in the following sections.

Grade	Forecast based on year 6 CAT tests		Forecast based on Fischer Family Trust data		YELLIS forecast (year 9)		Gg GCSE 3 year rolling mean (historic)		Teacher targets set at start of year 10		National GCSE results 2003	
	No of students	%	No of students	%	No of students	%	%	No of students	No of students	%		
A*	0	0	3	3	2	2	8	-	6	5	7.3	-
A	2	2	29	26	6	5	20	-	13	12	13.3	-
B	19	18	31	28	22	20	30	-	32	29	16.8	-
C	42	38	17	15	25	23	18	-	37	34	23.9	-
D	26	24	14	13	31	28	12	-	18	16	16.1	-
E	16	15	11	10	17	15	7	-	3	3	10.1	-
F	6	6	3	3	6	5	4	-	1	1	6.2	-
G	0	0	3	3	1	1	1	-	0	0	3.4	-
U	0	0	0	0	0	0	0	-	0	0	2.9	-
	%A*-G	100	%A*-G	100	%A*-G	100	%A*-G	100	%A*-G	100	%A*-G	97.1
	%A*-C	57	%A*-C	73	%A*-C	50	%A*-C	76	%A*-C	80	%A*-C	61.3

Figure 4 | *Predicted grades for a whole GCSE Geography cohort, prepared using Excel.*

Having constructed a spreadsheet it is then easy to incorporate any additional information as and when it becomes available. To make such data more readily accessible and to facilitate analysis, the data can quickly be graphed. This then becomes a useful tool which can be used to continuously monitor progress towards targets. Figure 5 shows the cohort data from Figure 4 as a bar chart, with the internal year 10 examination results added. It shows at a glance that students are still falling significantly short of the more challenging targets generated by the three-year rolling mean for the department and the Fischer Family Trust-based forecast.

Although setting up spreadsheets and generating charts may be initially time-consuming, once this is completed for one cohort it can be copied and used for successive cohorts simply by in-putting data for the next cohort the following year.

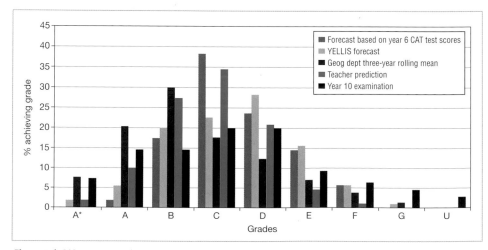

Figure 5 | *GCSE target setting and tracking data for a cohort at the end of year 10.*

Stage 1: How well is the department doing?
Building a picture of your department's performance
- How do our results compare with other subjects in my school?
- What is the three-year trend for our results, *e.g. A*-C passes at GCSE or level 5+ at key stage 3 ... and how does it compare with other subjects?*
- Do all students perform equally well ... What about gender, different ability groups, students from different ethnic backgrounds, classes with different teachers?

Figure 7 shows a departmental spreadsheet analysis of students' performance in geography in one cohort, when compared with their other GCSE results. It shows clearly that the lowest achieving students performed much better overall in their other GCSEs than they did in geography and presents an issue that the department wants to resolve.

Stage 2: How do we compare with geography departments in other schools?
Broadening the picture of your department's performance
- The *Autumn Package* provides benchmark data which allows national comparisons of GCSE and key stage 3 results to be made with geography departments in other similar schools.
- *PANDAs* provide benchmark data enabling departments to compare their student's attainment to other similar schools.
- Examination boards provide data including GCSE A*-C, A*-G, average points and average marks for each paper/component.

Stage 5: Taking action and reviewing progress
Monitoring progress towards targets (for cohorts and individual students)
Information that can be used to inform these processes includes:
- Trial GCSE examinations and other tests
- Ongoing teacher assessment tasks

This information should be reviewed by the department on a regular basis to inform future planning (see stage 4) and should be discussed with individual students.

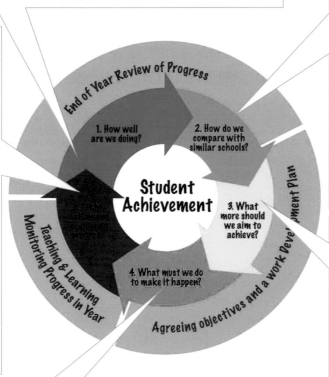

Stage 3: What more should we aim to achieve?
Forecasting and target setting. Using assessment information to plan for the future
Set key stage 3 and key stage 4 student and departmental targets using the range of data listed on the next page.

Stage 4: What must we do to make it happen?
Linking numerical target setting to curricular target setting and to teaching and learning
- Short-term 'gap closing' strategies include: *identification and mentoring of underachievers, use of IEPs (see Chapters 26 and 31), revision sessions for GCSE.* Student tracking data, for example the information shown in the spreadsheets in Figures 2 and 3, can be very useful in identifying which students to focus on. For example, Connor Dixon, in Figure 3, was doing less well at the end of year 8 than he was at the end of year 6. Alternatively, the data can be transformed into graphs (Figure 8) which clearly track progress to targets for individual students.
- Longer-term strategies for improvement include: *the development of assessment for learning techniques such as sharing learning objectives and outcomes, high quality oral and written feedback, student-friendly success criteria to support peer- and self-assessment, the use of writing interventions.*

The section on 'Target getting – how do we make it happen?' expands on these suggestions.

Figure 6 | *DfES's five-stage cycle for school improvement annotated with possible departmental activities (see also text on previous pages).*

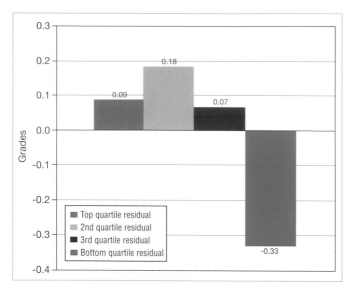

Figure 7 | *The differences in one cohort's GCSE attainment in geography compared with their attainment in other GCSE subjects.*

The role of target setting in departmental development

Continuous and planned departmental use of relevant national, LA and school data can be very powerful in informing teachers' expectations of their students. The DfES's five-stage cycle for school improvement shown in Figure 6 can provide a useful framework for geography departments seeking to improve their use of performance data. This approach is also likely to raise professional development training needs for individuals or whole departments.

So how might this actually operate within a geography department? Figure 7 indicates the difference between one cohort's GCSE attainment in geography compared with the same students' attainment in their other GCSEs. This type of information is often provided by LAs but can also be generated within a school. It is extremely valuable in informing development planning and teacher CPD. This analysis indicates that the higher achieving students in this department performed better in geography than in their other GCSE subjects overall. However the 'bottom' quartile had achieved less well. The teachers were, therefore, able to implement several strategies designed to support the lower achievers.

'Student/teacher friendly' graphs (Figure 8) can inform teacher planning and can also be used in regular student 'self-evaluation' sessions. When used in a sensitive manner this type of information can help to create a positive 'self-improvement' culture among students.

Target getting: making it happen

If target setting is to lead to improvement then *stage 4* of the five-stage cycle for departmental improvement is of paramount importance. Effective target setting cannot rely solely on 'number crunching'. There is also the danger that, in focusing on improving examination performance, attainment-raising strategies may become 'reactive' and short term in focus. In order to meet or exceed departmental targets the process should include a balance of long-, medium- and short-term strategic planning together with support for teacher professional development needs or opportunities that become apparent. Figure 9 suggests a range of possible long-, medium- and short-term strategies that a geography department might implement, via its development plan, to improve student and departmental attainment. Some are more appropriate to key stage 4 than key stage 3.

Gap-closing strategies are the types of activities required to respond to identified weaknesses or underachievement for individuals or small groups of students. They may also arise in response to unforeseen circumstances such as a portion of the cohort missing a series of lessons because of a residential visit for another subject area.

These can be extremely worthwhile in improving the attainment of individuals. However, gap-closing activities will not improve a department's performance long term. To achieve this, it is necessary to plan for and implement a range of strategies that will **improve the quality of teaching and learning** across the geography department. The following sections explore the role curricular target setting, when accompanied by assessment for learning (AfL) processes, can play in improving teaching and learning over the longer term.

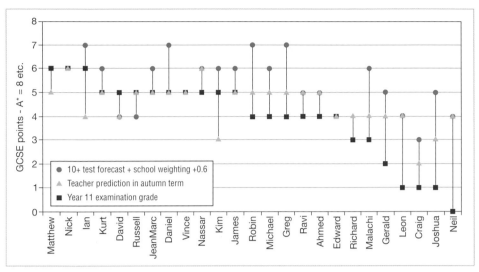

Figure 8 | *Individual student tracking data based on predicted and forecasted grades and year 11 trial examination results.*

Curricular target setting

" *A curricular target expresses in words, supported by data, a specific aspect of the curriculum as a focus for improvement. It is identified for a range of sources of evidence as an area of weakness in students' learning. They state what students need to do to demonstrate achievement over the longer term (DfES, 2004).*

SHORT TERM	MEDIUM TERM	LONG TERM
▪ Mentor or coach underachieving (in relation to predicted grades or levels) students	▪ Track individual student attainment via range of predicted grades/levels and use information to inform planning	▪ Planned use of the five-stage cycle of departmental improvement linked to teacher professional development
▪ Implement and monitor IEPs	▪ Develop 'extension' and 'support' activities in schemes of work	▪ Cycle of departmental improvement is informed by departmental record keeping which enables the tracking of performance data
▪ Issue revision activities booklet (KS4)	▪ Improve diagnostic feedback from first piece of GCSE coursework to inform second coursework item	▪ Identification and use of curricular target setting to target areas for improvement
▪ Lunchtime or breakfast club revision classes (KS4)	▪ Provide 'report' and 'explanation' genre writing frames for GCSE coursework	▪ Develop assessment for learning processes including:
▪ Booster classes during year 11 study leave	▪ Provide examination performance student self-evaluation sheets (Figure 13)	• Objective-led learning
▪ Secure parental involvement in coursework requirements and deadlines		• High quality oral and written feedback
		• Peer- and self-assessment informed by success criteria
		▪ Develop independent 'enquiry' based learning
		▪ Explicit teaching of different genres of writing

CLOSING GAPS ◀──────────▶ **IMPROVING TEACHING AND LEARNING**

Figure 9 | *Examples of short-, medium- and long-term strategies for raising student attainment.*

With the increasing tendency for school senior leaders to require departments to generate termly or half termly grades, levels or even sub-levels for students in order to track their progress towards targets it is easy to lose sight of the real purpose of all this data. The research evidence collated by Black and Wiliam (1998) indicates that feedback in the form of grades or levels does little to increase student motivation or foster improvement in their work. Rather it is the carefully constructed oral or written feedback that teachers can provide about how individuals are currently performing and how they might improve their work that can have the most significant impact on students.

Therefore, if teachers are to help improve student attainment by closing 'learning gaps' then it is essential that moving targets are translated into curricular targets, and curricular targets into shoprt term learning outcomes. That way meaningful student feedback can be provided about their work.

To identify their curricular targets a geography department should first gather evidence to help them to identify aspects of learning that students do less well in for a particular key stage. Evidence which can usefully inform this process includes:

- student work samples
- teacher assessment task and examination answers
- lesson observation information
- student questionnaires and interviews
- Ofsted inspection reports.

Having gathered suitable evidence geography teachers then need to analyse it to identify strengths and weaknesses and to formulate curricular targets. It is important to cross-reference these to the national curriculum level descriptions and/or key stage 4 examination criteria for geography.

Because curricular targets are long term it is important to 'layer' them so that they can be translated, first into year group targets, then into class targets, and finally into individual or group targets for individual lessons which would be expressed as learning outcomes. The following case study shows how a geography department went about identifying a key stage curricular target and planning to improve student performance in it.

Case study

The department began by sampling a year 8 end-of-unit assessment task. The task and one example from the student work sample used to determine curricular targets is shown in Figure 10. The 'call outs' record comments made by the teachers when they analysed this piece of work. The scrutiny of students' work revealed a number of 'gaps' between the **intended learning outcomes** and what the students actually achieved based on **observed outcomes**. These are summarised in Figure 10.

The department discovered that most students only engaged with the first of the progressively more challenging learning outcomes. This prevented many of them from attaining national curriculum levels 5 and 6 for the assessment task. Following their analysis of the work sample, the department felt they should focus curricular targets on written extended explanations, specifically focusing on why people have different views and how different people's values and attitudes can affect people and places.

They took national curriculum level 5 as a benchmark for this curricular target and used the relevant element of the national curriculum level descriptions to identify the explicit indicators of progression for explaining differing viewpoints (Figure 11a). The department then used this information to develop a layered curricular target that they would focus on in their long-, medium- and short-term

End-of-unit assessment task

Use the sources you have collected to write a report that discusses whether Aston Villa should expand their football ground. Consider which people will benefit, and who will lose out. Try to describe and explain why people have different views on this matter and what effects this will have on them.

**Should Aston Villa
Expand their Football Ground?**

You've copied too directly from the text here try to write in your own words.

Aston Villa started in 1874 and moved to their ground called Villa Park in 1897. It was at the edge of the city at the time in the north of Birmingham City. It was quickly surrounded by terraced housing and is now within the city and not near its edge. It's quite rough their now with high unemployment. There are some shops nearby along Witton Lane and some parking. The ground has a capacity of 39,339 but the owners want to make it bigger into a 50,000-seater stadium.

They have asked the local council for planning permission to extend the ground to make it bigger for European games. Although Aston Villa doesn't paly many European games, the club wants to extend the North stand and Trinity Road stand and redevelop the Holte Pub into a 140-bed hotel. They want to close the road and use the children's playground and park for car park space turning it into a concrete jungle. The directors say they will make lots of new jobs for the locals but won't say how many. I think they will just make the club richer.

You make some good points but try to expand them more

The locals are not happy and they make a protest by forming a human chain with 2000 people all linking arms. They think that they are imprisoners in their own home. The fans take over causing pollution and throwing rubbish like chip rappers and coke cans everywhere. Some old people are locked in their homes on match days because football fans are loud and aggressive shouting all the time.

I think that although the expansion of the ground will make more jobs and help local shopkeepers, we don't know how many jobs would be made, it could just be only twenty. Also the children will lose their play area and the fans cause too much pollution. Therefore I think that Aston Villa should definitely not expand their ground.

Try to link your views and explain how the expansion will impact on the community positively or negatively

The student presents opposing viewpoints, but is largely descriptive, and does not satisfactorily explain why people have differing views.
The department identified that students often recognised opposing viewpoints and were able to select appropriate information from the textbooks but they rarely linked ideas together to explain why people have differing viewpoints. It decided to focus its curricular target on the difference between description and explanation as this had the potential to impact on the attainment of students currently achieving levels 4 and 5.

You've just described how the club want to expand without saying how the community will benefit! How will co-operation be improved? How will local businesses benefit?

The teacher gives indication of how the work could be improved but misses the opportunity to highlight strengths in the work such as the important use of the connective 'because' which helps move the descriptions into explanations.
This would help to move the student towards the 'Most are …' learning outcome identified for the lesson.

Intended learning outcomes	Observed learning outcomes
All are able to describe their own views and those of others as to whether the expansion of the football ground is a good or a bad idea. **Most** are able to explain why people have different views about the location of the new football ground. **Some** will be able to compare and contrast different views and be able to explain how people's values and attitudes affects people and places in the community.	**All** students were able to extract basic relevant information from the text sources. These were generally copied or re-phrased. **Most** students were able to describe their own views and select information that enabled them to describe those of others. **A few** students gave basic reasons as to why some people have differing viewpoints, but these explanations were underdeveloped and tended to offer simple statements in support of opinions. Although a minority of students did identify links between pieces of information, these were poorly supported by evidence.

Figure 10 | *The task set, and a student response, for a year 8 end-of-unit assessment task.*

(a)

Element of geography	Level 5	Level 6	Level 7
Views, values and attitudes	Suggest explanations for the ways in which human activities cause changes to the environment and the different views people hold about them.	Explain how different values and attitudes, including their own, result in different approaches that have different effects on people and places.	Understand that many factors, including people's values and attitudes, influence decisions made about places and environments. Use this understanding to explain the resulting changes.

(b)

	Layered curricular target
Individual student or group	I can write about my own and others' different points of view and explain why people have them.
Whole class	You will be able to explain why you and other people have different points of view about a geographical issue.
Year group	In extended writing students should be able to use appropriate topic sentences and connectives to support their explanations of people's views, values and attitudes about a geographical issue.
Key stage	Students need to improve their written explanations of their own and others' views, values and attitudes in relation to named geographical features, patterns and processes.

Figure 11 | (a) Level indicators for explaining different viewpoints, transposed into (b) layered curricular targets for key stage 3.

planning and which would, they hoped, impact on student standards at key stage 3 (Figure 11b).

To address the curricular target in their medium-term planning the department focused specifically on developing literacy strategies aimed at scaffolding non-fictional writing together with using peer and self opportunities. The curricular target was made explicit to students through lesson learning objectives and outcomes, formative written feedback on extended writing tasks, and oral feedback. Source: DfES, 2005a.

Having identified a curricular target the next step for a department, as the case study suggests, is to incorporate it into curriculum planning. Planning for progression towards the curricular target across the key stage will be important and is likely to be expressed in the teaching objectives within the scheme of work. These would then be further refined into learning objectives and outcomes for individual lessons.

'Closing the gaps' to curricular targets

Going back to Royce Sadler's quote at the start of this chapter; what he says is fundamental to securing independent student learning. Although students need support from their teachers to determine the gap between the *desired goal*, and their *present position*, if they are to become more independent learners they need to take increasing responsibility for identifying and closing the gaps for themselves.

If students are to know and recognise the standards they are aiming for, and how to get there, then it is essential that their teachers develop a deeply rooted understanding of progression in the concepts and skills that underpin learning geography. Only then will they be able to communicate steps towards the *'desired goals'* to students. Teachers, therefore, need to establish frameworks, either on paper or in their heads, that describe progression in the use of those concepts and skills which are key to improving performance in the curricular targets they have identified.

An approach to creating scaffolds of this kind was developed by a group of Staffordshire teachers as part of a Best Practice Research Scholarship project. Their work focused on improving students' written geographical descriptions and explanations. By analysing many student descriptions and explanations the team were able to identify those characteristics that make one description or explanation better than another. They expressed their findings in two models: a 'scaffold for better descriptions' and a 'scaffold for better explanations', both written in 'student speak' (see Figure 7, Chapter 32, page 429).

Scaffolds such as these become even more powerful when used as tools to promote independent learning, when they are shared with and understood by students. For this to happen teachers need to integrate them into lessons so that students can learn how to make effective use of the success criteria they describe. Scaffolds such as these can be used by students in lessons:

- to judge the quality of an exemplar piece of writing;
- for peer- or self-assessment of drafted work before improving it;
- to help articulate how they arrived at their 'grading' decisions, within class discussion;
- to set targets for improvement for future work.

They can also help teachers to provide focused and specific oral and written feedback to students in relation to their curricular targets. The teachers involved in the research project (DfES, 2005b) found that the following factors helped students to use the scaffolds most effectively:

- Expressing the description of each 'stage' in quality in 'student speak'.
- Asking students to underline the parts of their work they felt illustrated the highest level they had achieved and then label this with key words from the generalised statements.
- Asking students to focus on particular sentences rather than going straight for an overall assessment of their work enabled them to assess their own work more easily.
- Sometimes the students were unable to bridge the gap between the generalisation of the statements and the specific aspects of the context addressed in their work so teachers gave written examples of how each level applied to the context that they were studying.
- Combining words and pictures to appeal to both right- and left-brain-dominant learners.
- Encouraging students to justify how they arrived at their 'grading' decisions in pairs and using this as a basis for a short class discussion.

Once teachers have a secure understanding of progression in the geographical skills or areas of understanding that they have identified as curricular targets, there is a range of strategies they might use to support students in achieving them with some independence. These include:

- **Modelling:** for example, where the teacher models the use of a skill or procedure and invites students to contribute to the process or, alternatively, students are asked to model in groups or pairs.

Good point, but try to back up your predictions with evidence to support your statement

The teacher highlights the quality of the **description** but asks the student to extend his response, to meet the third learning outcome, by **providing evidence** from the image to support the annotation.

the picture is showing how landuse is changing here. I think that old buildings are being knocked down to make way for housing. This means that the population could be getting more.
Useful point, summarising well

This office block looks like it was built in the 1970s or 1960s. It is being demolished. This may also be used for houses or maybe a school.

There are no houses in the distance which shows that this place is on the edge of a city. ✓

Modern housing project that could be replacing older slum housing. ✓

New roads make better transport links. Why is this attractive for new industry?

The student **describes** the impact new roads may have on the area. The teacher's comment encourages a response that provides an **explanation as** specified in the third learning outcome.

porta cabins and parked cars and a working crane all show that the site is being built on. ✓

Evidence of tipping waste on derelict land. This could be due to crime or lack of facilities.

The teacher credits the quality of the students answer and unpicks it to highlight why it is good. She could have been more specific in the use of language to relate this to the intended outcomes and to reinforce the learning goals. For example by using the terms **description**, **explanation** and **the use of evidence.**

This is a brownfield site. It may have had an old factory on it or maybe slum houses. The factory could have closed down due to foreign imports, competition, lack of space or poor transport links. Superb answer you have made an excellent prediction and justified your answer by backing it up with evidence

You've clearly made progress and made an effort to add explanation and justification to your annotations, well done ☺

The teacher acknowledges the progress made and makes a clear reference to standards of attainment, using the same language of the objectives and outcomes for the lesson.

Figure 12 | *Sample marking of an annotated photograph.*

■ **Questioning:** for example, where the teacher encourages students to ask their own challenging questions and displays a list of question stems, for different levels of thinking, for them to choose from.

■ **Using staged success criteria**, like those in Figure 7 in Chapter 32, then gradually removing the 'scaffold' to promote independence.

■ **Analysing model answers** to identify success criteria, with or without teacher support.

■ **Sequencing from best to worse and analysing student work** to identify success criteria.

■ **Oral teacher feedback:** for example, where the teacher uses questions which encourage reflection for example, 'If I look at this criterion and this part of your work what do you think I am going to say?'

■ **Written teacher feedback**, where the teacher specifically references the learning outcomes in their written comments on students' work. An example of marked work, from a department that had identified improving students' 'geographical descriptions and explanations' as curricular targets, is shown in Figure 13. The lesson, from a year 8 unit of work on 'Urban land use', focused on two main **learning objectives:**

• to develop the skills of photograph interpretation

• to describe and explain how the decline of industry impacts on the urban landscape and land use.

GCSE EXAM STUDENT SELF EVALUATION

Name _____ Form _____ Date _____

	No of marks lost	Comment or details
YEAR 10 EXAM PERCENTAGE & GRADE		
YEAR 11 EXAM PERCENTAGE & GRADE		
Areas in which marks were lost		
Question **misinterpreted** or **misread**		
Vocabulary in question not known (list) _____		
Didn't pay enough attention to the **number of marks** available		
Did not support answer with relevant **example** or **case study**		
Answers not developed or **contextualised**		
Detailed **linkages** and the **inter-relationships** between factors not included		
Answer not in the correct sequence		
Incorrect or careless use of **map**, **graph** or **other skills** (say which skills)		
Did not follow the instruction to **describe** or **explain**		
Work **not understood**		
Work **not revised** or not known		
Ran out of **time**		
Other reasons _____		

Targets for improvement (e.g. more detail needed in classwork/homework, revision skills, organisation of file, catching up on missed work, 'past paper' practice)

Figure 13 | *GCSE students' self-evaluation sheet.*

Teacher plans and delivers lessons which focus on identified areas

Teacher is able to prioritise areas for future individual and class improvement

Students sit an internal examination which is marked by the teacher

Teacher reads the students' self-evaluation sheets

Teacher provides oral examination feedback and specific marking criteria and model answers

Students calculate where most marks were lost and generate targets for improvement

Students create a tally of the number of marks lost (Figure 13) and provide details to contextualise

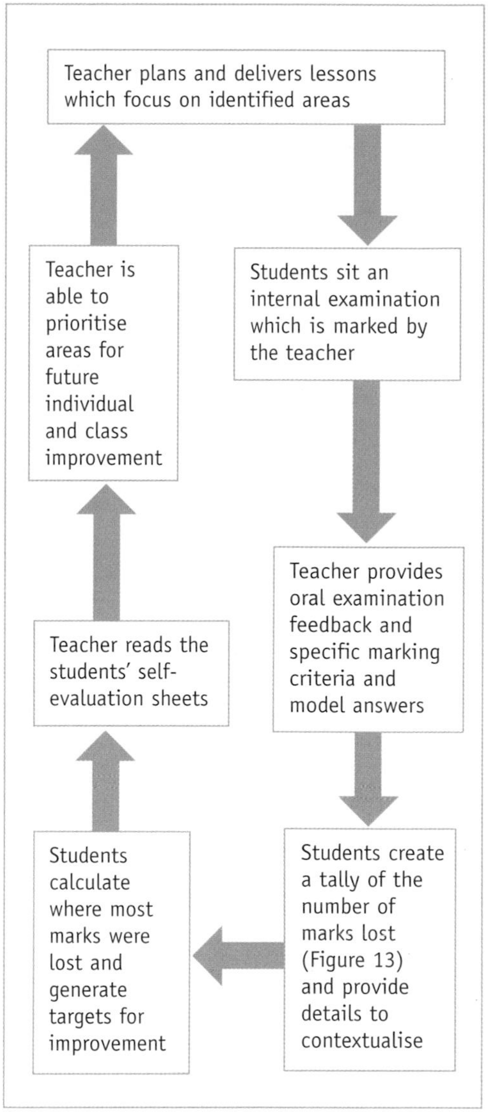

Figure 14 | *Student self-evaluation improvement cycle.*

The **learning outcomes** were to have:
- recognised, identified and described the key features of urban re-development and land use;
- explained how industrial change impacts on urban land use;
- selected evidence from the photograph and from personal experiences to support explanations of changing land use.

The speech bubble comments identify the strengths and weaknesses of the teacher feedback in relation to the learning objectives and outcomes identified for the lesson.

Self assessment at key stage 4

The strategies described above apply equally to key stages 3, 4 and beyond. This final section considers approaches specific to trial examination outcomes. By involving students formally in monitoring, evaluating and tracking their own examination performances they are more likely to engage with *'What must I do to make it happen?'*

One way of getting students actively involved in identifying their own weaknesses so that they know how to improve is through the use of an 'examination self-evaluation sheet'. (see e.g. Figure 13). This self-evaluation sheet is designed to inform the process of student target setting and teacher short- and medium-term planning. Figure 14 suggests a small-scale cycle of improvement that can promote the effective use of such self-evaluation sheets.

The process described in Figure 14 can help teachers to identify actual weaknesses in their students' examination performance and, thus, allow them to plan future individual, group or class support on specific aspects of the specification or on examination technique. Meanwhile the students are able to identify and actively respond to areas of weakness they have identified for themselves. They should also be able to recognise the reasons underpinning future lesson objectives planned by their geography teacher and be able to link these directly to their own learning needs.

And finally ...

Departmental target setting is not about LA or national trend lines and targets, it is about real students, in real classrooms and the processes that enable the individuals we teach to do the best they can ... adding real value. Within these processes the setting of individual and cohort numerical targets serves important purposes. By setting student targets, teachers go beyond departmental data and evidence to identify the true potential of the individuals they teach. They can then use these targets as a means of tracking progress and as a tool to motivate and direct learning. Cohort targets enable teachers to look beyond their own classrooms to compare the performance of their students with other geography departments and to judge whether their expectations should be higher.

All the number crunching and numerical target setting in the world will not lead to improved student standards. To move from 'target setting' to 'target getting' numerical targets must become inextricably linked to departmental processes for improving teaching and learning, through teacher professional development.

'Target setting' sets the scene for a dynamic dialogue with students about improving their learning, while 'target getting' involves teachers and their students in a dialogue which focuses on determining success, by recognising the goals to be aimed for, identifying the present position, and understanding and agreeing how the gap between the two might be closed.

Acknowledgements

The author wishes to acknowledge the work of Nigel Bielby and Richard Hicks (Secondary National Strategy Consultants for Cheshire LA) in the 'Curricular target setting' and 'Written feedback' geography exemplification from DfES, 2004b.

Implications for practice

(a) Use a range of different types of assessment data to inform individual student target setting.

Collect different types of data in your school for key stages 3 and 4. Try to enlist the support of your school data manager who may be able to save you time and energy. Have a go at entering the individual student data into a spreadsheet (or other data management system) like those shown in Figures 2 and 3. You will find that some data sources provide forecasts or inform predictions that are more accurate than others. Experiment to discover those which can inform challenging but realistic targets for your students. Once you have established a range of individual student forecasts and predictions have a go at amalgamating them to provide whole-cohort forecasts and targets like those shown in Figure 4.

(b) Target setting processes can usefully inform ongoing departmental development.

Try to build the five-stage cycle for departmental development (Figure 6) into your departmental calendar for the next 12 months. (Download from the Standards site the DfES booklet which explains how to get the most out of the Autumn Package.) Use the national data to determine how well your department is doing when compared with geography departments in other schools. Try to identify the short-, medium- and long-term strategies that your department might adopt to improve student attainment. Use Figure 9 to prompt departmental discussions.

(c) In order to close students' 'learning gaps' it is essential to translate numerical targets into curricular targets.

After reading the departmental case study on pages 442-4, work with your department to identify a curricular target for either key stage 3 or key stage 4. Once this is done, work collaboratively to identify steps in progression towards the curricular target by constructing a scaffold like those shown in Figure 10. Experiment with using the scaffold in a variety of ways with students.

References

Black, P. and Wiliam, D. (1998) *Inside the Black Box: Raising standards through classroom assessment.* London: School of Education, Kings College.

Black, P., Harrison, C., Lee, C., Marshall, B. and Wiliam, D. (2003) *Assessment for Learning: Putting it into practice.* Oxford: Oxford University Press.

DfES (2004) Key Stage 3 Strategy: *'Assessment for learning: whole school training materials'* (Ref 0043-2004 G). London: DfES.

DfES (2005a) *Key Stage 3 Strategy: 'Assessment for learning: subject development materials'* (second edition, Ref 1101-2005 CD). London: DfES.

DfES (2005b) *Key Stage 3 Strategy: 'Assessment for learning: whole school development materials'* (second edition, Ref 1098-2005 DVD). London: DfES. (Includes a video of a teacher using the 'scaffold for better descriptions'.)

George, J., Clarke, J., Davies, P. and Durbin, C. (2002) 'Helping students to get better at geographical writing', *Teaching Geography*, 27, 4, pp. 156-9.

Standards – www.standards.dfes.gov.uk/performance/recporgposters/?version=1

Chapter 34

Teacher assessment in geography

Nic Howes

Before reading this chapter consider the following questions:

- Why do we have teacher assessment in geography at key stage 3?

- What evidence supports your teacher assessed levels at key stage 3?

- How are students involved in your teacher assessment of their key stage 3 levels?

- How can good practice in teacher assessment at key stage 3 support teaching and learning in later key stages?

The need for teacher assessment at key stage 3

The national curriculum places a statutory requirement on schools to report a level in geography for each student at the end of the three years of key stage 3; the level must be reported to parents and to the Department for Education and Skills. There is no statutory requirement to report levels in year 7 or year 8; any attempt to do so runs contrary to QCA advice. QCA makes clear that the level descriptions can only be applied to a range of work produced over three years. Teacher assessment refers to a level of attainment judged by a student's teachers as opposed to a level arrived at after the student sits an external examination (standard assessment test or SAT). The mechanism for arriving at a key stage 3 level in geography for each student is solely teacher assessment; there are no additional statutory SATs as is the case in English, mathematics and science. There is also no statutory requirement to report a level in geography at the ends of key stages 1 and 2.

There were early attempts to devise statutory SATs for geography but they were abandoned, much to the relief of most experienced professionals in geography education. Timed assessment of students' learning of the whole programmes of study (PoS) at the end of the three years of key stage 3 is problematic for a range of reasons, these include:

- the wide-ranging content of the PoS and assessment criteria (level descriptions);
- the importance of assessing whether students have learned to take a synoptic view;
- the importance of geographical enquiry, which was emphasised in the revised national curriculum and which cannot easily be assessed under timed conditions;
- the danger of assessment overload for students at the end of key stage 3;
- it is better to assess attainment over a long period of time rather than in a short 'spot' assessment that may be externally marked with no allowance for an 'off day'.

The above reasons indicate that there is a need for teacher assessment that is much more than an end-of-key-stage examination. Teacher assessment is a continuous process for students and their teachers throughout key stage 3; it should incorporate good practice that has assessment for learning embedded in it (see Chapter 32) and makes use of a range of assessment techniques throughout the key stage. Teacher assessment should provide opportunities for individual student enquiry to be assessed and could include use of the non-statutory *Optional Tests and Tasks* published by QCA and ACCAC. Therefore, it is necessary for teachers to devise assessment that:

- is manageable for teachers and students in the context of their overall workload;
- is understood clearly by students;
- allows for inclusion so that all students can show what they have learned;
- improves learning;
- does not dominate the curriculum and stifle new approaches to learning (such as thinking skills – see Chapters 16 and 40).

Gathering evidence

It is important to collect evidence of students' experiences and achievements in key stage 3 geography to support Teacher Assessed levels, in order to:

- monitor progress and set targets for improvement (see Chapter 33);
- provide a basis for writing annual reports and for discussing progress with individual students and their parents;
- support end-of-key-stage judgements;
- maintain fair and consistent assessment standards among teachers through time.

The range of evidence available in geography is considerable, and it is good practice to plan for as much variety as possible, to provide all students with opportunities to demonstrate positive achievement. Retainable evidence may be categorised as direct evidence, indirect evidence and ephemeral evidence.

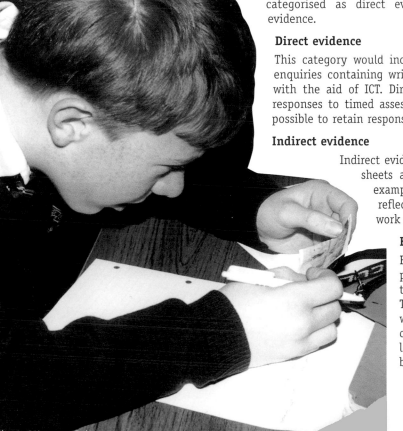

Direct evidence

This category would include exercise books and individual student enquiries containing written and visual material, possibly produced with the aid of ICT. Direct evidence should also include individual responses to timed assessments such as end-of-unit tests. It is also possible to retain responses by pairs and groups of students.

Indirect evidence

Indirect evidence might include students' self-evaluation sheets and/or teacher observations and notes. An example evaluation sheet with space for student reflection and a discussion regarding pieces of work are shown in Figures 1 and 2.

Ephemeral evidence

Ephemeral evidence may or may not be physically recorded but includes important teacher knowledge of individual students. This may include observations on students who make frequent, perceptive oral contributions to lessons but do not match the level of these in their written work, or it may be discussions with students (Figure 3).

Photo: ©Margaret Roberts.

(a) Teacher's comments

Literacy
Good spelling and vocabulary. Please check all sentences are full sentences and read well. Some sentences are too long.

Numeracy
Accurate and carefully analysed

Understanding
Good understanding - work is logical and rational.

Decision making
Well reasoned, sensible decisions made. Choices reasoned and justified. Clear evidence of careful decisions made in the light of all available information. Good.

General comment
Very good work

Mark A

(b) Student's comments

Having read the comments on your work, choose two things that you think you need to work on to improve over the next term.

I think that I am always writing my sentences too long. I tend to use a lot of commas instead of full stops. I don't think I explain them very well.

I also don't think I am very good at graphs. I tend to forget to label the axes.

Figure 1 | *A completed assessment sheet for a year 7 activity on routes to schools. Note: the mark is based on level descriptor grades A-D devised by the school.*

Teacher-researcher: *Are there things about doing this piece of coursework that you're unhappy about?*

Emma: *Well, I found that my teacher ... It's not his fault, but ... there wasn't always time for him to talk to all of us and help us with specific things. Like I was the first to do a piece on a model seaside resort, but I asked for help and there wasn't enough time in the lesson, so I didn't end up including that piece.*

Teacher-researcher: *And if you had, that would have helped with your marks, do you think?*

Emma: *That's what sir said. He said it could have bumped them up a little bit. He said I would still have got a 'C' but more of a 'C'.*

Figure 2 | *Extracts of discussions can also act as 'indirect evidence' in portfolios.*

James can explain things, but as soon as it comes to putting something down on paper and having to record his findings in that way, he struggles and doesn't have some of the techniques needed – the grammar especially ...

Keith is an interesting case – although his Edinburgh Reading Test score is high, his literacy skills are very weak. Little of his writing here is sustained and many key words are mis-spelt. Work was probably rushed and not checked.

Figure 3 | *Examples of teacher observations about individual students.*

A portfolio is a collection of evidence that exemplifies students' standards of work. There is no statutory requirement for schools to produce portfolios of any kind but many schools choose to do so because they find them useful. Portfolios may be divided into two broad categories:

1. The school or departmental portfolio that exemplifies standards of attainment at each end-of-key-stage 3 level including borderlines between levels.
2. The individual student portfolio that builds up samples of work through key stage 3, providing a basis for considerations of progress and, ultimately, evidence to support teacher assessment of the student's key stage 3 level.

At the John Kyrle High School the individual student portfolio is a cardboard pocket folder into which the teacher places assessed work from the student concerned. The geography department has agreed key pieces of work for selection but teachers are free to select additional pieces if they feel that these are helpful to the process of teacher assessment. The key pieces of work include a minimum of five individual student enquiries (carried out as extended homework) and a series of end-of-unit tests (completed in school). The importance of geographical enquiry was such that it was made a major focus for assessing QCA's 'aspects of performance'.

Used in conjunction with students' exercise books, the portfolios enable teachers to make a summative assessment of each student's end-of-key-stage 3 attainment against the level descriptions to reach a 'best fit' level. Teacher assessment must be criterion-referenced, with the criteria coming from the level descriptions; any attempt to assign levels along a normal distribution curve at the end of year 9 – or following the pattern of SAT results in core subjects – is bad practice. The formative nature of teacher assessment means that students are familiar from the outset with the process of assembling their portfolios and understand how important the contents are in determining their key stage 3 levels (see also Chapters 32, 33 and 35).

Each geography classroom has a bank of open-fronted wooden shelves in which portfolios are stored for students currently in key stage 3. The departmental portfolio is stored elsewhere and is made up from a selection of individual student portfolios from previous years that exemplifies standards of attainment at each end-of-key-stage 3 level including borderlines between levels; it is updated each year to include better examples and to take account of changes in assessment criteria (as may occur with reviews of the national curriculum). The department is not obsessive about retaining evidence once students have moved beyond key stage 3; portfolios provide a good example of sustainable development in practice: unless they are required for the departmental portfolio, the contents are returned to students and the folders are reused.

The departmental portfolio enables teachers to demonstrate standards in the department on the numerous occasions on which the need arises, for example:
- annual moderations of key stage 3 levels;
- induction of new teachers in the department;
- informing parents of standards;
- delivering in-service training;
- talking to senior management, advisers, inspectors and other education professionals.

Involving students

To enable all students to demonstrate positive achievement it is essential that they are involved in the process of teacher assessment. The first step is to share the assessment criteria, so that students understand what is expected from them. There are various ways in which this may be achieved:
- To help understanding of the assessment of individual student geographical enquiries, it is good practice to draw up student-friendly versions of the 'aspects of performance' from QCA, and display them in classrooms, as a link on the school website, or distribute copies to individual students (Figure 4).
- Provide students with written guidance on how to succeed. This may be regarding an approach to learning (Figure 4a) or related to specific skills used in a particular geographical enquiry (Figure 4b).
- Provide students with a framework of content to revise before a test.
- Add 'signposts' on test papers to explain how marks will be awarded. For example: *Describe the effects of an earthquake [3 marks] (marks will be awarded for reference to named, located examples and for development of points to give details).*

(a)

Preparation

- Think hard about your questions – focus them on the theme of the investigation and act on your teacher's advice.
- Remember it's about gathering new information, not about writing down what you already know (which is – understandably – very little on some issues).
- Make an effort to seek information – listen to your teacher's advice and act on it.

Gathering information

- When you ask for information – by writing or speaking – use several clearly focused short questions, for example:
  What causes footpath erosion?
  Where is footpath erosion a problem in the national park?
  What strategies do you use to manage footpath erosion?
  Rather than:
  Tell me about conflicts in your area.
- Be prepared to change your questions if you find that it is difficult to answer them.
- Learn how to use a search engine on the internet and an index/contents in a book; ask your teacher if you don't know how to do these things.
- Look for case-studies which give you information about specific events and places.
- Always look for opportunities to write about sustainable development.

Writing it

- Do not copy another person's text – use your own words.
- Use a word-processor if you have access to one.
- Do not use fancy typefaces like this.
- Use a question/answer approach: write your first question, leave a line, answer the question fully and then write the next question and so on and so on.
- Remember to use question marks after questions.
- Avoid writing long descriptions.
- Divide your work up into paragraphs and make use of bullet points and/or headings.
- Avoid writing conversationally, e.g. don't begin an answer with *Well* ...
- It is a good idea to include at the end of your enquiry a list of books and people from whom you obtained information.
- Do not present your work with each page in a separate plastic pocket (it is very time-consuming to mark).
- Become a good editor of your own writing: remove errors in typing, spelling, grammar and punctuation.
- To reach the highest national curriculum levels you will need to evaluate your sources of evidence: are they reliable? accurate? biased?

Illustrations (maps, photographs, drawings, diagrams, tables, etc.)

- Make good use of diagrams – and don't forget to use maps to show the location of the places you write about (remember it is geography).
- Number all illustrations and refer to them by number in your writing.
- Photographs are particularly good if you annotate (label) them, so the reader knows what she/he is meant to look at.
- Draw diagrams to help explain things.
- Use tables to summarise information.

Remember – you will be expected to gather information and write a report on many occasions in education and employment; it is worth learning enquiry skills at an early age – ask an older person!

Figure 4 | *Providing student-friendly assessment information: (a) general, and (b) in relation to specific pieces of coursework. Sources: (a) John Kyle High School; (b) Jo Gant, Hertswood School.*

(b) Producing a rainforest display: year 9 coursework

You have been asked by the British Museum to help design a room for a new display area. The display is to be on tropical rainforests – their natural beauty, deforestation and sustainable development. With this display they would also like you to design a variety of educational posters to explain what your model shows (see below).

What do I have to do?

■ Build a small-scale model, which shows and explains the causes and effects of deforestation on the Yanomani tribe and the rainforests of Brazil. The model should be divided into two sections, showing the rainforest before and after deforestation.
■ Create a series of educational posters that explain the following:
  • What the original primary forest looks like, how it works (nutrient cycle) and how the Yanomani live their lives (shifting cultivation)
  • Who is deforesting the area and why
  • The meaning of 'sustainable development'. How this idea could be used to help protect the rainforest and develop the area for its people.

How am I going to do this?

You will be given four lessons and homework to complete this task. The geography department will provide you with paper, pens, scissors, glue, etc. However, you will have to collect and bring in the rest of the materials you think will help you to make your models and posters. Students who have done this task in the past have used cardboard, wood, plastic, soil, plants, toy trucks and animals to complete their models.

What level do I need to achieve and how will I know if I am doing this right?

You should be aiming for at least a national average of level 5. Below is a mark scheme to help you make sure that you reach this level. Use it as a checklist to ensure that you have covered everything.

Level	Description
3	A basic model with few labels. The model labels include canopy, under-canopy, buttress, roots, etc., and one or two human impacts. The posters have little written material and very limited explanations of how and why deforestation occurs. No attempt to explain sustainable development.
4	A model with a variety of labels that cover the main structure of the forest. No mention of the nutrient cycle. Several impacts are shown. The posters describe the structure of the rainforest, with limited explanation of how and why deforestation occurs. A definition of sustainable development is given.
5	A model that has a variety of labels that cover the main structure of the forest. The nutrient cycle is briefly mentioned. A variety of impacts are shown. The posters describe and begin to explain the structure of the rainforest and how plants have adapted to the climate. An explanation is given of the main uses of the rainforest. Links sustainable development to the Yanomani as well as giving a definition.
6	Detailed knowledge of the main structure of the forest is labelled on the model. The posters have information on the rainforest's nutrient cycle. A variety of impacts are shown on the model. The posters begin to explain the advantages and disadvantages of deforestation. The Yanomani's life is described with reason for why it is sustainable.
7	Detailed knowledge of the main structure of the forest and how the nutrient cycle works is given on the model. Posters showing how deforestation can affect the nutrient cycle. A variety of impacts are shown on the model. The posters describe and explain the structure of the rainforest and how plants have adapted to the climate. The posters explain the advantages and disadvantages of deforestation. The Yanomani's life is described with reasons for why it is sustainable.

Good luck. Remember this work will go towards your final level at the end of this year. Use the mark scheme to get the level you wish. Don't forget to pop into the coursework club on Thursdays if you need extra help.

Student's geographical enquiry planning sheet

Student's name:

Write down your questions

_____

_____

Teacher approval (initials):   Date:

Describe how you intend to collect your evidence:

_____

_____

What help will you need?

_____

_____

Figure 5 | *An example enquiry planning sheet.*

A simple planning sheet (Figure 5) is an effective tool for teachers to use to direct individual student enquiries towards positive achievement. Assessment for learning takes place when students' work is returned to them with comments written in the framework of aspects of performance; the comments should include suggestions for improvement in future pieces of work. At the point of receiving their assessed work it is useful for students to reflect on their attainment by completing a self-evaluation sheet, such as that shown in Figure 2.

At the John Kyrle High School, students have open access to their portfolios: they may take them home overnight to show their parents if they wish. The students are responsible for adding assessed work and self-evaluations to their portfolios, and are therefore able to review their own progress.

Teacher assessment should take place within a whole-school policy of target setting for individual students; each student should know her/his end-of-key-stage target level in every subject and these will form the basis of discussions on progress. The individual target is a great motivator for most students, and many will want advice from their teacher on how to exceed it.

Teacher assessment beyond key stage 3

Teacher assessment should be a positive experience for key stage 3 students and their teachers; it is therefore important to extend its principles into key stage 4 and at post-16 where external examinations – and their potential flaws as an assessment method – feature more prominently.

Students may be helped towards examination success by using the following aspects of teacher assessment:

- teachers share examination assessment criteria with students;
- students attempt written responses to past examination questions and teachers assess with formative comments;
- teachers share good written responses to examination questions with students;
- teachers use assessment to assist students to improve their 'examination technique';
- teachers support students to carry geographical enquiry skills forward to success in examination coursework.

Implications for practice

(a) Carry out an audit of your current assessment practice throughout key stage 3.

There should be opportunities – including differentiated geographical enquiries and short tests – for all students to demonstrate positive achievement in accordance with the range of knowledge, understanding and skills referred to in the level descriptions and aspects of performance. Take action to improve areas that need it after identification in the audit (e.g. opportunities for students to demonstrate their understanding and knowledge of sustainable development).

(b) Consider building up individual student portfolios or just a departmental portfolio to exemplify standards.

Decide how you will manage storage and how long you will retain students' work. Come to an agreement on a manageably sized range of key assessments that you wish to include in your portfolios. Specify the resource implications that need to be addressed for successful teacher assessment and take them to your management team.

(c) Decide how you will mark students' work and how you will inform them about their marks.

This may be to show students about their progress towards – or movement beyond – their key stage 3 target level. Aspects of performance are useful for informing students of their strengths and areas for improvement, and avoid the awkward issue of attempting to assign a distinct national curriculum level to one piece of work.

(d) Consider your students' involvement in teacher assessment and introduce measures to improve it ...

... where necessary; for example, individual target-setting, preferably part of a whole-school policy. Use teacher assessment as a purposeful process that provides answers to the ubiquitous questions:

- How is student X making progress? What aspects of her/his work need improvement?
- What evidence do you have of standards and student progress in the geography department?
- How does the department maintain conformity in its assessments in key stage 3?
- How are all students provided with opportunities to show positive achievement?

Related publications from the Geographical Association:
- Butt, G. (2002) *Theory Into Practice: Extending writing skills*.
- Butt, G., Lambert, D. and Telfer, S. (eds) (1995) *Assessment Works*.
- Hopkin, J., Telfer, S. and Butt, G. (eds) (2000) *Assessment in Practice: Raising standards in secondary geography*.
- 'Assessment Matters' – a regular feature in the GA's secondary journal *Teaching Geography*.

References

George, J., Clarke, J., Davies, P. and Durbin, C. (2002) 'Helping students to get better at geographical writing', *Teaching Geography*, 27, 4, pp. 156-9.

Martin, F. (2004) 'It's a crime', *Teaching Geography*, 29, 1, pp. 43-7.

Owen, C. (2001) 'Developing literacy though key stage 3 geography', *Teaching Geography*, 26, 4, pp. 160-6.

Reid, A. and Jones, M. (2002) 'Learning from GCSE coursework', *Teaching Geography*, 27, 3, pp. 120-5.

Roberts, M. (2003) *Learning Through Enquiry: Making sense of geography in the key stage 3 classroom*. Sheffield: Geographical Association.

Wood, P. (2001) 'Bridging key stages 2 and 3', *Teaching Geography*, 26, 1, pp. 40-2.

Wood, P. and Sutton, A. (2002) 'Decision-making exercises and assessment in post-16 geography', *Teaching Geography*, 27, 2, pp. 69-73.

Chapter 35

Developing key skills through geography

Emma Gobourn

> **Before reading this chapter consider the following questions:**
>
> ■ Which key skills are developed as your students learn geography?
>
> ■ To what extent do you provide opportunities for each key skill to be developed? (How could considering progression, differentiation and assessment improve these opportunities?)
>
> ■ How does the development of your students' key skills improve their learning in geography?

Geography is a subject full of opportunities for students to use a variety of skills and develop their competency in areas such as literacy, numeracy and working with others. The key skills naturally addressed by the study of geography include:
■ Application of number
■ Communication
■ Information and communications technology (ICT)
■ Improving own learning and performance
■ Problem solving
■ Working with others.

Developing proficiency in these skills is a gradual process with clear progression through the key stages, during post-16 study and beyond. The transferable nature of key skills and concepts such as lifelong learning have become increasingly significant in educational thinking.

Geography is an excellent vehicle for key skills development. The interdisciplinary nature of the subject ensures that programmes of study and schemes of work include many topics and activities which involve an interweaving of skills. This diversity of tasks and subject matter ensures that key skills development can be integrated naturally into geography work rather than discretely taught, consequently being more relevant and effective. Students can also benefit from gaining additional qualifications in key skills while studying geography. Key skills work through geography has become increasingly prominent but is not a new facet of the discipline. Developing transferable skills has to some extent been a hidden agenda in the past but is now highlighted and accepted as an intrinsically essential part of the study of geography.

Photo: ©Emma Gobourn.

In order to maximise the benefits of improved key skills proficiency, active planning for key-skills-rich activities is essential. Planning ahead for key skills can ensure that aspects such as communication or ICT ability are highlighted before beginning a task. Students can be directed towards developing their skills, which should in turn improve their geography. For example, discussing what makes a good report before students begin work can encourage them to express their ideas in a fluent, organised and accurate manner. When students develop their key skills competency they benefit from becoming independent and effective learners. In this way, they become better geographers and attainment levels are increased. There are two-way benefits of promoting key skills development: geographical study can improve students' skills and, in turn, improved skills can improve students' geography performance. Improving students' key skills can help them to gather and analyse geographical information, and communicate and present their findings more effectively. Thinking-skills-based activities provide many key skills development opportunities (see Chapter 16). Enquiry-based teaching and learning and many coursework tasks have key skills as their foundation (see Chapter 9). For example, a decision-making exercise can involve students in discussing issues while working with others, reading and synthesising information from different sources, analysing data and presenting a report of their findings using ICT. These key skills are the necessary tools needed for students to access geographical ideas independently and effectively.

Planning for key skills development in geography

Actively planning tasks and activities which support key skills development is important to maximise the benefits for geographers without distracting from the curriculum content. Integrated tasks are more efficient and effective than bolt-on and discrete activities. Planning for key skills development should not be about additionality but about getting the most from every activity or lesson.

Throughout the key stages and in post-16 study, progression in key skills proficiency can be planned for and assessed, whether internally or formally, through key skills qualifications and specification requirements. A geography department key skills policy should provide an overview of strategies and approaches to key skills but this needs to be followed through with practical planning. It is beneficial to plan for key skills when auditing and reviewing schemes of work. Whole-school key skills strategies and the framework of key skills qualifications may need to be considered and geography teachers' decisions need to be made in the context of what is happening elsewhere in the school. There may, for example, be the opportunity for cross-curricular projects. For example, a geography and biology microclimate project could involve students working in groups collecting data from several sites around the school grounds and the results analysed using ICT. While working through the enquiry process and collecting, presenting and analysing data, and producing the final report students would have many opportunities to develop a range of key skills including application of number, ICT, and working with others.

Key skills opportunities should be identified in schemes of work. Specification documents may signpost suitable parts of the course and existing development opportunities should be highlighted. The extracts in Figure 1 show how key skills can be planned for at GCSE and A-level.

(a) GCSE

Theme	Focus questions	Teaching and learning strategies	Key skills
Coastal erosion	How can coasts be protected? What conflicts of interest arise?	Case study of Holderness coast. Decision-making exercise: should the coastline south of Mappleton be protected? Students to produce a report using ICT.	*Communication* – reading and synthesising, writing *ICT* – word processing of final report, annotation of digital images *Problem solving*

(b) AS-level

Theme	Focus questions	Teaching and learning strategies	Key skills
Tourism	What are the major patterns and flows in world tourism? What are the impacts of these trends?	Mapping of data to identify patterns. Statistical analysis of spreadsheet data to test hypotheses. Research task in pairs to consider impacts based on a particular case study. (Task includes contacting relevant organisations by e-mail and gathering information from websites.) Presentation of findings to rest of group.	*Application of number* *ICT* *Communication*

Figure 1 | *Extracts from schemes of work which incorporate key skills in (a) GCSE and (b) AS-level studies.*

It is important to remember that one opportunity to address a key skill is unlikely to be enough for every student to become proficient (or produce evidence for a key skills qualification). Therefore, practise of key skills is essential and needs to be built into schemes of work, and skills need to be revisited at suitable intervals. Differentiation should be considered to meet students' varying needs and if they are to be entered for formal key skills tests, baseline assessment may be valuable to ascertain the current skills proficiency of each individual.

Key skills development can be part of any geography activity including class work, homework, group work, research tasks, coursework and fieldwork. Several key skills may be addressed during each lesson or task, without necessarily being highlighted to students.

Activities such as the fieldwork shown in Figure 2 provide rich opportunities to develop key skills through geography:

- **Working with others** and **Problem solving** – students work in groups to determine field methods and the questionnaire is designed collectively.
- **Communication skills** – a group discussion is held to decide on a hypothesis and suitable methods. Students carry out surveys with members of the public and produce final report of findings. Students also prepare a presentation of main conclusions.
- **Application of number** – students analyse questionnaire survey results and carry out calculations such as range and averages. Statistical techniques such as standard deviation are also used.
- **ICT** – data are entered into a spreadsheet package and graphs produced. The final report is word processed. Digital camera images are used for annotation. Websites are accessed to gain supporting research information and organisations are contacted via e-mail.

Geography courses include a rich diversity of skills-based opportunities. Examples of activities undertaken as a natural part of the study of geography and how they may develop key skills are identified in Figure 3.

Figure 2 | *Key skills and urban fieldwork in action (Communication and Working with others). Photo: ©Emma Gobourn.*

Many key skills are developed through geography whether they are explicitly highlighted or not. Wide-ranging activities and topics depend upon students using skills such as communication and therefore it is important for geography teachers to facilitate the development of students' skills. Integrating skills development into existing geography tasks is the most effective strategy and minimises extra workload. Improved key skills proficiency is not just an indirect extra benefit of studying geography but actually improves the standard of students' achievement in geography. This poses the question: does skills proficiency follow from geographical attainment or does geographical attainment depend on skills being developed first? With either scenario, developing key skills is not a fringe activity in geography, rather it is an essential aspect of the discipline and should therefore be planned carefully.

Assessing key skills through geography

Planning to develop key skills through geography needs to consider when and how they will be assessed (Flinders, 2000). The focus should be to accredit existing good practice rather than to create artificial assessment opportunities. Sharing assessment criteria with students is important when facilitating their key skills development. For example, before an assessed presentation or discussion students could share ideas about what makes a good presentation or discussion and consider effective techniques as well as the geography subject matter. Similarly, before writing an essay students should be directed towards thinking about how they can improve their written communication skills. Sharing the assessment criteria with students can be informal and verbal or could be formal and based around external key skills qualifications. Placing the emphasis on students to organise for their own portfolio of evidence where relevant can also share the responsibility.

Assessing key skills through geography can provide a focus and structure for key skills development. Geography provides an excellent vehicle for generating portfolio evidence for generic key skills qualifications as well as geography-specific skills.

Assessment of key skills through geography can be external (by test or portfolios) and be based on the specification requirements of awarding bodies. Issues here include the role of other subject areas and baseline testing to determine an appropriate level of entry. Diagnostic tests are available, or students could be asked to complete a self assessment. It is important to recognise that individual students may have varying levels of competency between the key skills. For example, a student may have effective and fluent communication skills but struggle with application of number work.

Teacher assessment could be informal and internal, although structured criteria-referenced assessment is likely to be most focused and support student progression (see

Activity	Example	Key skills developed
Research	Pair-work research into a volcanic eruption – presentation of a written report	**Communication** – reading and synthesising, writing fluently and accurately **ICT** – use of internet, e-mail and CD-Roms **Working with others**
Extended writing	Essay about the impacts of tourism	**Communication** – reading and synthesising, writing
Enquiry-based task	Coursework investigation: How has counter-urbanisation affected the village of Hartlebury?	**Application of number** – statistical analysis of field data **Communication** – carrying out questionnaire surveys with members of the public and production of a written report **ICT** – spreadsheet used to enter and present data and word processing of report **Problem solving**
Decision-making exercise	Group exercise: Should a town's bypass be approved?	**Problem solving** **Working with others** **Communication** – discussing issues and writing conclusions
Presentation	Presentation about an earthquake case study using ICT and images	**Communication** **ICT** – importing images from the internet and CD-Roms, and using a presentation software package such as *PowerPoint* to produce supporting slides
Discussion	Group discussion about the advantages and disadvantages of coastal defences for a particular stretch of coastline	**Working with others** **Communication** – preparatory research (reading and synthesising). Expressing opinions and concepts fluently to others while moving the discussion on and drawing conclusions
Role play	Conflicts of interest in the Amazon rainforest role play: should a new mine be developed?	**Working with others** **Problem solving**
Statistical analysis	Statistical analysis of world population spreadsheet data including the use of techniques such as standard deviation	**Application of number** – selecting and using an appropriate technique and relating quantitative results to qualitative geographical theory **ICT** – using spreadsheets to sort and summarise data
Cartography	Mapping land use from fieldwork notes and use of GIS package	**Working with others** to gather data **ICT** – GIS software
ICT tasks	Contacting organisations via e-mail as part of coursework data collection Analysis of quantitative data	**ICT** ■ researching (using e-mail contacts, websites and CD-Roms) ■ presentation of graphs and maps and photographic images ■ spreadsheet-produced graphs and tables ■ word processing
Case studies	Industrial change and redevelopment in Glasgow – tasks including research, data analysis and report writing	**Application of number** – analysis of data using techniques such as Spearman's Rank Correlation Co-efficient **Communication** – reading and synthesising, writing
Revision	Producing a revision plan, setting own targets and reviewing progress	**Improving own learning and performance** – organising and monitoring performance and raising achievement

Figure 3 | *Key skills in geography.*

GCSE – Human geography *How successful has the London Docklands redevelopment been?*	Adapting this approach for other topics:
Aims and context As part of the settlement topic, students have studied land use models, urban change and problems in inner cities. This unit of work is designed for students to consider how effective one response to inner city problems has been and students are encouraged to reach balanced conclusions. The unit takes 3-4 lessons plus homework to complete.	**GCSE – Physical geography** *How successful have the Holderness coast defences been?* While studying coasts, students study erosion, transportation and deposition. This unit aims to encourage students to consider and evaluate coastal management strategies and the impact of leaving some areas unprotected.

Tasks

(a) Students research, read and synthesise from a variety of sources including textbooks, websites and video clips about the London Docklands redevelopment. Each student produces a summary sheet which answers the following:
- What problems were there in the London Docklands area before redevelopment?
- Why did these problems exist?
- How has the area been redeveloped? (Consider jobs, housing, transport and environmental change.)

(b) A role play is used to consider the impacts of the London Docklands redevelopment on groups such as:
- local people (original residents)
- professionals living in luxury apartments (new residents)
- former dock workers
- businesses relocating to new Docklands offices.

The role play is concluded with a discussion about what is meant by a *successful redevelopment*.

(c) Students produce a word-processed report to sum up their findings using their research summary sheet and role play conclusions. The report must include text, images and a map.

Skills developed

Reading and synthesising evidence from several sources
Applying geographical terminology to a case study
Considering bias of sources, organising ideas and presenting a balanced evaluation
Developing verbal communication and role-play skills
Using ICT to present text, images and a map

Assessment

Students can be given a grade for their contribution to the role play.
The final report is assessed and feedback given.
Students make at least two suggestions of how they could improve their own learning and performance when they next carry out similar work.

As with the London Docklands tasks, students carry out research and a role play. This is in preparation for producing a newspaper-style article about defending the Holderness coast. Students are encouraged to write in a style appropriate to the purpose and use ICT software to produce their newspaper article which is then assessed.

A-level – Population
A comparison of the population characteristics of Brazil and the UK
Case studies of the UK and Brazil are used to consolidate learning about natural increase, population pyramids and migration.

Students work in pairs and use atlases, textbooks, websites and video clips to find out about population structure and change through time. Their completed report should include description, explanation and comparison.

Key skills developed include reading and synthesising, ICT skills (such as presenting population pyramids), and working with others (researching one country each and then working together for the final report and comparison).

Assessment of the final report is most effective if each student clearly identifies their contribution.

Figure 4 | *Examples of tasks with integrated key skills development.*

Chapters 32 and 33). Key skills can be assessed with qualitative statements or matched against quantitative levels. However key skills are assessed, providing formative feedback to move students on is essential (see Chapter 32). For example, feedback about student performance with application of number skills in an enquiry project may be brief and verbal or students could be given detailed written feedback after a written assignment. Peer and self assessment could also be used: students can be given either an awarding body's assessment criteria for particular key skills or agreed internal criteria to assess work. Students could be asked to audit their own skills at the start of the course and review them regularly to help improve their own learning and performance skills. This can be effectively incorporated into the target-setting process and be an important part of formative assessment. Student-led assessment of key skills also encourages them to

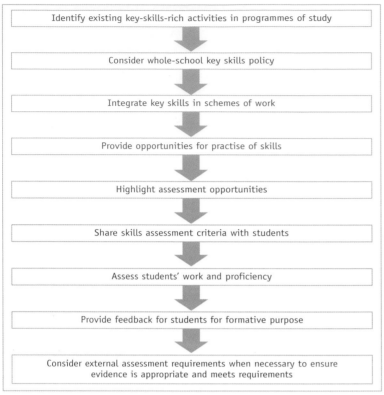

Figure 5 | *Developing and assessing key skills activities.*

become active learners with responsibility for their own learning.

Geography is a good source of key skills proficiency evidence (Figure 4). The great variety of tasks undertaken include coursework, statistical analysis, essays and ICT work. Fieldwork reports address many key skills and provide opportunities for the practise and development of skills. The type of evidence required for portfolios should be considered and shared with students if key skills are to be formally assessed. For example, to show evidence of reading and synthesising, students can be asked to photocopy and annotate a section of each source used. Verbal work such as presentations and discussions can be assessed. Completing observation sheets when observing these activities can formalise situations and structure activities and feedback. These could be completed by the teacher or as a peer- or self-assessment exercise. Witness statements about the use of key skills can also provide evidence. With externally assessed key skills, the awarding body may provide the necessary paperwork, or geography departments may wish to develop their own.

Points to consider when planning to develop and assess key skills through geography are shown in Figure 5.

There are many benefits of developing key skills through geography. As a discipline, geography naturally addresses and depends upon skills-based activities. Active planning to develop and assess key skills should enable students to become effective learners who can apply their skills as better geographers.

Active research ideas

■ Review and revise schemes of work to plan for key skills
■ Develop a departmental key skills policy, considering progression, differentiation and assessment
■ Investigate the opportunities for students to gain external qualifications in key skills through their study of geography
■ Set up cross-curricular projects or activities which develop a range of key skills
■ Design a student self-assessment sheet which includes a review of key skills developed
■ Consider key skills development when setting targets for students.

Related publications from the Geographical Association:
■ Broad, J. (2001) *A-Z Advancing Geography: Key Skills.*
■ Holmes, D. and Farbrother, D. (2000) *A-Z Advancing Geography: Fieldwork.*

Implications for practice

(a) **Planning for key skills development in geography ensures that lessons incorporate a variety of teaching and learning styles.**

Student-centred, active learning and enquiry-based tasks are particularly effective in facilitating key skills development. Key-skills-based activities should be integrated within geography not taught discretely. By increasing students' proficiency in skills such as communication, ICT and working with others, understanding and attainment will improve. Key skills are the tools necessary for learning.

(b) **Key skills should be openly addressed during teaching and learning activities.**

Rather than key skills development being a hidden agenda, key skills can be planned for, highlighted and possibly assessed. Students need guidance and feedback for progression to take place. For example, discussing what makes a good presentation with a class can help students to improve. Some activities such as fieldwork are particularly skills-rich. Relevant key skills to be developed can be identified while sharing objectives, setting targets and evaluating learning.

(c) **Assessment for learning (see Chapter 32) can support progression in key skills development.**

Self assessment and peer assessment can encourage students to improve their own learning and performance. Students of all abilities benefit from improving their key skills. Differentiation must consider students' individual needs for each particular skill to facilitate progress.

(d) **Geography can be promoted as a subject which encourages students to develop a range of valuable transferable skills.**

This can help to ensure healthy option numbers at GCSE and A-level. Highlighting the transferable skills which are developed through the study of geography and the value of a geography qualification for employability can attract students. Key skills reinforced in geography will support students' achievement across the curriculum.

References

Print

Bland, K. *et al.* (2000) *Key Skills in A-level Geography*. National Extension College. (Pack contains activities and suggestions for developing key skills through geography.)

Flinders, E. (2000) 'Assessing key skills through geography: a practical approach', *Teaching Geography*, 25, 2, pp. 96-8.

Electronic

Supporting materials and other information is available from the following awarding bodies and key skills websites:

- AQA – www.aqa.org.uk/
- DfES – www.dfes.gov.uk/keyskills
- Edexcel – www.edexcel.org.uk/
- OCR – www.ocr.org.uk/
- QCA – www.qca.org.uk/keyskills
- WJEC – www.wjec.co.uk/

Chapter 36

Preparing for public examinations

Sue Warn

Before reading this chapter consider the following questions:

- How can you manage the 'treadmill' of external assessment?

- How can you meet the targets set for my students' performance yet still follow an enquiry-based approach to learning?

- What strategies are there for incorporating assessment imaginatively into your students' learning?

Introduction

The world of the secondary school geography teacher is perceived by many as one which is constrained by a straightjacket of largely external assessment, with a series of summative assessment at key stage 3, key stage 4 (GCSE) and AS followed by A2. As these various stages were developed diachronously, with the Curriculum 2000 framework for post-16 and the review of key stage 3 pre-dating the GCSEs, it is hardly surprising that teachers and their students are faced with a bewildering patchwork of knowledge, understanding and skills, and proscribed content through which they have to develop an effective and imaginative pathway.

It is possible to develop a hierarchy of assessment for teachers to use when setting internal examinations – see Figure 1, which is based on thinking developed by senior examiners.

However, the reality is that the picture is far more blurred than the information in Figure 1 indicates because of the range of specifications and related assessment packages on offer. Of equal concern is the resulting piecemeal diet which students can receive from the 'space, place, environment' triangle if teachers do not give considerable thought to case study choice. Currently, many students have a very stereotyped and narrow view of the world, almost never studying countries in Eastern Europe or those belonging to the Commonwealth of Independent States, focusing instead upon the rainforests of Amazonia, or urban squatter settlements, and often revisiting the same places and topics a number of times at different stages.

Geography teachers are invariably enthusiastic about their subject, but this enthusiasm can sometimes lead to 'fat file syndrome' and the notion persists among

	GCSE Foundation	GCSE Higher	AS	A2
Knowledge	*Student offers...* ... basic definitions and examples ... and simple processes	*Student provides...* ... basic definitions with some short case studies which are usually well defined in the specification ... range of basic processes	*Student uses...* ...wider range of definitions ... extended case studies ... terminology of A-level *And demonstrates ...* ... more advanced knowledge of physical and human processes	*Student demonstrates knowledge of ...* ... geographical terminology, i.e. it is used habitually as part of knowledge base ... extended case studies ... processes across field of geography ... distributional inter-linkage ... a wide range of sources, and synthesises them
Under-standing	*Student offers...* ... one or two clearly identified concepts ... clearly identified contexts	*Student provides...* ... range of concepts ... limited awareness of theory and applies it to clearly identified contexts ... occasionally transfers these to new contexts	*Student demonstrates...* ... conceptual understanding ... application of theory ... ability to transfer theory to new contexts	*Student is able to ...* ... apply theory widely ... demonstrate an understanding of interlinked concepts ... offer alternative explanations – i.e. critical understanding ... frequently apply critical understanding to new concepts ... demonstrate complex understanding
Command words	*Student is able to ...* state describe identify outline	*Student is able to ...* describe and suggest reasons	*Student is able to ...* describe in detail examine assess explain	*Student is able to ...* analyse critically assess evaluate discuss
Complexity of task	*Examination papers are ...* ... totally structured with a series of short questions	*Examination papers are ...* ... usually structured open-ended short end-piece often worth 6-8 marks	*Examination papers comprise ...* ... partially structured open-ended (at end) questions, frequently with some guidance ... two or three part essays ... extended writing worth 10+ marks possible (often 1 hour 20 minutes)	*Examination papers are ...* ... open-ended ... unlikely to include a structured essay (student usually has to generate own structure and synthesise) (often 2-2.5 hours)
Resource analysis Skills and techniques	*Students are expected to analyse ...* ... simple single resources ... information which is largely provided for direct lift-off ... simple cartoons, clear photos and simple maps	*Students are expected to analyse ...* ... some straightforward resources with possible comparison of or linkage to two clear clues *There is also ...* ... an occasional requirement to draw a sketch map, often with a framework supplied	*Students are expected to analyse ...* ... a more complex range of resources, with frequent comparison/ linkage required ... questions that are largely data-response involving interpretation *And...* ... student has to generate own sketch maps and diagrams	*Students are expected to analyse ...* ... a wide range of resources – many complex (e.g. satellite images or synoptic charts) ... questions that are often data stimulus which require them to develop their own interpretations technical resources from journals *And ...* ... student is expect to generate own sketch maps and diagrams as part of answer, to enhance quality

Figure 1 | *Levels of examining and expectation of students at GCSE and A-level. Photo: Bananastock Ltd.*

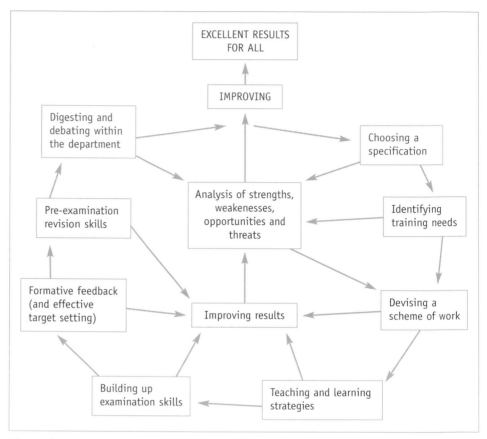

Figure 2 | *Developing the virtuous circle of assessment-led learning.* ©*Sue Warn.*

students that geography is relatively hard, endlessly worthy (yes, even sustainability can be overdone), has onerous coursework and is not especially 'cool'. The natural breadth of the subject is reflected in the overloaded content of many public examination specifications, especially at GCSE and AS-level, so this requires careful management.

There are considerable pressures on teachers to achieve results – both high grades in absolute terms, and significant value-added scores from the most recent benchmarks. While accepting that high grades are what matter most for the majority of students, and a good end-result makes them more forgiving of indifferent teaching or semi-arid learning environments, we as teachers of geography need to look at how we can develop a 'virtuous circle' of assessment-led learning (Figure 2) which addresses some of the fundamental underlying issues.

Establishing a framework

First, select your specification

In order to achieve the end-goal of 'excellent results for all' (see Figure 2), it is vital for teachers to devise an overall, appropriate framework for their public examination work. While ACCAC/QCA monitoring is designed to ensure that standards are maintained across the whole range of examination specifications and that no awarding body's examinations are easier or harder than others, there is no doubt that some assessment packages suit certain groups of students better than others, according to, for example, gender, or ability mix. The awarding bodies usually offer a range of specifications at both GCSE and Advanced level (A-level) with very different assessment packages, derived from within common QCA subject criteria. Specifications from the same awarding body must be significantly different to justify their existence, and usually reflect so-called traditional or modern approaches.

While student performance is one criterion for choice, teacher preference and resource availability also are key factors. Choosing the GCSE and A-level courses to ensure vertical geographical progression is also a vital factor. Achieving a balance between building on GCSE concepts, yet encouraging students to explore new topics pre-university, requires considered judgement from teachers. The question has to be asked, 'Is it worth doing this for the minority of students progressing through key stage 4 to A-level and on to higher education when those students represent perhaps only 2-3% of the original cohort?'

Identifying training needs

Once you have selected your specification it is important to 'get inside the system'. Initially this can be done by consulting teachers' guides published by the awarding body, and obtaining sets of past papers, mark schemes and examiners' reports – often best done by liaising with a nearby centre which already covers that specification.

Contact the awarding body to see what help and training is available for new centres. Awarding body training usually varies from basic feedback to more detailed courses on raising achievement in problem units, such as synoptic ones. Perhaps the best sort of training of all is to get various members of the departmental team to act as assistant examiners for a variety of papers at GCSE, AS and A2. This experience is particularly useful for newly-qualified teachers, or those hoping to achieve promotion to posts of responsibility. It also provides extremely useful training on how to improve your own students' performance.

Devising a scheme of work

Far too many teachers play safe and use the chosen awarding body's specification as the scheme of work, frequently reinforced by the standard awarding body-sponsored textbooks (see Chapter 13). However, teachers can devise their own schemes of work which can be used as a basis for diverse teaching and learning strategies with a rationalised policy of skills development, and which with careful use of case studies and examples, can provide a balanced areal coverage at a variety of scales and in countries at different states of development.

At A-level, care must be taken not to do the same studies as at GCSE, to avoid monotony and to ensure a richness of geographical experience. It is much better to refer to these *en passant* to make comparisons and contrasts. The aim has to be the successful incorporation of assessment (the development of skills) into teaching and learning (assessment-led learning).

Teaching and learning strategies

Much research material is now avaiable free of charge on the internet or at low cost in pre-digested form (e.g. *Geofile*) and this can be assessed in terms of its coherence, relevance and up-to-datedness, all of which are significant in terms of motivating students. To achieve both coherence and coverage it is worth developing checklists or spider diagrams such as that shown in Figure 3.

There is absolutely no reason why imaginative teaching and the exploration of, for example, 'mysteries' should cease with key stage 3. There is also scope for developing personal research skills using both primary and secondary techniques in a well-structured

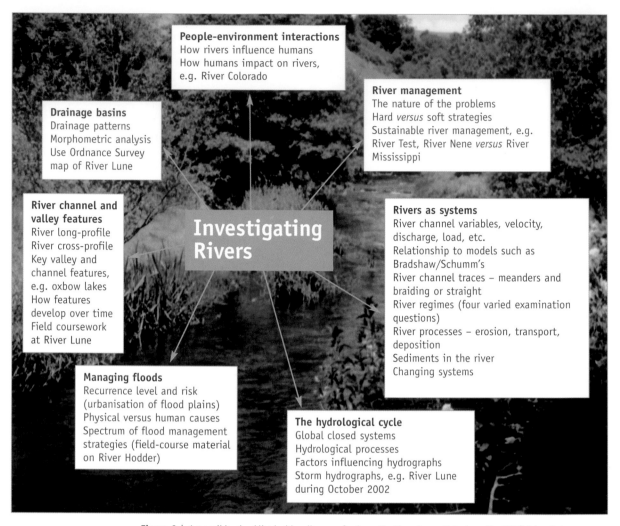

People-environment interactions
How rivers influence humans
How humans impact on rivers,
e.g. River Colorado

River management
The nature of the problems
Hard *versus* soft strategies
Sustainable river management, e.g.
River Test, River Nene *versus* River
Mississippi

Drainage basins
Drainage patterns
Morphometric analysis
Use Ordnance Survey
map of River Lune

**River channel and
valley features**
River long-profile
River cross-profile
Key valley and
channel features,
e.g. oxbow lakes
How features
develop over time
Field coursework
at River Lune

**Investigating
Rivers**

Rivers as systems
River channel variables, velocity,
discharge, load, etc.
Relationship to models such as
Bradshaw/Schumm's
River channel traces – meanders and
braiding or straight
River regimes (four varied examination
questions)
River processes – erosion, transport,
deposition
Sediments in the river
Changing systems

Managing floods
Recurrence level and risk
(urbanisation of flood plains)
Physical versus human causes
Spectrum of flood management
strategies (field-course material
on River Hodder)

The hydrological cycle
Global closed systems
Hydrological processes
Factors influencing hydrographs
Storm hydrographs, e.g. River Lune
during October 2002

Figure 3 | *A possible checklist/spider diagram for investigating rivers. Note how the UK fieldwork is incorporated as an in-depth case study and how use is made of a variety of comparative case studies. Photo: ©Diane Wright.*

case study development programme. For example, a spreadsheet can be put together of a group's research on individual hurricane events in order to look at hurricane occurrence spatially as well as temporally and to relate damage and deaths to the actual magnitude of the events.

Similarly, group and collaborative work, if managed effectively to ensure quality presentations and useful outcomes in terms of assessment offers diversity in the classroom (these are discussed in detail in Chapter 25). Groups can look at, for example, varying rates of erosion along cliff profiles (Figure 4), or possible choices from the spectrum of coastal management options for a particular stretch of coastline, using cost-benefit analysis as the major technique, as well as potential environmental impact.

Maximising diversity in learning strategies will help improve student knowledge, understanding and skills, all of which are vital components to success in public examinations.

Activities	
1. Each group to produce a five-minute presentation describing and explaining the features shown on one profile.	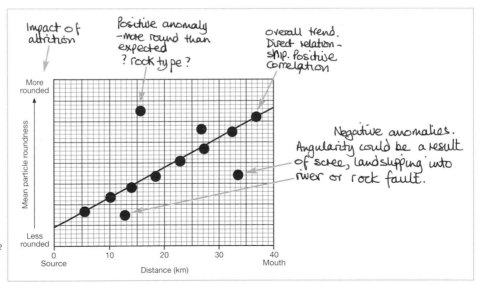
2. Groups use the profiles to undertake a ranking exercise: from 1: least eroded to 5: fastest/most rapid rate of erosion.	
3. Individual task to write a justification for overall ranking, offering reasons.	
4a. Summarise features leading to variable rates of cliff erosion 4b. Summarise key terminology 4c. Look at a map sequence to measure rates of erosion over time, or contrasting photographs before and after a major storm.	

Figure 4 | *Activities relating to varying rates of erosion along cliff profiles.*

Figure 5 | *Using simple graphs for data response questions.*

Building up examination skills

It is worth looking closely at assessment demands made by the examination (both as class and homework tasks) – essentially students need to learn how to analyse and interpret data such as graphs, maps, diagrams and photographs. They also need to know how to respond to a variety of question styles such as structured short-answer questions

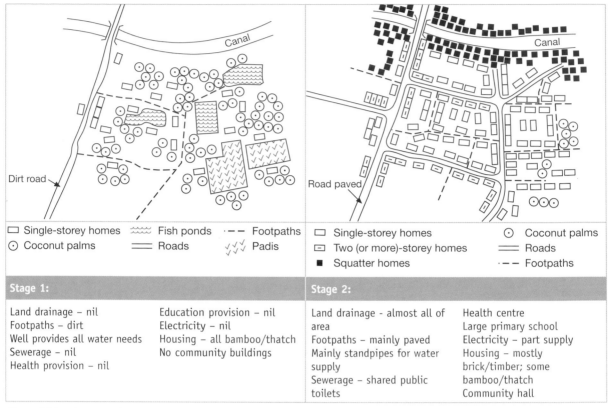

Stage 1:	
Land drainage – nil	Education provision – nil
Footpaths – dirt	Electricity – nil
Well provides all water needs	Housing – all bamboo/thatch
Sewerage – nil	No community buildings
Health provision – nil	

Stage 2:	
Land drainage - almost all of area	Health centre
Footpaths – mainly paved	Large primary school
Mainly standpipes for water supply	Electricity – part supply
Sewerage – shared public toilets	Housing – mostly brick/timber; some bamboo/thatch
	Community hall

Figure 6 | *Development of urban neighbourhoods in Indonesia. Source: Hornby and Jones, 1991.*

and essays, as well as decision-making and issues-analysis exercises. Some of this work can be done as homework. Managing homework effectively is crucial to students' success in public examinations: little and often seems to work well at GCSE and AS – with tasks which encourage students to read and to consolidate notes taken in the lesson.

One strategy for ensuring success in **data response** questions is to cut up past examination papers and to organise them to fit your scheme of work. Use photographs of physical and human landscapes because these are often more complex for students to analyse and describe. Use basic techniques, e.g. orientating the direction in which the photograph was taken, or measuring scale or angle of slope. A simple graph such as that shown in Figure 5 can be used not only to indicate how students should describe trends and relationships on graphs (always quote the data in the answer) but also to reinforce understanding of river erosion and the index of roundness or wear. A practical session with a stone board of carefully selected pebbles could reinforce the concept, possibly using statistical techniques such as Spearman Rank or Chi-square or Zinng's index to develop the study further.

One of the main difficulties that students experience is to describe change over time from a series of diagrams or maps. Here practice with the thought bomb and brief plan sequence as shown below can be very helpful. In describing changes to an area on the edge of a city in Indonesia – shown in Figure 6 – many students adopted a piecemeal approach. For example, they described the loss of coconut palms, rather than taking an overview and looking at a combination of factors, e.g. rapid urbanisation on the edge of the city over a given period and its links to the economic development of the country as a whole.

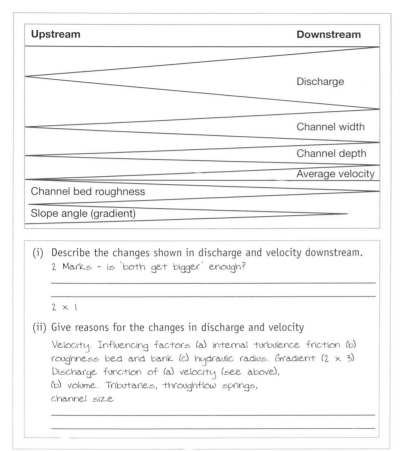

Upstream	Downstream
	Discharge
	Channel width
	Channel depth
	Average velocity
Channel bed roughness	
Slope angle (gradient)	

(i) Describe the changes shown in discharge and velocity downstream.
2 Marks - is 'both get bigger' enough?

_____

_____

2 × 1

(ii) Give reasons for the changes in discharge and velocity

Velocity. Influencing factors (a) internal turbulence friction (b) roughness bed and bank (c) hydraulic radius. Gradient (2 × 3)
Discharge function of (a) velocity (see above),
(b) volume. Tributaries, throughflow springs,
channel size

_____

_____

Figure 7 | Annotated examination questions. Source: Edexcel B specification.

Competence in relation to data-response activities can be worth around an extra 15% of marks in many GCSE and AS-level examinations. At A2 the approach is usually data stimulus, whereby students must analyse the implications of the data and use the findings in their answer.

The ability to answer **short structured questions** is of paramount importance for GCSE/AS-level papers. What is needed is to ensure that a student avoids the situation where he or she consistently loses marks through each sub-section because of a lacklustre performance. Figures 7 and 8 illustrate two ways of improving students' perform-ance, i.e. by annotating the questions with key advice. If done early on in the course, this kind of prompting technique is a very helpful device for steering students in the right direction and boosting their confidence. In time, the dissection of each question, with command words (what do they really mean?) and key words should become second nature.

Of equal importance is the use of **mark schemes** from the beginning, as part of self- and peer-assessment of performance. Questions are marked using a combination of **points** (for structured questions) and **levels** where more extended writing is required (see also Chapters 32, 33 and 37). Each level is characterised by a particular **quality** of performance, such as the degree of detailed exemplification, or range of ideas introduced. Familiarity with the demands of the mark scheme enhances student performance greatly, and helps them to develop a critical approach towards improving it.

Developing an appropriate geographical **vocabulary** is another essential skill for preparing students for public examinations. Most awarding bodies publish lists of vocabulary at GCSE, and some do for AS. Students should never be without a good geographical dictionary, and imaginative ways of building up essential vocabulary need to be devised because it helps students to understand the demands of questions, define terms accurately for knowledge marks, and enhances their essay performance. One way to do this is to generate crosswords and quizzes for them to practice on – older students should have some fun and games in lessons too!

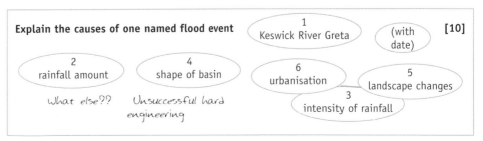

Explain the causes of one named flood event [10]

1 Keswick River Greta (with date)

2 rainfall amount

4 shape of basin

6 urbanisation

5 landscape changes

3 intensity of rainfall

What else??

Unsuccessful hard engineering

Figure 8 | An example thought bomb and one line plan sequence for answering a question on flood events.

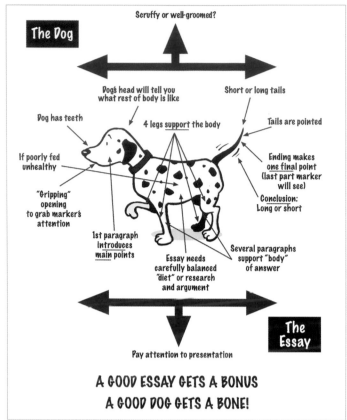

The Dog

Scruffy or well-groomed?

Dog's head will tell you what rest of body is like

Short or long tails

Dog has teeth

4 legs support the body

Tails are pointed

If poorly fed unhealthy

Ending makes one final point (last part marker will see)

"Gripping" opening to grab marker's attention

Conclusion: Long or short

1st paragraph introduces main points

Several paragraphs support "body" of answer

Essay needs carefully balanced "diet" or research and argument

Pay attention to presentation

The Essay

**A GOOD ESSAY GETS A BONUS
A GOOD DOG GETS A BONE!**

Figure 9 | *Comparing an essay with a dog. Source: A. Jeanes, Simon Langton Boys School, Canterbury.*

As Figure 1 shows, a hierarchy of **extended writing** exists between GCSE Foundation, through Higher to AS and to A2 where most questions are **essay style**. Clearly a strategy for building up essay skills has to be developed, especially when stepping up from AS to A2. At AS all specifications demand some extended answers – usually the last part of each structured question is worth between 6 and 10 marks. The first skill students need is to thought bomb and sequence a basic one line **plan**, for example, on a flood event as shown in Figure 8.

Even at GCSE, mini essay titles can be more sophisticated, therefore students need to learn to plan by *concept* with supporting case studies and examples, rather than merely writing descriptive case studies one after the other. For more sophisticated AS/A2 essays it is useful to develop the writing frame idea of introduction, main body, and conclusion. Figure 9 shows a model which compares an essay with a dog, to help students understand this idea, and Figure 10 provides an example of a writing frame for an essay on famine.

Some students develop complexes, believing that they will never be successful essay writers, or never be able to do issues analysis. To prevent this happening a structured programme of communal planning and organisation, initially with gradual stepped development of the students' own skills in employing the tactics described here and in Chapter 37, is essential.

A variety of different presentations throughout the course can improve writing skills (see Chapter 11). A parallel programme should be developed to build up students ability to draw **simple maps and diagrams** to support and enhance their extended answers. For many students, simple conceptual diagrams, e.g. of a U-shaped valley, can enhance their understanding considerably. Equally, developing good annotational skills is very important; and something that can be done effectively on field courses, or as part of group work. For example, when studying a river basin such as that of the Mississippi the class can split into four groups, each being given a **design brief** to annotate a basic pre-drawn sketch map to show features such as flooding, management, variations in discharge, or economic uses of the Mississippi basin, and potential conflicts. These question-related designer maps are so much more useful than over-complex generic maps which do not focus on the question. As with any successful group work, the end-result should be high-quality products (perhaps computer drawn, see Chapter 10).

Formative feedback

It is absolutely vital that students of all abilities receive honest yet supportive feedback as to how they are performing. There are many commercial systems available, such as YELLIS (year 11) and ALIS (post-16), which forecast likely student performance and enable a process of individual target setting to be embedded in teaching (see Chapters 32-34). With unit structures such as those for A-level, opportunities exist for purposeful

The root causes of famine lie in physical geography. Discuss.

Introduction

- Definition of famine with relation to chronic hunger – an acute crisis. Extreme significance of famine as a killer, in spite of general increase in global food supplies (statistics).

- Consideration of the issue – what exactly is a root cause (underlying cause) as opposed to an immediate trigger?

Causal analysis of famine is complex – can depend on whether the fundamental cause is seen as food availability decline/deficit (FAD). Likely to be triggered by physical factors such as drought, climate change, floods, cyclones, pests and war, which affect food supplies.

A food entitlement deficit (FED) likely to be related to social and political factors in particular poverty, or land ownership issues. These affect food factors, in particular poverty or land ownership issues, which affect food security (could be root cause of colonisation). Range of case studies to show variety of location and famine type (famine can happen with or without major death tolls. Some historic, some current).

Main body

Use cards or post-its to summarise key features

Major sections		Case study choice
Major paragraph, actions, physical, farmers (FAD) range of factors	Pests / Drought	Irish potato famine (pests trigger) physical causes, locust in Niger
Social and political factors affecting FED. Role of wars and refugees		Famine in Wollo district, Ethiopia (recurring) or Niger
Supporting factors current crises, HIV/AIDS, climate change – increasing stress	Political issues / Political issues – targeted recipient	Current famines in sub-Saharan Africa, Tanzania, Sudan drought, climate change
Reassessment, cumulative factors, clearly many triggers, concentration, yet underlying causes of poverty		Famine in north Korea? political issues Famine in Zimbabwe, land reform, political instability, colonialism
Paragraph, evaluating and reviewing Conclusion – increasing triggers but really tied to poverty	Decline in famine / Increased food security/decline of poverty	India's famine pre green revolution affected very poor, now no problem

Conclusion

Famine related to a number of causes, climatic, demographic, sociological, economic and political. Identifying both triggers but a lot underlying root causes (make case study links). Include summary diagram. Not all physical hazards lead to famine, famine is economically selective. Role of capital and technology in overcoming it. Root causes now increasingly social and political and above all impacts on those below the povery line (diagram of crunch model).

Figure 10 | *Tackling extended writing/essays at A-level: The writing frame concept applied to a famine question.*

With reference to a named rural area, examine the factors influencing its landscape and character

A Named rural area: Brittany in France

The land use in Brittany changed dramatically in the 1970s. As traditional farming methods declined the high-technology intensive farming methods took over the farming industry.

Small farms were condensed and the field size increased. The blockages were removed and the fields opened out. These were to occupy larger intensive farming units such as pigs and chickens to provide meat and eggs for the general public. The farming units result in pollution from the manure and fertilizers used on the fields. Eutrophication then occurs as nitrates and chemicals are absorbed into the rivers and cause conflict between the fishermen and farmers. The algae that occurs from eutrophication then grows on the surface of the water causing problems for fishermen.

The area is no longer consisting of small farms with a local community. These instead have been replaced by the larger units and the number of farms has decreased.

Hedges have been removed which has resulted in the loss of habitat for some wildlife.

B Named rural area: Harefield, Middlesex

Harefield is a large village in Middlesex on a rural urban fringe. It is a village that has changed due to urbanisation and people migrating to the rural areas from urban cities or towns. Harefield is surrounded by fields and woodland which makes it give the impression of being idyllic and away from big cities.

However on our field trip to Harefield I discovered that although it is a large village it is segregated into two parts. New developments give the impression that Harefield is merging into a small town. However on our fieldtrip I discovered central Harefield is very much in character with people's ideas of how a rural settlement should be. The services in the centre are 'typical' village services with bakers, post office etc. The village green in the heart of the village also gives the impression as an idyllic village.

However in my fieldwork I discovered Harefield's character has been altered by the fact that Junction 17 on the M25 is less than half an hours walk from the village centre. The landscape of Harefield is surrounded by fields and is hilly which gives the idea of being quite remote but with the M25 and other major roads leading to and from Harefield it gives the village a character very different from most of a 'typical' village. During my fieldwork 'villagers' often said that the community character was altered by the continuous urbanisation that Harefield has suffered, but the surrounding landscape would not give that impression.

Figure 11 | Example answers for students to 'mark'. They should mark (with a red ring) the facts and figures in each answer and (where necessary) offer comments on ways in which the answers could be improved.

individual progress interviews, and there is no better time for counselling than when the latest results have been received. A variety of factors get in the way of student success, many not directly related to the geography lesson. Of vital importance is the need to seek a second opinion from an experienced tutor or another member of the geography department, to provide enhanced support for specific students.

Pre-examination revision skills

Pre-revision and revision skills are vital (see also Chapter 37). It is always useful to go over the difficult areas (get the previous year's students to recommend the problem concepts) and also to spend time on whole-paper and individual question analysis. Now that awarding bodies make copies of candidates' scripts available, a useful post-examination activity is for the departmental team to look at a range of students' performances to identify areas for improvement. (Common pitfalls include students using rubric errors and not employing good time management during examinations.) This post-examination script analysis, combined with consideration of examiners' reports, informs teachers very effectively.

It is when choosing the executing of case studies that candidates also often fall short. Examples of students' answers from examiners' reports are useful in this context. Get the students to act as exam markers, in particular using the 'red ring' test (encircling words or phrases in red pen) to indicate where the answer includes precise facts and figures related to a particular case study. Figure 11 provides two examples for students to practise on.

In short, ensure that the revision period is not too extensive, provide assessment-based learning throughout the course and bear in mind that it is only necessary for students to hone skills and consolidate all the lessons learnt to achieve success.

Digesting and debating with the department

It is very important for the departmental team to allow time to digest and analyse the flow of useful information and support on examinations that 'rains down' on their desks. They should also take the opportunity to debate strategies for teaching and learning about revision. There is no doubt that departments that use collaborative-thinking approaches enjoy greater success in preparing their students for public examinations, and as a consequence, achieve better results. The secret is to make assessment fun and help all learners to win.

Implications for practice

(a) **Assessment forms a vital part of learning.**

Drip feed assessment into the overall learning process. This should allow your students to develop a range of skills and confidence over time.

(b) **Use assessment to monitor student's individual progress.**

As both a formative and a diagnostic tool although it is used summatively to grade a students performance in public examinations. It is therefore vital that you avail yourself of all data available from, for example, Ofsted, PANDAS and Fischer Family Trust data. These show how good overall performance is in a national context and a similar schools context as well as looking at progression from one key stage to another (value added data).

(c) **Public examinations.**

Assessment by public examinations has developed into a far more transparent process. It is vital that you avail yourself of the different types of support available and maximise these opportunities.

Related publications from the Geographical Association:
- Butt, G. (2002) *Theory Into Practice: Extending writing skills*.
- Roberts, M. (2003) *Learning through Enquiry: Making sense of geography in the key stage 3 classroom*.
- The regular 'Assessment Matters' pages in *Teaching Geography*.

Reference and further reading

Ferretti, J. and Greasley, B. (2001) *Geography: GCSE Revision Notes*. Deddington: Philip Allan Updates.
GeoFile online – www.nelsonthornes.com/secondary/geography/geofile/
Hornby, W.F. and Jones, M. (1991) *An Introduction to Settlement Geography*. Cambridge: Cambridge University Press.
Raw, M. (2000) *Geography: AS/A-level Revision Notes*. Deddington: Philip Allan Updates
Staffordshire Learning Net – www.sln.org.uk/geography

Chapter 37

'Gotta get thru this' – GCSE examination

Russell Chapman and Bob Digby

Before reading this chapter consider the following questions:

- How can you prepare your students for revision?

- What means can you use to prepare students for their GCSE examinations?

- How can you make best use of 'pre-release' materials, particularly those related to decision making?

Chapter 36 emphasises the importance of choosing a specification appropriate to our needs, and of using imaginative approaches to teaching in preparation for public examinations. In this chapter, the focus is on preparing students for GCSE, with the aim of providing them with two years of enjoyable and imaginative learning, ideally leading to success in the examinations. As Roberts notes (2003), the purpose of all learning – and that includes learning for revision – is 'making sense'.

Preparing students for revision

There are several generic revision guides on the market, and all are obtainable from booksellers. Although such guides sell well and may have a role to play, in our view they have serious shortcomings in terms of their approach to examinations, as follows:

(a) They are essentially 'crammer guides', designed to provide students with all they need to know in a few brief pages.

(b) They assume that all specifications are the same, and that geography can be expressed in general, place-less terms.

(c) They do not help students to *make sense of* the course that they have studied, only provide generalised information that can be transmitted in the short term, and that has little long-term value.

(d) They do not encourage students to think in terms of relevance and issues, and about things that affect people and the environment they live in.

(e) They encourage students to believe that rote learning is a valid means of education.

Examination paper	Type of examination	Marks	Examination length
Either Paper 1F (Foundation - grades C-G) *Or* Paper 3H (Higher - grades A*-D)	A decision-making exercise based on pre-released resources issued during May, and with an examination about 3-4 weeks later	25%	1 hour 15 minutes
Either Paper 2F (Foundation tier) *Or* Paper 4H (Higher tier)	A written examination during June based upon learning during the course	50%	2 hours
Coursework	An investigation based on primary data to be carried out at some time during the course	25%	Is not examined once complete

Figure 1 | *Examination structure for one Edexcel assessment procedure in geography.*

We believe that if students *understand* their course they should be able to handle any question that examiners set. How, then, can we as geography teachers prepare our students for examinations in ways that encourage understanding?

Knowing what examinations lie ahead

GCSE examinations are tiered; that is, they are levelled according to student abilities. The Foundation tier (coded 'F' in Figure 1) is targeted at students of average ability and below who are not expected to achieve above Grade C. Higher tier examinations (coded 'H' in Figure 1) are aimed at students expected to achieve at between Grade D and A*. The decision about which tier is most appropriate for which student will need to be made at the time of examination entries (usually 4-6 months prior to the examination).

Getting to know the specification

Clearly, it is vitally important to be thoroughly acquainted with the specification of your choice. Given busy schedules and heavy workloads, it is all too easy to read and absorb a specification in September, then to find when you open it some months later that much of it has faded from memory. While specifications should not dictate our teaching strategies, a disciplined attitude towards time allocation for each component of the specification will ensure that all areas receive equal coverage and balance.

Just as important is students' own knowledge of the specification that they have been taught. Most students study nine or ten GCSEs and have to know the rigours of each; no two subjects are exactly alike. Students will therefore need some kind of guidance (preferably written) about their course, and how what they are being taught will translate into examination experience. Figure 2 shows advice given by a school about their GCSE course and how it is divided up into core and optional units.

Students should also know where *general* understanding is required, as opposed to *specific* case study knowledge. In the specification, look carefully for case studies (or appropriate scales of study) which *must* be carried out; these are studies that students will be asked to recall in the examination. Specification writers and examiners do this so that students – and teachers! – can keep learning to a manageable level by limiting places studied. Candidates should always be able to refer to case studies, because credit is given for examples.

Preparing for the examination

Revision is a personal thing, because people learn in different ways. Too many students are given revision to do but with little guidance as to how to do it; yet there are several things that can be done to help students. Most advice suggests that everything should be broken into small pieces or 'sound-bite' equivalents. Most BBC revision programmes allow 12-15 minutes per topic. This should be a guide for teachers in terms of suggesting how students should revise. Small study 'chunks' are often better as a tool for preparation than lengthy, unbroken periods of time.

Aiding the revision process

No matter how imaginative the teacher or department, some GCSE preparation is

Core units	
Unit titles	**Themes**
A1: Providing for population change	Population dynamics Population and resources
A2: Planning for change	Settlement Employment
A3: Coping with environmental change	Coasts Hazards

These units will be examined by:
- ■ The decision-making paper (paper 1F or 3H)
- ■ Section A of the written paper (paper 2F or 4H)

One unit will be examined in the decision-making paper. Whichever unit is examined in this paper will not be re-tested in Section A of the written paper 2F or 4H. The remaining two units will be assessed in Section A.

Each of the two questions in Section A
- ■ Counts for 30 marks. Allow 30% of the time per question – 36 minutes per question
- ■ Consists of structured questions, ranging from short answers (1-2 marks) to longer extended answers (8-9 marks). The longest answers demand case study knowledge.

In addition, there are four option units, from which you have studied two.

Option units
Either Unit B4: Water   **or**   Unit B5: Weather and climate **And either** Unit C6: Farming   **or**   Unit C7: Recreation and tourism
These units will be examined by Sections B and C of the written paper (paper 2F or 4H). There will always be a question on the Options you have studied. Each of the two questions in Section B counts for 20 marks. Allow 20% of the time per question – 24 minutes per question. Again, there is a mix of short and long answers.

Figure 2 | A summary of content for one Edexcel specification for GCSE Geography.

simply drill testing, and does not necessarily of itself improve students' geographical understanding. However, if focused and explicit, the following strategies may help in assisting teachers in preparing students for examinations in ways that complement good teaching. The list is not exhaustive (see also Chapter 32), and teachers need not feel that they have to do all of these with every student – some strategies will suit some students more than others.

Lesson activities

■ **Regular testing**
throughout the course, with questions that mirror what students can expect to meet in the GCSE. This might be based on past examination papers, where these exist, but a good department should be able to construct its own series of tests on topics.

■ **Focused testing:** Some questions require learned knowledge, while others ask students to interpret data and demonstrate understanding. Some tests should be short, with quick-fire questions, while others should be longer and require some extended writing. Others could assess geographical skills such as Ordnance Survey map work or data-handling skills. Make it clear to students what they are being expected to do, and how this is mirrored in the examination.

■ Include lessons that focus upon aspects of **question skills** – e.g. getting to know command words, timed answers, or planning longer extended written answers.

■ Help students to gain an understanding of **mark schemes**, particular to recognise which questions will be marked by point marking (where one correct point is given one mark) and which by levels of response (where generic criteria are constructed to assess level of understanding or explanation). Students should be familiar with what is required for Levels 1, 2 and 3. Use published mark schemes from each year's cycle of examinations; these are usually available and in schools by October following that year's June examinations.

■ Some awarding bodies publish model answers, or have marking exercises as part of their teacher in-service training and feedback from the examination cycles in different years. Use the same marking exercises with students, so they begin to understand how and why examiners mark as they do. Place them in the role of **markers** of actual **examination extracts**.

Outside lessons

- **Mock examinations:** These are commonly held in year 11, usually some time between mid-December and March, and serve as a concentrated way of preparing students for an intensive examination period. These are essential as a means of collecting evidence. You could be asked to provide evidence of student achievement if they missed the June examination through illness, and a completed mock examination is an invaluable source. However, they are of limited value if there is little or no prior preparation, since students will be working on the course (and other coursework in some subjects) right up until the mock examinations.
- **After-school lessons:** These are particularly useful for students who may be struggling and for whom there is insufficient time in class. They are also helpful for students going over particular topics.
- **Specific revision homeworks**, targeted at revision of particular topics. These are all the more useful if teachers provide short guidelines of, for instance, terminology that students need to know, or trial questions of the kind that they could be asked in their test.
- **Booklets of past questions** for students to work on during the Easter holidays, or as homework. These are especially helpful when used in conjunction with revision exercises in class and homework. They can be a useful follow-up to aid students' knowledge and understanding.
- **E-mail contact:** As a teacher, you should not feel that you have to give your personal e-mail address to students, but you could set up a 'work-only' e-mail so that students can contact you with questions about their revision. This is especially helpful when students e-mail you attached answers, but it is even more useful in helping to clarify topics about which students have little understanding.

Advising students about revision

Everyone revises in different ways, largely because, historically, few teachers have given much advice about *how* to revise – only *what* to revise! Also, different teachers make different suggestions. In terms of revision time, quantity by no means guarantees quality. The strategy of 'making notes on notes' – i.e. using index cards to abbreviate notes – is of questionable value; students' notes might be brief already, or inaccurate! How much better if students are able to learn by understanding.

Constructing a revision timetable

Before Easter, encourage students to construct a revision timetable and allocate subjects and topics to slots. In Figure 3a every revision day has three sessions, but students only use two of these, and each session comprises three one-hour units. An example is shown in Figure 3b. Students should be encouraged to build in breaks from work every day.

Developing frameworks for understanding

To help students to prepare case studies in some detail, it is possible to use a framework that is applicable regardless of topic. Most geographical case studies can be broken down in manageable portions that build into the complete picture. It encourages students to think 'What, where, why, how and with what consequences?' (see Figure 4). They should then be ready to try out timed exercises, and past examination papers.

Pre-release examination materials

Decision-making papers are based upon issues analysis – that is, students are assessed on their ability to make a decision from a number of options about a problem or issue, for which there are proposed solutions. In general terms, the examination itself:

- will consist of structured questions, ranging from short answers (worth 1-3 marks) to one final question that requires extended writing and is worth about 12 marks. For students taking the Foundation tier, longer 12-mark questions are split into shorter questions worth fewer marks
- will assess a specific part of the specification, which is not re-assessed elsewhere
- will be based upon resource materials, in the form of a booklet, that awarding bodies issue several weeks before the examination. Students are not normally allowed to take any notes into the examination.

It is also assumed that lesson and homework time is spent in preparation by reading and analysing the resources.

(a) A revision timetable (yellow blocks indicate free time)

Time	Monday	Tuesday	Wednesday	Thursday	Friday	Saturday	Sunday
9-12	Subject 1						
2-5		Subject 3					
7-10	Subject 2	Subject 4					

(b) Putting it all into action

Advice given to GCSE students in a London school

R – revising to learn activities One hour at a time (1 unit)	For the first hour of the first session read through the selected topic from your file and books. ■ Copy out the sub-headings onto a clean sheet of file paper as you read, and leave spaces beneath them. Using headings that you are already familiar with will help to reinforce your order of thinking. ■ In the space that you create, pose your own questions from your notes and link them to the relevant pages in your book or file. ■ Think like an examiner. Test yourself. Try the 'What, where, why, how, consequences' routine each time (see Figure 4).
T = testing your understanding activities	Return to your sheets of headings, sub-headings and spaces. Now start to fill them in, without using your notes or books. See how much you can achieve. Force yourself to write things down. Time will pass rapidly. Don't worry about the ones you cannot answer. When you have finished you will finally have an idea of what you know and what you don't! If you have left gaps, you now know where they are and they will be easy to look up, because they are all in the same order as your files/books. Go back to these and read them again.

(c) Knowing your strong and weak topics

Prioritise revision topics according to your level of understanding	Make a list of your strong and weak areas based upon your marks or grades in homeworks and tests, mocks, etc. Know where the gaps are!
Allocate topics to your revision timetable	Make session 1 of your stronger topics. You'll cover this one quickly and feel all the better for it. Go to the hardest one next time around and then fill your schedule up, balancing good with bad.

Figure 3 | *Advice given to GCSE Geography students: (a) a revision timetable, (b) putting it into action, and (c) working on strong and weak topics. Adapted from: Digby et al., 2004.*

Preparing for the examination

This approach is based upon the four 'Rs' – Read, Recognise, Reconstruct and Review.

1. Read

Teachers should check through the resources with students and highlight words and phrases that are likely to pose difficulties. What are the key words and definitions that students need to know?

2. Recognise

The second stage is to recognise how the resources fit the course as described in the specification. Students should be able to recognise:
- What the problem is about
- How it fits in with the course
- Which part of the specification it is testing
- What knowledge and revision will enable understanding of the materials.

Be sure, too, that students actually read the resources to find out the following:
- data about the place, the problem, and the causes of the problem
- the effects of the problem
- the possibilities for solving the problem
- what decision will have to be made.

3. Reconstruct

This stage involves students taking each of the resources stage by stage. Consider the following questions:
- What is the place like?
- What are the issues affecting the place?
- Who is involved? How and why are they involved?
- Why does the problem exist? How have the causes arisen?
- What impacts is the problem having? Upon whom is it having the greatest impacts?
- What are the proposed solutions to the problem?
- What are the implications of each solution, if it were to be adopted?
- What are the costs and benefits of each proposal?
- Are there conflicts involved in each proposal? Would a conflict matrix help?

To help students through this process, teachers can use the frameworks suggested in Figures 5a and 5b.

4. Review

This stage involves reaching a decision, after reviewing all of the material.
- Review each of the proposed solutions and the analysis of each one, using Figures 5a and 5b.
- Which solution seems to be the 'best' and why? Is there one single solution, or would a combination of more than one work best?
- Which is the weakest? Why? Why can some solutions be rejected?

Summary

Revision is not a bolt-on process, nor does it occur accidentally or naturally. Preparation for any examination involves knowledge of what to be expected, a review of what has been taught, and an application of knowledge and understanding to new situations. Students should be taught the strategies outlined in this chapter as an integral part of their course, so that they can become familiar with, for instance, cost-benefit analysis as an analytical tool. In the same way that teachers prepare for good teaching and learning during the GCSE course, so we should prepare for revision. Whatever the course, we

Case study	Population change in Malawi
What? *Define the issue that is being discussed in the case study. This involves **description** only and is a low-level but important skill.*	**What is happening in Malawi?** ■ It has a youthful population ■ It has experienced considerable growth ■ It has a high birth rate of 38 and a death rate of 22 per 1000, a low life expectancy (37 years) and high infant mortality (122 per 1000) ■ The population is expected to grow from 10 million in 2000 to 14 million by 2010
Where? *This involves **description** only and is again only a low-level skill but it establishes evidence of understanding.*	**Where is Malawi and what is it like?** Students could try to draw a basic sketch map to show the location and learn basic details of distances, sizes and place names.
Why? How? *Try to explain the reasons for the current situation. This should mean that you include some details on the **factors** and the **processes** that have allowed it to occur. This involves the use of geographic terminology and is a higher-level skill than description.*	**Why is the population growing?** Birth rate is higher than death rate because: ■ the use of medicines from Aid programmes has reduced infant mortality; more children survive to adulthood; ■ vaccines and inoculations have reduced the age of death, so life expectancy increases; ■ the role of women has an impact on development. Traditional customs together with the status of women and value of children mean that births have not yet fallen quickly. Children remain assets and family size is high, especially in rural areas; ■ the youthful population is the reason that the population continues to grow. Children born today are 'parents' of tomorrow; children born 15 years ago are on the verge of being parents.
Consequences? *Level 3 at GCSE considers the effects of geographical events. Examiners assess the ability to use data to draw conclusions, and to explain how ordinary events become serious issues.* *Consequences are grouped as:* *Social: how people's lives are changed in both positive and negative senses* *Economic: the way the economy changes; positive and negative multiplier effects* *Environmental: the positive and negative impacts on the local and wider environments.*	**What are the consequences for Malawi?** High rates of population growth ■ put pressure on resources and reinforce the conditions of poverty; ■ are a symptom of poverty – because low levels of welfare and economic well-being make children **assets** to families. Young family members help to rear babies; older ones work the land and support elderly parents where no pensions exist. **Socially:** family size is decided locally but leads to growing populations as babies survive into parenthood; more hands to work but more mouths to feed! **Economically:** the workforce grows, but the amount of wealth generated has to be shared among more people. Relative poverty increases. **Environmentally:** more land has to be used to feed people and results in over-use of poorer land if the best land has already been used. If crops fail, the land may suffer desertification and people are forced to migrate to cities in hope of survival.

Figure 4 | *What, where, why, how and with what consequences? A framework for learning about population issues in Malawi. Adapted from: Digby et al., 2004.*

(a) Analysing the proposal – based on a scenario of four proposed solution

	Social impacts	Economic impacts	Environmental impacts
Scheme 1			
Scheme 2			
Scheme 3			
Scheme 4			

(b) Analysing the costs and benefits of each proposal

	Costs	Benefits
Scheme 1		
Scheme 2		
Scheme 3		
Scheme 4		

Figure 5 | *Frameworks for analysing proposals. Adapted from: Digby et al., 2004.*

believe that 'cramming' – however common it may be – is likely to lead to a false sense of security, and to a view of learning as something that has a short-term, utilitarian purpose. Such learning defeats the purpose of good teaching, which is surely about *making* sense.

Implications for practice

(a) Revision is an integral part of the process of learning.

Revisiting work done is a necessary part of learning. Reference back to ideas and concepts, and to the particular value of places and themes in enabling the development of geographical understanding has a significant place in student learning. This is likely to be most successful where students are encouraged to think geographically in this process of learning, rather than adopting a utilitarian stance and telling students 'you will need this for the exam'.

(b) Preparing for public examinations may involve some drill, but this should not be at the expense of understanding and of making sense.

'Drill' has some value in the development of life skills – such as being able to focus thought and to write in a concentrated period of time, to respond to a stimulus quickly, to synthesise ideas, and to revisit knowledge, understandings and skills. However, these should be developed in this light and not just as a part of a process of 'getting through'. In how many other areas of life will students ever be asked to drill themselves? Far more useful to them will be the ability to think and consider ideas in a geographical framework.

(c) Avoid situations that result in short-term 'cramming'.

Most published revision guides aim for short-term cramming and focus little upon understanding. Knowledge gained in such a way is likely to have short-term value only, and is unlikely to help students to develop a framework for thinking. Preparation for examinations which is based upon analysis, thinking and understanding is likely to have a better long-term impact upon students.

Related publication from the Geographical Association:
■ Roberts, M. (2003) (see below).

References

Digby, B., Bowes-Jones, C., Chapman, R., Fitzgerald, S. and Howard, E. (2004) *It's a World Thing Revision Guide*. Oxford: Oxford University Press.

Roberts, M. (2003) *Learning through Enquiry: Making sense of geography in the key stage 3 classroom*. Sheffield: Geographical Association.

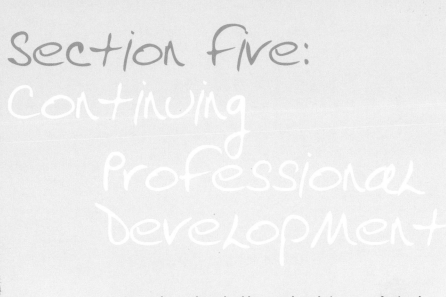

Section five: Continuing Professional Development

Geography teachers should not neglect their own professional practice and should continue the process of developing their pedagogic knowledge that they began during their initial training. Professional growth requires attitude, a willingness to be flexible, imaginative and take risks, as much as knowledge, understanding and skills.

" A renewed professionalism may ultimately be the best way to balance and moderate the demands of a centralised curriculum... The linked questions of subject definition, subject professionalism, scholarship and curriculum development are crucial elements in the macro-level policy equation as well as in the micro-level arenas of teaching and learning (from Rawling, E. (2001) *Changing the Subject*. Sheffield: GA, p. 177-8).

" The role of research in supporting teaching and learning in geography is greater than providing information on what works in the classroom. It also has a role in challenging assumptions, in identifying underpinning values and in asking critical questions about purposes. Research into geographical education can help us see things differently and freshly. It can empower teachers to construct their own understandings, to clarify their own values and to have professional confidence to make changes in classroom practices (from Roberts, M. (2000) 'The role of research in supporting teaching and learning' in Kent, A. (ed) *Reflective Practice in Geography Teaching*. London: Paul Chapman Publishing, p. 293).

" Geography, I believe, has a future. It will be a future determined not only by curriculum developers and teachers, not only by academics and environmentalists, not only by politicians and the public. It will be a future determined by the way children perceive our knowledge base and the sensitivity and utility it offers to a worthwhile understanding of the world (from Slater, F. (1995) 'Geography into the future', *Geographical Education*, 8, 3, p. 6)

Chapter 38

Building on young people's experience of geography in primary schools

Phil Wood

Before reading this chapter consider the following questions:

- What are the main features of your students' geographical experiences during the primary phase?

- How do you manage the transition between key stages 2 and 3 to ensure that there is continuity and progression in students' learning in geography?

> *it seems that geography is weakest at the points of interface between key stages and sectors ... Nowhere is this weakness more evident than at the point of transition from primary to secondary school – from key stage 2 to key stage 3* (Carter, 1999, p. 289).

> *It is no longer acceptable for geography teachers in secondary schools to ignore what pupils have learnt in primary schools* (Bennetts, 1995, p. 75).

Both of the above quotes point to an important issue that affects all geography departments within secondary schools. What is the past experience of students at primary level and how should this affect the style, approach and content of the subject at the start of key stage 3? There is a clearly identified 'dip' in performance by students at the start of key stage 3, perhaps due to a wide variation in primary provision but also due to a lack of consideration by secondary specialists of what has gone before. This variation in provision at primary school level may be due to a number of factors, including the development of schemes of work within the subject by non-specialists, the medium through which the subject is taught, i.e. as a separate subject or through 'humanities projects', and using a different focus for studies, primaries often taking 'place' as their main approach (Fry and Schofield, 1993). However, whilst it is tempting for secondary departments to focus on unequal provision and experience at primary level, they need to acknowledge that they have a very important part to play in ensuring continuity across the key stages.

Photo: © Tina Horler, Abbey Primary School, Leicester.

As Chapman (2001) highlights, many secondary departments develop schemes of work with no consideration of what students have already covered at key stage 2. Expectations are often low and students find themselves repeating work they have already covered. This results in a lack of continuity, in consequence some students may become de-motivated.

This highlights an important issue for both primary and secondary teachers and departments. How can the 'divide' between key stages 2 and 3 be bridged to ensure clear continuity and, as a result, more rapid progress? Much of what follows here is a discussion of the issues highlighted by Marsden:

> what is sorely needed for key stage 3 is a recognition of where children are at the beginning of year 7 ... based on the principles of transition, liaison, continuity, consistency, and pedagogical structure. In sum, there should be a bottom-up rather than a top-down approach to continuity between the primary and secondary phases of schooling (1997, p. 70).

In other words, if students are to succeed and reach their full potential at key stage 3, the work they follow must take account of where they have come from and how what they have done can be expanded and pursued further.

Primary geography – curriculum and pedagogy

To understand the elements of geography that students should have covered by the time they arrive at secondary school, the first document to consult is obviously the national curriculum orders for geography. A helpful summary of the work that should be covered is offered by Catling (1998) and is shown in Figure 1.

As Figure 1 shows, by the end of the primary phase, students will have covered a wide range of geographical issues. First, they should have studied both their local environment and localities in the wider world. In this context, it is worth noting that the ActionAid study packs on Chembakolli and Bangalore (1991, 1993), both in India,

Aspects of geography...		
... to introduce, develop and extend across key stages 1 and 2	**... to *broaden* in key stage 2**	**... to *introduce* in key stage 2**
1 Place ■ local area, including school grounds ■ other localities ■ land and building use ■ the character of localities ■ comparing places: commonalities and diversity ■ sense of the wider world: local and global	**1 Place** ■ changes in localities ■ connections and links between places ■ locational knowledge	**1 Place** ■ changes in places
2 Natural and human environment ■ features of the environment ■ features of settlements ■ change in environments ■ weather ■ personal and people's views on the environment ■ environmental sustainability and improvement	**2 Natural and human environment** ■ weather and seasons ■ topical local and global awareness ■ environmental issues ■ land use and variety issues	**2 Natural and human environment** ■ settlement size ■ economic activity in settlements ■ rivers ■ explaining patterns in the environment
3 Geographical methods ■ use of enquiry/investigative process ■ fieldwork ■ mapping skills, large scale to globes/atlases ■ use of secondary sources on places and environment, including photographs and software packages	**3 Geographical methods** ■ use of 'geographical' instruments and techniques	

Figure 1 | *A summary of the areas to be covered at key stages 1 and 2. Source: Catling, 1998.*

continue to be popular in primary schools and often provide the basis for comparative studies with home locations. Figure 1 also highlights the fact that at primary school pupils will have developed skills in making comparisons and in considering both similarities and diversity in locations. Therefore place knowledge will have been developed and a general understanding of differences and similarities identified.

The further development of place often occurs through the use of fieldwork and enquiry skills. For example, use is made of both the school grounds and the local area for data collection; the latter often being explored in terms not only of its historical growth and functions but also in terms of the economic activities found there. This leads to a more in-depth understanding of place, as well as of the skills and techniques required to measure and understand the features found.

River studies are popular in primary schools and help students to gain an understanding of a physical environment at first hand, thus also encountering and developing relevant skills. The same is true of weather studies, through which students gain a basic understanding of the features and measurement of weather as well as climate. As Figure 1 shows, by the end of the primary stage students should have covered the basics of map work, including the use of globes, atlases and Ordnance Survey maps, though the extent of coverage will vary depending on the level of resourcing available in individual schools.

Curriculum culture characteristics	Upper primary (years 5 and 6)	Lower secondary (years 7 and 8)
Ideology	Progressive, child-centred, strong welfare orientation	Classical, subject-centred and vocational
Curriculum design	Topic- or theme-centred, subject integration	Subject-centred
Classroom ecology	Open, generalist classrooms, mobile furniture	Specialist, subject-specific classrooms, static furniture
Preferred pedagogy	Projects and topics, active experimental learning with many opportunities for fieldwork, multiple learning resources, mixture of work and play	Subject-focused, much use of textbooks and teacher prepared worksheets, fewer opportunities for fieldwork
Teacher	Generalist, trained through four-year undergraduate (BEd) or one-year PGCE teacher-training course	Specialist, trained principally through one-year PGCE teacher-training course

Figure 2 | *Contrasts in the culture of primary and secondary school. Source: Williams, 1997.*

The 'environment' features largely in the key stage 1 and 2 orders, with consideration of issues relating to the environment, people's views about these issues, and the environment in general. Pupils are introduced to the idea of sustainability and a sense of a wider global community and how this can lead to environmental improvement at the local as well as the global scale.

As the above summary demonstrates, by the time students reach secondary school they will have had considerable exposure to the subject, and as Carter adds, they 'will have had six of their nine years of entitlement to geography' (1999, p. 289). However, as important as the content might be, it is also useful to have some understanding of how the subject is approached. Generally, primary geography is seen as part of a wider, active primary curriculum (Figure 2).

Figure 2 gives the impression of a primary approach which is active and enquiry based, making much use of projects and first-hand experience. Since the publication of Williams' article, in which this figure appeared, some changes have begun which blur the pedagogies to a degree. At primary level, the more extensive use of highly structured lessons through the introduction of the literacy and numeracy hours has led to a more varied approach. These lessons are structured with both formal and more informal parts to each lesson with clearly defined objectives, and a short plenary at the end of each lesson to gauge levels of learning. At the same time many secondary departments are becoming more active in their approach, with a greater emphasis on enquiry-led learning and assessment for learning.

A useful way for secondary teachers to gain an impression of how primary colleagues might teach the subject is to download examples of the Qualifications and Curriculum Authority (QCA) exemplar schemes of work for primary geography from the internet (see DfES website). Many primary schools follow these schemes to a greater or lesser degree and as well as indicating how the subject is taught, they also give an excellent idea of the level of work covered.

In summary, although it is certainly the case that the experience of students will vary considerably, even in the different feeder schools of a single secondary, what they will all have is a wealth of experience on which to draw, and this must surely be taken into account when they start their key stage 3 work. While the outline above provides an indication of what students might have accomplished, any secondary department that is keen to ensure a smooth transition between phases must play a pro-active role.

Secondary schools – how do we make the link?

The most obvious reason for secondary school geography departments to spend time on making primary links is the tangible benefits that these can bring by ensuring continuity and progression for students. As has been stated above, it is all too easy to assume that students lack understanding and knowledge and to write schemes of work in isolation from what has gone before. To do so is bound to cause problems. The feeling of excitement in engaging in life in a new school soon dissipates if students find that their work is merely a repeat of what has gone before, or is totally different and does not build on earlier experience. At its worst this could potentially lead to poor behaviour, and certainly to a lack of motivation. By spending time on initiating links, the transition period between schools can be turned into a positive experience, allowing teachers and students to move forward together and leading to both enjoyment and motivation for students early in their secondary careers.

Cross-phase links can be developed in many different ways and it very much depends on the local situation as to which form of link works best. Some secondary schools will have a relatively small number of feeder primaries in close proximity, others might have a large number spread over a wide geographical area, especially in some rural locations. What follows is an outline of some of the ways in which links can be made, starting with those that involve the least time and resources and moving on to ways that take a greater amount of time and focus but which can bring some of the biggest rewards (for practical examples, see Chapman, 2001).

1. Making use of key stage 2 SATs

There is no assessment evidence available for secondary teachers which relates to geography as such. However, by asking for both English and mathematics standard assessment task (SAT) data it is possible to gain a fair impression of basic levels of reading, writing and mathematics which departments will want to exploit in the first year of secondary school. Having an overall idea of students' ability in these areas will allow teachers to target resources in a more focused way, rather than having to depend on trial and error or wait until CAT scores become available later in the year (by which time the ability of individual students will have been gauged within geography).

2. Swapping schemes of work

By swapping schemes of work with feeder primaries, teachers in secondary departments and their feeder primary schools can see how both prior and subsequent experiences fit together. This simple link enables knowledge of both content, and perhaps as importantly, pedagogy, to be built up. It can act as a focus for departmental meetings, explicitly tracking subject content, skills development and understanding to ensure that clear routes for progression exist. It will also highlight where particular groups of students may have a hole in their understanding.

3. Cluster meetings

A termly or half-termly meeting which brings together primary feeders and a secondary department can be very potent in forging links and taking work forward. Jones (1999) highlighted some of the important issues involved in ensuring that such groups are successful in the long term. He noted weaknesses in some groups due to such things as the timing of meetings, which often had to occur at the end of a busy school day, poor attendance, a lack of focus for the meetings, or other curricular demands. However, if weaknesses due to organisational issues can be overcome, then meetings can allow for fruitful discussion of schemes of work and pedagogy, and in some cases may even allow for the development of resources and common approaches, as well as providing an opportunity for secondary schools to offer resources or expertise to the feeder primaries if they require them.

4. Sharing examples of work

The vast majority of secondary departments will have portfolios of work that act as exemplars for different national curriculum levels. By comparing these with work produced at primary level a genuine and informed discussion regarding pedagogy and standards can be developed between the two phases so that there is a deeper understanding of how work is assessed and commented upon. It is also an opportunity for primary colleagues to see how their former pupils have progressed and so to obtain some useful feedback.

5. Observations

It might be possible for some departments, if they can feed the work they are doing into departmental development plans, to carry out some observations in their primary feeders. Direct observation of lessons will provide a huge amount of information to departments about pedagogy, classroom management and the work of students which does not appear in written form. Again, this can be extremely useful for departmental meetings as it might act as a catalyst for rethinking classroom management in the first term of year 7 to ease transition if there are very different classroom climates at primary and secondary level. If it is possible to return the invitation for gaining time for primary colleagues to 'follow' their former pupils into year 7 by observing them in action, then this is an added bonus.

6. Joint projects

Developing cross-phase enquiries or projects successfully takes the greatest amount of time and resourcing of all six ways of making links, but the potential gains are considerable. Taking an issue of common interest, perhaps something in the news, or local to the schools involved, is a good starting point for work with primary schools. Such an issue allows for a common strand of learning to be developed between the two phases and therefore leads to continuity: it allows students to start work at secondary level that they have already met and feel confident with. This will have positive effects on their work, allowing them to develop from familiar ideas developed at key stage 2 to new concepts and methods introduced at the start of key stage 3. Such projects are best completed after SATs tests in year 6 when more time might be available to undertake work. At the start of year 7 the projects can then also play a pivotal part in initial assessments. Cross-phase project work would be appropriate as a basis for deciding on an initial national curriculum level for students, acting as a baseline but also as both a diagnostic assessment (establishing strengths and weaknesses in knowledge, conceptual understanding and skills development) and a formative assessment (used to shape and improve students' work, often by the setting of targets) (see Chapters 32 and 33). The completion of the project therefore allows a teacher to discuss and agree areas for improvement with students. This allows focused development of understanding and skills at an early stage, which should act as a great motivator for students from the beginning of year 7. It also ensures that the teacher can set appropriate and challenging work from the outset.

An example of such a link project is one on transport that was undertaken by a cluster of schools in and around Horncastle, Lincolnshire (Wood, 2001). Transport is an important issue in the Horncastle area as it is rural in character and many of the pupils and students travel to school by means of either public or private transport. Figure 3 outlines the transport work covered at key stage 2 and 3.

As Figure 3 shows, there is a clear progression in both content and understanding from one level to another, so that at key stage 3, for example, principles of catchment and spheres of influence can be introduced. The work undertaken ended in a simple decision-making exercise so that students could use the information they had collected to a practical end. Feedback on the completed work was given to students in the form of a summary comment and mark from teachers; this then acted as the basis for discussion and target setting at key stage 3.

Key stage 2	Key stage 3
 This unit of work concentrated on the journey to school which pupils make, and the level of safety around their school. The walk was focused around the following questions: ■ How do we get to school? ■ Why do we choose to come that way? ■ How big an issue is traffic around our school? ■ Could we close any roads around our school? ■ What other things could we do to reduce traffic problems around our school?	 This extends the scope of the work completed at key stage 2 by asking the following questions: ■ How do we get to secondary school? ■ How does the journey compare with the one we took to primary school? ■ How does traffic vary across our area? ■ What things can we do to reduce traffic problems around our area?

Figure 3 | *Key stage 2 and key stage 3 units of work on transport in the Lincolnshire Link Project. Source: Wood, 2001.*

All of the above points show different ways in which secondary schools can be pro-active in creating and strengthening links with their primary feeders. They are all aimed at bridging the 'gap' between key stages 2 and 3 so that a potential weakness can become a major strength.

Final thoughts

The examples outlined here have emphasised the value of supporting the transition between key stages 2 and 3 through linking with primary schools. A huge amount of time is spent in departments on considering how to maximise the time we have in the curriculum to help our students progress as far as possible. However, if we are to do this throughout key stage 3, it is vital that the work developed is challenging from the start of year 7. This is only possible if we engage with the experiences students have had before they reach us at secondary school. By doing this we are not only making the transition easier for the students but also enabling them to progress to their potential and beyond in geography.

Related publications from the Geographical Association:
From Scoffham, S. (2004) (see below): Bowles, R. 'Chapter 17: Weather and climate', Catling, S. 'Chapter 6: Understanding and developing primary geography', Krause, J. and Millward, J. 'Chapter 25: The geography subject leader', Richardson, P. 'Chapter 22: Planning the geography curriculum'
■ *Primary Geographer* (the GA's termly magazine for primary teachers)
■ *Teaching Geography* – articles reporting on research and practice in continuity (see below for examples)

References

ActionAid (1991) *Chembakolli: Life and change in an Indian village*. Chard: ActionAid.
ActionAid (1993) *Bangalore: Life and change in an Indian city*. Chard: ActionAid.
Bennetts, T. (1995) 'Continuity and progression', *Teaching Geography*, 20, 2, pp. 75-9.
Carter, R. (1999) 'Connecting geography', *Geography*, 84, 4, pp. 289-97.
Catling, S. (1998) 'Geography in the national curriculum and beyond' in Carter, R. (ed) *Handbook of Primary Geography*. Sheffield: Geographical Association, pp. 28-41.
Chapman, S. (2001) 'Researching cross-phase liaison between key stages 2 and 3', *Teaching Geography*, 26, 3, pp. 122-6.
DfES (Department for Education and Skills – www.standards.dfes.gov.uk/schemes
Fry, P. and Schofield, A. (eds) (1993) *Geography at Key Stage 3: Teachers' experience of national curriculum geography in year 7*. Sheffield: Geographical Association.

Jones, B. (1999) 'Continuity in the key stage 2-3 geography curriculum', *Teaching Geography*, 24, 1, pp. 5-9.

Marsden, B. (1997) 'Continuity after the national curriculum', *Teaching Geography*, 22, 2, pp. 68-70.

Scoffham, S. (ed) (2004) *Primary Geography Handbook*. Sheffield: Geographical Association.

Williams, M. (1997) 'Progression and transition in a coherent geography curriculum' in Tilbury, D. and Williams, M. (eds) *Teaching and Learning Geography*. London: Routledge, pp. 59-68.

Wood, P. (2001) 'Bridging key stages 2 and 3', *Teaching Geography*, 26, 1, pp. 40-2.

Implications for practice

(a) It is important to gain a knowledge and understanding of what students have undertaken during their primary school years.

You can approach this in a number of ways. It may be as simple as reading through the national curriculum orders for both key stages 1 and 2. This will give you the bare 'facts' of what should have been covered prior to key stage 3. A more developed understanding can come from reading some, or all, of the QCA schemes of work for key stages 1 and 2 (see DfES website). These are widely used by primary schools and will give you a more detailed impression of the content *and* possible approaches. Finally, the *Primary Geography Handbook* (companion publication to this book: Scoffham, 2004) offers a detailed overview of many important aspects of primary level geography.

(b) Links between primary and secondary schools are important in that they foster both continuity and progression in students' work.

Continuity and progression are important if we are to encourage students to reach their full potential and these can most easily be fostered between key stages 2 and 3 by developing practical links. Discussion in your departmental meetings focusing on year 7 might be an initial way to consider the issues, and where those issues are identified they might act as the first point of contact with primary colleagues. This will demonstrate a genuine interest in developing links.

(c) Links can take a number of forms and need to be carefully planned.

Links can take a series of forms, and the level at which your department will want to operate at depends on a number of other factors. These factors include other elements of a departmental development plan and their time commitment, the size of your department, and the interests of its individual members. Whatever links are considered, they must be carefully planned for as it is better to have a small-scale but successful link than a large-scale link that disintegrates quickly: getting your colleagues interested a second time might not be so easy.

(d) There are many benefits from developing links with primary schools.

Links can provide a lot of data and information which otherwise would not be available. You can use SATs data as a source of information on basic levels of numeracy and literacy which may help to indicate the level of resources that will suit students. Schemes of work can be used in your departmental meetings as a starting point in discussing issues of progression, ensuring that year 7 is used to its fullest. Meetings, once organised, can take many of these issues forward. It is always helpful to ensure that the focus for meetings is explicit and agreed ahead of time to allow for positive and informed discussions. A useful first focus might be a round-table discussion of key stage 2 and key stage 3 schemes of work. Potentially, the use of link projects will also allow you to provide early feedback and target setting with students if the work is used as a focus for formative and diagnostic assessment. It also informs your planning to produce work of a realistic and challenging level.

Chapter 39

Supporting non-specialist teachers of geography

Bob Jones, Janet Lewis, Diane Swift and Dennis Vickers

Before reading this chapter consider the following questions:

■ Who are the non-specialist teachers of geography?

■ Does it matter whether or not your students are taught by non-specialists?

■ How can curriculum development projects support the development of non-specialist geography teachers?

■ Does your confidence about the curriculum raise standards in the classroom?

> *An increasing number of lessons in years 7 to 9 are taught by non-specialists. Their strengths as teachers not withstanding, in general they do not have the technical subject knowledge to explain geographical concepts or an understanding of the quality of work required to reach the higher levels. The lack of professional development opportunities available for geography teachers frequently compounds this problem* (Ofsted, 2004, p. 6).

This statement contains several ideas worthy of further investigation. It suggests that quality teaching is dependent on secure subject knowledge, and that non-specialists are not up-to-date with recent geographical thinking. Additionally, the QCA *Monitoring Report 2001-02*, stated that: 'the extent of non-specialist teaching in key stage 3 geography continues to give cause for concern in relation to the quality of key stage 3 geography and the possible impact on take-up of the subject at key stage 4' (QCA, 2002). This chapter explores how the authors – three teachers in Stone (a small town in Staffordshire) – developed a continuing professional development project to support 'non-specialist' colleagues teaching geography, with Diane Swift.

As a group of teachers we wanted to develop our subject knowledge through a school-based curriculum development project. We focused on a year 8 scheme based on the theme of settlement, and intended to implement this through a curriculum initiative that emphasised a futures perspective. (The previous scheme was textbook based and used a range of examples, none of them local.)

As we discussed our approach it soon became difficult to identify the non-specialists amongst us. Through his whole-school special needs role, Dennis was confident of different pedagogies but had limited specialist geography knowledge; Janet was familiar with the subject knowledge that underpinned the previous scheme; Bob has a strong local knowledge and years of geography teaching experience; and Diane had experience of using futures thinking approaches (Hicks, 2001). However, we enjoyed the challenge of participating in this project – and we are not alone. According to Matthew Horne's research on why teachers must transform teaching: 'For many teachers, the challenge of improving performance through learning from experience is one of the most rewarding processes of the job' (2001, p. 44). But, to refer back to Ofsted's concerns, we were beginning to reveal the complexity of the non-specialist issue. Secure subject knowledge is not simply the province of the specialist geography teacher and insecure subject knowledge is not necessarily the main challenge facing the non-specialist. In our, and many other situations, we found ourselves becoming co-learners – sharing our very different experiences; a situation that was appropriate for our professional development. Both Janet and Dennis had timetables dominated by geography teaching and were planning to teach geography for some time to come. This is not always true of non-specialist teachers.

Who are the non-specialists?

Identifying non-specialist teachers is not as straightforward as it sounds. All teachers bring to the classroom a variety of skills and expertise. Within a geography context students are entitled to a full national curriculum experience within key stage 3. It is ultimately the responsibility of the head of department to support colleagues in delivering the best geography teaching that they can. Students have a right to expect this of us. However, each and every geography department is different; and those staffed only by specialist geographers are few and far between.

Also, thankfully in the minority (although a reality for some), are those departments staffed by a team of teachers, each member teaching a few periods of geography. Some may be specialists, but other school responsibilities compete with their geographical expertise. Others may have no geography background. This situation demands a different set of strategies from those explored in this chapter, and for which there is insufficient space to do them justice.

Most departments will at some time, support a colleague who was not trained to teach geography, but who has a contribution to make to the department. Nationally, the non-specialist situation is fuelled by two demands. First, the Teacher Training Agency's (TTA) attempt to recruit one-fifth of all geography graduates onto postgraduate certificate of education (PGCE) courses is challenging at a time when geography graduate unemployment is low. Second, the fact that half of newly-qualified teachers will leave the occupation within five years of starting (Horne, 2001) can create staffing shortages, which are often met by non-specialists who may feel that their subject knowledge is insecure.

As Dawson *et al.* (2004) indicate, there are several practical ways in which you can make non-specialists feel that they are part of the geography team: approaches which will benefit both the department and the non-specialist.

> ■ *Make sure your department has straightforward schemes or units of work.*
> ■ *Have a good bank of resources available. Let non-specialists know what work you are doing and share materials. Do this frequently rather than just at the beginning of each term.*
> ■ *Monitor their lesson planning. Provide support where they need to be more thorough.*
> ■ *Observe non-specialists as part of your department observation schedule.*
> ■ *As part of their continuing professional development, make time for them to observe geography specialists.*

> ■ *Where non-specialists have difficulty with a particular class, arrange for them to watch that class in another subject area and talk through their observations. Come up with a plan of action for enabling them to work with the class in future.*
> ■ *Help them manage difficult students by offering support. Where possible, have the more challenging students in your lessons.*
> ■ *Monitor their marking, assessment and setting of homework.*
> ■ *Suggest homework activities as part of a departmental programme.*
> ■ *Demonstrate how to use databases for assessment, as appropriate.*
> ■ *Include them in your school/departmental training, especially using current initiatives such as the development of thinking skills.*
> ■ *Give them a balanced timetable – do not give them all bottom sets or groups.*
> ■ *Make them feel valued. Listen to and act upon their ideas for delivering particular parts of the curriculum.*
> (Dawson *et al.*, 2004, p. 89)

Why does subject knowledge matter?

> *Teaching is good overall in two thirds of schools, but remains better at key stage 4 than at key stage 3. Teachers' expectations are lower than in most other subjects and weaknesses in subject knowledge are linked to the use of non-specialist teachers in key stage 3* (Ofsted, 2004, p. 2).

Here Ofsted makes a clear link between the quality of students' work and the teacher's confidence about their subject. In other words, when a teacher with substantial expertise is delivering lessons, it is likely that the students will perform better. Perhaps unsurprisingly, recent research concerning teachers' own development reached a similar conclusion. The TTA evaluation of the New Opportunities Fund ICT training (NOFT) programme found that teachers who had participated in subject specific courses had a far better experience than those who had participated in generic training (Ofsted, 2002). When we teach we need to be well versed in the most recent thinking about pedagogy, but we need to teach students *about* something. The synergy between pedagogy and content is one of the key ingredients in effective geography classrooms.

No one individual teacher, no matter how talented and charismatic, can possess complete knowledge about their curriculum area and the appropriate pedagogy, hence the importance of continuing professional development (CPD). The rest of this chapter will concentrate on the Stone CPD-led project as a way of supporting non-specialists with a substantial geography commitment. We agree with the statement:

> *As we strive for a high equity, high excellence education system, it is the continuing professional development (CPD) of teachers that is at the heart of the response. Put simply, unless teachers see their continuing development as an essential part of their professionalism the system will be unable to make the next big step forward in standards of learning and achievement* (Hopkins, 2005, p. 4).

Role of CPD

Our work was school-based, facilitated by Best Practice Research Scholarship (BPRS) awards, which have now been phased out (to be replaced by devolution of CPD to schools – see Chapter 41). However, there are various other ways of gaining financial support to enable school-based curriculum development work. These include teacher sabbaticals, professional bursaries and other similar opportunities, details of which can be found on the TeacherNet website. The British Council also has funding related to international experiences, and for the more adventurous there are Higher Education and Research Opportunities (see websites). School-based CPD was significant in this example:

> *To make any lasting and noticeable difference to teachers' performance, their individual CPD must be long term and classroom focused, involving both pupils and expert advice. It must meet their individual learning needs and preferences and it must provide an appropriate mixture of learning opportunities within and outside the classroom* (Brown et al., 2001).

For the Stone work it was important that the teachers had time to work together and funds to produce classroom materials. Both teachers and students thought the existing settlement unit was a 'jumping through hoops' activity rather than one that engaged and motivated the students. The BPRS award enabled the teachers to meet and discuss geography content and teaching and learning strategies and to consider how these could be used to improve students' classroom experiences. This school-based ownership was highly significant:

> *In order to thrive on change in schools, teachers must be able to help shape it. To achieve this, continuous learning must become the central characteristic of teacher professionalism and an integral part of any overall approach to change across the school system* (Horne, 2001, p. 10).

Stone curriculum development project

'At first sight teaching about the future might seem to be a ridiculous proposition, certainly from the teaching as telling perspective' (Fisher, 1998, p. 79). Incorporating a futures dimension into the curriculum involves an understanding of both the content and the pedagogy. In order to become familiar with what we would be asking the students to think about we used David Hicks' (2001) 'probable futures' frame ourselves. Figure 1 demonstrates the frame as applied to interpretations of the geography national curriculum. We found the frame challenging in that it supported us in some deep thinking. Inevitably, perhaps, the probable futures were generally pessimistic and the preferred futures were optimistic. The 'actions necessary' section made us think that we could take positive steps to inform future thinking. We were eager to use this strategy in the classroom so we developed our familiarity with this approach by reading *Citizenship for the Future – A practical classroom guide* (Hicks, 2001).

The revised Stone scheme involved students in undertaking an eight-week unit of work which included the use of a Mystery activity to consider how Stone developed as a settlement, and the use of 'Maps from memory' applied to an outline map of Stone High Street (see Chapter 16 and Leat and Nichols, 2001). The 'Maps from memory' approach proved to be one of the students favourite activities and supported the development of their spatial literacy.

Having built up a familiarity with Stone's past and present we then wanted the students to consider their town's future. In order for them to do this in a structured and meaningful way, we wanted to support their thinking by grounding it in reality: we were aiming for their descriptions to be realistic and not about green Martians landing in Stone high street. What we liked about the futures frame was that it not only structured students thinking about the future but also supported them in considering actions to make the probable into the preferred. The futures frame was then used as a scaffold to a piece of extending writing (Figure 2), thus tackling head-on Ofsted's concern about quality classroom work in geography being underpinned by subject expertise.

While valuing this experience hugely and being convinced of its role and value in supporting non-specialist teachers, we recognise that it is not an activity to be entered into lightly. The project was spread over an academic year, and it has taken the best part of another year to reflect upon the experiences. If you venture into similar experience, expect to do the work over an 18-month period to secure real value from the learning. It has had big rewards for us: our own reflections on the experience were positive, and more importantly – as Figure 3 indicates – so were the students'.

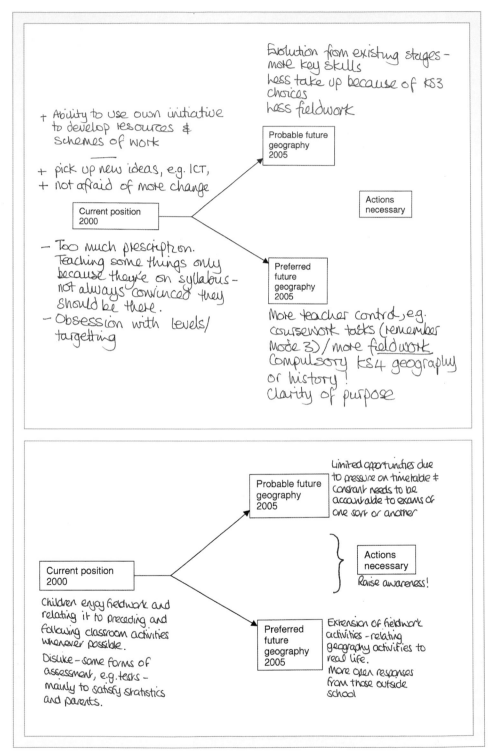

Figure 1 | *In April 2000 teachers were asked to imagine what their school of geography curriculum might look like in 2005. Here are two responses.*

What i would like to see in Stone & My village

I would like to see in Stone a shopping centre because if this happened it could bring more people into shop and it would make more money for it. Then again it would also cause more pollution in the air because of the cars, lorries & vans etc.

If there was a new hospital built this would mean that people wouldn't have to go so far to get to the other hospitals, for e.g Stafford. Public might not live near the hospitals and would have to drive or go via bus and might be an inconvenience to the public.

Stone would have more space to spread out, because of the countryside it would slowly be increased outwards and upwards. Some people might like this change but also some might be against it for one reason, people like the view of the countryside and enjoy walks.

I would like to see something being done about Stone because I don't think it is very full, and there are a lot of spaces to be filled up what do you mean. If there was a shopping centre then there wouldn't be more shops inside it so people would like to walk around that shop or other shops.

In my village maybe a place for the children could be built So that the children would have something to do and the older people might be satisfied because they might not feel scared about the children at night. I think that they should get something like westbridge Park where the children could play tennis/badminton and other sports.

Also I think that they should build a some sort of shopping centre or shopping park, because then both adults and children can shop around.

As we will be around 18-19 then I think we should have a local Hospital. This is because we will be getting into fights in bars, car crashes and all kinds of dangerous/stupid things. Therefore, we will definitely need a local Hospital (I hope not Ros!!)

Stone in five years [possible]

In stone in five years, there will definitely be some new houses in Walton and new factories also in Walton. There will also be some spare land where the old hospital is, as it will soon be demolished. There are also rumours that the library will be moved to Westbridge, but as I say this is just a rumour.

Before demolition old Hospital   After
cloud of dust + then

CHANGES IN STONE

How Stone has changed in the last few years:

In the last few years, Stone has had a by-pass built so that the high street could be pedestrianised [except for delivery lorries/vans]. Last year [2000] a "Safeway's" store and petrol station was erected alongside the by-pass to give the people of Stone and the surrounding area a wider selection/range of foods.

Petrol Station

New houses have been built in the North, West End of Walton near the common land and in the West End of Stone opposing the Walton Inn next to the A34. The roundabouts at the BP garage have been re-done for more convenience to drivers.

BP Garage

There have also been new Restaurants such as "Decks" and "The Foundation" built in Stone. These give People a wider choice of places to eat and drink.

Stone in 5 years [preferred]

In Stone in five years I would love to see better books and organisation in the local library, as it was very disorganised last time I went there so I never went back as I glanced around the shelves I didn't see any books that looked in the slightest bit interesting.

I think there should also be more things for young people to do. Like an under 20's club for the under 20's. I also think there should be a local Cinema so we don't have to go all the way to Festival Park [the Stafford Cinema is rubbish].

There should also be a McDonalds or K.F.C or something other than Fish+Chips and Curry.

new Shopping centre

Figure 2 | *Two examples of students' extended writing about the future of Stone, Staffordshire.*

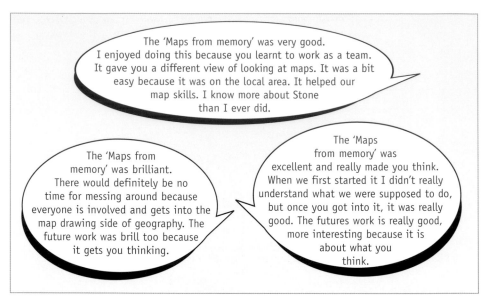

Figure 3 | *Students' comments on the activities.*

A researcher interviewed members of the class with the teachers sitting in, which proved (unexpectedly) to be one of the most useful CPD elements of the project. The teachers were delighted at the quality and depth of their students' responses.

As a result of their involvement in this CPD-led curriculum development project, the quality of student achievement in the classroom was raised. Follow-up has included presenting the work at training sessions, and to improve his subject knowledge, Dennis undertook a geography degree through the Open University. While the latter might be taking things a little too far for many of us, we would urge you to have a go at school-based curriculum development work with the 'specialist' and 'non-specialist' as co-learners.

Related publications from the Geographical Association:
- *Theory into Practice* series (1999-present)
- Research File pages in *Teaching Geography* (1998-present)
- Valuing Places webpages (see below)

References

Print

Brown, S., Edmonds, S. and Lee, B. (2001) *Continuing Professional Development, LEA and School Support for Teachers*. NFER, LGA Education Research Programme, Report 23.

Dawson, G., Lodge, R. and Roberts, D. (2004) 'Enhancing students' experience of geography', *Teaching Geography*, 29, 2, pp. 84-9.

Fisher, T. (1998) *Developing as a Teacher of Geography*. Cambridge: Chris Kington Publishing.

General Teaching Council (2001) *Corporate Plan, 2001*. London: GTC.

Hicks, D. (2001) *Citizenship for the Future: A practical classroom guide*. Guildford: WWF-UK.

Hopkins, D (2005) *Creating Powerful Learning Experiences* (GTC's Learned Paper Series). London: GTC.

Horne, M. (2001) *Classroom Assistance: Why teachers must transform teaching*. London: DEMOS.

Leat, D. and Nichols, A. (1999) *Theory into Practice: Mysteries Make You Think*. Sheffield: Geographical Association.

Ofsted (2001) *Continuing Professional Development for Schools* (Ref: HMI 416). London: Ofsted.

Ofsted (2002) *ICT in Schools: Effect of government initiatives*. London: Ofsted.
Ofsted (2004) *Ofsted Subject Report – 2002/03 – Secondary, Geography* (ref: HMI 1985) (available online: www.ofsted.gov.uk/publications).
Ofsted (1998) *Geography in Secondary Education 1993-7*. London: Ofsted.
QCA (2002) *Autumn Term Update*. London: QCA.

Electronic

British Council – www.britishcouncil.org/learning.htm
General Teaching Council – www.gtc.org.uk/CPD and www.gtce.org.uk/CPD_home/
Teacher Training Agency – Can Teach – www.canteach.gov.uk
TeacherNet – www.teachernet.gov.uk
Valuing Places – www.geography.org.uk/vp

Implications for practice

(a) All teachers are specialists at something.

Whether your forte is pedagogy, curriculum development or subject knowledge, consider ways in which you could explore these specialisms with colleages. Do this either in your department or across subject areas or as part of wider meetings with colleagues in other schools and at other phases, or all three. The experiences of the Valuing Places project indicate that it is possible (see website for more information).

(b) Size matters – to an extent!

There are helpful curriculum ideas that are small and practical, in contrast to big curriculum development projects, and both have a role to play.

(c) Consider school-based projects with all teachers as learners.

Choose a topic and a learning approach from one of the chapters in this book, or an area not mentioned here. Link it to an area that needs developing anyway, and plan an 18-month project. Be prepared to make mistakes. Involve students in the feedback and review – have fun and your students will too.

Q2: What response do trainee teachers get from their students?

The response of students to the strategy is generally positive:

> Even members of the class who normally appeared slightly apathetic were spurred on by the friendly competition between groups ... Spirits of the class were high ... as they enjoyed the novelty of the experience.

> Overall I thought the activity was successful and the students did enjoy it, making comments such as 'It's not like learning – you learn things without realising it'.

However, there were instances where the initial student response was negative. On these occasions, because trainee teachers know that the activity usually 'works', they were encouraged to persevere:

> When introducing the lesson I was almost immediately met with hostility from a small number, who questioned the necessity and value of such a lesson ... It is a defence mechanism ... due to poor self-esteem. [As there is] a tendency for poor behaviour at the school, a 'chalk and talk' approach to teaching is often used, because activities which require group work, movement around the classroom or independent talk can be very difficult to manage [but this young teacher worked on overcoming the doubters:] What I found most encouraging was that those who had objected to the lesson initially, very quickly became engaged and motivated ... In this respect I thoroughly enjoyed teaching thinking; it gave each individual an opportunity to take part in the lesson.

Sufficient numbers of experienced teachers have related their successful use of 'Maps from Memory', inspiring confidence and encouraging perseverance when trainees encounter difficulties. Powerful pedagogical strategies such as this are designed to have such an effect. An intrinsic part of their pathology is to excite and engage students, which is one of their great benefits as teaching tools. Unless teachers see a positive impact in students as a result of introducing new initiatives, they tend not to persevere. An improvement in GCSE results perhaps two or three years away is not what fuels teachers' cognitive and emotional systems – it is how their students behave, light up, switch on, talk. It is part of the reason why it can be hard to enact change through large-scale curriculum projects, where the first experiences do not provide that certain 'buzz'.

Q3: How do teachers interpret the experience?

In their reflections, almost all trainee teachers expressed satisfaction with their initial attempts with 'Maps from Memory', and considered ways of overcoming the difficulties. Their evaluations appeared to lead to two distinct outcomes: some trainees were provoked by their experience to enquire further into the strategy's potential; others, having added the strategy to their repertoire, worked on 'embedding' it by refining their use of it.

One trainee teacher reflected on what he thought students had practised (working in a group, decision making, organising and identifying their strengths and weaknesses) and what they had learnt (a better understanding of the process of longshore drift). In his lesson evaluation he identified problems with class management and the frustration of trying to debrief the activity when the students appeared over-stimulated. As a result, this trainee resolved to manage the task differently next time:

> The first thing I have to address is ... having the classroom prepared ... I feel that the students may have been more settled if I had been ready [and] I felt that as I was explaining the activity most of the class were not listening and this was because of the students getting into groups. If I was to carry out this exercise again I would explain it first and then ask the students to get themselves into groups.

Another trainee used 'Maps from Memory' with a year 11 class as a recap for work on the location of natural hazards. She reported that 'the lesson went well as it was first period in the day and students had not experienced this activity before, so it was *different*'. Each student was given a blank outline map of the world on which they recorded the location of various hazards. It transpired that:

> *The finished products were very detailed and clear and as a result I encouraged them to stick the maps into their exercise books and use it as revision for the global location of volcanoes and earthquakes.*

This is a good use of the strategy within a subject context, with every prospect – as witnessed by many of the reports – that the students had processed a visual source and committed it to their long-term memory. 'Maps from Memory' is now part of this trainee's repertoire for more effective and motivating teaching.

The reflective process outlined in both of these cases was concerned primarily with classroom management and readily observed outcomes, but they fall short of really sparking off observations or questions about learning. For other trainee teachers the questions raised by teaching thinking skills in general and 'Maps from Memory' in particular, were about being able to use the strategy with confidence. However, some also had particular concerns, as the following trainee's comments indicate:

> *At first, teaching thinking lessons seemed a daunting task to plan because they seemed a different style to 'normal' lessons … Although the planning seemed daunting at first, the more thinking-skills lessons that I did, the easier they were to plan and the more confident I became in their delivery … My other area of concern was that of questioning in the debrief phase.*

And in concluding her reflections, this trainee concentrated on her ability to teach in a style that 'makes learning fun and interesting … I hope to continue to improve my delivery of lessons'. In some cases a different style of reflection is apparent – one associated with an alternative approach to the trainee's own professional development. Trainees in this category are looking out for the unexpected – they want to enquire. One trainee built this aspect of his own learning into the observations he asked his mentor to make:

> ■ *Who worked/was actively involved?*
> ■ *What roles did students take in their teams?*
> ■ *What were the teams observing and remembering first?*
> ■ *What did the teams think was important information and what was not?*

The mentor's account of the lesson is full of observations:

> *From the first number called, students looking at the map commented: 'Eh! How am I supposed to remember all that'. Once back to their tables … the teams asked students who had been to the front 'What's the picture?/What are we supposed to draw?'*
>
> *The second number called drew the response: 'Ah, I see!' And, by the time the third number was called, teams were suggesting what to look for when next at the front – in particular the images and words of the examples in each section … students spent less and less time at the map; presumably they were looking for very specific features and not at the whole picture.*

This trainee later tested students on recall of the visual representation and analysed what parts had and had not been remembered. He read copiously on the subject of visual memory in order to make sense of his analysis, and reflected on what he had learned about the class, particularly in terms of interpersonal relationships.

Q4: What impedes a more sophisticated use?

There are several factors that impede more sophisticated use of powerful pedagogical strategies. These include: students' conceptions of learning, apprenticeship as a student, and pedagogical content knowledge.

1. Students' conceptions of learning

Some students have conceptions of learning and conceptions of themselves as learners that run counter to the very nature of the activity. Research comparing the attitudes of students in North East England with ones in Kentucky and St Petersburg found that most of the students in North East England viewed school in strictly utilitarian terms (Elliott *et al.*, 1999). According to the students sampled, school is about getting qualifications to get a job or to go on to higher or further education; there is little intrinsic value attached to schooling. There is no value placed on being an educated person for its own sake. The same was true of students in Kentucky (USA), but not in St Petersburg (Elliott *et al.*, 1999).

The dominant experience of students in school is relative success or failure in curriculum tasks, which define one as a learner. There is considerable evidence of the poor self-concept of many students at the end of key stage 2, with some evidence to show that national testing has exacerbated this (Davies and Brember, 1997). This trend towards the visible importance to all of examination results has been termed 'performativity'.

2. Apprenticeship as a student

Teachers are affected by the ways in which they themselves were taught. This ingrained behaviour is variously described in the literature in terms of images (Calderhead and Robson, 1991) and biographies (Knowles, 1992). There is not sufficient space here to discuss this issue as fully as it deserves, but in simple terms the way students are taught and the way classrooms operate is an accident of history. Classrooms and teaching could be very different, but we are stuck in a rut. Apprenticeship to be a teacher through being a student recycles increasingly redundant teaching behaviours. The automatic behaviour of many trainee teachers is to stand at the front, ask questions, hand out textbooks and/or worksheets and do battle over misdemeanours, even when they harbour very different ambitions.

3. Pedagogical content knowledge

Strategies like 'Maps from Memory' can help create memorable lessons. The above evidence would suggest, however, that the full potential is not being realised and learning is being lost. Collating our observations with those made by trainee and experienced teachers helps to indicate what that potential may be. All of the observations indicate what better-performing groups and individual students did when compared with peers. These include the following:

1. The better-performing groups of students planned more. A plan is a pre-determined course of action to achieve a goal (Hayes-Roth and Hayes-Roth, 1979). However, planning is not predominantly a pre-task process. When we start to plan something complex we do not know all we need to know, so we do not start with an overall plan and then successively fill in the detail, rather we jump around between stages or levels. Our total plans have decisions going in both directions – detail being developed in response to a refining of the 'big picture' or purpose, and the big picture being refined as the detail develops. Planning is not unidirectional, proceeding from the main template to the fine grain. New information comes to light and tentative

decisions become firmer or become overturned as alternative plans are generated and considered. Poorer-performing groups do not plan as much.

2. Better-performing groups of students are more systematic in attending to the fine detail. They develop strategies for making sure that they do not miss information and that it links together coherently as in the original. For example, in a history lesson where groups were reproducing a collage of drawings depicting features of the Roman army, only one group counted the number of component drawings and compared their relative sizes. This kind of approach greatly assists planning. Poorer-performing groups are more haphazard, do not develop these reference points and therefore do not have ways of checking what they have done.

3. Better-performing groups exhibited good helping behaviours. Although this was rarely planned, they are silent when the observers return and allow them a few seconds, without distraction, to disgorge all the information that they can remember. Then they gradually ask questions to jog the observers' memory or watch to see if the emerging detail further prompts their memory. This is a form of external support for metacognition – someone else is providing the prompts to help you think and remember. Less successful groups interact much less and can be critical towards their peers, blaming them for memory lapses.

4. Better-performing groups use their existing knowledge to make sense of the emerging picture. An analogy is having the picture on the box top when you are trying to complete a jigsaw, which confers significant advantages. First, it allows students/groups to predict what they will see. Second, it allows them to interpret and remember what they see. Third, it allows them to check what they think they have seen – does it make sense in terms of the whole? Poorer-performing groups struggle to gather the pieces of the jigsaw, having no clear picture of what it all means.

5. Some individuals have powerful visual memories and can hold on to more spatial information than others. Memory has a visuo-spatial component, which applies to both long-term memory and working memory (often referred to as the visuo-spatial sketchpad). There are strong parallels between the understanding of graphics and their properties and the development of grammatical competence in children. Visual memory should be considered alongside language memory in terms of importance.

Pedagogical content knowledge is a concept developed to represent that form of subject knowledge which teachers develop as they learn to teach, in order to get their subject across to students (Wilson *et al.*, 1987). It is the stories, explanations, introductions, stimulating activities, everyday examples and current affairs snippets that help students make meaning from teaching. The problem is that pedagogical content knowledge applies differentially to declarative knowledge (what) rather then procedural knowledge (how). Few experienced teachers have more than a superficial knowledge of student learning. They do not have a starting point for making best use of powerful learning experiences, although this chapter indicates how some trainee teachers have the enquiring disposition to quarry out the learning potential as best they can.

Conclusion

The trainee teachers sampled found the 'Map from Memory' strategy relatively straightforward to use in the geography classroom, although they were aware of the need for careful planning. As the quotes indicate, teacher motivations varied but for most it revolved around capturing attention, improving student motivation and self-esteem, and dealing with the perceived issue of unsatisfied learning styles – in particular the roles of kinaesthetic and visual learning.

Learning to teach is a highly demanding activity, creating great emotional stress. Trainee teachers feel a great need to create classrooms in which students co-operate and are interested, and they understand that these conditions allow the flowering of human relationships between teacher and learner. Trainees' needs, like those of the majority of teachers, are relatively basic and where students will not co-operate the natural tendency is to feel a failure. If, however, students can be motivated and interested the trainee teacher can feel a sense of achievement and satisfaction. As Askew *et al.* (1999) argue, when trying something new in the classroom the touchstone is student response.

The danger is that the enjoyment becomes an end in itself, and without a sharp purpose the activity becomes stale. Some trainees were working in schools where 'Maps from Memory' was used in a number of departments so students were encountering it in several different lessons. One student observed that the teachers must have all been on the same training day as this was the third time that he had experienced the strategy. The fact that the novelty was beginning to wear off is an indication of a lack of progression in learning resulting from the strategy.

Implications for practice

(a) In using powerful pedagogic strategies teachers should try to devote more energy and attention to watching and listening to students as they engage in the tasks.

One's mindset should not be Have they got it right? What grade or mark should I give them? Have they learned it? Instead it should be How are they doing it? Who is doing it well? How do we all learn from that? How can I help the poorer performers do it better? This process needs as much support as possible whether through mentors, tutors, performance managers or peers. Teachers need encouragement to take risks and learn. It is through enquiring into student learning that we are most likely to develop our practice.

(b) Teachers rarely expect or encourage transfer from teaching-thinking lessons into other lessons.

Thinking seems to be for thinking-skills lessons rather than for learning generally. If teachers intend students to understand that 'Maps from Memory' improved their processing and learning of diagrams or improved planning generically, then they need to be encouraging students to apply that learning in ordinary contexts. Strategies such as 'Maps from Memory' therefore need to be embedded into teaching plans and not used as 'add ons' or special treats!

(c) Teachers who are skilled in making powerful learning events count need to be trained as coaches to support the development of classroom practice in others.

Coaching is a powerful professional developmental process, which can help change thinking and beliefs and the relevant materials are available to all secondary schools in England from the Department for Education and Skills (DfES, 2003).

Related publications from the Geographical Association:
- Leat, D. and Nichols, A. (1999) *Theory into Practice: Mysteries Make You Think.*
- McPartland, M. (2001) *Theory into Practice: Moral Dilemmas.*
- Roberts, M. (2003) *Learning through Enquiry: Making sense of geography in the key stage 3 classroom.*

References

Askew, M., Brown, M., Rhodes, V., Johnson, D. and Wiliam, D. (1997) *Effective Teachers of Numeracy.* London: Kings College, London.

Calderhead, J. and Robson, M. (1991) 'Images of teaching: student teachers' early conceptions of classroom practice', *Teacher and Teacher Education,* 7, pp. 1-8.

Davies, J. and Brember, I. (1997) *Attitudes to School and the Curriculum in Year 2, Year 4 and Year 6: A longitudinal study over four years.* Manchester: University of Manchester.

DfES/QCA (2001) *Geography: The national curriculum in England (KS1-3).* London: DfES/QCA.

DfES (2003) *Sustaining Improvement: A suite of modules on coaching, running networks and building capacity.* London: DfES.

Elliott, J., Hufton, N., Hildreth, A. and Illushin, L. (1999) 'Factors influencing educational motivation: a study of expectations, attitudes and behaviour of children in Sunderland, Kentucky and St Petersburg', *British Educational Research Journal,* 25, pp. 75-94.

Hayes-Roth, B. and Hayes-Roth, F. (1979) 'A cognitive model of planning', *Cognitive Science,* 3, pp. 275-310.

Knowles, J. (1992) 'Models for understanding pre-service and beginning teachers' biographies' in Goodson, I. (ed) *Studying Teachers' Lives.* London: Routledge, pp. 99-152.

Leat, D. and Higgins, S. (2002) 'The role of powerful pedagogical strategies in curriculum development', *The Curriculum Journal,* 13, pp. 71-85.

Nichols A. and Kinninment, D. (2001) *More Thinking Through Geography.* Cambridge: Chris Kington Publishing.

Wilson, S., Shulman, L. and Richert, A. (1987) '"150 different ways" of knowing: representations of knowledge in teaching' in Calderhead, J. (ed) *Exploring Teachers' Thinking.* London: Cassell, pp. 104-124.

Chapter 41

Research in geographical education

Rachel Lofthouse and David Leat

Before reading this chapter consider the following questions:

- What opportunities exist for you to try new approaches to teaching in a supportive environment, which might really challenge your thinking and practice?

- Can you recognise the importance of social learning in your development as a teacher? How can your opportunities for social learning be developed?

- What feedback do you get in school? Is it broadly judgemental or is it challenging, thought provoking and developmental?

- What access do you to have to new ideas and frameworks that have a good evidence base, or to other teachers' good practice?

This chapter starts with a pastiche. It may not represent your experience but it makes an important point about the experience of many teachers. Figure 1 compares experience during initial teacher training and the early years of teaching in school. It is almost certainly more true of the past than the present, as recent arrangements for induction should have improved the early years of teaching as a professional experience.

The point that we wish to emphasise is that PGCE courses are, for most people, periods of intense professional learning. The peer group is vital as it provides emotional support, a chance to share resources and ideas, a safe place to discuss failures and painful experiences and a group of people with whom you can identify. Often it generates lasting relationships. As a trainee teacher once reflected at the end of her course:

> I have never learned so much in a year. It has been hard ... and so many things to think about, but every time you think it is getting too much, there has been someone, the mentor, other teachers, tutors and especially the [other students] to get you going again with some idea or just cheering you up.

For some fortunate people this is replicated in their first year of teaching if there is a good induction programme, but more often the experience is impoverished by comparison. Thereafter, there is the danger of being swamped by school work. There is no absolute reason why professional learning should trail off so sharply. It is not that you stop learning altogether but it is more likely that one is learning how to make lessons and administration run more smoothly, to become more efficient.

In the British Educational Research Association bulletin *Research Intelligence* (2002), Matthew Horne reports on research undertaken for Demos, a think tank that had

PGCE course	In school
■ Frequent observation with developmental focus ■ Encouragement to reflect ■ Close support from peers ■ Engagement with literature and research ■ Many new teaching ideas related to subject ■ Focus on development ■ Balance between teaching and professional learning	■ Infrequent observation with judgemental focus ■ Too busy to reflect ■ Relative isolation ■ Engagement with school and subject documentation ■ Limited access to new ideas ■ Focus on surviving ■ Teaching and professional learning out of balance

Figure 1 | *Comparison of learning opportunities in initial teacher training and early years in school.*

interviewed 150 teachers. Horne states that the most important factor in determining whether teachers stay in the profession is their perception of the quality of their working conditions and 'their opportunities for professional creativity and autonomy' (Horne, 2001, p. 9). Taking a wider international perspective Joyce *et al.* put the view that teachers are doing the best they can and that 'applying pressure without opportunity for study and training will simply not work' (Joyce *et al.*, 1997, p. 149). This was reiterated in a story in the *Times Educational Supplement* in July 2001 which was headlined 'Young staff flee factory schools'. It reported teachers in their twenties and early thirties being driven out of schools, complaining of a new style of aggressive management, obsessed with targets but unwilling to support teachers' daily work. Our argument is not just that research is important to help teachers improve their practice, rather it is a broader one. We believe that research plays a critical part in creating the working conditions that will make teaching a job with satisfaction. That teachers' learning and satisfaction are important is well-captured by Sarason, 'it is virtually impossible to create and sustain over time conditions for productive learning for students when they do not exist for teachers' (1990, p. 45).

The national curriculum, despite its undoubted merits, did encourage a somewhat mechanistic approach to continuing professional development. Summarising a number of surveys, Helsby and Knight (1997) found that in the experience of most teachers, in-service training opportunities had become geared towards implementing national policies with little attention being given to individual needs. By contrast, the picture that emerges from research on effective teachers in key stage 2 is of the importance of sustained professional development. 'Twenty day' courses were the epitome of this, offering a chance to stand back from teaching and look closely at the quality of students' learning through analysis of their work, classroom observation or interviewing. This is enhanced if the teacher has had a chance to work with other teachers.

The 'wrong' role for research

When schools and teachers are casting around for help when they are under pressure it is tempting to go for 'quick fixes'. The school effectiveness movement has offered just such a temptation. However it is important to distinguish between school effectiveness and school improvement, for the latter has offered some valuable support to schools. The problem with school effectiveness is that it is based substantially on correlations, and is based on research that has found a link between certain teaching behaviours and a measure of better results. Thus, for example, David Reynolds (1998) suggests the following list of effective teacher behaviours from research in 'other countries':

Cameo: research-driven teacher training

Julia McGrane completed her geography PGCE in the early 1990s, teaching first at Heaton Manor School in Newcastle then became head of department at St Thomas More RC High School in North Shields, and later a facilitator for the National College of School Leadership's Networked Learning Communities programme. Julia was a founder member of the Thinking Through Geography group and has contributed substantially to its writing and research. She was also involved in a Teacher Training Agency-funded teacher research project and a school-based research consortium.

Throughout her career as a teacher Julia was constantly trying new approaches and ideas in her teaching and helping others to do the same. She researched and developed her practice in a very critical way. This included planning innovations, videoing herself in the classroom, watching others, interviewing students, administering and analysing questionnaires and working with other teachers to make sense of data. It also involved asking herself difficult questions. This engagement with research in the classroom, both hers and others, has created a thirst for knowledge on Julia's part in relation to research.

As a consequence of her involvement she has created a desire to explain and understand events in the classroom. Thus, Julia has become a consumer as well as a producer of research.

Figure 2 | *How one teacher's career has evolved in relation to her involvement in research.*

- Lesson clarity
- Instructional variety
- Teachers' effective time management
- High student levels of time on task
- Maintaining a high success rates.

There are at least two substantial problems with this approach to using research in teaching. First, the measurement of better results is usually through fairly straightforward (therefore reliable) tests of English and mathematics (Hill, 1998), rather than wider tests of problem solving, application and motivation (which are generally more valid). Second, it is very difficult for teachers to change their teaching on the basis of the very general correlations. How exactly do you go about getting students to spend more time on their work? There is every chance that students spending more time on task is an effect of better teaching, rather than a cause of better learning.

In reviewing the potential role of formative assessment in improving motivation and achievement, Black and Wiliam (1998) offer a partial solution to the problem of linking research findings to practical activity. They state that teachers will not take up research-based ideas if they are presented as general principles, leaving teachers with the task of translating them into practice – teachers are too busy. They require 'a variety of living examples of implementation, by teachers with whom they can identify and from whom they can derive both conviction and confidence' (Black and Wiliam, 1998, p. 16). Research cannot offer a menu of solutions, but it can provide the basis for initiating change that is transformational. The cameo shown in Figure 2 helps to indicate how a teacher's teaching can become research driven.

The 'right' role for research

If school effectiveness is a blind alley, is there a better avenue for exploring the relationship between research and teacher professionalism? The most promising would seem to be variants of action research. This avoids the notion that a generalised research finding can be readily copied by teachers. As Hannon observes, 'Teachers do not use research as a cookbook but as a resource in constructing their view of what is worth aiming for and likely ways to get it' (quoted in Roberts, 2002, p. 283). Action research is best thought of as a cyclical process that moves through planning, action, observation and reflection with progressive focusing through successive cycles of research, usually focused on the classroom. Elliott (1991) has presented one of the most elaborate forms of this model. However, a number of valid criticisms have been levelled at action research. In a particularly stinging attack on government-funded teacher research, Foster (1999) questions some of the fundamentals of such research – controls, validity, methods, etc.

One way of considering the relationship between research and practice is in terms of the source of the research initiative. Top-down research, as epitomised by school effectiveness, develops golden rules which teachers have to implement, the critical weakness being that there is no opportunity for teachers to develop a sense of ownership. On the other hand, teacher-led research, or the bottom-up approach, has also been criticised as being introverted and insubstantial, as the teacher may pursue matters that are potentially trivial. A balance needs to be achieved where top-down structures provide support and resources, dissemination and challenge, while the bottom-up element means that teachers have choice and can pursue issues of substantial relevance to their context and personal interests (see Chapters 39 and 40). Huberman (2001) draws a distinction between closed individual cycles at one extreme of teacher learning through enquiry, and open collective cycles at the other. The latter is open to outside inputs from facilitators who might work in a university, subject association, interest group or local authority. The facilitator can provide frameworks within the work, good ideas to try, and research to help teachers make sense. They are collective in that several teachers from the same or related institutions work together. The open collective cycle is a model which crystallises the advantages of action research which achieves the balance between top-down and bottom-up. From our experience of working with teachers doing action research, and in the light of the above, we would highlight four essential conditions:

- being challenged,
- learning socially,
- getting feedback, and
- making connections.

1. Being challenged

It is important to understand why challenging oneself is so important. It should be recognised that part of the process of learning to teach is about making lessons more manageable. For the trainee teacher, lessons are potentially chaotic – there are so many things to think about that can go wrong and one is always striving to establish routines. However, routine can quickly become an unexamined straightjacket, where getting through textbook tasks or worksheets without mishap or poor behaviour is the unspoken goal. Teachers have to take risks in order to learn and improve their practice. In the words of one teacher-researcher: 'It's actually trying things that helps – going outside your comfort zone'. For another teacher it was a chance to step out of their view of teaching as it 'forced me to look at other people's perspectives'. Jill Jackson, a regional co-ordinator for the Valuing Places project, describes her experience of the project as follows:

> *The Valuing Places project is different because its emphasis is on people's self development and there is a genuine desire to provide time to plan and implement then evaluate and reflect ... To me, the recognition that reflection and review are essential elements of developing and improving learning programmes is true CPD. It is also highly motivating and satisfying in that learning takes place for teachers and students alike* (Jackson, 2005, p. 29).

It is clear from these teachers' experiences that self-development can bring satisfaction. Similarly, as found in his study of Swiss teachers, Huberman (1998) found that the level of satisfaction was higher among teachers who engaged in 'productive tinkering' than those who did not. The 'tinkering' involved carrying out small-scale experiments such as trying new material, or different student groupings.

2. Learning socially

In the United States it has been argued that schools and school districts are social organisations, in which knowledge is generated through talk and social interaction (Cousins and Leithwood, 1993). Where teachers research the same or inter-related topics they can compare practice, ask questions, clarify meaning, exchange ideas and inspire one another. Professional development takes place through the medium of conversation. It focuses on the particulars of teaching, learning, subject matter and students. Being critical is a crucial component as it rises above sharing and encouragement. It has been stressed (Ball and Cohen, 1999) however that professional development is best achieved through the use of teaching artefacts such as videotapes, curricular materials and samples of work, as they provide a concrete focus for discussion. The use of this type of specific evidence helps develop a more descriptive and meaningful language for communication and knowledge generation about teaching. As one of our teacher colleagues put it:

> *Discussion helps. Watching videos and debating what it was we were looking at, what it was that was going on. I didn't realise that I planned as much as I do, I thought it just happened, and it helps you verbalise what you do.*

A feeling of safety is an important component of learning for teachers. In the discussions that take place in planning projects, viewing videos, as well as during observations and in analysing data, there can be an openness about practice. In relation to group dynamic theory, Wallach *et al.* (1962) suggest that experimenting groups of teachers are more likely to take risks than individuals without mutual support. Teachers that we have worked with have exchanged experiences that included lessons which felt like failures and had been video-recorded for posterity. As Huberman notes, 'since what is being tried out is new to all, temporary difficulties, even failures, are socially legitimate' (2001, p. 153) Action research can be the embodiment of risk – stepping out of the known.

3. Getting feedback

Watkins (2000) has made the point that most feedback that teachers get is highly evaluative (e.g. Ofsted inspections, performance management) and is normally couched in terms of judgements. Watkins argues that if teachers behave towards each other as hostile witnesses they put at risk the trust and learning orientation required to build professional communities.

Teachers involved in action research can get very vivid and immediate feedback, such as video recordings and comments from students in interviews, which may illuminate much about their teaching behaviour and persona and the impact of these on their students. Drawing on Chi, Watkins (2000) argues that in a collaborative approach, many parties interact and continuously produce and receive feedback. In one project, a teacher-researcher noted that, apart from what she learnt during discussion, there were four types of feedback that really made her think:
- watching how someone else did their debriefing at the end of lessons,
- interviewing students for other teachers (which made her reflect on her own teaching),
- reading transcripts from her own students, and
- watching herself on video.

She commented: 'I got more idea about the effects of my teaching and teaching generally in three months than I had got in the previous three years – by a mile'. Another teacher said that seeing himself on video and reading transcriptions of interviews had made the most impact on his thinking. In summary, meaningful learning is enriched by feedback, but not necessarily where it is sharply evaluative and embedded in a power relationship.

4. Making connections

Once teachers have been able to articulate their practice they are in a position to benefit from more generalised research perspectives as they set their view of that practice against the theoretical frames. Wood and Bennett (2000) worked with a group of reception class teachers, examining the match between their stated theories and their actual practice. The teachers reflected on practice, watched video tapes of their teaching and developed a thirst for new theoretical insights from other research. Transforming one's practice from the mass of unarticulated particulars to some form of generalisation puts it into a form where it can be understood within a much wider frame and it can be connected to many other issues and agendas. Doherty and Elliott (1999) have also found that when staff report back the findings of their action research they are provoked into exploring how those findings could be interpreted through reference to research literature. Baumfield and McGrane (2000) go further and suggest that the catalyst for engagement *with* research is basically engagement *in* research. The process of using action research to transform implicit knowledge into some explicit statement of principles about teaching can create a readiness in teachers for wider thought and engagement. This seems to be associated with a shift in enquiry focus from their performance to wider issues about teaching and learning. It may even be connected to the process of shifting out of one's classroom and being able to see teaching and learning from other perspectives, both in other teachers' classrooms and other contexts such as discussions and conferences. Distancing oneself from one's routine environment helps to remove the blinkers on thinking, opening the way to a broader view of teaching and learning.

The case study of 'Teacher-researchers in action' – written by Pauline Marsden, Stacey Kalamzi and Diane Swift – below illustrates various aspects of the above discussion.

Case study: Teacher-researchers in action

Pauline Marsden, Head of Geography, and Stacey Kalamzi, who was then a newly-qualified teacher at Sandon High School, Stoke on Trent, worked with Diane Swift to explore GeoVisions thinking and its impact on geography teaching and learning in the classroom. Much of Stacey's mentoring was based around this BPRS-funded curriculum development project. Thus, two teachers (one with substantial classroom experience and one in his first year of teaching) became teacher researchers supported by the GeoVisions BPRS team. The key challenge of the research was to explore how to teach about the European Union in a meaningful way.

Revisiting enquiry

For our work on re-fashioning the enquiry approach, we re-worked Adey and Shayer's (1994) Cognitive Acceleration in Science Education model for geography (Figure 3).

The intention was to bring depth to each unit by weaving one major place study through the enquiry. This helps to challenge learners to access higher order thinking about place. The study will generally be at the local scale (often, but not exclusively, someone else's local). The original scheme of work was expanded by developing a spatial understanding of the European Union, and by personalising it through the use of case study material that linked the EU with places in Stoke on Trent using the GeoVisions enquiry route shown in Figure 3.

Use of the internet as a resource

Because all of the GeoVisions BPRS teachers[1] were dissatisfied with the textbooks they were working with, most turned to the internet and became confident and critical users. To make the material on Stoke on Trent accessible, a Mystery was used (Leat and Nichols, 1999). This strategy generated student engagement with the complex factors connected with EU funding. Students mediated and refined their understanding though talk, and we witnessed much evidence of peer tutoring. Stacey observed that:

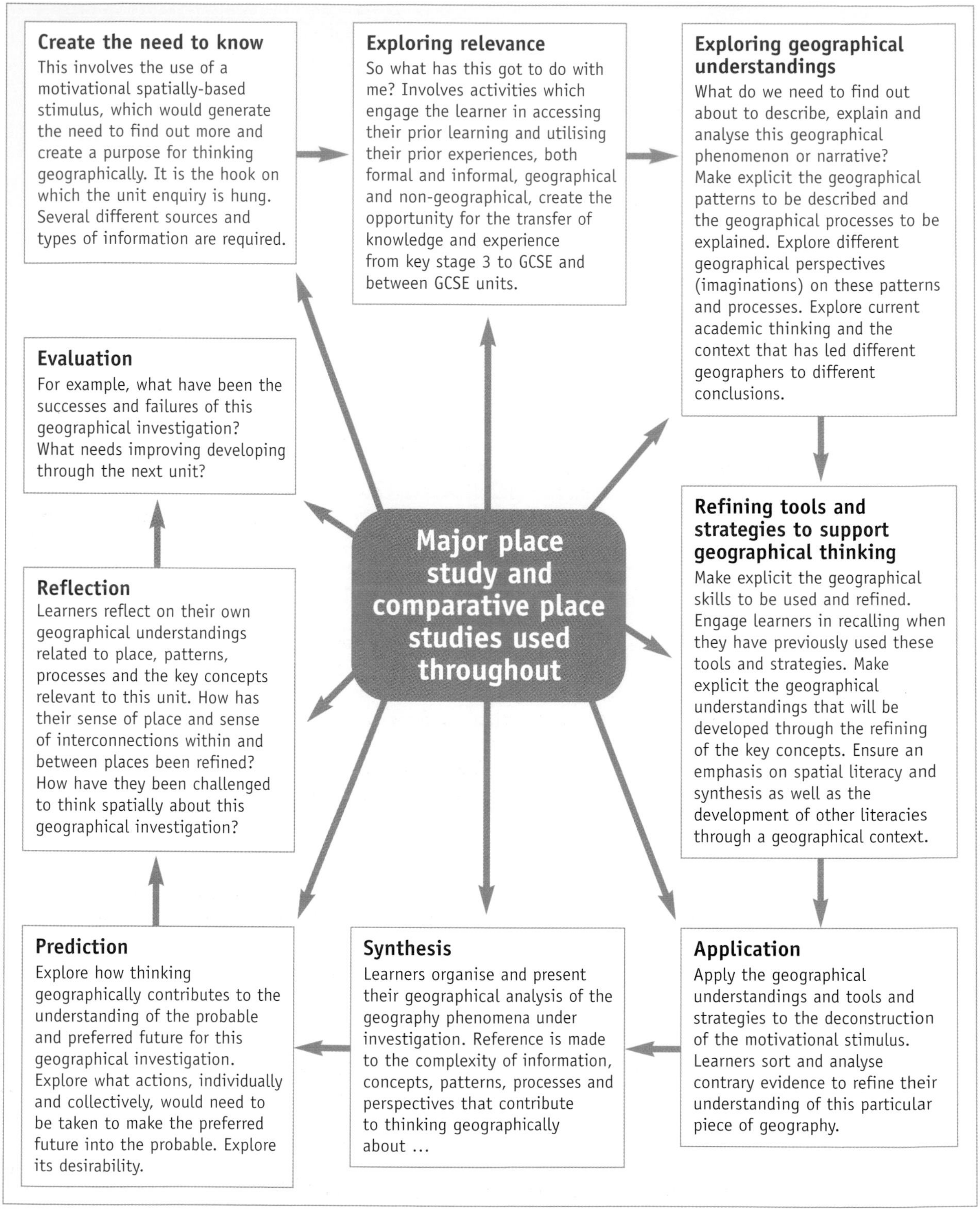

Create the need to know

This involves the use of a motivational spatially-based stimulus, which would generate the need to find out more and create a purpose for thinking geographically. It is the hook on which the unit enquiry is hung. Several different sources and types of information are required.

Exploring relevance

So what has this got to do with me? Involves activities which engage the learner in accessing their prior learning and utilising their prior experiences, both formal and informal, geographical and non-geographical, create the opportunity for the transfer of knowledge and experience from key stage 3 to GCSE and between GCSE units.

Exploring geographical understandings

What do we need to find out about to describe, explain and analyse this geographical phenomenon or narrative? Make explicit the geographical patterns to be described and the geographical processes to be explained. Explore different geographical perspectives (imaginations) on these patterns and processes. Explore current academic thinking and the context that has led different geographers to different conclusions.

Evaluation

For example, what have been the successes and failures of this geographical investigation? What needs improving developing through the next unit?

Reflection

Learners reflect on their own geographical understandings related to place, patterns, processes and the key concepts relevant to this unit. How has their sense of place and sense of interconnections within and between places been refined? How have they been challenged to think spatially about this geographical investigation?

Major place study and comparative place studies used throughout

Refining tools and strategies to support geographical thinking

Make explicit the geographical skills to be used and refined. Engage learners in recalling when they have previously used these tools and strategies. Make explicit the geographical understandings that will be developed through the refining of the key concepts. Ensure an emphasis on spatial literacy and synthesis as well as the development of other literacies through a geographical context.

Prediction

Explore how thinking geographically contributes to the understanding of the probable and preferred future for this geographical investigation. Explore what actions, individually and collectively, would need to be taken to make the preferred future into the probable. Explore its desirability.

Synthesis

Learners organise and present their geographical analysis of the geography phenomena under investigation. Reference is made to the complexity of information, concepts, patterns, processes and perspectives that contribute to thinking geographically about ...

Application

Apply the geographical understandings and tools and strategies to the deconstruction of the motivational stimulus. Learners sort and analyse contrary evidence to refine their understanding of this particular piece of geography.

Figure 3 | *The enquiry route for GeoVisions geography. After: Adey and Shayer, 1994.*

> *Students enjoyed the Mystery based on the ceramic industry of Stoke on Trent. A longer session would have allowed key concepts to be developed. Thinking skills were developed and students had to read out their cards and listen to one another, so group-working skills were developed as well.*

Development of spatial intelligence

Several map-based activities supported the students in developing confidence about the locality and familiarity with the outlines of European countries, as well as about maps as a way of representing information. Significant improvements in students' spatial abilities were observed during this unit:

> *Donna thought it was good, a fun way of learning members of the EU and recognising countries. I thought that the lesson required good teacher management of the groups and resources. Excellent learning environment. All students actively involved on task.*

Did we make a difference?

Reviewing the work included looking at students' work, teachers logs, interviews with the teachers and students, and by comparing students' achievements with other year 8 groups. Students developed a sound knowledge of the EU. When they were interviewed three months after the topic, the students' recall and use of geographical terminology was impressive. At the end of year 8, the students sat an internal examination, which included a question on the EU; it was answered better than ever before. This suggested that by making transparent their connections with the EU, the topic had given the EU meaning.

Although this work took eight weeks rather than three, by completing the topic in depth, the students accessed higher-order thinking skills that should transfer to other aspects of their geography. Giving the students the opportunity to talk in a structured way helped them to refine their thinking with their peers before they wrote their responses. This became a significant factor across all schools involved in the research (eight in total). Pauline Marsden is now undertaking further research about the quality of students' writing in geography. So yes, the work did make a difference.

Note

1. BPRS teachers and their research schools: Dennis Vickers, Alleynes High School; Gary Dawson, Fair Oak High School; Richard Lycett, Kingsmead High School; Janet Rundle, Paulet High School; Gill Brown, Perton Middle School; Pauline Marsden, Sandon High School; Linda Hack, St Edwards Middle School; Janet Lewis, Walton Priory Middle School.

Appropriate support for research

The North East School-Based Research Consortium was a co-ordinated action research network linking Newcastle University with six local schools (Heaton Manor and Walker Schools in Newcastle, Prudhoe Community High and St Benet Biscop in Northumberland, and Longbenton and St Thomas More in North Tyneside). Analysis of teacher diaries has enabled us to identify the research support needed as teachers progress through their enquiry into their efforts to change their practice (Figure 4).

Support needed	Role of research and higher education researchers
Good ideas to get started and motivated	Providing research outcomes which have practical starting points for teachers who wish to innovate in relation to a particular topic
Practical help to get going in the classroom	Supporting planning and implementation of ideas, perhaps through coaching or collaboration
Advice in dealing with scaling up issues	Help in collecting, analysing and presenting data and advising on problems, talking to senior managers or school audiences in support of emergent ideas
Helping teachers to connect their changing practice to new issues which offer the next step in their development	Suggesting or drip-feeding research write-ups or summaries of research which help make connections or move thinking on
Support in disseminating the work through the spoken and written word, video and the internet	Commissioning or joint-authoring articles, organising conferences with teachers as speakers or workshop leaders, spreading the word about good ideas and practice

Figure 4 | *Research support required over time by teachers doing action research.*

The changing professional development landscape

The supportive structures that are being outlined here do not exist in all schools, in fact they are relatively rare. Perhaps five years ago one might ponder the four questions at the start of this chapter, conclude that the landscape for professional development informed by research, in the broadest sense, was depressing, and sigh in resignation. In the early twenty-first century the situation is different; one should have higher expectations and be more assertive. New teachers should expect a high quality induction, where their interests and needs dominate the agenda, and they should not be forced to jump through hoops unless their practice is demonstrably weak. The Key Stage 3 Strategy

Figure 5 | *DfEE outline of activities that impact on classroom practice. Source: DfEE, 2001. Photo: ©Diane Swift.*

1. Opportunities to learn from and with other teachers, in their own or other schools:
   - By observing colleagues teaching and discussing what they have observed;
   - Through collaborative enquiry into real school improvement problems, drawing on best practice in developing solutions;
   - By taking part in coaching or mentoring.

2. High quality focused training on specific skill areas, underpinned by excellent teaching materials and direct support to apply their learning back in the classroom.

Furthermore research shows that successful professional development is characterised by:
   - the chance to experiment with new ideas
   - the opportunity to understand the rationale behind those ideas
   - the opportunity to have explicit coaching and feedback
   - the chance to reflect on practice
   - support by headteachers
   - participation in wider teacher networks.

(now known as the Secondary National Strategy) provides money, training materials and consultant support for developmental projects for those departments that are selected. The National College for School Leadership is operating a Networked Learning Communities programme which funds groups of schools to develop leaders in learning with popular foci being assessment for learning and thinking skills. Teachers are increasingly being appointed onto panels and committees to advise on research funding, strategies and implementation.

Further, in 2001 the DfEE (now DfES) launched *Learning and Teaching: A strategy for professional development* (2001a,b). This document represented a considerable shift in policy towards learning from classroom experience as a mainstay of professional learning. It had much to recommend it (e.g. Figure 5).

From 2005 considerable funding for continuing professional development (CPD) is being devolved to schools. This is not 'ring fenced' and teachers are encouraged, from the bottom up, to make demands on the school to provide funds for collaborative CPD.

As we move forward with a greater sense of professional autonomy, as well as accountability, we should be happy for our schools and geography departments to be judged on the level of CPD and/or research activity as much as on examination results.

Conclusion

One of the fundamental conditions for professional development to flourish is trust. Teachers need to work together to solve problems related to teaching and learning. Trust can be in short supply in schools because of regimes of accountability, inspection and competition. Teachers rarely have genuine opportunities to learn from and with each other. They stay in their subject bunkers and get on with delivering their bit of the curriculum. Trust is a product of professional and personal relationships. If you know other teachers well from working and from socialising with them, not only do you benefit from some of their knowledge and expertise, you may also create new knowledge and be more likely to ask for their help and advice when you need support. The more teachers work together in action research mode the more they trust each other and, in turn, the more likely they are to work together again. This developing resource, inherent in strong social networks, is sometimes referred to as social capital (Hargreaves, 2003). Just as material capital is important in developing economies, so social capital, built on trust, is pivotal for professional development.

The effect of collaborative CPD is described in the Evidence for Policy and Practice Information review by Cordingley *et al.* (2003) which demonstrated such impacts on teachers as greater confidence, greater belief to make a difference for students, greater enthusiasm for collaborative working, and a greater willingness to try new things and change practice. From 2005 there will be a national framework for coaching and mentoring, which should help to consolidate the growing trend towards collaborative action research, which creates the conditions in which teachers both contribute to knowledge about teaching and learning, and draw on existing research by academics and practitioners.

Research should not be solely in the hands of academics, universities and 'big' names, although they play an important part. It should permeate the life of any profession, otherwise its claim to professionalism will be less than secure and convincing. Research is not something to be handed down to teachers to be implemented, it should be part of the lifeblood of schools, where practice is examined and developed through a process of collective enquiry. The key aims should be to ask questions of yourself, of your practice and of your students' learning, and to take an interest in how the rest of the world can answer those questions.

Implications for practice

(a) **Geography teachers will increasingly need to access their own 'CPD needs' and to interact with research in geographical education.**

(b) **Being a 'consumer' and/or a 'producer' of research.**

The role of consumer can involve reading and then adapting and adopting new practices, ideas and approaches. As a producer you may be engaged with research towards a dissertation, or work on collaborative projects.

(c) **Look for opportunities for research-led CPD.**

This can lead to curriculum or pedagogic development, can bring enormous professional satisfaction and can rejuvenate your practice. It is hard work and, of course, can be accredited or receive professional recognition.

(d) **It is important to consider where there may be conflicts of priorities.**

Sometimes a conscious effort is needed to ensure that CPD or research time is not swallowed up by 'preparing for Ofsted-'type activities. Managers may need to be helped to understand your needs, rather than impose their priorities on you. Now is the time to be proactive.

Related resources from the Geographical Association:
- The *Theory into Practice* series (1999 - present).
- Research File pages in *Teaching Geography* (1999 - present).
- The web-based Register of Research – www.geography.org.uk/research

References

Print

Adey, P. and Shayer, M. (1994) *Really Raising Standards*. London: Routledge.

Ball, D.L. and Cohen, D.K. (1999) 'Developing practice, developing practitioners: towards a practice-based theory of professional education' in Sykes, G. and Darling-Hammond, L. (eds) *Teaching as the Learning Profession: Handbook of policy and practice*. San Francisco: Jossey-Bass.

Baumfield, V. and McGrane, J. (2000) 'Teachers using evidence and engaging in and with research: one school's story'. Paper given at the BERA conference, Cardiff, September.

Black, P. and Wiliam D. (1998) *Inside the Black Box: Raising standards through classroom assessment* London: King's College.

Cordingley, P., Bell, M., Rundell, B., Evans, D. and Curtis, A. (2003) *The Impact of Collaborative CPD on Classroom Teaching and Learning*. University of London: EPPI-Centre.

Cousins, J. and Leithwood, K. (1993) 'Enhancing knowledge utilisation as a strategy for school improvement', *Knowledge: Creation, Diffusion, Utilization*, 14, pp. 305-33.

DfEE (2001a) *Learning and Teaching: A strategy for professional development*. London: DfEE.

DfEE (2001b) *Continuing Professional Development Video Case Studies*. London: DfEE.

Doherty, P. and Elliott, J. (2000) 'Engaging teachers in and with research: the relationship between context, evidence and use'. Paper given at the BERA conference, Cardiff, September.

Elliott, J. (1991) *Action Research for Educational Change*. Buckingham: Open University Press.

Foster, P. (1999) 'Never mind the quality, feel the impact: a methodological assessment of teacher research sponsored by the Teacher Training Agency', *British Journal of Educational Studies,* 57, pp. 380-98.

Hargreaves, D. (2003) *Working Laterally: How innovation networks make an education epidemic.* London: DfES.

Helsby, G. and Knight, P. (1997) 'Continuing professional development and the national curriculum' in Helsby, G. and McCulloch, G. (eds) *Teachers and the National Curriculum.* London: Cassell.

Hill, P. (1998) 'Research-driven school reform', *School Effectiveness and School Improvement*, 9, pp. 419-26.

Horne, M. (2001) *Classroom Assistance - Why teachers must transform teaching.* London: Demos.

Huberman, M. (1989) 'The professional life cycle of teachers', *Teachers College Record*, 91, pp. 31-58.

Huberman, M. (2001) 'Networks that alter teaching: conceptualization, exchanges and experiments' in Soler, J., Craft, A. and Burgess, H. (eds) *Teacher Development: Exploring our own practice.* London: Paul Chapman Publishing.

Jackson, J. (2005) 'Sharing places', *Teaching Geography (Valuing Places special)*, 30, 1, pp. 28-31.

Joyce, B., Calhoun, E. and Hopkins, D. (1997) *Models of Learning: Tools for teaching.* Buckingham: Open University Press.

Leat, D. and Nichols, A. (1999) *Theory Into Practice: Mysteries make you think.* Sheffield: Geographical Association.

Reynolds, D. (1998) *Teacher Effectiveness: Better teachers, better schools*, Annual Teacher Training Agency Lecture. London: TTA.

Roberts, M. (2002) 'The role of research in supporting teaching and learning' in Smith, M. (ed) *Teaching Geography in Secondary Schools.* London: Routledge Falmer.

Sarason, S. (1990) *The Predictable Failure of Educational Reform: Can we change course before it's too late?* San Francisco: Jossey Bass.

Smith, A. (1999) *Accelerated Learning in the Classroom.* Stafford: Network Educational Press Ltd.

Times Educational Supplement (2001) 'Young staff flee factory schools', 20 July, p. 1.

University of Newcastle, School of Education (1995) *Improving Students Performance, A Guide to Thinking Skills in Education and Training.* Newcastle Upon Tyne: Tyneside TEC.

Wallach, M., Kogan, N. and Bem, D. (1962) 'Group influence on individual risk-taking', *Journal of Abnormal and Social Psychology*, 65, pp. 75-86.

Watkins, C. (2000) 'Feedback between teachers' in Askew, S. (ed) *Feedback for Learning.* London: Routledge Falmer.

Wood, E. and Bennett, N. (2000) 'Changing theories, changing practice: exploring early childhood teachers' professional learning', *Teaching and Teacher Education*, 16, pp. 635-47.

Electronic

National College for School Leadership Networked Learning Communities – www.ncsl.org.uk/index.cfm?pageID=randd-nlg-index

Teacher Learning Academy – www.gtce.org.uk/cpd_home/TLA/

Postgraduate Diploma in Learning and Teaching at the Institute of Education, University of London – www.ioe.ac.uk/pdlt

Open University Teaching and Learning Resources – www.open.ac.uk

Chapter 42

Sustaining school geography

David Balderstone and David Lambert

> **Before reading this chapter consider the following questions:**
>
> - How do you want your students to experience learning geography?
> - In what ways does the subject contribute to your professional development?

Capturing interest and maintaining relevance

> *Why do you bother doing this job, Mr Brook?*
> *Seriously. What is the point?* (Cowan, 1996, p. 27).

In Andrew Cowan's novel *Common Ground*, Euan Elliot, a disaffected sixth-former, stops his geography teacher (Ashley Brook) in his tracks during a lesson about urban land-use models that we are all likely to recognise:

> *These are attempts to represent the structure of cities in the form of diagrams, the earliest of which was devised by an American called Burgess in the 1920s and was based on Chicago. You could say it resembles a target – like so* (Cowan, 1996, p. 23).

In first encounters with urban land-use models, sometimes lengthy descriptions of each model are followed by a discussion of their 'limitations'. Success in this part of the human geography course is achieved through recognition of some patterns of land-use, recall of examples and reasons why the models might not work after all. No wonder another student in Ashley Brook's class yawns! The somewhat embattled geography teacher responds with a familiar retort:

> *But there's loads more of this stuff to get through. We're supposed to discuss prevailing winds and the rise in car ownership. There's Ullman and Harris, and a man called Mann. All vital for your personal development* (Cowan, 1996, p. 23).

Let's try to unpick the situation in Ashley Brook's classroom. He feels that he has lots of 'stuff' to get through and is mindful of the context of the school he is teaching in. He tries to bring the subject alive with an energetic exposition with diagrams, analogies and reference to his students' local area which consists of a variety of new estates overlooked by high-rise tower blocks, and an area of former council homes.

But at the same time he hints at a possible source of disillusionment with what he is teaching, namely, that he is doing it just because 'it is on the syllabus'. To what extent had Ashley Brook really tried to make connections with Euan's world or enabled Euan to make connections with wider perspectives in geography? Clearly, it does not have to be this way and we might question whether Ashley Brook has a very dynamic view of geography as a subject. What is of more concern is the fact that the lesson material described so vividly in this story has become established, standard content, almost as if it were beyond question the authorised curriculum! Even if we accept that selected land-use models are worth studying and that the descriptive and analytical skills associated with such study have value, there are difficult questions to ask about the content of the geography curriculum. Indeed, as a student in geography classrooms nearly 30 years ago, one of the authors was already wondering 'why are we bothering to study this model if it "does not work" and only really applied to certain North American cities nearly a century ago?'

Many new entrants to the profession, with much creative energy and enthusiasm, start out by claiming the value of geography as a dynamic subject in schools – 'It's about the real world and is relevant to our everyday lives'. Yet, they find themselves teaching lessons like the one described above, because 'it's on the curriculum'. 'Watered-down' versions of this lesson are frequently delivered to students as young as 12 and 13 years of age due to some mistaken belief that these urban land-use models should be taught to young people at this, a crucial stage in their education, when their views about what is interesting and worthwhile to study are being shaped. There is also every chance that they will experience a similar lesson at the age of 15, and again at 17, though perhaps with a little more detail thrown in.

So what we teach in geography is important, as are the ways in which we enable young people to engage with its different aspects. We need to maintain a strong sense of direction in the subject, always keeping in mind the principle of 'fitness for purpose' when deciding what is relevant, worthwhile and motivating for young people to learn through geography, and how we intend them to learn about these things:

> *In other words, we may establish what we would like students to learn, and the way we would prefer them to learn it, but why do we want students to learn these things in these ways?* (Lambert, 2004, p. 80).

The scholarship of teaching?

The idea of the scholarship of teaching came originally from the USA, at first in the context of higher education. However, we think it can be applied to school teaching and has great potential benefit – not least in differentiating very clearly the functions and responsibilities, as well as the skills and knowledge base, of teachers and teaching assistants.

The majority of teachers have a contribution to make to subject leadership. In doing so, they can call on several forms of 'scholarship', and should do so openly. The attributes of scholarship derive from their own success and continued commitment to learning.

The scholarship of teaching requires day-to-day teaching to be more thoughtful, so informed it becomes adventurous (being prepared to risk failure and setback), and less instinctive, habitual and routine. For example, we may suggest that if teaching became more oriented to 'curriculum making' (rather than 'curriculum delivery') it would become not only more effective, but also more satisfying. It is hard to imagine one without the other.

What the scholarship of teaching implies is a kind of 'going meta' about the job, in which you and your colleagues get better and better at asking questions about what students are learning, and how this is being organised and arranged. You also become committed to deepening and broadening the learning, so that geography becomes a fantastically motivating mental 'climbing frame', the use of which enables young minds to make better sense of the modern world.

In contrast, an *absence* of scholarship in teaching can result in a loss of heart, and a *demoralisation* of teaching, which becomes too formulaic and repetitive, and often fails to inspire interest. It is possible that Mr Brook in the fictional example described earlier lacked opportunities or incentives to extend his scholarship. The perceived need to 'cover' what comes to be regarded as the authorised content results in many teachers inadvertently becoming *curriculum transmitters*, rather than the *curriculum developers* envisaged by this handbook.

The teaching geography 'tripod'

Scholarship of teaching sits on a tripod of three connected areas of expert knowledge:

- Practical knowledge of teaching
- Knowledge about learning
- Synoptic capacity for geography.

The first two items in the list can be acquired to some extent 'generically'. Initiatives such as the Secondary National Strategy, have focused on 'teaching and learning', with materials disseminated into schools to support teachers. Effective learning, it is argued, is supported by good teaching which is based on knowledge of students and an understanding of the learning process. This is true. But we think that this methodology is limited by its lack of concern for the subject and *what* is taught.

The third item in the list, 'synoptic capacity for geography', refers to the teacher's ability to think creatively and productively about the subject. Teachers with a well-developed synoptic capacity have a clear sense of purpose and know the educational potential of the subject – where it can take you and why it is significant. It is the ability of a teacher to 'think big' about the subject and move beyond considerations about the content to be covered. Our synoptic capacity includes our knowledge of the principles that bind the subject together.

Thus, the subject becomes a distinctive means to desirable ends. It provides stimulating and useful resources which can be organised in such a way as to stir curiosity and motivate worthwhile learning. The learning is described and directed by carefully selected educational goals. The selection is based on what we think education is for, what kind of experiences and encounters students should have, and where we think the subject resource can take us. Thus, the questions we need to address are:
- What concepts can be grown and developed within this subject?

- What knowledge can be acquired and in what way is it known, and is useful to know?
- Which skills can be developed and refined with this subject?
- How can the subject help us make sense of the world and engage with it more intelligently?

Developing the subject

If we want to develop geography's role in equipping young people for 'sustainable futures', then we can use geography to help us think creatively about the nature of economic security and prosperity, how to imagine social justice in this context and (at the same time) realise the significance of environmental limits and fragility. Geography is a subject with such potential.

In different ways, the geography curriculum projects of the 1970s and early 1980s emphasised critical enquiry, the gathering and use of evidence, the significance of reasoning with data and decision making (Rawling, 2001; Chapter 8). In more recent years, geography educationists have not been afforded the time, space and encouragement to build on these projects. (The GA is now trying to redress this balance through its 'teacher-led curriculum development' projects (see GA website.) But the GYSL and 16-19 projects in particular broke new ground in values education strategies, recognising that people's values and perceptions are in themselves essential variables to understanding the world (see also Chapters 14, 15 and 30). We can take a lot from this and be confident that we can, and must, be even bolder and inventive with students – for example, using technology and the outdoor classroom to ensure learning is relevant and authentic (see also Chapters 7, 10, 17, 6, 18 and 31 respectively).

To do this we need to be clear about the scope of geography. In brief:

- School geography insists on the inseparability of *physical environments* and *human-created worlds* in which we live. This is a profound and potentially powerful outcome (see Chapter 5).
- *Interdependence* is therefore a key idea, underpinning the concept of *sustainable development* (see Chapter 23).
- Geography is concerned with the *study of places,* the diverse manifestations of the *human occupation of space* (see Chapter 14).
- Place study also develops through a deepening understanding of *scale,* the zoom lens through which geographical study is undertaken. 'Local communities' are all connected to a *global world* and successful local communities are both conscious of and comfortable with this; a perspective that is at the heart of *global citizenship* (see GA/DEA, 2004; Chapter 39).
- At its best, school geography recognises the agency of students themselves, drawing from their own *geographical imaginations* and experiences, and learning to project their understandings into the future (see Chapters 4 and 23).

'Geo-literacy' and informed citizenship

Geography is sometimes said to be concerned with *making sense of the world*. In literal terms, doing geography means Earth-writing, or writing the world. The study of geography also enables students to 'read the world' more intelligently; thus, we can think of the subject as contributing to a form of literacy making a curriculum without modern geography one that is seriously impoverished.

Geography has an extensive body of facts – its *vocabulary*. It has structures and theoretical perspectives – its *grammar* and syntax. Just as in the learning of any 'language', simply knowing the vocabulary is not enough. On the other hand, the grammatical structures remain largely inert and useless without vocabulary. (The idea of geography being a form of language has also been described in the USA context - see Gersmehl, 2005.) And of course, there is nothing that can replace using and practising the language if it is to be learned well. Similarly, geography is a resource that needs to be used, wherever possible in authentic settings, but always with a clear sense of purpose. A 'geo-literate' person acquires a good knowledge of the world at a range of scales, but also an understanding of how it works 'in the round' or as a whole – using structures and theoretical perspectives from, for example, economics, sociology, politics, biology, physics and psychology. Such a person is in a good position to exercise holistic judgements concerning the future.

One of the overarching purposes of practising geography is the exploration of sustainable development and developing the knowledge, understanding and skills for building sustainable communities. In this way, geography can contribute powerfully to a critical, active and informed citizenship (see Chapter 30).

Learning through geography and the future

Crystal-ball gazing is notoriously risky, especially in a handbook of this kind. But let us try just one prediction: no matter how powerful the technology (access to Google Earth on your mobile phone may well have the power to change school geography for ever!), no matter how wacky the design of new school buildings, no matter how many teaching assistants are employed ... there will be an enduring need for young people to learn geography. This may take place in new ways and (as yet) unknown curriculum structures, but there will always be a need to learn how to orient oneself, and to relate to the rest of the world. Therefore there will be an enduring need for geography teachers.

Lest this sounds complacent, however, let us return you to the tale described at the start of this chapter. Geography may wither away unless it can show, constantly, that it is relevant to young people, that it is worthwhile, and that it motivates them to learn.

Clearly, such aims are not exclusive to geography, as David Buckingham argues:

> *While the social and cultural experiences of children have dramatically transformed over the past 50 years, schools have singularly failed to keep pace with change. The classrooms of today would easily be recognisable to the pioneers of public education of the mid-nineteenth century: the ways in which teaching and learning are organised, the kind of skills and knowledge that are valued in assessment, and a good deal of the actual curriculum content, have changed only superficially since that time* (Buckingham, 2003).

Exploring the 'residuals' of geography at school, using adults' recollections, often reinforces these observations. During interviews with Chris Durbin on the subject, teachers' said they associated geography with:

> - *Learning trivial facts that seem a long way from modern reality.*
> - *Learning about maps but not applying them to real situations.*
> - *The lack of challenge and remoteness from reality.*
> - *Too much that is mundane and depressing.*
> - *Lack of direct experience* (Durbin, 2004, p. 82).

Responding to this may require listening to students more than we have perhaps been accustomed to doing in the past. It is hard work, as Anoop Nayak notes in describing how difficult it is to explain the conditions of 'being young':

> *That we can stand apart from, and coolly record our observations about youth in the certain knowledge that 'we were once young but no longer are' becomes something of a silent shibboleth ... In somewhat teasing fashion, the harder we try to explain the conditions of 'being young', the more estranged we can become from these experiences. The rational can only ever approximate the experiential* (Nayak, 2003, p. 3).

But just as geography teachers probably need to rediscover themselves as 'curriculum makers', they may need to find ways to tune into young people and their geographies. This does not mean somehow 'pandering' to students' preoccupations or 'dumbing down' the subject. It means understanding where children are coming from. It is for this reason above all that geography teachers need good 'synoptic capacity'.

Surveys of the attitudes of young people contrast sharply with the picture painted of them by commentators. Summerskill (2002) found that young British adolescents are 'optimistic, positive and principled', which contrasts sharply with the popular stereotype of a 'selfish generation high on drugs and soft on the work ethic'. In this survey Summerskill noted that participants had high levels of trust in parents and teachers and low levels in politicians and journalists. Even though the views expressed suggested that they felt disconnected from party politics, there was evidence of young people's concern for the world around them, through support for charities and environmental groups as well as through involvement in voluntary work. Demetriou (2004) noted similar levels of optimism in a study in 15 cities across Europe. In this survey the teenagers indicated increased levels of political activism; and the survey used the term 'sunshine teens' to describe a generation concerned with a range of social, political, environmental and ethical issues. This increase in political activity among teenagers was attributed partly to recent global events, notably those of 11 September 2001 in the US, and the Iraq conflict. It is likely that the devastating tsunami of 2004, or Hurricane Katrina, the Pakistani earthquake, hunger in West Africa and Live 8 – all occurring in 2005 – may produce similar responses.

Reviews of learning and student reflection on experiences in geography can provide insights into what motivates them, how they are learning and what they value. There is a growing body of research into the value of student voices in transforming learning and raising achievement (Ruddock, 1996; Fielding, 2001; Barratt *et al.,* 2005). Fielding recognises that transforming learning is an enterprise that should involve teachers and learners:

> *Teachers cannot create new roles and realities without the support and encouragement of their students; students cannot construct more imaginative and fulfilling realities of learning without a reciprocal engagement with their teachers. We need each other to be and become ourselves to be and become both learners and teachers of each other together* (2001, p. 108).

We need not only look to educationists for guidance. In geography research has focused on how young people's identities are constructed, how they use, interpret and contest spaces and how they are often excluded from adult spaces (Holloway and Valentine, 2000). Such lines of inquiry can help geographers to address questions about how people are represented in society, whose identity is included and whose excluded (Jackson, 2000). In 2005 the GA/CABE project 'Where will I live?' (see GA website) noted that, while young people could shape informed views on the design and layout of new settlements, they were not confident that their views would be 'listened to'.

The terminology we use to describe young people may itself be problematic. Nayak (2003) reminds us that children, youth, young people and teenagers are social constructs that have different meanings in different times and places. The street may be the only place where young people feel 'included' yet 'hanging about in the street' is frequently portrayed as 'a threat to public order' (Skelton and Valentine, 1998, p. 7).

There is a risk of course that research into young people's lives is evaluated in terms of *particular* adults' own experiences and perceptions of being young. It will produce controversial material which will yield many differing responses from teachers. We may simply be able to agree that considering students' lives – their experiences and their geographical imaginations – is part of the complex mix for curriculum making.

Developing as geography teachers

The need to reassert geography teachers' role as 'curriculum makers' is a core message running throughout this book. It is true that there is much generic skill to be learned in teaching. But the teaching is a job characterised by its moral purpose, as discussed in the early chapters in this book. What's the point of being a 'good teacher' if what you are teaching is possibly out of date, irrelevant or wrong? The curriculum has to be made and remade continuously by 'activist professionals' (Sachs, 2003), which should be the focus for much of teachers' professional development.

What form of professional learning will make this possible?

> *Every teacher now has the opportunity, under the performance management arrangements, to discuss their learning and development needs annually with their line manager and to set one or more development objectives* (DfES, 2002).

The 'opportunity' referred to here is very significant. But it requires great skill to articulate 'development objectives', partly because there is often a tension between what your department or school wants from your development, and what you value.

From 2005, the government has promoted 'new professionalism' which moves us ever closer to a system that expects all teachers to engage in systematic and continuous professional development (CPD). Again, this raises some questions:

- What kind of CPD is valued?
- For what purpose is CPD valued?
- Whose interests does CPD serve?

The Geographical Association's enduring mission is 'to further the learning and teaching of geography'. Looking to the future of geography in schools great store is attached to *teacher-led curriculum development*. In other words, the case is made here for CPD which is focused on 'curriculum making'. Our position, which in essence is that teachers need to think of themselves as creative curriculum makers, is summed up well by the 'cook, chill and reheat' analogy. The *reheated* geography curriculum cannot be avoided and is useful, but like fast food, should be reserved only for emergencies, rather than being the staple diet.

Subject leadership

Even though the managerial aspects of being a head of department or subject co-ordinator are important, it is subject leadership responsibilities that perhaps define the role. Establishing and articulating a vision for geography is one of the key responsibilities of subject leaders. This vision should ensure that the geography curriculum is stimulating, current, relevant, challenging and worthwhile. Above all, it should clearly be seen to contribute to a high-quality educational experience – and attainment – for all students.

A subject leader's role is to ensure that the departmental team has a shared moral purpose and the skills to make this vision for the subject a collective one. The main idea here is that the department finds ways to pull together with a shared view of how to make the curriculum experience for students matter to them. In this sense, a subject leader needs to develop a departmental culture and ethos that is conducive to the department working as a team (collegiality). Departmental culture might be usefully defined as 'the way we do things around here', and elsewhere (see GA website) Fred Martin provides a helpful discussion of the importance of developing an effective departmental ethos.

This does not mean all teaching is or should be the same, but all teachers of geography can – indeed must - contribute to this process. It is important that it happens locally, in school. Various CPD programmes devised externally and from central agencies often fail in this respect. Indeed, national teacher development programmes have often been so concerned with teaching teachers generally that they have, in recent years, failed even to engage seriously with the subject.

Thus, school-based professional development (inservice training (inset) days and departmental meetings) – or better still, local consortia of schools – can focus on *curriculum making*. Activities and discussions can incorporate issues such as 'assessment for learning' and 'thinking skills', but the goal is to ensure creative curriculum making, focused on new lesson ideas, students' work and an occasional look at what is current in the wider discipline.

Building a 'community of practice'

The vision we have for the way in which school geography might develop in the future does not depend on a centrally driven teacher development programme or on the agency of dedicated and innovative individuals. 'Solutions' to the curriculum and the pedagogic challenges that abound are rarely simple and hardly ever of a 'one size fits all' character, but they can be worked out by practitioners on the ground in the company of others. Collaboration, the sense that 'we are working on this and learning together', and dialogue between practitioners (thinking together) play a critical role in sustaining the development of the subject. Such professional development can be stimulated from outside through a 'community of practice' such as those supported by the subject association.

Professional development under this kind of rubric can be entirely localised, for it may not be prudent to wait for the course or inset pack to be brought to your door. Research indicates that when it comes to CPD, the challenge is how to maintain personal interest and motivation (DfES, 2003). For us, the way to do this is to 'take ownership'. If you assume CPD is something *done to you,* or you wait for CPD to *provide you* with 'the answer' then you can become dissatisfied or frustrated. The challenge for you, therefore, is to find out and decide what you would like to do, or try out. This may come from talking to other teachers, from reading an article, attending a lecture or workshop, or from talking to your students.

The point is that teachers' thinking about the curriculum does not take place in a vacuum. It is stimulated, shaped and inspired by 'what's going on elsewhere'. It is now widely believed that one of the most useful attributes a teacher can have is to be able to model the characteristics of a genuine learner. In this sense, a professional community of practice of teachers is a learning community *par excellence.*

The 'teacher as learner' is perhaps easiest to imagine in the context of coming to something new altogether, such as a new location for fieldwork. However, in an 'information soaked' world it applies to all settings. A teacher as learner is confident enough to be uncertain, and therefore to be seen to be in the process of learning. Such a teacher is not only skilful at getting students to think and talk about their learning, but can analyse his or her own professional learning.

Using this frame of reference, CPD becomes just another (usually very positive) opportunity to contribute to the process of professional learning – by provoking a new thought, or by looking at the familiar in a new way. The value of the CPD may therefore rest on what *you bring* to the experience as much as the experience itself. This is the thinking behind much of the Geographical Association's approach to funded project work, namely teacher-led curriculum development (see GA website).

'Local solutions' emphasise the ability of teachers themselves, with appropriate challenge, stimulus, leadership and support, to find solutions to curriculum and pedagogic issues. Bringing subject specialists together, with a real sense of purpose for their own professional development, and providing them with opportunities to think together provides a creative resource. Geography teachers are given the opportunity to think deeply about the subject's important concepts and distinctive contribution to students' learning. The projects section of the GA website provides a flavour of such local solutions.

Conclusion

Teachers' professional development hinges on their growing appreciation of learning. The subject knowledge acquired through higher education or from elsewhere has to be reworked before it can be taught effectively to students. This reworking process begins in initial teacher training, but continues throughout a teaching career. Sustained engagement with the dynamics of students' learning uniquely guides the way that existing subject knowledge has to be reconfigured locally if it is to be to be taught successfully in schools. Thus, what teachers know about their subject has to be reworked on site, and such is teachers' agency that they will always have a key role in shaping curriculum subjects. In this sense, teachers are learners too. They are key players in curriculum development, or as we have called it here, curriculum making.

Related resources from the Geographical Association:
- GA website 'Projects' section – www.geography.org.uk/projects
- Rawling, E. (2001) (see below).

References

Barratt, R., Scott, W. and Barratt Hacking, E. with Nicholls, D., Davies, K. and Talbot, W. (2005) 'Listening to children (L2C): a collaborative school-based research project', *Teaching Geography*, 30, 3, pp. 137-41.

Buckingham, D. (2003) *Media Education: Literacy, learning and contemporary culture*. Cambridge: Polity Press.

Cowan, A. (1996) *Common Ground*. New York: Harcourt Brace.

Demetriou, D. (2004) 'Optimistic, responsible and political: the face of today's teens', *The Independent*, 31 March.

DfES (2002) 'Introduction' to Standards Framework (available online: www.teachernet.gov.uk/Standards_Framework/standard).

Durbin, C. (2004) 'The good and the bad in geography', *Teaching Geography*, 29, 2, pp. 82-3.

Fielding, M. (2001) 'Beyond the rhetoric of student voices: new departures or new constraints in the transformation of 21st century schooling?', *Forum*, 43, 2, pp. 100-9.

Geographical Association website – www.geography.org.uk

GA/DEA (2004) *The Global Dimension*. Sheffield/London: GA/DEA.

Gersmehl, P. (2005) *Teaching Geography*. New York: Guilford Press.

Holloway, S. and Valentine, G. (2000) *Children's Geographies: Living, playing, learning*. London: Routledge.

Jackson, P. (2000) 'New directions in human geography' in Kent, A. (ed) *Reflective Practice in Geography Teaching*. London: Paul Chapman Publishing, pp. 50-6.

Lambert, D. (2004) 'Geography' in White, J. (ed) *Rethinking the School Curriculum: Values, aims and purposes*. London: Routledge Falmer, pp. 75-85.

Nayak, A. (2003) *Race, Place and Globalization: Youth cultures in a changing world*. Oxford: Berg.

Rawling, E. (2001) *Changing the Subject: The impact of national policy on school geography 1980-2000*. Sheffield: Geographical Association.

Ruddock, J. (1996) *School Improvement. What can pupils tell us?* London: David Fulton.

Sachs, J. (2003) *The Activist Teaching Profession*. Buckingham: Open University Press.

Skelton, T. and Valentine, G. (1998) *Cool Places: Geographies of youth cultures*. London: Routledge.

Summerskill, B. (2002) 'Teenagers: young, free and very nice', *The Observer*, 21 July.

Implications for practice

(a) **Continually reflect on the educational purpose of your geography lessons – what constitutes 'worthwhile learning'?**

Ask these questions of your geography lessons (or a short sequence of lessons!)
What makes this lesson a geography lesson?
In what ways is this lesson...
... enjoyable?
... worthwhile?
... relevant?
What did the students make of this lesson?
The purpose of these questions is to force the issue of curriculum goals – what we have called moral purpose. Is the purpose of the geography curriculum experience clear? Does it measure up to what students expect and deserve? Will geography serve them well in their futures?

(b) **Ensure that geography, the subject, continues to occupy a central role in your professional learning as a teacher.**

Geography teachers are learners too. The geography curriculum should be seen as a creative act of interpretation and interaction – *curriculum making* rather than transmission. Relevant intellectual and creative experiences in geography education are an important part of your professional development. Participation in relevant 'learning communities' can make a significant contribution to this process of professional learning.

Index

Photo: ©Steve Banner